ACCOUNTING APPLICATIONS

A SYSTEMS APPROACH

RON COUGLER, B.A., C.M.A.
Business Head
Glendale High School
Tillsonburg, Ontario

CONTRIBUTING AUTHOR:

NORMAN J. SHOEMAKER, B. Ed.
Head, Business Education
Sir Winston Churchill Secondary School
Vancouver, British Columbia

WILEY

John Wiley & Sons

Toronto   New York   Chichester   Brisbane   Singapore

To my wife, Elaine, and our children, Kevin and Beth. Thanks again for your patience and understanding during the preparation of this textbook.
R.C.

To those who are the true constants in my life:
My Mom and Dad
My sons, Scott and Rob
N.S.

Canadian Cataloguing in Publication Data

Cougler, Ronald A.
   Accounting applications

ISBN 0-471-79611-5

1. Accounting.   I. Shoemaker, Norman J., 1942–   II. Title.

HF5635.C68 1991   657'.042   C91-094701-5

DEVELOPMENTAL EDITOR: Marg Bukta
COPY EDITOR: Ann Downar
DESIGN: Brant Cowie / ArtPlus Limited
PAGE MAKE-UP: Heather Brunton / ArtPlus Limited
FILM OUTPUT: TypeLine Express Limited

Printed and bound by T.H. Best

10 9 8 7 6 5 4 3 2 1

Table of Contents

CHAPTER 4 Cash Control and Banking 205

CHAPTER 5 Accounts Receivable 271

Acknowledgements

I acknowledge with thanks the constructive comments and suggestions of the following reviewers of this textbook:

Heather Doyle
F.W. Johnson Collegiate
Regina, Saskatchewan

John Emery
Saunders Secondary School
London, Ontario

Linda Engh
Springbrook Community High School
Calgary, Alberta

Howard Lear
Killarney Secondary School
Vancouver, British Columbia

Bill Lum
Vancouver Technical Secondary School
Vancouver, British Columbia

I would also like to thank Paul McLean, a student at Annandale High School, for volunteering to test the Bedford material, and Ann Downar for her meticulous attention to detail. And a special thanks to Marg Bukta for her constructive suggestions on improving the quality of this text, and to my contributing author, Norman Shoemaker, for preparing the Bedford material.

Finally, I wish to express my sincere appreciation to Mr. Robert J. Lindquist, B. Comm, C.A., Partner, Peat Marwick, Lindquist, Holmes, who contributed all of the material necessary to prepare the forensic accounting cases. This was indeed a highlight of the manuscript stage of this text.

To the Teacher

Accounting Applications: A Systems Approach provides students opportunities to develop the accounting skills required to enter the job market immediately following this course or as a basis for further study. The text provides an in-depth study of the accounting techniques and practices used in today's business offices. By first establishing the manual procedures and then the computerized use of those skills, the text assists students in understanding and applying modern applied accounting systems.

Accounting Applications: A Systems Approach presents each new skill in a contextual, meaningful framework. Thus, the students not only learn the accounting skill but also understand its relevance in the real world of accounting. By giving students ample opportunities and examples to learn the system manually, the text enhances understanding of the underlying systems involved. The students begin the computer-related activities only after they have mastered the skill manually.

Accounting Applications: A Systems Approach challenges students at all levels of ability through graded and creative activities. Many of these activities take the students beyond the classroom and into the community for field assignments. Thus, through the use of community businesses, the students see the direct application of the material they are studying. This immediacy increases student motivation, classroom interest, and student productivity.

One special feature of the text is *Crimebusters*. By studying how actual crimes have been tracked down and solved through accounting procedures, the students see a different application of the skills they are learning. These cases also introduce into the classroom a vehicle for class discussions and debate regarding the various values, value conflicts, and ethical concerns often faced by workers in accounting-related careers.

Chapters 2-9 each deal with a specific application, such as the accounting system for a service business and accounts receivable, and each is a stand-alone unit. That is, it may be presented at any point in the course that best suits the needs of the students. This enables the teacher to design a course that focuses very directly on the needs of a particular class. Teachers may, therefore, sequence the material to meet their planning needs, the special requirements of the students, and the changing business community environment.

The work within each chapter is divided into lesson sections. Each of these discreet sections is followed by a set of activities that allow the students to demonstrate their understanding of the material — an immediate check of the concepts and skills presented. These activities are review based and can be completed in a short period of time, even those that take the students beyond the immediate textual material.

The activities at the end of each chapter tie the information from the entire chapter together and ask the students to go beyond. Here the students must analyze, synthesize, create field reports, flowcharts, prepare reports, select relevant data, and transfer information and ideas from one activity to another. These activities, graded from least to most involved, require the student to show an understanding of the system being studied. Not every activity at the end of each chapter will be done by every student. The teacher is provided with enough material to choose those activities that best suit the needs and skills of individual students and the time available.

Many of the activities throughout the text can be incorporated into a collaborative learning strategy. These types of cooperative activities familiarize the students with the work environment found in most offices today. It is important that students learn to work in a cooperative environment. The group activities are designed to encourage problem solving and the development of communication skills. Further, they encourage the students to develop respect for others' abilities as well as to recognize their own self worth.

Each set of accounting skills presented manually to the students is reinforced by *Accounting Applications: A Systems Approach* using the computer. Thus, the students investigate and practise the skills prior to being introduced to them in computer form. The data disk that accompanies the Teacher's Resource Package allows the students to spend their computer time working on accounting problems, not inputting background data.

The computer activities are specific to the chapter. Thus, each chapter contains a complete set of both manual and computer instructions and exercises. This program has the additional benefit of allowing the students to see the difference between manual and computer accounting procedures. They have the opportunity of evaluating the steps eliminated, those added, the necessary preparation of data, and the types of information generated.

In both the manual and the computer materials, the students work from replicas of source documents. This type of material gives the lessons the realism needed to make the course interesting, meaningful, and business-related for the students.

Accounting Applications: A Systems Approach focuses on the practical applications of accounting skills that students have acquired in other courses. This practical, hands-on text maintains high student interest and involvement through both the type and style of presentation of the materials and its realistic approach to the problems. The computer applications prepare the students for many accounting-related jobs. This text also helps students take control of the many accounting-related aspects of their personal lives.

THE TEACHER'S RESOURCE PACKAGE

The Teacher's Resource Package reproduces, with answers, the Student Working Papers. The teacher can have the students check their own work or put the answers on an overhead projector for whole class discussion and teaching.

All answers for the computer application activities are provided in the same screen format that the students will see them. Thus, the students and the teacher see the answers in a final print-out format.

THE STUDENT WORKING PAPERS

For every chapter in the text, there is a related chapter in the Working Papers. Every accounting form required by the students to complete the activities and exercises in the text is provided in a well-labelled format in the Working Papers. Each page is serrated, three-holed punched.

THE PROGRAM

Accounting Applications: A Systems Approach is comprised of the text, the Student Working Papers, a Teacher's Resource Package, and a data disk. The program is designed to facilitate classroom use. It presents real problems to students preparing to enter accounting-related careers. Further, the text provides the skills needed for those students wishing to go further in their studies of accounting. Its modular setup allows students to move smoothly from the manual exercises to their computer counterparts. We hope you enjoy using this text and wish you success with your course.

To the Student

Accounting Applications: A Systems Approach contains nine chapters. Each chapter follows the same format.

Chapter Opener: The first page of each chapter gives its title (which specifies the accounting area to be studied), the chapter number, a mini table of contents showing the sections of the chapter, the specific *Crimebusters* case, and the career profile highlighted in the chapter.

The first page of each chapter has the chapter's objectives listed down the left-hand side. These objectives are stated as tasks that you will learn to accomplish in this chapter.

The first numbered section of each chapter is an Overview, setting out the purpose and key elements of the chapter. This is the only section of the chapter that is not followed by a set of questions or activities.

Each chapter presents information through a series of lessons or sections. The sections are numbered for easy reference, as are all illustrative material, source documents, and other graphic elements.

At the end of each section there is a set of questions that refer to the material presented in that section. These questions are review oriented and are quite specific in their focus.

Each chapter includes a section using the ACCPAC Bedford Integrated Accounting software. The Bedford Exercise is specific to the skills taught in the chapter.

At the end of each chapter is a Dictionary of Accounting Terms in which all the new terms, concepts, and vocabulary items introduced in the chapter are defined.

The end-of-chapter activities begin with a set of manual exercises. Every accounting form needed to complete these manual activities is found in the Student Working Papers.

COMPUTER ACTIVITIES

Following the manual exercises in each chapter is a set of computer activities. They are presented in a generic format and can be used with any software package that is available. There are five types of computer activities and many questions within each type.

The five types presented are:

SS	=	spreadsheet
DB	=	data base
G	=	graphics
WP	=	word processing
I	=	Integrated package

CRIMEBUSTERS

Each chapter features a special crime that has been solved using forensic accounting procedures and skills. These cases provide the background, the crime, and how the crime was solved. The final court disposition of the case is also given. Following each case there is a series of questions. Forensic accounting is an exciting and quite unusual aspect of accounting that most students and teachers find fascinating. The cases are all Canadian and most are quite recent.

CAREER PROFILES

This feature presents a variety of different careers that require or use accounting information and skills. They range from a mechanical engineer (Chapter 2) to a golf pro (Chapter 5). Each profile outlines the career path taken by the person and how knowledge of accounting systems were required or helped in that career development. As well, after each career profile there are discussion questions to help you think about the role of accounting in day-to-day business activities and in that specific career.

INDEX

At the back of the text is an index of terms, ideas, and concepts for quick reference by the students and teacher. The index can be used for easy reference or for more research-oriented tasks.

We hope you enjoy using this text and wish you good luck in this course and in your future endeavours.

1

Systems Approach to Accounting

At the end of this chapter, you should be able to:

- Understand the relationships among the various accounting systems of the accounting process.

- Explain how manual and computer-assisted methods are used in accounting work.

- Know the basic operation of a microcomputer setup and its usefulness to accounting in terms of spreadsheet, graphics, database, and word processing software.

- Journalize source documents and prepare financial statements on a computer using the ACCPAC Bedford Integrated Accounting software.

1.0

Overview

The process of accounting is made up of several accounting systems: cash, accounts receivable, accounts payable, inventory, payroll, and cost accounting. Each of these systems impact on the general ledger of a business. The general ledger is then used to prepare year-end financial statements. Chapter 1 describes these accounting systems briefly, and then shows how accounting data is recorded, both manually and with the help of microcomputers.

1.1

Accounting Systems

Several accounting systems can be identified in the accounting process. A **system** is an individual accounting topic such as accounts receivable. Figure 1-1 indicates some of the essential accounting systems. The focal point of the accounting process is the **general ledger**, from which it is possible to prepare the **income statement** and the **balance sheet** at the business year end.

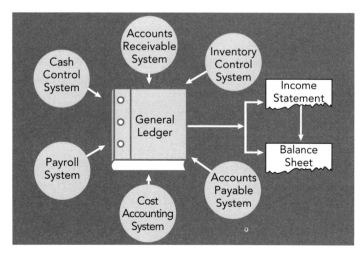

FIGURE 1-1   Flowchart of the accounting process

The circles in Figure 1-1 indicate the areas of accounting activities usually found in larger businesses. Not all systems will be found in all businesses. Here is a brief description of the accounting systems outlined in Figure 1-1.

CASH CONTROL SYSTEM

Because cash is the most liquid of assets, it is extremely important for a business to install a proper method to handle cash receipts and deposits to the business bank account. Other equally important controls include the regular reconciliation of the bank account, and a proper setup for the authorization of cash payments. A good cash control system encompasses both physical and accounting controls over cash handling.

ACCOUNTS RECEIVABLE SYSTEM

A good accounts receivable system ensures that customers are billed correctly, and that payments received from customers are properly recorded. This system provides reports that analyse accounts receivable balances, and keeps them to a minimum. It also indicates to management when to take action on overdue accounts either by charging interest or by initiating proper debt collection procedures.

ACCOUNTS PAYABLE SYSTEM

The accounts payable system ensures that supplier accounts are paid on time, that discounts on purchases are taken before due dates, and that only those goods actually received are paid for. An accounts payable system requires good control over the receipt of goods and the approval for payment. In some businesses a vouchers payable system replaces the accounts payable system.

INVENTORY CONTROL SYSTEM

Inventory control involves recording inventory transactions in the ledger accounts as well as having control over the physical handling of these assets. The need for strict inventory control varies from one business to another. In merchandise businesses, such as jewellery stores, inventory control is critical; in some service businesses, such as travel agencies, it is not a significant accounting concern. Inventory control should safeguard stock on hand and keep inventory balances to a reasonable and cost-efficient level.

Payroll System

The payroll system must work perfectly. Employees demand to be paid the exact wage or salary owing to them on pay day. The government wants the deductions from employees' paycheques to be accurately calculated and submitted on time. And business managers need exact payroll costs entered into general ledger accounts at the end of each time period so that they can make good management decisions.

Cost Accounting System

Cost accounting involves the calculation of labour, materials, and overhead costs for a specific job. Manufacturing concerns, and some service businesses, need a formal cost accounting system. If set up properly, the cost accounting system ensures proper job pricing and, therefore, profitability. Cost accounting systems are essentially job cost or process cost systems.

Q U E S T I O N S

1. Name the basic accounting systems found in accounting.

2. Look at Figure 1-1 and indicate which of the systems is involved in the following accounting operations.
   (a) calculating the correct wage for an employee
   (b) computing interest on a customer's account
   (c) making a daily bank deposit
   (d) calculating an amount owing to a supplier
   (e) re-ordering stock for a retail store
   (f) determining if a certain job will be profitable

3. Name the two main financial statements produced by the accounting process.

4. Select one, or more, of the accounting systems in Figure 1-1 that would be important for each of these businesses. Explain your answer(s).
   (a) a jewellery store
   (b) an auto repair garage
   (c) a fast food outlet
   (d) a department store

5. Visit a retail store in your community to find out which of the accounting systems are used by that store. Of those used, which system does the owner regard as the most important? Prepare a brief report on your findings.

1.2

Manual Accounting

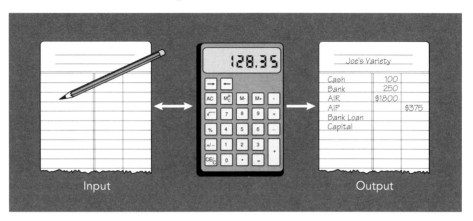

Input

Output

FIGURE 1-2   Manual accounting

When the practice of accounting was originally developed, entries were made by hand; even today many books are still kept using pencil and paper. This method is referred to as a manual method of accounting because all accounting transactions are recorded by hand. The development of the modern calculator considerably speeded up the processing of accounting data. And during the last two decades, calculators have shrunk in size from desktop models to powerful, hand-held electronic models. Some of these small calculators can generate printed tapes, which are very useful for checking inputted data.

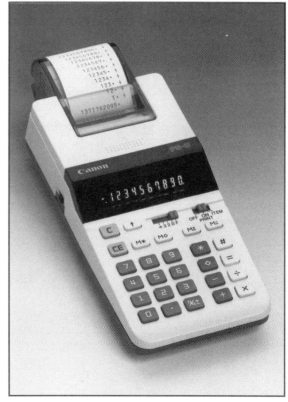

FIGURE 1-3
A printing calculator

Businesses that make accounting entries by hand but use a calculator to assist with the number crunching are still using a manual accounting method.

Calculators do speed up the processing of accounting data, but they do not guarantee that figures are accurate or that the books will balance. A good accountant will still use some estimating skills to determine if answers done with the aid of a calculator appear to be reasonable.

Many small businesses use a manual method called *one-write* for processing accounting data. The *one-write* produces three documents with *one writing* application. The accounting documents are mounted on a pegboard, one on top of the other. The documents are coated on the back so that when accounting information is written on the first document, the data is simultaneously transferred to the second and third documents. This reduces the amount of writing and is very efficient for a smaller business with few transactions.

Figure 1-4 shows a one-write application for accounts payable. When the accounting clerk writes out the creditor's cheque, the data is transferred to a cash flow report and to the purchases journal for the business. This saves time, since otherwise a clerk would have to write each of these documents out separately, transfering the data from one document to another.

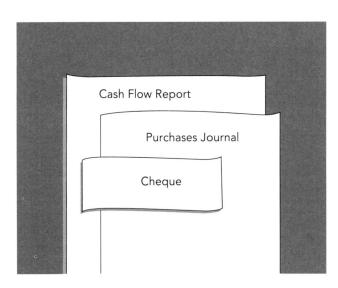

FIGURE 1-4   A one-write application

Q U E S T I O N S

6. What does the term *manual accounting* mean?

7. What is a "printing" calculator?

8. If people use calculators for accounting, will their work always be perfect? Explain.

9. Why must a person who uses a calculator also use estimating skills?

10. Why is it better to use a calculator with a tape, rather than just a display window, for your accounting work?

11. What is the advantage of the *one-write* method?

1.3

Computer Accounting

It is now a fairly common practice for many businesses to use a microcomputer for some aspect of their business operations. Because it is only natural that the use of microcomputers will increase, it is important for you to become familiar with this hardware, and with the computer software application packages that are used with microcomputers.

Figure 1-5 shows a microcomputer setup that consists of three main devices: an **input** device, a **central processing unit,** and an **output** device.

In the computer setup shown in this photograph, the input device is a keyboard. Computer keyboards are similar to ordinary typewriter keyboards because they have the same central layout of keys.

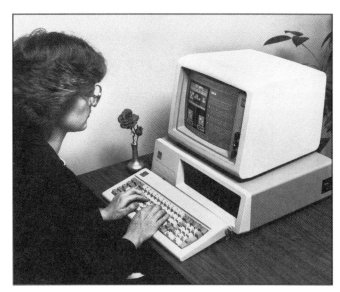

FIGURE 1-5
A microcomputer setup

In addition, computers usually have function keys, and a numeric keypad. Figure 1-6 gives a close-up of two popular styles of keyboard for a microcomputer.

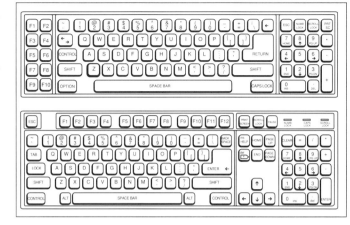

FIGURE 1-6   *Two popular styles of computer keyboard*

Notice the keys labelled F1 through F12. Depending on the software used, these function keys perform different operations. One key, for instance F10, might be used to save a file; another key, for instance F7, might be used to exit a program. Users will have to know their software to understand the uses of the various function keys.

The processing unit has two parts to it: the main memory and the central processing unit. Main memory consists of electronic parts (chips) that store the input data (numbers, letters, and special characters) received from the keyboard. The instructions needed to process the data, once it has been entered, are stored in the central processing unit. This unit receives information from the software and directs it to all other parts of the computer setup, including the screen and the printer.

Microcomputers have three types of disk drives. In Figure 1-7, you can see the two drives labelled 5 1/4″ and 3 1/2″. The third drive, the hard drive, is contained inside the computer. A hard drive that is said to have a storage capacity of 20 megabytes of information will hold about 20 000 000 characters of data.

FIGURE 1-7   *Disk drives*

The monitor, also called a video display terminal or screen, is similar to a television except that it can only display messages and prompts from the program plus information entered by the user. Monitors can be monochrome (one colour), or colour, with the clarity of the image depending on the quality of the monitor.

FIGURE 1-8   *A monitor*

"When you go to the bank tomorrow, you should find an extra $50,000 in your savings account."

A microcomputer setup is not really complete until it has a printer attached to it to make printouts (hard copy). Many home users of microcomputers do not buy a printer immediately, but later find the need to have a hard copy of the screen output. Businesses using a computer for accounting must have a printer to produce hard copies of statements and reports. Printers are of two types: dot matrix, with near-letter quality (NLQ), and laser. Dot matrix printers have print heads with pins that print dots to form letters, while laser printers use a technology similar to the one used in a photocopier. Laser printers have a print quality approaching the one in this textbook.

FIGURE 1-9   *A dot matrix printer*

The most advanced operations, of course, are those that use **computer accounting software** to record, save, and retrieve accounting data. Businesses that use microcomputers for their accounting may select an integrated software program that has these five main features:

1. Spreadsheet
2. Graphics
3. Database
4. Word Processing
5. Telecommunications

Microsoft Works, Lotus 1-2-3, and *First Choice,* for example, are integrated software packages that have spreadsheet, graphics, database, word processing, and telecommunication components; plus the ability to transfer data from one to another.

Because the first four applications listed above are very important, they will be discussed in more detail in the following sections. Included also will be examples of how each of these programs can be used in accounting.

QUESTIONS

12. Name the three main hardware devices found in a microcomputer setup.

13. How does a keyboard for a microcomputer differ from a typewriter keyboard?

14. What are the other names for a computer monitor?

15. What are the two functions of a processing unit in a microcomputer?

16. Name the three common types of disk drives that could be found in a microcomputer setup.

17. Explain, briefly, the difference between dot matrix output and laser output.

18. Check a newspaper to see if you can find the names of some computerized accounting packages being sold for businesses.

1.4

Spreadsheets / Graphics

An electronic **spreadsheet** is produced on a computer and is a useful accounting tool. It is comprised of rows, columns, and cells. A spreadsheet computer screen looks like Figure 1-10.

A **row** is an area of information that runs horizontally on a spreadsheet. A **column** is an area of information that runs vertically on a spreadsheet. A **cell** is located at the intersection of a row and a column, and is referred to by its proper column letter and row number. (A cell can also be referred to as an address.) In the diagram, only cell B2 has been highlighted, but every point of intersection between columns and rows represents a cell, or address, on a spreadsheet.

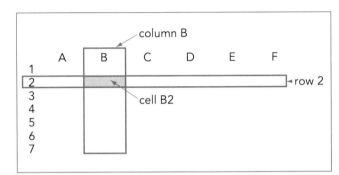

FIGURE 1-10
Features of a spreadsheet

Into each cell, you may enter either alphabetic information (such as a column heading) or numeric data (such as sales figures). Numeric data can be a positive value such as 20 000, a negative value such as 1 500–, or a decimal value such as 8.50. A cell can also be programmed with a formula, such as C6+C7+C8, that calculates an answer automatically.

An electronic accounting spreadsheet can take the place of manually prepared accounting tables. Let's examine an example of a manually prepared sales analysis that shows the sales figures of a business for the first three months of the year.

Sales Analysis For the First Quarter, 19 –				
	JAN.	FEB.	MAR.	TOTAL
Product A	25 000 –	27 000 –	28 000 –	80 000 –
Product B	30 000 –	25 000 –	20 000 –	75 000 –
Product C	27 000 –	26 000 –	27 000 –	80 000 –
Totals	82 000 –	78 000 –	75 000 –	235 000 –

FIGURE 1-11   *A manually prepared sales analysis*

Here is the same sales analysis as it would appear on the computer screen in spreadsheet form.

```
        A           B          C          D          E          F
 1   Sales Analysis
 2   For the First Quarter, 19-
 3
 4                   JAN        FEB        MAR       TOTAL
 5
 6   Product A      25000      27000      28000      80000
 7   Product B      30000      25000      20000      75000
 8   Product C      27000      26000      27000      80000
 9                 ------     ------     ------     ------
10   Totals         82000      78000      75000     235000
11                 ======     ======     ======     ======
12
```

FIGURE 1-12   *A sales analysis spreadsheet*

Numeric data is automatically right justified when entered onto a spreadsheet. Any alphabetic data is left justified. In this example, the column headings have been adjusted to line up with the numeric data in each column. Cell B10 has been programmed to add the numbers in B6, B7, and B8. Cells C10, D10, and E10 have also been programmed to add their columns of data. Cells E6, E7, and E8 have all been programmed to add across the spreadsheet. Cell E6 contains the formula B6+C6+D6. Figure 1-12 highlights the cells that have been programmed on this spreadsheet.

Like the accountant's manual worksheet, a computer spreadsheet consists of rows and columns. But the computer spreadsheet is a much better accounting tool because it automatically performs mathematical calculations on columns or rows of figures, when programmed with a **formula** to do so.

Any cell can be programmed with a formula that depends on data in other cells. This principle of cells being related to other cells is what gives the spreadsheet its power. It will automatically recalculate all answers affected by any change, using the formulas built into it. This is called the "what if" scenario in accounting. For example, in the spreadsheet above you could say, "What if Product A had sales of $30 000 in January?" When you enter the new sales figure, the following result will automatically appear on the computer screen.

	A	B	C	D	E	F
1	Sales Analysis					
2	For the First Quarter, 19-					
3						
4		JAN	FEB	MAR	TOTAL	
5						
6	Product A	30000	27000	28000	85000	
7	Product B	30000	25000	20000	75000	
8	Product C	27000	26000	27000	80000	
9						
10	Totals	87000	78000	75000	240000	
11						
12						

FIGURE 1-13   *A revised spreadsheet sales analysis*

When the 25 000 sales figure in cell B6 is changed to 30 000, the totals in cells B10, E6, and E10 will change automatically.

Spreadsheets have other powers that make them far more efficient than manually prepared accounting documents:

- You can expand the width of columns, depending on the software, to 40 or more characters. Also, some columns can be set wider than others.
- Columns can be set to automatically enter the decimal point if you enter dollar amounts on the spreadsheet.
- Dollar signs can be inserted beside any row or column of numbers that you wish.
- Formulas can be replicated quickly by the spreadsheet. Replication means that a formula only has to be entered once, and it can be automatically placed in other cells with the correct cell designations.
- Some spreadsheets allow you to sort the columns in ascending or descending order.
- Most spreadsheets have graphics capabilities which can be called upon to produce line graphs, bar graphs, or pie graphs at the stroke of a key.
- All spreadsheet programs allow users to print the contents of a spreadsheet. Users have to remember, however, that many printers will only accept paper that is 85 columns wide. Some spreadsheets will turn sideways, though, so that they print lengthwise on the paper.

Spreadsheets are a powerful tool when used for the correct accounting application. As you progress through the text, you will see several examples and problems using spreadsheet theory.

Graphics software is a program that presents spreadsheet data in picture form. For many of us, pictures convey a stronger, more lasting impression of things; a statistical table, on the other hand, has to be carefully studied to understand what it is trying to say. Let's explore this idea by looking at a table of data and then seeing the same table in picture form. Here is a manually prepared monthly sales commission report for eight real estate salespersons who work in a small firm.

When this data is fed into a computer using a graphics package, several graph styles can be produced. Three such graphs would be a bar graph, a line graph, and a pie graph (pie chart). The table in Figure 1-14 was converted to the bar graph, Figure 1-15.

Monthly Sales Commissions September 19–	
Ambert	$3 600
Davis	5 700
Dinsmore	1 400
Henhawk	4 300
Kingsley	5 000
Monroe	8 700
Seth	6 200
Wong	5 600

FIGURE 1-14
A manually prepared monthly sales commission report

FIGURE 1-15
A computer-generated bar graph.

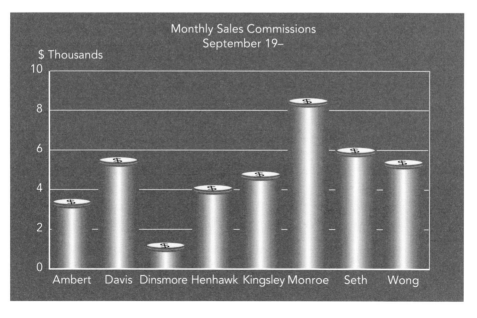

Think about which of these two forms of reporting creates a stronger impression. On the bar graph, Monroe clearly stands out as the top salesperson, yet reading the data in the table format does not create as strong an impression. It is also very evident that Dinsmore's sales are extremely low and some managerial action is called for with this salesperson.

Graphics are an important means of presenting accounting information. They are also used to help sell or promote a product or idea. Business presentations to salespersons, customers, creditors, and management frequently include graphics.

Here are two samples of the other types of graphs, the line graph and the pie graph, using the same monthly sales commission data.

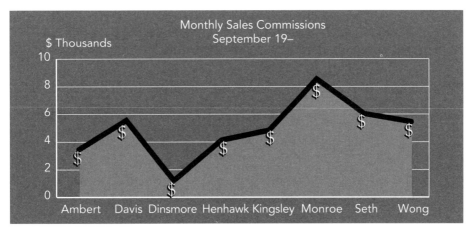

FIGURE 1-16   A line graph

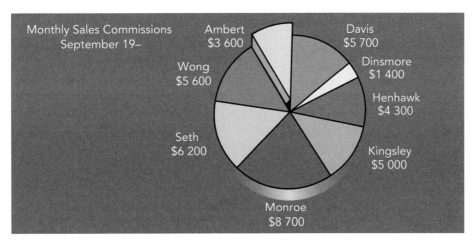

FIGURE 1-17   A pie graph

A line graph is especially useful for showing the progression or trend of sales over a year, or even several years. The pie graph in Figure 1-17 uses different shading to separate the sections of the pie. On all three graphs, colour can be used most effectively to enhance the impact of the accounting data presented to viewers.

Q U E S T I O N S

19. How are spreadsheets labelled for columns? for rows?

20. What two names are used to identify the point at which a row and a column intersect?

21. What three types of numbers can be placed onto a spreadsheet?

22. What does the term "what if" refer to when using spreadsheets?

23. Explain, in your own words, seven features that are fairly common to all spreadsheets.

24. Most graphics packages will print at least three basic types of graphs. What are they?

25. How can graphs be enhanced, i.e., made more attractive to read?

26. Of the three graph samples shown in this section, which one do you think is easiest to read? Be prepared to defend your answer.

1.5

Databases

Businesses have a great need to file accounting information, and a database is a useful computer tool for this purpose. Some accounting files needed, for example, might be payroll information about employees, addresses for customers, product listings for creditors, or inventory descriptions. The word **database** refers to one or more files of information that are accessed using database management software.

In manual record keeping, information about individual debtors is often recorded on separate sheets or cards. These cards contain information about customers of a business and are arranged in alphabetical order and filed, along with other customer cards, in a book or drawer in the Accounts Receivable department.

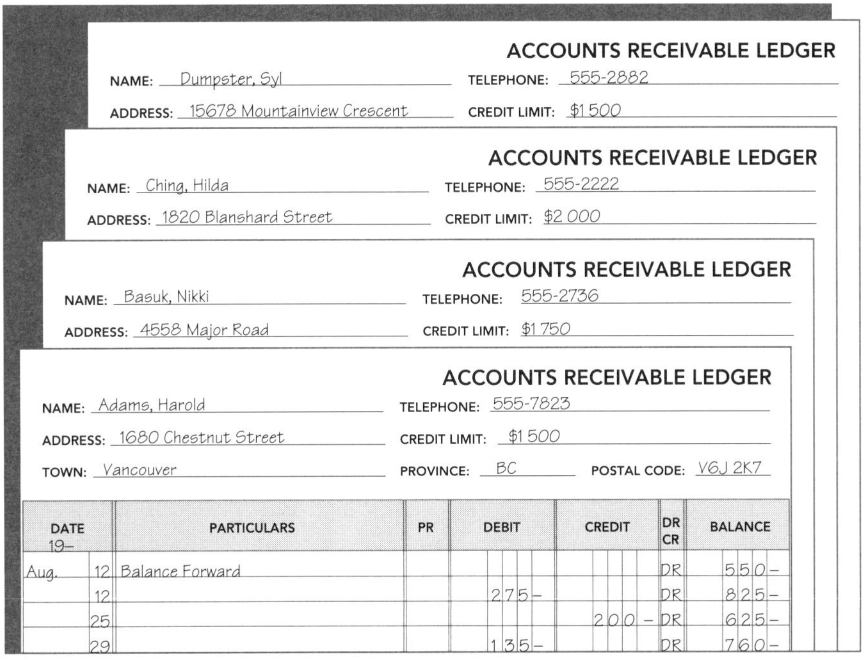
ACCOUNTS RECEIVABLE LEDGER
NAME: Dumpster, Syl TELEPHONE: 555-2882
ADDRESS: 15678 Mountainview Crescent CREDIT LIMIT: $1 500

ACCOUNTS RECEIVABLE LEDGER
NAME: Ching, Hilda TELEPHONE: 555-2222
ADDRESS: 1820 Blanshard Street CREDIT LIMIT: $2 000

ACCOUNTS RECEIVABLE LEDGER
NAME: Basuk, Nikki TELEPHONE: 555-2736
ADDRESS: 4558 Major Road CREDIT LIMIT: $1 750

ACCOUNTS RECEIVABLE LEDGER
NAME: Adams, Harold TELEPHONE: 555-7823
ADDRESS: 1680 Chestnut Street CREDIT LIMIT: $1 500
TOWN: Vancouver PROVINCE: BC POSTAL CODE: V6J 2K7

DATE 19–		PARTICULARS	PR	DEBIT	CREDIT	DR CR	BALANCE
Aug.	12	Balance Forward				DR	550–
	12			275–		DR	825–
	25				200 –	DR	625–
	29			135–		DR	760–

FIGURE 1-18 *Accounts receivable cards*

In Figure 1-18 there are four customer cards. Each card is called a record. A **record** is a collection of related fields about one customer. Each record has seven fields of information about a customer at the top of the card, e.g., name, street, town, province, postal code, telephone number, and credit limit. This information is relatively permanent and can easily be stored in database form. A **field** is one piece of information about a customer, e.g., name. The whole set of records is referred to as a customer **file**.

In a computerized system, the file of records above would be stored on either a hard disk or on floppy disks. The setup would look like this.

CUSTOMER FILE

Name	Address	Town	Prov.	PC	Telephone	Credit
Adams, Harold	1680 Chestnut St.	Vancouver	BC	V6J 2K7	555-2736	$1 500
Basuk, Nikki	4558 Major Road	Vancouver	BC	V7J 3L3	555-2763	$1 750
Ching, Hilda	1820 Blanshard	Vancouver	BC	V5G 2N9	555-2222	$2 000
Dumpster, Syl	15678 Mountainview	Vancouver	BC	V6K 3L5	555-2882	$1 500

FIGURE 1-19 *Printout of an accounts receivable file*

In this customer file there are four records, each with seven fields of data. In order to store this information on a disk, you would have to name the file and give it a defined structure. You tell the computer:

1. the field headings
2. the field size
3. the data types (may be optional)

The field headings used are Name, Street, Town, Prov., PC, Telephone, and Credit. The field sizes are 14 spaces for Name, 18 spaces for Street, 10 for Town, 5 for Prov., 7 for PC, 9 for Telephone, and 7 for Credit. Most software will allow users to change field widths after data is entered. The term **data type** indicates whether data is alphabetic, numeric, or alphanumeric (a combination of numbers, letters, and/or special characters). If numeric, it could be integer data, that is with no decimal places, or it could contain decimals. The telephone number entered above is alphanumeric because of the special character (the dash).

Once you have created a database, you can enter the customer information. Any record can be changed at any time. You can add records, delete records, or select certain records. This process is called editing the file. The word **edit** means to make changes to the data in a record, file, or database.

Databases usually have several powerful commands that you can access. Here are some examples of operations that can be performed on the data you have stored.

- Sort records into ascending or descending alphabetical order, e.g., by customer name.
- Select certain records for viewing, e.g., all customers whose outstanding balances are over $500.00.
- Calculate such answers as the total balance owing by all your customers.

Some databases are program-driven and need keyed-in commands to perform; for instance, SORT NAME might sort the records by last name. TOTAL might total any field that you indicate, and SELECT might look for certain customer records you want to see. The commands used vary, of course, from one database program to another.

Other databases are menu-driven. A **menu** is a list of choices shown on a computer screen. Figure 1-20 is an example of a screen menu.

Menu-driven software is referred to as user-friendly software, but the fact that it is termed so does not guarantee ease of use. A person using accounting software will be better prepared if he or she knows a lot of accounting theory.

```
┌─────────────────────────────────┐
│  ████████████████████████████   │
│  █   Accounts Receivable File   │
│  ████████████████████████████   │
│    1. ADD new customer records. │
│    2. DELETE old customers.     │
│    3. EDIT (change) records.    │
│    4. SORT the customer file.   │
│    5. SELECT certain customers. │
│    6. EXIT the A/R file.        │
│                                 │
└─────────────────────────────────┘
```

FIGURE 1-20
The screen menu for an accounts receivable file

Q U E S T I O N S

27. What is the difference between a database and a file?

28. In an accounts receivable system, what constitutes a file? a record? a field?

29. What does the phrase *data type* mean?

30. Indicate which data type each of the following fields would be (i.e., alphabetic, alphanumeric, or numeric).

(a) a customer's telephone number
(b) a customer's name
(c) a customer's balance owing
(d) a customer's address

31. Research a database program and describe some of the operations you can perform on data using the program.

1.6

Word Processing / Integrated Software

Word processing software is a writing tool for preparing letters, reports and other accounting documents. Word processing may not be used as extensively in accounting as the other four types of software packages discussed here. Nevertheless, it is important to recognize that there are several accounting-related documents that can be keyed in and stored on a word processor for later use.

Consider the following document. It is part of a report issued by an auditing firm at the conclusion of its work on a business.

Auditor's Report

We have examined the balance sheet of The Primrose Inn as at December 31, 19– and the statements of income and changes in financial position for the year then ended.

Our examination was made in accordance with generally accepted auditing standards and included such tests and other procedures as we considered necessary in the circumstances.

In our opinion these financial statements present fairly the financial position of The Primrose Inn as at December 31, 19– and the results of its operations and the changes in its financial position for the year then ended, in accordance with generally accepted accounting principles applied on a basis consistent with that of the preceding year.

Clarkson, Gordon & Co.   February 28, 19–

By storing this document on disk, the auditing firm does not have to retype it each year. It can be accessed, and amended if need be, the dates can be changed, and a new copy can be printed.

Word processing is also used effectively in accounting applications where certain form letters are sent out regularly. For instance, amounts overdue from customers will often generate a reminder letter. The master can be stored on disk and recalled whenever it is necessary to contact a tardy customer.

After you have read the following letter, consider what changes would have to be made before a similar letter could be sent to another customer.

Once the letter has been printed, the disk copy can be stored and used for any customer who is delinquent. The only items that need to be changed are the date, address, salutation, and amount owing. By using a word processor, this task can be completed quickly and efficiently. A word processor has these advantages over a typewriter:

• Error correction on word processed documents is effortless.
• When words have to be added, they are merely inserted and the original text shifts automatically to make room.
• Sections of the original text can be easily deleted.
• Storage of accounting documents on disk is very compact yet the documents are easily accessible.

September 10, 19–

Ms. Angie Coro
230 Huron St.
Saskatoon, SK
S7N 2J2

Dear Ms. Coro

On reviewing our accounts receivable records at the end of our fiscal year, we noticed that your account is 90 days past due. We are sure that this is merely an oversight on your part, and would appreciate receiving the amount owing by return mail.
    Your balance outstanding as of August 31 was $120.
    A stamped, self-addressed envelope is enclosed for your convenience in remitting the balance to us.

Yours truly

Wayne Caslick
Credit Officer
Encl.

This first chapter should leave you with the impression that computers and the software run on them play an important part in accounting. The applications that follow will reinforce this idea, as well as review important accounting principles.

You can take all of the component parts of an integrated package and link them together to produce output. Assume that you want to send a congratulatory letter to the top salesperson for last year, Bert Rush. The letter will include a spreadsheet of his sales, and a graph showing the sales in bar graph form. Bert's name and address will be taken from the company database file of employee information. This project integrates the computer components discussed in this systems chapter:
 1. Spreadsheet $\rightarrow$ Bert's sales table for one year
 2. Graphics $\rightarrow$ the bar graph of sales data
 3. Database $\rightarrow$ Bert's mailing address
 4. Word Processing $\rightarrow$ the letter to Bert

By using the four programs in an integrated package, you can maximize the use of a computer system for accounting purposes. Here is the letter sent to Bert. Notice the four components as they are highlighted in Figure 1-21.

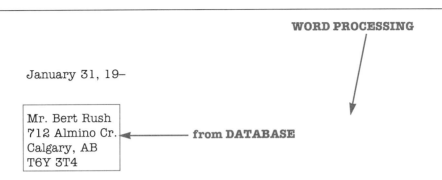

January 31, 19–

Mr. Bert Rush
712 Almino Cr. ◄——————— from **DATABASE**
Calgary, AB
T6Y 3T4

Dear Bert

Congratulations on achieving the status of top salesperson for our company this past year. Your sales record was a remarkable achievement. According to our records, this is the summary of your sales for the year 19–, as summarized for each sales quarter:

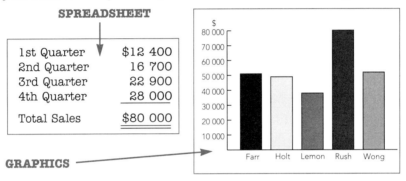

SPREADSHEET

1st Quarter	$12 400
2nd Quarter	16 700
3rd Quarter	22 900
4th Quarter	28 000
Total Sales	$80 000

GRAPHICS

When compared, in graph form, with other salespersons, you will note that your record stands out as an example for others to aim for. A bonus cheque of $1 000 is being mailed to you in appreciation of your efforts. Keep up the good work.

Yours truly

J. Gladstone, President
SECURITY SYSTEMS LTD.

FIGURE 1-21
An integrated letter

Another example of integration in accounting using the computer would be to combine a list of customer names, addresses, and overdue balances (from a customer database), with a covering letter (using word processing). Figure 1-22 shows this.

More applications will be displayed in subsequent chapters of the text.

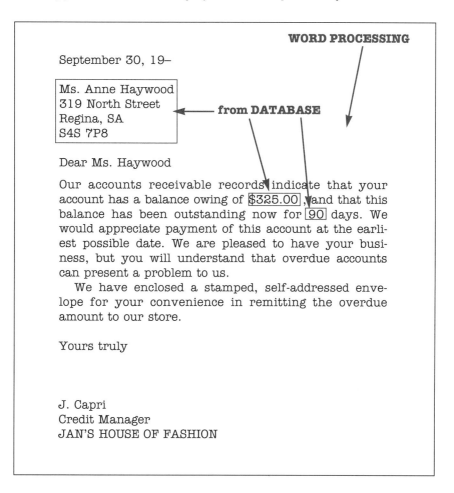

WORD PROCESSING

September 30, 19–

Ms. Anne Haywood
319 North Street
Regina, SA
S4S 7P8

from DATABASE

Dear Ms. Haywood

Our accounts receivable records indicate that your account has a balance owing of $325.00, and that this balance has been outstanding now for 90 days. We would appreciate payment of this account at the earliest possible date. We are pleased to have your business, but you will understand that overdue accounts can present a problem to us.

We have enclosed a stamped, self-addressed envelope for your convenience in remitting the overdue amount to our store.

Yours truly

J. Capri
Credit Manager
JAN'S HOUSE OF FASHION

FIGURE 1-22
A customer overdue letter

Q U E S T I O N S

32. Why is a word processing package an important piece of software in accounting?

33. Assume that you have saved on disk a letter to a customer reminding her about her outstanding balance. What information would you change to use this same letter format for another customer?

34. There are many excellent word processing software packages being sold for microcomputers today. Check a daily newspaper to find the names of at least five.

1.7

Bedford Exercise 1 — The Musicman

General ledger software handles accounting transactions from journalizing source documents through to the preparation of financial statements. You will find that working with this type of software package will enable you to quickly and accurately enter accounting data, thus allowing the program to process that information in a number of ways. This powerful tool also allows you, with a few keystrokes, to quickly access useful information any time it is needed. You will generally find that accounting packages are user-friendly, but they do have some very strict protocols that must be followed to obtain the best results and minimize frustration. *ACCPAC Bedford Integrated Accounting* is one of several accounting packages that is suitable to the needs and requirements of small businesses.

GETTING STARTED

The explanations in this section are for three systems on which *Bedford* may be installed.

If your computer system has two floppy disk drives, drive A is for the program disk, and drive B is for the data disk.

If your computer system has a hard drive, or is part of a Local Area Network (LAN), you can use the hard disk (drive C), or fileserver, to store both the program and the data. However, it is a good data processing procedure to backup your data on a floppy disk. In the case of a LAN, the program is installed by a person designated as the SYSOP (System Operator). For security reasons, the SYSOP is the only person allowed to perform this function. On many systems, space designated on the fileserver to hold programs is commonly referred to as drive F, and space set aside to store the data files is commonly referred to as drive H. Users of programs on a LAN must also have clearance from the systems operator by using an identification code and password to gain access to the system.

Access the *Bedford* file. Your teacher will tell you how to do this. The following will appear on your screen:

GENERAL	PAYABLE	RECEIVABLE	PAYROLL	INVENTORY	JOBCOST	SYSTEM

Company...d:\[path]

FIGURE 1-23   *Status line with path*

BEDFORD DATA FILES

The company files for each of the nine chapters in this text have already been saved for you on a data disk. You will be accessing the company files and making accounting entries to change the accounting data for the companies you work with. The company for this chapter is called The Musicman, a disc jockey service operated by a recent college graduate.

The Musicman is a sole proprietorship owned by Troy Winkworth and based in his home in Edmonton, Alberta. Dance revenue for The Musicman has been growing for some time and Troy has decided to use *ACCPAC Bedford Integrated Accounting* software to computerize his accounting records.

All of the account balances for The Musicman are stored on the data disk that accompanies this textbook. The business has just completed a fiscal year and the trial balance for the business as of the first day of the first month of the next fiscal year is:

The Musicman
Trial Balance
as at 1st day of next fiscal year

No.	Account	Debit	Credit
110	Bank	$ 8 000	
120	A/R — Bowman S.S.	800	
121	A/R — Valley Heights S.S.	0	
122	A/R — Terry Fox S.S.	0	
123	A/R — College Ave. S.S.	0	
130	Music Supplies	3 000	
180	Van	25 000	

185	Music Equipment	17 000	
210	Bank Loan		6 500
220	A/P — Elite Sound Service		3 500
221	A/P — Nethercott Printing		0
222	A/P — Bell Canada		0
310	T. Winkworth, Capital		43 800
315	T. Winkworth, Drawings	0	
410	Dance Revenue		0
510	Advertising Expense	0	
520	Bank Charges	0	
530	Miscellaneous Expense	0	
540	Telephone Expense	0	
550	Van Expense	0	
		$ 53 800	$ 53 800

Documented now are *Bedford* instructions that will show you how to:
(1) access the general ledger accounts for The Musicman;
(2) journalize several transactions for the business; and
(3) prepare a set of financial statements for the business.

Follow the instructions carefully, step by step! As you work through the entire exercise for The Musicman, you may want to refer back to the trial balance above for help in journalizing the accounting transactions.

ACCESSING THE MUSICMAN GENERAL LEDGER

Insert your data disk into drive B (the one on the right or on the bottom).
To retrieve the general ledger for The Musicman, you use the file name **musicman**. Key in the letter of the drive that contains your data file, followed by a colon, backslash, and the file name. That is, key in
b:\musicman
Even when you key in a lower case letter for the drive name, it will appear as an upper case letter. See Figure 1-24.

GENERAL	PAYABLE	RECEIVABLE	PAYROLL	INVENTORY	JOBCOST	SYSTEM

Company: B:\musicman.......................................d:\[path]

FIGURE 1-24   *Status line with company name*

Press [Enter] (or [↵]). The following will appear on screen:

GENERAL	PAYABLE	RECEIVABLE	PAYROLL	INVENTORY	JOBCOST	SYSTEM

FIGURE 1-25   *Status line*

As previously mentioned, the accounts and all of the historical balances have been entered onto a data disk for you. The accounting system only has to be set in the **Ready** mode. To do this you select **SYSTEM**, **Default**, **Module**, and **General**, as follows:

1. Press [→] to highlight **SYSTEM** and then press [↓] to access the

    SYSTEM module. The following appears on screen:

GENERAL	PAYABLE	RECEIVABLE	PAYROLL	INVENTORY	JOBCOST	SYSTEM

Status
Save
Finish
Advance
Default
Integrate
Purge

FIGURE 1-26   *Status line showing* **SYSTEM** *options*

2. Press [↓] to **Default** and [→] for access to **Default** options.

GENERAL	PAYABLE	RECEIVABLE	PAYROLL	INVENTORY	JOBCOST	SYSTEM

Module
Display
Print
Export

FIGURE 1-27   **Default** *options*

3. Press ⟦→⟧ to select **Module**.

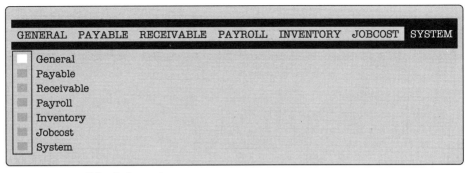

FIGURE 1-28 **Module** *options*

4. Press ⟦→⟧ to select **General**.

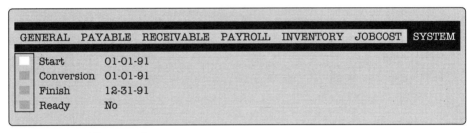

FIGURE 1-29 **General** *options*

5. Using the information provided by your teacher, enter the **Start**, **Conversion**, and **Finish** dates available on your *Bedford* program. Be sure you have entered the dates correctly following the mmddyy (month/day/year) sequence, since once the program is in the **Ready** mode it is not possible to make further changes to these dates.

   Finally, move your cursor down beside **Ready** and press ⟦→⟧ .

6. Press ⟦←⟧ once to save your changes, and twice more to return to

   SYSTEM options. Your screen will look like Figure 1-30, with **Default** highlighted.

   Press ⟦↑⟧ to get to **Finish**. Then press ⟦→⟧ to exit the program.

   Note that the program automatically saves all changes when you exit. Watch for the

   * * * **saving** * * *

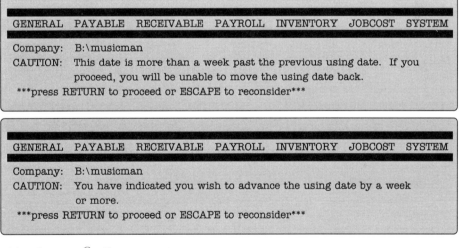

GENERAL PAYABLE RECEIVABLE PAYROLL INVENTORY JOBCOST SYSTEM

Status
Save
Finish
Advance
Default
Integrate
Purge

FIGURE 1-30   Status line showing Default highlighted

7. Now load *Bedford* again. Key in **b:\musicman** and press ⌜Enter⌝. You will be asked for the **Using** date. Enter the **Using** date provided by your teacher. Remember the sequence, mmddyy. *Bedford* will respond with two cautions that the date you have chosen is for a time period of more than a week. See Figure 1-31. You can ignore these messages and proceed, by pressing ⌜Enter⌝ or ⌜↵⌝ as suggested on the screen.

GENERAL PAYABLE RECEIVABLE PAYROLL INVENTORY JOBCOST SYSTEM

Company: B:\musicman
CAUTION: This date is more than a week past the previous using date. If you
           proceed, you will be unable to move the using date back.
 press RETURN to proceed or ESCAPE to reconsider

GENERAL PAYABLE RECEIVABLE PAYROLL INVENTORY JOBCOST SYSTEM

Company: B:\musicman
CAUTION: You have indicated you wish to advance the using date by a week
           or more.
 press RETURN to proceed or ESCAPE to reconsider

FIGURE 1-31   Cautions

The main status line now appears across the top of your screen.

GENERAL PAYABLE RECEIVABLE PAYROLL INVENTORY JOBCOST SYSTEM

FIGURE 1-32   Status line

JOURNALIZING TRANSACTIONS

You are now ready to journalize transactions.

1. Press ⬇ to use the **GENERAL** module.

The following appears on screen.

GENERAL	PAYABLE	RECEIVABLE	PAYROLL	INVENTORY	JOBCOST	SYSTEM

☐ Ledger
▨ Journal
▨ Display
▨ Print
▨ Export
▨ Import

FIGURE 1-33   **GENERAL** *options*

2. Press ⬇ to select **Journal**.

3. Press ➡ to access the **Journal** option.

The following appears on screen.

GENERAL	PAYABLE	RECEIVABLE	PAYROLL	INVENTORY	JOBCOST	SYSTEM

☐ Comment...
▨ Source
▨ Date
▨ Account
▨   Amount
▨ Project
▨   Amount

FIGURE 1-34   **Journal** *option*

You are going to enter the transaction to record a sales invoice dated the 3rd of this month. Sales invoice M344 is the source document that is evidence of a sale of services performed for Bowman Secondary School, for $650 for another school dance. A/R—Bowman S.S. (account 120) is debited, and Dance Revenue (account 410) is credited, $650.

4. The **Comment** line is used for recording the explanation for each transaction for example, sales invoice. A maximum of 26 characters may be used for an explanation. Notice that the beginning letter in each word is capitalized automatically.
Key in: sales invoice

Press Enter

5. The **Source** line is used to record the number of the source document.
Key in: M344

Press Enter

6. The **Date** line is used to record the date of the source document.
Key in: mm03yy (Remember to enter the month (mm) and the year (yy) you are using.)

7. Key in: 120
The **Account** name is printed automatically as soon as the last number

of the code is put in. (Press the down cursor ↓ to see all the accounts.)

Do not press Enter .

8. On the **Amount** line, it is not necessary to key in the dollar sign, or decimals if there are no cents.
Key in: 650

Press Enter

9. You will be prompted for the account again.
Key in: 410
The name of the account affected appears on the account line of the

screen. There is no need to press Enter .

10. You will see a prompt ▌650▌ beside the entry place for the amount. To use it and place it quickly into the amount area:

Hold down Shift and press Enter . This is called the default option.

11. Check the accuracy of your transaction before you post it.

Press: F2 to see your general journal entry.

Press: F2 to return to the original screen.

You may use the F2 key to review a transaction at any time. If you have made an error in journalizing the transaction, use the escape key

Esc to return to step 3.

12. The posting procedure involves two key strokes:

    i) Press ⌷Enter⌷ . This moves the cursor to the left of the word **Comment**.

    ii) Press ⌷←⌷ to post the entry.

You are now ready to journalize the remaining transactions. For each transaction, follow steps 3 to 12. Enter debits first, and credits second, as you would in manual accounting.

TRANSACTIONS

2. Cash Receipt 176   Dated: mm03yy
   From Bowman S.S., paying their account in full, $1 450.
   You must enter a minus sign (–) before or after an amount that
   decreases an account.

3. Cheque 111   Dated: mm03yy
   To the Bank of Montreal $1 576; of this amount $76 is for interest on
   the bank loan, the rest a reduction of the principal.
   (Note: You must enter a minus sign for the debit to Bank Loan and a
   minus sign for the credit to the Bank account, since we are decreasing
   these accounts; the debit to Bank Charges is normal.)

4. Sales Invoice M345   Dated: mm10yy
   To Valley Heights S.S., $700 for a school dance.

5. Cheque 112   Dated: mm10yy
   To Carillion Music Centre, $450 for music supplies.

6. Cheque 113   Dated: mm10yy
   To City Garage, $210 for gasoline for the van.

7. Sales Invoice M346   Dated: mm17yy
   To Terry Fox S.S., $800 for a dance.

8. Purchase Invoice 3489   Dated: mm17yy
   From Nethercott Printing, $465 for advertising brochures.

9. Cheque 114   Dated: mm17yy
   To Elite Sound Service, $500 payment on account.

10. Sales Invoice M347   Dated: mm24yy
    To College Avenue S.S., $1 000 for a dance.

11. Billing Statement 1133   Dated: mm30yy
    From Bell Canada, $218.50 for telephone bill.

12. Cheque 115   Dated: mm30yy
    To Terry's Garage, $465 for van repairs.

13. Cheque 116   Dated: mm30yy
    To the owner for drawings, $850. (Drawings is a minus entry, because it
    eventually decreases capital.)

DISPLAYING

Press ⬇ to move from **Journal** to **Display**.

Press ➡ to access any of the six **Display** options.

The following will appear on screen.

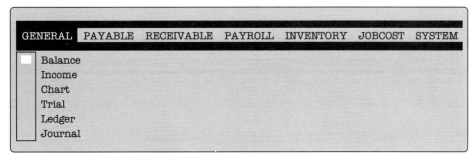

GENERAL	PAYABLE	RECEIVABLE	PAYROLL	INVENTORY	JOBCOST	SYSTEM
Balance
Income
Chart
Trial
Ledger
Journal

FIGURE 1-35   **Display** *options*

Access each of the above menu items to bring up a **Balance** sheet, an
Income statement, a **Chart** of accounts, a **Trial** balance, the general
Ledger accounts, and the general **Journal**. You may be prompted for
dates. Remember, a date is entered in the sequence mmddyy (month/
day/year).

PRINTING

Press ⬇ to move from **Display** to **Print**.

Press ➡ to access any of the six **Print** options.

Figure 1-36 will appear on screen.

You may access and print any of these. You may be prompted for dates.
Remember, a date is entered in the sequence mmddyy (month/day/year).

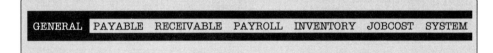


```
GENERAL  PAYABLE  RECEIVABLE  PAYROLL  INVENTORY  JOBCOST  SYSTEM
   Balance
   Income
   Chart
   Trial
   Ledger
   Journal
```

FIGURE 1-36   **Print** *options*

FINISHING A SESSION

Press ⎡Esc⎦ one or more times until the status line appears:

```
GENERAL  PAYABLE  RECEIVABLE  PAYROLL  INVENTORY  JOBCOST  SYSTEM
```

FIGURE 1-37   *Status line*

Press ⟶ until **SYSTEM** is highlighted.

Press ⟱ to access the **SYSTEM** module.

The following appears on screen.

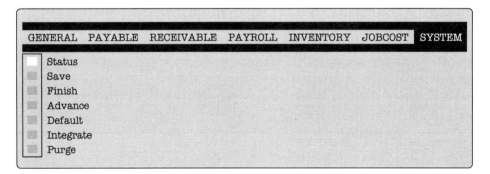

```
GENERAL  PAYABLE  RECEIVABLE  PAYROLL  INVENTORY  JOBCOST  SYSTEM
   Status
   Save
   Finish
   Advance
   Default
   Integrate
   Purge
```

FIGURE 1-38   **SYSTEM** *options*

Press ⟱ to select **Finish** option and ⟶ to exit the program.

Again, note that the program automatically saves all changes when you exit.

1.8

Dictionary of Accounting Terms

Accounts Payable System   The accounting controls necessary for accurate handling of supplier accounts.

Accounts Receivable System   The accounting controls necessary for accurate handling of customer accounts.

Cash Control System   The physical and accounting controls over cash handling.

Cell   The point of intersection of the row and the column on a spreadsheet.

Column   An area of information that runs vertically on a spreadsheet.

Computer Accounting   The use of a microcomputer to record, save, and retrieve accounting data.

Cost Accounting System   Calculating material, labour, and overhead costs for a job to ensure profitability.

Database   One or more computer data files.

Data Type   Indicates whether data is numeric, alphabetic, or alphanumeric.

Edit   To change the data in a record, file, or database.

Field   One piece of information about someone or something, e.g., a customer's name.

File   A group of records.

Formula   A program built into a specific cell by the user of a spreadsheet to perform calculations automatically.

General Ledger Software   A program that handles accounting transactions from journalizing source documents through to the preparation of financial statements.

Graphics   A computer program that presents data in graph form.

Inventory Control System   Involves recording inventory transactions in the ledger accounts, and having control over the physical handling of these assets.

Manual Accounting   Recording accounting transactions by hand.

Menu   A list of choices shown on a computer screen.

One-write   A method of producing several documents using only one writing entry.

Payroll System   The accounting controls that ensure accurate payment to employees.

Record   A number of fields of information about one person or thing.

Row   An area of information that runs horizontally on a spreadsheet.

Spreadsheet   A computer program that uses columns, rows, and cells to store data.

System   A term used to refer to the way individual accounting operations are performed.

Word Processing   A computer program that is a writing tool for preparing letters, reports, or other documents.

MANUAL EXERCISES

1. What are the missing system names in Figure 1-39?

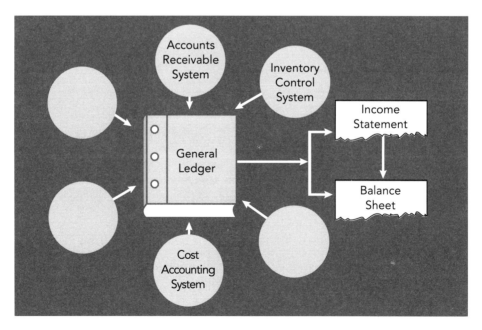

FIGURE 1-39

2. Match the terms on the left to their definitions on the right.

(a) Cash Control System		(1)	Keeps stock balances to efficient levels.
(b) Accounts Receivable System		(2)	Ensures that employees are paid accurately.
(c) Inventory Control System		(3)	Controls amounts owing from customers.
(d) Payroll System		(4)	Calculates the expected profit of a job.
(e) Accounts Payable System		(5)	Controls the most liquid asset of the business.
(f) Cost Accounting System		(6)	Controls amounts owing to suppliers.

3. For each of these situations, indicate to the owner of the business which accounting system needs to be changed.
   (a) The customers are allowing 60 days to pass without paying their accounts.
   (b) One of the cashiers has embezzled $2 000 from the business.
   (c) The business lost $1 000 on the last job it completed.
   (d) Two suppliers offered trade discounts to the business, but the invoices were paid too late to take advantage of the discounts.
   (e) An employee claims that too much income tax was deducted from her last paycheque.
   (f) The owner discovered that two expensive portable televisions were missing from the showroom floor.

4. Which of the six accounting systems would be most important for each of these businesses?
   (a) a swimming pool contractor
   (b) a ticket booth at a movie theatre
   (c) a retail store that sells leather coats
   (d) a telephone company

5. Indicate if these statements are true or false.
   (a) The systems described in this chapter are found in all businesses.
   (b) The main focus of the accounting process is to produce an income statement for the business.
   (c) Accounts receivable is the most liquid asset in any business.
   (d) Inventory control is important for merchandise businesses, but not service businesses.
   (e) One of the reasons to monitor accounts payable is to take advantage of supplier discounts.

(f) Not all businesses need a special cost accounting system.

(g) An accounting operation is designed to suit the business using it.

(h) The payroll system in a business is important only because the government demands careful recordkeeping.

(i) Accounting systems are separate and do not tie into the general ledger.

6. Total these accounting summaries using a hand-held or desktop calculator. See if you can beat the suggested time for each problem.

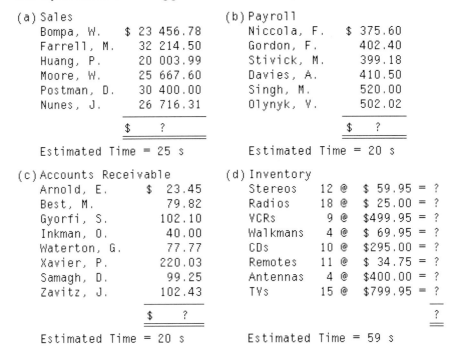

(a) Sales

Bompa, W.	$ 23 456.78
Farrell, M.	32 214.50
Huang, P.	20 003.99
Moore, W.	25 667.60
Postman, D.	30 400.00
Nunes, J.	26 716.31
	$?

Estimated Time = 25 s

(b) Payroll

Niccola, F.	$ 375.60
Gordon, F.	402.40
Stivick, M.	399.18
Davies, A.	410.50
Singh, M.	520.00
Olynyk, V.	502.02
	$?

Estimated Time = 20 s

(c) Accounts Receivable

Arnold, E.	$ 23.45
Best, M.	79.82
Gyorfi, S.	102.10
Inkman, O.	40.00
Waterton, G.	77.77
Xavier, P.	220.03
Samagh, D.	99.25
Zavitz, J.	102.43
	$?

Estimated Time = 20 s

(d) Inventory

Stereos	12 @	$ 59.95 = ?
Radios	18 @	$ 25.00 = ?
VCRs	9 @	$499.95 = ?
Walkmans	4 @	$ 69.95 = ?
CDs	10 @	$295.00 = ?
Remotes	11 @	$ 34.75 = ?
Antennas	4 @	$400.00 = ?
TVs	15 @	$799.95 = ?
		?

Estimated Time = 59 s

7. The answers that follow were all written manually by a senior accounting student who had used a hand-held calculator to do the calculations. He did not use estimation skills to see if the answers were reasonable. Can you estimate, and say which answers are not reasonable?

Monthly Sales

Jan.	$28 456.08
Feb.	32 614.50
Mar.	10 003.90
Apr.	25 667.60
May.	32 400.40
June	26 716.30
	$98 459.18

Payroll Summary

Adachi	$ 400.00
Brenner	389.90
Farmer	345.62
Jackson	430.75
Overdon	412.12
Parker	456.02
	$2 434.41

Accounts Payable

Hayes Garage	$ 321.00
Bell Canada	34.10
PUC	110.00
Websters	50.00
King Mfg.	440.00
OHIP	75.00
	$5 230.10

8. Name the hardware devices shown in Figure 1-40, a computer setup diagram.

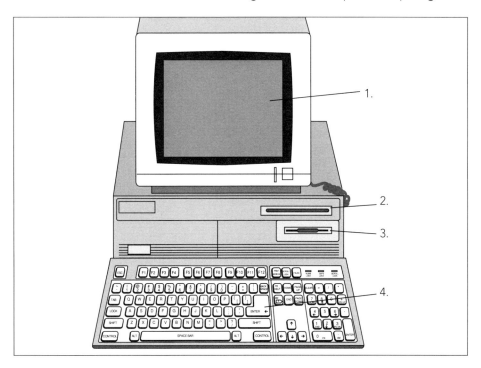

FIGURE 1-40

9. Name the parts of this computer keyboard.

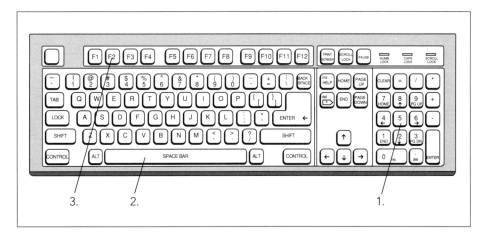

FIGURE 1-41

10. To review the parts of a microcomputer setup used for accounting, rewrite these sentences and complete them.
    (a) A microcomputer consists of a(n) _____ device, such as a keyboard, a(n) _____ unit, and a(n) _____ device such as a screen.
    (b) The place on a keyboard where all the number keys are is called the _____.
    (c) Most keyboards have ten keys, labelled F1 through F10. These are called _____ keys.
    (d) Another name for the computer screen is the _____.
    (e) Computer monitors can be either colour monitors or _____ monitors.
    (f) The instructions needed to process data on a computer are found in the _____.
    (g) Microcomputers can have three types of disk drives: a 5 1/4" floppy, a 3 1/2" floppy, and a(n) _____ drive.
    (h) A 40-megabyte hard disk drive holds approximately _____ characters.
    (i) Printers for computers vary, but most can be described either as _____ or as laser printers.

11. Use a calculator for the following accounting exercise.

	Assets	=	Liabilities	+	Capital
(a)	$ 20 500	=	$ 7 200	+	$?
(b)	$ 50 000	=	$?	+	$ 21 600
(c)	$?	=	$ 18 725	+	$ 40 275
(d)	$ 60 120	=	$ 15 790	+	$?
(e)	$ 92 784	=	$?	+	$ 10 354
(f)	$?	=	$ 52 344	+	$ 47 901
(g)	$?	=	$ 127 675	+	$ 67 325
(h)	$ 320 000	=	$?	+	$ 75 825
(i)	$ 567 218	=	$ 102 673	+	$?
(j)	$?	=	$ 245 666	+	$ 433 001

12. Calculate the balances for each of the T-accounts. Prepare a formal trial balance of the ledger. The date to be used is March 31, 19–, and the firm is J. Szabo Home Renovations.

GENERAL LEDGER

Bank		Accounts Receivable		Equipment	
2 345.69	400.00	400.00	200.00	900.00	
2 500.00	875.40	335.00		350.00	
400.00	175.00			502.34	
1 983.01	1 000.00				
200.00	200.00				
3 000.00	27.19				
	700.00				
	748.38				
	26.00				

Automobile		Bank Loan		Accounts Payable	
20 000.00		400.00	1 250.00	875.40	875.40
		1 000.00	2 500.00		350.00
					502.34
					36.92
					93.25

J. Szabo, Capital		J. Szabo, Drawings		Sales	
	22 293.93	125.00			887.67
	3 000.00	175.00			735.00
		200.00			1 983.01

Bank Charges		Car Expense		Rent Expense	
14.50		23.95		700.00	
26.00		36.92		700.00	
		27.19			

Utilities Expense		Wages Expense	
93.25		797.86	
		748.38	

13. Calculate the balances for each of the T-accounts. Prepare a formal trial balance of the ledger. The date to be used is August 31, 19–, and the firm is CanWest Programs.

GENERAL LEDGER

Bank	
11 726.45	800.00
1 000.00	750.00
1 775.00	325.00
700.00	556.65
	701.00
	701.00
	575.00
	900.00
	325.00
	27.50

Accounts Receivable	
700.00	700.00
870.00	

Computer Equipment	
4 900.00	
575.00	

Furniture & Fixtures	
2 000.00	
1 800.00	

Bank Loan	
750.00	3 000.00

Accounts Payable	
556.65	556.65
575.00	575.00
	1 000.00
	102.48
	66.49
	187.50

K. Toluda, Capital	
	15 679.73

K. Toluda, Drawings	
300.00	
325.00	
325.00	

Sales	
	1 990.07
	1 870.00
	1 775.00

Bank Charges	
50.00	
27.50	

Computer Expense	
50.00	
102.48	
66.49	

Rent Expense	
900.00	
900.00	

Utilities Expense	
187.50	

Wages Expense	
600.00	
701.00	
701.00	

14. Calculate the balances for each of the T-accounts, and prepare a formal trial balance of the ledger. The date to be used is October 31, 19–, and the firm is Crystal's Beauty Salon.

GENERAL LEDGER

Bank		A/R		Shop Equipment	
7 993.40	740.00	2 500.00	1 200.00	2 600.00	
866.33	1 000.00	500.00	700.00	740.00	
1 200.00	314.14			375.63	
971.28	285.00				
349.90	620.00				
700.00	825.00				
	302.08				
	900.00				
	35.00				

Office Equipment		Bank Loan		A/P	
1 800.00	260.00	1 000.00	4 000.00	314.14	314.14
620.00				620.00	100.00
285.00					620.00
					375.63

C. LeBlanc, Capital		C. LeBlanc, Drawings		Sales	
	11 579.66	800.00			900.22
		825.00			866.33
		260.00			971.28
					849.90

Advertising Expense		Bank Charges		Rent Expense	
75.00		50.00		900.00	
100.00		35.00		900.00	

Utilities Expense	
75.62	
302.08	

15. Using your knowledge from an earlier course in accounting and the information below, manually prepare a 6-column year-end worksheet for Richardson Tax Service. Extend, balance, and rule the worksheet.

No.	Account	Debit	Credit
	Richardson Tax Service		
	Trial Balance		
	April 30, 19-		
110	Bank	$ 4 850	
115	Accounts Receivable	13 990	
150	Equipment	25 750	
202	Bank Loan		$ 5 000
215	Accounts Payable		3 975
310	G. Richardson, Capital		12 576
315	G. Richardson, Drawings	12 000	
410	Sales		98 449
510	Advertising Expense	550	
515	Bank Charges	375	
520	Rent Expense	9 600	
525	Wages Expense	52 885	
		$120 000	$120 000

16. Manually prepare a 6-column year-end worksheet for Murray Graphics. Extend, balance, and rule the worksheet.

No.	Account	Debit	Credit
	Murray Graphics		
	Trial Balance		
	November 30, 19-		
100	Bank	$ 7 435	
110	Accounts Receivable	26 339	
120	Land	20 000	
130	Building	50 000	
140	Equipment	12 700	
200	Bank Loan		$ 12 000
220	Accounts Payable		15 004
300	D. Murray, Capital		65 664
310	D. Murray, Drawings	10 000	
400	Sales		112 332
500	Advertising Expense	1 429	
510	Bank Charges	215	
520	Office Supplies Expense	4 000	
530	Telephone Expense	1 082	
540	Utilities Expense	6 800	
550	Wages Expense	65 000	
		$205 000	$205 000

17. Using the data provided prepare a 6-column year-end worksheet for Benson Consulting as of July 31, 19–. Extend, balance, and rule the worksheet.

No.	Account	Balance
110	Bank	$ 3 021
115	Accounts Receivable	19 667
150	Office Equipment	28 500
215	Accounts Payable	7 827
310	G. Benson, Capital	42 511
315	G. Benson, Drawings	24 000
410	Sales	248 326
510	Advertising Expense	3 201
515	Automobile Expense	3 449
520	Office Supplies Expense	11 501
525	Rent Expense	14 400
530	Telephone Expense	925
535	Wages Expense	190 000

18. Using the data provided, prepare a 6-column year-end worksheet for Thompson Tool and Die as of March 31, 19–. Extend, balance, and rule the worksheet.

No.	Account	Balance
110	Bank	$ 11 202
115	Accounts Receivable	18 773
145	Office Equipment	3 000
150	Shop Equipment	82 774
155	Truck	32 000
210	Bank Loan (current)	4 000
215	Accounts Payable	3 006
250	Bank Loan (long-term)	12 000
310	T. Thompson, Capital	64 236
315	T. Thompson, Drawings	15 000
410	Sales	184 448
510	Advertising Expense	1 212
515	Bank Charges	2 972
520	Equipment Repairs Expense	4 950
523	Raw Materials Expense	20 000
525	Rent Expense	5 600
530	Supplies Expense	1 750
535	Telephone Expense	1 003
540	Truck Expense	4 003
545	Utilities Expense	6 681
550	Wages Expense	56 770

19. Prepare an income statement and a balance sheet for Richardson Tax Service using the worksheet you completed for exercise 15.
20. Prepare an income statement and a balance sheet for Murray Graphics using the worksheet you completed for exercise 16.
21. Prepare an income statement and a balance sheet for Benson Consulting using the worksheet you completed for exercise 17.
22. Prepare an income statement and a balance sheet for Thompson Tool & Die using the worksheet you completed for exercise 18.

COMPUTER EXERCISES

SS1   Use a spreadsheet to produce this accounting sales summary. Program the spreadsheet to calculate the total sales in cell B9. Save your solution on disk under the file name CH1SS1.

	A	B
1	SALES SUMMARY	
2	Brock, W.	23 456.78
3	Duong, N.	32 214.50
4	Holt, P.	20 003.99
5	Moti, W.	25 667.60
6	Post, D.	30 400.00
7	Quinn, J.	26 716.31
8		
9	Total	?
10		

SS2   Use a spreadsheet to produce this accounting payroll summary. Increase the width of column A to 15 characters. Program the spreadsheet to calculate the Gross Pay in column D (Column B * Column C). Insert dollar signs beside the Gross Pay figures, and program the spreadsheet to calculate the total Gross Pay in cell D9. Save your solution on disk under the file name CH1SS2.

	A	B	C	D
1	PAYROLL SUMMARY			
2	Skouros, F.	40	10.00	$?
3	Graham, F.	40	11.10	$?
4	Bonet, M.	38	10.05	$?
5	Van Meer, A.	25	10.20	$?
6	Sulu, M.	40	10.50	$?
7	Olin, V.	40	10.75	$?
8				
9			Total	$?
10				

SS3   (a) Create a 6-column worksheet for Monogram Plus, as shown in
Figure 1-42. Set columns A and B to a width of 10. Set columns C
through H to a width of 8. Program the spreadsheet (worksheet) as indicated and produce a printout. Save the template under the file name
CH1SS3. Note: Cell references and general program suggestions have
been provided. The program you use will require very specific instructions in order to pick up material from other cells or for performing
mathematical calculations. Follow the software instructions carefully.

	A	B	C	D	E	F	G	H
1	MONOGRAM PLUS		WORKSHEET			FOR THE YEAR ENDED MAY 31, 19-2		
2								
3	ACCOUNTS		TRIAL BALANCE		INCOME STATEMENT		BALANCE SHEET	
4								
5	Bank		500				C5	
6	Accounts Receivable		18000				C6	
7	Van		22500				C7	
8	Equipment		12600				C8	
9	Accounts Payable			2300				D9
10	Bank Loan			3700				D10
11	H. Dye, Capital			26000				D11
12	H. Dye, Drawings		12000				C12	
13	Sales			98000		D13		
14	Advertising Expense		1250		C14			
15	Bank Charges		450		C15			
16	Rent Expense		14400		C16			
17	Telephone Expense		965		C17			
18	Wages Expense		47335		C18			
19								
20			130000	130000	SUM	F13	SUM	SUM
21								
22	Net Income				F20-E20			E22
23								
24	BALANCING TOTALS				E20+E22	F20	G20	H20+H22
25								
26								

FIGURE 1-42

(b) Create an income statement for Monogram Plus in file CH1SS3 which you have just set up. Follow the format shown in Figure 1-43. Program the spreadsheet as indicated and produce a printout. Save your work under file name CH1SS3.

	A	B	C	D	E	F	G	H
33								
34								
35	MONOGRAM PLUS							
36	INCOME STATEMENT							
37	FOR THE YEAR ENDED MAY 31, 19-2							
38								
39	REVENUE							
40	Sales			F13				
41								
42	EXPENSES							
43	Advertising		E14					
44	Bank Charges		E15					
45	Rent		E16					
46	Telephone		E17					
47	Wages		E18	SUM				
48								
49	NET INCOME			D40-D47				
50								
51								

FIGURE 1-43

(c) Create a balance sheet for Monogram Plus, in file CH1SS3. Follow the format shown in Figure 1-44. Program the spreadsheet as indicated and produce a printout. Save your work under the file name CH1SS3.

```
      A         B         C         D         E         F         G         H
54
55  MONOGRAM PLUS
56  BALANCE SHEET
57  MAY 31, 19-2
58
59  ASSETS
60  =======
61  CURRENT ASSETS
62  Bank                                      G5
63  Accounts Receivable                       G6
64                                                 _____
65   Total Current Assets                              E62+E63
66
67  FIXED ASSETS
68  Van                                       G7
69  Equipment                                 G8       E68+E69
70                                                 _____
71  TOTAL ASSETS                                       F65+F69
72                                                     ========
73
74  LIABILITIES
75  ========
76  CURRENT LIABILITIES
77  Accounts Payable                          H9
78  Bank Loan                                 H10  _____
79
80  TOTAL CURRENT LIABILITIES                          E77+E78
81
82
83  OWNER'S EQUITY
84  ========
85  H. Dye, Capital
86    Balance, June 1, 19-1                   H11
87    Add: Net Income                         E22
88    Less: Drawings                          G12
89                                                 _____
90  Balance, May 31, 19-2                              E86+E87-E88
91
92  TOTAL LIABILITIES + OWNER'S EQUITY                 F80+F90
```

FIGURE 1-44

SS4   Recall the worksheet template you saved under the file name CH1SS3, and enter the new company name and account balances shown for Grabb Delivery. Save your work under the file name CH1SS4. Produce a printout of the spreadsheet (worksheet, income statement, and balance sheet).

```
                      Grabb Delivery
                      Account Balances
                       May 31, 19-2

     Account                  Debit          Credit
     Bank                   $ 4 700
     Accounts Receivable     12 600
     Van                     18 000
     Equipment                7 200
     Accounts Payable                      $  1 500
     Bank Loan                                8 500
     L. Grabb, Capital                       50 000
     L. Grabb, Drawings      25 000
     Sales                                  120 000
     Advertising Expense      3 140
     Bank Charges               690
     Rent Expense            24 000
     Telephone Expense        1 200
     Wages Expense           83 470
```

DB1   Create a customer database for Stubbe's Furniture. Define the following fields for your file.

Name	=	20 columns
Street	=	15 columns
Town	=	10 columns
Postal Code	=	7 columns
Balance Owing	=	8 columns

Enter the raw data shown below, and program the database to add up the customer balances.

Anderson, W.	303 Avon St.	Regina	S4V 1L8	$314.15
Becker, B.	7 Ryan Rd.	Regina	S4S 6X9	101.09
Cheng, C.	11 Cullum Pl.	Regina	S4R 8B8	667.67
Daignard, D.	2400 Gordon Rd.	Regina	S4S 4M4	556.56
Ewaschuk, O.	Levene Cr.	Regina	S4X 1N4	400.00

DB2   Create an employee database for Silverthorne Concrete. Define the following fields for your file.

Name	=	15 columns
Department	=	2 columns
Hourly Rate	=	5 columns
Gross Wage	=	7 columns

Enter the raw data shown below, and program the database to add up the employees' gross wages.

Harrelson, W.	A	$17.50	$667.80
Poloshcuk, E.	B	18.00	513.24
Urqhuart, T.	C	17.75	690.81
Lemon, F.	A	18.50	802.02
Wong, W.	B	19.00	760.00

DB3   Create a supplier database for Rita's Carpet. Define the following fields for your file.

Supplier Name	=	20 columns
Town	=	10 columns
Terms	=	10 columns
Amount Owing	=	9 columns

Enter the raw data shown below, and program the database to add up the amount owing to the suppliers.

Harding Carpet	Brantford	Net 30	$14 567.98
York Fibres	Toronto	2/10,n/30	13 445.16
Burlington Mills	Toronto	3/10,n/30	27 889.56
Canada Carpet	Montreal	Net 30	5 229.46
Hanover Carpet	Hanover	Net 30	2 110.10

DB4   Create an inventory database for the Edmonton Stereo Warehouse. Define the following fields for your file.

Product Description	=	20 columns
Stock Code Number	=	7 columns
Quantity	=	5 columns
Unit Price	=	7 columns

Enter the raw data shown below, and program the database to find the value of each item (Quantity * Unit Price), and to add up the total value of the store inventory.

B/W TVs	667000	112	$ 75.00
B/W TVs	667001	180	125.00
B/W TVs	667002	300	250.00
Colour TVs	668000	230	380.00
Colour TVs	668001	400	675.00

DB5 Create a cheque register for the Western Stetson Co. Define the following fields for your file

Date	=	8 columns
Payee	=	20 columns
Cheque No.	=	5 columns
Amount (Bank Credit)	=	10 columns

Enter the raw data shown below, and program the database to add up the Amount (Bank Credit) column.

06 01 91	Towne Garage	0078	$345.67
06 02 91	P.U.C.	0079	681.03
06 05 91	A. Fisher	0080	13.54
06 07 91	H. Johnson	0081	120.20
06 09 91	Standard Glass	0082	87.78

DB6 Create a database for J. Ferris Holdings. Julie has a small portfolio of stocks that she watches carefully, since the stock gains must be declared for income tax purposes. Define the following fields for her database:

Description (Name)	=	25 columns
No. of Shares	=	5 columns
Bought at	=	6 columns
Sold at	=	6 columns
Total Gain	=	7 columns

Enter the sample data shown below. Program the database to find the total gain (or loss) for each stock, and the overall gain (or loss) on the stock portfolio.

Royal Bank of Canada	200	$54.70	$75.00	?
Brascan	400	72.10	82.25	?
Moore Business Forms	275	37.00	42.75	?
Offshore Oil	4 500	.32	.38	?
Northern Gold Mines	8 000	.34	1.29	?

DB7 Abbs Construction uses a job costing system to prepare a quotation on a job. It also keeps a database of certain cost data for easy reference when quoting. Define the following fields:

Job Description	=	25 columns
Material Cost	=	9 columns
Labour Cost	=	9 columns
Overhead Cost	=	9 columns
Total Cost	=	9 columns

Enter this raw data and program the database to calculate the Total Cost for each job.

Tool Shed #1	$ 345.80	$ 667.82	$123.43	?
Tool Shed #2	456.75	712.03	176.35	?
Pool Decking	1 546.70	450.00	235.70	?
Split Fence	4 500.00	900.00	350.00	?
Carport	5 889.32	2 478.98	804.73	?

G1   Create a bar graph for this sales data. Your vertical axis should read 100, 120, 140, 160, 180, 200, and 220.

The Computer Store
Sales Data in Units

Complete Systems	170
Printers	150
Ribbons	200
3 1/2" Disks	220
5 1/4" Disks	140
Hard disk drives	110

G2   Create a line graph for this sales data. Your vertical axis should read 12 000, 16 000, 20 000, and so on, up to 32 000.

The Widget Company
Sales Data

January	$12 000
February	14 000
March	20 000
April	15 000
May	24 000
June	30 000

G3   Create a pie graph for this sales data.

Northern Sales Ltd.
Sales Data by Salesperson

Michelle Smith	$ 25 000
Fred Otten	13 500
Janet Slagers	32 000
Julie Dewachter	6 000
Jennifer Arthur	19 500
Beth Cougler	40 000
Total Sales	$135 000

WP1 Use the model auditor's report in section 1.6 of this chapter to produce another auditor's report making these changes:
(a) The business is Alexander Real Estate Limited.
(b) The auditing firm is Hyde, Houghton Chartered Accountants.
(c) The reporting date is March 14, 19–.

WP2 Use the model customer letter in section 1.6 to send a similar letter making these changes:
(a) The customer is Ms. P. Caffyn, 290 Jackson Drive, Saskatoon, SK, S9H 4M7.
(b) The account is 60 days past due.
(c) The amount owing is $2 478.19.

WP3 Prepare this letter to one of your sales people.

September 25, 19–

Joan Majid
234 37th Street
Calgary, AB
T2N 1N6

Dear Joan

I have just finished my reading of the company sales report for the first half of this year. You are leading our company in sales for the second straight year and I offer my sincere congratulations.

As you know, the position of National Sales Manager will have to be filled at the year end. Your track record so far makes you a prime candidate for that promotion.

Yours truly

W. Van Wyk, President Tech Basics Ltd.

R. v. BOON

BACKGROUND

The West Harrow branch of the Ontario Eye Bank Society was formed in the late 1970s. This charitable organization assists patients in arranging eye transplant operations and finances individual patients who cannot afford the operation. The office manager of the West Harrow branch was Mr. Franklin K. Boon.

The office manager was to prepare budgets each year, supervise office staff, and act as the signing authority for the society's financial operations. Mr. Boon reported to a voluntary board of directors consisting of twelve citizens in the township. Financial reports, by law, were to be filed with both Revenue Canada and the federal government.

In 1985, Ministry of Health auditors performed a routine audit of the accounting records of the society.

INVESTIGATION

The auditors' investigation revealed the following document (Figure 1-45), a cash register tape from Woolco, that was claimed as a business expense by Mr. Boon. Look at this document and the related information to see if you can determine what is wrong with Mr. Boon's expense claim.

DEPARTMENT	CODE
Candy	010
Music	212
Toys	235
Sports	239
Clothing	410
Stationary	421

```
        6050        10/25/85
          60        No Sale
        2664        6:24PM

              .00
           161.92    TOTAL
            11.99    TAX
   239     36.95
   239      4.50
   421       .75
   239     36.95
   239      4.50
   010      3.57
   010      1.69
   010      3.98
   010      5.07
   410     13.41
   212      8.99
   010      3.34
   010      1.87
   010      1.77
   010      1.87
   010      4.77
   235     15.95

        2663         6:20PM
```

FIGURE 1-45   Woolco cash register tape and coding summary

FRAUD

Mr. Boon was claiming personal expenses as expenses of the Eye Society. It is hard to imagine Mr. Boon using candy, clothing, sporting goods, tapes, or toys in his job with the Eye Society.

Therefore, the Eye Society was paying expenses that did not legitimately pertain to it. In addition to this, the auditors also found that Mr. Boon had claimed these same expenses on reports to the Ministry of Health. In other words, he had claimed illegitimate expenses twice.

SENTENCE

As a result of the audit, Mr. Boon was charged with fraud, an indictable offence under the Criminal Code of Canada. His case was heard in Provincial Court in Chatham, and he was sentenced to a year in prison for his crime. He was also ordered to make restitution to the Eye Society for the total amount of the false expense claims made by him, approximately $15 000. He was, in addition, dismissed as the office manager for the Eye Society, and disgraced in the eyes of the community for his breach of trust.

QUESTIONS

1. Was Mr. Boon's crime serious enough to have him sent to prison?
2. Should the Board of Directors have checked up on Mr. Boon more often?
3. How does an organization, like the Eye Society, ensure that it is hiring honest people as employees?
4. Is there any way that the Eye Society could have protected itself against this kind of theft happening?

NAME

NO.

Career Profile

Danny Williams operates a chain of 25 sporting goods stores in western Canada called *Let's Play Ball*. The stores are located in all major cities and towns from Winnipeg, Manitoba, to Victoria, British Columbia. *Let's Play Ball* is a successful business that relies on Danny's knowledge of the sporting goods industry and the market for sporting goods sales. His background includes a career in pro ball with the Canadian Football League. Danny was a star quarterback with the Toronto Argonauts for four consecutive seasons, winning several trophies for excellence on the football field.

Few people know that while playing football, Danny was at an eastern university majoring in Business Administration, and specializing in accounting. This knowledge (along with his sports knowledge) provided Danny with the know-how to make his business grow. Shortly after graduation Danny saw the need in western Canada for a sporting goods store that would provide quality goods at affordable prices, particularly in the teenage market where funds are limited. Danny computerized his first store to handle accounts receivable and inventory on an efficient basis. He was able to buy quality goods cheaply and keep inventory levels to a minimum.

As the business expanded, Danny linked all his franchise stores by computer terminals. He was then able to transfer goods (inventory) from one store, where sales were down, to other stores where those items could be sold more quickly. By using an integrated accounting package, Danny has access to daily financial reports on sales, profit levels, and return on investment. Customer records (accounts receivable) are kept using a database software program. The program prepares a weekly schedule of overdue accounts and automatically charges interest on these accounts.

A spreadsheet program is used for sales reports of product lines, reports of sales by individual stores, and sales by sales personnel. At the touch of a key, the computer will also use this sales data to prepare graphs of the sales — bar graphs, line graphs, and pie charts, broken down any way Danny wants to analyse company sales.

Danny no longer worries about the financial side of his business since he has a full accounting staff comprised of a professional accountant and some bright community college graduates who majored in accounting. As his business grew, Danny decided to turn the accounting over to young people who understood the exciting use to which computers could be put in a business operation.

Danny now spends most of his time visiting the stores in his capacity as president of the company. In this way he can keep a close ear to the market to stay on top of customer trends. Store managers are trained at head office now, and one of the most important courses they are exposed to is the Computer Accounting course.

Danny will always appreciate his accounting background and what it did to make his *Let's Play Ball* a successful franchise.

For Discussion

- Danny bought a computer for his first sporting goods store. Why did this help him with his business at the start?
- How often does Danny get computer updates about his stores? Is this often enough?
- Is the store chain using all of the computer software discussed in this chapter, i.e. spreadsheets, graphics, databases, word processing and telecommunications?
- What is the main reason for Danny's success?

2

The Accounting System for a Service Business

2.0

Overview

A service business relies on the personal skills of the owner, and/or employees, for its source of income. Some good examples of service businesses are a collision service, a hairdressing salon, a carpenter, and an interior decorator. In each of these businesses, the owner has developed a marketable skill, and then built a business around that skill. This chapter describes in detail the total accounting process associated with a specific service business, Bukta Collision Service.

"C'mon, Dave! I saw him first."

2.1

Source Documents and Journalizing

Marg Bukta owns and operates a small business called Bukta Collision Service with four full-time employees. Bukta Collision Service repairs cars, trucks, and vans for people who have been in accidents, or does repairs for those people who simply want to maintain their vehicles in good condition.

In order to keep proper records for the accounting process of her business, Marg has four basic categories of **source documents**. Figure 2-1 shows how these source documents are used as input to the overall accounting process of the business.

Now read about each of these key source documents and, as you read, keep the picture of the Bukta Collision Service accounting cycle in your mind.

SALES DOCUMENTS

For Marg's business, the sales invoice is a basic source document used for several types of accounting transactions. The first two types of transactions discussed in this section are the charge sale, and the credit invoice.

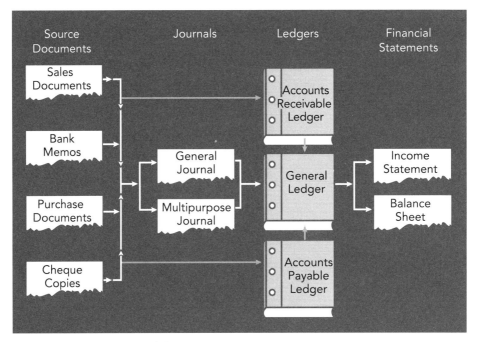

FIGURE 2-1   A flowchart of the accounting process

The Charge Sale

A **charge sale** is a sale on account to a customer. When a sales invoice is used for a charge sale, the box labelled "Charge" is marked off on the sales invoice.

As of January 1991, many businesses in Canada are required to pay a 7% federal tax on goods and services they buy, and to collect a 7% tax on goods and services sold. Provinces differ in the manner in which they handle the collection of federal and provincial taxes — some provinces integrate these two taxes, others charge provincial sales tax on the federal tax, and some charge taxes separately on the basic invoice amount.

On this invoice there are two tax items, the federal **GST** (Goods and Services Tax) at 7% of the sub total; and the **PST** (Provincial Sales Tax) at 8% of the sub total. The 7% GST applies to all of Canada, while provincial sales tax rates vary from province to province. Also, depending on the province, PST may be calculated on the base price plus GST. In Ontario, the PST rate is 8% and the tax is calculated on the base price only.

A charge sale is recorded as a debit to the Accounts Receivable control account in the general ledger (and the customer's account in the subsidiary ledger), a credit to Sales, a credit to GST Payable, and a credit to PST Payable.

		519-555-2927
B C S	**BUKTA COLLISION SERVICE**	**Marg Bukta, Prop.**

5 Stover St. S.
Norwich, Ontario N0J 1P6

Date <u>Nov. 1</u>   19<u>–</u>

Name <u>Gordon Stone</u>

Address <u>16 Marshall Drive</u>

Town <u>Norwich, Ontario</u>   Postal Code <u>N0J 1P0</u>

Quantity	Description	Price	Amount
1	New bumper installed for 1987 Buick	260–	260–
	Labour costs 1 hour @ $40		40–

Cash/Cheque	Charge X	Credit Invoice	Sub Total	300–
Credit Card #			GST	21–
Invoice # 1670	Terms: net 30 days 2% per month on overdue		PST	24–
			Total	345–

FIGURE 2-2   *A charge sales invoice*

GENERAL JOURNAL
PAGE <u>111</u>

DATE 19–	PARTICULARS	PR	DEBIT	CREDIT
Nov. 1	A/R— Gordon Stone		3 45 –	
	Sales			3 00 –
	GST Payable			2 1 –
	PST Payable			2 4 –
	To record a charge sale Inv. 1670			

FIGURE 2-3   *The general journal entry for a charge sale*

Notice in Figure 2-3 that the short form A/R has been used for Accounts Receivable. This is acceptable accounting practice. This entry includes the customer's name so that the debit side of the entry can be posted to the customer's account in the accounts receivable subsidiary ledger.

For those customers who charge their work, the amount owing is due in 30 days (net 30), or there is an interest charge of 2% per month on overdue accounts. Some businesses offer discount terms, e.g. 2/10, n/30, to customers who pay accounts early. Customers who pay within 10 days may take a 2% discount on the bill (2/10). If the discount is not taken, the bill must be paid within 30 days (n/30). Bukta Collision Service's terms of net 30 indicate that they do not offer discounts to customers.

The Credit Invoice

The sales invoice document is also used as a credit invoice when a customer's account has to be adjusted. Let's assume that a customer, Diane Tribe, was overcharged $70 for parts on a recent repair bill. This would result in a credit invoice being issued to Diane for $80.50, the $70 overcharge on the part price plus $4.90 for GST and $5.60 for PST.

This invoice is labelled "Credit Invoice" so that it will be recorded correctly by the bookkeeper. In addition, the box labelled "Credit Invoice" is marked off. See Figure 2-5.

The general journal entry to record this credit invoice is a debit to Sales (or Sales Returns and Allowances), a debit to GST Payable, a debit to PST Payable, and a credit to the Accounts Receivable control account in the general ledger (and the customer's account in the subsidiary ledger).

GENERAL JOURNAL

PAGE 111

DATE 19–	PARTICULARS	PR	DEBIT	CREDIT
Nov. 2	Sales		70 –	
	GST Payable		4 90	
	PST Payable		5 60	
	A/R— Diane Tribe			80 50
	To record credit invoice for parts			
	overcharge Inv. 1672			

FIGURE 2-4   *The general journal entry for a credit invoice*

B C S	**BUKTA COLLISION SERVICE**		519-555-2927 Marg Bukta, Prop.	

5 Stover St. S.
Norwich, Ontario N0J 1P6

Date _Nov. 2_   19–___

Name _Diane Tribe_

Address _R.R. 1_

Town _Norwich, Ontario_   Postal Code _N0J 1P0_

Quantity	Description	Price	Amount
	CREDIT INVOICE		
	Overage on parts re		
	repair job, Oct. 31		70 –

Cash/Cheque	Charge	Credit Invoice X	Sub Total	70 –
			GST	4 90
Credit Card #			PST	5 60
Invoice # 1672	Terms: net 30 days 2% per month on overdue		Total	80 50

FIGURE 2-5   *A credit invoice*

Two other sales-related transactions are cash receipt entries. A **cash receipt** is a cash sale or a receipt on account from a customer.

The Cash Sale

If repair work is performed on a customer's car and the customer pays cash, then the sales invoice acts as a cash receipt, and the box labelled "Cash/Cheque" is marked off. Figure 2-6 shows a cash sale in the amount of $172.50, including the GST and the PST.

B C S	BUKTA COLLISION SERVICE		519-555-2927 Marg Bukta, Prop.

5 Stover St. S.
Norwich, Ontario N0J 1P6

Date Nov. 3   19–

Name __Bill Smith__

Address __24 South Street__

Town __Norwich, Ontario__   N0J 1P2

Quantity	Description	Price	Amount	
	Replace windshield on			
	1987 Dodge Van		130	–
	Labour costs: 1/2 hour @ $40		20	–

Cash/Cheque X	Charge	Credit Invoice	Sub Total	150	–
Credit Card #			GST	10	50
Invoice # 1674	Terms: net 30 days 2% per month on overdue		PST	12	–
			Total	172	50

FIGURE 2-6   *A cash sale*

GENERAL JOURNAL

PAGE __111__

DATE 19–		PARTICULARS	PR	DEBIT	CREDIT
Nov.	3	Bank		1 72 50	
		Sales			1 50 –
		GST Payable			1 0 50
		PST Payable			1 2 –
		To record a cash sale Inv. 1674			

FIGURE 2-7   *The general journal entry for a cash sale*

Whenever cash is received by Bukta Collision Service it is deposited daily into the business bank account.

Cash Received on Account

If the customer is making a payment on account to the business for an amount owing from previous work, then the box labelled "Cash/Cheque" is marked off.

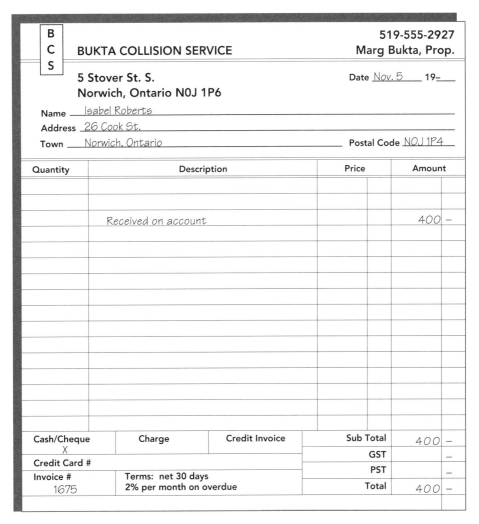

FIGURE 2-8   *A receipt on account*

In this example a customer, Isabel Roberts, is making a $400 payment to Bukta Collision Service on her account. There is no federal tax (GST) nor provincial tax (PST) on a receipt on account, because a sale is not being made. These taxes were included in the original sale.

The general journal entry for a receipt on account is:

GENERAL JOURNAL

PAGE 112

DATE 19—		PARTICULARS	PR	DEBIT	CREDIT
Nov.	5	Bank		400 –	
		A/R— Isabel Roberts			400 –
		To record cash received on account			
		Invoice 1675			

FIGURE 2-9   The general journal entry for a receipt on account

BANK MEMOS

The Bank Credit Memo

Bank credit memos are more unusual than debit memos. A **bank credit memo** is a document detailing money deposited into a bank account by the bank. One of the ways a bank credit memo is used is for a business loan. When the owner of a business agrees to a loan, the bank often deposits the money into the customer's bank account and then notifies him or her by sending out a bank credit memo. If Bukta Collision borrows $5 000, the bank would put the money into the business bank account and send out a notice like Figure 2-10.

"$84 for labor! Wow, what an honor! Johnny Carson changed my plugs."

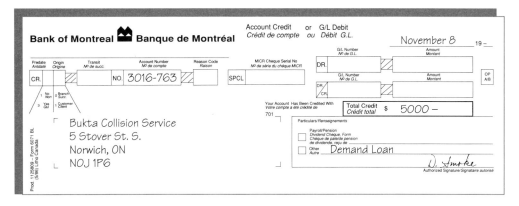

FIGURE 2-10   *A bank credit memo*

When Bukta Collision receives the bank credit memo, it makes the following journal entry into its books:

GENERAL JOURNAL

PAGE 112

DATE 19–		PARTICULARS	PR	DEBIT	CREDIT
Nov.	8	Bank		5000 –	
		Bank Loan			5000 –
		To record a bank credit memo			
		received regarding a loan			

FIGURE 2-11   *The general journal entry for a bank credit memo*

The Bank Debit Memo

It is common practice for banks to charge directly (deduct from) their customers' accounts for service charges and/or interest on bank loans. The bank makes the appropriate accounting entry at a set date, transfers the funds out of the customer's account, and then sends a debit memo to its customer so that the customer can record the transaction in his or her books of account. A **bank debit memo** is a document detailing money deducted from a bank account for interest or service charges. The monthly bank charges for the past month were in the amount of $47.92. Therefore, the bank has debited Bukta Collision Service's bank account in the amount of $47.92, the interest for one month. The bank then mailed the following debit memo to Bukta Collision Service, to inform the business of the deduction from its bank account.

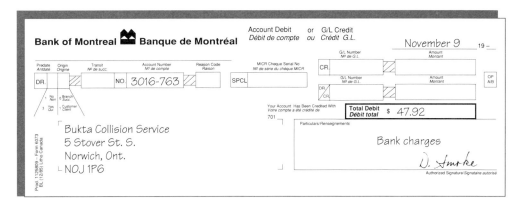

FIGURE 2-12   A bank debit memo

The bank debit memo received by Bukta Collision Service resulted in the following general journal entry:

GENERAL JOURNAL

PAGE 112

DATE 19–		PARTICULARS	PR	DEBIT	CREDIT
Nov.	9	Bank Charges		47 92	
		Bank			47 92
		To record a bank debit memo			
		received for bank charges			

FIGURE 2-13   The general journal entry for a bank debit memo

PURCHASE DOCUMENTS

Bukta Collision Service also receives purchase invoices, and credit invoices, from businesses that supply it with goods and services.

The Purchase Invoice

The source document below is a **purchase invoice** (a document received when goods or services are bought on account) from the Peter Paint Company. Bukta Collision Service has purchased a supply of paint for the body shop. Notice that the invoice from Peter Paint Company has terms of 3/10, n/30 written at the top. This means that Bukta Collision Service may take a 3% discount if this bill is paid in 10 days. If no discount is taken, the bill must be paid in 30 days (net 30). Obviously, it is to Bukta Collision's advantage to pay the bill within the 10 days so that the discount can be taken.

Peter Paint Company 170 Concession Street Cambridge, Ontario N1R 2H7		519-555-2767	Invoice # PPC3615 Date Nov.12/–
To: Bukta Collision Service 5 Stover Street S. Norwich, ON NOJ 1P6			**Tel:** 555-2927 **Att:** Marg Bukta

Your Order **Number:** 110	Our Order **Number:** 5625	Salesperson F. Curry	**Terms:** 3/10, n/30 **f.o.b.:** Destination
Date Shipped: Nov. 12/–		**Shipped Via:** Purolator	

Qty Ordered	Qty Shipped	Description	Unit Price	Amount
4	4	Basic Black Paint #6673	23.75	95 –
2	2	Sky Blue #6681	22.50	45 –
3	3	Cloud Grey #6690	20.00	60 –
			Sub Total	200 –
			GST	14 –
			PST	16 –
			Total	230 –

FIGURE 2-14   *A purchase invoice*

When a purchase invoice is received by a business it will have a GST amount on it. Because the items purchased are used to earn income by the business, this tax becomes an **input tax credit** to the buyer, and the amount stated for GST is debited into an account called GST Recoverable, a current asset.

Whenever it is time to send GST to the government, the balance in the GST Recoverable account is subtracted from the balance in the GST Payable account. This net amount is sent to the Receiver General.

Here is the general journal entry, including the treatment for the input tax credit for Bukta Collision Service.

GENERAL JOURNAL

PAGE 112

DATE 19–		PARTICULARS	PR	DEBIT	CREDIT
Nov.	9	Paint Expense		2 1 6 –	
		GST Recoverable		1 4 –	
		A/P— Peter Paint Co			2 3 0 –
		To record the purchase of paint;			
		Inv. PPC3615, at full invoice price			

FIGURE 2-15   *The general journal entry showing input tax credit*

The accounting entry includes the supplier's name so that the credit side of the entry can be posted to the supplier's account in the accounts payable subsidiary ledger.

The term *purchase invoice*, for Bukta Collision Service, refers to invoices that cover three main types of transactions:
(1) the purchase of supplies for the business
(2) bills received for other expenses, e.g. advertising
(3) the purchase of assets

The Credit Invoice

Bukta Collision Service sometimes has to return goods to suppliers for credit when they are defective, or when they are not exactly what was ordered in the first place. The supplier then issues a credit invoice to Bukta Collision Service. A **credit invoice** is an invoice received from a supplier which reduces Bukta's accounts payable.

When goods are returned to a supplier, the journal entry must reduce the balance in the GST Recoverable account. The general journal entry for the credit invoice is shown in Figure 2-17.

Peter Paint Company 170 Concession Street Cambridge, Ontario N1R 2H7		Credit Invoice # CR112	
	519-555-2767	Date Nov.8/–	

To: Bukta Collision Service
5 Stover Street S.
Norwich, ON   NOJ 1P6

Tel: 555-2927
Att: Marg Bukta

Your Order Number: 110	Our Order Number: 5625	Salesperson F. Curry	Terms: 3/10, n/30 f.o.b.: Destination
Date Shipped: Nov. 12/–		Shipped Via: Purolator	

Qty Shipped	Description	Unit Price	Amount
2	Sky Blue #6681	22.50	45 –
	Sub Total		45 –
	GST		3 15
	PST		3 60
	Total		51 75

FIGURE 2-16   A credit invoice

GENERAL JOURNAL

PAGE 112

DATE 19–		PARTICULARS	PR	DEBIT	CREDIT
Nov.	18	A/P— Peter Paint Co.		5 1 75	
		GST Recoverable			3 15
		Paint Expense			48 60
		To record goods returned to the			
		supplier			

FIGURE 2-17   The general journal entry for a credit invoice

CHEQUE COPIES

When Marg's bookkeeper pays a bill for the business, she writes out a cheque. A **cheque** is a document indicating payment to buy an asset, to reduce a liability, or to pay an expense. The cheque has two parts, a stub to record the details of the cheque, and the cheque itself which is given to, or mailed to, the recipient.

| No: 1215 | | | B BUKTA COLLISION SERVICE | 1215 |

No: 1215

Date: _Nov. 30/–_

To: _Norwich PUC_

For: _Heat & Light_

Bal Fwd	$	1575–
Deposit	$	ø
Balance	$	1575–
Amount	$	150–
Balance	$	1425–

B
C BUKTA COLLISION SERVICE   1215
S 5 Stover Street S.
Norwich, ON N0J 1P6

Date: _Nov. 30_ **19–**

Pay to the
Order of: _Norwich PUC_ $ 150.00

— _One Hundred and Fifty_ ———————— xx **Dollars**
                                         100

Bank of Montreal
Norwich, Ontario

Peg Bradford
M. Bukta

3 0 ⺊ ⺊ 7 ⺊ 3

FIGURE 2-18   *A cheque and stub*

This particular cheque is charged to the business expense account, Heat and Light. Therefore the general journal entry is:

GENERAL JOURNAL

PAGE 11

DATE 19–		PARTICULARS	PR	DEBIT	CREDIT
Nov.	30	Heat & Light Expense		1 4 0 19	
		GST Recoverable		9 81	
		Bank			1 5 0 –
		To record payment to the PUC			
		Cheque 1215			

FIGURE 2-19   *The general journal entry for a payment by cheque*

The cheque is a source document for a journal entry into the books of account. Both the bookkeeper and the owner, Marg Bukta, sign cheques for better cash control. Cheques are usually written for one of four types of business transactions:

(1) a cash payment to a supplier on account
(2) a cash payment of an expense
(3) a cash purchase of an asset
(4) a cash withdrawal by the owner

QUESTIONS

1. Name five examples of service businesses.

2. Name the four types of sales-related transactions.

3. The sales invoice for Bukta Collision Service can be used for four types of accounting transactions. Name them.

4. Does Bukta Collision Service charge customers for amounts overdue?

5. If a supplier invoice listed terms of 2/7, n/15, what would this mean?

6. Indicate whether each of these accounting transactions would be a bank debit memo or a bank credit memo.
   (a) The bank has transferred $10 000 from the owner's personal account to the business bank account.
   (b) Monthly interest of $240 was charged on a bank loan and deducted from the business bank account.

7. What do the initials GST stand for on an invoice?

8. If the sub-total on an invoice is $250, what is the invoice total after the 7% GST and an 8% PST (calculated on the base price) are added?

9. What happens to the two parts of a business cheque?

10. If a business issues a cheque, what four types of payments could it be making?

2.2

Using a Multipurpose Journal

All of the sample transactions in section 2.1 were shown in general journal form to keep the illustration simple. Now let's look at the same transactions as they would be entered into the multipurpose journal that Bukta Collision Service actually uses. A **multipurpose journal** is a multi-columned book of account used to record balanced accounting transactions. The multipurpose journal in Figure 2-20 covers the month of November for the business. The entries described in section 2.1 are highlighted for easy recognition.

The multipurpose journal is the main book of original entry for Bukta Collision Service. Most of the source documents used by the business can be entered into this journal. There is also a general journal which is used for entries that do not fit easily into the multipurpose journal, and/or for special entries to be made at the year-end — adjusting entries and closing entries.

#	DATE 19–		CUSTOMER/SUPPLIER	NO.	CASH DR	CASH CR	ACCOUNTS RECEIVABLE DR	ACCOUNTS RECEIVABLE CR	✔
1	Nov.	1	Gordon Stone	1670			345 –		✔
2		1	Brian Garner	1671			115 –		✔
3		2	Diane Tribe	1672				80 50	✔
4		3	Jim Clement	1673	17 25 –				
5		3	Bill Smith	1674	17 2 50				
6		5	Norwich Gazette	1211		250 –			
7									
8		5	Isabel Roberts	1675	400 –			400 –	✔
9		6	John Kupisz	1676			5750 –		✔
10		8	Bank of Montreal	CM	5000 –				
11		9	Auto Supply Co.	951					
12									
13		9	Jackie Potters	1677			920 –		✔
14		9	Bank of Montreal	DM		47 92			
15		10	Laurie Lewis	1678			690 –		✔
16		10	Martin Wylie	1679			4025 –		✔
17		11	Bell Canada	1212		125 31			
18									
19		12	Jane Cossar	1680	16 10 –				
20		12	Peter Paint Co.	3615					
21									
22		18	Peter Paint Co.	112					
23									
24		19	Peter Paint Co.	1213		172 90			
25		20	Wayne Smith	1681	575 –				
26		21	Robin Vankerrebroeck	1682			1380 –		✔
27		24	Peg Caffyn	1683	37 95 –				
28		28	Wages	1214		5000 –			
29		30	Norwich PUC	1215		150 –			
30									
31					13 27 750	5 74 613	13 2 25 –	4 80 50	

FIGURE 2-20   *Multipurpose journal for November*

In this multipurpose journal there were three blank columns to the left of the Other Accounts section. These three columns have been used for Sales, GST Payable, and PST Payable. If there had been other blank columns, they would have been used for any accounts with frequently occurring transactions in the month. One business, for example, might pay weekly wages and want to label the blank column "Wages." This use of blank columns for frequently used accounts cuts down the writing of account names by the bookkeeper.

The two columns labelled "Other Accounts" at the right of the multipurpose journal are miscellaneous columns. Not every account used by Bukta

MULTIPURPOSE JOURNAL
PAGE NO. ___11___

ACCOUNTS PAYABLE DR	ACCOUNTS PAYABLE CR	✔	SALES CR	GST PAYABLE CR	PST PAYABLE CR	ACCOUNT	PR	OTHER ACCOUNTS DR	OTHER ACCOUNTS CR	
			300 –	21 –	24 –					1
			100 –	7 –	8 –					2
			(70 –)	(490)	(560)					3
			1500 –	105 –	120 –					4
			150 –	1050	12 –					5
						Advert. Expense		233 64		6
						GST Recoverable		16 36		7
										8
			5000 –	350 –	400 –					9
						Bank Loan			5000 –	10
	642 –	✔				Parts Expense		600 –		11
						GST Recoverable		42 –		12
			800 –	56 –	64 –					13
						Bank Charges		47 92		14
			600 –	42 –	48 –					15
			3500 –	245 –	280 –					16
						Telephone Expense		117 68		17
						GST Recoverable		7 63		18
			1400 –	98 –	112 –					19
	230 –	✔				Paint Expense		216 –		20
						GST Recoverable		14 –		21
5175		✔				Paint Expense			48 60	22
						GST Recoverable			3 15	23
17825		✔				Discounts Earned			5 35	24
			500 –	35 –	40 –					25
			1200 –	84 –	96 –					26
			3300 –	231 –	264 –					27
						Wages Expense		5000 –		28
						Heat & Light Expense		140 19		29
						GST Recoverable		9 81		30
230 –	872 –		18280 –	12 79 60	14 62 40			6445 23	5057 10	31

Collision Service can have its own column in the multipurpose journal. Therefore the Other Accounts section is necessary for transactions that do not have their own special column.

If you want to record an opposite entry into the multipurpose journal, you can circle the debit or credit to change the entry. On November 2, for example, a credit invoice was issued to Diane Tribe. The accounting entry to record this was a debit to the Sales account, a debit to the GST Payable, a debit to PST Payable and a credit to Accounts Receivable. The debits to Sales, GST Payable, and PST Payable are each circled since they are debits placed in credit columns. These entries are sometimes written in red instead of circled.

	DATE 19–	CUSTOMER/SUPPLIER	NO.	CASH DR	CASH CR	ACCOUNTS RECEIVABLE DR	ACCOUNTS RECEIVABLE CR	✔
1	Nov. 1	Gordon Stone	1670			345 –		✔
2	1	Brian Garner	1671			1 15 –		✔
3	2	Diane Tribe	1672				80 50	✔
4	3	Jim Clement	1673	1 7 25 –				
5	3	Bill Smith	1674	1 72 50				
6	5	Norwich Gazette	1211		250 –			
7								
8	5	Isabel Roberts	1675	400 –			400 –	✔
9	6	John Kupisz	1676			57 50 –		✔
10	8	Bank of Montreal	CM	5 000 –				
11	9	Auto Supply Co.	951					
12								
13	9	Jackie Potters	1677			9 20 –		✔
14	9	Bank of Montreal	DM		47 92			
15	10	Laurie Lewis	1678			6 90 –		✔
16	10	Martin Wylie	1679			40 25 –		✔
17	11	Bell Canada	1212		1 25 31			
18								
19	12	Jane Cossar	1680	1 6 10 –				
20	12	Peter Paint Co.	3615					
21								
22	18	Peter Paint Co.	112					
23								
24	19	Peter Paint Co.	1213		1 72 90			
25	20	Wayne Smith	1681	5 75 –				
26	21	Robin Vankerrebroeck	1682			13 80 –		✔
27	24	Peg Caffyn	1683	37 95 –				
28	28	Wages	1214		50 00 –			
29	30	Norwich PUC	1215		1 50 –			
30								
31				13 2 77 50	5 7 46 13	13 2 25 –	4 80 50	
				(110)	(110)	(120)	(120)	

FIGURE 2-21 *Multipurpose journal with posting notations*

Bukta Collision Service uses a multipurpose journal because it cuts down on posting time, in that fewer individual entries have to be written into ledger accounts. The names of the most frequently used accounts appear at the top of the columns where data is accumulated. Only the final totals are posted to the ledger accounts.

POSTING THE MULTIPURPOSE JOURNAL

Posting to the General Ledger

Before posting, the multipurpose journal is totalled and balanced at the end of each month. The totals of all the columns, except the two Other

MULTIPURPOSE JOURNAL

PAGE NO. ___11___

ACCOUNTS PAYABLE DR	ACCOUNTS PAYABLE CR	✓	SALES CR	GST PAYABLE CR	PST PAYABLE CR	ACCOUNT	PR	OTHER ACCOUNTS DR	OTHER ACCOUNTS CR	
			300 –	21 –	24 –					1
			100 –	7 –	8 –					2
			(70 –)	(4 90)	(5 60)					3
			1500 –	105 –	120 –					4
			150 –	10 50	12 –					5
						Advert. Expense	502	233 64		6
						GST Recoverable	130	16 36		7
										8
			5000 –	350 –	400 –					9
						Bank Loan	210		5000 –	10
	642 –	✓				Parts Expense	542	600 –		11
						GST Recoverable	130	42 –		12
			800 –	56 –	64 –					13
						Bank Charges	506	47 92		14
			600 –	42 –	48 –					15
			3500 –	245 –	280 –					16
						Telephone Expense	544	117 68		17
						GST Recoverable	130	7 63		18
			1400 –	98 –	112 –					19
	230 –	✓				Paint Expense	540	216 –		20
						GST Recoverable	130	14 –		21
51 75		✓				Paint Expense	540		48 60	22
						GST Recoverable	130		3 15	23
178 25		✓				Discounts Earned	518		5 35	24
			500 –	35 –	40 –					25
			1200 –	84 –	96 –					26
			3300 –	231 –	264 –					27
						Wages Expense	580	5000 –		28
						Heat & Light Expense	520	140 19		29
						GST Recoverable	130	9 81		30
230 –	872 –		18280 –	1279 60	1462 40			6445 23	5057 10	31
(220)	(220)		(410)	(230)	(231)					

Accounts columns, are posted to their correct ledger accounts. The entries in the Accounts Receivable and Accounts Payable columns are posted to the subsidiary ledgers daily so that customer and supplier accounts are always current. The Other Accounts column entries must be posted individually to the correct accounts.

The purpose behind cross-referencing is to assist the bookkeeper or accountant in tracing entries later, if necessary. Figure 2-21 shows the multipurpose journal after the columns and the Other Accounts have been posted to the general ledger. (The **general ledger** contains all the accounts of a business needed to prepare the financial statements.)

The posting process may be very familiar to you at this point. But, just to be sure, here is the Bank account from the general ledger for Bukta Collision

Service with the multipurpose journal posted for the month. You will remember that, in posting, the journal and the ledger are cross-referenced with account numbers and page numbers. The Bank columns of the multipurpose journal are posted to account #110, and this account number is written below the debit column and the credit column in brackets. When the Bank debit and credit totals are posted into the Bank account, the PR (**posting reference**) notation in the Bank account is MPJ11 (multipurpose journal, page 11).

GENERAL LEDGER

ACCOUNT Bank							NO. 110	
DATE 19–	PARTICULARS	PR	DEBIT		CREDIT	DR CR	BALANCE	
Nov. 30	Bal. Fwd.					DR	6 9 2 4 88	
30		MPJ11	13 2 7 7 50		5 7 4 6 1 2	DR	14 45 6 26	

FIGURE 2-22   *Bank account with PR notation*

Once the multipurpose journal is posted then the general ledger should be checked to see if it is still in balance. This will be done in the next section of this chapter when a worksheet is prepared for the business.

Posting to the Accounts Receivable Ledger

Because entries that affect the accounts receivable subsidiary ledger are made into the multipurpose journal each day, these must be posted to the individual customer accounts. Each debit or credit in the Accounts Receivable columns is posted to the subsidiary ledger as of the date of the transaction. A tick is placed in the special tick column (by the Accounts Receivable columns) to show that the amount has been posted. (Many businesses will post daily directly from the sales invoices and receipts on account.) The accounts receivable ledger is comprised of individual ledger cards for each customer, and contains mailing information for sending monthly statements to the customer. It also shows the customer's credit limit, which is the maximum amount that the customer is allowed to charge on his or her account. This card provides a perpetual record of invoices charged, payments received, and the balance owing by the customer to Bukta Collision Service on any given date. A final point to note is that there are no account numbers on the accounts receivable ledger cards because they are filed alphabetically.

Notice that when you post to the accounts receivable ledger card, it is important to write the number of the sales invoice (#1675) in the Particulars column, for later reference if necessary.

ACCOUNTS RECEIVABLE LEDGER							
NAME: Isabel Roberts **ADDRESS:** 26 Cook St. **TOWN:** Norwich **PROVINCE:** Ont.					**TELEPHONE NO.:** 555-3705 **CREDIT LIMIT:** $ 3 000 **POSTAL CODE:** NOJ 1P4		
DATE 19–		**PARTICULARS**	**PR**	**DEBIT**	**CREDIT**	**DR CR**	**BALANCE**
Oct.	31	Bal. Fwd.				DR	4 0 0 –
Nov.	5	Invoice 1675	MPJ11		4 0 0 –	–	∅

FIGURE 2-23   *An accounts receivable ledger card*

Posting to the Accounts Payable Ledger

As entries that affect the accounts payable subsidiary ledger are made into the multipurpose journal each day, these must be posted to the subsidiary ledger accounts. Each debit or credit in the Accounts Payable columns is posted to the subsidiary ledger as of the date of the transaction. A tick is placed in the special column (by the Accounts Payable columns) to show that the amount has been posted. (Many businesses will post daily directly from the purchase invoices and cheque copies.) The accounts payable ledger is comprised of individual ledger cards for each supplier, and contains mailing information for sending monthly payments to the supplier. This card provides a perpetual record of goods and services purchased, payments made, and the balance owing to the supplier by Bukta Collision Service on any given date. As with accounts receivable, there are no account numbers on the accounts payable ledger cards because they are filed alphabetically.

Notice again the invoice reference in the Particulars column on the accounts payable ledger card.

ACCOUNTS PAYABLE LEDGER							
NAME: Peter Paint Company **ADDRESS:** 170 Concession St. **TOWN:** Cambridge **PROVINCE:** Ont.					**TELEPHONE NO.:** 555-2767 **POSTAL CODE:** N1R 2H7		
DATE 19–		**PARTICULARS**	**PR**	**DEBIT**	**CREDIT**	**DR CR**	**BALANCE**
Oct.	31	Bal. Fwd.				–	∅
Nov.	12	Invoice 3615	MPJ11		2 3 0 –	CR	2 3 0 –
	18	Cr. Inv. 112	MPJ11	5 1 75		CR	1 7 8 25
	19	Cheque 1213	MPJ11	1 7 8 25		–	∅

FIGURE 2-24   *An accounts payable ledger card*

Both the accounts receivable ledger and the accounts payable ledger are balanced monthly and checked against their control accounts in the general ledger. Trial balances are prepared of each subsidiary ledger to prove that they do agree with their control accounts.

QUESTIONS

11. What is the sales tax rate for the province in which you live?

12. Why is a credit entry made to GST Payable and PST Payable?

13. What do the short forms A/R and A/P stand for in accounting?

14. Match the accounting source document to the proper description.
    (1) Cash Sales Invoice
    (2) Charge Sales Invoice
    (3) Credit Invoice
    (4) Purchase Invoice
    (5) Bank Debit Memo

    a. Customer's account decreased.
    b. Customer doesn't pay the bill immediately.
    c. You bought something on account.
    d. Bank deducted service charges.
    e. Customer paid immediately.

15. Name the two subsidiary ledgers that must agree with their control accounts in the general ledger.

16. Explain the difference between a bank debit memo and a bank credit memo.

17. How would you record a debit to the Sales account in the multipurpose journal?

18. Why are there two columns labelled "Other Accounts" on the multipurpose journal?

19. Why does a multipurpose journal save posting time?

20. Which columns on the multipurpose journal are posted to both control accounts and subsidiary ledger accounts?

21. Where are account numbers placed when totals are posted from the Bank columns in the multipurpose journal?

22. Where are the posting reference notations made in a multipurpose journal for other accounts? Explain this fully.

23. When you post to the accounts receivable and accounts payable ledgers from the multipurpose journal, what kind of posting notation is used to show you have posted to these sub-ledgers?

2.3

The 8-Column Worksheet and Adjustments

Most accountants will take a trial balance on a worksheet. The worksheet below is an 8-column worksheet and the Trial Balance columns have been prepared using the year-end balances from the general ledger for Bukta Collision Service.

WORKSHEET

Bukta Collision Service   FOR THE _Year_____   ENDED _Dec. 31_ **19 –**

	ACCOUNTS	ACCT. NO.	TRIAL BALANCE DR	TRIAL BALANCE CR	ADJUSTMENTS DR	ADJUSTMENTS CR	INCOME STATEMENT DR	INCOME STATEMENT CR	BALANCE SHEET DR	BALANCE SHEET CR	
1	Bank	110	24 800 –								1
2	Accounts Receivable	120	10 000 –								2
3	All. for Doubtful Accounts	121		Ø							3
4	GST Recoverable	130	200 –								4
5	Prepaid Insurance	140	4 500 –								5
6	Building—Brick	150	120 000 –								6
7	Acc. Dep.—Building	151		6 000 –							7
8	Equipment	160	40 000 –								8
9	Acc. Dep.—Equipment	161		8 000 –							9
10	Tow Truck	170	20 000 –								10
11	Acc. Dep.—Tow Truck	171		6 000 –							11
12	Bank Loan	210		6 000 –							12
13	Accounts Payable	220		3 000 –							13
14	GST Payable	221		1 200 –							14
15	PST Payable	222		800 –							15
16	M. Bukta, Capital	310		166 000 –							16
17	M. Bukta, Drawings	315	48 000 –								17
18	Sales	410		200 000 –							18
19	Advertising Expense	502	3 600 –								19
20	Bad Debts Expense	504	Ø								20
21	Bank Charges	506	1 500 –								21
22	Dep. Exp.—Building	510	Ø								22
23	Dep. Exp.—Equipment	512	Ø								23
24	Dep. Exp.—Tow Truck	514	Ø								24
25	Discounts Earned	518		3 000 –							25
26	Heat & Light Expense	520	14 000 –								26
27	Insurance Expense	522	Ø								27
28	Miscellaneous Expense	530	900 –								28
29	Office Expense	535	400 –								29
30	Paint Expense	540	7 000 –								30
31	Parts Expense	542	41 000 –								31
32	Telephone Expense	544	1 100 –								32
33	Truck Expense	560	3 000 –								33
34	Wages Expense	580	60 000 –								34
35			400 000 –	400 000 –							35
36											36

FIGURE 2-25   An 8-column worksheet

Before this worksheet can be completed, there are some year-end adjustments that must be made in the Adjustments columns of the worksheet.

Adjustments are changes in account balances that need to be made at year end to meet generally accepted accounting principles. These adjustments can be grouped into three types, and these will be discussed in detail for you.

PREPAID INSURANCE

Prepaid insurance is an amount paid that will usually benefit a future time period. Bukta Collision has an account called "Prepaid Insurance" with an account balance of $4 500. This represents the premium on a one-year insurance policy on the fixed assets, which was paid on July 1st. A policy year for insurance does not necessarily coincide with the fiscal year of the business, therefore half of this amount will have to be expensed out at the year end.

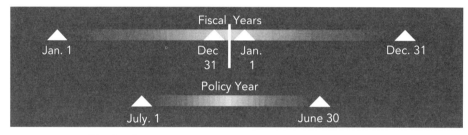

FIGURE 2-26   Timeline for insurance coverage

There are two ways a business can record the purchase of insurance in its books of account, when it pays the insurance premium:
  (a) debit an asset account, Prepaid Insurance
  (b) debit the expense account, Insurance Expense
Here is an explanation of each possible accounting option.

Debiting Prepaid Insurance
If a business uses this method, when it buys insurance, Prepaid Insurance will be debited and Bank will be credited.

GENERAL JOURNAL

PAGE _82_

DATE 19–		PARTICULARS	PR	DEBIT	CREDIT
July	1	Prepaid Insurance		4500 –	
		Bank			4500 –
		To record the purchase of a one-year			
		insurance policy			

FIGURE 2-27   Recording prepaid insurance as an asset

The adjusting entry at year end then credits Prepaid Insurance $2 250 and debits the Insurance Expense account $2 250. This is the actual amount of insurance "used up" from this policy. The other $2 250 will be the opening balance in the Prepaid Insurance account at the start of the next year. This adjustment for insurance will be entered on the worksheet later as adjusting entry #1.

Debiting Insurance Expense

The business could have debited all of the $4 500 to the Insurance Expense account when the insurance was originally bought. That is, the accounting entry would have debited Insurance Expense and credited Bank.

GENERAL JOURNAL

PAGE 82

DATE 19–		PARTICULARS	PR	DEBIT	CREDIT
July	1	Insurance Expense		4500 –	
		Bank			4500 –
		To record the purchase of a one-year			
		insurance policy			

FIGURE 2-28   *Recording prepaid insurance as an expense*

In this case the adjusting entry would be to credit the Insurance Expense account $2 250 and debit Prepaid Insurance $2 250. Whichever method is chosen, the end result is the same: the insurance expense is $2 250.

DEPRECIATION

Fixed assets in a business are depreciated, or written off, over a period of time, in an attempt to match costs to revenue. **Depreciation** is a method of allocating an asset's cost over its useful life. This is the Generally Accepted Principle of Matching. (**Generally Accepted Accounting Principles** are guidelines set down by professional accounting bodies for the preparation of financial statements.) Bukta Collision Service has three fixed assets that it has to depreciate at year end: the building, the equipment, and the tow truck. The cost of these assets has to be spread over a number of years since the assets are useful over a number of years. The two most common ways that depreciation can be calculated are the straight-line method, and the declining-balance method. Some businesses will use straight-line deprecia-tion for their books, and declining-balance depreciation for income tax pur-poses. Declining-balance depreciation, however, is the only method allowed for income tax purposes by Revenue Canada. The tax department uses the term *capital cost allowance*, rather than depreciation.

Straight-Line Depreciation

Straight-line depreciation produces an equal amount of asset depreciation for each fiscal period. It is most useful when the asset being depreciated is used evenly over its life. Salvage value must be taken into consideration when straight-line depreciation is used. Salvage value is the amount a busi-ness thinks it will get for an asset at the end of its useful life. For the straight-line depreciation example that follows, Bukta Collision Service has equipment that cost $40 000. Assume that its estimated salvage value is $5 000 and its useful life is five years. The formula and calculation for straight-line depreciation is:

$$\text{Annual Depreciation} = \frac{\text{Asset Cost} - \text{Salvage Value}}{\text{Estimated Useful Life}}$$

$$= \frac{\$40\ 000 - \$5\ 000}{5\ \text{Years}}$$

$$= \$7\ 000/\text{Year}$$

In the example above, the equipment would be depreciated by $7 000 every year for five years. At the end of five years, the equipment which would be of no further use to the business would be fully depreciated, or written off the books, and sold for its salvage value. These funds are not treated as sales revenue, but rather as an exchange of one asset for another.

Declining-Balance Depreciation

Declining-balance depreciation is the method used by most businesses, since it is the only one allowed on income tax returns in Canada. This method is also popular because it allows for higher depreciation in the early years of ownership of an asset. With this method of accelerated deprecia-tion, the same fixed percentage (or rate of depreciation) is used every year. Depreciation is calculated on the net book value of assets each year, their original cost less their depreciation to date. (Salvage values are not taken into consideration for this method of depreciation. Any scrap value can be considered near the end of the asset's life.)

When the declining-balance method of depreciation is used, fixed per-centages are used for different groups, or classes of assets. The word **class** refers to an asset grouping established by the government for purposes of depreciation. Some of the fixed asset classes allowed by Revenue Canada are:

Class	Description	Rate of Depreciation
3	BUILDINGS — brick buildings	5%
8	MACHINERY, EQUIPMENT, FIXTURES	20%
10	AUTOMOTIVE — cars, vans, trucks, tractors, stable equipment; computers	30%
16	RENTAL VEHICLES & COIN MACHINES — taxicabs, car rental business vehicles, video games, pinball machines	40%
17	SURFACE CONSTRUCTION — roads, parking lots, sidewalks, airplane runways	8%

Bukta Collision Service uses the declining-balance method of depreciation for its three fixed assets, buildings (class 3), equipment (class 8), and trucks (class 10). To calculate depreciation on each fixed asset, find the net book value of the asset on the worksheet, and apply the declining-balance rate of depreciation allowed by the government (in the table above). Here are the depreciation calculations for the three fixed assets owned by Bukta Collision Service.

Buildings (Class 3)

Building — Brick	$120 000
Accumulated Depreciation — Building	(6 000)
Net Book Value	114 000
Rate of Depreciation — Class 3	× .05 (5%)
Depreciation Expense — Building	$ 5 700

The adjustment on the worksheet is a debit to the account Depreciation Expense — Building, and credit to the account Accumulated Depreciation — Building. This depreciation will be entered on the worksheet later as adjusting entry #2.

Equipment (Class 8)

Equipment	$40 000
Accumulated Depreciation — Equipment	(8 000)
Net Book Value	32 000
Rate of Depreciation — Class 8	× .20 (20%)
Depreciation Expense — Equipment	$ 6 400

The adjustment on the worksheet is a debit to the account Depreciation Expense — Equipment and credit to the account Accumulated Depreciation — Equipment. This depreciation will be entered on the worksheet later as adjusting entry #3.

Tow Truck (Class 10)	
Tow Truck	$20 000
Accumulated Depreciation — Tow Truck	(6 000)
Net Book Value	14 000
Rate of Depreciation — Class 10	×.30 (30%)
Depreciation Expense — Tow Truck	$ 4 200

The adjustment on the worksheet is a debit to the account Depreciation Expense — Tow Truck and credit to the account Accumulated Depreciation — Tow Truck. This depreciation will be entered on the worksheet later as adjusting entry #4.

No matter what system of depreciation is used, the book value of the asset has no bearing on its market value. Depreciation is a method of allocating the cost of an asset over its useful life. In the case of fixed assets, you are spreading their cost over a number of years, not trying to guess how much they are worth each year. Accountants emphasize that depreciation is a method of allocation, not of valuation.

BAD DEBTS

The third type of adjustment relates to customers who have left their accounts outstanding for a very long time. Amounts in this category are regarded as uncollectible bad debts of the business. **Bad Debts** are customer amounts deemed to be uncollectible at the year end. An adjusting journal entry has to be made in the books. There are several approaches that can be taken in calculating this figure. The method used by Bukta Collision Service is to calculate a percentage of accounts receivable.

Percentage of Accounts Receivable

A business such as Bukta Collision Service often uses an aging analysis of its accounts receivable to calculate its bad debts at year end. The balances owing by customers are divided into time periods and then a percentage figure is applied to these balances to determine the estimated bad debts. Here is the aging analysis for Bukta Collision Service:

```
                         Aging Analysis

                                   % Estimated to    Estimated
             Age         Balance   be Uncollectible  Bad Debts
      1 - 30 Days        $8 000          1%            $ 80
     31 - 60 Days        $1 000         10%            $100
     61 - 90 Days        $  800         25%            $200
     Over 90 Days        $  200         60%            $120

                                                      $500
```

The adjusting entry on the worksheet is to debit Bad Debts Expense and credit Allowance for Doubtful Accounts (a contra account that offsets Accounts Receivable.)

GENERAL JOURNAL

PAGE 120

DATE 19–		PARTICULARS	PR	DEBIT	CREDIT
Dec.	31	Bad Debts Expense		500 –	
		Allowance for Doubtful Accounts			500 –
		To set up the allowance at year end			

FIGURE 2-29   *The general journal entry for bad debts*

This is the method that Bukta Collision uses, and this figure for bad debts will be entered on the worksheet later as adjusting entry #5.

You have learned two new contra accounts in this text, Accumulated Depreciation, and Allowance for Bad Debts.

There are five adjustments that have been made to the accounts on the worksheet. Here are the details:

(1) The insurance policy was bought on July 1st and lasts for one year. The premium paid was $4 500.00. Therefore, $2 250 has to be transferred from Prepaid Insurance to Insurance Expense.

(2) The building has to be depreciated $5 700. The building is a class 3 asset and is depreciated at 5% of net book value.

(3) The equipment has to be depreciated $6 400. The equipment is a class 8 asset and is depreciated at 20% of net book value.

(4) The tow truck has to be depreciated $4 200. The tow truck is a class 10 asset and is depreciated at 30% of net book value.

(5) The Percentage of Accounts Receivable method of calculating bad debts shows that the allowance for bad debts should be $500.

These adjustments are entered onto the worksheet and are shown for you in Figure 2-30. Each adjustment is numbered so that you can follow it logically. Once the adjustments are recorded the worksheet can be extended, totalled, and cross-balanced.

WORKSHEET

Bukta Collision Service

FOR THE _Year_ ENDED _Dec. 31_ 19 –

	ACCOUNTS	ACCT. NO.	TRIAL BALANCE		ADJUSTMENTS		INCOME STATEMENT		BALANCE SHEET		
			DR	CR	DR	CR	DR	CR	DR	CR	
1	Bank	110	24800 –						24800 –		1
2	Accounts Receivable	120	10000 –						10000 –		2
3	All. for Doubtful Accounts	121		Ø		⑤ 500 –				500 –	3
4	GST Recoverable	130	200 –						200 –		4
5	Prepaid Insurance	140	4500 –			① 2250 –			2250 –		5
6	Building—Brick	150	120000 –						120000 –		6
7	Acc. Dep.—Building	151		6000 –		② 5700 –				11700 –	7
8	Equipment	160	40000 –						40000 –		8
9	Acc. Dep.—Equipment	161		8000 –		③ 6400 –				14400 –	9
10	Tow Truck	170	20000 –						20000 –		10
11	Acc. Dep.—Tow Truck	171		6000 –		④ 4200 –				10200 –	11
12	Bank Loan	210		6000 –						6000 –	12
13	Accounts Payable	220		3000 –						3000 –	13
14	GST Payable	221		1200 –						1200 –	14
15	PST Payable	222		800 –						800 –	15
16	M. Bukta, Capital	310		166000 –						166000 –	16
17	M. Bukta, Drawings	315	48000 –						48000 –		17
18	Sales	410		200000 –				200000 –			18
19	Advertising Expense	502	3600 –				3600 –				19
20	Bad Debts Expense	504	Ø		⑤ 500 –		500 –				20
21	Bank Charges	506	1500 –				1500 –				21
22	Dep. Exp.—Building	510	Ø		② 5700 –		5700 –				22
23	Dep. Exp.—Equipment	512	Ø		③ 6400 –		6400 –				23
24	Dep. Exp.—Tow Truck	514	Ø		④ 4200 –		4200 –				24
25	Discounts Earned	518		3000 –				3000 –			25
26	Heat & Light Expense	520	14000 –				14000 –				26
27	Insurance Expense	522	Ø		① 2250 –		2250 –				27
28	Miscellaneous Expense	530	900 –				900 –				28
29	Office Expense	535	400 –				400 –				29
30	Paint Expense	540	7000 –				7000 –				30
31	Parts Expense	542	41000 –				41000 –				31
32	Telephone Expense	544	1100 –				1100 –				32
33	Truck Expense	560	3000 –				3000 –				33
34	Wages Expense	580	60000 –				60000 –				34
35			400000 –	400000 –	19050 –	19050 –	151550 –	203000 –	265250 –	213800 –	35
36	Net Income						51450 –			51450 –	36
37							203000 –	203000 –	265250 –	265250 –	37
38											38

FIGURE 2-30   *The worksheet extended and balanced*

At this point, the adjustments on the worksheet must be journalized into a general journal and posted to the general ledger. The entries are journalized for you in Figure 2-31.

GENERAL JOURNAL

PAGE 120

DATE 19–		PARTICULARS	PR	DEBIT	CREDIT
		ADJUSTING JOURNAL ENTRIES			
		①			
Dec.	31	Insurance Expense	522	2250 –	
		Prepaid Insurance	140		2250 –
		To adjust for insurance expense			
		②			
	31	Dep. Expense—Building	510	5700 –	
		Acc. Dep.—Building	151		5700 –
		To adjust for depreciation			
		③			
	31	Dep. Expense—Equipment	512	6400 –	
		Acc. Dep.—Equipment	161		6400 –
		To adjust for depreciation			
		④			
	31	Dep. Expense—Tow Truck	514	4200 –	
		Acc. Dep.—Tow Truck	171		4200 –
		To adjust for depreciation			
		⑤			
	31	Bad Debts Expense	504	500 –	
		Allowance for Doubtful Accounts	121		500 –
		To adjust for bad debts			

FIGURE 2-31   *Adjusting journal entries*

Although the general ledger is not shown, you can tell from the PR column in the general journal that these adjusting entries have been posted into the ledger. The worksheet will be used to prepare the financial statements in section 2.4.

QUESTIONS

24. List ten fixed assets that can be depreciated each year if owned by a business.

25. What does the term *net book value* mean? Does it mean the same as *market value*? Explain.

26. Find the yearly depreciation for five years on a $20 000 truck using:
    (a) straight-line depreciation
    (b) declining-balance depreciation
    The truck has a salvage value of $4 000 and will last five years.

27. Calculate the depreciation on a $14 000 photocopier for three years using:
    (a) straight-line depreciation
    (b) declining-balance depreciation
    The photocopier has a salvage value of $2 000 and is expected to last six years.

28. Calculate the depreciation on a $50 000 frame tool shed for five years using:
    (a) straight-line depreciation
    (b) declining-balance depreciation
    The tool shed has a salvage value of $5 000 and is expected to last twenty years.

29. Accumulated Depreciation — Truck is a contra account. What does *contra* mean?

30. Use the government depreciation tables provided to find the depreciation rates for these assets:
    (a) a brick warehouse
    (b) a computer system
    (c) an automobile
    (d) a lathe
    (e) shop tables
    (f) fencing

2.4

Preparing the Financial Statements

Once the 8-column worksheet has been extended, totalled, and balanced, it can be used to prepare the financial statements for the business. The two main statements you are concerned with for a small service business, such as Bukta Collision Service, are the income statement and the balance sheet. The income statement is prepared first because the net income figure has to flow through to the owner's equity section of the balance sheet.

The income statement for Bukta Collision is prepared directly from the Income Statement debit and credit columns on the worksheet:

Bukta Collision Service
Income Statement
For the Year Ended December 31, 19–

Revenue:		
Sales	$200 000	
Discounts Earned	3 000	
Total Revenue		$203 000
Expenses:		
Advertising	3 600	
Bad Debts	500	
Bank Charges	1 500	
Depreciation — Building	5 700	
Depreciation — Equipment	6 400	
Depreciation — Tow Truck	4 200	
Heat & Light	14 000	
Insurance	2 250	
Miscellaneous	900	
Office	400	
Paint	7 000	
Parts	41 000	
Telephone	1 100	
Tow Truck	3 000	
Wages	60 000	151 550
Net Income		$ 51 450

Once the income statement is prepared, you can use the Balance Sheet columns on the worksheet to prepare the formal balance sheet for the business. The net income from the income statement is transferred to the owner's equity section of the balance sheet and added to the capital balance. A net profit for the business increases the owner's equity in the business. Conversely, a net loss would be subtracted from the old capital amount since it would decrease the owner's equity.

Bukta Collision Service
Balance Sheet
December 31, 19–

Current Assets:

Bank			$ 24 800
Accounts Receivable		$ 10 000	
Less: Allowance for Bad Debts		500	9 500
GST Recoverable			200
Prepaid Insurance			2 250
Total Current Assets			36 750

Fixed Assets:

	Cost	Acc. Dep.		
Building	$120 000	$11 700	108 300	
Equipment	40 000	14 400	25 600	
Tow Truck	20 000	10 200	9 800	143 700
Total Assets				$180 450

Current Liabilities:

Bank Loan		$ 6 000	
Accounts Payable		3 000	
GST Payable		1 200	
PST Payable		800	
Total Current Liabilities			$ 11 000

Owner's Equity

Opening Balance	166 000	
Add: Net Income	51 450	
	217 450	
Less: Drawings	48 000	
Closing Balance		169 450
Total Liabilities and Owner's Equity		$180 450

There are different formats that can be used for financial statement presentation. Formats used depend on the accountant who prepares the financial statements, and/or the computer software program that might be used to prepare the statements. This will become evident in section 2.7 when the *ACCPAC Bedford Integrated Accounting* program is used.

2.5

Closing Entries

Once the income statement and the balance sheet have been prepared, a business must close out its books. Closing out the books means that all Revenue and Expense accounts and Drawings must be brought to zero, since all of these accounts keep information for only one year. At the end of a fiscal year, they must be emptied so that they are ready for the next year.

Closing entries are journal entries which close out certain accounts to nil balances at year end. To follow this process through from start to finish, you will begin with the trial balance after adjustments. See Figure 2-32.

The accounts are going to be closed out in this order:

1st: all Revenue accounts to the Income Summary
2nd: all Expense accounts to the Income Summary
3rd: the Income Summary account to the Capital account
4th: the Drawings account to the Capital account

The Income Summary account is just a temporary account used during the closing out (journalizing) process. The important thing to understand is that eventually the profit (or loss) of the business gets added to (or charged against) the owner's Capital account. Figure 2-33 shows the closing journal entries in the order just mentioned. They are numbered for your convenience in cross-referencing.

		Bukta Collision Service Trial Balance December 31, 19–		
110	Bank		$ 24 800	
120	Accounts Receivable		10 000	
121	Allowance for Doubtful Accounts			$ 500
130	GST Recoverable		200	
140	Prepaid Insurance		2 250	
150	Building (Brick)		120 000	
151	Accumulated Depreciation — Building			11 700
160	Equipment		40 000	
161	Accumulated Depreciation — Equipment			14 400
170	Tow Truck		20 000	
171	Accumulated Depreciation — Tow Truck			10 200
210	Bank Loan			6 000
220	Accounts Payable			3 000
221	GST Payable			1 200
222	PST Payable			800
310	M. Bukta, Capital			166 000
315	M. Bukta, Drawings		48 000	
410	Sales			200 000
502	Advertising Expense		3 600	
504	Bad Debts Expense		500	
506	Bank Charges		1 500	
510	Depreciation Expense — Building		5 700	
512	Depreciation Expense — Equipment		6 400	
514	Depreciation Expense — Tow Truck		4 200	
518	Discounts Earned			3 000
520	Heat & Light Expense		14 000	
522	Insurance Expense		2 250	
530	Miscellaneous Expense		900	
535	Office Expense		400	
540	Paint Expense		7 000	
542	Parts Expense		41 000	
544	Telephone Expense		1 100	
560	Tow Truck Expense		3 000	
580	Wages Expense		60 000	
			$416 800	$416 800

FIGURE 2-32   *Trial balance after adjustments*

GENERAL JOURNAL

PAGE 121

DATE 19–		PARTICULARS	PR	DEBIT	CREDIT
		CLOSING JOURNAL ENTRIES			
		①			
Dec.	31	Sales		2 0 0 0 0 0 –	
		Discounts Earned		3 0 0 0 –	
		Income Summary			2 0 3 0 0 0 –
		To close out Revenue accounts			
		②			
	31	Income Summary		1 5 1 5 5 0 –	
		Advertising Expense			3 6 0 0 –
		Bad Debts Expense			5 0 0 –
		Bank Charges			1 5 0 0 –
		Depreciation Expense—Building			5 7 0 0 –
		Depreciation Expense—Equipment			6 4 0 0 –
		Depreciation Expense—Tow Truck			4 2 0 0 –
		Heat & Light Expense			1 4 0 0 0 –
		Insurance Expense			2 2 5 0 –
		Miscellaneous Expense			9 0 0 –
		Office Expense			4 0 0 –
		Paint Expense			7 0 0 0 –
		Parts Expense			4 1 0 0 0 –
		Telephone Expense			1 1 0 0 –
		Tow Truck Expense			3 0 0 0 –
		Wages Expense			6 0 0 0 0 –
		To close out Expense accounts			
		③			
	31	Income Summary		5 1 4 5 0 –	
		M. Bukta, Capital			5 1 4 5 0 –
		To close out Income Summary			
		account			
		④			
	31	M. Bukta, Capital		4 8 0 0 0 –	
		M. Bukta, Drawings			4 8 0 0 0 –
		To close out Drawings account			

FIGURE 2-33   *Closing journal entries*

Once the closing entries have been journalized, they must be posted into the appropriate accounts in the general ledger.

The Post-Closing Trial Balance

Once the closing entries have been posted to the general ledger accounts, a trial balance should be taken to ensure that the ledger is still in balance. There are essentially three ways to take the trial balance:
(1) a zero proof tape trial balance
(2) a balanced ledger tape trial balance
(3) a formal trial balance
In the first option, the zero proof, a calculator tape is taken of all of the account balances left after closing. The accounts are listed in the order they appear in the ledger, and when the tape is totalled it should show a "0" balance. The second option is a listing of all debit account balances and a total, followed by a listing of all the credit account balances and a total — the totals for the debits and credits should equal each other. The third option is a formal trial balance where all of the accounts in the ledger are listed along with their final balances. Figure 2-34 shows the formal trial balance for Bukta Collision Service.

Bukta Collision Service
Trial Balance
December 31, 19–

110	Bank	$ 24 800	
120	Accounts Receivable	10 000	
121	Allowance for Doubtful Accounts		$ 500
130	GST Recoverable	200	
140	Prepaid Insurance	2 250	
150	Building (Brick)	120 000	
151	Accumulated Depreciation — Building		11 700
160	Equipment	40 000	
161	Accumulated Depreciation — Equipment		14 400
170	Tow Truck	20 000	
171	Accumulated Depreciation — Tow Truck		10 200
210	Bank Loan		6 000
220	Accounts Payable		3 000
221	GST Payable		1 200
222	PST Payable		800
310	M. Bukta, Capital		169 450
		$217 250	$217 250

FIGURE 2-34   *Post-closing trial balance*

Take another look at Figure 2-34. Notice that all of the Revenue and Expense accounts and the Drawings account are missing. They have been emptied so that they are ready for the next fiscal period. The Drawings account has been charged against the Capital account and the profit for the year has been added to the Capital account. The accounts are now ready for the next accounting period to begin.

This completes the accounting cycle for this service business. The next section will explain how a computer can be used for accounting work in a service business.

2.6

Using the Computer

There are many ways in which a computer can be useful in a service business. This section will provide several examples of business forms or reports that can be made using spreadsheet, graphics, and database software.

Spreadsheets

A **spreadsheet** is a computer document consisting of rows and columns which can be programmed with formulas. An Accounts Receivable summary can be produced using a spreadsheet program. Here is a sample Accounts Receivable summary for Bukta Collision Service that has been prepared using a spreadsheet program.

	A	B	C	D	E
1	Bukta Collision Service				
2	ACCOUNTS RECEIVABLE				
3					
4	Month	Balance			
5					
6	Jan	2100			
7	Feb	3800			
8	Mar	12000			
9	Apr	14200			
10	May	9800			
11	Jun	10000			
12	Average	8650			
13					
14					
15					
16					

FIGURE 2-35   *A spreadsheet accounts receivable summary*

Some of the information on a spreadsheet can be permanent, such as the heading "Accounts Receivable", the sub-heading "Bukta Collision Service", and the column labels. When a new spreadsheet is drawn up, the permanent areas will not have to be changed. New accounts receivable data will simply have to be inserted into the correct cells in the Balance column. The spreadsheet has been programmed to average the Balance column automatically. This pre-programming feature of the spreadsheet is what gives the spreadsheet its power and usefulness.

Graphics

The word **graphics** refers to computer software which presents accounting data in graph form. Once a spreadsheet has been stored on disk, it is usually easy to have the computer print a graph of the data from the spreadsheet. Most integrated software packages have this feature. And usually once the spreadsheet is stored, you can go directly to the production of a graph. There are different styles of graphs, with the three most common being bar graphs, line graphs, and pie charts. The example for Bukta Collision is a bar graph showing the Accounts Receivable for the business for the last six months. The graph gives a quick visual impression of the Accounts Receivable balances over the time period selected.

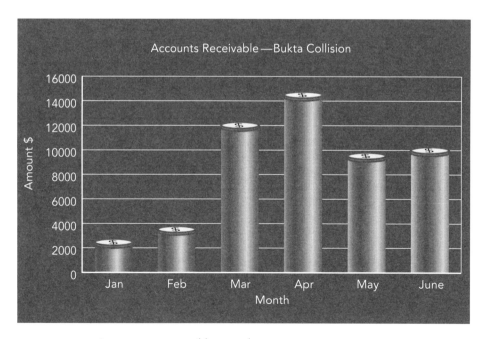

FIGURE 2-36   *A computer-generated bar graph*

With this software, you label the graph as well. The balance owing is scaled on the y-axis on the left, and the months are shown on the x-axis along the bottom. The data for the graph is taken from a spreadsheet which the computer has in its memory.

Databases

A **database** is one or more files of accounting information. One example of a database which might be useful to Bukta Collision Service is a list of suppliers.

```
Name:   Fairway Supply
Address:   279 Blucher St.
Town:   Kitchener
PC:  N2H 5V8
Terms:   2/15, n/30
```
one record

```
ACCOUNTS PAYABLE FILE
```

Name	Address	Town	PC	Terms
Auto Supply Parts	1210 Dundas St.	London	N5W 3A9	n/30
C.M. Peterson	75 Adelaide St. S.	London	N5Z 3K3	n/30
Fairway Supply	279 Blucher St.	Kitchener	N2H 5V8	2/15, n/30
Border Parts	4420 Drummond St.	Niagara Falls	L2E 6E6	1/10, n/30
Peter Paint Company	170 Concession St.	Cambridge	N1R 2H7	3/10, n/30
Breck Auto Parts	1216 Dundas St.	London	N5W 3A9	n/15

FIGURE 2-37   *A supplier file*

The top part of Figure 2-37 shows the form used when the database is set up and stored. The lower part is an up-to-date listing of all of the suppliers who sell goods and services to Bukta Collision, and includes their names, addresses, and terms. Once this file is saved in the computer, it is easy to get certain printouts, e.g., all suppliers who offer a discount of 2% or more. The computer is very good at sorting, selecting, and printing specific information once the original file has been stored.

2.7

Bedford Exercise 2 — Bluebuoy Houseboats

The company in this chapter is called Bluebuoy Houseboats, a houseboat rental service operated by a man with 25 years of experience on major cruise lines.

Bluebuoy Houseboats is a sole proprietorship owned by John Cook. The main office is in Vancouver, BC, but the houseboat rentals take place on Shuswap Lake. The sole source of income for the business is from the rental of houseboats on a daily, weekend, or weekly basis. Although this is a seasonal business and most of the revenue is earned in the summer months, the start of the fiscal year is January 1. Because the business has tripled in size in the last three years, the owner has decided to computerize the accounting records using the *ACCPAC Bedford Integrated Accounting* software. The business has completed six months of operations. The trial balance after six months is as shown.

The accounts and all of the historical balances have been entered onto a disk for you, and the computer accounting system only has to be set to **Ready** mode. The instructions for using *Bedford* and entering data are outlined in Chapter 1.

No.	Account	Debit	Credit
	Bluebuoy Houseboats		
	Trial Balance after 6 months		
110	Bank	$ 22 006	
130	GST Recoverable	560	
140	Supplies	2 015	
180	Houseboats	425 000	
190	Furniture & Equipment	6 040	
210	Bank Loan		$ 11 200
220	A/P Otter Marine Engines		4 200
230	GST Payable		800
235	PST Payable		1 800
240	CPP Payable		202
241	UI Payable		324
242	Income Tax Payable		2 372
243	Provincial Medical Payable		188
310	J. Cook, Capital		430 000

315	J. Cook, Drawings	4 000	
356	Retained Earnings		0
410	Houseboat Rental Income		50 000
510	Accounting & Legal Expense	1 000	
520	Advertising Expense	2 925	
530	Bank Charges	975	
535	CPP Expense	101	
540	Heat & Light Expense	2 299	
550	Houseboat Expenses	8 500	
560	Miscellaneous Expense	315	
570	Rent Expense	6 000	
580	Telephone Expense	750	
585	UI Expense	100	
590	Wages Expense	18 500	
		$501 086	$501 086

ACCESSING THE BLUEBUOY HOUSEBOATS GENERAL LEDGER

To retrieve the general ledger for Bluebuoy, you use the file name **bluebuoy**. Key this name into the computer, insert the dates provided by your teacher, and set the program to **Ready**, as described in Chapter 1.

Enter the **Using** date provided by your teacher. Remember the sequence, mmddyy. As before, ignore the cautions and proceed.

JOURNALIZING TRANSACTIONS

To journalize general ledger transactions, access the **GENERAL** module and the **Journal** option.

TRANSACTIONS

1. Cash Receipt 398   Dated: mm01yy
   Cash sale $1 130; Houseboat Rental Income $1 000 plus GST Payable $70, and PST Payable $60.

2. Cash Receipt 399   Dated: mm01yy
   Cash sale $1 356; Houseboat Rental Income $1 200 plus GST Payable $84, and PST Payable $72.

3. Cheque 439   Dated: mm01yy
Rent Expense, $12 000 plus GST Recoverable $840; cheque for $12 840 to Shuswap Properties.

4. Cheque 440   Dated: mm02yy
Bank loan payment, $1 000 plus Bank Charges (interest) $98; cheque for $1 098 to the Toronto-Dominion Bank.

5. Cheque 441   Dated: mm05yy
Supplies, $600 plus GST Recoverable $39.62; cheque for $639.62 to the Bayshore Marina.

6. Cash Receipt 400   Dated: mm06yy
Cash received, $3 955; Houseboat Rental Income $3 500 plus GST Payable $245, and PST Payable $210.

7. Cash Receipt 401   Dated: mm07yy
Cash sale $1 356; Houseboat Rental Income $1 200 plus GST Payable $84, and PST Payable $72.

8. Cheque 442   Dated: mm08yy
Advertising Expenses, $420 plus GST Recoverable $29.40; cheque for $449.40 to CPC Printing.

9. Purchase Invoice T7000   Dated: mm10yy
Supplies, $810 plus GST Recoverable $53.49; on account from Thunderbird Marine; total $863.49.

Note: This requires a new A/P account in the ledger for Thunderbird Marine. To insert a new account, access **GENERAL**, **Ledger**, and **Insert**. Key in this information:

       Account: A/P Thunderbird Marine
       Number: 221
       Type: R
       Suppress: Y

10. Cash Receipt 402   Dated: mm12yy
Cash sale $1 356; Houseboat Rental Income $1 200 plus GST Payable $84, and PST Payable $72.

11. Cash Receipt 403   Dated: mm13yy
Cash sale $4 746; Houseboat Rental Income $4 200 plus GST Payable $294, and PST Payable $252.

12. Cheque 443   Dated: mm14yy
    CPP Payable (Dr) $202; UI Payable (Dr) $324; Income Tax Payable
    (Dr) $2 372; Bank (Cr) $2 898.
    (Note: Don't forget to add a minus sign after these figures because you
    are decreasing these account balances.)

13. Cheque 444   Dated: mm15yy
    Wages Expense (Dr) $4 250; CPP Payable (Cr)$81; UI Payable (Cr)
    $42; Income Tax Payable (Cr) $1 186; Provincial Medical Payable (Cr)
    $94; Bank (Cr) $2 847.

14. Memo 121   Dated: mm15yy
    Employer's payroll contributions; CPP Expense (Dr) $81; UI Expense
    (Dr) $67; CPP Payable (Cr) $81; UI Payable (Cr) $67.

15. Cash Receipt 404   Dated: mm16yy
    Cash sale $1 356; Houseboat Rental Income $1 200 plus GST Payable
    $84, and PST Payable $72.

16. Cash Receipt 405   Dated: mm18yy
    Cash sale $1 243; Houseboat Rental Income $1 100 plus GST Payable
    $77, and PST Payable $66.

17. Cash Receipt 406   Dated: mm20yy
    Cash sale $5 650; Houseboat Rental Income $ 5 000 plus GST Payable
    $350, and PST Payable $300.

18. Cash Receipt 407   Dated: mm21yy
    Cash sale $904; Houseboat Rental Income $800 plus GST Payable $56,
    and PST Payable $48.

19. Cheque 445   Dated: mm23yy
    Provincial Medical Payable, $282; paid in full.

20. Cash Receipt 408   Dated: mm27yy
    Cash sale $9 040; Houseboat Rental Income $8 000 plus GST Payable
    $560, and PST Payable $480.

21. Purchase Invoice 5009   Dated: mm29yy
    Houseboat Expenses, $5 800 plus GST Recoverable $383.02; on
    account from Pace Marine; total $6 183.02.

    Note: This requires a new account in the ledger for Pace Marine. To
    insert a new account, access **GENERAL**, **Ledger**, and **Insert**. Key in
    the following information.

Account: A/P Pace Marine
Number: 222
Type: R
Suppress: Y

22. Cheque 446   Dated: mm30yy
Wages Expense (Dr) $4 250; CPP Payable (Cr) $81; UI Payable (Cr)
$42; Income Tax Payable (Cr) $1 186; Provincial Medical Payable (Cr)
$94; Bank (Cr) $2 847.

23. Memo 122   Dated: mm30yy
Employer's payroll contributions; CPP Expense (Dr) $81; UI Expense
(Dr) $67; CPP Payable (Cr) $81; UI Payable (Cr) $67.

24. Cheque 447   Dated: mm30yy
J. Cook, Drawings $4 000.

DISPLAYING AND PRINTING

Select **Display**. Your teacher will advise you which of the six options to
preview. You may be prompted for dates. Remember, a date is entered in
the sequence mmddyy (month/day/year).

Print any statements requested by your teacher. Again, you may be
prompted for dates.

FINISHING A SESSION

Access the **SYSTEM** module and select the **Finish** option.

2.8

Dictionary of Accounting Terms

Adjustments   Changes in account balances that need to be made at year
end to meet generally accepted accounting principles.

Bad Debt   A customer account deemed to be uncollectible at year end.

Bank Credit Memo   A notice mailed by the bank when it puts money into
your bank account.

Bank Debit Memo   A notice mailed by the bank when it deducts money from your bank account.

Cash Receipt   A cash sale or a receipt on account from a customer.

Charge Sale   A sale whereby a customer agrees in writing to pay on a later date for goods or services received.

Cheque Copy   A document indicating payment to buy an asset, to reduce a liability, or to pay an expense.

Class   An asset grouping established by the government for purposes of depreciation.

Closing Entries   Journal entries which close out certain accounts to nil balances at year end.

Credit Invoice   A document received from a supplier which reduces accounts payable, or issued to a customer to reduce accounts receivable.

Depreciation   A method of allocating an asset's cost over its useful life.

General Ledger   All of the accounts of a business needed to prepare the financial statements.

Generally Accepted Accounting Principles   Guidelines set down by professional accounting bodies for the preparation of financial statements.

GST   The federal goods and services sales tax.

Input Tax Credit   The GST paid for purchases which can be subtracted from the GST otherwise payable.

Multipurpose Journal   A multi-columned book of account used to record balanced accounting transactions.

Posting Reference   An account number or page number which indicates that an accounting entry has been posted.

Prepaid Insurance   Insurance which will benefit a future time period.

PST   A provincial retail sales tax applied (where used) to goods and services.

Purchase Invoice   An accounting document received when goods or services are bought on account.

Source Documents   Documents which are used to make accounting entries in the books of account.

MANUAL EXERCISES

1. Journalize these accounting transactions for Ralph's Cleaning Service (which is located in Ontario), on page 8, in a multipurpose journal. Add, balance, and rule the multipurpose journal.

Jan. 2: Cheque Copy
           Paid rent for the month to Alf Lossing, $425.00 plus $29.75 GST Recoverable; cheque #320.
       3: Cash Sale
           Cash sale of services, $310.00 plus $21.70 GST Payable; invoice #1900.
           (Note: All cash received is deposited immediately into the business bank account.)
       5: Charge Sale
           Sold services on account to Jim Poach for $250 plus $17.50 GST Payable; invoice #1901. Terms net 30.
       5: Cash Receipt
           Received on account, $200 from Karen Jansen.
       8: Cash Sale
           Cash sale of services, $650 plus $45.50 GST Payable; invoice #1902.
       9: Purchase Invoice
           Bought supplies on account from Canadian Paint, $234 plus $15.17 GST Recoverable (charge to Supplies Expense); invoice #C373.
      12: Cheque Copy
           Paid $175.00 plus $12.25 GST Recoverable to CJJN for radio advertising; cheque #321.
      13: Cash Sale
           Cash sale of services, $520 plus $36.40 GST Payable; invoice #1903.
      14: Purchase Invoice
           Bought supplies on account from Lamer Wholesale, $117 plus $7.58 GST Recoverable; invoice #667.
      16: Cheque Copy
           Truck repairs, $302 plus $19.57 GST Recoverable; cheque #322 to King Bros.
      17: Charge Sale
           Sold services on account to Helen Graham, $350 plus $24.50 GST Payable; invoice #1904. Terms net 30.
      21: Cash Sale
           Cash sale of services, $610 plus $42.70 GST Payable; invoice #1905.

22:   Cheque Copy
      Made a $500.00 payment on the current portion of the bank loan
      to the Bank of Montreal, cheque #323.

23:   Cash Sale
      Cash sale of services, $1 400 plus $98 GST Payable; invoice #1906.

24:   Cash Receipt
      Jim Poach paid his account in full; invoice #1901.

25:   Bank Memo
      A bank debit memo was received from the Bank of Montreal for
      $220; interest on the bank loan.

27:   Cheque Copy
      Purchased $390.00 worth of supplies from Bendix Cleaning plus
      $25.28 GST Recoverable; cheque #324.

29:   Cheque Copy
      The owner, Ralph Misquita, withdrew $500.00 from the business
      for his personal use. Cheque #325.

30:   Charge Sale
      Sold services on account to Chang Duong, $450 plus $31.50 GST
      Payable; invoice #1907. Terms net 30.

30:   Cash Sale
      Cash sale of services, $725 plus $50.75 GST Payable; invoice #1908.

31:   Purchase Invoice
      Bought a new electronic sander, on account, for the business from
      Black and Decker, $480 plus $31.11 GST Recoverable; invoice #973.
      Charge to the Equipment (asset) account.

31:   Cash Receipt
      Helen Graham paid her account in full (invoice #1904).

2. Journalize these transactions for Pam's Portrait Studio (which is located in
   Alberta), on page 1, in a multipurpose journal. Add, balance, and rule the
   multipurpose journal. Post to the general ledger, and take a trial balance of
   the ledger.

   Nov. 2:   Opening Entry
              Pam Chan opened the business with $10 000 cash and
              equipment worth $3 750.

         2:   Charge Sale
              Sold services on account to Chris Black, $420 plus GST Payable
              $29.40; invoice #001. Terms net 30.

         3:   Purchase Invoice
              Bought a computer from Land of Software, $2 500 plus $175 GST
              Recoverable. Their invoice #812, net 30. Charge to Equipment.

4:   Cheque Copy
Wrote a cheque to Landon Holdings for the monthly rent, $920 plus $64.40 GST Recoverable; cheque #101.

7:   Cash Sale
Cash sale $525 plus $36.75 GST Payable; invoice #002.
(Note: Cash received is always deposited directly into the bank account. All cash received is deposited immediately into the business bank account.)

8:   Bank Credit Memo
Borrowed $18 000.00 from Canada Trust at 10.5%. The money was deposited in the bank account.

8:   Cheque Copy
Bought a new van from Spalding Motors, invoice #565, $16 750 plus $1 172.50 GST Recoverable; cheque #102.

11:   Charge Sale
Invoice #003 to Charlene Calvert, $825 plus $57.75 GST Payable. Terms net 30.

12:   Cash Receipt
Chris Black paid his account in full, $449.40.

14:   Purchase Invoice
Bought developing chemicals on account from Murray Photo, $1 020.16 plus $71.41 GST Recoverable; invoice #891. Terms are 2/15, n/30. Charge to Supplies Expense.

14:   Cash Sale
Cash sale, $900 plus $63 GST Payable; invoice #004.

18:   Purchase Invoice
Purchase invoice #116 from Hobb Papers for envelopes for pictures, $176.31 plus $12.34 GST Recoverable. Terms net 30.

20:   Charge Sale
Sale on account to Steve Gergich, $300 plus $21 GST Payable; invoice #005. Terms net 30.

21:   Charge Sale
Sale on account to Darrell Marshall, $680 plus $47.60 GST Payable; invoice #006. Terms net 30.

21:   Cash Sale
Cash sale, $1 100 plus $77 GST Payable; invoice #007.

22:   Cheque Copy
Cheque #103 to Canada Trust, $1 000.00, to partially reduce the principal of the bank loan.

22:   Cheque Copy
      Cheque #104 to Murray Photo Supply to pay invoice #891 in full,
      less the 2% discount on the invoice.
25:   Cash Sale
      Cash sale $450 plus $31.50 GST Payable; invoice #008.
27:   Cheque Copy
      Paid the telephone bill, $128.75 plus $9.01 GST Recoverable;
      cheque #105.
28:   Cash Receipt
      Steve Gergich paid invoice #005 in full.
29:   Cheque Copy
      Wrote cheque #106 to Land of Software, $2 675.
30:   Charge Sale
      Sale on account to Karen Codling, $575 plus $40.25 GST Payable;
      invoice #009. Terms net 30.
30:   Cash Receipt
      Darrell Marshall paid his account in full; invoice #006.
30:   Bank Debit Memo
      Interest on the bank loan at Canada Trust, $113.89.

3. Find the net book value and depreciation for these fixed assets. Use the
   government table of depreciation rates.

Asset	Balance	Accumulated Depreciation
Frame Shed	$25 000	$ 2 500
Video Games	$48 000	$16 400
Parking Lot	$14 000	$ 8 500
Delivery Van	$19 500	$ 0

4. Find the annual depreciation on the assets below, using straight-line
   depreciation:

Asset	Cost	Salvage Value	Estimated Life
Automobile	$24 000	$4 000	5 years
Shop Lathe	$ 8 200	$1 200	10 years
Frame Shed	$28 000	$4 000	8 years
Trailer	$12 000	$1 200	6 years

5. Find the annual depreciation on the assets below, using straight-line depreciation:

Asset	Cost	Salvage Value	Estimated Life
Automobile	$18 000	$3 000	5 years
Furniture	$10 000	$ 500	10 years
Computer	$ 4 800	$ 800	4 years
Dental Equipment	$32 000	$4 000	8 years

6. Calculate and journalize, on page 9 of a general journal, the annual depreciation for each of the following assets using the declining-balance method of depreciation, as of December 31, 19–.

Asset	Cost	Rate
Photocopiers	$ 18 000	20%
Boiler	$ 60 250	20%
Building	$375 000	5%
Trucks	$128 400	30%

7. Calculate and journalize, on page 12 of a general journal, the annual depreciation for each of these assets using the declining-balance method of depreciation, as of December 31, 19–.

Asset	Cost	Rate
Snowplow	$ 82 000	30%
Combine	$130 000	30%
Furniture	$ 18 800	20%
Shop Building	$ 90 000	5%

8. Calculate and journalize, on page 17 of a general journal, the adjustment for these insurance policies. Your company has a December 31st year end. The policies were originally charged to Prepaid Insurance.

Company	Premium	Policy Date	Term
Aetna	$1 200	Apr. 1st	3 years
Western	$ 600	Aug. 1st	2 years
Gore	$4 800	Feb. 1st	1 year

9. Calculate and journalize, on page 22 of a general journal, the adjustment for the following insurance policies. Your company has a December 31st year end. The policies were originally charged to Prepaid Insurance.

Company	Premium	Policy Date	Term
Aetna	$4 500	Jul. 1st	3 years
Western	$3 000	Nov. 1st	2 years
Gore	$ 960	Dec. 1st	1 year

10. Find the adjusting entry for bad debts.

Age	Balance	% Estimated to be Uncollectible	Estimated Bad Debts
1 – 30 Days	$6 000	7%	
31 – 60 Days	$4 000	10%	
61 – 90 Days	$1 800	30%	
Over 90 Days	$ 450	60%	

Journalize the adjusting journal entry for the bad debts, on page 17 in a general journal, as of June 30, 19–.

11. Find the adjusting entry for bad debts.

Age	Balance	% Estimated to be Uncollectible	Estimated Bad Debts
1 – 30 Days	$6 200	7%	
31 – 60 Days	$2 300	10%	
61 – 90 Days	$ 700	30%	
Over 90 Days	$ 200	60%	

Journalize the adjusting journal entry for the bad debts, on page 9 in a general journal, as of September 30. 19–.

12. The trial balance for Schmidt Enterprises is:

Schmidt Enterprises
Trial Balance
December 31, 19–

No.	Account	Debit	Credit
110	Bank	$ 4 750	
120	Accounts Receivable	1 750	
121	Allowance For Doubtful Accounts		$ 0
130	GST Recoverable	200	
140	Prepaid Insurance	900	
150	Building (Brick)	58 705	
151	Acc. Dep. — Building		0
160	Office Equipment	15 000	
161	Acc. Dep. — Office Equipment		0

210	Bank Loan		3 000
220	Accounts Payable		3 600
230	GST Payable		400
310	S. Schmidt, Capital		75 000
315	S. Schmidt, Drawings	23 500	
410	Consulting Fees		118 000
502	Advertising Expense	475	
504	Bad Debts Expense	0	
505	Bank Charges	280	
508	Dep. Exp. — Office Equipment	0	
510	Insurance Expense	720	
512	Supplies Expense	800	
514	Telephone Expense	2 900	
516	Utilities Expense	7 700	
518	Wages Expense	82 320	
		$200 000	$200 000

(a) Transfer this data to an 8-column worksheet and record these adjustments at year end, December 31st.
   (i) Fixed assets are depreciated using (government) declining-balance rates; building 5%, equipment 20%.
   (ii) Prepaid insurance is to be credited $450 and expensed.
   (iii) The bad debts will be 1% of the accounts receivable.
(b) Prepare an income statement and a balance sheet at year end.

13. The trial balance for Jim's Ski School is shown below.

Jim's Ski School
Trial Balance
April 30, 19–

No.	Account	Debit	Credit
110	Bank	$ 2 290	
120	Accounts Receivable	5 375	
130	GST Recoverable	375	
140	Prepaid Insurance	2 280	
150	Ski Equipment	38 400	
151	Acc. Dep. — Ski Equipment		$ 0

151	Acc. Dep. — Ski Equipment		$ 0
160	Van	24 000	
161	Acc. Dep. — Van		0
210	Bank Loan		4 075
220	Accounts Payable		2 200
230	GST Payable		525
310	J. Peters, Capital		35 000
315	J. Peters, Drawings	18 320	
410	Lesson Income		228 200
502	Advertising Expense	5 000	
504	Bad Debts Expense	0	
506	Bank Charges	670	
508	Dep. Exp. — Ski Equipment	0	
510	Dep. Exp. — Van	0	
512	Equipment Repairs	13 450	
514	Insurance Expense	0	
516	Rent Expense	35 000	
518	Supplies Expense	2 400	
520	Telephone Expense	900	
522	Utilities Expense	6 210	
524	Van Expense	2 830	
526	Wages Expense	112 500	
		$270 000	$270 000

(a) Transfer this data to an 8-column worksheet and record these adjustments at year end, April 30, 19–.
   (i) The ski equipment and the van are depreciated using (government) declining-balance rates; equipment 20%, van 30%.
   (ii) The prepaid insurance has been used up. Expense it!
   (iii) The bad debts will be 1% of the accounts receivable. Add the appropriate account for this item.
(b) Prepare an income statement and a balance sheet at year end for the business.
(c) Journalize the adjusting entries in a general journal, page 15.
(d) Journalize the closing entries for the business.

COMPUTER EXERCISES

SS1   Set up a spreadsheet template for the following sales invoice. Save it under the file name CH2SS1.

```
        A            B           C          D          E          F
 1  BUD'S INCOME TAX SERVICE                                   INVOICE
 2  55 DUNDAS STREET
 3  FLIN FLON, MANITOBA
 4
 5  Name:
 6  Address:
 7  Town:
 8  Postal Code:                          Date:                   19
 9
10
11
12
13
14
15                                                   TOTAL
16
17  INVOICE NO:               OVERDUE INTEREST: 2% PER MONTH
18
```

SS2   Call up the template saved as CH2SS1 and prepare an invoice for this transaction. Save your work under the file name CH2SS2.

Name: Paul McQuiggin
Address: 1200 North Street
Town: Churchill Falls, Manitoba
Postal Code: R4G 1B6   Date: April 10, 19–
    Preparation of personal income tax return including an
    Investment Income Schedule.   Total: $ 85.00
Invoice No: 467

SS3   Change the template saved as CH2SS1 and prepare an invoice for the
data given. Save under the file name CH2SS3.

> Burt's Tree Removal
> R.R. 2
> Flin Flon, Manitoba R6Y 2N9
> Name: Ms. Heather Chapman
> Address: R.R. 3
> Town: Flin Flon, Manitoba
> Postal Code: R6Y 2N8   Date: July 20, 19–
>   Removal of 2 tree stumps in front yard $75.00
>   Replacement of 6 fence posts in back yard $90.00
> Invoice No: B88-374

SS4   Use a spreadsheet to produce this sales summary for The Mane Event,
a hairdressing salon. Save under the file name CH2SS4.

	A	B	C	D	E	F
1	SALES SUMMARY					
2						
3	JAN	12000				
4	FEB	14000				
5	MAR	18000				
6	APR	15000				
7	MAY	20000				
8	JUN	25000				
9	TOTAL	?				

SS5   Use a spreadsheet to produce this payroll summary for The Quick
Construction Company. Save under the file name CH2SS5.

	A	B	C	D	E	F
1	PAYROLL SUMMARY					
2						
3	ADAMS	550				
4	COSTA	575				
5	HILLIS	600				
6	MEHDI	480				
7	TAKACS	500				
8	TOTAL	?				

SS6   Use a spreadsheet to produce the following accounts receivable summary
for The Weed Crew, a lawn repair service. Interest on account balance is
calculated at 2% of the account balance. Save under the file name CH2SS6.

	A	B	C	D	E	F
1	ACCOUNTS RECEIVABLE					
2	CUSTOMER		BALANCE		INTEREST	
3	ANDERSON, W.		540.00		?	
4	GONOZ, K.		1 280.00		?	
5	MONIZ, A.		120.00		?	
6	MUELLER, P.		180.00		?	
7	PIOMBO, A.		330.00		?	
8	TOTAL		?		?	

DB1 Prepare a customer database for Hiawatha Insurance Co. using these five customers as an example.

Name	Address	Town	Balance
J. Dewaele	34 Friar Lane	Kingston	$456.50
S. Martens	12 Holt St.	Cornwall	$760.60
S. Cattle	200 Canon Ave.	Kingston	$210.00
C. Calvert	6 Gordon St.	Cornwall	$ 50.00
H. Chapman	456 John St.	Napanee	$304.08

Prepare an alphabetical list of the file, with the balances totalled.

DB2 Prepare a customer database for Anne's Sewing Shop using these five customers as an example.

Name	Address	Town	Balance
B. Vermeeren	1210 Allen Pkwy.	Regina	$2 402.50
J. Grant	823 Farrell St.	Regina	$1 002.90
H. Wallington	16 Grey St.	Regina	$ 80.25
H. Den Dekker	231 Drew St.	Regina	$4 235.74
J. Strome	2828 Tomm Ave.	Regina	$ 465.65

Prepare an alphabetical list of the file, with the balances totalled.

DB3 Prepare a payroll database for Henderson Recreation using these five employees as an example.

No.	Name	Dept.	Hourly Rate
1.	B. Molnar	A	$10.25
2.	M. Vallee	B	$10.16
3.	S. Waite	A	$10.80
4.	J. Torres	B	$ 9.75
5.	R. Serrador	B	$10.90

Prepare a list of the file, with the employees ranked from the highest hourly rate to the lowest.

DB4   Prepare a payroll database for Malahide Township using these five employees as an example.

No.	Name	Hourly Rate	Hours
1.	H. Schmidt	$10.50	40
2.	S. Townsend	$11.00	38
3.	D. Marshall	$12.00	35
4.	D. Hawley	$ 9.10	40
5.	C. Eisele	$11.82	40

Program the database to find each employee's gross pay, and then prepare a list of the file, with the employees ranked from the highest gross pay to the lowest.

DB5   Prepare an accounts payable database for Rick's Electronics Shop using these five suppliers as an example.

Name	Address	Town	PC	Balance
Grey Co.	121 Dundas St.	London	N6A 3F2	$4 500.00
Websters	23 Town Line	Dutton	N7B 2G5	$ 812.37
Dart Ltd.	400 Adelaide St.	London	N6A 3G6	$2 356.02
Eatonia	2323 Fifth Ave.	Windsor	N9H 5Y5	$1 445.16
King Bros.	R.R.1	Chatham	N8G 1G1	$ 432.70

Sort the file alphabetically by supplier name, program the database to find the total balance owing to all suppliers, then prepare a list of the file.

DB6   Prepare an accounts payable database for Essex Fertilizers using these five suppliers as an example.

Name	Address	Town	PC	Balance
Aldrich Ltd.	R.R.2	Harley	N7A 4F2	$5 112.67
Green Feed	R.R.3	Dutton	N7B 2G5	$2 110.54
CIL	R.R.1	Leamington	N2H H2P	$7 443.32
Dow Chemical	R.R.2	Sarnia	N9l 6L2	$6 223.48
Nutra Fill	R.R.1	Tilbury	N9N 3M3	$3 567.95

Select any suppliers whose balance is over $3 000 and print an alphabetical list of those suppliers.

GR1   Create a bar graph for Raymore Microfilming Service using this sales data. Your vertical axis should read 1 000, 1 200, 1 400, 1 600, 1 800, 2 000, and 2 200.

Raymore Microfilming Service
Sales Data — First Half 19–

January	$1 010
February	$1 200
March	$1 750
April	$1 440
May	$1 590
June	$2 090

GR2   Create a line graph for the Sunset Motel using this sales data. Your vertical axis should read 10 000, 12 000, 14 000, 16 000, 18 000, 20 000, and 22 000.

Sunset Motel
Sales Data — Second Half 19–

July	$21 800
August	$20 400
September	$12 300
October	$10 100
November	$14 600
December	$17 740

GR3   Create a pie graph for Canada Real Estate salespersons using this sales data.

Canada Real Estate
Commissions by Salesperson

Fischer, M.	$3 000
Seth, A.	$4 500
Pratt, T.	$7 800
Wallace, M.	$5 000
Zadow, A.	$6 150

GR4   Graph the data for exercise SS4 above.

GR5   Graph the data for exercise SS5 above.

GR6   Graph the data for exercise SS6 above.

WP1   Your best customer has an account overdue in the amount of $280.00. Prepare this letter on your word processor to jog her memory about the account. Save it under the file name CH2WP1.

August 23, 19–

Ms. Veronica Anstee
34 Lisgar Avenue
Burnaby, BC
V6K 1K9

Dear Ms. Anstee

We are sure it is an oversight, but your account balance of $280.00 is now 60 days overdue. You have been a valuable customer of our business, but we would appreciate remittance of this amount owing as soon as possible. If the amount is not correct, according to your records, please call me at the business number (555-2593), so that we may discuss this matter.

Yours truly

Your Name

Credit Manager

WP2   Use the file CH2WP1 and send another letter, making these changes:
a. The customer is Stephanie Mudge
b. The account is 90 days overdue.
c. The balance owing is $95.10.

WP3   Assume you are Veronica (WP1). Use your word processor to draft a letter to Morrow Manufacturing, explaining why you are late with the payment on your account. Indicate that payday is not for another week, and ask if your payment can be delayed another two weeks.

R. v. PILFER

CASE SOLVED

BACKGROUND

Formaldahide Township has many suppliers from whom it buys goods and services. In 1986 one of the accounting clerks who processed supplier invoices for payment became suspicious about a company called Staten Supplies. The clerk had never seen a salesperson from this company visit the township offices. Nor had the company ever phoned the township offices or even sent a Christmas card. The clerk began to wonder if this company even existed. So she expressed her concerns to her supervisor, the Township Clerk. He promised to investigate, but six months later nothing had been said. The accounting clerk then went to the Mayor and explained her concerns. The Mayor called in a team of forensic accountants to investigate the case.

INVESTIGATION

The accountants found that the following situation existed:
1. The telephone number for Staten Supplies always had a tape recorded message, "Sorry, we cannot take your call....".
2. All the Staten Supplies invoices were for under $500. All orders over $500 had to be tendered, by policy.
3. All cheques to Staten Supplies were always under $2 000. Cheques over $2 000 had to be approved by the Township Treasurer and signed by hand.
4. The Township Clerk always hand-delivered the cheques to Staten Supplies.
5. On examining the records, it was found that no cheques for Staten Supplies were ever issued when the Township Clerk was on vacation.
   Do you suspect that something fishy is going on here? Read on!

FRAUD

The forensic accountants talked to the receiver in the warehouse and found that no deliveries had ever been received from Staten Supplies at the township warehouse. Further investigation revealed that no company named Staten Supplies was registered with the Ministry of Consumer and Corporate Affairs.

It was obvious that supplier invoices were being prepared, billing the township for goods that were never shipped to or received by the township. The fraud scheme was designed by the Township Clerk. An outside partner, Albert Diaz, banked the cheques from the township and kept the records for the phony business.

It was revealed that, over a period of time, the Township Clerk, R. Pilfer, and Albert Diaz had defrauded the township of $64 000 by issuing these phony supplier invoices.

SENTENCE

Albert Diaz admitted to his part in the fraudulent scheme when questioned by the police. He told them that the profits were split evenly between the two men, and that he, Albert, kept the records and banked the money into two personal bank accounts. Albert testified at the trial of the Township Clerk, R. Pilfer, who was also convicted of fraud under the Criminal Code of Canada. Albert received a six-month sentence and had to pay $100 000 restitution. The Township Clerk was convicted and sentenced to fifteen months in jail.

QUESTIONS

1. When did the accounting clerk begin to suspect that something was wrong with the accounting records?
2. Could the Mayor have investigated this problem without outside help?
3. Should a business, or township, check out the background of every supplier it deals with?
4. What should the township do to make sure this kind of fraud doesn't happen again in the future?

Career Profile

Michelle Duguay owns a machine shop in a small town in southern Alberta. From her business which is attached to her house, she produces and sells specialized gears and moulds. Michelle graduated from university with a degree in mechanical engineering. She worked for an engineering firm for two years, but didn't like the rigid hours, or the work. She wanted to try running her own business. In particular she was interested in producing workable products for specialized needs. She had discovered there was a market for these during her time at the engineering firm. After she had been open a year, Michelle took a night school course in introductory accounting at the local community college. She knew how to handle the engineering side of her business, but she needed to have some knowledge of accounting as well.

Michelle took two year-long courses, Accounting Fundamentals in the first year, and Computer Accounting the next year. The introductory course taught her the basic accounting cycle from journalizing documents through to financial statements. And the computer course trained her in the use of a special accounting package called *ACCPAC Bedford Integrated Accounting*. By earning high marks in each of these courses, Michelle felt that she had enough accounting knowledge to handle the books for her business.

Michelle uses *Bedford* for the general ledger, the accounts payable, and the accounts receivable for the business. She does not have a very large inventory, so she keeps track of it using a computer spreadsheet program. Michelle does not use the payroll part of the *Bedford* package since she and her husband are the only employees of the business. Since her husband only works a few hours each week, his pay can easily be calculated by hand.

The *Bedford* accounting package provides Michelle with a classified balance sheet and a classified income statement at the end of each month. Michelle and her accountant talk once each month about these financial statements and he advises her about the tax side of the business.

Michelle also uses a spreadsheet for her business. She charts the production and sales each week on a spreadsheet, and the program automatically prepares a bar graph so that she can see sales results in a visual form. By studying this chart, she has a good idea when her peak season will be, and she can quickly see whether there is an improvement in sales from one week to the next. She also uses the spreadsheet to keep track of inventory. The names of the parts are all stored on the spreadsheet, along with prices. All Michelle has to do is to enter the quantity of each on hand; the spreadsheet calculates the extended inventory value and totals the inventory automatically.

Her computer system has a database program as well. Michelle likes to keep an updated list of customer names and addresses because she sends a regular newsletter to her customers, updating them on products, prices, and trends in the industry. The database provides a mailing list at the push of a button, and it is easy to add and delete customers. The database allows Michelle to select certain customers if she wants, and will sort the list alphabetically; it will even select customers in a certain geographical area.

Michelle has seen her business grow steadily for the last five years. She attributes her success to her knowledge of mechanics, her drive to provide quick customer service, and her knowledge of accounting fundamentals and computer accounting.

FOR DISCUSSION

- Michelle Duguay is an engineer. Did she really need to take some extra accounting courses to run her business?
- What did Michelle learn from the introductory accounting course?
- Of all the computer programs we have learned about in this chapter, which ones is Michelle using for her business?
- What useful kinds of information does Michelle have for her business now that she uses a computer?

3

The Accounting System for a Merchandise Business

- **Journalize source documents using special journals and post to ledger accounts.**

- **Complete an 8-column worksheet with adjustments.**

- **Prepare classified financial statements.**

- **Journalize closing entries for the appropriate accounts.**

- **Relate the uses of the computer to the needs of a small merchandise business by completing spreadsheet, graphics, database, word processing, and integrated accounting exercises.**

- **Journalize source documents and prepare financial statements on a computer using ACCPAC Bedford Integrated Accounting software.**

3.0
Overview

A merchandise business is distinguished from a service business by the fact that it sells merchandise, as opposed to offering skilled services or the use of facilities. There are numerous examples of merchandise businesses: drug stores, clothing stores, jewellery stores, hardware stores, etc. Merchandise businesses deal in inventory and this presents special accounting problems that are not found with service businesses. This chapter deals with a small retail business called Medieval Glass that sells stained glass and stained glass products to its customers.

3.1
Source Documents and Journalizing

Jim McLellan owns a small business called Medieval Glass, and operates it as a single proprietorship. He retails glass to hobbyists; and sells finished stained glass products — lamps, suncatchers, ashtrays, and mirrors. Jim will also make special custom stained glass products, for example stained glass windows for new or old houses.

In order to keep proper accounting records for his business, Jim has five types of source documents which will be described in detail. **Source documents** are documents which are used to make accounting entries in the books of account.

Figure 3-1 shows how the source documents are used as input to the overall accounting process of the business.

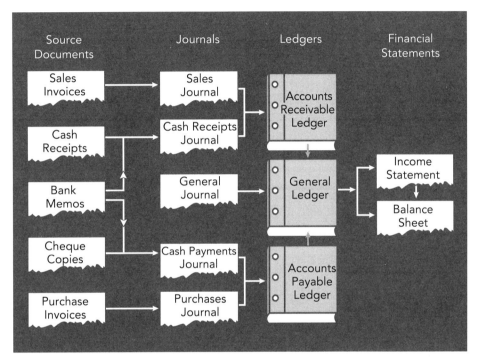

FIGURE 3-1   *A flowchart of the accounting process*

Now read about each of these key source documents and, as you read, keep the picture of the Medieval Glass accounting cycle in your mind.

SALES INVOICES

For Medieval Glass, the sales invoice is a basic source document used for several types of accounting transactions. Two of these transactions are the charge sale, and the credit invoice.

The Charge Sale

A **charge sale** is a sale on account to a customer. When a sales invoice is used for a charge sale, the box labelled "Sales Invoice" is marked off on the invoice.

Medieval Glass Company			Invoice	

Medieval Glass Company
12 Renaissance Avenue
Kitchener, ON N2G 1G3
Tel: 1-519-555-8202
Fax: 519-555-9980

Date Nov. 1   19–

Name Mr. Richard Thurtell

Address 83 Blackwell Rd.

Town Kitchener   Postal Code N2N 1P4

Quantity	Description	Price		Amount	
12 pcs	#56 Rose Glass	2	50	30	–
10 pcs	#110 Lavender Flat	2	80	28	–
5 pcs	#60 Deep Red	2	40	12	–

Sales Invoice ✔ Cash Sale ☐	Sub Total	70	–
Credit Invoice ☐ On Account ☐	GST	4	90
Number	Terms: 2/10, net 30	PST	5	60
425	2% per month on overdue	Total	80	50

FIGURE 3-2   *A sales invoice*

On invoices for Medieval Glass there are two tax items, the federal **GST** (Goods and Services Tax) at 7% of the sub-total; and the provincial **PST** (Sales Tax) at 8% of the sub-total. The GST applies to all of Canada, while the provincial tax rates vary from province to province.

Also, depending on the province, PST may be integrated with GST, calculated on the base price alone, or on the base price plus GST. In Ontario, the PST rate is 8% and the tax is calculated on the base price only.

For those customers who charge their work, there is a 2% discount if the bill is paid within 10 days (2/10). If the discount is not taken, the amount owing is due in 30 days (net 30). If accounts go beyond the 30 days, there is an interest charge of 2% per month on overdue accounts. When a customer takes a discount, that discount is calculated on the total invoice price.

A charge sale is recorded as a debit to the Accounts Receivable control account in the general ledger (and the customer's account in the accounts receivable subsidiary ledger), a credit to Sales, a credit to GST Payable, and a credit to PST Payable. The credits to GST Payable and PST Payable increase the firm's liability to the federal and provincial governments, since Medieval Glass acts as a tax collector in both cases.

GENERAL JOURNAL

PAGE 41

DATE 19–		PARTICULARS	PR	DEBIT	CREDIT
Nov.	1	A/R—Richard Thurtell		80 50	
		Sales			70 –
		GST Payable			4 90
		PST Payable			5 60
		Sales Invoice 425			

FIGURE 3-3   *The general journal entry for a charge sale*

Notice in Figure 3-3 that the short form A/R has been used for Accounts Receivable. This is acceptable accounting practice. This entry includes the customer's name so that the debit side of the entry can be posted to the customer's account in the accounts receivable subsidiary ledger.

The Credit Invoice

The sales invoice document is also used as a credit invoice when a customer's account has to be adjusted. Yesterday, one of Jim's customers, Ellen Hutchinson, returned a small suncatcher because the solder was too loose. Jim has decided to issue Ellen a credit invoice. She is pleased and has placed a new order for a larger suncatcher. Figure 3-4 shows the credit invoice issued to Ellen.

Medieval Glass Company			**Invoice**	
12 Renaissance Avenue				
Kitchener, ON N2G 1G3				
Tel: 1-519-555-8202			Date _Nov. 3_ 19_–_	
Fax: 519-555-9980				

Name _Ellen Hutchinson_

Address _9 Water Dr._

Town _Kitchener_   Postal Code _N2G 1Z6_

Quantity	Description	Price		Amount	
	CREDIT INVOICE				
1	Sun catcher — Bluebird	8	–	8	–

Sales Invoice ☐ Cash Sale ☐	Sub Total	8	–
Credit Invoice ☑ On Account ☐	GST		56
Number	Terms: 2/10, net 30	PST		64
427	2% per month on overdue	Total	9	20

FIGURE 3-4   *A credit invoice*

The words "Credit Invoice" are written at the top and the "Credit Invoice" box in the lower left corner is checked off. The accounting entry is a debit to Sales (or Sales Returns and Allowances), a debit to GST Payable, a debit to PST Payable, and a credit to Accounts Receivable (and the customer's account in the accounts receivable subsidiary ledger). The GST Payable account and the PST Payable account both have to be debited since the original sales taxes no longer have to be paid to the federal or provincial governments.

GENERAL JOURNAL

PAGE 41

DATE 19–		PARTICULARS	PR	DEBIT	CREDIT
Nov.	3	Sales		8 –	
		GST Payable		56	
		PST Payable		64	
		A/R— Ellen Hutchinson			9 20
		Credit Invoice 427			

FIGURE 3-5   *The general journal entry for a credit invoice*

CASH RECEIPTS

The two other uses of the basic sales invoice are the cash sale or cash received on account from a customer. The term **cash receipt** can refer to either of these types of transaction.

The Cash Sale

The invoice form is used by Medieval Glass as a cash receipt by checking the "Cash Sale" box in the lower left hand corner of the invoice. See Figure 3-6. The document is then completed for the cash sale, including the GST calculation, and the PST calculation.

The general journal entry for a cash sale is shown in Figure 3-7.

Whenever cash is received by Medieval Glass, Jim deposits it at the end of the day into the business bank account for good internal cash control.

The Receipt on Account

If the business is receiving cash from a customer for an amount owing from a previous sale on account, then the box labelled "On Account" is checked off. See Figure 3-8.

In this example a customer, Kim Farkas, is making a $200 payment to Medieval Glass on her account. There are no federal (GST) or provincial (PST) taxes on a receipt of cash on account.

The general journal entry for a receipt of cash on account is shown in Figure 3-9.

Medieval Glass Company   Invoice
12 Renaissance Avenue
Kitchener, ON N2G 1G3
Tel: 1-519-555-8202   Date _Nov. 5_ 19–
Fax: 519-555-9980

Name _Jim Barrow_

Address _86 Westwood Cr._

Town _Kitchener_   Postal Code _N2N 268_

Quantity	Description	Price	Amount
1	Tiffany Lamp—As per	180 –	180 –
	description on the		
	estimate form		

Sales Invoice ☐ Cash Sale ✔	Sub Total	180 –
Credit Invoice ☐ On Account ☐	GST	12 60
Number	Terms: 2/10, net 30	PST	14 40
429	2% per month on overdue	Total	207 –

FIGURE 3-6   *A cash sale*

GENERAL JOURNAL

PAGE _42_

DATE 19–	PARTICULARS	PR	DEBIT	CREDIT
Nov. 7	Bank		2 0 7 –	
	Sales			1 80 –
	GST Payable			1 2 60
	PST Payable			1 4 40
	Cash sale Invoice 429			

FIGURE 3-7   *The general journal entry for a cash sale*

Medieval Glass Company			Invoice
12 Renaissance Avenue			
Kitchener ON N2G 1G3			
Tel: 1-519-555-8202		Date _Nov. 8_____ 19–___	
Fax: 519-555-9980			

Name __Kim Farkas_____

Address _111 Vanier St._____

Town ___Kitchener_____   Postal Code _N2G 1J6__

Quantity	Description	Price	Amount
1	Received on account		200 –

			Sub Total	200 –
Sales Invoice ☐	Cash Sale ☐			
Credit Invoice ☐	On Account ☑		GST	
Number	Terms: 2/10, net 30		PST	
432	2% per month on overdue		Total	200 –

FIGURE 3-8   *A receipt on account*

GENERAL JOURNAL

PAGE _42_

DATE 19–		PARTICULARS	PR	DEBIT	CREDIT
Nov.	8	Bank		200 –	
		A/R—Kim Farkas			200 –
		Receipt on account			

FIGURE 3-9   *The general journal entry for a receipt on account*

BANK MEMOS

The Bank Debit Memo

It is common practice for banks to charge directly (deduct from) their customers' accounts for service charges and/or interest on bank loans. The bank makes the appropriate accounting entry at a set date, transfers the funds out of the customer's account, and then sends a debit memo to its customer so that the customer can record the transaction in his or her books of account. A **bank debit memo** is a document detailing money withdrawn from a client's bank account by the bank. Jim does not have a bank loan outstanding for his business at this time. But the bank did charge him $14.50 for service charges on his business bank account. When the bank deducts service charges, they send a bank debit memo to explain the service charge. A sample bank debit memo is illustrated in Figure 2-12 in Chapter 2.

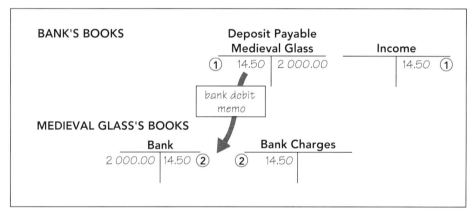

FIGURE 3-10   T- accounts used for a bank debit memo

The bank debits their liability account Deposits Payable — Medieval Glass, because they deduct the $14.50 directly from Jim's account, and credit their Income account. When Jim receives the bank debit memo he debits Bank Charges and credits his Bank account.

GENERAL JOURNAL

PAGE 43

DATE 19–		PARTICULARS	PR	DEBIT	CREDIT
Nov.	12	Bank Charges		14 50	
		Bank			14 50
		To record a bank debit memo			

FIGURE 3-11   The general journal entry for a bank debit memo

The Bank Credit Memo

A **bank credit memo** is a document detailing money deposited into a client's bank account by the bank. Jim has decided to borrow $1 500 from the bank so he will have enough money to purchase a new glass-cutting machine for his business. The bank has just put the money into the account of Medieval Glass and has sent Jim a credit memo to advise him of this deposit.

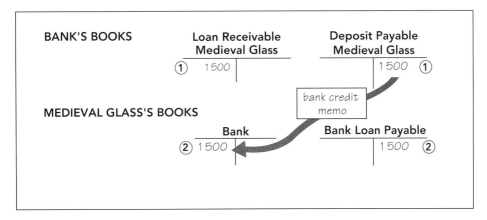

FIGURE 3-12   *T-accounts used for a bank credit memo*

When Medieval Glass receives the bank credit memo, it makes the following journal entry into the books:

GENERAL JOURNAL

PAGE 44

DATE 19–		PARTICULARS	PR	DEBIT	CREDIT
Nov.	15	Bank		1500 –	
		Bank Loan Payable			1500 –
		To record a bank credit memo			

FIGURE 3-13   *The general journal entry for a bank credit memo*

PURCHASE INVOICES

Medieval Glass also receives purchase invoices, and credit notes, from businesses that supply it with goods and services.

The Purchase Invoice

The source document shown in Figure 3-14 is a purchase invoice received from North American Glass. A **purchase invoice** is an accounting document received when goods or services are bought on account. Medieval Glass has purchased a supply of stained glass. Notice that the invoice from North American Glass has terms of 1/10, n/30 in the top right corner. This means that Medieval Glass may take a 1% discount if this bill is paid in 10 days (1/10). If no discount is taken, the bill must be paid in 30 days (n/30).

A purchase invoice is recorded into the books of account using the full invoice amount. When a purchase invoice is received by a business it will show a GST amount on it. This tax becomes an **input tax credit** to the buyer, and the amount stated for GST on the invoice is debited into a GST Recoverable account on the books of the buyer.

Whenever it is time to send GST to the government, the balance in the GST Recoverable account is subtracted from the balance in the GST Payable account. This net amount is sent to the Receiver General.

Figure 3-15 shows the general journal entry, including the treatment for the input tax credit for Medieval Glass.

This entry includes the supplier's name so that the credit side of the entry can be posted to the supplier's account in the accounts payable subsidiary ledger.

The term *purchase invoice*, as used by Medieval Glass, refers to invoices that cover three main types of transactions:
  (1) the purchase of merchandise for resale
  (2) bills received for other expenses, e.g. advertising
  (3) the purchase of assets

The Credit Invoice

Medieval Glass sometimes has to return goods to suppliers for credit when they are defective, or when they are not exactly what was ordered in the first place. The supplier then issues a credit invoice to Medieval Glass. A **credit invoice** is an invoice received from a supplier which reduces the accounts payable. The credit invoice shown in Figure 3-16 is for defective glass which Medieval Glass had to return to the supplier.

North American Glass		Invoice # 912	
16167 Industrial Drive		Terms: 1/10, n/30	
Kitchener, Ontario			
M9W 2L1	519-555-5555	Date: Nov. 16, 19 –	

Sold To:	Medieval Glass	Ship To:	Same
	1245 King W.		
	Kitchener, ON		
	N2G 1G3		

Qty Ordered	Qty Shipped	Description	Unit Price	Amount
5	5	#156 Rose Glass	40.00	200 –
4	4	#123 Royale Blue	22.00	88 –
12	12	#018 Pink Opaque	26.00	312 –
			Sub Total	600 –
			GST	42 –
			PST	
			Total	642 –

FIGURE 3-14   A purchase invoice

GENERAL JOURNAL

PAGE _44_

DATE 19–		PARTICULARS	PR	DEBIT	CREDIT
Nov.	16	Purchases		600 –	
		GST Recoverable		42 –	
		A/P—North American Glass			642 –
		To record supplier invoice 912			

FIGURE 3-15   The general journal entry based on full invoice price

NORTH AMERICAN GLASS 16167 Industrial Drive Kitchener, Ontario M9W 2L1		519-555-5555	Credit Invoice # CR75 Date Nov. 20, 19 –	
Sold To: Medieval Glass 1245 King W. Kitchener, ON N2G 1G3			Sold To: Same	

Qty	Description	Unit Price	Amount	
1	#156 Rose Glass	40.00	40	–
	Sub Total		40	–
	GST		2	80
	PST			
	Total Credit		42	80

FIGURE 3-16   *A credit invoice*

When goods are returned to a supplier, the entry must recognize that the GST input tax credit must be reversed in the GST Recoverable account.

The general journal entry for the credit invoice therefore is as shown in Figure 3-17.

GENERAL JOURNAL

PAGE 46

DATE 19–		PARTICULARS	PR	DEBIT	CREDIT
Nov.	20	A/P—North American Glass		42 80	
		GST Recoverable			2 80
		Purchases Returns and Allowances			40 –
		To record credit invoice CR75			

FIGURE 3-17   *The general journal entry for a credit invoice*

CHEQUE COPIES

Each cheque has two parts, a stub to record the details of the cheque, and the cheque itself which is given to, or mailed to, the payee.

No. 200	MEDIEVAL GLASS		200
Date: _Nov. 20/19–_	12 Renaissance Avenue Kitchener, ON N2G 1G3		Date: _Nov. 20_ **19–**
To: _K-W Record_			
For: _Advertising_	Pay to the Order of: _The K-W Record_		$ _133.00_
Bal Fwd $ _1650–_	— _One Hundred and Thirty-Three_ —————— xx **Dollars**		
Deposit $ _Ø_		100	
Balance $ _1650–_	Bank of Nova Scotia		
Amount $ _133–_	Westmount Branch Kitchener, Ontario	_J. McLellan_	
Balance $ _1517–_	3 0 1 2 4 5 5	_D McLellan_	

FIGURE 3-18 *A cheque and stub*

This particular cheque is charged to the expense account, Advertising. Therefore the general journal entry is:

GENERAL JOURNAL

PAGE _46_

DATE 19–		PARTICULARS	PR	DEBIT	CREDIT
Nov.	20	Advertising Expense		1 2 4 30	
		GST Recoverable		8 70	
		Bank			1 3 3 –
		To record cheque 200			

FIGURE 3-19 *The general journal entry for a cheque*

A cheque is one of the main source documents that is entered into the books of account. Cheques are written for one of four types of business transactions:

(1) a cash payment to a supplier on account
(2) a cash payment of an expense
(3) a cash purchase of an asset
(4) a cash withdrawal by the owner

QUESTIONS

1. (a) What is a merchandise business?
   (b) How does a merchandise business differ from a service business?

2. Name the five types of source documents used by Medieval Glass.

3. The sales invoice form for Medieval Glass can be used for four accounting transactions. Name them.

4. Does Medieval Glass charge customers for amounts overdue? Does it offer a discount?

5. If a supplier invoice lists terms of 2/15, n/30, what does this mean?

6. Indicate whether the source document for each of the following accounting transactions is a bank debit memo or a bank credit memo.

   (a) A new supply of cheques was issued to the customer and the $10.00 cost charged against her/his bank account.
   (b) A $5 000 loan was put into the customer's bank account.

7. What do the letters GST stand for? Is this tax imposed by the federal or the provincial government?

8. What is the PST rate for your province?

9. If the sub-total on an invoice is $710, what is the invoice total after the 7% GST and an 8% PST are added? (PST is calculated on the base price.)

10. What kinds of payments do businesses make by cheque? Give four specific examples for a bakery.

3.2

Using Special Journals

All of the sample transactions in section 3.1 were shown in general journal form to keep the illustration simple. Medieval Glass uses the five-journal system for its business, namely:
- sales journal
- cash receipts journal
- cash payments journal
- purchases journal
- general journal

The Sales Journal

The **sales journal** is a book of original entry used to record the sale of merchandise bought on account. Most entries in this journal are a debit to Accounts Receivable (and the customer's account in the accounts receivable subsidiary ledger), a credit to Sales, a credit to GST Payable, and a credit to PST Payable.

If a credit invoice is issued to a customer, Accounts Receivable will be credited and Sales, GST Payable, and PST Payable will be debited. This is shown in the entries on the 3rd and the 21st of the November sales journal.

If you want to record an opposite entry into any of the special journals, you can circle the debit or credit to change the entry. On November 3, for example, a credit invoice was issued to Ellen Hutchinson. The accounting entry to record this was a debit to the Sales account, a debit to GST Payable, a debit to PST Payable, and a credit to Accounts Receivable. The debits to Sales, GST Payable, and PST Payable, and the credit to Accounts Receivable, are all circled since they are opposing entries to the column headings. These can also be written in red.

An alternative to debiting Sales would be to debit an account called Sales Returns and Allowances. It is called a contra revenue account because eventually the total in this account is deducted from the total of the Sales account, to arrive at a net sales figure. Due to the nature of the business, Medieval Glass does not feel it needs to use this contra revenue account.

The Cash Receipts Journal

Any transaction that causes an increase in cash is recorded in the **cash receipts journal**. The four types of transactions that are entered here, therefore, are:
- a cash sale
- a cash receipt on account
- a bank loan
- a personal cash investment by the owner

	DATE 19–		PARTICULARS	INV. NO.	OTHER ACCOUNTS CR				
					ACCOUNT	PR	AMOUNT		
1	Nov.	1	Richard Thurtell	425					
2		3	Ellen Hutchinson	427					
3		6	Les Peter	430					
4		10	Dace Zvanitas	433					
5		11	Theresa Deroo	434					
6		17	Dennis Noonan	437					
7		21	Les Peter	439					
8		22	Bob Marsden	440					
9		25	Sue Lowrie	442					
10		28	John Clement	443					
11		30	Debbie Giesbrecht	444					
12									
13									

FIGURE 3-20 *Sales journal*

	DATE 19–		PARTICULARS	INV. NO.	OTHER ACCOUNTS CR				
					ACCOUNT	PR	AMOUNT		
1	Nov.	1	Dick MacKenzie	426					
2		4	Veronica Magyar	428					
3		5	Jim Barrow	429					
4		6	Ted Koza	431					
5		8	Kim Farkas	432					
6		12	Connie Bray	435					
7		15	Bank of Montreal	C M	Bank Loan		1500 –		
8		17	Dace Zvanitas	436					
9		20	Theresa Deroo	438					
10		22	Bruce Bell	441					
11		28	Richard Thurtell	445					
12									
13									

FIGURE 3-21 *Cash receipts journal*

SALES JOURNAL

FOR THE _Month_ ENDED _November 30_ 19 – PAGE _16_

	SALES CR	GST PAYABLE CR	PST PAYABLE CR	✔	ACCOUNTS RECEIVABLE DR	
	70 –	490	560	✔	8050	1
	(8 –)	(56)	(64)	✔	(920)	2
	40 –	280	320	✔	46 –	3
	25 –	175	2 –	✔	2875	4
	310 –	2170	2480	✔	35650	5
	200 –	14 –	16 –	✔	230 –	6
	(40 –)	(280)	(320)	✔	(46 –)	7
	12 –	84	96	✔	1380	8
	100 –	7 –	8 –	✔	115 –	9
	850 –	5950	68 –	✔	97750	10
	160 –	1120	1280	✔	184 –	11
						12
						13

CASH RECEIPTS JOURNAL

FOR THE _Month_ ENDED _November 30_ 19 – PAGE _21_

SALES CR	GST PAYABLE CR	PST PAYABLE CR	DISCOUNTS ALLOWED DR	ACCOUNTS RECEIVABLE CR	✔	BANK DR	
50 –	350	4 –				5750	1
120 –	840	960				138 –	2
180 –	1260	1440				207 –	3
80 –	560	640				92 –	4
				200 –	✔	200 –	5
400 –	28 –	32 –				460 –	6
						1500 –	7
			58	2875	✔	2817	8
			713	35650	✔	34937	9
400 –	28 –	32 –				460 –	10
				8050	✔	8050	11
							12
							13

	DATE 19–		PARTICULARS	CH. NO.	OTHER ACCOUNTS DR				
					ACCOUNT	PR	AMOUNT		
1	Nov.	2	Wilson Stationers	194	Office Exp.		10 5 93		
2		5	Sean McLellan	195					
3		7	Rainbow Glass	196					
4		12	Bank of Montreal	D M	Bank Chgs.		1 4 50		
5		15	Craig Mfg. Co.	197	Equipment		1 3 7 1 1 3		
6		18	Rainbow Glass	198					
7		19	Kitchener PUC	199	Utilities Exp.		1 9 6 26		
8		20	K.W. Record	200	Advert. Exp.		1 2 4 30		
9		22	Imperial Oil	201	Car Exp.		7 4 77		
10		24	North American Glass	202					
11		28	Bell Canada	203	Teleph. Exp.		7 0 09		
12									
13									

FIGURE 3-22   *Cash payments journal*

	DATE 19–		PARTICULARS	INV. NO.	OTHER ACCOUNTS DR				
					ACCOUNT	PR	AMOUNT		
1	Nov.	2	Laidlaw	759					
2		5	Grabb Bag Co.	310					
3		12	Rainbow Glass	R198					
4		16	North American Glass	912					
5		20	North American Glass	75	Purch. Ret. & Allow.		40 –		
6		28	Renaissance Glass	R212					
7									
8									

FIGURE 3-23   *Purchases journal*

CASH PAYMENTS JOURNAL

FOR THE __Month__ ENDED __November 30__ 19__–__ PAGE __24__

DISCOUNTS EARNED CR	GST RECOVERABLE DR	PURCHASES DR	WAGES DR	ACCOUNTS PAYABLE DR	✔	BANK CR	
	6 87					1 1 2 80	1
			50 –			50 –	2
	16 36	233 64				2 50 –	3
						14 50	4
	88 87					14 60 –	5
	19 63	280 37				3 00 –	6
	13 74					2 10 –	7
	8 70					1 33 –	8
	5 23					80 –	9
5 99				59 9 20	✔	5 93 21	10
	4 91					75 –	11
							12
							13

PURCHASES JOURNAL

FOR THE __Month__ ENDED __November 30__ 19__–__ PAGE __11__

FREIGHT-IN DR	MISCELL. EXPENSE DR	OFFICE EXPENSE DR	PURCHASES DR	GST RECOVERABLE DR	✔	ACCOUNTS PAYABLE CR	
16 82				1 18	✔	18 –	1
	70 09			4 91	✔	75 –	2
			300 –	21 –	✔	3 21 –	3
			600 –	42 –	✔	6 42 –	4
				(2 80)	✔	(4 2 80)	5
			400 –	28 –	✔	4 28 –	6
							7
							8

The Cash Payments Journal

Any transaction that causes a decrease in cash is recorded in the **cash payments journal**. The four types of transactions that are entered here are:
- a cash payment to a supplier on account
- a cash payment of a business expense
- a cash purchase of an asset
- a cash withdrawal by the owner

The Purchases Journal

The **purchases journal** is a book of original entry used to record the purchase of any item bought on account. Most entries in this journal are a credit to Accounts Payable. The debit side of the entry could be for:
- a charge to Purchases and GST Recoverable
- a charge to an expense account
- a charge to an asset account

If a credit invoice is received from a supplier, Accounts Payable will be debited and the other accounts involved in the transaction will be credited. This is shown in the entry for November 20th of the purchases journal.

The General Journal

The general journal is used for the rare entries that do not fit easily into the four special journals, and for the adjusting entries and closing entries made at year end. These entries are shown later.

Some of the special journals have blank columns in them. These blank columns can be used for any accounts which have frequently occurring transactions in the month. One business, for example, might pay regular freight bills and want to label the blank column "Freight-In". This use of blank columns for frequently used accounts cuts down the writing of account names, and posting, by the bookkeeper.

The column labelled "Other Accounts" at the left of each journal is a miscellaneous column. Not every account used by Medieval Glass can have its own column in the journals. Therefore the Other Accounts section is necessary for transactions that do not have their own special column.

Medieval Glass uses special journals because there are a reasonably large number of accounting entries each month and these journals cut down on posting time, in that fewer individual entries have to be written into ledger accounts. The use of special journals also makes balancing easier at month end since four smaller journals are balanced instead of one large multipurpose journal. Only the final totals, and the individual amounts in the "Other Accounts" columns, are posted to the ledger accounts.

POSTING FROM THE SPECIAL JOURNALS

Posting to the General Ledger

The word **posting** refers to transferring entries from the journals to a ledger. Before posting, each of the four special journals (not the general journal) is totalled and balanced at the end of the month. The totals of the columns are then posted into the general ledger, except for the Other Accounts column. Each individual account in the Other Accounts column must be posted since the accounts all differ. The total of the Other Accounts column is not posted. The special journals do not have to be posted in any given order. However, posting the sales and purchases journals first, followed by the cash receipts and cash payments journals helps to prevent temporary negative balances in the Accounts Receivable, Accounts Payable, and Cash accounts.

The phrase **Posting Reference** is an account number or page number that indicates that an accounting entry has been posted. Notice the account numbers in brackets beneath each column, and in the PR columns, to indicate that posting has taken place.

The purpose behind cross-referencing is to assist the bookkeeper or accountant in tracing entries later, if necessary. Figures 3-24 to 3-27 show the four special journals after they have been totalled and balanced, and the Other Accounts column has been posted to the general ledger.

The Bank account will be used to illustrate the posting process from the cash receipts journal, and the cash payments journal, to the general ledger. You will remember that, in posting, the journal and the ledger are cross-referenced with account numbers and page numbers. The Bank debit column in the cash receipts journal is posted to account #110, and this account number is written below the debit column in brackets. The Bank credit column in the cash payments journal is posted to account #110, and this account number is written below the debit column in brackets. In Figure 3-28, the Bank account PR column shows that the entries came from the cash receipts journal, page 21 (CRJ21), and the cash payments journal, page 24 (CPJ24).

Once the four special journals, and the general journal, are posted, the general ledger should be checked to see if it is still in balance. This will be done in the next section of this chapter when a worksheet is prepared for the business. A **worksheet** is a paper used to adjust account balances before preparing financial statements.

The Accounts Receivable and Accounts Payable columns are posted to the **subsidiary ledger** so that customer and supplier accounts always agree with their control accounts in the general ledger.

	DATE 19–		PARTICULARS	INV. NO.	OTHER ACCOUNTS CR				
					ACCOUNT	PR	AMOUNT		
1	Nov.	1	Richard Thurtell	425					
2		3	Ellen Hutchinson	427					
3		6	Les Peter	430					
4		10	Dace Zvanitas	433					
5		11	Theresa Deroo	434					
6		17	Dennis Noonan	437					
7		21	Les Peter	439					
8		22	Bob Marsden	440					
9		25	Sue Lowrie	442					
10		28	John Clement	443					
11		30	Debbie Giesbrecht	444					
12									
13									

FIGURE 3-24   Completed sales journal

	DATE 19–		PARTICULARS	INV. NO.	OTHER ACCOUNTS CR				
					ACCOUNT	PR	AMOUNT		
1	Nov.	1	Dick MacKenzie	426					
2		4	Veronica Magyar	428					
3		5	Jim Barrow	429					
4		6	Ted Koza	431					
5		8	Kim Farkas	432					
6		12	Connie Bray	435					
7		15	Bank of Montreal	C M	Bank Loan	210	1 5 0 0 –		
8		17	Dace Zvanitas	436					
9		20	Theresa Deroo	438					
10		22	Bruce Bell	441					
11		28	Richard Thurtell	445					
12									
13							1 5 0 0 –		

FIGURE 3-25   Completed cash receipts journal

SALES JOURNAL

FOR THE Month ENDED November 30 19– PAGE 16

		SALES CR	GST PAYABLE CR	PST PAYABLE CR	✔	ACCOUNTS RECEIVABLE DR	
		70 –	4 90	5 60	✔	80 50	1
		(8 –)	(56)	(64) ✔		(9 20)	2
		40 –	2 80	3 20	✔	46 –	3
		25 –	1 75	2 –	✔	28 75	4
		3 10 –	21 70	24 80	✔	35 6 50	5
		200 –	14	16 –	✔	2 30 –	6
		(40 –)	(2 80)	(3 20) ✔		(46 –)	7
		12 –	84	96	✔	13 80	8
		1 00 –	7 –	8 –	✔	1 15 –	9
		8 50 –	59 50	68 –	✔	9 77 50	10
		1 60 –	11 20	12 80	✔	1 84 –	11
		17 19 –	1 20 33	1 37 52		19 76 85	12
		(410)	(221)	(222)		(110)	13

CASH RECEIPTS JOURNAL

FOR THE Month ENDED November 30 19– PAGE 21

SALES CR	GST PAYABLE CR	PST PAYABLE CR	DISCOUNTS ALLOWED DR	ACCOUNTS RECEIVABLE CR	✔	BANK DR	
50 –	3 50	4 –				57 50	1
1 20 –	8 40	9 60				1 38 –	2
1 80 –	12 60	14 40				2 07 –	3
80 –	5 60	6 40				92 –	4
				2 00 –	✔	2 00 –	5
4 00 –	28 –	32 –				4 60 –	6
						15 00 –	7
			58	28 75	✔	28 17	8
			7 13	35 6 50	✔	34 9 37	9
4 00 –	28 –	32 –				4 60 –	10
				80 50	✔	80 50	11
12 30 –	86 10	98 40	7 71	6 65 75		35 72 54	12
(410)	(221)	(222)	(508)	(120)		(110) –	13

	DATE 19–		PARTICULARS	CH. NO.	OTHER ACCOUNTS DR		
					ACCOUNT	PR	AMOUNT
1	Nov.	2	Wilson Stationers	194	Office Exp.	516	1 0 5 93
2		5	Sean McLellan	195			
3		7	Rainbow Glass	196			
4		12	Bank of Montreal	D M	Bank Chgs.	504	1 4 50
5		15	Craig Mfg. Co.	197	Equipment	160	1 3 7 1 13
6		18	Rainbow Glass	198			
7		19	Kitchener PUC	199	Utilities Exp.	526	1 9 6 26
8		20	K.W. Record	200	Advert. Exp.	502	1 2 4 30
9		22	Imperial Oil	201	Car Exp.	505	7 4 77
10		24	North American Glass	202			
11		28	Bell Canada	203	Teleph. Exp.	524	7 0 09
12							1 9 5 6 98
13							

FIGURE 3-26   *Completed cash payments journal*

	DATE 19–		PARTICULARS	INV. NO.	OTHER ACCOUNTS DR		
					ACCOUNT	PR	AMOUNT
1	Nov.	2	Laidlaw	759			
2		5	Grabb Bag Co.	310			
3		12	Rainbow Glass	R198			
4		16	North American Glass	912			
5		20	North American Glass	75	Purch. Ret. & Allow.		40 –
6		28	Renaissance Glass	R212			
7							40 –
8							

FIGURE 3-27   *Completed purchases journal*

ACCOUNT Bank							NO 110	
DATE 19–		PARTICULARS	PR	DEBIT	CREDIT	DR CR	BALANCE	
Nov.	30	Balance Forward	–			DR	7 4 9 82	
	30		CRJ21	3 5 7 3 01		DR	4 3 2 2 83	
	30		CPJ24		3 2 7 8 51	DR	1 0 4 4 32	

FIGURE 3-28   *Bank account*

CASH PAYMENTS JOURNAL

FOR THE _Month_ ENDED _November 30_ 19– PAGE _24_

DISCOUNTS EARNED CR	GST RECOVERABLE DR	PURCHASES DR	WAGES DR	ACCOUNTS PAYABLE DR	✔	BANK CR	
	6 87					1 1 2 80	1
			50 –			50 –	2
	1 6 36	2 3 3 64				2 50 –	3
						1 4 50	4
	8 8 87					1 4 60 –	5
	1 9 63	2 8 0 37				3 00 –	6
	1 3 74					2 1 0 –	7
	8 70					1 3 3 –	8
	5 23					8 0 –	9
5 99				5 9 9 20	✔	5 9 3 21	10
	4 91					7 5 –	11
5 99	1 6 4 31	5 1 4 01	5 0 –	5 9 9 20		3 2 7 8 51	12
(510)	(130)	(518)	(528)	(220)		(110)	13

PURCHASES JOURNAL

FOR THE _Month_ ENDED _November 30_ 19– PAGE _11_

FREIGHT-IN DR	MISCELL. EXPENSE DR	OFFICE EXPENSE DR	PURCHASES DR	GST RECOVERABLE DR ✔	ACCOUNTS PAYABLE CR	
1 6 82				1 18 ✔	1 8 –	1
	7 0 09			4 91 ✔	7 5 –	2
			3 00 –	2 1 – ✔	3 2 1 –	3
			6 00 –	4 2 – ✔	6 4 2 –	4
				(2 80) ✔	(4 2 80)	5
			4 00 –	2 8 – ✔	4 2 8 –	6
1 6 82	7 0 09	Ø	1 3 00 –	9 4 29	1 4 4 1 20	7
(5 1 1)	(5 1 4)		(5 1 8)	(130)	(2 2 0)	8

Posting to the Accounts Receivable Subsidiary Ledger

When entries that affect accounts receivable are made into the sales journal or the cash receipts journal they should be posted to the accounts receivable subsidiary ledger. A tick is placed in the column provided to show the posting to the subsidiary ledger. Each debit or credit in the Accounts Receivable columns is posted to the subsidiary ledger as of the date of the transaction. The accounts receivable ledger is comprised of individual ledger cards for each customer which contain mailing information for sending monthly statements. Each card shows the customer's credit limit, which is the maximum amount that the customer is allowed to charge on his or her account. Most importantly, this card provides a perpetual record of charge sales, payments received, and the balance owing by the customer to Medieval Glass on any given date. A final point to note is that there are no account numbers on the accounts receivable ledger cards because they are filed alphabetically. See Figure 3-29.

ACCOUNTS RECEIVABLE LEDGER							
NAME: Richard Thurtell					**TELEPHONE NO.:** 555-6739		
ADDRESS: 83 Blockwell Rd.					**POSTAL CODE:** N2N 1P4		
TOWN: Kitchener		**PROVINCE:** Ontario			**CREDIT LIMIT:** $500		
DATE 19–	PARTICULARS	PR	DEBIT	CREDIT	DR CR	BALANCE	
Nov. 1	Invoice 425	–	80 50		DR	80 50	

FIGURE 3-29   *An accounts receivable ledger card*

Notice that when you post to the accounts receivable ledger card, it is important to write the number of the sales invoice in the Particulars column of the ledger account, for later reference if necessary.

Posting to The Accounts Payable Subsidiary Ledger

When entries that affect accounts payable are made into the purchases journal or the cash payments journal they should be posted to the accounts payable subsidiary ledger. A tick mark is placed in the column to show the posting to the subsidiary ledger. Each debit or credit in the Accounts Payable columns is posted to the subsidiary ledger as of the date of the transaction. The accounts payable ledger is comprised of individual ledger cards for each supplier, and contains mailing information for contacting suppliers if necessary. This card provides a perpetual record of goods and services purchased, payments made, and the balance owing to a supplier by Medieval Glass on any given date. As with accounts receivable, there are no account numbers on the accounts payable ledger cards because they are filed alphabetically.

Notice again the invoice reference in the Particulars column on the accounts payable ledger card. Both the accounts receivable ledger and the accounts payable ledger are balanced monthly and checked against their control accounts in the general ledger. Trial balances are prepared of each subsidiary ledger to prove that they do agree with their control accounts.

ACCOUNTS PAYABLE LEDGER							
NAME: Laidlaw Transport				TELEPHONE NO.: 555-3668			
ADDRESS: 115 Lancaster St. E.				POSTAL CODE: N2M 1M7			
TOWN: Kitchener PROVINCE: Ontario				TERMS: Net 30			
DATE 19–	PARTICULARS	PR	DEBIT	CREDIT	DR CR	BALANCE
Nov. 2	Invoice 759	–		18 –	CR	18 –

FIGURE 3-30   *An accounts payable ledger card*

Q U E S T I O N S

11. Why is a credit entry made to GST Payable and PST Payable?

12. Name the two most common subsidiary ledgers in a business.

13. Match the source document to the description.

    (1) Cash Sales Invoice
    (2) Charge Sales Invoice
    (3) Credit Note
    (4) Purchase Invoice
    (5) Bank Credit Memo
    a. Bank loaned us money.
    b. Sale on account to customer.
    c. Bought merchandise for resale.
    d. Returned goods to supplier.
    e. Customer paid immediately.

14. How does a business know if its subsidiary ledgers are in balance?

15. Give two reasons for a bank to issue a bank debit memo.

16. Why is there an Other Accounts column in each special journal?

17. Indicate which special journal is used for each transaction:
    (a) Sold goods on account.
    (b) Wrote a cheque to pay the monthly rent.
    (c) Returned goods to a supplier for credit.
    (d) Bought goods for resale on account.
    (e) A customer returned goods for credit.
    (f) A payment for heat and light was charged to the telephone account in error.

18. In what order are the special journals posted to the ledger?

3.3

The 8-Column Worksheet and Adjustments

Trial balances taken at the end of a fiscal year are usually done on an 8-column worksheet because there are year-end adjustments that have to be made on the company books. (Any trial balances calculated more frequently can be done on the 6-column worksheet.) The worksheet (Figure 3-31) is an 8-column worksheet and the trial balance columns have been prepared using the general ledger for Medieval Glass.

Before this worksheet can be completed, there are four year-end adjusting entries to make in the Adjustments columns of the worksheet. Some adjustments are made through the use of vouchers. A **voucher** is a document that itemizes the accounts to be debited and credited for the adjustment. **Adjustments** are changes in the account balances that need to be made at year end to meet **Generally Accepted Accounting Principles**, guidelines set down by professional accounting bodies for the preparation of financial statements. These adjustments are now discussed in detail.

PREPAID SUPPLIES

Prepaid Supplies are supplies already purchased that will benefit a future time period. Prepaid Supplies is an asset account that contains the value of all office and shipping supplies purchased during the year plus any supplies on hand at the beginning of the year (if this was not the first year of operation for the business). Medieval Glass has a balance of $2 350 in its Prepaid Supplies account. This figure represents the sum paid for supplies during the year ($2 050) and the opening inventory ($300). At the end of the year, however, not all of these supplies will still be on hand. An inventory count of supplies will yield the true figure.

Medieval Glass has counted its supplies at year end and found that $350 worth are still on hand. Therefore, $2 000 of supplies were used up and must be expensed out at year end.

This requires an adjustment on the worksheet that debits the Supplies Expense account $2 000 and credits Prepaid Supplies $2 000. This will be entered on the worksheet later as adjusting entry #1.

There are two ways a business can record the purchase of supplies in its books of account:

(a) debit the asset account, Prepaid Supplies

(b) debit the expense account, Supplies Expense

Medieval Glass

WORKSHEET
FOR THE Year   ENDED Nov. 30 19 –

	ACCOUNTS	ACCT. NO.	TRIAL BALANCE DR	TRIAL BALANCE CR	ADJUSTMENTS DR	ADJUSTMENTS CR	INCOME STATEMENT DR	INCOME STATEMENT CR	BALANCE SHEET DR	BALANCE SHEET CR	
1	Bank	110	10770 –								1
2	Accounts Receivable	120	3000 –								2
3	GST Recoverable	121	230 –								3
4	Merchandise Inventory	130	12000 –								4
5	Prepaid Supplies	140	2350 –								5
6	Equipment	160	10500 –								6
7	Acc. Dep.—Equipment	161		2100 –							7
8	Bank Loan	210		5000 –							8
9	Accounts Payable	220		4100 –							9
10	GST Payable	221		600 –							10
11	PST Payable	222		800 –							11
12	J. McLellan, Capital	310		25000 –							12
13	J. McLellan, Drawings	315	14000 –								13
14	Sales	410		80000 –							14
15	Advertising Expense	502	600 –								15
16	Bank Charges	504	130 –								16
17	Dep. Expense—Equipment	506	Ø								17
18	Discounts Allowed	508	550 –								18
19	Discounts Earned	510		800 –							19
20	Heat & Light Expense	512	3400 –								20
21	Miscellaneous Expense	514	770 –								21
22	Office Expense	516	930 –								22
23	Purchases	518	50000 –								23
24	Purchases Ret. & Allow.	520		1600 –							24
25	Supplies Expense	522	Ø								25
26	Telephone Expense	524	770 –								26
27	Wages Expense	526	10000 –								27
28			120000 –	120000 –							28
29											29
30											30
31											31
32											32
33											33

FIGURE 3-31   *An 8-column worksheet*

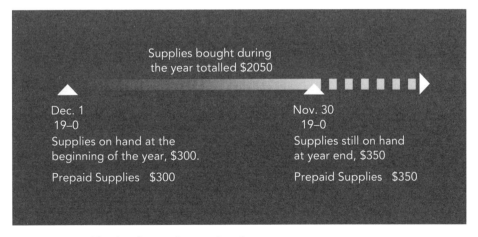

FIGURE 3-32   *Timeline for supplies purchased*

Here is an explanation of each possible accounting option.

Debiting Prepaid Supplies

If a business uses this method, when it buys supplies, Prepaid Supplies will be debited and Bank will be credited. See Figure 3-33.

DATE 19–		PARTICULARS	PR	DEBIT	CREDIT
Jan.	25	Prepaid Supplies		2050 –	
		GST Recoverable		143 50	
		Bank			2193 50
		To record purchase of supplies			
		Cheque 94			

FIGURE 3-33   *The general journal entry for prepaid supplies*

The adjusting entry at year end then credits Prepaid Supplies $2 000 and debits the Supplies Expense account $2 000. This is the actual amount of supplies used up in the year. The remaining $350 will be the opening balance in the Prepaid Supplies account at the start of the next year.

Debiting Supplies Expense

The business could have charged all of the $2 350 to the Supplies Expense account when the supplies were originally bought. That is, the accounting entry would have debited Supplies Expense and credited Bank (Figure 3-34).

DATE 19–		PARTICULARS	PR	DEBIT	CREDIT
Jan.	25	Supplies Expense		2050 –	
		GST Recoverable		143 50	
		Bank			2193 50
		To record purchase of supplies			
		Cheque 94			

FIGURE 3-34   *The general journal entry for supplies expense*

In this case the adjusting entry would be to credit the Supplies Expense account $50 and debit Prepaid Supplies $50. (Remember, there were $300 worth of prepaid supplies on hand at the beginning of the year.) Whichever method is chosen, the end result is the same: the supplies expense for the year is $2 000.

DEPRECIATION

Depreciation is a method of allocating an asset's cost over its useful life. Fixed assets in a business are depreciated, or written off, over a period of time, in an attempt to match costs to revenue. This is the Generally Accepted Accounting Principle of Matching.

Medieval Glass has one fixed asset that it has to depreciate at year end: the equipment. The cost of this asset has to be spread over a number of years since the equipment is used over a number of years. Depreciation is the process of spreading the cost of an asset over its estimated useful lifetime. The two most common ways of calculating depreciation are the straight-line method, and the declining-balance method. Some businesses will use straight-line depreciation for their books, and declining-balance depreciation for income tax purposes. Declining-balance depreciation, however, is the only method allowed for income tax purposes by Revenue Canada. The tax department uses the term *capital cost allowance*, rather than depreciation.

Straight-Line Depreciation

Straight-line depreciation produces an equal amount of asset depreciation for each fiscal period. It is most useful when the asset being depreciated is used evenly over its life. Salvage value must be taken into consideration when straight-line depreciation is used. Salvage value is the amount a business thinks it will get for an asset at the end of its useful life. For the straight-line depreciation example that follows, Medieval Glass has equipment that cost $10 500. Assume that its estimated salvage value is $500 and its useful life is five years. The formula and calculation for straight-line depreciation is as follows.

$$\text{Annual Depreciation} = \frac{\text{Asset Cost} - \text{Salvage Value}}{\text{Estimated Useful Life}}$$

$$= \frac{\$10\ 500 - \$500}{5\ \text{Years}}$$

$$= \$2\ 000/\text{Year}$$

In the example above, the equipment would be depreciated by $2 000 every year for five years. At the end of five years, the equipment, which would be of no further use to the business, would be fully depreciated, or written off the books and sold for its salvage value. These funds are not treated as sales revenue, but rather as an exchange of one asset for another.

Declining-Balance Depreciation

Declining-balance depreciation is the method used by most businesses, since it is the only one allowed on income tax returns in Canada. This method is also popular because it allows for higher depreciation in the early years of ownership of an asset. With this method of accelerated depreciation, the same fixed percentage (or rate of depreciation) is used every year. Depreciation is calculated on the net book value of assets each year, their original cost less their depreciation to date. (Salvage values are not taken into consideration for this method of depreciation. Any scrap value can be considered near the end of the asset's life.)

When the declining-balance method of depreciation is used, different fixed percentages are used for different groups, or classes of assets. The word **class** refers to an asset grouping established by the government for purposes of depreciation. Some of the fixed asset classes allowed by Revenue Canada are:

Class	Description	Rate of Depreciation
3	BUILDINGS — brick buildings	5%
8	MACHINERY, EQUIPMENT, FIXTURES	20%
10	AUTOMOTIVE — cars, vans, trucks, tractors, stable equipment; computers	30%
16	RENTAL VEHICLES & COIN MACHINES — taxicabs, car rental business vehicles, video games, pinball machines	40%
17	SURFACE CONSTRUCTION — roads, parking lots, sidewalks, airplane runways	8%

Medieval Glass uses the declining balance method of depreciation for its equipment (class 8). To calculate depreciation on the equipment, find the net book value of the asset on the worksheet, and apply the declining-balance rate of depreciation allowed by the government (in the table above). Here is the depreciation calculation for the equipment owned by Medieval Glass.

Equipment (Class 8)

Equipment	$10 500
Accumulated Depreciation — Equipment	(2 100)
Net Book Value	8 400
Rate of Depreciation — Class 8	× .20 (20%)
Depreciation Expense — Equipment	$ 1 680

The adjustment on the worksheet is a debit to the account Depreciation Expense — Equipment and credit to the account Accumulated Depreciation — Equipment.

GENERAL JOURNAL

PAGE 48

DATE 19–		PARTICULARS	PR	DEBIT	CREDIT
Nov.	30	Depreciation Expense—Equipment		1680 –	
		Acc. Dep.—Equipment			1680 –
		To record annual depreciation,			
		using the declining-balance method			

FIGURE 3-35   *The general journal entry for depreciation*

This depreciation will be entered on the worksheet later as adjusting entry #2.

No matter what system of depreciation is used, the book value of the asset has no bearing on its market value. Depreciation is a method of allocating the cost of an asset over its useful life. In the case of fixed assets, you are spreading their cost over a number of years, not trying to guess how much they are worth each year. Accountants emphasize that depreciation is a method of allocation, not of valuation.

ACCRUED WAGES

Accrued Wages are wages owing to employees which have not yet been paid by year end. The fiscal year end for Medieval Glass was on Thursday, November 30, 19–. Since employees are paid every two weeks, they do not get paid again until Friday, December 8, the regular payday. As of November 30, therefore, there are 4 days wages owing to employees for their work. This amount is called an **accrual** and must be set up in the business books as an amount owing at year end. Figure 3-36 may explain this situation more clearly.

The payroll on Friday, December 8th was $500 for part-time wages. The accrued wages at year end then are:

$$\frac{4 \text{ days accrued}}{10 \text{ days payroll}} \times \$500 = \$200$$

November/December				
Mon	Tue	Wed	Thu	Fri
27	28	29	30 year end	1
4	5	6	7	8 payday

FIGURE 3-36   *Calendar*

The accounting entry to adjust for the wage accrual is to debit the Wages Expense account $200, and credit an account called Accrued Wages. Note that Accrued Wages had to be added to the worksheet. (See Figure 3-38.)

GENERAL JOURNAL

PAGE _48_

DATE 19–		PARTICULARS	PR	DEBIT	CREDIT
Nov.	30	Wages Expense		200 –	
		Accrued Wages			200 –
		To set up wage accrual at the			
		year end			

FIGURE 3-37   *The general journal entry for accrued wages*

This is recorded as adjusting entry #3 on the worksheet.

MERCHANDISE INVENTORY

The final adjustment for Medieval Glass is the easiest to make but the hardest to understand. When a business buys merchandise, an entry is made to debit Purchases and credit Bank or Accounts Payable. The merchandise inventory account balance is not changed until the end of the year. This is called the **periodic system of inventory**. This system, and another system called **perpetual inventory** are dealt with fully in Chapter 7, Inventory Control.

If a business uses the periodic system, it only counts its inventory once a year, at the end of the fiscal year. You have probably seen signs in store windows saying, "Closed for Inventory". The store is counting its inventory so that it can adjust its books at year end.

The adjustment for inventory is not entered into the Adjustments column. Instead, on the worksheet, the old inventory ($12 000) is entered in the debit column of the Income Statement columns on the Merchandise Inventory line. Then the new inventory figure ($16 000) is written in the credit column of the Income Statement columns, and the debit column of the Balance Sheet columns.

The debit in the Income Statement columns is there because you assume that the old inventory is sold during the year and you are really charging the inventory to the income statement. The new inventory is recorded as a credit in the Income Statement columns because you are reducing inventory costs when there is still inventory left over at the end of the year. The new inventory also is a current asset from which the business will benefit during the next fiscal period.

Look carefully at the inventory adjustment shown for Medieval Glass. This is adjusting entry #4 on the worksheet but it is not usually numbered.

There are four adjustments that have been made to the accounts on the worksheet. Here are the details:

(1) The supplies bought during the year totalled $2 350. Ending inventory was $350. Therefore, $2 000 worth of supplies must be expensed out at year end i.e. transferred from Prepaid Supplies to Supplies Expense.
(2) The equipment has to be depreciated $1 680. The equipment is a class 8 asset and is depreciated at 20% of net book value.
(3) There are accrued wages of $200.
(4) The old merchandise inventory ($12 000) has to be adjusted to reflect the new balance of merchandise inventory on hand for the next fiscal period ($16 000).

Once the adjustments are recorded the worksheet can be extended, totalled, and cross-balanced.

WORKSHEET

Medieval Glass

FOR THE _Year_   ENDED _Nov. 30_ 19 _—_

#	ACCOUNTS	ACCT. NO.	TRIAL BALANCE DR	TRIAL BALANCE CR	ADJUSTMENTS DR	ADJUSTMENTS CR	INCOME STATEMENT DR	INCOME STATEMENT CR	BALANCE SHEET DR	BALANCE SHEET CR	#
1	Bank	110	10770 -						10770 -		1
2	Accounts Receivable	120	3000 -						3000 -		2
3	GST Recoverable	121	230 -						230 -		3
4	Merchandise Inventory	130	12000 -				(4)12000	(4)16000 -	16000 -		4
5	Prepaid Supplies	140	2350 -			(1)2000 -			350 -		5
6	Equipment	160	10500 -						10500 -		6
7	Acc. Dep.—Equipment	161		2100 -		(2)1680 -				3780 -	7
8	Bank Loan	210		5000 -						5000 -	8
9	Accounts Payable	220		4100 -						4100 -	9
10	GST Payable	221		600 -						600 -	10
11	PST Payable	222		800 -						800 -	11
12	J. McLellan, Capital	310		25000 -						25000 -	12
13	J. McLellan, Drawings	315	14000 -						14000 -		13
14	Sales	410		80000 -				80000 -			14
15	Advertising Expense	502	600 -				600 -				15
16	Bank Charges	504	130 -				130 -				16
17	Dep. Expense—Equipment	506	0		(2)1680 -		1680 -				17
18	Discounts Allowed	508	550 -				550 -				18
19	Discounts Earned	510		800 -				800 -			19
20	Heat & Light Expense	512	3400 -				3400 -				20
21	Miscellaneous Expense	514	770 -				770 -				21
22	Office Expense	516	930 -				930 -				22
23	Purchases	518	50000 -				50000 -				23
24	Purchases Ret. & Allow.	520		1600 -				1600 -			24
25	Supplies Expense	522	0		(1)2000 -		2000 -				25
26	Telephone Expense	524	770 -				770 -				26
27	Wages Expense	528	10000 -		(3) 200 -		10200 -				27
28			120000 -	120000 -							28
29	Accrued Wages	230				(3)200 -				200 -	29
30					3880 -	3880 -	83030 -	98400 -	54850 -	39480 -	30
31	Net Income						15370 -			15370 -	31
32							98400 -	98400 -	54850 -	54850 -	32
33											33

FIGURE 3-38   *The worksheet extended and balanced*

At this point, the adjustments on the worksheet (except for the inventory adjustment) must be journalized into a general journal and posted to the general ledger. The entries are journalized for you in Figure 3-39.

Although the general ledger is not shown, you can tell from the PR column that these adjusting entries have been posted into the ledger. The worksheet will be used to prepare the financial statements in section 3.4.

GENERAL JOURNAL

PAGE 47

DATE 19–		PARTICULARS	PR	DEBIT	CREDIT
		ADJUSTING JOURNAL ENTRIES			
		①			
Nov.	30	Supplies Expense	522	2000 –	
		Prepaid Supplies	140		2000 –
		To adjust for supplies expense			
		②			
	30	Dep. Expense—Equipment	506	1680 –	
		Acc. Dep.—Equipment	161		1680 –
		To adjust for depreciation			
		③			
	30	Wages Expense	528	200 –	
		Accrued Wages	230		200 –
		To adjust for accrued wages			

FIGURE 3-39   *Adjusting journal entries*

QUESTIONS

19. What two accounting choices does a business have to record the purchase of supplies?

20. A firm bought $900 worth of supplies and charged them to Prepaid Supplies. At year end there was $100 worth of supplies on hand. What is the adjusting entry?

21. A firm bought $1 225 worth of supplies and charged them to Supplies Expense. At year end there was $75 worth of supplies on hand. What is the adjusting entry?

22. What does the term *classes of assets* refer to?

23. Give the class and rate for these assets: cement sidewalk; video machine; taxi; van; brick store.

24. Calculate the depreciation on a $22 000 car for two years using:
    (a) straight-line depreciation
    (b) declining-balance depreciation
    The car has a salvage value of $2 000 and is expected to last six years.

25. Calculate the depreciation on a $2 000 grinder for four years using:
    (a) straight-line depreciation
    (b) declining-balance depreciation
    The grinder has a salvage value of $200 and is expected to last four years.

26. Accumulated Depreciation — Truck is a contra account. What does *contra* mean?

27. Which depreciation method must be used for tax purposes?

28. Find the accrued wages for a December 31st year end, if the bi-weekly payroll paid on Friday, January 4th was $800.

29. Find the accrued wages for a December 31st year end, if the monthly payroll paid on Friday, January 11th was $2 500.

3.4

Preparing the Financial Statements

Once the 8-column worksheet has been extended, totalled, and balanced, it can be used to prepare the financial statements for the business. The two main statements we are concerned with for a small service business, such as Medieval Glass, are the income statement and the balance sheet. The income statement is prepared first because the net income figure has to flow through to the owner's equity section of the balance sheet.

The income statement for Medieval Glass is prepared directly from the Income Statement debit and credit columns on the worksheet:

Medieval Glass
Income Statement
For the Year Ended November 30, 19–

Revenue:			
Sales			$80 000
Cost of Goods Sold:			
Opening Inventory		$12 000	
Purchases	$50 000		
Less: Purch. Ret. & Allow.	1 600	48 400	
Goods Available for Sale		60 400	
Closing Inventory		16 000	
Cost of Goods Sold			44 400
Gross Income on Sales			35 600

Expenses:		
Advertising	600	
Bank Charges	130	
Depreciation — Equipment	1 680	
Heat & Light	3 400	
Miscellaneous	770	
Office	930	
Supplies	2 000	
Telephone	770	
Wages	10 200	20 480
Net Operating Income		15 120
Other Items:		
Discounts Earned	800	
Less: Discounts Allowed	550	250
Net Income		$15 370

Once the income statement is prepared, you can use the Balance Sheet columns on the worksheet to prepare the formal balance sheet for the business. The net income from the income statement is transferred to the owner's equity section of the balance sheet and added to the capital balance. A net profit for the business increases the owner's equity in the business. Conversely, a net loss would be subtracted from the old capital amount since it would decrease the owner's equity. See overleaf.

There are different formats that can be used for financial statement presentation. Formats used depend on the accountant who prepares the financial statements, and/or the computer software program that might be used to prepare the statements. This will become evident in section 3.7 when the *ACCPAC Bedford Integrated Accounting* program is used.

Medieval Glass
Balance Sheet
November 30, 19–

Current Assets:				
Bank			$10 770	
Accounts Receivable			3 000	
GST Recoverable			230	
Merchandise Inventory			16 000	
Total Current Assets				$30 000
Prepaid Expenses:				
Supplies				350
Fixed Assets:				
	Cost	Acc. Dep.		
Equipment	$10 500	$3 780		6 720
Total Assets				$37 070
Current Liabilities:				
Bank Loan			$5 000	
Accounts Payable			4 100	
GST Payable			600	
PST Payable			800	
Accrued Wages			200	
Total Current Liabilities				$10 700
Owner's Equity				
J. McLellan, Capital				
Opening Balance			25 000	
Add: Net Income			15 370	
			40 370	
Less: Drawings			14 000	
Closing Balance				26 370
Total Liabilities and Owner's Equity				$37 070

3.5

Closing Entries

Once the income statement and the balance sheet have been prepared, a business must close out its books. **Closing entries** are journal entries which close out certain accounts to nil balances at year end. Closing out the books means that all revenue and expense accounts and the drawings account are brought to zero. At the end of a fiscal year they must be emptied so that they are ready for the next year.

Also, the closing entry to delete the old merchandise inventory and set up the new merchandise inventory is journalized.

Closing entries are done in a logical order, and are usually journalized in the general journal. To follow this process through from start to finish, we will begin with the trial balance after the entries in the adjustments column. The trial balance is as shown.

Medieval Glass
Trial Balance
November 30, 19–

110	Bank	$ 10 770	
120	Accounts Receivable	3 000	
121	GST Recoverable	230	
130	Merchandise Inventory	12 000	
140	Prepaid Supplies	350	
160	Equipment	10 500	
161	Accumulated Depreciation — Equipment		$ 3 780
210	Bank Loan		5 000
220	Accounts Payable		4 100
221	GST Payable		600
222	PST Payable		800
230	Accrued Wages		200
310	J. McLellan, Capital		25 000
315	J. McLellan, Drawings	14 000	
410	Sales		80 000
502	Advertising Expense	600	
504	Bank Charges	130	
506	Depreciation Expense — Equipment	1 680	
508	Discounts Allowed	550	

510	Discounts Earned		800
512	Heat & Light Expense	3 400	
514	Miscellaneous Expense	770	
516	Office Expense	930	
518	Purchases	50 000	
520	Purchases Returns & Allowances		1 600
522	Supplies Expense	2 000	
524	Telephone Expense	770	
528	Wages Expense	10 200	
		$121 880	$121 880

FIGURE 3-40   *Trial balance with adjustments*

The accounts are going to be closed out in this order:

1st: The Merchandise Inventory adjustment is made.
2nd: The Sales account is closed to the Income Summary.
3rd: All Expense accounts are closed to the Income Summary.
4th: The Income Summary account is closed to Capital.
5th: The Drawings account is closed to Capital.

The Income Summary account is just a temporary account used during the closing out (journalizing) process. The important thing is to understand that eventually the profit (or loss) of the business gets added to (or charged against) the owner's Capital account. The closing journal entries in the order just mentioned are shown in Figure 3-41. They are numbered for your convenience in cross-referencing.

Once the closing entries have been journalized, they must be posted into the appropriate accounts in the general ledger.

THE POST-CLOSING TRIAL BALANCE

Once the closing entries have been posted to the general ledger accounts, a trial balance should be taken to ensure that the ledger is still in balance. There are essentially three ways to take the trial balance:
(1) A *zero proof* tape trial balance.
(2) A *balanced ledger* tape trial balance.
(3) A *formal* trial balance.

GENERAL JOURNAL

PAGE 120

DATE 19–		PARTICULARS	PR	DEBIT	CREDIT
		CLOSING JOURNAL ENTRIES			
		①			
Nov.	30	Merchandise Inventory	130	16000 –	
		Merchandise Inventory	130		12000 –
		Income Summary	600		4000 –
		To close out old inventory and			
		set up new inventory			
		②			
	30	Sales	410	80000 –	
		Income Summary	600		80000 –
		To close out Revenue account			
		③			
	30	Income Summary	600	68630 –	
		Discounts Earned	510	800 –	
		Purchases Returns & Allowances	520	1600 –	
		Advertising Expense	502		600 –
		Bank Charges	504		130 –
		Dep. Expense—Equipment	506		1680 –
		Discounts Allowed	508		550 –
		Heat & Light Expense	512		3400 –
		Miscellaneous Expense	514		770 –
		Office Expense	516		930 –
		Purchases	518		50000 –
		Supplies Expense	522		2000 –
		Telephone Expense	524		770 –
		Wages Expense	528		10200 –
		To close out Expense accounts			
		④			
	30	Income Summary	600	15370 –	
		J. McLellan, Capital	310		15370 –
		To close out Income Summary account			
		⑤			
	30	J. McLellan, Capital	310	14000 –	
		J. McLellan, Drawings	315		14000 –
		To close out Drawings account			

FIGURE 3-41   *Closing journal entries*

In the first option, the zero proof, a calculator tape is taken of all of the account balances left after closing. The accounts are listed in the order they appear in the ledger, and when the tape is totalled it should show a "0" balance. The second option is a listing of all debit account balances and a total, then a listing of all the credit account balances and a total. The totals for the debits and credits should equal each other. The third option is a formal trial balance where all of the accounts in the ledger are listed along with their final balances. Figure 3-42 shows the formal trial balance for Medieval Glass.

Medieval Glass
Trial Balance
November 30, 19–

110	Bank	$10 770	
120	Accounts Receivable	3 000	
121	GST Recoverable	230	
130	Merchandise Inventory	16 000	
140	Prepaid Supplies	350	
160	Equipment	10 500	
161	Accumulated Depreciation — Equipment		$ 3 780
210	Bank Loan		5 000
220	Accounts Payable		4 100
221	GST Payable		600
222	PST Payable		800
230	Accrued Wages		200
310	J. McLellan, Capital		26 370
		$40 850	$40 850

FIGURE 3-42   *Post-closing trial balance*

Take another look at Figure 3-42. Notice that all of the Revenue and Expense accounts and the Drawings account are missing. They have been emptied so that they are ready for the next fiscal period. The Drawings account has been charged against the Capital account and the profit for the year has been added to the Capital account. The accounts are now ready for the next accounting period to begin.

This completes the accounting cycle for this merchandise business. The next section will explain how a computer can be used for accounting work in a merchandise business.

3.6

Using the Computer

There are several ways in which a computer can be useful in a merchandise business. This section will provide some examples of business forms or reports that can be made using spreadsheet, graphics, and database software.

Spreadsheets

A **spreadsheet** is a computer document consisting of rows and columns which can be programmed with formulas. A good use of a spreadsheet for a merchandise business, like Medieval Glass, is the sales summary listing that can be prepared at year end.

	A	B	C	D	E
1	Medieval Glass				
2	Sales Summary 19-				
3					
4	Month	Sales	Lamps	Windows	Other
5					
6	Jan	5000	3000	1500	500
7	Feb	4000	1000	2000	1000
8	Mar	3500	1000	2500	
9	Apr	6000	3000	3000	
10	May	9000	1800	6000	1200
11	Jun	12500	2000	8000	2500
12	Jul	2000	600	600	800
13	Aug	2000		2000	
14	Sep	5000	400	3600	1000
15	Oct	6500	4200	1500	800
16	Nov	8500	3000	4000	1500
17	Dec	16000	7500	4500	4000
18					
19	Totals	80000	27500	39200	13300
20					

FIGURE 3-43   *A spreadsheet sales summary*

Some of the spreadsheet content is permanent: the title "Sales Summary", the sub-headings in row 4 "Month .... Other", and the months in column A. The new sales data can be inserted in columns C, D, and E. This spreadsheet has been programmed to total the monthly sales in column B and to total the sales for the year in cells B19, C19, D19, and E19. The spreadsheet could also be programmed to calculate percentages of sales for each of the three categories.

The secret to the successful use of a spreadsheet is to find a business application that involves calculations that can be programmed into the computer. This saves doing them by hand, of course, and this is the purpose of using the computer as an accounting tool.

Graphics

The word **graphics** refers to computer software which presents accounting data in graph form. Once a spreadsheet has been stored on disk, it is usually easy to have the computer print a graph of the data from the spreadsheet. Most integrated software packages have this feature. And usually once the spreadsheet is stored, you can go directly to the production of a graph. There are different styles of graphs with the three most common being bar graphs, line graphs, and pie charts. The example for Medieval Glass is a bar graph showing the sales for the year, broken down by month and product line. The graph gives a quick visual impression of the sales over a period of one year.

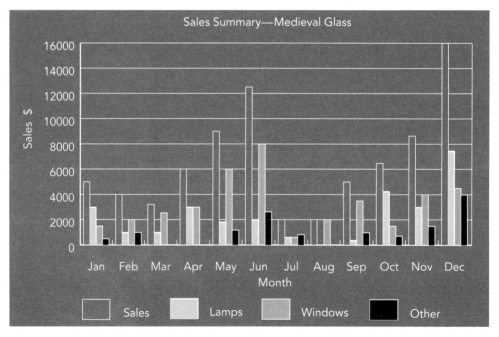

FIGURE 3-44   A computer-generated bar graph

The dollar amounts are scaled on the y-axis on the left, and the total sales and product breakdowns are shown on the x-axis along the bottom. With this software, you can label the graph as well. The data for the graph is taken from the spreadsheet in Figure 3-43, which the computer has in its memory.

Databases

A **database** is one or more files of accounting information. One example of a database which might be useful for Medieval Glass is a customer database, or an accounts receivable file.

```
Name: Marsden, Bob
Address: 130 Glen Park Cr.
Town: Kitchener                        one record
PC: N2N 1G2
Telephone No: 555-3385
Credit Limit: $1500
```

ACCOUNTS RECEIVABLE FILE

Name	Address	Town	PC	Tel. No.	Credit Limit
Deroo, Theresa	25 Clarence Place	Kitchener	N2H 2L1	555-2093	$ 500
Hutchinson, Ellen	24 Hill Street	Kitchener	N2H 5T1	555-9901	$ 750
Marsden, Bob	130 Glen Park Cr.	Kitchener	N2N 1G2	555-3385	$1500
Peter, Les	152 Millwood Cr.	Kitchener	N2P 1M4	555-4433	$ 500
Thurtell, Richard	83 Blackwell Rd.	Kitchener	N2N 1P4	555-6739	$ 500
Zvanitas, Dace	1 Westgate Walk	Kitchener	N2M 2T7	555-1829	$ 750

FIGURE 3-45   A customer file

The top part of Figure 3-45 shows the form used when the database is set up and stored. The lower part is a listing of the file showing customer name, address, town, postal code, telephone number, and credit limit. Once the file has been stored, a business can manipulate it in several ways, e.g., print an alphabetical listing of the file, select certain customers, or create mailing labels.

3.7

Bedford Exercise 3 — The Lumber Barn

The company in this chapter is called The Lumber Barn.

You have taken a position as accounting clerk for The Lumber Barn located in Moncton, New Brunswick. You are to commence your duties the first day of the new fiscal year. The arrangement is that you are to work with the present accounting clerk until his departure at the end of the month. During this time you will become sufficiently acquainted with the firm's accounting records and company procedures to enable you to assume full responsibility for the accounting system using microcomputer equipment. Initially, the company has decided to use the *Bedford* **General** ledger module only. Provincial Sales Tax is currently at 11% and is levied on the base price plus GST for all sales. The 7% GST (Federal Goods and Services Tax) affects all sales and purchases.

The trial balance at the start of this new fiscal year is as shown.

The Lumber Barn
Opening Trial Balance

No.	Account	Debit	Credit
105	Petty Cash	$ 100.00	
110	Bank	19 760.28	
120	A/R Builder's World	1 140.50	
121	A/R Gunter's Fine Cabinets	1 938.92	
122	A/R Home Building Ltd.	2 166.03	
123	A/R Kell Construction Ltd.	569.58	
124	A/R MJD Construction Ltd.	1 595.99	
125	A/R Pioneer Designs	684.74	
126	A/R Reliable Construction	456.77	
127	A/R Eastern Contracting Ltd.	1 709.66	
130	GST Recoverable	418.20	
135	Merchandise Inventory	36 812.47	
140	Prepaid Supplies	700.00	
141	Prepaid Insurance	4 800.00	
180	Office Equipment	6 200.00	
181	Acc. Dep. — Office Equipment		$ 2 232.89
185	Trucks	45 000.00	
186	Acc. Dep. — Trucks		22 450.73
190	Building	140 000.00	
191	Acc. Dep. — Building		26 600.39
195	Land	60 000.00	
210	Bank Loan		15 000.00
220	A/P Allwood Industries		2 568.24
221	A/P Grove Cedar Products		1 498.01
222	A/P Tyee Forest Products		2 354.92
223	A/P Weststar Timber		6 312.88

230	GST Payable		2 940.00
231	PST Payable		4 943.40
240	CPP Payable		168.86
241	UI Payable		200.03
242	Income Tax Payable		1 486.35
243	Provincial Medical Payable		187.62
244	Company Pension Payable		933.67
310	R. Falkenburg, Capital		234 175.15
315	R. Falkenburg, Drawings		0.00
356	Retained Earnings		0.00
410	Sales		0.00
411	Sales Ret. & Allowances	0.00	
412	Sales Discounts	0.00	
501	Beginning Inventory	0.00	
502	Purchases	0.00	
503	Freight-In	0.00	
504	Purchases Ret. & Allowances		0.00
505	Purchases Discounts		0.00
506	Ending Inventory		0.00
510	Advertising Expense	0.00	
512	Company Pension Expense	0.00	
515	CPP Expense	0.00	
520	Dep. Exp. — Office Equipment	0.00	
521	Dep. Exp. — Trucks	0.00	
522	Dep. Exp. — Building	0.00	
550	Insurance Expense	0.00	
555	Interest Expense	0.00	
560	Maintenance Expense	0.00	
565	Miscellaneous Expense	0.00	
570	Salaries Expense	0.00	
575	Supplies Expense	0.00	
580	Telephone Expense	0.00	
585	Truck Expense	0.00	
590	UI Expense	0.00	
595	Utilities Expense	0.00	
		$324 053.14	$324 053.14

The accounts and all of the historical balances have been entered onto a data disk for you, and the computer accounting system only has to be set to **Ready** mode. The instructions for using *Bedford* and entering data are outlined in Chapter 1.

ACCESSING THE LUMBER BARN GENERAL LEDGER

To retrieve the general ledger for The Lumber Barn, you use the file name **lumbbarn**. Key this name into the computer, insert the dates provided by your teacher, and set the program to **Ready**, as described in Chapter 1.

Enter the **Using** date provided by your teacher. Remember the sequence, mmddyy. As before, ignore the cautions and proceed.

JOURNALIZING TRANSACTIONS

To journalize general ledger transactions, access the **GENERAL** module and the **Journal** option.

TRANSACTIONS

All credit sales are on a 2/10, n/30 basis.

1. Sales Invoice S1014   Dated: mm01yy
   Sale on account to Home Building Ltd., $7 601.28. Sales $6 400, GST Payable $448, and PST Payable $753.28.

2. Cash Receipt L101   Dated: mm02yy
   Received $1 938.92 on account from Gunter's Fine Cabinets.
   (Note: When you need to decrease an account, enter a minus sign before or after your amount.)

3. Cheque 125   Dated: mm05yy
   Payment on account to Allwood Industries, $2 568.24.

4. Purchase Invoice 3456   Dated: mm07yy
   Purchased merchandise, $1 500, GST Recoverable $105, on account from Grove Cedar Products. Total owing, $1 605.

5. Sales Invoice S1015   Dated: mm08yy
   Sale on account to Eastern Contracting Ltd., $4 988.34. Sales $4 200, GST Payable $294, and PST Payable $494.34.

6. Sales Invoice S1016   Dated: mm08yy
   Sale on account to Gunter's Fine Cabinets, $4 038.18. Sales $3 400,
   GST Payable $238, and PST Payable $400.18.

7. Cheque 127   Dated: mm09yy
   Amount owing to Tyee Forest Products, $2 354.92. Payment was
   $2 307.82, Purchases Discounts $47.10.

8. Cheque 128   Dated: mm09yy
   Paid company pension deductions for December to Galt & Associates,
   $933.67.

9. Purchase Invoice L876   Dated: mm10yy
   Purchased merchandise, $6 200, GST Recoverable $434, on account
   from Allwood Industries. Total owing $6 634. Terms net 30.

10. Cheque 129   Dated: mm11yy
    Freight-In $426.36 and GST Recoverable $29.85 to pay CP Rail.

11. Cash Receipt L102   Dated: mm11yy
    Received $9 571.96; Sales Discounts $195.35. Home Building Ltd. paid
    their account in full. Amount of invoices, $9 767.31.

12. Cash Receipt L103   Dated: mm12yy
    Received $1 595.99 on account from MJD Construction Co. Account
    paid in full. Too late for the discount.

13. Cash Receipt L104   Dated: mm13yy
    Received $1 709.66, on account from Eastern Contracting Ltd. Too late
    for the discount.

14. Purchase Invoice 8765   Dated: mm14yy
    Purchased merchandise, $1 400, GST Recoverable $98, on account
    from Weststar Timber. Total owing $1 498. Terms net 30.

15. Cheque 130   Dated: mm15yy
    Amount owing to Weststar Timber, $6 312.88. Paid invoice 4567 in full.
    Too late for the discount.

16. Cheque 131   Dated: mm15yy
    Remitted for provincial sales taxes collected in December. Cheque
    made out to Provincial Treasurer.

17. Cheque 132   Dated: mm15yy
    Debit CPP Payable $168.86, UI Payable $200.03, and Income Tax
    Payable $1 486.35. Total $1 855.24 sent to Receiver General of Canada
    for payroll deductions.

18. Sales Invoice S1017   Dated: mm16yy
    Sale on account to MJD Construction Co., $5 700.96. Sales $4 800,
    GST Payable $336, and PST Payable $564.96.

19. Sales Invoice S1018   Dated: mm16yy
    Sale on account to Pioneer Designs, $6 888.66. Sales $5 800, GST
    Payable $406, and PST Payable $682.66.

20. Cash Receipt L105   Dated: mm18yy
    Received $4 888.57; Sales Discounts $99.77. Received on account from
    Eastern Contracting Ltd. Amount of original sale $4 988.34.

21. Cash Receipt L106   Dated: mm18yy
    Received $3 957.42; Sales Discounts $80.76. Received on account from
    Gunter's Fine Cabinets. Amount of original sale $4 038.18.

22. Sales Invoice S1019   Dated: mm19yy
    Sale on account to Home Building Ltd., $6 176.04. Sales $5 200, GST
    Payable $364, and PST Payable $612.04.

23. Cheque 133   Dated: mm21yy
    Amount owing to Grove Cedar Products, $1 498.01. No discount.

24. Cheque 134   Dated: mm21yy
    Miscellaneous Expense $25.71, Maintenance Expense $33.53, Supplies
    Expense $31.30, and GST Recoverable $5.67. Cheque issued to Lisa
    Ellis to replenish the petty cash fund.

25. Credit Invoice C100   Dated: mm23yy
    Amount owing to Allwood Industries was reduced by $535. GST
    Recoverable was reduced by $35 and Purchases Ret. & Allowances was
    increased by $500, invoice L876. (Remember to use the minus sign.)

26. Sales Memo SM 50   Dated: mm25yy
    Debit Sales Ret. & Allowances $600, GST Payable $42, and PST
    Payable $70.62. Issued to Home Building Ltd., $712.62. Unsuitable
    lumber returned by customer.

27. Cheque 135   Dated: mm29yy
    Telephone Expense $241.81 and GST Recoverable $15.24. Payment to
    NB Telephone Company.

28. Cheque 136   Dated: mm30yy
    R. Falkenburg, Drawings $2 500.

29. Cheque 137   Dated: mm30yy
Salary Expense $9 340, CPP Payable $185, UI Payable $174, Income Tax Payable $2 384, Provincial Medical Payable $94, Company Pension Payable $560. Cheque to payroll account, $5 943.

30. Bank Debit Memo   Dated: mm30yy
Interest Expense $162.50, automatically withdrawn from account.

31. Voucher 001   Dated: mm30yy
CPP Expense $185, and UI Expense $278. CPP Payable $185, and UI Payable $278. Employer's share of deductions.

32. Voucher 002   Dated: mm30yy
Company Pension Expense, $560. Company Pension Payable, $560.

33. Voucher 003   Dated: mm30yy
Lisa Ellis, office clerk, submitted an inventory list totalling $250 for office supplies still on hand at month end. Make the appropriate adjusting entry.

34. At the end of the business day the closing inventory of lumber products as determined by a physical count was $34 500. Two entries are needed to adjust the inventory.

Voucher 004   Dated: mm30yy
Transfer the beginning inventory to the Cost of Goods Sold section by debiting Beginning Inventory $36 812.47 and crediting Merchandise Inventory by the same amount.

Voucher 005   Dated: mm30yy
Enter the ending inventory by debiting Merchandise Inventory $34 500, and crediting Ending Inventory by the same amount.

35. Voucher 006   Dated: mm30yy
Record the adjusting entry for Insurance Expense, $600.

36. Voucher 007   Dated: mm30yy
Record adjusting entries for estimated depreciation on:
Office Equipment $66.00; Trucks $564.00; and Building $1 890.00.

DISPLAYING AND PRINTING

Select **DISPLAY**. Your teacher will advise you which of the six options to preview. You may be prompted for dates. Remember, a date is entered in the sequence mmddyy (month/day/year).

Print any statements requested by your teacher. Again, you may be prompted for dates.

FINISHING A SESSION

Access the **SYSTEM** module and select the **Finish** option.

3.8

Dictionary of Accounting Terms

Adjustments   Changes in account balances that need to be made at year end to meet generally accepted accounting principles.

Accrued Wages   Wages owing to employees which have not yet been paid by year end.

Bank Credit Memo   A notice mailed by the bank when it puts money into your bank account.

Bank Debit Memo   A notice mailed by the bank when it deducts money from your bank account.

Cash Payments Journal   A book of original entry used to record all transactions that cause a decrease in cash.

Cash Receipt   A cash sale or a receipt on account from a customer.

Cash Receipts Journal   A book of original entry used to record all transactions that cause an increase in cash.

Charge Sale   A sale whereby a customer agrees in writing to pay on a later date for goods or services received.

Cheque Copy   A document indicating payment to buy an asset, to reduce a liability, or to pay an expense.

Class   An asset grouping established by the government for purposes of depreciation.

Closing Entries   Journal entries which close out certain accounts to nil balances at year end.

Credit Invoice   A document received from a supplier which reduces accounts payable, or issued to a customer to reduce accounts receivable.

Depreciation   A method of allocating an asset's cost over its useful life.

Generally Accepted Accounting Principles   Guidelines set down by professional accounting bodies for the preparation of financial statements.

GST   The federal goods and services sales tax.

Input Tax Credit   The GST paid for purchases which can be subtracted from the GST otherwise payable.

Posting Reference   An account number or page number which indicates that an accounting entry has been posted.

Prepaid Supplies   Supplies purchased which will benefit a future time period.

PST   A provincial retail sales tax applied (where used) to goods and services.

Purchase Invoice   An accounting document received when goods or services are bought on account.

Purchases Journal   A book of original entry used to record the purchase of goods or services bought on account.

Sales Journal   A book of original entry used to record all charge sales and credit invoices issued to customers.

Source Documents   Documents which are used to make accounting entries in the books of account.

Subsidiary Ledger   A ledger that contains accounts related to a general ledger account. The most common are the accounts receivable and accounts payable ledgers.

MANUAL EXERCISES

1. Journalize these accounting transactions for the month of October 19– into the appropriate journal: sales journal (page 18), cash receipts journal (page 12), cash payments journal (page 14), purchases journal (page 16). The GST is 7% and the PST is 12% and is calculated on the base price.

Oct. 1:   Cash Receipt
              #380 from Bud Wirth, $500 received on account.
       1:   Sales Invoice
              #540 to Carol Dedecker, $300, plus taxes.

2: Cheque Copy
#1210 to Maritime Supply on an account balance of $1 673.34, less a 2% discount.

3: Sales Invoice
#541 to Beth Taylor, $470, plus taxes.

3: Credit Invoice Issued
#CR40 to Beth Taylor, $30, plus taxes, for defective goods on invoice #541.

4: Purchase Invoice
From Maritime Supply, $1 450 of merchandise for resale plus GST. Terms 2/10, n/30. Invoice MM882.

7: Sales Invoice
#542 to Tom Morrissey, $1 270, plus taxes.

8: Sales Invoice
#543 to Bill Woods, $650, plus taxes.

8: Cash Receipt
#381 from Carol Dedecker, paying invoice #540 in full, less a 2% discount.

9: Cheque Copy
#1211 to Atlantic Outerwear on account balance $1 554.67, less a 2% discount.

10: Purchase Invoice
From Harding & Lowe, $2 365.48, merchandise for resale plus GST. Terms 2/10, n/30. Invoice #4466.

11: Cheque Copy
#1212 to Maritime Supply to pay invoice MM882 less discount.

11: Credit Note Received
From Harding & Lowe, $235.00 for defective merchandise, plus GST.

11: Cash Receipt
#382 from the owner, Lorraine Greaves, $4 000; a cash investment into the business.

12: Cash Receipt
#383 from Beth Taylor, paying invoice #541 less credit invoice CR40, less a 2% discount.

14: Cash Receipt
#384 from a cash sale $2 500, plus taxes.

14: Sales Invoice
#544 to Maureen Declerc, $840, plus taxes.

16: Cheque Copy
#1213 to Atlantic Freight for freight charges, $202.05 plus GST.

17: Cheque Copy
#1214 to Maritime Bell for the monthly telephone bill, $210.34 plus taxes.

18: Purchase Invoice
From Wilson Stationers for $380.80 for paper for the laser printer, plus GST Recoverable $23.80. Invoice #667. Terms net 30.

18: Cheque Copy
#1215 to Harding & Lowe for invoice #4466 less the discount.

20: Cash Receipt
#385 from Maureen Declerc paying invoice #544 in full, less a 2% discount.

21: Sales Invoice
#545 to Deb Giesbrecht $190, plus taxes.

21: Credit Invoice Issued
#CR41 to Deb Giesbrecht, $20, plus taxes for overcharge on goods billed on invoice #545.

22: Purchase Invoice
From Work Wearhouse, $3 002.92, for merchandise purchase of resale plus GST. Invoice #W-991. Terms net 30.

24: Cheque Copy
#1216 to Urqhuart Bros. on account, $700.

24: Sales Invoice
#546 to Ellen Cadotte, $130, plus taxes.

24: Cash Receipt
#386 from The Toronto Dominion Bank, a loan of $15 000.

27: Purchase Invoice
From Urqhuart Bros., $2 660, for the purchase of merchandise for resale plus GST. Terms 2/10, n/30.

28: Cheque Copy
#1217 to Polanksi Outfitters, $940 on account, less a 2% discount.

28: Purchase Invoice
From Maritime Supply, MM891, $673.63 for the purchase of merchandise for resale plus GST. Terms 2/10, n/30.

28: Sales Invoice
#547 to Gae Brown, $1 440, plus taxes.

29: Purchase Invoice
From Thompson Transport, $410.70 for freight charges plus GST. Invoice #4444.

30: Cheque Copy
#1218 to Petro Canada for gas and oil, $236.57 plus GST.

2. Journalize these accounting transactions for the month of August 19– into the appropriate journal: sales journal (page 7), cash receipts journal (page 6), cash payments journal (page 4), purchases journal (page 5). The GST is 7% and the PST is 7% calculated on the base price plus GST.

Aug. 1:   Sales Invoice
           #1221 to Mark Cassone, $320.50, plus taxes.
      1:   Purchase Invoice
           From Twilight Supply, $818.18 plus $53.53 GST Recoverable; invoice T444; net 30.
      2:   Cash Receipt
           #800 from Lisa Lawless on account, $450, less a 2% discount.
      2:   Cash Receipt
           #801 from Jackie Bauer on account, $810, less a 2% discount.
      3:   Cheque Copy
           #410 to Office Supply, $310.78 plus $20.33 GST Recoverable. (Charge to Prepaid Office Supplies.)
      3:   Cheque Copy
           #411 to the Royal Bank, $2 000, a mortgage payment. Interest of $14.92 is included in this amount.
      3:   Sales Invoice
           #1222 to Norm Collins, $507, plus taxes.
      4:   Cheque Copy
           #412 to Bradford Mfg. on account, $700.
      4:   Purchase Invoice
           #907 from Hall Bros., $612 plus GST; purchase of merchandise for resale. Terms 1/15, n/30.
      5:   Cash Receipt
           From Mark Cassone, paying invoice #1221 in full, less a 2% discount.
      8:   Purchase Invoice
           From Thompson Transport, $376.67 plus GST, freight on incoming goods; invoice #3169. Terms 2/10, n/30.
     10:   Credit Note Received
           From Twilight Supply, $55, plus GST; credit note 77.
     10:   Purchase Invoice
           From Allied Mfg. Ltd., $1 456.83 plus GST; invoice #665; purchase of merchandise for resale; net 30.
     12:   Cheque Copy
           #413 to Hall Bros. for invoice #907 less the discount.

12: Sales Invoice
     #1223 to Troy Winkworth $715.40, plus taxes.
13: Cash Receipt
     #802 from Andrea Harper, on account, $640.50.
15: Cheque Copy
     To Office Supply, $312.65 plus 20.45 GST Recoverable;
     new office desk; #414.
16: Cheque Copy
     #415 to Thompson Transport for invoice #3169 less the discount.
16: Cash Receipt
     #803, cash sale, $775.20, plus taxes.
17: Cash Receipt
     #804 from Troy Winkworth paying invoice #1223 in full, less a
     2% discount.
18: Purchase Invoice
     From Ookpik Ltd., $1 130 plus GST; invoice 2211;
     purchase of merchandise for resale. Terms net 30.
19: Sales Invoice
     #1224 to Dave Gradisch, $904.15, plus taxes.
19: Sales Invoice
     #1225 to Derek Barnard, $182.20, plus taxes.
22: Purchase Invoice
     From Gerrards Ltd., $1 094.92 plus GST; invoice #90-87;
     for the purchase of merchandise for resale.
23: Cheque Copy
     #416 to SaskTel, $127.52 plus taxes, for the phone bill.
24: Cheque Copy
     #417 to the SaskEnergy, $312.46 plus GST.
     Charge to Heat & Light Expense.
24: Sales Invoice
     #1226, to Elaine Wallington, $333.33, plus taxes.
25: Bank Debit Memo
     The bank deducted $23.75 from the business bank account for
     monthly service charges.
25: Purchase Invoice
     #932, from Hall Bros., $998 plus GST; purchase of merchandise
     for resale. Terms 1/15, n/30.
26: Credit Invoice Issued
     CR65, $45.00 plus taxes, to Derek Barnard for defective goods on
     our sales invoice dated August 19th, less GST and PST.

28:   Cash Receipt
      #805 from a cash sale $1 825, plus taxes.
29:   Bank Credit Memo
      Borrowed $18 000 from the Royal Bank. The funds were deposited
      into the business bank account.
30:   Sales Invoice
      #1227 to Jan Valcke, $404.04, plus taxes.
31:   Purchase Invoice
      From Allied Mfg., $3 029.18 plus GST; invoice #682; net 30;
      goods for resale.

3. Calculate this year's depreciation and the new net book value for these fixed
   assets. Use the government table of depreciation rates.

Asset	Balance	Accumulated Depreciation
Warehouse	$90 000	$ 0
Delivery Truck	$18 000	$9 180
Pizza Oven	$ 4 000	$1 952
Cash Register	$ 2 500	$ 500

4. Find the annual depreciation on the assets below, using straight-line
   depreciation:

Asset	Cost	Salvage Value	Estimated Life
Typewriter	$ 800	$ 200	4 years
Grinder	$12 600	$1 600	8 years
Desk	$ 750	$ 150	15 years
Alarm System	$ 4 200	$ 800	8 years

5. Find the annual depreciation on the assets below, using straight-line
   depreciation:

Asset	Cost	Salvage Value	Estimated Life
Equipment	$24 000	$6 000	6 years
Furniture	$10 000	$2 000	10 years
Camcorder	$ 2 400	$ 400	4 years
Garage	$50 000	$5 000	20 years

6. Calculate and journalize, on page 7 of a general journal, the annual depreciation for each of these assets using the declining-balance method of depreciation, as of December 31, 19–.

Asset	Cost	Rate
Cars	$ 60 000	30%
Furnace	$ 15 000	20%
Paint Guns	$ 28 400	20%
Building	$128 400	5%

7. Calculate and journalize, on page 10 of a general journal, the annual depreciation for each of these assets using the declining-balance method of depreciation, as of December 31,19–.

Asset	Cost	Rate
Tractor	$42 000	30%
Spreader	$18 000	20%
Wagon	$ 9 000	20%
Shed	$28 000	10%

8. Find the accrued wages for a business as of its year end, December 31st. The pay period is bi-weekly (every two weeks). The payroll, $12 000, was paid on Friday, Jan. 7th.

9. Find the accrued wages for a business as of its year end, November 30th. The pay period is bi-weekly (every two weeks). The payroll, $18 000, was paid on Friday, Dec. 3rd.

10. Find the accrued wages for a business as of its year end, October 31st. The pay period is monthly. The payroll, $32 480, was paid on Friday, Nov. 11th.

11. Sandhya Chari operates a small business called Ident-A-Shirts. She sells t-shirts to clubs and her trial balance as of December 31st is as shown.
    (a) Transfer this data to an 8-column worksheet and record these adjustments at year end, December 31st.
        (i) Fixed assets are depreciated using (government) declining-balance rates; building 5%, equipment 20%.
        (ii) Prepaid supplies is to be credited $1 800 and expensed.
        (iii) There were wages of $800 paid on Friday January 4th. The payroll is bi-weekly.
        (iv) The year-end inventory is $16 050.
    (b) Prepare an income statement and a balance sheet at year end for the business.

Ident-A-Shirts
Trial Balance
December 31, 19–

No.	Account	Debit	Credit
110	Bank	$ 1 115	
120	Accounts Receivable	3 835	
130	GST Recoverable	550	
135	Merchandise Inventory	13 500	
140	Prepaid Supplies	2 000	
150	Building (Brick)	100 000	
151	Accumulated Depreciation — Building		$ 5 000
160	Store Equipment	25 000	
161	Accumulated Depreciation — Store Equipment		5 000
210	Bank Loan		7 500
220	Accounts Payable		7 000
230	GST Payable		1 500
235	Accrued Wages		0
260	Mortgage Payable		60 000
310	S. Chari, Capital		77 400
315	S. Chari, Drawings	24 000	
410	Sales		96 600
411	Sales Returns and Allowances	1 900	
502	Advertising Expense	1 225	
503	Bank Charges	7 400	
504	Depreciation Expense — Building	0	
506	Depreciation Expense — Store Equipment	0	
508	Discounts Allowed	1 400	
509	Discounts Earned		800
510	Purchases	50 000	
512	Supplies Expense	0	
514	Telephone Expense	1 667	
516	Utilities Expense	8 753	
518	Wages Expense	18 455	
		$260 800	$260 800

12. Bits and Bytes is a small computer store operating on the main street of Kamloops, B.C. The trial balance as of June 30, 19– is:

Bits and Bytes
Trial Balance
June 30, 19–

No.	Account	Debit	Credit
110	Bank	$ 4 632	
120	Accounts Receivable	22 000	
130	GST Recoverable	1 446	
135	Merchandise Inventory	26 556	
140	Prepaid Supplies	1 410	
150	Delivery Van	20 000	
151	Accumulated Depreciation — Delivery Van		$ 9 800
160	Store Equipment	18 320	
161	Accumulated Depreciation — Store Equipment		6 595
210	Bank Loan		11 700
220	Accounts Payable		9 000
230	GST Payable		2 005
231	PST Payable		2 850
235	Accrued Wages		0
310	T. Brizio, Capital		74 250
315	T. Brizio, Drawings	18 000	
410	Sales		165 150
411	Sales Returns and Allowances	1 860	
502	Advertising Expense	3 457	
503	Bank Charges	1 450	
504	Depreciation Expense — Delivery Van	0	
506	Depreciation Expense — Store Equipment	0	
508	Discounts Allowed	2 440	
509	Discounts Earned		1 200
510	Purchases	78 220	
512	Rent Expense	22 400	
513	Supplies Expense	0	
514	Telephone Expense	1 821	
516	Utilities Expense	11 738	
517	Van Expense	6 800	
518	Wages Expense	40 000	
		$282 550	$282 550

(a) Transfer this data to an 8-column worksheet and record these adjustments at year end, June 30.

 (i) Fixed assets are depreciated using (government) declining-balance rates; equipment 20%, van 30%.

 (ii) Prepaid supplies is to be credited $1 375 and expensed.

 (iii) There were wages of $1 200 paid on Friday July 3rd. The payroll is bi-weekly.

 (iv) The closing inventory is $28 956.

(b) Prepare an income statement and a balance sheet at year-end for the business.

13. Surf N Turf in Halifax specializes in selling fresh seafood. (Their products are tax exempt.) The trial balance at the end of September, 19– is:

Surf N Turf
Trial Balance
September 30, 19–

No.	Account	Debit	Credit
110	Bank	$ 13 000	
120	Accounts Receivable	32 000	
135	Merchandise Inventory	50 000	
140	Prepaid Supplies	3 800	
150	Equipment	62 000	
151	Accumulated Depreciation — Equipment		$ 30 000
160	Van	24 000	
161	Accumulated Depreciation — Van		12 000
210	Bank Loan		54 075
220	Accounts Payable		2 725
230	Accrued Wages		0
310	J. McLeod, Capital		77 520
315	J. McLeod, Drawings	18 320	
410	Sales		288 635
411	Sales Returns and Allowances	4 760	
502	Advertising Expense	4 455	
504	Bank Charges	467	
506	Depreciation Expense — Equipment	0	
508	Depreciation Expense — Van	0	
509	Discounts Allowed	4 200	
510	Discounts Earned		1 380

512	Equipment Repairs	13 454
514	Insurance Expense	960
516	Purchases	135 000
518	Rent Expense	22 500
520	Supplies Expense	0
522	Telephone Expense	1 210
524	Utilities Expense	7 776
526	Van Expense	2 830
528	Wages Expense	58 603
		$466 335 $466 335

(a) Transfer this data to an 8-column worksheet and record these adjustments at year end, September 30.
  (i) The ski equipment and the van are depreciated using (government)
      declining-balance rates; equipment 20%, van 30%.
  (ii) The prepaid supplies have been used up. Expense them!
  (iii) The accrued wages are $1 400.
  (iv) The closing inventory is $35 000.
(b) Prepare an income statement and a balance sheet at year end for the
business.
(c) Journalize the adjusting entries in a general journal, page 15.
(d) Journalize the closing entries for the business.
(e) Prepare a post-closing trial balance.

COMPUTER EXERCISES

SS1   Set up a spreadsheet template that looks like this for a sales invoice. Here, PST is calculated on base price only. Insert the programs to calculate the amounts required. Save the template under the file name CH3SS1.

```
              A         B          C                 D           E
    1   CANADA'S WORK WEARHOUSE              Invoice #
    2   1010 QUEENS AVENUE
    3   BRANDON, MANITOBA, R2T 4M7
    4
    5   Name:
    6   Address:
    7   Town:
    8   Postal Code:                         Date:            19
    9
   10   QTY    DESCRIPTION                    PRICE       AMOUNT
   11
   12
   13
   14
   15                                      SUB TOTAL
   16                                         7% GST
   17                                         7% PST
   18                                          TOTAL
```

SS2   Use the template created in question SS1 and prepare an invoice (#467) for this transaction. Save under the file name CH3SS2.

Name: Chad Nevill
Address: 820 Peel Street
Town: Brandon, Manitoba
Postal Code: R4S 1L9
Date: April 10, 19–

QTY	DESCRIPTION	PRICE
12	Work Shirts	$15.00
12	Work Pants	$35.00
36	Pairs Work Socks	$ 4.50

SS3   Use the template created in question SS1 and prepare an invoice (#468) for this transaction. Save under the file name CH3SS3.

Name: Brent Bates
Address: 750 Franklin Street
Town: Brandon, Manitoba
Postal Code: R7A 5R3
Date: April 11, 19–

QTY	DESCRIPTION	PRICE
10	Work Shirts	$15.00
15	Work Pants, Medium	$35.00
12	Pairs Work Socks	$ 4.50
8	Handkerchiefs	$ 2.75

SS4   Use a spreadsheet to produce this sales summary for The Tacky T-Shirt Company. Insert a program to calculate the total. Save your work under the file name CH3SS4.

	A	B	C	D	E	F
1	SALES SUMMARY					
2						
3	JAN	13 456.90				
4	FEB	18 775.01				
5	MAR	20 000.30				
6	APR	30 337.55				
7	MAY	40 784.11				
8	JUN	42 389.66				
9	TOTAL	?				

SS5   Use a spreadsheet to produce this depreciation table for The Computer Emporium. Set column A to 15 characters and program the C.C.A column. (C.C.A. = Closing Balance * Rate) Save your work under the file name CH3SS5.

	A	B	C	D	E
1	DEPRECIATION TABLE				
2		Closing			
3	Asset	Balance	Class	Rate	C.C.A.
4	Automobile	22 400	10	.30	
5	Equipment	67 845	8	.20	
6	Furniture	14 820	8	.20	
7	Building	248 000	3	.05	

SS6   Recall the spreadsheet saved as CH3SS5 and enter this data on the same spreadsheet template. Save your work under the file name CH3SS6.

Asset	Closing Balance
Automobile	$ 77 350
Equipment	$142 420
Furniture	$ 28 450
Building	$416 300

DB1   Prepare a customer database for Dan the Record Man using these five customers as an example.

Name	Address	Town	Balance
T. Wedlake	1800 Vista Cr.	Calgary	$867.34
C. Cadman	200 Skyline Cr.	Calgary	$223.44
M. Koike	12 Oakmoor Dr.	Calgary	$789.32
M. Pratt	190 Marwood St.	Calgary	$ 56.87
J. Balazs	12 Hawk Crt.	Calgary	$354.00

Prepare an alphabetical list of the file, with the balances totalled.

DB2   Prepare a customer database for Hunter's Hardware using these five customers as an example.

Name	Address	Town	Balance
A. Locker	320 Tronson St.	Kelowna	$1 005.46
K. Carter	1800 Windsor Rd.	Kelowna	$ 903.45
K. McLaughlin	4 Bell Rd.	Kelowna	$2 376.44
T. Sage	2800 Alcan Dr.	Kelowna	$3 001.01
J. Burwell	1458 Fife Rd.	Kelowna	$ 278.38

Prepare an alphabetical list of the file, with the balances totalled.

DB3   Prepare a payroll database for Buck's Supermarket using these five employees as an example.

No.	Name	Dept.	Hourly Rate
1	N. Hagerman	Grocery	$ 9.25
2	T. Burwell	Grocery	$ 9.25
3	T. Nigh	Deli	$ 8.75
4	J. Craigwell	Meat	$12.15
5	A. Gorvett	Grocery	$10.10

Prepare a list of the file, with the employees ranked from the lowest hourly rate to the highest.

DB4   Prepare a payroll database for the Canadian Tire Place using these five employees as an example.

No.	Name	Hourly Rate	Hours
1	Trevor Waite	$10.25	40
2	Regan Zilic	$ 9.80	38
3	Jay Friesen	$ 8.75	35
4	Kelly Burns	$12.40	40
5	Jamie Hind	$12.60	40

Program the database to find each employee's gross pay, and then prepare a list of the file, with the employees ranked from the highest gross pay to the lowest.

DB5   Prepare an accounts payable database for The Classy Clothier using these five suppliers as an example.

Name	Address	Town	PC	Balance
John Forsyth	280 Dundas St.	London	N6A 3F2	$3 555.77
Imported Silk	44 Bryant Ave.	London	N7B 5G2	$8 777.02
Biltmore Hats	1 Bilt Drive	Guleph	N1H 7B9	$7 094.23
Eatonia	2323 Fifth Ave.	Windsor	N9H 5Y5	$6 354.23
Smithsons	700 Dieppe Ave.	Cornwall	K6H 3K1	$4 004.09

Sort the file alphabetically by supplier name, program the database to find the total balance owing to all suppliers, then prepare a list of the file.

DB6   Prepare an accounts payable database using these five suppliers as an example.

Name	Address	Town	PC	Balance
Paul Emile	400 rue Dante	Quebec	G2T 1J9	$2 998.78
Olivier Mfg.	50 rue Dublin	Quebec	G4C 3Y9	$6 344.20
J.A. Sagard	4 rue Lavoie	Quebec	G3W 2J7	$3 675.08
Pierre Masse	90 ave Royal	Quebec	G4A 2M6	$1 111.19
P. Louis Ltd.	34 ave Willow	Quebec	G1V 2N7	$4 534.76

Select any suppliers whose balance is over $3 000 and print an alphabetical list of those suppliers.

GR1   Create a bar graph for Gourmet Kitchen Utensils using this sales data. Your vertical axis should read 10 000, 14 000, 18 000, 22 000, 26 000, 30 000, and 34 000.

Gourmet Kitchen Utensils
Sales Data — First Half 19–

January	$12 485
February	$16 776
March	$16 848
April	$27 485
May	$30 040
June	$32 444

GR2   Create a line graph for Brazilian Shoes using this sales data. Your vertical axis should read 10 000, 14 000, 18 000, 22 000, 26 000, 30 000, and 34 000.

Brazilian Shoes
Sales Data — Second Half 19–

July	$18 400
August	$22 700
September	$28 750
October	$13 000
November	$17 000
December	$32 100

GR3   Create a pie graph for this data for Magic Moments Children's Wear salespersons, using this sales data.

Magic Moments Children's Wear
Salespersons Commissions

Kent Cooper	$1 800
Eric Klaassen	$2 400
Vicki Walker	$3 600
Wayne DeJong	$1 970
Dennis Donais	$2 850

GR4   Graph the data for exercise SS4 above.

GR5   Graph the data for exercise SS5 above.

GR6   Graph the data for exercise SS6 above.

WP1   One of your branch hardware stores has been neglecting to take advantage of purchase discounts by paying vendor statements too late. Send the store manager this letter. Save it under the file name CH3WP1.

November 26, 19–

Ms. Sheila Matychuk

c/o The Hardware Trader
529 Victoria Street
Midland, Ontario
L4R 1A3

Dear Ms. Matychuk

The president has read your monthly accounts payable report and has asked me to write you concerning your late payment practices. You are losing the advantage of generous supplier discounts by not paying invoices and statements when due. This has resulted in a loss to us of almost $1 000 in the month of September alone.
This practice is a major violation of company policy which encourages store managers to take advantage of cash discounts from creditors. Please take corrective action on this matter immediately.

Yours truly

Your Name

Vice-President

WP2   Use the file CH3WP1 and send another letter, making these changes:
a. The store manager is Jamie Toth.
b. The store address is 210 Wall St., Pembroke, Ontario K8A 2W2.
c. The amount being lost is closer to $2 000.

WP3   Assume you are Sheila Matychuk (WP1). Draft a letter to the vice-president explaining why you are late with the payments on vendor accounts. Indicate that you have been installing a new computer system and it still has a few "bugs".

R. v. GIBSON

BACKGROUND

Jannette Gibson was the bookkeeper for the Lindwood Pet Care Centre. Her duties included handling all cash receipts, making bank deposits, and reconciling the bank account for the business at month end. In short, she had total control of all cash handling activities within the business. The partner owners of the Centre became suspicious when bank deposits were not as high as could be expected during a particularly busy month. They hired a team of forensic accountants to investigate the cash practices of the Lindwood Pet Care Centre.

INVESTIGATION

The owners, the police, and the forensic accountants reviewed all source documents for the month of September and found:

1. 180 customer copies of sales invoices showed a "total charge" amount higher than the figures entered into the cash receipts journal, by $2 600.
2. 520 office copies of sales invoices showed a "total charge" amount higher than the figures entered into the cash receipts journal, by $8 900.
3. 100 office copies had been altered so that the "total charge" agreed to the lower amount entered into the cash receipts journal. This caused an understatement of $500 in cash receipts.

The total amount misappropriated during the time period analysed was, therefore, $12 000, as shown by this summary.

	No. of Invoices	Original Charge	Charge Per the CRJ	Discrepancy
1.	180	$ 4 040	$1 440	$ 2 600
2.	520	$13 200	$4 300	$ 8 900
3.	100	$ 2 860	$2 360	$ 500
	800	$20 100	$8 100	$12 000

FRAUD

To uncover the fraud, investigators compared the customer copies of sales invoices, filed alphabetically, to the individual entries for each customer in the cash receipts journal. Here is a sample comparison to show the individual discrepancies.

Invoice Number	Amount Per Customer Invoice	Amount Recorded in Cash Receipts Journal	Discrepancy
	R. v. Gibson		
	Schedule of Fraudulent Invoices		
52592	$ 10	$ 6	$ 4
52226	10	5	5
52178	12	4	8
52443	14	5	9
28796	12	4	8
28891	20	10	10
52364	46	26	20
52102	25	5	20
52709	42	12	30
	$5 800	$3 200	$2 600

FIGURE 3-46   *The fraudulent invoice schedule*

Some of the individual invoices (see Figure 3-47) were altered to show lesser amounts than had been billed to the customers. The lesser amounts were recorded in the cash receipts journal and the difference pocketed by the bookkeeper.

SENTENCE

Trial was held in County Court because the amount of fraud involved in the case exceeded $1 000. Evidence was heard that Ms. Gibson had stolen to support her husband

52397	Linwood Pet Care Centre	

Dr. K. Ration
Dr. P. Patterson
Dr. Y. Chow   Invoice

Linwood, NB
E5E 3K9
555-8888

Client: _G. Tebus_   Tel.#: _555-3131_
Address: _1274 Fair Cr_   Town: _Moncton_
Postal Code: _E5E 678_   Credit Limit: $ _1000_

Services	Amount
X Ray	45 –

Comments	Sub Total	45 –
Next Visit: _____ 19 ___	GST	
at _____	PST	
Cash ☐ Charge ☐ am pm	Total	45 –

FIGURE 3-47 *An altered invoice*

who was unemployed and her two small children aged 7 and 10. After hearing the pre-sentence report, Judge Graham ordered Ms. Gibson to make restitution for the embezzled funds, and placed her on probation for two years. She was fired from her bookkeeping job and will not be able to be bonded to handle any future jobs handling cash.

QUESTIONS

1. Why do you think it took the employers a long time to discover the fraud?
2. What internal control procedure might have prevented this fraud?
3. Should Ms. Gibson's family and financial background have been heard in court as relevant to this case?
4. Was the sentence appropriate in this case? Did Ms. Gibson "get off lightly"?

Career Profile

Elaine Cooper is an English teacher at a small high school, and has been teaching for the past ten years. Last year she decided to take a break from her teaching duties. She went half-time and on her days off launched a new business venture called *Monogram Magic*. The business consisted of monogramming shirts, sweaters, hats, and blankets using an expensive computerized monogramming machine.

The sewing machine is programmed to produce perfect sewing. It has various font (printing) styles and sizes, and there is a data disk containing several symbols that can be sewn on the products. Elaine felt confident about her sewing skills and believed there was a market for a quality product that could be guaranteed perfect. She had some great ideas for a mail promotion campaign as well.

The bank needed a cash flow forecast for the business before they would approve a new loan for $30 000. So Elaine used a spreadsheet program to produce a cash flow projection for the bank.

The banker was impressed and granted the loan to Elaine. The business began operating in June and sales have been steadily increasing as word of mouth spreads about the quality of work being produced. The last concern Elaine had was the bookkeeping aspect of the business. She had kept the household records for many years, but she felt that preparing records manually would be too time consuming for the business. So she bought a copy of the *ACCPAC Bedford Integrated Accounting* program and transferred all the records onto the computer. She worked through the *Bedford* learning tutorial, and she attended a night school course given by a local professional accountant. Her income statement and her balance sheet for *Monogram Magic* were prepared automatically by the *Bedford* program. The banker is impressed by the increasing sales and profit margins of the business, and by the role which the computer has played in the prosperity of the business.

There is only one question remaining in Elaine's mind after operating successfully for one year, and being her own boss — should she return to full-time teaching?

```
Monogram Magic    Cash Flow Forecast

                             May     Jun     Jul     Aug     Sep     Oct
Estimated Sales (Monthly)      0     200    1000    2000    2000    3000

Cash Receipts
  Cash from Sales              0     200    1000    2000    2000    3000
  Cash Equity Contribution 15000       0       0       0       0       0
  New Ventures Loan        15000       0       0       0       0       0
  Small Business Loan       5000       0       0       0       0       0
                          ------   -----   -----   -----   -----   -----
  Total                    35000     200    1000    2000    2000    3000

Cash Disbursements
  Equipment                27000
  Repairs Expense — Shop    1000
  Labour Expenses              0
  Personal Drawings            0
  Materials                 2500     100     500    1000    1000    1500
  Licences & Insurance       200
  Advertising Expense        200     900     900     100     100     150
  Selling Expense            123      20     100     200     200     300
  Office Expense              30      30      30      30      30      30
  Office Equipment           200
  Loan Repayment —
    Ventures Loan Interest   181     181     181     181     181     181
    Principal                  0
  Loan Repayment —
    Sm. Bus. Ln.             123     123     123     123     123     123
  Loan Repayment  — LOC      123     123     123     123     123     123
                          ------   -----   -----   -----   -----   -----
  Total                    31680    1477    1957    1757    1757    2407

Surplus (Deficit)           3320   -1277    -957     243     243     593

Cumulative                  3320    2043    1086    1329    1572    2165
```

FIGURE 3-48   *A spreadsheet cash flow forecast*

FOR DISCUSSION

- Do you think Elaine should return to full-time teaching?
- What kinds of reports can Elaine prepare for her business, using her *Bedford* program?
- Do you think she should take an accounting course?

4

Cash Control and Banking

- **Journalize and post cash receipts transactions, and understand control procedures for cash receipts.**

- **Journalize and post cash payments transactions, and understand control procedures for cash payments.**

- **Set up and maintain a petty cash system.**

- **Understand the role of the electronic cash register in cash handling.**

- **Prepare a bank reconciliation for a business and journalize the accounting entries related to it.**

- **Use computer software for handling cash activities.**

4.0

Overview

The cash control system in a business is one of the major accounting systems that are important to any business.

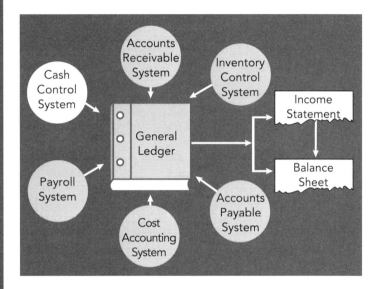

FIGURE 4-1   Flowchart of the accounting process

Cash is the most liquid asset that a business can own, and therefore steps must be taken to safeguard its control. This chapter describes source documents and accounting entries associated with cash; control over cash receipts and discounts allowed to customers; and control over cash payments and discounts earned from suppliers. There is also a complete outline of how a petty cash system operates; how electronic cash registers are used; and a study of bank reconciliations and their importance in cash control. In addition, there will be a detailed look at how cash transactions can be handled using computer software and the *ACCPAC Bedford Integrated Accounting* software.

4.1

Source Documents and Journalizing

Jim Alexander operates a movie rental business called Action Video, as a proprietorship in Kingston, Ontario. The main source of revenue of the business is the rental of movies, although other revenue comes from sales of movies, posters, t-shirts, compact discs, and cassette tapes.

CASH RECEIPTS — SOURCE DOCUMENTS

Cash is received into most businesses from five basic types of business transactions:

    (1) cash sales
    (2) cash received (from customers) on account
    (3) cash investment by the owner
    (4) cash borrowed from the bank
    (5) cash sale of an asset

Cash sales and customer receipts occur practically every day at Action Video, while investment, borrowings, and sale of assets by the owner are less frequent events.

Cash Sales

Each customer who comes into Action Video to rent a movie is issued a cash sales slip. A **cash sales slip** is a document issued to a customer as proof that he or she has paid cash to a business. Most sales are cash, and therefore the design of a cash sales slip is relatively straightforward.

ACTION VIDEO
1200 Main Street
Kingston, Ont.
K7K 3Y8

555-1234

Date May 1 19 –

Name Heather Lemon
Address 2352 Cedar St. Town Kingston
Postal Code K2K 3Z2 Telephone Number 555-3611

Quantity	Description	Price		Amount	
1	Back to the Future	3	99	3	99
1	War Games	3	99	3	99
		Sub Total		7	98
		GST			56
		PST			64
		Total		9	18

CASH [X] CHARGE [ ] Invoice # 4769

FIGURE 4-2 *A cash sales slip*

Movie rentals are subject to the 7% federal **GST** (goods and services tax), and 8% **PST** (provincial sales tax), calculated on base price only.

The cash sales slips are serially numbered so that numeric control can be obtained and each sales slip accounted for by the owners. More will be said on this control aspect in section 4.2.

The general journal entry for the cash sales slip is:

GENERAL JOURNAL

PAGE 17

DATE 19–		PARTICULARS	PR	DEBIT	CREDIT
May	1	Bank		9 18	
		Rental Income			7 98
		GST Payable			56
		PST Payable			64
		To record the rental of 2 movies			

FIGURE 4-3   *The general journal entry for a cash sales slip*

Cash Received (from customers) on Account

Action Video Club members are allowed to charge their movies, if they wish, and then be billed monthly for their movie rentals. When they remit the balance owing, a receipt is made out and handed to them, or mailed to them if their payment has been received in the mail.

ACTION VIDEO
1200 Main Street
Kingston, Ont.

555-1234   K7K 3Y8   555-1234

Cash Receipt No.   567   Date   May 7   19 –

RECEIVED FROM   Denise Durst

Forty-Three -- 75 /100 Dollars

Account Balance Before Payment $ 45.90
Amount Paid $ 43.60
Discount Allowed $ 2.30 $ 45.90
                    Balance Due $ Ø

Initials   B.K.

FIGURE 4-4   *A receipt on account*

Note that cash receipt slips are also serially numbered for control purposes.

When money is received on account, there are no new sales taxes. Sales taxes are charged at the original time of the movie rental.

Club members are allowed to take a discount of 5% off the total owing on their bills if paid within 10 days of receipt of the monthly statement. The next journal entry illustrates a club member paying her account and taking the 5% discount allowed.

The accounting entry for this receipt on account is a debit to Bank, a debit to Discounts Allowed, and a credit to Accounts Receivable (and the customer's account in the subsidiary ledger).

GENERAL JOURNAL

PAGE 18

DATE 19–		PARTICULARS	PR	DEBIT	CREDIT
May	7	Bank		43 60	
		Discounts Allowed		2 30	
		A/R—Denise Durst			45 90
		To record receipt on account			

FIGURE 4-5   *The general journal entry for a receipt on account*

Cash Investment by the Owner

The owner of Action Video has decided to make an additional cash investment into the business of $10 000. This type of transaction requires a receipt being issued to the owner for the cash invested into the business. The accounting entry for the additional cash investment by Jim is:

GENERAL JOURNAL

PAGE 18

DATE 19–		PARTICULARS	PR	DEBIT	CREDIT
May	10	Bank		100 00 –	
		J. Alexander, Capital			100 00 –
		Cash Investment by owner			

FIGURE 4-6   *The general journal entry for a cash investment*

Cash Borrowed From the Bank

Because of the growth prospects, Jim has borrowed $20 000 from the Bank of Montreal. The money was deposited directly into the business bank account through a bank credit memo. (A **bank credit memo** is a notice mailed by the bank when it puts money into your bank account.) The following accounting entry is made in the books of Action Video.

GENERAL JOURNAL

PAGE 19

DATE 19–		PARTICULARS	PR	DEBIT	CREDIT
May	12	Bank		2000 0 –	
		Bank Loan			2000 0 –
		Borrowed money from the bank @			
		14.5% interest rate			

FIGURE 4-7   *The general journal entry for a bank loan*

Cash Sale of a Fixed Asset

Selling an asset of a business is a transaction which may not occur very often. Assume, however, that the business had a six-month-old VCR that they used to show movies in the store. The VCR originally cost $500. They decided to sell it for $200 because it had been heavily used.

The accounting entry must delete the VCR from the books ($500), recognize the money lost on it ($300) and the GST adjustment, and record the amount of the cheque ($200 plus GST and PST). Here is the accounting entry:

GENERAL JOURNAL

PAGE 20

DATE 19–		PARTICULARS	PR	DEBIT	CREDIT
May	15	Loss on Sale of Equipment		300 –	
		Bank		230	
		GST Payable			14 –
		PST Payable			16 –
		Equipment			500 –
		Sale of used VCR			

FIGURE 4-8   *The general journal entry for the sale of the VCR*

The only other cash source document needed by the business is the daily deposit slip. The **daily deposit slip** is a document prepared for cash which is being deposited into the business bank account. For the purpose of control, cash received is deposited at least once a day, and more often if cash receipts are especially high on any given day. Here is the deposit slip for a typical day at Action Video:

FIGURE 4-9 A deposit slip

Cash Payments — Source Documents

Cash payments from the business are made mostly by cheque. A cheque will usually have a **cheque stub** attached which lists the details of the cheque and keeps a running bank balance. Payments cover five types of transactions for the business:

(1) cash payments for expenses
(2) cash payments (to suppliers) on account
(3) cash withdrawals by the owner
(4) cash payments of a bank loan
(5) cash purchase of assets

Cash Payments for Expenses

All major expenses of the business are paid for by cheque. Each cheque has a stub with details of the payment, and the cheque itself. Here is the cheque used by Action Video:

FIGURE 4-10   A cheque with stub

The stub contains a running balance of the bank account so that cheques will not be written if there are not sufficient funds to cover the amount of the cheque. Also, the stub is another record of the cheque if it needs to be traced later on.

Cash Payments (to suppliers) on Account

Cheques are often written to suppliers for goods which have been purchased on account. Figure 4-11 shows an example of a bill for the purchase of some t-shirts by Action Video. Notice that the supplier has offered a discount of 2/10, n/30 off the invoice total.

GARNER DISTRIBUTING CO. LTD.	Invoice
30 Aberdeen St.	G2288
Kingston, Ont. K7L 3N2	
555-9283	
Terms: 2/10, n/30	Date _May 15_ 19–

Name _Action Video_

Address _1200 Main St. W._   Town _Kingston_

Postal Code _K7K 3Y8_   Telephone Number _555-1234_

Quantity	Description	Price		Amount	
24	t-shirts with cresting	5	98	143	52
	"Action Video"				
		Sub Total		143	52
		GST		10	05
CASH ☐ CHARGE [X] COD ☐		PST			Ø
		Total		153	57

FIGURE 4-11   A supplier's invoice

GENERAL JOURNAL

PAGE _20_

DATE 19–		PARTICULARS	PR	DEBIT	CREDIT
May	15	Purchases		1 4 3 52	
		GST Recoverable		1 0 05	
		A/P—Garner Distributing			1 5 3 57
		To record purchase invoice G2288			

FIGURE 4-12   The general journal entry for a supplier's invoice

When a business buys goods and services, it is allowed an input tax credit for the full amount of the GST figure on the purchase invoice. This amount is debited to a GST Recoverable account in the general ledger. This account will later be offset against the GST Payable account when the business remits the GST collected to the federal government. Notice that PST was not charged since these goods were bought for resale.

The bookkeeper for Action Video has to watch to make sure that any discounts offered by the creditors are taken by Action Video. It is a good business practice to take advantage of supplier discounts, and Action Video always tries to pay these accounts before the discount period expires. The journal entry for the payment to this supplier, with the discount taken, is:

GENERAL JOURNAL

PAGE 23

DATE 19–		PARTICULARS	PR	DEBIT	CREDIT
May	23	A/P—Garner Distributing		1 5 3 57	
		Bank			1 5 0 50
		Discounts Earned			3 07
		To record payment of invoice G2288			
		less a 2% discount			

FIGURE 4-13   *The general journal entry for a cheque to a supplier*

Not all suppliers offer cash discounts, but they are usually offered when large quantities of goods are being purchased.

Cash Withdrawals by the Owner
Any owner of a business usually needs money to live on and pay personal expenses. These amounts are called "Drawings" and constitute a withdrawal of capital by the owner. The accounting entry each time an owner makes a withdrawal of money will be similar to Figure 4-14.

Cash Payment of a Bank Loan
Bank loans usually require regular monthly payments of principal and interest on the loan. When these cheques are written, the accounting entries are a debit to Bank Loan, a debit to Interest Expense, and a credit to Bank. See Figure 4-15.

GENERAL JOURNAL

PAGE 23

DATE 19–		PARTICULARS	PR	DEBIT	CREDIT
May	24	J. Alexander, Drawings		850 –	
		Bank			850 –
		To record cheque 105; owner has			
		withdrawn funds for personal use			

FIGURE 4-14   *The general journal entry for drawings*

GENERAL JOURNAL

PAGE 25

DATE 19–		PARTICULARS	PR	DEBIT	CREDIT
May	31	Bank Loan		300 –	
		Interest Expense		200 –	
		Bank			500 –
		To record the monthly payment on			
		the bank loan			

FIGURE 4-15   *The general journal entry for a bank loan payment*

In some cases the payment will be automatically deducted from the business account through a bank debit memo. (A **bank debit memo** is a notice mailed by the bank when it has deducted money from an account.)

Cash Purchase of Assets

Whenever assets are bought by the business, a cheque is written and one of the asset accounts must be debited. Assume that Action Video has just bought a new computer system so that the owner can use *Bedford* to computerize the accounting work. The accounting entry for the purchase of the new computer is shown in Figure 4-16.

Action Video will debit the GST Recoverable account for the input tax credit when it buys the computer. The GST Recoverable account will be offset against the GST Payable account.

The most frequent entries for cash payments are the payment of expenses and the payment to suppliers for goods and services bought on account.

GENERAL JOURNAL

PAGE 25

DATE 19–		PARTICULARS	PR	DEBIT	CREDIT
May	31	Office Equipment		2 1 9 5 64	
		GST Recoverable		1 5 3 69	
		Bank			2 3 4 9 33
		To record the purchase of a new			
		computer; cheque 120			

FIGURE 4-16   *The general journal entry for the purchase of a computer*

QUESTIONS

1. Why are cash sales slips serially numbered?

2. Two types of cash receipt transactions are the most common in most businesses. Which ones are they?

3. Two types of cash payment transactions are the most common in most businesses. Which ones are they?

4. Why is it advantageous to have stubs attached to cheques?

5. What does the phrase *input tax credit* mean?

4.2

Journalizing and Posting Cash Receipts / Internal Control

Although cash receipts can be recorded in a general journal, it is more efficient to use a cash receipts journal for any accounting transactions that require a debit to Bank. The **cash receipts journal** is a book of original entry in which all cash receipts of a business are first recorded (along with bank credit memos). The design of a cash receipts journal depends on the specific business using it, but Figure 4-17 shows a good sample of what a cash receipts journal might look like.

The cash receipts journal has special columns for the accounts used most frequently in a business, so that these account names need not be written each time a cash transaction takes place. Only the totals of the special columns have to be posted into the general ledger accounts.

Section 4.1 listed five typical cash receipt transactions:

(1) cash sales
(2) cash received (from customers) on account
(3) cash investment by the owner
(4) cash borrowed from the bank
(5) cash sale of an asset

To study how a cash receipts journal is used by a business, assume that Action Video had the following sample transactions in the first week of October, 19–.

Oct. 1: Cash sale for $575; $500.00 sale, plus GST, and PST; invoice #420.
      2: Received on account from Ainsley Roose, $42.75. The monthly statement was $45.00 but the customer deducted a 5% discount; receipt #555.
      3: The business borrowed $5 000 from the Bank of Montreal. The money was deposited immediately into the bank account; credit memo.
      4: The owner, J. Alexander, invested $15 000 cash into the business from personal funds; receipt #556.
      5: An old electric cash register was sold for $75 plus GST and PST. Its depreciated value was $75; receipt #557.

	DATE 19–		PARTICULARS	INV. NO.	OTHER ACCOUNTS CR				
					ACCOUNT	PR	AMOUNT		
1	Oct.	1	Cash sale	420					
2		2	Ainsley Roose	555					
3		3	Bank of Montreal	CM	Bank Loan		5000	–	
4		4	Owner invested	556	J. Alexander, Cap.		15000	–	
5		5	Sold cash register	557	Equipment		75	–	
6									
7									

FIGURE 4-17   *Cash receipts journal with entries*

Figure 4-17 shows how these transactions are journalized in a cash receipts journal.

For the first two entries, you can use the special columns. The third transaction requires a credit to the Bank Loan account and since there is no special column for this, use the Other Accounts columns. The fourth transaction needs a credit to Capital and again, use the Other Accounts column. Finally, the last transaction is selling off an asset at its depreciated cost. This entry too has to be recorded using the Other Accounts columns.

If you look at the cash receipts journal again, you will notice that every entry in the journal has a debit to the Bank account. Therefore, whenever there is an accounting transaction that must debit the Bank account, it will have to be entered into the cash receipts journal.

Figure 4-18 shows the same cash receipts journal as it would appear at the end of the month with column totals.

At the end of the month all of the columns are totalled and the cash receipts journal is cross-balanced. The totals of all of the debit columns must equal the totals of all of the credit columns.

Once the journal is balanced, the total of each of the special columns is posted to its account in the general ledger. Therefore, Bank, Discounts Allowed, Accounts Receivable, Sales, GST Payable, and PST Payable totals are all posted to the general ledger. The posting reference appears at the bottom of each column inside brackets. Thus, the Bank column has been posted to account #110, the Bank account. The amounts in the Other Accounts column must be posted individually to the correct account. Notice the three account numbers in the PR column for Other Accounts.

CASH RECEIPTS JOURNAL

FOR THE ___Month___ ENDED ___Oct. 31___ 19 – PAGE ___10___

SALES CR	GST PAYABLE CR	PST PAYABLE CR	DISCOUNTS ALLOWED DR	ACCOUNTS RECEIVABLE CR	✔	BANK DR	
5 0 0 –	3 5 –	4 0 –				5 7 5 –	1
			2 25	4 5 –		4 2 75	2
						5 0 0 0 –	3
						15 0 0 0 –	4
	5 25	6 –				8 6 25	5
							6
							7

	DATE 19–		PARTICULARS	INV. NO.	OTHER ACCOUNTS CR			
					ACCOUNT	PR	AMOUNT	
1	Oct.	1	Cash sale	420				
2		2	Ainsley Roose	555				
3		3	Bank of Montreal	CM	Bank Loan	210	50 00 –	
4		4	Owner invested	556	J. Alexander, Cap.	310	150 00 –	
5		5	Sold cash register	557	Equipment	180	75 –	
22		29	Cash sale/rental	443				
23		30	Mike Pokorny	567				
24		31	Vicki Walker	568				
25							240 00 –	
26								
27								
28								

FIGURE 4-18   *Cash receipts journal for October*

The entries in the Accounts Receivable column must be posted to the subsidiary accounts for each customer. These accounts are filed in the accounts receivable subsidiary ledger and must be kept up-to-date during the month so that if customers question their account balances, the business has up-to-date information and can respond accurately to customer questions. Notice the ticks in the column next to the Accounts Receivable column, to show that these amounts have been posted. The month-end total is posted to the Accounts Receivable control account.

Discounts Allowed

Discounts Allowed is a percentage applied to an invoice total to reduce the payment owed by a customer. When customers pay their accounts within a specified time period, they are entitled to take a discount before payment. Action Video Club members are allowed a 5% discount if accounts are paid within 10 days of the end of month; 5/10 e.o.m. See the example of a monthly statement, Figure 4-19.

There are two viewpoints on the treatment of Discounts Allowed. In the first, Discounts Allowed is treated as a contra-revenue account. Because discounts offset revenue from a sale, the entry is a debit and the account balance appears on the income statement in the Revenue section where it is deducted from Sales to arrive at Net Sales.

CASH RECEIPTS JOURNAL

FOR THE Month ENDED Oct. 31 19 — PAGE 10

SALES CR	GST PAYABLE CR	PST PAYABLE CR	DISCOUNTS ALLOWED DR	ACCOUNTS RECEIVABLE CR	✔	BANK DR	
500 —	35 —	40 —				575 —	1
			1 87	45 —	✔	42 75	2
						5 000 —	3
						15 000 —	4
	5 25	6 —				86 25	5
30 —	2 10	2 40				34 50	22
		(31)	3 91	85 78	✔	85 79	23
		(24)	3 04	66 72	✔	66 73	24
8206 —	57442	65648	2570	550 —		33961 20	25
							26
(410)	(221)	(222)	(508)	(120)		(110)	27
							28

MONTHLY STATEMENT

ACTION VIDEO
1200 Main Street
Kingston Ont.
K7K 3Y8

5/10 e.o.m.

555-1234

555-1234

To: Joan Scholten
415 Friar Crescent
Kingston, Ont. K7L 4T5

$ _____

Please detach and return upper part with payment.

- -

Date	Charges	Balance
Sept. 08	Movie rental; invoice #435	4.59
15	Movie rental; invoice #498	4.59
22	Movie rental; invoice #522	4.59
22	Poster; invoice #523	4.08
30	Movie rental; invoice #565	4.59
	Total	22.44

FIGURE 4-19   A monthly statement

According to the other view, Discounts Allowed is an expense account; it is a cost of doing business. Again, the account has a debit balance. Discounts Allowed, in this case, may be shown on the income statement as an expense of the business, or as an extraordinary item at the bottom of the income statement, after the operating net income is calculated. Figures 4-20 and 4-21 show these two accounting treatments of discounts on an income statement.

Name
Model Income Statement
For the year Ended December 31, 19–

Revenue:		
Sales		$20 000
Expenses:		
Advertising	$ 200	
Discounts Allowed	850	
Insurance	440	
Telephone	720	
Wages	12 290	14 500
Net Income		$ 5 500

FIGURE 4-20   *Discounts Allowed as an expense*

Name
Model Income Statement
For the year Ended December 31, 19–

Revenue:		
Sales		$20 000
Expenses:		
Advertising	$ 200	
Insurance	440	
Telephone	720	
Wages	12 290	13 650
Operating Income		$ 6 350
Discounts Allowed		850
Net Income		$ 5 500

FIGURE 4-21   *Discounts Allowed as an extraordinary expense*

INTERNAL CONTROL

The phrase **internal control** refers to the methods used to safeguard assets and ensure the accurate recording of cash receipts in the books of account. There are two ways in which a business controls its cash receipts: accounting controls, and physical controls.

Accounting Controls

Accounting Controls are checks which are placed in an accounting system to ensure that cash receipts and payments are accurately recorded.

There are three accounting controls that Action Video has put into place to ensure that cash paid to the business actually finds its way into the business bank account:

(1) Use serially numbered cash receipts slips.

A serially numbered cash receipt should be filled out every time cash is received in a business.

All cash sales slips are numbered. When a customer pays at the cash register, a copy of the receipt is placed with the others that have been issued. At the end of the day, the owner of the business checks the numbers turned in at the cash register against the books issued to the sales personnel. If any slips are not accounted for, it could indicate fraud by an employee.

(2) Separate cash handling and recording.

Another technique for controlling cash is to separate cash handling from cash recording. That is, the person who receives cash from a customer is not allowed access to the company books, particularly the accounts receivable ledger. An employee who received $100.00 cash from a customer and kept it might be able to falsify the books if he or she had access to the accounts receivable ledger.

"I've quit my job at the bank."

(3) Reconcile the bank account regularly.

A third accounting control over cash handling is to reconcile the bank account for the business once a month. This is an important concept and it will be covered in detail in section 4.5.

Businesses should not assume that banks do not make mistakes with their money, and the bank reconciliation will check the accuracy of the bank records against the business records.

Physical Controls

The term **physical controls** relates to devices such as cash registers, locks, safes, and alarm systems which protect assets from being stolen. Physical controls over cash are most important since cash is very liquid, easy to steal and easy to spend. Here are three examples of physical cash controls:

(1) Make daily deposits.

Cash received in a business should be deposited into the business bank account daily, or more frequently if a large amount of cash is handled. A fast food hamburger outlet, for example, might want to make two or three deposits a day so that a minimal amount of cash is on hand. Deposits can be made using overnight deposit and quick deposit forms supplied by most banks. Action Video makes deposits only once a day unless cash receipts are particularly high. The bank's night depository is used for deposits made after banking hours.

(2) Use an in-store cash safe.

A business owner who has trouble getting to the bank should consider an in-store safe for cash. Safes are often set in the front window of the business, in full view of the public, to cut down the risk of burglaries. There are also armoured car companies, Brinks for example, that will drive to a business and pick up large amounts of cash, under armed guard.

(3) Use an electronic cash register.

The cash registers used by stores are a means of physically controlling cash. Most machines have drawers with special money slots for coins and bills. This helps employees make the right change for customers; and in fact modern computerized cash registers tell employees exactly how much to pay out to the customer for change. This cuts down on cash losses. In addition, cash registers can be locked for control. If at all possible, each employee should be supplied with his or her own cash tray. Then at the end of the shift each cash tray should be balanced off. This topic will be discussed more fully in section 4.4 of this chapter.

QUESTIONS

6. Why is it more efficient to use a cash receipts journal for a business rather than a general journal?

7. Why is there a special column called Other Accounts in a cash receipts journal?

8. What is the cash receipts journal column labelled GST Payable used for?

9. Which columns on the cash receipts journal have only their totals posted to ledger accounts?

10. Which column on the cash receipts journal has entries posted to a subsidiary ledger?

11. What does the phrase *serially numbered* mean?

12. What is the difference between accounting controls and physical controls?

13. Name the three accounting controls that can be used for handling cash receipts.

14. Name the three physical controls that can be used for handling cash receipts.

4.3

Journalizing and Posting Cash Payments / Internal Control

The cash payments journal is very similar to the cash receipts journal described in section 4.2. A cash payments journal is a book of original entry in which all cheques issued by a business are first recorded (along with bank debit memos). Every accounting transaction entered into a cash payments journal is a credit to the Bank account. Cash payments journals vary in format depending on the particular business where they are being used. The model in Figure 4-22 is fairly typical because the special columns shown are used by most businesses.

The cash payments journal has special columns for the accounts used most frequently when cash payments are made by the business. The account names need not be written each time a cash payment transaction takes place. In addition, only the totals of the special columns have to be posted into the general ledger accounts.

Section 4.1 listed five typical cash payment transactions:
(1) cash payments for expenses
(2) cash payments (to suppliers) on account

(3) cash withdrawals by the owner

(4) cash payments of a bank loan

(5) cash purchase of assets

To study how a cash payments journal is used by a business, assume that Action Video had the following sample transactions in the first week of October, 19—.

Oct. 1:   Paid immediately for posters bought from Argus Posters; their invoice J282 in the amount of $250 plus GST less a 5% discount; cheque #100.

2:   Paid Canadian Shirts on account; cheque #101 for $156, The original invoice was for $150 plus GST ($10.50) but Action Video earned a 3% discount ($4.82) by paying within 15 days.

3:   Wrote cheque #102 to the Bank of Montreal for $1 000, a payment on the loan with them. Interest Expense $400; loan reduction $600.

4:   The owner, J. Alexander, made a withdrawal of $500 for his personal use; cheque #103.

5:   Bought a new display for the business that cost $1 296 (charge to Equipment) plus GST Recoverable $84; cheque #104 to The Shelving People.

6:   Paid the monthly telephone bill to Bell Canada, $126.36 plus GST Recoverable $8.19; cheque #105.

Figure 4-22 shows how these transactions are journalized in a cash payments journal.

	DATE 19–		PARTICULARS	CH. NO.	OTHER ACCOUNTS DR			OFFICE EXPENS DR
					ACCOUNT	PR	AMOUNT	
1	Oct.	1	Argus Posters	100				
2		2	Canadian Shirts	101				
3		3	Bank of Montreal	102	Bank Loan		600 –	
4					Interest Exp.		400 –	
5		4	Owner withdrawal	103	J. Alexander, Draw.		500 –	
6		5	The Shelving People	104	Equipment		1296 –	
7		6	Bell Canada	105	Telephone Exp.		12636	
8								
9								

FIGURE 4-22   *Cash payments journal with entries*

For the first two entries, you can use the special columns. The next four entries do not fit into the special columns, and therefore you use the Other Accounts section. Every accounting transaction entered into the cash payments journal is a credit to the Bank account. In addition, you record all of the cheque numbers so that you can reconcile the bank account at the end of the month.

Figure 4-23 shows the same cash payments journal as it would appear at the end of the month.

At the end of the month all columns are totalled and the cash payments journal is cross-balanced. The totals of all the debit columns must equal the totals of all the credit columns.

Columns must be balanced before the cash payments journal can be posted to the general ledger accounts. Once the journal is balanced, the total of each of the special columns is posted to its account in the general ledger. Therefore, Bank, Discounts Earned, GST Recoverable, Accounts Payable, Purchases and Wages are all posted to the general ledger. The posting reference appears at the bottom of each column inside brackets. Thus, the Bank column has been posted to account #110, the Bank account. The accounts in the Other Accounts column must be posted individually to the correct account. Notice the account numbers in the PR column beside the Other Accounts.

The entries in the Accounts Payable column must be posted daily to the accounts payable subsidiary ledger accounts for each customer. These accounts must be kept up-to-date so that if the owner questions any supplier account balances, the business has up-to-date information and can initiate

CASH PAYMENTS JOURNAL

FOR THE Month ENDED Oct. 31 19 – PAGE 10

DISCOUNTS EARNED CR	GST RECOVERABLE DR	PURCHASES DR	WAGES DR	ACCOUNTS PAYABLE DR	✔	BANK CR	
1 3 38	1 7 50	2 5 0 –				2 5 4 12	1
4 82				1 6 0 50	✔	1 5 5 68	2
						1 0 0 0 –	3
							4
						5 0 0 –	5
	8 4 –					1 3 8 0 –	6
	8 19					1 3 4 55	7
							8
							9

| | DATE 19– | | PARTICULARS | CH. NO. | OTHER ACCOUNTS DR | | | OFFICE EXPENSE DR |
					ACCOUNT	PR	AMOUNT	
1	Oct.	1	Argus Posters	100				
2		2	Canadian Shirts	101				
3		3	Bank of Montreal	102	Bank Loan	210	600 –	
4					Interest Exp.	530	400 –	
5		4	Owner withdrawal	103	J. Alexander, Draw.	315	500 –	
6		5	The Shelving People	104	Equipment	180	1 296 –	
7		6	Bell Canada	105	Telephone Exp.	565	1 26 36	
22		29	D. Stone	118				
23		30	Movie Distributors	119				
24		31	Kingston PUC	120	Utilities Exp.	570	85 –	
25							10 1 89 50	3 7 1
26								
27								(5 4 0
28								

FIGURE 4-23   Cash payments journal for October

inquiries to the suppliers. The ticks in the column next to the Accounts Payable column show that these amounts have been posted.

Discounts Earned

Discounts Earned is a percentage applied to a purchase to reduce the amount paid to a supplier. Some of the suppliers used by Action Video offer a cash discount if their invoice is paid within a specified time period; as does Action Video with accounts receivable. In the supplier invoice shown earlier, the terms were 2/10, n/30. This means that there was a 2% discount if the bill was paid within 10 days of the date of issue. The total bill was expected to be paid within 30 days if the discount is not taken.

The Discounts Earned account may be shown on the income statement as a deduction from Purchases, or as an item that affects expenses, or as another item of income at the bottom of the statement. In any case, the account normally has a credit balance. If Discounts Earned is deducted from the Purchases figure or if it affects expenses, then Discounts Earned is

CASH PAYMENTS JOURNAL

FOR THE Month   ENDED Oct. 31   19 – PAGE 10

DISCOUNTS EARNED CR	GST RECOVERABLE DR	PURCHASES DR	WAGES DR	ACCOUNTS PAYABLE DR	✔	BANK CR	
1338	1750	250 –				25412	1
482				16050	✔	15568	2
						1000 –	3
							4
						500 –	5
	84 –					1380 –	6
	819					13455	7
			34 –			34 –	22
	1582	226 –				24182	23
	595					9095	24
216 –	23150	2855 –	834 –	3215 –		174 8020	25
(420)							26
	(125)	(560)	(580)	(230)		(110)	27
							28

known as a contra account. When Discounts Earned is offset against Purchases, that calculation takes place in the Cost of Goods Sold section of the income statement. Figures 4-24 and 4-25 show possible treatments of the account Discounts Earned on an income statement.

INTERNAL CONTROL

There are two ways in which a business controls its cash payments: accounting controls, and physical controls.

Accounting Controls
(1) Make payments by cheque.
Cash payments should only be made by cheque, if at all possible. A cheque provides a record of the transaction when cashed and returned to the business by the bank. It is written proof that a payment was made, and is regarded as external evidence of a transaction for audit, or legal purposes.

Name		
Model Income Statement		
For the Year Ended December 31, 19–		
Revenue:		
Sales		$20 000
Expenses:		
Advertising	$ 200	
Discounts Earned	(650)	
Insurance	440	
Telephone	720	
Wages	12 290	13 000
Net Income		$ 7 000

FIGURE 4-24   *Discounts Earned as part of expenses*

Name		
Model Income Statement		
For the year Ended December 31, 19–		
Revenue:		
Sales		$20 000
Expenses:		
Advertising	$ 200	
Insurance	440	
Telephone	720	
Wages	12 290	13 650
Operating Income		6 350
Discounts Earned		650
Net Income		$ 7 000

FIGURE 4-25   *Discounts Earned as extraordinary income*

(2) Prepare cheques.

Cheques should be authorized by one person, based on the source document that triggers the transaction; prepared by a second person, and then signed by a third person as a means of control.

(3) Reconcile the bank account.

Bank accounts should be reconciled monthly to determine if cheques issued by the business were eventually cashed and deducted from the business bank account. Bank reconciliations are covered in detail in section 4.5 of this chapter.

Physical Controls

Physical controls over cash payments can also involve three types of controls:

(1) Operate a petty cash system.

A **petty cash fund** is a small change fund used for small payments. A petty cash fund typically would have from $50 to $200. Money is not handed out unless a bill is tendered to the person operating the fund. When the fund becomes depleted, it is replenished and an accounting entry made for the payments out of the fund. The word **replenish** means to fill a petty cash fund back up to its original amount after the supporting vouchers are examined. This is covered in detail in section 4.4 of this chapter.

(2) Do not sign blank cheques.

Businesses are often asked to give blank cheques to employees to cover the purchase of business items. This will occur where the employee does not know the exact amount of the purchase she/he is about to make. This is a bad accounting practice and should never be allowed by a business. It can be avoided by using company credit cards or just by having the employee charge the purchase to the company name.

(3) Obtain receipts.

Every payment made by a business must be supported by a purchase invoice which supports the amount paid. The best support vouchers will come from sources outside the business. Invoices should be filed alphabetically so that they are readily accessible to management and auditors should a question arise about any particular payment by the business. Revenue Canada requires that receipts be produced for any expense claimed as a deduction for tax purposes.

QUESTIONS

15. Why is it more efficient to use a cash payments journal for a business rather than a general journal?

16. Why is there a special column called "Other Accounts" in a cash payments journal?

17. Every entry in a cash payments journal has one thing in common. What is that?

18. Which columns in the cash payments journal have only their totals posted to ledger accounts?

19. Which column in the cash payments journal has entries posted to a subsidiary ledger?

20. What is the difference between accounting controls and physical controls?

21. Name three accounting controls that can be used for handling cash payments.

22. Name three physical controls that can be used for handling cash payments.

4.4

Petty Cash Funds / Electronic Cash Registers

Most firms have small payments that must be made immediately: stamps, stationery items, lunches, taxis, etc. It is inconvenient, inefficient, and costly to write a cheque for each one of these small payments. Therefore, many companies operate a petty cash fund. The fund contains a limited amount of cash, e.g. $100, and is maintained for the purchase of small items that require immediate payment. One person is selected to be in charge of the fund so that control and accountability rest with only one employee. A cheque is written to establish the fund.

The cash is placed into a locked drawer or a special petty cash box. The person in charge of the fund (petty cashier) must keep good records. Payments should only be made from the fund if a Petty Cash Voucher is filled out requesting payment from the fund. The voucher indicates to whom payment is made, the amount paid, the particulars, the account to be charged, the payment date, and the signature of the person receiving the cash.

GENERAL JOURNAL

PAGE 48

DATE 19–		PARTICULARS	PR	DEBIT	CREDIT
Nov	1	Petty Cash		100 –	
		Bank			100 –
		To set up the fund			

FIGURE 4-26   *The general journal entry to set up a petty cash fund*

Some businesses require the person responsible for the petty cash to complete a petty cash record. The signed vouchers are used to complete the record. The headings on the columns depend on the particular business and its needs. Let's examine an illustration of the Action Video petty cash record. The owner of the business set up a $100 petty cash fund on November 1.

The following payments were made from the petty cash fund during the month.

FIGURE 4-27
A petty cash voucher

NO.:	1
Date:	November 1 / 19 –
Amount:	19.00
Paid to:	C. Hedecker
Signature:	
Explanation:	Postage stamps
Authorized by:	J. Potters
Charge to Account:	Postage Expense
	GST Recoverable

Nov. 1:   Set up fund with $100.
    1:   Bought $19.00 worth of postage stamps. Price includes GST of $1.24.
    4:   Bought stationery supplies costing $12.00, including GST of $.73.
    7:   Bought office supplies, $6.10, including GST of $.37.
   12:   The Sales Manager submitted taxi claim for $10.00, including GST of $.65.
   17:   The owner withdrew $5.00 for his personal use.
   18:   Bought a new computer cartridge, $9.95, including GST of $.61.
   20:   Paid Purolator Courier for a package, $9.50, including GST of $.62.
   27:   Paid $10 to the local high school for a yearbook ad. (Note that this ad is GST exempt. Total ad sales will be well below the $30 000 level at which GST must be charged.)
   30:   Took a customer to lunch, $8.25, including GST of $.50.
   30:   Bought some scratch pads for the office, $5.20, including GST of $.32.

These payments have been recorded by an office clerk in a petty cash record.

PETTY CASH RECORD

FOR THE Month ENDED November 30 19___

DATE 19–	DESCRIPTION	PC VO. NO.	RECEIPTS	PAYMENTS	FREIGHT IN	OFFICE EXP.	GST RECOV.	SUNDRY ACCOUNT	AMOUNT
Nov. 1	Received cash	–	100 –						
1	Postage stamps	1		19 –			1 24	Postage Expense	17 76
4	Stationery supplies	2		12 –		11 27	73		
7	Office supplies	3		6 10		5 73	37		
12	Taxi	4		10 –			65	Misc. Expense	9 35
17	Owner withdrawal	5		5 –				Drawings	5 –
18	Computer cartridge	6		9 95		9 34	61		
20	Purolator invoice	7		9 50	8 88		62		
27	H.S. Yearbook	8		10 –				Advertising Expense	10 –
30	Lunch	9		8 25			50	Misc. Expense	7 75
30	Scratch pads	10		5 20		4 88	32		
			100 –	95 –	8 88	31 22	5 04		49 86
	Balance			5 –					
			100 –	100 –					

FIGURE 4-28 *Petty cash record*

The record has been cross-balanced for the month. Since the total spent is $95.00, the Petty Cash Fund has to be replenished. The vouchers are submitted to the accountant who makes out a cheque for $95.00 to replenish the fund. When the reimbursement cheque is cashed, the $95.00 is put back into the petty cash box. (Note that the Petty Cash account balance remains at $100, even though the amount of actual petty cash on hand decreases with each payment made out of the funds.) The following general journal entry is made in the books to record the monthly expenses.

GENERAL JOURNAL

PAGE 53

DATE 19–	PARTICULARS	PR	DEBIT	CREDIT
Dec. 1	Freight-In		8 88	
	Office Expense		31 22	
	GST Recoverable		5 04	
	Postage Expense		17 76	
	Miscellaneous Expense		17 10	
	J. Alexander, Drawings		5 –	
	Advertising Expense		10 –	
	Bank			95 –
	To replenish petty cash fund			

FIGURE 4-29 *The general journal entry to replenish petty cash*

It is possible for the petty cash fund to be out of balance. If this happens, any shortage is debited to Cash Short (expense), or credited to Cash Over (income). If there are significant shortages or overages, an investigation would be necessary.

   If the amount of the petty cash fund is too low, it can be increased at any time. Assume that Action Video wants to increase its petty cash fund to $150. The general journal entry to do this is shown in Figure 4-30.

GENERAL JOURNAL

PAGE _53_

DATE 19–		PARTICULARS	PR	DEBIT	CREDIT
Dec.	1	Petty Cash		50 –	
		Bank			50 –
		To increase the petty cash fund			

FIGURE 4-30   *The general journal entry to increase the petty cash fund*

ELECTRONIC CASH REGISTERS

Modern electronic cash registers have several cash handling and control features that are useful to businesses — GST and PST calculation keys, discount capabilities, currency conversion, paid out and received on account functions, etc.

   Electronic cash registers display the change required so that clerks do not have to calculate it. For example, a total of $77.88 is rung up on the cash register, and the customer remits $100; the cash register will compute the change as $22.12. This considerably reduces cash handling errors by store clerks.

FIGURE 4-31
An electronic cash register

These cash registers, of course, calculate sales tax automatically. For example, on a $250 sale, the cash register will calculate the GST, and the PST where applicable. Both of these totals are printed at the end of the day as part of the management report tape produced by the cash register.

Cash registers can be linked to computer systems and programmed to automatically update accounts receivable, inventory, and sales figures. Printed reports can then be obtained at the end of each day showing the customer's new account balances, the latest inventory levels, and the total cash and charge sales for that day.

All electronic cash registers provide a management report tape when requested. This tape has a summary of all transactions entered through the cash register for the day: cash sales, charge sales, GST collections, PST collections, receipts on account, refunds, etc. Here is a sample management report tape:

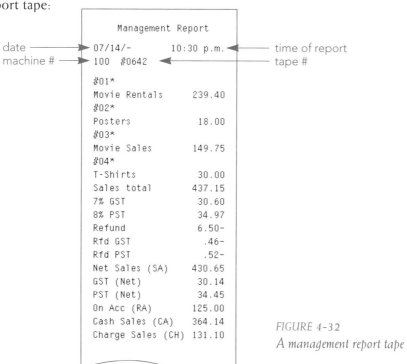

```
              Management Report

date ──────▶ 07/14/-      10:30 p.m. ◀────── time of report
machine # ─▶ 100  #0642 ◀─────────────────── tape #

             #01*
             Movie Rentals    239.40
             #02*
             Posters           18.00
             #03*
             Movie Sales      149.75
             #04*
             T-Shirts          30.00
             Sales total      437.15
             7% GST            30.60
             8% PST            34.97
             Refund            6.50-
             Rfd GST             .46-
             Rfd PST             .52-
             Net Sales (SA)   430.65
             GST (Net)         30.14
             PST (Net)         34.45
             On Acc (RA)      125.00
             Cash Sales (CA)  364.14
             Charge Sales (CH) 131.10
```

FIGURE 4-32

A management report tape

The data on the management report tape is used to prepare a daily cash balance form for the business. This form determines whether there is a cash shortage or overage for the day. Figure 4-33 gives a sample form.

Compare the management report tape to the cash daily balance form to see where all of the balancing figures come from. Not all the figures on the

DAILY CASH BALANCE FORM

ACTUAL CASH IN DRAWER				DEBIT	CREDIT
17 X	2.00 = $	34.00			
8 X	5.00 = $	40.00			
6 X	10.00 = $	60.00			
12 X	20.00 = $	240.00	BANK	48794	
2 X	50.00 = $	100.00			
X	100.00 = $		ACCTS. REC. (CH)	13110	
TOTAL BILLS =		474.00	CASH SHORT	120	
CHANGE =		13.94			
TOTAL	$	487.94	ACCTS. REC. (RA)		125 –
CASH SUMMARY			SALES (SA)		43065
CASH SALES (CA)		36414	GST PBL		3014
REC'D ON ACC'T. (RA)		125 –	PST PBL		3445
CASH COUNT SHOULD BE		48914	CASH OVER		
ACTUAL CASH IN DRAWER		48794	TOTALS	62024	62024
CASH (SHORTAGE) OVER		120			

FIGURE 4-33   Daily cash balance form

tape are needed to balance the cash each day. Other information is provided about daily transactions which will be useful to management; for example, the sales breakdown by category, and the refund data.

Some stores use electronic hand scanners to input data to a cash register. The markings on the product are referred to as a **UPC**, or universal product code, and consist of black bars of varying widths.

QUESTIONS

23. Why do businesses bother with a petty cash fund?

24. Describe in your own words how a petty cash fund operates.

25. What headings are used on a petty cash record?

26. How often is a petty cash fund reimbursed?

27. What information is contained on a petty cash voucher?

28. Name five special functions of an electronic cash register.

29. List some of the totals provided on a typical management report tape.

30. Is a cash shortage a debit, or a credit? Why?

31. What is the main function of the daily cash balance form?

32. What is a scanner?

4.5

Bank Reconciliations

When a business receives its monthly bank statement, it should prepare a bank reconciliation to ensure that the balance in the Bank account in the general ledger agrees with the cash balance reported on the bank statement. The objectives of this reconciliation process are to:

- identify transactions that the bank has processed through the bank account that the business has not yet recorded on its books and to journalize these transactions on the books.
- trace deposits to the bank statement to ensure that these funds have actually been deposited to the bank account.
- determine which cheques written by the business are still outstanding at month end.
- find the exact bank balance that the company has at month end.
- detect and correct errors in the books.
- detect errors made by the bank and to notify the bank of them.

A **bank reconciliation** is an accounting form which is used to calculate the true balance of a bank account. The **true balance** is the actual amount of money in a bank account after making adjustments for outstanding items. There are six main reconciling items found in most bank reconciliations:

(1) *Outstanding Cheques:* An **outstanding cheque** is one which the business has written out, journalized in its cash payments journal, and then sent to the payee. If a cheque is not cashed by the payee and processed by the bank by month end, it becomes an outstanding cheque and it must be deducted from the balance reported by the bank on the bank statement.

(2) *Outstanding Deposits:* **Outstanding deposits** have not yet been received by the bank for processing. Deposits can be made by businesses by taking them to the bank, mailing them in, or depositing them in the overnight depositories found on the outside of banks. If a deposit is mailed or sent on the last day of the month, and the bank does not process it until the beginning of the next month, it becomes an outstanding deposit on the bank reconciliation. Outstanding deposits must be added to the balance reported by the bank on the bank statement.

(3) *Bank Service Charges:* Banks levy service charges for various banking activities — writing cheques, making deposits, bank interest on loans, etc. These charges are usually deducted from the business bank account, and the busi-

ness may not be notified of these charges until the month end when the bank statement is received. The charges will then have to be deducted from the business book balance at month end on the bank reconciliation.

(4) *Bank Collections:* Banks sometimes collect receivables for businesses and deposit the money to the credit of the business. The amount collected may appear on the bank statement but not on the company books. This means that the amount collected has to be added to the business book balance at month end when the reconciliation is performed.

(5) *NSF Cheques:* It is not unusual for a business to be given a cheque from a customer which subsequently proves to be uncashable. These cheques are called NSF (or Non-Sufficient Funds) cheques. If a cheque is **NSF** this means there are insufficient funds in a bank account to cover the cashing of a specific cheque. When the NSF cheque is first deposited the bank treats it as an increase in cash. But when the bank discovers that the issuer does not have enough money to cover the cheque, the bank deducts the value of the cheque plus NSF

"Maybe we're over-drawn!"

charges from the depositor's account. This amount must then be deducted from the bank balance on the bank reconciliation.

(6) *Book Errors:* It is possible for an error to be made in the books when a deposit or cheque is recorded. For example, assume that a cheque to Harper Bros. for repairs and maintenance was recorded as $345.69 instead of $543.69. This discrepancy would show up when the bank cashed the cheque for the correct amount, $543.69, and the bank account was reconciled. When two digits are reversed in order, the error is called a transposition error.

Transposition errors are easy to detect because the difference in the two numbers is always evenly divisible by 9 (543.69 − 345.69 = 198). This difference, 198, is evenly divisible by 9.

Errors made by a business must be adjusted on the books through general journal entries. Errors made by the bank should be brought to the attention of the bank so that they can correct their records (and that of the business account) as soon as possible.

A Bank Reconciliation Illustration

Action Video has just received its bank statement for the end of December 19–. The accountant has gathered the following information for the reconciliation:

- The balance per the bank statement is $2 655.42.
- The bank balance per the general ledger is $2 805.00.
- A deposit for $344.58 was made on December 31 in the night depository and not recorded by the bank until January 3rd; it is therefore outstanding.
- There are three cheques written by the owner that have not been received and cashed by the bank:

        #345 . . . . . . $25.10
        #348 . . . . . . $46.90
        #355 . . . . . . $58.00

- An NSF cheque for $52.00 given to Action Video by a customer, Ernie Avilla, was deducted from the account by the bank after it bounced.
- The bank statement indicates that a service charge was deducted by the bank in the amount of $8.00.
- $125 owing to the business by Nghia Duong was collected by the bank and deposited into the business bank account.

Bank reconciliations can take different forms. The example shown here is a report form reconciliation.

Action Video Bank Reconciliation Statement December 31, 19–			
Balance per Bank Statement			$2 655.42
Add: Outstanding Deposit			344.58
			3 000.00
Less: Outstanding Cheques:			
	#345	$25.10	
	#348	46.90	
	#355	58.00	130.00
True Balance			$2 870.00
Balance Per Books			$2 805.00
Add: Account Collected (Nghia Duong)			125.00
			2 930.00
Less: NSF Cheque (Ernie Avilla)			(52.00)
Service Charge			(8.00)
True Balance			$2 870.00

FIGURE 4-34   *A bank reconciliation statement*

Now that the bank reconciliation is complete you know what the true balance of the bank account is. The adjustments to the bank books will eventually take care of themselves. Outstanding cheques will be presented to and cashed by the bank, and the outstanding deposit will be credited to the business bank account at the first of the next month. The three reconciling items for the business books will have to be recorded in the business books through a general journal entry. The note collected has to be added back and credited to the customer's account, the NSF cheque has to be charged back to the customer since it has not been paid, and the service charge will have either to be charged to bank charges or to Ernie Avilla's account. The journal entries that are prepared after the reconciliation are:

GENERAL JOURNAL

PAGE _57_

DATE 19–		PARTICULARS	PR	DEBIT	CREDIT
Dec.	31	Bank		125 –	
		A/R—Nghia Duong			125 –
		To record account collected by the			
		bank			
	31	A/R—Ernie Avilla		52 –	
		Bank			52 –
		To record an NSF cheque			
	31	Bank Charges		8 –	
		Bank			8 –
		To record sevice charges			

FIGURE 4-35   *The general journal entries for reconciling items*

QUESTIONS

33. Why are bank reconciliations necessary?

34. Explain these bank reconciliation terms: outstanding cheque; outstanding deposit; service charge; NSF.

35. What do the words *true balance* mean?

36. Does every reconciling item on a bank reconciliation statement have to be journalized to correct the books?

37. Could reconciling items be made in any of the special journals, instead of the general journal? Which journal(s)?

4.6

Using the Computer

A computer can be useful in processing cash handling activities. This section will provide some examples of business forms or reports that can be made using spreadsheet, graphics, and database software for cash handling activities.

Spreadsheets

A good use of a spreadsheet for a cash handling activity would be a petty cash record. Section 4.4 described the function of the petty cash record and gave a detailed example of the document itself. Figure 4-36 shows the same document produced on a computer with a spreadsheet program.

Some of the spreadsheet information is permanent, such as the title of the spreadsheet, and the column headings. The spreadsheet has been programmed to calculate the sums of all the columns, to calculate the balance of petty cash on hand in cell E18, and to give the balancing totals in cells D20 and E20. Any cash receipt or cash payment application which uses formulas could potentially be programmed on a spreadsheet.

	A	B	C	D	E	F	G	H	I	J
1	PETTY CASH RECORD						For the Month of November 19–			
2										
3	Date	Description	No.	Rec'd	Paid	Fr. In	Off.	GST	Sundry	Amount
4										
5	1	Rec'd cash	–	100.00						
6	1	Stamps	1		19.00			1.24	Post. Exp.	17.76
7	4	Stationery	2		12.00		11.27	.73		
8	7	Off. Supplies	3		6.10		5.73	.37		
9	12	Taxi	4		10.00			.65	Misc. Exp.	9.35
10	17	Owner's draw	5		5.00				Drawings	5.00
11	18	Computer cart.	6		9.95		9.34	.61		
12	20	Purolator inv.	7		9.50	8.88		.62		
13	27	H.S. Yearbook	8		10.00				Ad. Exp.	10.00
14	30	Lunch	9		8.25			.50	Misc. Exp.	7.75
15	30	Scratch pads	10		5.20		4.88	.32		
16										
17				100.00	95.00	8.88	31.22	5.04		49.86
18										
19		Balance			5.00					
20										
21				100.00	100.00					
22										

FIGURE 4-36   *A spreadsheet petty cash record*

Graphics

Once a spreadsheet has been stored on disk, it is usually easy to have the computer print a graph of the data from the spreadsheet. Most integrated software packages have this feature. And usually once the spreadsheet is stored, you can go directly to the production of a graph. There are different styles of graphs. The three most common are bar graphs, line graphs, and pie charts. The example shown in Figure 4-37 is a cash payments schedule showing the amounts paid by Action Video for utilities, over a two-year period. The line graph gives a quick visual impression of the amounts paid.

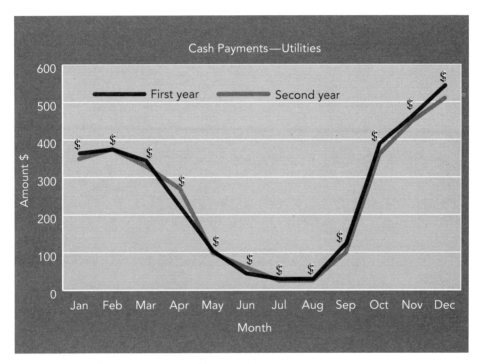

FIGURE 4-37   *A computer-generated line graph*

The dollar amounts are scaled on the *y*-axis on the left, and the months are shown on the *x*-axis along the bottom. The business is able to label and title the graph as well.

Databases

One example of a database which might be useful for Action Video is a listing of the customers who have become Action Video Club members.

```
Number:  5
Name:  Diane Black
Address:  20 Moore Cr.        one record
Town:  Kingston
PC:  K7M 3A9
```

```
MEMBERSHIP MAILING LIST
No.  Name                  Address          Town       PC
1    Allan, Beth           12 Second St.    Kingston   K7L 1H4
2    Arkona, Fred          44 Elm St.       Kingston   K7L 1M5
3    Axworthy, Tom         30 Politic Dr.   Kingston   K7L 4E5
4    Birdwell, Betty       120 Main St.     Kingston   K7M 8E2
5    Black, Diane          20 Moore Cr.     Kingston   K7M 3A9
6    Brownski, Lamont      121 Trinity Cr.  Kingston   K7P 2J7
7    Carr, Allan           78 Montana Dr.   Kingston   K7K 3Z4
8    Clipper, Henrietta    75 Fifth ave.    Kingston   K7M 2X2
```

FIGURE 4-38 A membership file

The top part of the Figure 4-38 shows the form used when the database is set up and stored. The lower part is a listing of the file showing the member's number, name, address, town, and postal code. Once the file has been stored, a business can manipulate it in several ways; e.g., print an alphabetical listing of the file, select certain customers, or create mailing labels.

4.7

Bedford Exercise 4 — Leon's on the Quay

The company in this chapter is called Leon's on the Quay, a restaurant owned by a person with varied hotel experience from Switzerland and Canada. The restaurant is located in Halifax, NS.

Leon's on the Quay has just become a reality. One of the more important operating decisions that Leon made (in addition to the menu selection) was to implement a computerized accounting system in order to generate the data he needed to control his cash flow. In order to get his restaurant ready for operation he has hired you to set up the computerized accounting system and to enter the transaction data for the first month.

The opening trial balance is as shown.

Leon's on the Quay
Opening Trial Balance

No.	Account	Debit	Credit
110	Bank	$20 000.00	
130	GST Recoverable	5 011.37	
140	Prepaid Restaur. Supplies	6 420.15	
141	Prepaid Food Supplies	6 419.85	
142	Prepaid Beverage Supplies	3 976.43	
143	Prepaid Insurance	0.00	
144	Prepaid Rent	4 000.00	
180	Furniture	29 160.00	
181	Acc. Dep. — Furniture	0.00	
185	Restaurant Equipment	40 687.10	
186	Acc. Dep. — Rest. Equipment	0.00	
190	Office Equipment	4 494.44	
191	Acc. Dep. — Office Equipment	0.00	
195	Leasehold Improvements	8 560.80	
210	Bank Loan		$15 000.00
220	A/P Bowes Food Equip. Ltd.		5 617.38
221	A/P Primo Foods Ltd.		3 887.96
222	A/P Wines & Things		4 779.20
223	A/P Seafood City		1 201.89
224	A/P Westbuild Contractors		9 499.63
230	GST Payable		0.00
235	PST Payable		0.00
240	CPP Payable		0.00
241	U I Payable		0.00
242	Income Tax Payable		0.00
243	Provincial Medical Payable		0.00
310	Leon Groenwold, Capital		88 744.08
315	Leon Groenwold, Drawings		0.00
356	Retained Earnings		0.00
410	Food Sales		0.00
420	Beverage Sales		0.00
510	Advertising Expense	0.00	
512	Beverage Supplies Expense	0.00	
515	CPP Expense	0.00	
520	Dep. Exp. — Furniture	0.00	
521	Dep. Exp. — Rest. Equipment	0.00	

522	Dep. Exp. — Office Equipment	0.00	
530	Food Supplies Expense	0.00	
535	Insurance Expense	0.00	
540	Interest Expense	0.00	
545	Rent Expense	0.00	
550	Repairs & Replacement Expense	0.00	
560	Restaurant Supplies Expense	0.00	
570	Salaries Expense	0.00	
580	Telephone Expense	0.00	
590	UI Expense	0.00	
595	Utilities Expense	0.00	
		$128 730.14	$128 730.14

The accounts and all of the historical balances have been entered onto a disk for you, and the computer accounting system only has to be set to **Ready** mode. The instructions for using *Bedford* and entering data are outlined in Chapter 1.

ACCESSING THE GENERAL LEDGER FOR LEON'S ON THE QUAY

To retrieve the general ledger for Leon's on the Quay, you use the file name **leonquay**. Key this name into the computer, insert the dates provided by your teacher, and set the program to **Ready**, as described in Chapter 1.

Enter the **Using** date provided by your teacher. Remember the sequence, mmddyy. As before, ignore the cautions and proceed.

JOURNALIZING TRANSACTIONS

To journalize general ledger transactions, access the **GENERAL** module and the **Journal** option.

TRANSACTIONS

The PST is 10%, calculated on the base price plus GST (7%).

1. Cheque 101   Dated: mm01yy
   Rent Expense, $4 000 plus GST Recoverable $280; rent paid to Westminster Quay Management Co. for monthly rental of restaurant premises.

2. Cheque 102   Dated: mm02yy
   Prepaid Insurance, $1 200 for one-year insurance policy from Great
   Pacific Insurance Company.

3. Purchase Invoice 443   Dated: mm03yy
   Prepaid Food Supplies, $3 100, bought on account from Primo Foods
   Ltd. Terms net 20. (There is no GST on food supplies.)

4. Purchase Invoice 2234   Dated: mm04yy
   Prepaid Beverage Supplies, $1 050 plus GST Recoverable $73.50.
   Bought wine on account from Wines & Things. Terms net 20.

5. Purchase Invoice 1102   Dated: mm05yy
   Prepaid Food Supplies, $1 500, bought on account from Seafood City.
   Terms net 30.

6. Cheque 103   Dated: mm07yy
   Advertising Expense, $540 plus GST Recoverable $37.80, for money paid
   to NewEast Publishing Co. for advertising the opening of the restaurant.

7. Cheque 104   Dated: mm07yy
   Paid on account to Bowes Food Equipment Ltd., $5 617.38.
   (Note: When you want to decrease an account, the amount must have a
   minus sign beside it.)

8. Cheque 105   Dated: mm08yy
   Paid on account to Primo Foods Ltd., $6 987.96.

9. Cash Receipts Summary 001   Dated: mm08yy
   Total weekly deposit $19 773.60; Food Sales $12 280, Beverage Sales
   $4 520, plus GST Payable $1 176 and PST Payable $1 797.60.
   The policy of the restaurant is to deposit daily all cash received and
   make an accounting entry on the Friday of each week.

10. Voucher 001   Dated: mm08yy
    Record the adjusting entry for supplies used: Restaurant Supplies,
    $1 344; Food Supplies, $5 176; Beverage Supplies $1 200.

11. Cheque 106   Dated: mm09yy
    Paid on account to Wines & Things, $4 779.20

12. Cheque 107   Dated: mm10yy
    Paid on account to Seafood City, $1 201.89.

13. Purchase Invoice 506   Dated: mm10yy
    Prepaid Food Supplies, $3 200, bought on account from Primo Foods
    Ltd. Terms net 20.

14. Cheque 108   Dated: mm13yy
    Payment on account to Westbuild Contractors, $9 499.63.

15. Purchase Invoice 2450   Dated: mm14yy
    Prepaid Beverage Supplies, $1 300 plus GST Recoverable $91. Bought
    wine on account from Wines & Things. Terms n/20.

16. Cash Receipts Summary 002   Dated: mm15yy
    Total weekly deposit $16 831.10; Food Sales $11 870, Beverage Sales
    $2 430, plus GST Payable $1 001 and PST Payable $1 530.10.

17. Voucher 002   Dated: mm15yy
    Record the adjusting entry for supplies used: Restaurant Supplies,
    $1 144; Food Supplies, $4 550; Beverage Supplies $1 026.

18. Purchase Invoice 1256   Dated: mm15yy
    Prepaid Food Supplies, $3 800, bought on account from Seafood City.
    Terms n/30.

19. Cheque 108   Dated: mm15yy
    Salaries Expense $12 000; CPP Payable $216, UI Payable $222, Income
    Tax Payable $2 640, Provincial Medical Payable $300; issued cheque for
    $8 622.

20. Voucher 003   Dated: mm15yy
    CPP Expense $216, and UI Expense $310.80. Employer's share of
    payroll deductions.

21. Purchase Invoice 613   Dated: mm17yy
    Prepaid Food Supplies, $3 800, bought on account from Primo Foods
    Ltd. Terms net 20.

22. Cheque 118   Dated: mm21yy
    Utilities Expense $246 plus GST $17.22, for gas consumption.

23. Cash Receipts Summary 003   Dated: mm22yy
    Total weekly deposit $21 303.70; Food Sales $15 070, Beverage Sales
    $3 030, plus GST Payable $1 267 and PST Payable $1 936.70.

24. Voucher 004   Dated: mm22yy
    Record the adjusting entry for supplies used: Restaurant Supplies,
    $1 448; Food Supplies, $5 792; Beverage Supplies $2 120.

25. Cheque 119   Dated: mm23yy
    Payment to Primo Foods Ltd., $3 200 on account.

26. Purchase Invoice 2567   Dated: mm24yy
    Prepaid Beverage Supplies, $1 400 plus GST Recoverable $98. Bought
    wine on account from Wines & Things. Terms n/20.

27. Cheque 120   Dated: mm24yy
    Paid to Wines & Things, $1 123.50 on account.

28. Purchase Invoice 1334   Dated: mm25yy
    Prepaid Food Supplies, $1 700, bought on account from Seafood City.
    Terms n/30.

29. Cheque 121   Dated: mm25yy
    Payment to Seafood City, $1 500 on account.

30. Purchase Invoice 751   Dated: mm27yy
    Prepaid Restaurant Supplies, $325 plus GST Recoverable $19.33,
    bought on account from Bowes Food Equipment Ltd. Terms n/30.

31. Cheque 122   Dated: mm28yy
    Telephone Expense $71.96 plus GST $4.28. Paid NS Telephone
    Company.

32. Cheque 123   Dated: mm29yy
    Salaries Expense $12 000; CPP Payable $216, UI Payable $222, Income
    Tax Payable $2 640, Provincial Medical Payable $300; issued cheque for
    $8 622.

33. Voucher 005   Dated: mm29yy
    CPP Expense $216, and UI Expense $310.80. Employer's share of
    payroll deductions.

34. Cash Receipts Summary 004   Dated: mm29yy
    Total weekly deposit $18 361.20; Food Sales $13 285, Beverage Sales
    $2 315, plus GST Payable $1 092 and PST Payable $1 669.20.

35. Voucher 006   Dated: mm29yy
    Record the adjusting entry for supplies used: Restaurant Supplies,
    $1 248; Food Supplies, $5 992; Beverage Supplies, $1 927.22.

36. Cheque 133   Dated: mm30yy
    Paid to Primo Foods Ltd., $3 800 on account.

37. Voucher 007   Dated: mm30yy
    Record the adjusting entry for insurance expense incurred, $100.

38. Voucher 008   Dated: mm30yy
Record the adjusting entry for estimated depreciation expense incurred: Furniture, $700; Restaurant Equipment, $550; Office Equipment, $105.

39. Voucher 009   Dated: mm30yy
Record the adjusting entry for estimated amortization of Leasehold Improvements, $142. (For this entry, debit Rent Expense and credit Leasehold Improvements.)

40. Cheque 134   Dated: mm30yy
To L. Groenwold, Drawings $4 000; personal use.

41. Bank Debit Memo   Dated: mm30yy
Payment on bank loan $2 000 and interest expense $178.

DISPLAYING AND PRINTING

Select **Display**. Your teacher will advise you which of the six options to preview. You may be prompted for dates. Remember, a date is entered in the sequence mmddyy (month/day/year).

Print any statements requested by your teacher. Again, you may be prompted for dates.

FINISHING A SESSION

Access the **SYSTEM** module and select the **Finish** option.

4.8

Dictionary of Accounting Terms

Accounting Controls   Checks which are placed in an accounting system to ensure that cash receipts and payments are accurately recorded.

Bank Credit Memo   A notice mailed by the bank when it puts money into your bank account.

Bank Debit Memo   A notice mailed by the bank when it deducts money from your bank account.

Bank Reconciliation   An accounting form which is used to calculate the true balance of a bank account.

Cash Payments Journal   A book of original entry in which all cheques issued by a business are first recorded, along with bank debit memos.

Cash Receipts Journal   A book of original entry in which all cash received by a business is first recorded, along with bank credit memos.

Cash Sales Slip   A document issued to a customer as proof that he or she has paid cash to the business.

Cheque Stub   A document attached to a cheque which lists the details of that cheque and which keeps a running bank balance.

Deposit Slip   A banking document prepared for cash which is being deposited into the business bank account.

Discounts Allowed   A percentage applied to a sale to reduce the payment made by a customer.

Discounts Earned   A percentage applied to a purchase to reduce the amount paid to a supplier.

Internal Control   The methods used to safeguard assets and ensure the accurate recording of transactions in the books of account.

NSF (Non-Sufficient Funds)   There are insufficient funds in a bank account to cover the cashing of a specific cheque.

On Account   Cash received by the business from customers who have previously charged goods or services to their account.

Outstanding Cheques   Cheques which have not yet been presented to the bank for payment.

Outstanding Deposits   Bank deposits which have not yet been processed by the bank.

Petty Cash   A small amount of money kept exclusively for the payment of small bills.

Physical Controls   Devices such as cash registers, locks, safes, and alarm systems which protect assets from being stolen.

True Balance   The actual amount of money in a bank account after making adjustments for outstanding items.

UPC   Universal Product Code, the bar marking on products used by scanners for computer data entry.

MANUAL EXERCISES

1. Record these transactions into a cash receipts journal for the month of November. The provincial tax rate is 7% and is calculated on the base price plus GST (7%). All sales are subject to PST and GST.

Nov. 1:   Cash sale $1 240, plus taxes; invoice #380.

     5:   Cash sale $772, plus taxes; invoice #381.

   10:   Owner, K. Fong, invested $6 000 into the business.

   12:   Customer, K. Chan, paid $49 on account; the original invoice was $50 less a sales discount of $1; invoice #366.

   14:   Cash sale $ 1 404, plus taxes; invoice #382.

   20:   Borrowed $3 500 from the Toronto-Dominion Bank.

   22:   Customer, Brian Rickard, paid $117.60; the original invoice was $120 less a sales discount of $2.40; invoice #298.

   25:   Customer, Jill Archibald, paid her account in full, $375. It was too late for the discount; invoice #302.

   28:   Cash sale $2 300, plus taxes; invoice #383.

2. Record these transactions into a cash receipts journal for the month of March. There is no provincial tax, and the GST is 7%.

Mar. 1:   Customer, Don Williams, paid $230.30; the original invoice was $235 less a 2% discount.

     5:   Cash sale $334, plus GST; invoice #75.

   10:   Customer, Ralph Bruce, paid his account in full, $470.40; $480 less a 2% discount.

   12:   Cash sale $317.17, plus GST; invoice #76.

   14:   Cash sale $990.40, plus GST; invoice #77.

   20:   Borrowed $7 000 from the Bank of Nova Scotia.

   20:   The owner, Ian McLaughlin, invested $8 000 into the business.

   22:   Customer, Janet Bell, paid her account in full, $686; the original invoice was $700 less a 2% discount.

   27:   Customer, John Eidt, paid $317.52; the original invoice was $324 less a 2% discount.

   30:   Sold the company car for $12 500 cash plus GST; its depreciated value was $13 800. (Charge to Loss on Sale of Asset.)

3. Record these transactions into a cash receipts journal for the month of December. The provincial tax rate is 10% and it is calculated on the base price plus GST (7%).

Dec. 1: Customer, Paul Kennedy, paid his account in full, $415.28. It was too late for the discount.

3: Cash sale, $505.05, plus taxes; invoice #900.

10: Cash sale, $774.38, plus taxes; invoice #901.

12: Customer, G. Brown, paid her account in full, $563.50; the original invoice was $575 less a 2% discount.

20: The owner, Paul Dore, invested $6 000 into the business from his savings account.

21: Paul borrowed $4 000 from National Trust.

25: Cash sale, $220.60 plus taxes; invoice #902.

26: Customer, Sharon Humphrey, paid on her account $666.40, $680 less the usual 2% discount.

30: Sold the business computer for $1 250 cash, plus taxes. Its depreciated value is $3 675.12. (Charge to Loss on Sale of Equipment.)

4. Record these transactions into a cash payments journal for the month of April. Provincial tax rate is 8% and is calculated on the base price only. GST is 7%.

Apr. 2: Cheque #200 to M. Anderson, for part-time wages, $45.

3: Cheque #201 to Murphy Distributing on account $1 285.60; invoice was $1 325.36 less a 3% discount.

8: Cheque #202 to Lawson Co, $775.17 on account; invoice was $790.99 less a 2% discount.

12: Cheque #203 to Hay Stationery for office stationery, $75.65, plus taxes.

18: Cheque #204 to the Bank of Montreal, payment of $750 on the bank loan outstanding. Interest of $265 included in the payment.

22: Cheque #205 to the owner, Jarrin Penny, drawings, $800.

27: Cheque #206 to Chad Westmacott, wages, $62.50.

29: Cheque #207 to Kelly Bock Mfg. on account $1 255.67; invoice was for $1 281.30 less a 2% discount.

30: Cheque #208 to Anderson Pontiac Buick, $22 500 for a new GMC delivery van, plus taxes.

5. Record these transactions into a cash payments journal for the month of September. Provincial taxes are 7%, calculated on the base price only. GST is 7%.

Sept. 1: Cheque #665 to Bennett Signs, a new sign for the delivery truck; $125.70, Advertising Expense, plus taxes.

  1: Cheque #666 to Phan Lan for part-time wages, $60.

  3: Cheque #667 to A. Lossing, for monthly rent, $990 plus GST.

  5: Cheque #668 to Fiber Mfg., on account $2 276.64; the original invoice was $2 323.10 (less a discount of 2%).

  12: Cheque #669 to Canada Trust, for the regular monthly payment on the mortgage, $1 150. The interest component of the payment is $663.25.

  14: Received a debit memo from the bank for service charges for August, $35.50.

  21: Cheque #670 to Liz Stone, for part-time wages, $125.

  24: Cheque #671 to Sominco Co. for purchases, $555.66 plus GST. Terms of sale were net 30.

  27: Cheque #672 to The Gazette, advertising, $210.25 plus GST.

  30: Cheque #673 to Harrison Trucking for freight-in on incoming goods, $125.30 plus GST.

6. Record these transactions into a cash payments journal for the month of July. PST is 8%, calculated on the base price. GST is 7%.

July 2: Cheque #001 to Bell Canada for phone installation, $120, plus taxes.

  2: Cheque #002 to Great West Insurance for insurance, $480 for 3 years. Charge to Prepaid Insurance.

  2: Cheque #003 to G. Peterson, rent for the month, $875 plus GST.

  7: Cheque #004 to Levi Strauss for purchases. The original invoice was $5 500 (less 1.5% discount).

  12: Cheque #005 to Overland Express for freight-in, $231.17 plus GST.

  14: Cheque #006 to Jim Grey, for part-time wages, $240.

  16: Cheque #007 to Wilson Stationers, $312.26 for letterhead, envelopes, etc. for the new business, plus taxes.

  22: Cheque #008 to Land of Software, $2 212.54, a new computer system for the business, plus taxes.

23: Cheque #009 to Farrel Mfg., on account. Their original invoice was $2 400; 2/10, n/30. Take the discount.

26: Cheque #010 to the owner, Shelly Snoddy, $1 700, drawings for the month.

7. Record these transactions in either a cash receipts journal, or a cash payments journal, for the month of May. The provincial tax rate is 11% calculated on the base price plus GST (7%).

May 1: Borrowed $12 000 from the Canadian Imperial Bank of Commerce.

1: Cash sale, $2 125.10, plus taxes; invoice #444.

1: Cheque #330 to King Realty for monthly rent, $1 400 plus GST.

3: Customer, Diane Black, paid her account, $320 less a 2% discount.

4: Cheque #331 to Kingsway Supply for purchases. The original invoice was $1 840 (less 2% discount).

5: Cheque #332 to DMT Transport, freight-in, $65.50 plus GST.

5: Cash sale, $3 050.60, plus taxes; invoice #445.

8: Customer, Cindy Neale, paid her account, $410 less a 2% discount.

9: Cash sale $4 450, plus taxes; invoice #446.

10: Cheque #333 to Multimedia Inc. for advertising, $800 plus GST.

12: Cheque #334 to Daniel VanWinden, drawings, $750.

15: Received a bank debit memo, service charges, $23.50.

15: Cheque #335, payment on the bank loan, $1 000. The amount going to loan reduction is $492.70.

17: Customer, Fred Gehring, paid his account, $900 less a 2% discount.

19: Customer, Kathy Gee, paid her account, $450 less a 2% discount.

22: The bank sent a credit memo for an account collected by them from Blair Chambers, $400; no discount.

23: Cheque #336, to Trudy Moore, part-time wages, $120.

25: Cheque #337, to King Syndicate for purchases. Original invoice was $3 456.17 less a 1% discount.

29: Cash Sale, $3 333.99, plus taxes; invoice #447.

31: Cheque #338, $1 250 for new office furniture, plus taxes.

8. Journalize these petty cash transactions on page 14 in a general journal.

Jan. 1: Set up a $200 petty cash fund. Cheque #1.
     24: Reimbursed the fund for these vouchers:

Office Expenses	$34.50	(GST Recoverable $2.10)
Freight-In	$65.98	(GST Recoverable $4.32)
Misc. Exp.	$42.50	(GST Recoverable $2.58)
Car Expenses	$50.00	(GST Recoverable $3.27)

     24: Increased the petty cash fund to $300. Cheque #9.

9. Journalize these petty cash transactions on page 21 in a general journal.

Mar. 1: Set up a $100 petty cash fund. Cheque #50.
     15: Reimbursed the fund for these vouchers:

Postage Expense	$39.00	(GST Recoverable $2.55)
Freight-In	$25.12	(GST Recoverable $1.64)
Misc. Exp.	$13.68	(GST Recoverable $0.89)
Van Expenses	$20.00	(GST Recoverable $1.31)

     16: Increased the petty cash fund to $200. Cheque #62.

10. Journalize these petty cash transactions on page 17 in a general journal.

Dec. 11: Reimbursed the fund for these vouchers, cheque #112.

Travel Expense	$41.87	(GST Recoverable $2.74)
Freight-In	$21.00	(GST Recoverable $1.37)
Gas & Oil	$55.00	(GST Recoverable $3.60)
Postage Expense	$78.00	(GST Recoverable $5.10)

     31: Increased the fund to $300 from $200. Cheque #130.

11. Given the information, complete a daily cash balance form for Okanagan Fruit as of July 31, 19–.

Cash Count
84 x $ 2.00
25 x $ 5.00
61 x $10.00
49 x $20.00
6 x $50.00
Coin: $41.29

FIGURE 4-39
Management report tape

Okanagan Fruit Management Report	
07/31/91	9:00 p.m.
212 #0078	
#01*	
Fruits	802.21
#02*	
Veggies	825.63
#03*	
Gifts	217.37
#04*	
Other	167.18
Sales Total	2 012.39
7% GST	26.92
6% PST	23.07
Refund	10.00
Rfd GST	.70
Rfd PST	.60
Net Sales (SA)	2 002.39
GST (Net)	26.22
PST (Net)	22.47
On Acc (RA)	250.00
Cash Sales (CA)	1975.12
Charge Sales (CH)	75.96

12. Given the information, complete a daily cash balance form for Bud's Burgers as of June 30, 19–.

Cash Count
22 x $ 2.00
6 x $ 5.00
11 x $10.00
18 x $20.00
8 x $50.00
Coin: $33.41

FIGURE 4-40
Management report tape

Bud's Burgers Management Report	
06/30/91	11:00 p.m.
667 #1001	
#01*	
Hot Foods	511.77
#02*	
Cold Foods	120.34
#03*	
Drinks	66.65
#04*	
Dairy	120.41
Sales Total	819.17
7% GST	57.34
10% PST	81.92
Refund	3.00
Rfd GST	.21
Rfd PST	.30
Net Sales (SA)	816.17
GST (Net)	57.13
PST (Net)	81.62
On Acc (RA)	40.00
Cash Sales (CA)	939.92
Charge Sales (CH)	15.00

13. Given the information, complete a daily cash balance form for Calgary Hats as of August 31, 19–.

Cash Count

40 x $ 2.00
18 x $ 5.00
44 x $ 10.00
37 x $ 20.00
21 x $ 50.00
Coin: $122.30

```
        Calgary Hats
      Management Report

08/31/91          11/59 p.m.
743   #1133

#01*
Stetson           2 134.78
#02*
Western             300.00
#03*
Range                40.00
#04*
Other                38.20
Sales Total       2 512.98
7% GST              175.91
Refund               72.00
Rfd GST               5.04
Net Sales (SA)    2 440.98
GST (Net)           170.87
On Acc (RA)         375.00
Cash Sales (CA)   2 101.85
Charge Sales (CH)   510.00
```

FIGURE 4-41
Management report tape

14. Given the following information for Harley's Arcade, complete a bank reconciliation for the business as of November 30th.

Balance Per Bank		$1 575.75
Outstanding Deposit		$ 420.82
Outstanding Cheques	#82	$ 12.15
	#83	$ 20.40
	#84	$ 32.00
	#87	$ 106.90
Balance per Books		$1 683.74
NSF Cheque (Paul Christo)		$ 40.00
Bank Credit Memo (account, from Ann Hong)		$ 200.00
Bank Debit Memo (service charges)		$ 18.62

15. Given the following information for Water World, complete a bank reconciliation for the business as of August 31st.

Balance Per Bank		$3 219.74
Outstanding Deposit		$2 654.33
Outstanding Cheques	#580	$1 403.76
	#582	$ 96.59
	#590	$ 442.12
	#594	$ 116.33
	#597	$ 202.87
Balance per Books		$4 531.21
NSF Cheque (Andy Potter)		$ 72.50
Interest on Bank Loan		$ 872.91
Bank Debit Memo (service charges)		$ 36.40
Error re our cheque #572 to Burnaby PUC, cheque was recorded in the books as $792.34; it should be $729.34		$ 63.00

16. Given the following information for Golf N' Putt, complete a bank reconciliation for the business as of July 31st.

Balance Per Bank		$1 015.55
Balance per Books		$ 883.46
Bank Debit Memo (service charges)		$ 20.12
Error re our cheque #112 to Bell Canada, cheque was recorded in the books as $58.66; it should be $85.66		$ 27.00
Interest on Bank Loan		$ 218.67
Account Collected (George Ireland)		$ 235.00
NSF Cheque (Paul Smith)		$ 50.00
Outstanding Deposit		$ 446.64
Outstanding Cheques	#102	$ 425.36
	#103	$ 106.06
	#110	$ 89.98
	#111	$ 23.00
	#118	$ 15.12

COMPUTER EXERCISES

SS1   Use a spreadsheet to produce this cash receipts summary. Program the spreadsheet to calculate the total of the Bank Dr. column. Save your solution on disk under the file name CH4SS1.

```
          A              B          C
 1   CASH RECEIPTS — Monday, October 5, 19-.
 2   Customer        Bank Dr.
 3   Armin, L.         214.00
 4   Chong, N.         100.00
 5   Fogel, B.          50.12
 6   Mintz, Q.         112.00
 7   Stang, P.         201.67
 8                    _____
 9   TOTAL               ?
10                    ========
```

SS2   Use a spreadsheet to produce this cash sales summary. Increase the width of column A to 15 characters. Program the spreadsheet to calculate values in the Bank Dr. column (Column E). Then program the spreadsheet to calculate the total of the Bank Dr. column. Save your solution on disk under the file name CH4SS2.

```
          A              B          C          D          E
 1   CASH SALES SUMMARY — Fred's Ice Cream Parlours
 2   Sales Item      Store 1    Store 2    Store 3    Bank Dr.
 3   Cones            342.50     445.30     202.10       ?
 4   Sundaes          112.30     334.47     102.98       ?
 5   Frozen Bars       23.45      34.50      10.65       ?
 6   Milk Shakes      277.09     321.09     445.23       ?
 7   Other Items      220.76     334.56     176.76       ?
 8                                                    _____
 9                                          TOTAL        ?
10                                                    ========
```

SS3   Create the following cash receipts table for Monogram Magic. Set column A to a width of 10. Set columns B through E to a width of 8. Program the spreadsheet to add columns B, C, D, and E. Insert dollar signs beside all numbers. Save the template under the file name CH4SS3.

	A	B	C	D	E
1	CASH RECEIPTS SUMMARY	— Monogram Magic			
2	Sales Item	Jan.	Feb.	Mar.	Bank Dr.
3	Tote Bags	1223.66	1333.78	2445.73	?
4	Shirts	3112.99	4656.88	5667.01	?
5	Sweatsuits	556.77	768.98	567.44	?
6	Pillows	221.32	333.00	212.78	?
7	Hats	5444.88	5666.77	5887.67	?
8		————	————	————	————
9		?	?	?	?
10					

SS4 Create a cheque register for Pine Ridge Golf Club. Program the spread-sheet to total the cheque register. Save your work under the file name CH4SS4.

	A	B	C
1	CHEQUE REGISTER — Week Ending Oct. 5/—.		
2	Payee	Ch. No.	Bank Cr.
3	Brent's Garage	273	607.08
4	Imperial Oil	274	330.17
5	T-D Bank	275	1500.00
6	T. Pevler	276	600.00
7	Brandon PUC	277	389.99
8			————
9		TOTAL	?
10			

SS5 Use a spreadsheet to produce this cash payments journal. Increase the width of column B to 15 characters. Program the spreadsheet to calcu-late the Bank Cr. column (Column C). Save your solution on disk under the file name CH4SS5.

	A	B	C	D
1	CASH PAYMENTS JOURNAL			
2	Date	Particulars	Bank Cr.	Account
3	June 1	D. Cohoe	450.00	Drawings
4	June 2	O. Cornwell	100.00	Wages
5	June 3	D. Pite	250.00	Wages
6	June 3	Bk. Montreal	2000.00	Bank Loan
7	June 5	King Ltd.	1278.45	A/P
8	June 7	XYZ Ltd.	990.30	A/P
9			————	
10		TOTAL	?	
11				

SS6 Use a spreadsheet to produce this template for a bank reconciliation statement. Save it under the file name CH4SS6.

```
            A                          B        C
 1  BANK RECONCILIATION STATEMENT
 2  Balance Per Bank                        X XXX.XX
 3  Add: O/S Deposit                          XXX.XX
 4  Less: O/S Cheques            #XX         XX.XX
 5                               #XX         XX.XX
 6                               #XX         XX.XX
 7                                          _____
 8  True Balance (Bank)                        ?
 9                                          ========
10  Balance Per Books                         XXX.XX
11  Add: Account Collected                    XXX.XX
12  Less: NSF Cheque                           XX.XX
13                                          _____
14  True Balance (Bank)                        ?
15                                          ========
```

SS7 Recall the spreadsheet form, CH4SS6. Insert these figures, and program the form to calculate the correct balance.

Balance Per Bank		$1 211.25
O/S Deposit		106.50
O/S Cheques	#65	66.43
	#68	87.12
	#70	42.50
Balance Per Books		969.65
Account Collected		210.00
NSF Cheque		57.95

SS8 Recall the spreadsheet form, CH4SS6. Insert these figures, and program the form to calculate the correct balance.

Balance Per Bank		$3 246.84
O/S Deposit		551.18
O/S Cheques	#18	831.46
	#44	1 516.75
	#45	102.12
Balance Per Books		199.49
Account Collected		1 500.00
NSF Cheque		115.00
Bank Debit Memo (service charges)		31.75
Bank Debit Memo (loan interest)		205.05

DB1 Create a customer database for Lights Unlimited. Define the following fields for your file.

```
Customer   = 16 columns
Balance    =  8 columns
Discount   =  5 columns
```

Enter the raw data shown below, and save under the file name CH4DB1.

Customer	Balance	Discount
Allan, D.	$450.00	2%
Bakos, K.	$128.95	1%
Cook, L.	$800.24	2%
Drew, M.	$230.30	3%
Euchuk, N.	$ 80.80	1%
Fox, R.	$444.44	2%

DB2 Retrieve CH4DB1 from your data disk. Program the database to find the net amount each customer can be expected to pay, after deducting the discount. Produce a listing of the file.

Customer	Balance	Discount	Net
X——X	XXX.XX	X.XX	XXX.XX

Program the listing to add the Net column.

DB3 Create a database bond portfolio for New Canada Life Insurance Co. Define the following fields for your file:

```
Description   = 25 columns
Amount        =  8 columns
Rate          =  6 columns
Maturity      = 10 columns
```

Enter the raw data shown below, and save under the file name CH4DB3. Print a listing of the file.

Description	Amount	Rate	Maturity
Gov't of Canada	$50 000	10%	Jan.1/95
Gov't of Canada	$30 000	11%	Jan.1/98
Gov't of Canada	$20 000	10.5%	Jan.1/99
Prov. of Saskatchewan	$40 000	9.8%	Jul.1/95
Prov. of Saskatchewan	$40 000	9.7%	Oct.1/94
City of Regina	$20 000	8.0%	Apr.1/96

G1 Create a bar graph for this cash sales data.

Igloo Ice Cream Bars
Cash Sales in Dollars August 7-12/–

Vanilla	$185
Cherry	$ 70
Fudge	$ 60
Chocolate	$ 95
Banana	$ 40
Other	$ 80

G2 Create a line graph for this cash sales data.

Anne's Fruit Market
Cash Sales

May	$ 1 550
June	$ 2 776
July	$18 445
August	$20 004
September	$12 221
October	$ 4 328

G3 Create a pie graph for this cash sales data.

Mt. Flintstone Ski Lodge
Cash Receipts

Tow Tickets	$140 500
Equipment Rental	$ 85 275
Equipment Sales	$ 45 668
Snack Bar	$126 450
Locker Rentals	$ 4 532
Miscellaneous	$ 1 205

WP1   Use your word processor to write this letter to one of your branch pizza outlets. Save this exercise as CH4WP1.

August 4, 19–

Pizza Dome
245 West 45th Street
Regina, Sask.
S6S 4G4

Attention: Lee Anderson, Store Manager

The size of your bank deposits for the last week of July would indicate that you are not making enough daily bank deposits. You are reminded that company policy states that once cash receipts are in excess of $5 000 a day, a deposit should be made. This is good internal control over cash. Your deposits for the month of August will again be monitored by head office to see that this situation improves.

Yours truly

J. Arthur
Controller, Pizza Dome

WP2   Retrieve CH4WP1, change the inside address and send another copy of the same letter to the store manager, Jamie DeJong, at 2303 North St. in Saskatoon, Saskatchewan, S7T 2R1.

WP3   Assume you are Lee Anderson (WP1). Draft a letter to the controller explaining why you have not been making more daily bank deposits. Indicate that you were short-staffed for that week, but that you have now hired more help.

R. v. THURGOOD

BACKGROUND

Auditors for a Canadian bank found that an amount in excess of $10 000 000 had been misappropriated from bank funds. The funds were embezzled by someone who had the authority to grant large loans without the necessity of higher approval. Proceeds of these loan advances, to fictitious companies, were directed to currency houses to be picked up as cash parcels, and to brokerage firms for the purchase of bonds.

INVESTIGATION

The bank auditors checked all bank personnel who had the authority to grant loans in excess of $100 000 without higher approval. Out of several candidates, they narrowed their investigation to Jason Thurgood, a loans manager. His personal living style was checked by bank staff and an investigative team of forensic accountants. Here are the investigation results:

1. Thurgood's annual salary was $75 000; high by banking standards but unusually low for a person living in a $500 000 home.
2. Thurgood made frequent trips to Atlantic City and Las Vegas in the course of the two-year period being examined.
3. The trips taken to the gambling cities were made in a private aircraft chartered by Mr. Thurgood from Toronto Island Airport.
4. A photo of Mr. Thurgood was recognized by gambling casino personnel as a frequent visitor to the gaming tables in those cities.

FRAUD

To uncover the specific amount of the fraud, investigators examined a report prepared by the Division of Gaming Enforcement, Department of Law and Public Safety, State of New Jersey. These records indicated that an account in

NAME

NO.

CRIMEBUSTERS

the name of Jason Thurgood sustained gambling losses of approximately $6 500 000 during the time period that funds disappeared from the bank.

Casino records indicated that massive amounts of cash and chips were won by Mr. Thurgood at the Caesar's Boardwalk Regency gambling casino. This evidence was obtained by court order.

The cash parcels had been placed on deposit with the California Clearing Corporation in Toronto and then transferred to gambling casinos, under Thurgood's direction, into accounts in his name. Thurgood then drew cash from the accounts to use in the various casinos at Atlantic City and Las Vegas.

SENTENCE

Trial was held in the Supreme Court of Ontario because of the excessive amount of the embezzlement i.e. over $10 000 000. Thurgood was found guilty of theft, under the Criminal Code of Canada. In spite of his family status, he was sentenced to ten years in prison for his crime. The penalty was severe because of the huge sums of money misappropriated and spent, but also because Thurgood was in a position of trust as a senior officer, and he schemed and plotted to by-pass the accounting controls of the bank.

QUESTIONS

1. Should anyone at the bank have wondered about Thurgood's extravagant lifestyle long before his thefts reached $10 000 000?
2. Under what conditions should forensic accountants, or the police, be allowed to examine personal bank accounts?
3. What kind of accounting controls might have prevented James Thurgood from stealing such a massive sum of money?
4. Was the sentence appropriate in this case? Should he have to pay back the money stolen from the bank?

Career Profile

Kevin and Bao were both looking for new jobs for the upcoming summer holidays. Kevin, 19, and Bao 17, both had part-time jobs for the winter months, but both felt the need for change. In addition, they wanted to be their own bosses. Bao had heard about the government Student Venture program which helped aspiring students with new business ventures. The government would loan up to $3 000 of capital to students who had a business idea but lacked the necessary financing.

Bao and Kevin reviewed the details of the program with their parents and applied for the funds. Their business idea was simple — they would offer a wide range of house and garden services to prospective clients: window washing, lawn and hedge trimming, driveway sealing, etc. Living in a small town of 5 000 people helped, since they felt they were well known. Their first step was to produce a cash flow forecast to show the government, and for their own information as well. They produced their cash flow forecast using a common spreadsheet program.

Their cash flow forecast had to be approved by the local Chamber of Commerce before the application could be submitted to the government for its approval. Both local business advisors and the government contact person were impressed. The loan was granted, and K & B House & Garden Services was under way. A month later, the government was looking for a financial report of operations to date. Bao turned to his computer once more for some accounting help. Since the cash flow forecast included a lot of the headings needed for the income statement, he was able to insert the actual data, and produce an income statement in minutes.

By the middle of the summer, K & B House & Garden Services was well established as a reliable, courteous business venture, and business was booming. The partnership had earned enough money to reimburse the government for its loan, and was beginning to make a considerable profit for the two student partners. Both Kevin and Bao feel that the computer was invaluable in putting their cash flow data in perspective and in helping them plan their financial operations.

```
                        CASH FLOW FORECAST

Date Loan Required: ASAP              Business:   K & B House &
Date Business                                     Garden Services
Operation Begins: May 1/-            Applicants:  Kevin Cougler
                                                  Bao Luong
Receipts           May     Jun     Jul     Aug     Sep    Total
Sales                0     400    1600    1600     700     4300
Loan              3000       0       0       0       0     3000
Other                0       0       0       0       0        0

Total             3000     400    1600    1600     700     7300

Disbursements
Tools/Equipment    600       0       0       0       0      600
Rentals              0      35      35      35       0      105
Labour               0       0       0       0       0        0
Drawings             0     200     200     200       0      600
Materials          175      40     160     160      75      610
Bus. Fees           50       0       0       0       0       50
Advertising        200      40      40      40       0      320
Insurance           50       0       0       0       0       50
Office              25      25      25      25      25      125
Car Expenses        30      60      60      60      30      240
Loan Repayment       0       0    1500    1500       0     3000

Total             1130     400    2020    2020     130     5700

Monthly Surplus   1870       0    -420    -420     570     1600

Cumulative        1870    1870    1450    1030    1600
```

FIGURE 4-42   *K & B cash flow forecast*

Kevin and Bao are starting to think about their second year of operations. Their financial plans include purchasing a used truck for the business, as well as a ride-on lawn mower. Both of these purchases will help them provide quicker and better service to their lawn customers. Bao has already started loading the cash flow data onto his computer, so that he will be ready for the banker next year when they apply for a larger loan. Since Bao is still in high school, he has decided to study computerized accounting next year, just in case they decide to franchise their successful venture across Canada.

```
K & B House & Garden Services
Statement of Cash Receipts and Disbursements
For the Period Ended June 30, 19–
Receipts
Sales                    $  600
Loan                      3 000
Other                         0
Total                                  $3 600
Disbursements
Tools/Equipment             600
Rentals                       0
Labour                        0
Drawings                      0
Materials                    45
Bus. Fees                    50
Advertising                 210
Insurance                    30
Office                       15
Car Expenses                 30
Loan Repayment                0
Total                                    980
Monthly Surplus                       $2 620

Prepared For: Student Venture Capital Program July 10, 19–
```

FIGURE 4-43   *K & B income statement*

FOR DISCUSSION

• Was it really necessary for Bao and Kevin to use a computer for their small business?
• Do you think Kevin and Bao got financial backing because they were able to use a computer to produce their cash flow forecasts?

5

Accounts Receivable

- Journalize and post accounts receivable transactions, and understand control procedures for charge sales.

- Understand accounts associated with the revenue category of a merchandising firm.

- Understand billing procedures and cycle billing.

- Understand analysis and reporting techniques for accounts receivable control.

- Journalize and post notes receivable transactions.

- Use computer software for handling accounts receivable activities.

5.0

Overview

Accounts receivable are amounts due to the business in the near future that arise from charge sales. A charge sale is a sale whereby the customer agrees in writing to pay for goods or services received on a later date.

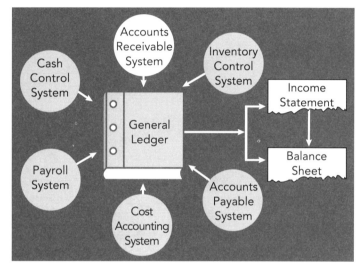

FIGURE 5-1   Flowchart of the accounting process

An accounts receivable clerk must be able to keep daily sales records, prepare (charge) sales invoices and credit notes, and know how to record transactions in a sales journal. A sales journal is a book of original entry for recording all charge sales. Sales invoices must be accurately prepared so that appropriate government sales taxes are levied and customers are billed the exact amount owing. Other accounts receivable tasks include handling customer payments, sales returns and allowances, and customer discounts. Statements must be sent out to customers on a monthly basis, and the business must be confident that the information on each customer statement is correct. Accounts receivable work will also entail analysis of accounts receivable by an aging schedule, and reporting to management on delinquent accounts. Analysing the credit status of prospective customers, assigning credit limits to customers, and collecting overdue accounts are also an important aspect of an efficient accounts receivable system.

5.1

Source Documents and Journalizing

Charles Stumpf owns and operates a successful computer retail store called Land of Software, in London, Ontario. The store retails microcomputer systems and software, and also earns income from computer repairs, and its training school operations. The business is operated as a sole proprietorship.

This section will describe the source documents used by Land of Software for handling accounts receivable activities. The accounting entries associated with the source documents will be journalized in general journal form; and in section 5.2, all the transactions affecting accounts receivable will be recorded in a sales journal, and in a cash receipts journal.

A **cash receipts journal** is a book of original entry in which all cash receipts of a business are first recorded, along with bank credit memos.

Charge sales are an important part of daily business operations for Land of Software. Many of the customers of the business are other businesses that are accustomed to charging purchases they make. As well, there are many individual customers who have dealt with Land of Software for some time and who are allowed to charge goods and services purchased.

The transactions and source documents associated with accounts receivable are:

(1) sales invoices
(2) credit invoices
(3) receipts on account
(4) monthly statements

SALES INVOICES

All customers who buy **on account** (buy goods or services and pay for them at a later date) from Land of Software are issued a (charge) sales invoice. Because this document will trigger a billing statement later in the month, it has several important features.

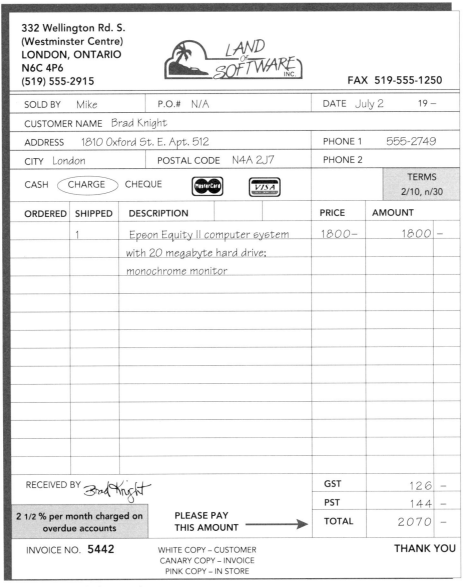

FIGURE 5-2   *A charge sales invoice*

Sales invoices are numbered for numerical control. The sales invoice used by Land of Software has three parts. Copy 1 (white), the original and the best copy, is given to the customer. Copy 2 (canary), is used to post to the customer's account. Copy 3 (pink), is filed by number for numerical control, to ensure that no invoices are missing.

The general journal entry for the charge sales invoice is:

GENERAL JOURNAL

PAGE 22

DATE 19–		PARTICULARS	PR	DEBIT	CREDIT
July	2	A/R—Brad Knight		2070 –	
		Computer Sales			1800 –
		GST Payable			126 –
		PST Payable			144 –
		To record charge sale inv. 5442			

FIGURE 5-3   *The general journal entry for a charge sales invoice*

CREDIT INVOICES

Credit invoices are issued to customers when defective goods are returned to the store, or when an error has been made on an original invoice and the customer's account must be given an allowance on the amount owing. Credit invoices, like the example Figure 5-4, are designated as such by writing "Credit Invoice" on the document. Many businesses use regular invoice forms for credit invoices; the forms are therefore numbered for control purposes.

Credit invoices, like sales invoices, have three parts: the original being given to the customer, the second used for posting to the customer's account, and the third used for numerical control.

It is important to note that when a credit invoice is issued, the GST Payable and the PST Payable have to be reversed. These amounts no longer have to be paid to the federal or provincial governments because part or all of the original sale has no longer been made.

There are two choices that can be made when a customer returns goods. The debit side of the entry can be charged directly to the Sales account. See Figure 5-5. If this approach is taken, the dollar volume of goods returned by customers will be buried in the Sales account, and important information about customer returns may be lost.

332 Wellington Rd. S. (Westminster Centre) LONDON, ONTARIO N6C 4P6 (519) 555-2915		*LAND OF SOFTWARE INC.*			FAX 519-555-1250	
SOLD BY Charles		P.O.# N/A		DATE July 4		19 –
CUSTOMER NAME Gary Waslewski						
ADDRESS 38 The Ridgeway				PHONE 1		555-1236
CITY London		POSTAL CODE N3B 2K4		PHONE 2		
CASH CHARGE CHEQUE		MasterCard VISA			TERMS 2/10, n/30	

ORDERED	SHIPPED	DESCRIPTION			PRICE	AMOUNT
	1	Defective software —			45 –	45 –
		Wheel of Fortune game				
		CREDIT INVOICE				

RECEIVED BY *Gary Waslewski*	GST	3	15
	PST	3	60
2 1/2 % per month charged on overdue accounts PLEASE PAY THIS AMOUNT	TOTAL	51	75

INVOICE NO. **5443**	WHITE COPY – CUSTOMER CANARY COPY – INVOICE PINK COPY – IN STORE	**THANK YOU**

FIGURE 5-4   A credit invoice

Another approach is to charge the dollar volume of returned goods to the **Sales Returns and Allowances** account, a contra account that will offset the Sales account on the income statement. See Figure 5-6.

GENERAL JOURNAL

PAGE 22

DATE 19–		PARTICULARS	PR	DEBIT	CREDIT
July	4	Sales		45 –	
		GST Payable		3 15	
		PST Payable		3 60	
		A/R—Gary Waslewski			5 1 75
		To record sales return Cr. Inv. 5443			

FIGURE 5-5   The general journal entry for a credit invoice (debit to Sales)

GENERAL JOURNAL

PAGE 22

DATE 19–		PARTICULARS	PR	DEBIT	CREDIT
July	4	Sales Returns and Allowances		45 –	
		GST Payable		3 15	
		PST Payable		3 60	
		A/R—Gary Waslewski			5 1 75
		To record sales return Cr. Inv. 5443			

FIGURE 5-6   The general journal entry for a credit invoice (charged to Sales Returns and Allowances)

This second method provides a record of the goods returned by customers in the course of one year. If the figure is high, it will be a signal to management that better control over the quality of goods, or service, being provided should be sought.

RECEIPTS ON ACCOUNT

Customers who charge their purchases often pay by mail since this is convenient for them. Those who pay by mail are not usually issued a cash receipt for their payment since they will see the credit on their next statement. Their cancelled cheque serves as a receipt. A **cash receipt** is a document issued to someone as proof that they have paid cash to the business. Customers who come into the store to pay part or all of their account are issued a cash receipt as proof of payment. Regular invoices are used as cash receipts by circling the word "Cash" on the sales invoice document and writing "Received on Account" on the invoice itself. Cash receipts are numbered for control, and the number sequence follows the regular invoice sequence.

332 Wellington Rd. S. (Westminster Centre) LONDON, ONTARIO N6C 4P6 (519) 555-2915	LAND of SOFTWARE INC.				FAX 519-555-1250	
SOLD BY		P.O.#		DATE July 12 19 –		
CUSTOMER NAME Brad Knight						
ADDRESS 1810 Oxford St. E. Apt. 512				PHONE 1	555-2749	
CITY London		POSTAL CODE N4A 2J7		PHONE 2		
(CASH) CHARGE CHEQUE MasterCard VISA					TERMS 2/10, n/30	

ORDERED	SHIPPED	DESCRIPTION			PRICE	AMOUNT	
		Received on account				2070	–
		Less: 2% Discount				38	88

RECEIVED BY			GST		
			PST		
2 1/2 % per month charged on overdue accounts	PLEASE PAY THIS AMOUNT ⟶		TOTAL	2031	12
INVOICE NO. 5501	WHITE COPY – CUSTOMER CANARY COPY – INVOICE PINK COPY – IN STORE			THANK YOU	

FIGURE 5-7   A cash receipt

Sales on account at Land of Software have terms of 2/10, n/30. This means that if the customer pays an invoice within ten days of the billing date, a 2% discount of the invoice price may be taken (2/10). If not, the total amount is due within 30 days (n/30).

For Brad Knight who bought an $1 800 computer from Land of Software, the total bill, with the GST and PST, was $2 070. Brad would calculate the discount allowed as follows:

Total Invoice	$2 070.00
Discount	41.40
Remittance	$2 028.60

The accounting entry needed to record the remittance of the original invoice amount less the discount is:

GENERAL JOURNAL

PAGE 25

DATE 19–		PARTICULARS	PR	DEBIT	CREDIT
July	12	Bank		2 028 60	
		Discounts Allowed		41 40	
		A/R—Brad Knight			2 070 –
		To record receipt on account			

FIGURE 5-8   *The general journal entry for a cash receipt less discount*

MONTHLY STATEMENTS

Customers who have charged goods or services during any given month are sent a statement of their account with Land of Software after the month end. The **monthly statement** shows a running balance of the account, all the debit entries (charges), and any credits (payments) made during the month. Here is a monthly statement:

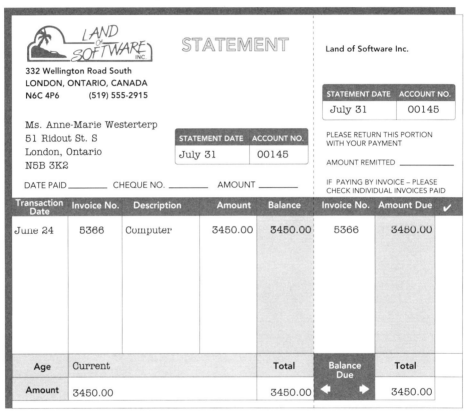

FIGURE 5-9   A monthly statement

Monthly statements usually have a return portion (or a return copy) for the customer to mail back in with the payment. This facilitates quick processing of the cash **receipt on account**. Land of Software's statements are processed on the computer, and the computer automatically prepares an aging analysis of the account at the bottom of the statement. An **aging analysis** is a table showing the accounts receivable of a business and the length of time these have been outstanding. More will be said on the aging of accounts receivable in section 5.4.

QUESTIONS

1. Why would a business decide to use a Sales Returns and Allowances account?

2. What defective goods have you or your family bought lately that had to be returned to the store for credit, or exchange?

3. What do these terms on invoices mean? 2/10, n/30; 1/15, n/30

4. An invoice is dated July 4 and has terms of 3/10, n/30. What is the last day for paying? receiving the discount?

5. What is the purpose of the return portion of a customer's statement?

5.2

Journalizing and Posting Sales Invoices / Internal Control

Land of Software uses a sales journal to record all charge sales invoices and credit invoices; and a cash receipts journal for receipts on account. The sales journal and the cash receipts journal used by Land of Software are typical of those found in many businesses, but they are tailored to suit the needs of this business. Standard journals could be used for sales and receipts, but an efficient business will shape the accounting records to its own needs.

THE SALES JOURNAL

Figure 5-10 shows the sales journal that was specially designed for Land of Software, and its particular type of revenue.

The sales journal for Land of Software has special columns for the accounts used most frequently: Sales, Accounts Receivable, GST Payable, PST Payable, Sales Returns and Allowances, and a special section for Other Accounts. This gives the owner a quick breakdown of monthly revenue once the totals are calculated and the sales journal balanced. (When the business is larger, sales will be broken down into the three components of retail, repairs, and training revenue.) The sales journal also has special columns for the sales invoice (or credit invoice) numbers, and a tick column which is checked when the accounts receivable debits are posted to the customers' accounts.

There are two types of accounting transactions that affect accounts receivable which are entered into the sales journal — charge sales and credit invoices issued.

	DATE 19–		PARTICULARS	INV. NO.	OTHER ACCOUNTS CR				
---	---	---	---	---	---	---	---		
					ACCOUNT	PR	AMOUNT		
1	Aug.	2	Rob Wood	5564					
2		4	Harold Ming	5566					
3		8	Rob Wood	5568					
4		12	John Calvert	5569					
5		18	Bob Newhouse	5570					
6		22	Edith Rice	5572					
7		25	Ellen Box	5573					
8		28	Keshav Chari	5575					
9		31	Grant Wettlauffer	5576					
10		31	Marnie Shultz	5577					
11									
12									
13									

FIGURE 5-10 *Sales journal with entries*

To study how the sales journal is used by the business, assume that Land of Software had these sample transactions in August.

Aug.
2: Sales Invoice #5564, to Rob Wood, $1 800, computer system, plus taxes.

4: Sales Invoice #5566, to Harold Ming, $349.00, sale of software, plus taxes.

8: Credit Invoice #5568, to Rob Wood, $50, plus taxes, for defective software.

12: Sales Invoice #5569, to John Calvert, $2 350, computer system, plus taxes.

18: Sales Invoice #5570, to Bob Newhouse, $40, plus taxes, for repairs to a hard disk drive.

22: Sales Invoice #5572, to Edith Rice, $3 400, computer system, plus taxes.

25: Sales Invoice #5573, to Ellen Box, $780, computer software, plus taxes.

28: Sales Invoice #5575, to Keshav Chari, $2 160, computer system, plus taxes.

SALES JOURNAL

FOR THE Month ENDED Aug. 31 19– PAGE 17

	SALES RETURNS AND ALLOWANCES DR	GST PAYABLE CR	PST PAYABLE CR	ACCOUNTS RECEIVABLE DR	✔	SALES CR	
		126 –	144 –	2070 –		1800 –	1
		24 43	27 92	401 35		349 –	2
	50 –	(3 50)	(4 –)	(57 50)			3
		164 50	188 –	2702 50		2350 –	4
		2 80	3 20	46 –		40 –	5
	238 –		272 –	3910 –		3400 –	6
		54 60	62 40	897 –		780 –	7
		151 20	172 80	2484 –		2160 –	8
		8 75	10 –	143 75		125 –	9
	250 –	(17 50)	(20 –)	(287 50)			10
							11
							12
							13

31: Sales Invoice #5576, to Grant Wettlauffer, $125, repair income, plus taxes.

31: Credit Invoice #5577, to Marnie Schultz, $250, plus taxes, for a defective modem.

These source documents are all entered into the sales journal for Land of Software. The credit invoices are opposite entries and (except for the entry to the Sales Returns and Allowances) amounts are entered in the appropriate columns of the sales journal with circles, or in red.

The columns labelled "Other Accounts" will seldom be used in this sales journal; only a very unusual transaction might trigger an entry here, such as the sale of a fixed asset on account.

Figure 5-11 shows how the sales journal for Land of Software would look after it had been balanced and posted at the end of the month.

The totals of the debit columns must equal the totals of all of the credit columns. All of the column totals except for Other Accounts are posted to their respective accounts in the general ledger of the business at the end of the month. Amounts in the Other Accounts column are posted individually.

	DATE 19–		PARTICULARS	INV. NO.	OTHER ACCOUNTS CR				
					ACCOUNT	PR	AMOUNT		
1	Aug.	2	Rob Wood	5564					
2		4	Harold Ming	5566					
3		8	Rob Wood	5568					
4		12	John Calvert	5569					
5		18	Bob Newhouse	5570					
6		22	Edith Rice	5572					
7		25	Ellen Box	5573					
8		28	Keshav Chari	5575					
9		31	Grant Wettlauffer	5576					
10		31	Marnie Shultz	5577					
11									
12									
13									

FIGURE 5-11   *Sales journal posted*

In addition, the individual entries in the Accounts Receivable column are all posted to the individual customer accounts in the subsidiary accounts receivable ledger. (As you will recall, the **accounts receivable ledger** is a group of accounts containing all the transactions for customers of the business.) This posting must be done on a daily basis so that the customer account totals in the subsidiary ledger are always current. The posting references for the individual postings to the customer accounts are a tick, while the references for the column totals are the general ledger account numbers inside the brackets at the bottom of each column.

Figure 5-12 gives a sample of 3-column accounts to show how the postings from the sales journal (and the cash receipts journal) are made to the general ledger control account, Accounts Receivable, and to the accounts receivable subsidiary ledger.

SALES JOURNAL

FOR THE ___Month___ ENDED ___Aug. 31___ 19_–_ PAGE _17_

	SALES RETURNS AND ALLOWANCES DR	GST PAYABLE CR	PST PAYABLE CR	ACCOUNTS RECEIVABLE DR	✔	SALES CR	
		1 26 –	1 44 –	20 70 –	✔	18 00 –	1
		24 43	27 92	401 35	✔	3 49 –	2
	50 –	(3 50)	(4 –)	(57 50)	✔		3
		164 50	1 88 –	27 02 50	✔	23 50 –	4
		2 80	3 20	46 –	✔	40 –	5
		2 38 –	2 72 –	39 10 –	✔	34 00 –	6
		54 60	62 40	8 97 –	✔	7 80 –	7
		151 20	172 80	24 84 –	✔	21 60 –	8
		8 75	10 –	143 75	✔	1 25 –	9
	2 50 –	(17 50)	(20 –)	(287 50)	✔		10
	3 00 –	749 28	856 32	1 23 09 60		110 04 –	11
							12
	(4 20)	(2 21)	(2 22)	(1 20)		(4 10)	13

GENERAL LEDGER

ACCOUNT Accounts Receivable   **NO** 120

DATE 19–		PARTICULARS	PR	DEBIT	CREDIT	DR CR	BALANCE
July	31	Balance Forward	–			DR	2 12 10 –
Aug.	31		SJ17	1 23 09 60		DR	3 35 19 60
	31		CRJ19		1 15 56 35	DR	2 19 63 25

ACCOUNTS RECEIVABLE SUBSIDIARY LEDGER

ACCOUNT Wood, Rob   **NO**

DATE 19–		PARTICULARS	PR	DEBIT	CREDIT	DR CR	BALANCE
July	31	Balance Forward	–			DR	Ø
Aug.	2		SJ17	20 70 –		DR	20 70 –
	8		SJ17		57 50	DR	2 01 2 50
	10		CRJ19		2 01 2 50	–	Ø

FIGURE 5-12   3-column accounts

	DATE 19–		PARTICULARS	INV. NO.	OTHER ACCOUNTS CR			
					ACCOUNT	PR	AMOUNT	
1	Aug.	2	Cash sale	5565				
2		6	Cash sale	5567				
3		10	Rob Wood	5564				
4		15	John Calvert	5569				
5		20	Cash sale	5571				
6		21	Bob Newhouse	5570				
7		23	Harold Ming	5566				
8		25	Cash sale	5574				
9		29	Edith Rice	5572				
10		31	Keshav Chari	5575				
11								
12								
13								

FIGURE 5-13   Cash receipts journal

THE CASH RECEIPTS JOURNAL

When customers pay their bills, the receipts are entered in the cash receipts journal for the business. Figure 5-13 shows a sample cash receipts journal for the month of August with discounts allowed recorded. **Discounts allowed** is a percentage applied to an invoice total to reduce the payment made by a customer. Receipts on account are highlighted for reference.

The total of the Accounts Receivable column is posted into the control account in the general ledger at end of the month. The **control account** is the main Accounts Receivable account in the general ledger. The other column totals are posted to their respective general ledger accounts as well, with the exception of the Other Accounts total. Any items recorded in the Other Accounts column are posted individually. The individual entries in the Accounts Receivable column have already been posted to the individual customer accounts in the accounts receivable subsidiary ledger. This posting must be done on a daily basis so that the customer account totals in the subsidiary ledger are always current. The posting references for the individual postings to the customer accounts are a tick, while the references for the column totals are the general ledger account numbers inside the brackets at the bottom of each column.

CASH RECEIPTS JOURNAL

FOR THE <u>Month</u>   ENDED <u>Aug. 31</u>   19 –   PAGE <u>19</u>

SALES CR	GST PAYABLE CR	PST PAYABLE CR	DISCOUNTS ALLOWED DR	ACCOUNTS RECEIVABLE CR	✔	BANK DR	
2000 –	140 –	160 –				2300 –	1
2570 70	179 95	205 66				2956 31	2
			40 25	2012 50	✔	1972 25	3
			54 05	2702 50	✔	2648 45	4
352 40	24 67	28 19				405 26	5
			92	46 –	✔	45 08	6
				401 35	✔	401 35	7
429 –	30 03	34 32				493 35	8
			78 20	3910 –	✔	3831 80	9
			49 68	2484 –	✔	2434 32	10
5352 10	374 65	428 17	223 10	11556 35		17488 17	11
							12
				(120)		(110)	13

Internal control refers to the methods used to safeguard assets and ensure the accurate recording of transactions in the books of account. Internal control for accounts receivable applications involves making sure that the original billing is accurate, and that collections from customers are correctly credited to the customers' accounts. Some internal control procedures are:

Arithmetic Accuracy
The original invoice must be extended properly (quantity × price), sales taxes (GST, and PST where applicable) must be correct, and addition must be accurate.

Subdivision of Duties
Clerks who receive cash in the business, to be credited to customers' accounts, should not be allowed to make entries in the accounts receivable subsidiary ledger. If they have access to the cash received and to the books, they can embezzle funds and falsify the accounts to cover up the theft. Employees will be discouraged from perpetrating fraud if they have to collaborate with another employee to do it.

Rotation of Employees

Rotation of employees from one job to another may strengthen internal control, since employees will be more likely to maintain records with care if they know that someone else may soon take over their duties.

Numbered Documents

If all source documents issued by a business are numbered, any missing number should be noticed and questions raised about the missing document.

Internal and External Audits

Larger firms have internal auditors who routinely check accounting work and establish controls over handling and recording of assets. Smaller firms do not always have controls such as those mentioned above, but have outside auditing firms perform test checks on the accounting system. Vigilance by the owner/manager is also an important factor in discouraging employee dishonesty.

Q U E S T I O N S

6. Why does Land of Software use two special journals for transactions affecting accounts receivable?

7. What are the three main sources of revenue for Land of Software?

8. What are the two ways for making unusual entries in a sales journal?

9. Explain the posting process that must be performed from a sales journal for accounts receivable entries.

10. Explain the posting process from a cash receipts journal for accounts receivable entries.

11. What does the term *internal control* mean?

12. Identify the five methods of establishing control over accounts receivable in a business.

13. Could a computer be used for any of the internal control measures used for accounts receivable? Explain.

5.3

Billing Procedures and Credit

Customers are billed for goods and services at the time of the sale. Many companies have followed a practice of sending out statements to customers at the end of each month. In this method of billing, all of the customers are billed at the same time. This practice has the advantage of being tidy and timely since customers are all notified at the same time that they have balances outstanding.

An alternative to this billing method is called **cycle billing**. Under this system, statements are mailed out on a cycle basis, i.e. the statements are staggered throughout the month. Assume that a business has 60 000 customers. If the business attempts to send out all of these statements at each month end, it may have an impossible task. If the statements are staggered throughout the month, say 2 000 a day, this spreads the billing workload evenly throughout the month. Customers will still receive monthly statements but they will be dated for the same day every month, e.g. the 23rd. The volume of accounts receivable that a business has will dictate how the business can handle the billing process most efficiently.

Although discount terms are very specific, as in 2/10, n/30, sellers often allow the discount even if payment is received after the ten-day time period because the flow of business documents is sometimes slow, in companies and in the mail. The purpose of the discount is to encourage customers to remit outstanding balances early. This improves the cash flow of the business. It would be unwise to refuse a customer payment because it is one day over the discount date.

Each customer is assigned a credit limit when buying at Land of Software. The credit limit is the maximum amount that the store will let a customer charge on his/her account. The normal level for approved individual customers is $2 500. If the owner is unsure about the reliability of a prospective customer and is having difficulty setting a credit limit, a credit check is run on the customer's financial background with the local Credit Bureau.

For larger corporate customers, a credit check is always run with the Credit Bureau, and the corporation may be asked for a recent set of financial statements. If these financial statements have been audited by public accountants they will, of course, be more reliable.

Once the credit limit for a customer has been established it can be reviewed on an annual basis. If a customer makes a habit of paying for goods within the 30-day time limit, then this enhances his/her credit rating and an increase in the credit limit may be in order.

Some accounts receivable may inevitably prove uncollectible, and must be written off as a **bad debt**. Regardless of how thoroughly a customer is investigated, bad debts do arise because of errors in judgment when assessing the credit limit, or because of unforeseen developments that make a customer suddenly risky. Establishing a credit limit for customers is a fine balance between avoiding losses by being too liberal, and rejecting profitable customers by being too conservative.

QUESTIONS

14. What is cycle billing?

15. Why does a business resort to cycle billing for its accounts receivable?

16. When would a business know that it should convert to cycle billing for its accounts receivable?

17. If you wanted to offer customers a 1% discount for paying their accounts within 15 days, how would this be written?

18. What does the term *credit limit* mean?

19. How does the owner of Land of Software decide what the credit limit will be for a particular customer? Try to think of three answers for this.

20. Should credit limits be adjusted often? Why? Why not?

5.4

Analysis and Reporting

The next important phases of accounts receivable work are analysing the balances in the accounts receivable ledger, determining the extent of uncollectible accounts, writing off bad debts, and reporting a fair figure for accounts receivable in the financial statements. The first step is to list the balances owing by individual customers.

ACCOUNTS RECEIVABLE TRIAL BALANCE

At the end of every month, an accounts receivable trial balance should be prepared. This is a listing of all customer accounts in the accounts receivable subsidiary ledger, and the balance due, which must match the balance in the Accounts Receivable control account. This schedule can be written with the same format heading as used for the trial balance of a general ledger.

```
                        Land of Software Inc.
                   Accounts Receivable Trial Balance
                        September 30, 19–

Ahmed, Jason                                    $ 2 080.80
Aziz, Barb                                         347.70
Beacon, Albert R.                               1 823.46
Bennett Signs                                   1 450.67
Coldwell, Lincoln                                 345.85
Craft Suppliers                                 3 220.19
```

Wong, Robert   887.63
Zaditz, Walter   2 080.80
Accounts Receivable Control Account   22 198.04

Total $22 198.04 $22 198.04

FIGURE 5-14   *Accounts receivable trial balance*

Accounts Receivable usually have a debit balance but occasionally a credit balance appears. This can occur when a customer overpays his/her account, returns merchandise for credit after paying for it, or is given a special allowance. The credit balance should theoretically be shown as a current liability. In practice, the credit is simply netted against the other debit balances in the trial balance, unless the credit balance was a significant amount and misrepresented the accounts receivable balance.

AGING ANALYSIS

Taking trial balance of the subsidiary ledger is a good method of making sure that the total of customer accounts agrees with the control account in the general ledger, but it does not indicate to the owner which accounts are more delinquent than others. This can be achieved through an aging of the accounts receivable balances. The length of time an amount has been outstanding has a bearing on whether or not it can be easily collected. An account 60 days past due is more likely to be collected than an account which is four months overdue.

An aging schedule is prepared by examining each customer's account and determining how old the balances are. Here is a partial schedule of the accounts receivable for Land of Software to illustrate what the aging schedule looks like:

			No. of Days Past Due			
Customer	Balance	Current	1 – 30	31 – 60	61 – 90	90+
Ahmed, Jason	$ 2 080.80	$ 2 080.80				
Aziz, Barb	347.70		$347.70			
Beacon, Albert R.	1 823.46	1 823.46				
Bennett Signs	1 450.67	1 450.67				
Coldwell, Lincoln	100.00					$100.00
Craft Suppliers	220.19				$220.19	
Wong, Robert	887.63	887.63				
Zaditz, Walter	2 080.80	2 080.80				
Total	$22 198.04	$21 184.30	$347.70	$345.85	$220.19	$100.00

Land of Software Inc.
Accounts Receivable Aging Schedule
September 30, 19–

FIGURE 5-15   Accounts receivable aging schedule

To understand how this aging analysis is prepared, Figure 5-16 shows a customer's statement with the actual entries for the past four months. This illustrates how the aging schedule is arrived at, based on the dates of the original invoices.

CALCULATION OF UNCOLLECTIBLE AMOUNT

Once the aging schedule has been prepared, it can be used to estimate what percentage of the older accounts will not be collected. See Figure 5-17. In many businesses this will be done by analysing the bad debt experience of previous years, or management intuition.

"If you miss a payment, I press this button and the unit self-destructs."

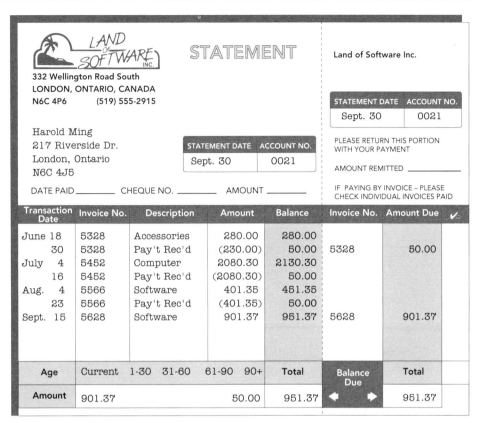

FIGURE 5-16 *Customer statement for four months*

Land of Software Inc.
Calculation of Uncollectible Amount
September 30, 19–

	Accounts Receivable	Estimated Loss Percentage	Uncollectible Amount
Current	$21 184.30	1%	$211.84
1 – 30 days	347.70	3	10.43
31 – 60 days	345.85	5	17.29
61 – 90 days	220.19	10	22.02
Over 90	100.00	40	40.00
	$22 198.04		$301.58

FIGURE 5-17 *Calculation of uncollectible amount*

The total of the Uncollectible Amount column should then be set up in the books as a debit to the Bad Debts Expense account and a credit to a contra account called Allowance for Doubtful Accounts.

DATE 19–		PARTICULARS	PR	DEBIT	CREDIT
Sept.	30	Bad Debts Expense		3 0 1 5 8	
		Allowance for Doubtful Accounts			3 0 1 5 8
		To set up allowance as per			
		uncollectible schedule			

FIGURE 5-18   The general journal entry for bad debts

WRITING OFF BAD DEBTS

Once the estimated uncollectibles have been calculated, any accounts receivable which are not subsequently collected must be written off to the Allowance for Doubtful Accounts account. When the original allowance is calculated at year end, the bad accounts remain in the ledger. When they are eventually officially recognized as bad debts, they are written off the books with a general journal entry. If we assume that Lincoln Coldwell will never pay his account balance, then we write off his account with this entry:

DATE 19–		PARTICULARS	PR	DEBIT	CREDIT
Oct.	12	Allowance for Doubtful Accounts		1 0 0 –	
		A/R—Lincoln Coldwell			1 0 0 –
		To write off a bad account			

FIGURE 5-19   The general journal entry to write off an account

RECOVERING AN ACCOUNT PREVIOUSLY WRITTEN OFF

Two months after the account was written off, Lincoln Coldwell paid his account in full. This means that the last entries for his account have to be reversed. The first entry sets up the $120 as an amount owing again:

GENERAL JOURNAL

PAGE 39

DATE 19–		PARTICULARS	PR	DEBIT	CREDIT
Dec.	15	A/R—Lincoln Coldwell		1 0 0 –	
		Allowance for Doubtful Accounts			1 0 0 –
		To reverse entry of Aug. 12 writing			
		off this account			

FIGURE 5-20   *The general journal entry to set up account receivable again*

Then the entry has to be made to record the collection of his account balance:

GENERAL JOURNAL

PAGE 39

DATE 19–		PARTICULARS	PR	DEBIT	CREDIT
Dec.	15	Bank		1 0 0 –	
		A/R—Lincoln Coldwell			1 0 0 –
		To record collection of bad debt			

FIGURE 5-21   *The general journal entry for account collection*

REPORTING

Accounts Receivable and the Allowance for Doubtful Accounts are shown as current assets on the balance sheet. The Allowance for Doubtful Accounts is a contra account because it has a credit balance and it belongs with the Accounts Receivable account. The difference between these two accounts is the net book value of the accounts receivable. This concept is similar to the net book value of fixed assets after the accumulated depreciation has been deducted. Figure 5-22 shows the balance sheet illustration.

```
                    Land of Software Inc.
                    Partial Balance Sheet
                    September 30, 19–

Current Assets:
  Bank                                                   $  13 990.36
  Accounts Receivable                      $22 198.04
    Less: Allowance for Doubtful Accounts     301.58      21 896.46

  Merchandise Inventory                                  164 113.18

  Total Current Assets                                   200 000.00
```

FIGURE 5-22   *Partial balance sheet*

Bad Debts are a normal expense of running a business and appear on the income statement.

```
                    Land of Software Inc.
                   Partial Income Statement
              For the Year Ended September 30, 19–

Revenue:
  Sales                                                  $240 000.00
    Less: Sales Returns and Allowances                     1 262.18

Net Sales                                                 238 737.82

Expenses:
  Advertising                              $3 621.12
  Bad Debts                                   301.58
  Bank Charges                              1 736.49
```

FIGURE 5-23   *Partial income statement*

QUESTIONS

21. What is an accounts receivable trial balance? How often is it prepared?

22. Assume that an accounts receivable trial balance has one account with a $45.00 credit balance. How would this be shown by the accountant on the financial statements?

23. Where does the data come from for an aging analysis?

24. How would the owner/manager of a business know what percentage of accounts will prove to be uncollectible?

25. What does the term *write off* mean when applied to accounts receivable?

26. If an account which has been written off is collected, what entries have to be made in the books to correct this?

27. What contra account appears on the balance sheet with the Accounts Receivable control balance?

5.5

Notes Receivable

Most businesses do not have Notes Receivable, since the purpose of service, merchandising, or manufacturing concerns is to sell goods and services, not to loan money. Notes receivable would be used where a business is willing to assist customers with the financing of a major purchase by financing it over a longer period of time than 30 days. Some examples would be businesses that sell high-priced durable goods such as farm machinery, heavy industrial machinery, or automobiles.

Let's assume, for an illustration on this point, that Land of Software received an order for 60 microcomputers for The Great Canadian Life Insurance Company. Because this order will be for approximately $180 000, it is a large sum to be paid at once. Land of Software has agreed to sell the goods and accept a note receivable for the total bill. A **note receivable** is a promise in writing to pay a certain amount at a future time for goods or services received. The note is for 90 days and bears interest at a rate of 14% per annum. The actual amount of the sale will be calculated this way:

60 Microcomputers @ $2 608.70 = $156 522.00
Plus 7% GST = $ 10 956.54
Plus 8% PST = $ 12 521.76

Total = $180 000.30

The balance owing is recorded as a note receivable instead of an account receivable because:

(1) the buyer has been given 90 days to pay instead of the usual 30 days allowed on ordinary accounts receivable,
(2) the rate of interest is 14% per annum, rather than the usual 2% interest charged on overdue accounts receivable,
(3) a note receivable requires a formal signed document, and
(4) the interest of 14% will be calculated and paid monthly by the buyer to Land of Software.

The accounting entry for this note, in general journal form is:

GENERAL JOURNAL

PAGE 39

DATE 19–		PARTICULARS	PR	DEBIT	CREDIT
Dec.	14	Note Receivable		180 000 30	
		Sales			156 522 –
		GST Payable			10 956 54
		PST Payable			12 521 76
		To set up note for invoice 5790			

FIGURE 5-24   *The general journal entry for a note receivable*

Notes receivable can be posted to an account directly in the general ledger because the notes will be filed by their due dates, and the notes will act as a subsidiary ledger.

The interest on the note is a form of revenue. Interest for the first month will be calculated as:

$180\ 000.30 \times 14\% \times \frac{1}{12} = \$2\ 100.00$

The journal entry for the interest will be:

GENERAL JOURNAL

PAGE 39

DATE 19–		PARTICULARS	PR	DEBIT	CREDIT
Jan.	14	Bank		2 100 –	
		Interest Income			2 100 –
		Interest on note receivable for			
		one month			

FIGURE 5-25   *The general journal entry for interest*

In three months this note will mature. Assuming that The Great Canadian Life Insurance Company pays the note and the final month's interest on that maturity date, the accounting entry would be:

GENERAL JOURNAL

PAGE 58

DATE 19–		PARTICULARS	PR	DEBIT	CREDIT
Mar.	14	Bank		1821 00 –	
		Note Receivable			1800 00 –
		Interest Income			21 00 –
		To record payment of note and last			
		month's interest			

FIGURE 5-26 *The general journal entry for payment of note + interest*

The topic of notes receivable is extensive, and this is only a cursory glance into the topic. The balance sheet presentation for notes receivable depends on the maturity date of the note. Notes due in less than a year are current and shown under the current assets section of the balance sheet. Notes due in more than a year should be shown under the heading Long-Term Investments.

QUESTIONS

28. Explain, briefly, how a note receivable differs from an account receivable.

29. What are some examples of goods that are financed through the issue of notes receivable?

30. Outline some of the characteristics of a note receivable.

31. How often is interest paid on a note receivable?

32. What does the term *maturity date* mean with regard to a note receivable?

33. A note receivable for $120 000 is to be paid back in four months. How will this amount be shown on the balance sheet of the business?

5.6

Using the Computer

The computer can be used to prepare special reports relating to accounts receivable by using an integrated software package that has spreadsheet, graphics, database, and word processing components.

Spreadsheets

An example of a spreadsheet activity in accounts receivable would be the preparation of a schedule showing the calculation of the uncollectible amounts. Here is an example that might be used for Land of Software:

```
             A              B           C             D
  1  Land of Software Inc.
  2  Calculation of Uncollectible Amount
  3  September 30, 19-
  4
  5                     Accounts       % Loss       Amount
  6  Current           21184.30          1          211.84
  7  1 - 30 days         347.70          3           10.43
  8  31 - 60 days        345.85          5           17.29
  9  61 - 90 days        220.19         10           22.02
 10  > 90 days           100.00         40           40.00
 11                   _____                   _____
 12  Total            22198.04                      301.58
 13                   =========                   =========
 14
```

FIGURE 5-27   *A spreadsheet schedule*

The headings are all a permanent part of the spreadsheet; only the data in column B will change each month (or each time the schedule is prepared). Once the new data is inserted in column B, the rest of the spreadsheet is calculated automatically and the new total for the uncollectibles arrived at.

Graphics

Spreadsheets are used to produce graphs on the computer. Most integrated software packages have this feature. Once the spreadsheet is stored, one of several types of graphs can be produced. The three main types would be a bar graph, a line graph, or a pie graph. The example shown in Figure 5-28 is a line graph. It shows the accounts receivable balances for Land of Software for the last three years, month by month.

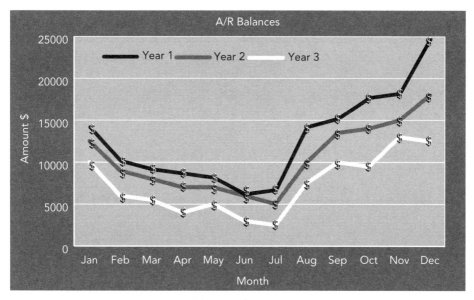

FIGURE 5-28   A computer-generated line graph

A quick look indicates that (assuming sales have been constant) the business has been quite successful in reducing the accounts receivable balances over the three-year period. The big advantage of graphs is the quick visual impression that owners or managers obtain from them.

Databases

A good example of a database for Land of Software is a list of those people who have requested to be on a mailing list for updated product information.

```
Name:  Becker, B.
Address:  44 Paul Street
Town:  London                         one record
PC:  N6H 1L2
User Code:  H
```

```
CUSTOMER MAILING LIST
Name                Address          Town      PC          User
Anderson, W.        401 Nelson St.   London    N6B 1A6      H
Becker, B.          44 Paul Street   London    N6H 1L2      H
Cooper Garage       705 Dundas St.   London    N5W 2Z4      C
Drew Street P.S.    88 Drew St.      London    N7T 2T9      E
Emerson S.S.        1013 Eren Ave.   London    N6E 2B3      E
```

The top part of the diagram shows the form used when the database is set up and stored. The lower part is a listing of the customers' names, addresses, towns, and postal codes, along with a code designating the type of user as commercial (C), educational (E), or home user (H). This code helps Land of Software direct computer and software information to specific users.

Word Processing

Land of Software has "A Friendly Reminder" that it mails to customers who have been somewhat delinquent in paying their overdue accounts.

LAND OF SOFTWARE
332 Wellington Road South
LONDON, ONTARIO N6C 4P6

(519) 555-2915

TO _____

A FRIENDLY REMINDER

CUSTOMER REPLY

☐ Full payment enclosed
☐ Partial payment enclosed in the amount of $ _____
☐ Payment previously mailed on _____ Cheque No. _____

➡ This is a reminder that there is a balance due on your account which may have been overlooked.

If your cheque is already in the mail, please accept our thanks. If not, please take a minute now and send us your payment. Thank you!

COMMENTS:
_____
_____
_____
_____
_____

DATE OF REMINDER

INVOICE NUMBER(S) _____
DATE PAYMENT DUE _____
AMOUNT DUE $ _____

SIGNED _____
DATE _____

FIGURE 5-29   *A friendly reminder*

The form is stored on the computer using a special form program that allows information to be word processed into the form. The operator merely adds the name and address of the customer, the invoice date, the date payment is due, and amount due. The form is then printed and mailed to the customer.

5.7

Bedford Exercise 5 — Jordan Landscaping

Jordan Landscaping is a small business owned by Cliff Jordan, a graduate of a community college landscaping program. The business is located in Ottawa. In the off-season, Cliff earns income by performing consulting services. He designs landscape projects for clients so that when the weather is favourable he can do the actual work. In this exercise, the income is all for consulting work. In Chapter 6, Cliff receives income for actual landscaping work performed.

You are a student in a two-year financial management program at a local junior college, and have been hired for the summer to assist in working with the *ACCPAC Bedford Integrated Accounting* software package.

The mid-year trial balance is as shown.

Jordan Landscaping
Mid-Year Trial Balance

No.	Account	Debit	Credit
110	Bank	$ 13 380.00	
120	Accounts Receivable	17 305.11	
130	GST Recoverable	200.00	
140	Prepaid Office Supplies	640.00	
141	Prepaid Drafting Supplies	1 260.00	
180	Drafting Equipment	35 800.00	
181	Acc. Dep. — Drafting Equipment		$ 7 160.00
190	Truck	22 000.00	
191	Acc. Dep. — Truck		6 600.00
210	Bank Loan		10 000.00
220	A/P Cano Drafting Supplies		3 905.50
230	GST Payable		876.61
240	CPP Payable		676.00
241	UI Payable		842.00
242	Income Tax Payable		2 142.00
310	C. Jordan, Capital		64 854.00
315	C. Jordan, Drawings	16 000.00	
410	Consulting Income		74 210.98

510	Advertising Expense	360.00	
515	CPP Expense	2 704.00	
520	Dep. Exp. — Drafting Equipment	2 386.72	
521	Dep. Exp. — Truck	2 200.00	
525	Drafting Supplies Expense	4 690.73	
530	Interest Expense	783.50	
540	Office Supplies Expense	979.68	
545	Rent Expense	10 000.00	
570	Salaries Expense	32 000.00	
580	Telephone Expense	520.00	
585	Truck Expense	4 000.00	
590	UI Expense	689.51	
595	Utilities Expense	3 367.84	
		$171 267.09	$171 267.09

The accounts and all of the historical balances have been entered onto a data disk for you, and the computer accounting system only has to be set to **Ready** mode. The instructions for using *Bedford* are outlined in Chapter 1.

ACCESSING THE JORDAN LANDSCAPING GENERAL LEDGER

To retrieve the general ledger for Jordon Landscaping, you use the file name **jordlan5**. Key this name into the computer, insert the dates provided by your teacher, and set the program to **Ready**, as described in Chapter 1.

Enter the **Using** date provided by your teacher. Remember the sequence, mmddyy. As before, ignore the cautions and proceed.

SETTING UP THE ACCOUNTS RECEIVABLE LEDGER

For this exercise, you will be using the **GENERAL** Ledger module and the Accounts **RECEIVABLE** Ledger module in *Bedford*.

The accounts receivable listing is as shown.

Jordan Landscaping
Accounts Receivable Listing

Howards, S. (Invoice S455)	$ 2 794.84
Locke, M. (Invoice S459)	3 577.01
Peterson, P. (Invoice S457)	3 905.50
Suttcombe, A. (Invoice S458)	4 996.90
Therault, C. (Invoice S456)	2 030.86
	$17 305.11

The **RECEIVABLE** module will have to be made ready before you start to journalize any transactions. This involves three steps.

Step 1 *Enter the balances above into the Accounts* **RECEIVABLE** *sub-ledger.*
  Select **RECEIVABLE**, **History**, and **Sale**.

Step 2 *Set the integration accounts.*
  Select **SYSTEM**, **Integrate**, **Receivable**, and key in the account numbers, as shown:

```
          Cash        110
          AccRec      120
```

Step 3 *Make the* **RECEIVABLE** *module ready.*
  Select **SYSTEM**, **Default**, **Module**, and **Receivable**. Change **Ready** to **Yes**. Return to the main status line.

JOURNALIZING TRANSACTIONS

To journalize general ledger transactions, access the **GENERAL** module and the **Journal** option.

To journalize accounts receivable transactions, access the **RECEIVABLE** module and the **Journal** option.

TRANSACTIONS

1. Cash Receipt (**RECEIVABLE, Journal, Payment**)   Dated: mm02yy
   Cheque received from S. Howards, $2 794.84; in full payment of invoice
   S455; their cheque 1210.

2. Cheque 549 (**GENERAL, Journal**)   Dated: mm02yy
   Cheque to Ontario Properties Ltd. for $2 500 plus GST $175, for the
   monthly rent.

3. To record this transaction, you will have to enter a new account in the
   RECEIVABLE sub-ledger. To do this, select **RECEIVABLE, Ledger**,
   and **Insert**; and key in this data:
   L. Novakowski: 6309 Baseline Road, Ottawa, Ontario, K3F 4B5,
   555-6767. (Answer Y to the **Purge** question and Y to the
   Statement question.)

   Sales Invoice S460 (**RECEIVABLE, Journal, Sale**)   Dated: mm03yy
   Invoice to L. Novakowski, $3 568 plus GST $249.76, for consulting
   income. Terms n/30.

4. Sales Invoice S461   Dated: mm03yy
   Invoice to C. Therault, $1 600 plus GST $112, for consulting income.
   Terms n/30.

5. Cheque 550   Dated: mm09yy
   Payment to Cano Drafting Supplies, $3 905.50 for their invoice L556.
   No discount available.

6. To record this transaction, you will have to enter a new account in the
   RECEIVABLE sub-ledger. To do this, select **RECEIVABLE, Ledger**,
   and **Insert**; and key in this data:
   M. Lawton: 6400 Cartier Avenue, Ottawa, Ontario, K5G 6T9;
   555-8000. (Answer Y to the **Purge** question and Y to the
   Statement question.)

   Sales Invoice S462   Dated: mm11yy
   Invoice to M. Lawton, $2 272 plus GST $159.04, for consulting income.
   Terms n/30.

7. To record this transaction, you will have to enter a new account in the
   GENERAL ledger. To do this, select **GENERAL, Ledger**, and
   Insert; and key in the following data:

Name: A/P Abblass Office Supply
Number: 221
Type: R
Suppress: Y

Purchase Invoice 223   Dated: mm12yy
Purchased office supplies from Abblass Office Supply, $486 plus $31.50
GST. Terms net 10.

8. Cheque 551   Dated: mm14yy
Paid Bell Canada for telephone expense, $180.30 plus GST $11.69.

9. Cheque 552   Dated: mm14yy
Payment to the Receiver General of Canada, $676.61, for net GST
collected in June. (GST Payable $876.61 less GST Recoverable $200.)

10. Cheque 553   Dated: mm14yy
Payment to the Receiver General of Canada, $3 660, for payroll
deductions from June; CPP Payable $676, UI Payable $842, Income Tax
Payable $2 142.

11. To record this transaction, you will have to enter a new account in the
RECEIVABLE sub-ledger. To do this, select **RECEIVABLE**,
Ledger, and **Insert**; and key in this data:
R. Lemieux: 6189 Champlain Drive, Ottawa, Ontario, K3T 6B3,
555-5070. (Answer Y to the **Purge** question and Y to the
Statement question.)

Sales Invoice S463   Dated: mm17yy
Invoice to R. Lemieux, $1 750 plus GST $122.50, for consulting
income. Terms n/30.

12. Cash Receipt   Dated: mm17yy
Cheque received from C. Therault, $2 030.86; in full payment of
invoice S456; their cheque 1111.

13. Cheque 554   Dated: mm20yy
Payment to Abblass Office Suppliers, $517.50. Full payment of
invoice 223.

14. Purchase Invoice 4496   Dated: mm21yy
Bought drafting supplies on account from Cano Drafting Supplies,
$2 098.44 plus $136.01 GST. Terms net 10.

15. Bank Debit Memo   Dated: mm21yy
    Payment made on bank loan to Bank of Nova Scotia, $2 000 plus
    interest $130.

16. Cash Receipt   Dated: mm23yy
    Cheque received from P. Peterson, $3 905.50; in full payment of invoice
    S457; their cheque 9339.

17. Cash Receipt   Dated: mm25yy
    Cheque received from A. Suttcombe, $4 996.90; in full payment of
    invoice S458; their cheque 2676.

18. Cash Receipt   Dated: mm27yy
    Cheque received from M. Locke, $3 577.01; in full payment of invoice
    S459; their cheque 0752.

19. Cash Receipt   Dated: mm27yy
    Cheque received from L. Novakowski, $3 817.76; in full payment of
    invoice S460; their cheque 2266.

20. Cheque 555   Dated: mm29yy
    Owner withdrew $3 000 from the bank for personal use.

21. Cheque 556   Dated: mm30yy
    Paid Ontario Hydro, $269 plus GST $18.83.

22. To record this transaction, you will have to enter a new account in the
    RECEIVABLE sub-ledger. To do this, select **RECEIVABLE**,
    Ledger, and **Insert**; and key in this data:
    S. Chang: 8008 Velcour Drive, Ottawa, Ontario, K4l 3Z5, 555-1712.
    (Answer Y to the **Purge** question and Y to the **Statement** question).

    Sales Invoice S464   Dated: mm30yy
    Invoice to S. Chang, $1 792 plus GST Payable $125.44, for consulting
    income. Terms n/30.

23. Voucher 109   Dated: mm30yy
    Adjust the accounts for office supplies used, $865; drafting supplies
    used, $2 106.

24. Voucher 110   Dated: mm30yy
    Adjust the accounts for estimated depreciation expense incurred:
    Drafting Equipment, $477; Automobiles, $385.

25. Voucher 111   Dated: mm30yy
    Record month-end payroll entry. Total Salaries Expense $9 000; CPP Payable $338, UI Payable $351, Income Tax Payable $2 142, net pay transferred to the payroll bank account, $6 169.

26. Voucher 112   Dated: mm30yy
    Record employer's payroll taxes; CPP Expense $338, UI Expense $491.40.

DISPLAYING AND PRINTING

Select **Display**. Your teacher will advise you which of the six options to preview. You may be prompted for dates. Remember, a date is entered in the sequence mmddyy (month/day/year).

Print any statements requested by your teacher. Again, you may be prompted for dates.

FINISHING A SESSION

Access the **SYSTEM** module and select the **Finish** option.

5.8

Dictionary of Accounting Terms

Accounts Receivable   Amounts due to the business in the near future that arise from charge sales, i.e. sales made on account.

Accounts Receivable Ledger   A group of accounts containing all the transactions for charge or credit customers of the business.

Aging Analysis   A table showing the accounts receivable of a business and the length of time these have been outstanding.

Bad Debt   A customer account deemed to be uncollectible at year end.

Cash Receipt   A cash sale or a receipt on account from a customer.

Cash Receipts Journal   A book of original entry in which all cash received by a business is first recorded, along with bank credit memos.

Charge Sale   A sale whereby the customer agrees in writing to pay on a later date for goods or services received.

Contra Account   An account which is paired with another account and has an opposing balance.

Control Account   The main Accounts Receivable account in the general ledger.

Credit Invoice   A document issued to a customer to reduce accounts receivable, or received from a supplier to reduce accounts payable.

Discounts Allowed   A percentage applied to a sale to reduce the payment made by a customer.

Internal Control   The methods used to safeguard assets and ensure the accurate recording of transactions in the books of account.

Monthly Statement   A report sent to a customer or received from a supplier showing the purchases and payments made during the past month.

Note Receivable   A promise in writing to pay a certain amount at a future time for goods or services received.

On Account   A term which refers to amounts owed by customers who buy goods or services and pay for them at a later date.

Receipt on Account   A source document prepared when cash is received to reduce a customer's balance owing.

Sales Journal   A book of original entry used to record all charge sales and credit invoices issued to customers.

Sales Returns and Allowances   A contra account which offsets the Sales account of a business.

MANUAL EXERCISES

1. Record these transactions on page 14 in a sales journal for the month of January. Total and balance the journal. There is no PST payable, as this business is in Alberta. The GST is 7%.

   Jan.   1:   Invoice #1125 to L. Lamb, $340 plus GST.
            3:   Invoice #1126 to H. Dykeman, $128 plus GST.
            5:   Credit Invoice #1127 to L. Lamb for defective goods, $75 plus GST.
          10:   Invoice #1128 to Jackie Chong, $85 plus GST.
          15:   Invoice #1129, $450 plus GST to M. McCann.
          18:   Invoice #1130, $1 240 plus GST to G. Overbaugh.

23: Credit Invoice #1131 to M. McCann, $25 plus GST.
24: Invoice #1132, $181.12 plus GST to D. Yates.
27: Credit Invoice #1133, $18.50 plus GST to D. Yates.
31: Invoice #1134 to C. Joshi, $1 012.12 plus GST.

2. Record these transactions on page 9 in a sales journal for the month of February. Total and balance the journal. PST of 7% is applied to the base price only. The GST is 7%.

Feb. 1: Invoice #660 to W. Zavitz, $75 plus taxes.
      3: Invoice #661 to B. Drake, $128 plus taxes.
      5: Credit Invoice #42 to P. Post for defective goods, $42.50 plus taxes.
     10: Invoice #662 to W. Kellar, $138 plus taxes.
     10: Credit Invoice #43, W. Zavitz, $12.40 plus taxes.
     15: Invoice #663, $125.60 plus taxes to Dr. J. Naranscik.
     16: Credit Invoice #44 to Dr. J. Naranscik for an overcharge of $12.00 plus taxes.
     15: Invoice #664, $210.10 plus taxes to L. Nye.
     18: Invoice #665, $48.50 plus taxes to G. Cheun.
     23: Credit Invoice #45, to G. Cheun, $22 plus taxes.
     27: Invoice #666, $88.88 plus taxes to A. Quay.
     28: Invoice #667, $55.55 plus taxes to T. Urolenut.

3. Record these transactions on page 16 in a sales journal for the month of March. Label an extra revenue column as "Repair Income". Total and balance the journal. PST is 6% and is applied to the base price only. The GST is 7%.

Mar. 2: To Rose Rockwell, $1 235.46 plus taxes; invoice #570. Credit to Sales.
      4: To Kal Kaunda, $776.68 plus taxes; invoice #571. Credit to Repair Income.
      6: To Dee Gagan, $313.31 plus taxes; invoice #572. Credit to Sales.
      9: To Anthony Cervini, $2 345.76 plus taxes; invoice #573. Credit to Sales.
     13: Credit Invoice #30 to Kal Kaunda, $35.12 for a defective part, plus taxes. Charge to Sales Returns and Allowances.
     16: To Fred Maxim, invoice #574, $212.16 plus taxes; for repairs.
     17: To Freda Browning, invoice #575, $304.04 plus taxes. Credit to Sales.

18:   Credit Invoice #31 to Fred Maxim, $44.44 for a defective part, plus taxes. Charge to Sales Returns and Allowances.

21:   Invoice #576, $18.95 plus taxes to Ann Gurd. Credit to Sales.

25:   Credit Invoice #32 to Ann Gurd, $18.95 for a defective part, plus taxes. Charge to Sales Returns and Allowances.

28:   Invoice #577, $102.08 to Phil Poole, plus taxes. Credit to Sales.

31:   Invoice #578, $80.80 plus taxes to Hilda Pye. Credit to Sales.

4. Record these transactions on page 16 in a cash receipts journal for the month of April. Total and balance the journal. The PST is 8% and is calculated on the base price only. GST is 7%.

Apr.   3:   Carol Pevler paid invoice #85, totalling $250, less 2% discount.

4:   Mary Miletic paid invoice #112, totalling $710, less 2% discount.

8:   The owner, Al Bruvelaitis, invested $8 000 in the business.

11:   Cash sale, $175 plus taxes; invoice #120.

11:   Mary Anne Verboom paid her account in full, $602.34. It was too late for any discount.

13:   Norbert Baertson paid his account in full, totalling $503.05, less 2% discount.

16:   Cash sale, $330 plus taxes.

20:   Borrowed $12 000 from National Trust.

21:   Bernd Stucke paid his account in full, $400. No discount.

30:   Gord Farqhuar paid his account, totalling $650, in full after deducting 2% discount.

5. Record these transactions on page 21 in a cash receipts journal for the month of May. Total and balance the journal. The PST rate is 10% and is calculated on the base price plus GST (7%).

May   2:   Received on account $124 less 2% discount, from Carol Steinberg.

4:   Received on account $145.90 less 2% discount, from Paul Drake.

4:   Cash sale, $712.20 plus taxes.

8:   Cash sale, $1 011.39 plus taxes.

11:   Received on account $232.18 less 2% discount, from D. Street.

12:   Received on account $924.48 less 2% discount, from Abigail Alabaster.

19:   Borrowed $4 500 from the Royal Bank.

21:   Cash sale, $556.83 plus taxes.

24:   Received on account $260.01 less 2% discount, from Harold Hill.

28:   Received on account $86.67 less 2% discount, from Jim Shaunessy.

29:    Received on account $346.68 less 2% discount, from Jane Powley.

31:    Received on account $113.25 less 2% discount, from Alan Khan.

6. Record these transactions on page 14 in a cash receipts journal for the month of June. Total and balance the journal. The PST rate is 11% and is calculated on the base price plus GST (7%).

June   1:   Cash sale $414.14 plus taxes.

2:    Owner Gail Godelie invested $4 000 in the business.

5:    Received on account $520.02 less 1% discount, from Tom Peazel.

8:    Received on account $837.81 less 1% discount, from Cornelius Van Der Woeden.

10:    Received on account $707.23 less 1% discount, from Jane Ryksen.

12:    Cash sale, $1 895.50 plus taxes.

15:    Cash sale, $2 214.75 plus taxes.

22:    Received on account $1 386.72 less 1% discount, from Carolyn Irving.

23:    Received on account $600.91 less 1% discount, from Dan Vanbesien.

24:    Cash sale, $236.85 plus taxes.

25:    Cash sale, $362.58 plus taxes.

29:    Received on account $462.24 less 1% discount, from Paul Hunyadi.

7. Record these transactions on page 27 in a sales journal or a cash receipts journal for the month of July. Terms are 2/10, n/30. There is no provincial tax applicable for this question. GST is 7%.

July   2:   Invoice #634, $125.25 plus GST to Greg Hilborn.

3:    Invoice #635, $501.01 plus GST to Ellen Avola.

5:    Cash sale, $114.56 plus GST, invoice #636.

5:    Received on account $1 072.40 less 2% discount, from Allyson Caslick.

8:    Cash invested into the business by the owner, Karen Gehring, $18 000.

10:    Invoice #637, $84.30 plus GST to Lonnie Hudson.

12:    Credit invoice #638 to Lonnie Hudson for defective goods, $48 plus GST.

12:    Invoice #639, $276.76 plus GST to Marlene Majernik.

15:    Invoice #640, $310.10 plus GST to Marg Freure.

17:    Cash sale, $615.15 plus GST; invoice #641.

19:    Received on account $624.02 from Don Dittmer, no discount.

22:   Received on account payment in full from Marg Freure for invoice #640, less 2% discount.

22:   Invoice #642, $18.98 plus GST to Ravi Ramashar.

23:   Received payment in full from Marlene Majernik for invoice #639, less 2% discount.

24:   Cash sale, $66.98 plus GST; invoice #643.

25:   Credit invoice #644 to Ravi Ramashar for defective goods, $18.98 plus GST.

26:   Borrowed $1 500 from the bank.

28:   Invoice #645, $830 plus GST to Gus Melapolis.

29:   Invoice #646, $1 020 plus GST to Yuri Gagarov.

31:   Received on account, $200 from Ravi Ramashar.

8. Indicate how these accounts would be classified. For each account state whether current or long term for assets and liabilities; and whether balance sheet or income statement.

(a) accounts receivable   (f) bad debts expense
(b) notes receivable (due in six months)   (g) interest income
(c) allowance for doubtful accounts   (h) sales returns and allowances
(d) interest receivable   (i) sales
(e) notes receivable (due in eighteen months)

9. Journalize these transactions on page 19 in a general journal.

Dec. 31:   Set up the allowance for doubtful accounts in the amount of $1 800.
Mar. 31:   Wrote off the account for Rae Rose, $238.50.
Apr. 30:   Wrote off the account for Helen Lamb, $180.20.

10. Journalize these transactions on page 23 in a general journal.

Dec. 31:   Set up the allowance for doubtful accounts in the amount of $2 800.
Mar. 31:   Wrote off the account for Janet Robb, $310.48.
Apr. 12:   Janet paid her account in full. (Hint: Two transactions.)

11. Journalize these transactions on page 24 in a general journal.

Dec. 31:   Increased the allowance for doubtful accounts balance to $1 800 from $1 400.
Mar. 31:   Wrote off the account for Sky Traher, $75.40.
      31:   Wrote off the account for Trevor Caldwell, $80.
Apr. 28:   Sky Traher paid her account in full.

12. Prepare a formal aging schedule for DeJong Pallets as of November 30th given this data:

Customer	Balance	Description
Amorey, C.	$ 209.09	Current
Bush, G.	$ 883.43	28 days
Foche, N.	$1 124.50	Current
Gibson, G.	$ 177.33	57 days
Ireland H.	$ 606.56	15 days
Jong, J.	$ 18.14	91 days
Lang, K.	$ 120.49	31 days
Monroe, F.	$ 25.00	75 days
Towne, T.	$ 850.00	Current

13. Use the data from exercise 12 and complete a formal schedule for uncollectible accounts:

Balances	% uncollectible
Current	1%
0 – 30 days	4%
31 – 60 days	10%
61 – 90 days	20%
Over 90 days	50%

14. Journalize these note receivable transactions for Land of Software on page 33 in a general journal. GST is 7%; PST is 8% calculated on base price only.

Jan.   2:   Sold 20 computers for $34 000 plus taxes; invoice #5200. Accepted a 90-day, 14% note receivable for the balance owing from Farkas Marketing.

Feb.   2:   Received the first cheque for interest on the note receivable.

Apr.   2:   The note matured and was paid in full plus the last month's interest owing.

15. Journalize these note receivable transactions for Land of Software on page 33 in a general journal. Taxes are as in exercise 14.

Feb.   1:   Sold 30 computers for $1 730.71 plus taxes; invoice #5432. (Round to whole dollars). Accepted a 6-month, 14% note receivable for the balance owing from Sulu Accounting Services.

Feb.   28:   Received the first cheque for interest on the note receivable.

Jul.   31:   The note was paid in full plus the last month's interest owing.

16. (a) Open an Accounts Receivable control account and subsidiary ledger
    accounts with the following balances: A/R control (120) $1 141.69;
    R. Cascia $577.80; M. Reisner $161.78; V. Vindasius $402.11. Other account
    balances include Cash (110) $16 742.90; GST Payable (221) $1 073.21;
    PST Payable (222) $1 123.21; I. Shenton, Capital (310) $68 692.74.
    Open further accounts as required.
(b) Record these transactions on page 17 in a sales journal, or on page 26
    in a cash receipts journal for August. The PST rate of 8% is applied to
    the base price only. GST is 7%.

Aug.   2:   Invoice #110, $257.67 plus taxes to Gloria Huang.
            All terms are 2/10, n/30.
       4:   Cash sale $111.99 plus taxes; invoice #111.
       6:   Received on account, $577.80 less 2% discount, from Rae Cascia.
       8:   Received on account payment in full from Gloria Huang,
            for invoice #110, less 2% discount.
      11:   Invoice #112, $48.98 plus taxes to Paul Christo.
      13:   Invoice #113, $374.20 plus taxes to Saul Rosenberg.
      14:   Cash sale $418.95 plus taxes; invoice #114.
      15:   Invoice #115, $98.00 plus taxes to Jack Glendinning.
      17:   Credit invoice #116 to Saul Rosenberg, for defective goods,
            $50 plus taxes.
      17:   Received on account payment in full from Paul Christo for
            invoice #112.
      18:   Invoice #117, $424.80 plus taxes to Cardy Wells.
      19:   Invoice #118, $600.00 plus taxes to Ron Ross.
      20:   Received on account $161.78 from Murray Reisner.
            No discount.
      21:   Cash invested into the business by the owner, Isabel Shenton,
            $9 000.
      21:   Cash sale $44.44 plus taxes; invoice #119.
      23:   Credit invoice #120 to Cardy Wells, adjustment on pricing error
            re invoice #117, $24.00 plus taxes.
      25:   Invoice #121, $32 plus taxes to Tony Cruzzea.
      27:   Invoice #122, $218.70 plus taxes to Bill Yaz.
      29:   Received on account payment on full from Saul Rosenberg.
            No discount.
      31:   Borrowed $6 000 from the bank.

(c) Take a trial balance of the subsidiary ledger.
(d) Post the journals to the appropriate ledger accounts, making the appro-
    priate posting references on the journals.

COMPUTER EXERCISES

SS1 Use a spreadsheet to produce this accounts receivable listing. Increase the width of column A to 15 characters. Program the spreadsheet to calculate the total of the A/R column. Save your solution on disk under the file name CH5SS1.

	A	B
1	ACCOUNTS RECEIVABLE	LISTING
2	AUGUST 31, 19-	
3	Customer	A/R Dr.
4	Bulaki, O.	1224.65
5	Dai N.	2345.19
6	Frank, P.	3554.09
7	Hiller, M.	2852.76
8	Harris, R.	998.40
9		————
10	TOTAL	?
11		═══

SS2 Use a spreadsheet to produce this accounts receivable listing. Increase the width of column A to 15 characters. Program the spreadsheet to calculate the total of the A/R column. Save your solution on disk under the file name CH5SS2.

	A	B
1	The Sandman	
2	ACCOUNTS RECEIVABLE	LISTING
3	June 30, 19-	
4	Customer	A/R Dr.
5	Anderson, L.	21242.50
6	Butkowski, B.	22333.76
7	Capriatti, J.	34556.74
8	Daignard, D.	18446.09
9	Eversham, T.	15665.49
10	Fong, W.	10401.04
11		————
12	Total	?
13		═══

SS3 Create this aging schedule template on the computer using a spreadsheet. Set the width of column A to 15 characters. Program the schedule to add the columns. Save the template under the file name CH5SS3.

	A	B	C	D	E	F	G
1	x----·x						
2	AGING SCHEDULE						
3	x----·x						
4	Customer	Balance	Curr.	1-30	31-60	61-90	Over
5	x----·x	xxx.xx					
6	x----·x	xxx.xx					
7	x----·x	xxx.xx					
8	x----·x	xxx.xx					
9	x----·x	xxx.xx					
10	x----·x	xxx.xx					
11							
12	Total	?	?	?	?	?	?
13							

SS4 Recall the aging schedule template CH5SS3 and insert this data. Print the resulting schedule on the printer.

	A	B	C	D	E	F	G
1	Bits and Bytes						
2	AGING SCHEDULE						
3	July 31, 19-						
4	Customer	Balance	Curr.	1-30	31-60	61-90	Over
5	Ault, D.	540.60	540.60				
6	Briggs, D.	222.31		222.31			
7	Cole Q.	345.09	245.09				100.00
8	Dipp, K.	28.10				28.10	
9	Eagle, M.	505.92		505.92			
10	Fitch, R.	101.83			101.83		
11							
12	Total	?	?	?	?	?	?
13							

SS5   Create this calculation of uncollectible amounts. Set column A to a width of 15 characters. Set columns B and D to a width of 10, and column C to a width of 6 places. Program the spreadsheet to do the required calculations, and save the template under the file name CH5SS5.

```
            A              B            C            D
 1   KRC Variety
 2   CALCULATION OF UNCOLLECTIBLE AMOUNTS
 3   August 31, 19-
 4                                             Uncoll-
 5                        A/R          Loss %   ectible
 6   Not Yet Due         6200            1         ?
 7   1-30 Days           1112            3         ?
 8   31-60 Days           445            5         ?
 9   61-90 Days           300           10         ?
10   Over 90 Days         175           40         ?
11                       _____         _____     _____
12   Totals                ?                       ?
13                       =====         =====     =====
```

SS6   Recall the calculation of uncollectible amount schedule, CH5SS6. Change the company name to KEC Manufacturing, and the date to September 30, 19–. Change Column B to these new figures. Print the new schedule on the printer.

	A/R
Not Yet Due	$23 445
1-30 Days	3 218
31-60 Days	1 667
61-90 Days	2 440
Over 90 Days	900

SS7   Create this notes receivable interest schedule. Program the spreadsheet to calculate the answers in column D (column A x column B). Save your spreadsheet under the file name CH5SS7.

```
         A              B            C
1    NOTES RECEIVABLE INTEREST SCHEDULE
2                                 Monthly
3       Amount        Rate %      Interest
4        15000        14.5           ?
5        28000        15.2           ?
6        50000        18.1           ?
7       128000        14.5           ?
8       212000        15.0           ?
9       250000        19.0           ?
```

SS8   Recall file CH5SS7 and change the Amount column to these figures. Print your new table on the printer.

```
   Amount
$ 24 500
$ 36 700
$110 000
$ 95 700
$ 66 000
$ 77 400
```

DB1   Create a customer database for The Basket Case. Define the following fields for your file.

```
Name            = 15 columns
Address         = 15 columns
Town            = 10 columns
Postal Code     =  7 columns
Balance Owing   = 10 columns
```

Enter the raw data shown below, and program the database to add up the customer balances.

Name	Address	Town	PC	Balance
Mackie, G.	12 South St.	Halifax	B2C 3H1	$1 309.07
Williams, R.	245 Sea Dr.	Halifax	B3F 4G4	$2 995.44
Hillner, R.	45 1st Ave.	Halifax	B2C 3H2	$ 865.76
Winrow, P.	300 Bridge Cr.	Halifax	B3J 2L2	$1 823.04
Crewe, D.	111 Fine Cr.	Halifax	B4D 1S3	$ 660.60
Aspen, O.	3 Ocean Dr.	Halifax	B1S 4T5	$2 002.48

DB2   Create a database for customers with a credit limit that is over $5 000. Use the following fields for your file.

Name	= 20 columns
Town	= 10 columns
Telephone	= 8 columns
Credit Limit	= 8 columns

Enter the raw data shown below and obtain a listing of the database.

Name	Town	Telephone	Credit Limit
Abbott Industries	London	555-0034	$ 6 000
Grew Bros.	Stratford	555-3352	$10 000
Jackson Co.	Chatham	555-2288	$ 7 500
Ontario Swine	Woodstock	555-3345	$10 000
Patterson Packers	London	555-4455	$ 6 000
W.O.B.I.	Woodstock	555-6674	$15 000

DB3   Create a database for customers who have notes outstanding. Define the following fields for your file.

Name	= 15 columns
Address	= 15 columns
Town	= 10 columns
Postal Code	= 10 columns
Balance of Note	= 9 columns

Enter the raw data shown below, and program the database to add up the amount owing by debtors.

Name	Address	Town	PC	Note
Buller, K.	125 1st. Ave.	Regina	S1Q 3F4	$25 000
Zavitz, K.	1020 Sea Dr.	Regina	S2B 2R3	$40 000
Pasquale, K.	300 1st Ave.	Regina	S4D 4T2	$65 000
Rigoni, M.	1456 Bridge Cr.	Regina	S5E 3H1	$38 200
Dagal, C.	32 Fine Cr.	Weyburn	S6D 6E7	$17 600
Spectre, A.	54 Ocean Dr.	Weyburn	S5F 7D6	$82 000

G1   Create a line graph for this sales data.

Hardware	Year 1	Year 2
Epson Equity II	$56 000	$57 000
Epson Equity IIe	$82 500	$94 000
Epson 286	$22 400	$42 500
Epson 386	$18 100	$36 770
Apex 440	$33 000	$12 000
Apex 580	$18 700	$32 500

G2   Create a bar graph for this accounts receivable data.

Store	Year 1	Year 2
London	$56 000	$57 000
Chatham	$82 500	$94 000
Hamilton	$22 400	$42 500
Kitchener	$18 100	$36 770
Woodstock	$33 000	$12 000
Stratford	$18 700	$32 500

G3   Create a pie graph for this accounts receivable data.

Store	
London	$128 956
Chatham	$ 56 778
Hamilton	$ 87 445
Kitchener	$ 66 002
Woodstock	$ 56 780
Stratford	$ 70 100

WP1   Use a word processor to send this letter to the manager of the Chatham store. Save your work under the file name CH5WP1.

December 31, 19–

The Locker Room
5 Pine Rd.
Chatham, Ontario
N7M 4H4

Attention: Donna Verbruggen, Store Manager

There is traditionally a lull in our sales after the Christmas holiday period. Last year we were not very effective in increasing our sales during this slack time. This year we will offer across-the-store discounts of 25% on all merchandise in an attempt to attract post-Christmas shoppers. Please use this letter as your authority to reduce merchandise prices accordingly.

Good luck on the sales campaign. We look forward to a positive sales report for January.

Yours truly

Peg Bradford
President
The Locker Room

WP2   Retrieve CH5WP1 and send a copy of the same letter to the store manager, George Amey, at 3511 Tecumseh Rd. W., Windsor, Ontario, N9C 2B6.

R. v. BUCKLEY

BACKGROUND

Anna Buckley started working for Upper Canada Transport and two years later she was promoted to the position of Accounts Receivable Supervisor, in charge of all customer accounts. She was able to train new billing clerks, and handle inquiries from customers in an efficient and pleasant manner. She was quick to learn about the new computer system when it arrived, and upgraded her knowledge on the system at a local community college. Anna was often complimented by her manager for the effort she put into the business, evidenced by the amount of work she frequently took home.

INVESTIGATION

Four years after her promotion, Mrs. Buckley became ill, quit her job and put her house up for sale. Upper Canada Transport hired a new Accounts Receivable Supervisor, Ms. Coyle, and she began collecting receivables immediately. She contacted one of the largest customers, Eastern Dairies, to request payment of their high balance owing to Upper Canada Transport. She advised the customer that their sales invoices were overdue, and asked if they were having any problems. Eastern Dairies informed Ms. Coyle that the invoices in question were all paid by cheques and that their account was current. When Upper Canada checked their reports they found that the Eastern cheques had been deposited but had been applied to pay older invoices of Eastern Dairies and other customers and not to the invoices submitted with the cheques. The outstanding invoices amounted to $47 000. The head office auditors were called in to investigate further. They found:

1. There were other customers who had outstanding invoices, according to Upper Canada Transport records, but who in fact had paid their old accounts in full.

2. The total amount that appeared to be outstanding, which had actually been paid by customers, was $116 028.65.
3. Upper Canada had fallen victim to a scheme commonly called "lapping". Cash and cheques were received at Upper Canada by Mrs. Buckley. The cash was removed for personal use while the cheques were applied to the invoices which were to have been paid by cash.

FRAUD

The accused had conducted a lapping scheme over several years. Each day her job was to balance the invoices with the cash received, and prepare a cash deposit. Incoming cheques were matched to invoice copies and another deposit slip prepared. The deposit slips and receivable reports were presented to the manager for his signature, along with customer cash and cheques in an envelope.

Supporting invoices were always in sealed and stapled envelopes for each report. The envelopes were not opened and verified by the manager. If the total of the bank deposit agreed with the receivable report, he would sign the report. Mrs. Buckley would often take the accounts receivable aging analysis home to work on it, because she was too busy during the day. When her manager questioned the Eastern Dairies balance, Mrs. Buckley said that the company was having difficulty switching to their new computer system and had asked Upper Canada Transport to be patient.

An analysis of the bank account of Mr. and Mrs. Buckley (Figure 5-31) showed deposit entries for a six-month period.

All customers of Upper Canada Transport were contacted when the lapping scheme first surfaced, and asked how much money was due to Upper Canada Transport. In total, Upper Canada's accounts receivable were overstated by $116 028.65.

Figure 5-32 is a summary of the accounts receivable which were not "receivable".

```
                    Deposits to the Bank Account of
                        Anna and Lorne Buckley
                           (six-month period)

Total Deposits                          .                    $113 227.04
Less: Known payroll deposits:
Family Allowances                            $232.00
Family Allowance Plan Loan               23 103.14
Transfer from a/c #1012                      232.00
U.C. Transport Credit Union                1 049.35
Bancardchek                                  920.00
Tax Refund                                   217.57
Not Sufficient Funds                       2 906.42
Loan                                       1 450.00
Ontario Credit Union                       1 000.00
Miscellaneous                                 10.11            31 120.59
                                                            $  82 106.45

Less: Known payroll deposits:
Mr. Buckley paycheques                   $29 570.08
Mrs. Buckley paycheques                    8 971.73           38 541.81

Balance of deposits, source unknown                         $  43 564.64
```

FIGURE 5-30   *Bank deposits*

```
Acc. No.        Customer                           Amount
3840            A.E.L. Ltd.                    $       8.75
4200            Allan Shoes Ltd.                      16.25
5064            Ally Mfg.                            237.62
5868            American Import Co.                  319.25
9570            Baja Canada Ltd.                   8 805.39
1087            Belleville Fasteners                  37.72
1175            Bradshaw Steel                       199.61
2230            Brown Forge                      16 562.61
13560           Buckthorp Leather                     93.01
27404           Crown Chocolate                       34.07
27775           Cutler's Distillery               2 349.42
30898           Deakin Bros.                         808.53
31264           Dillon Ltd.                          754.74
35952           Eastern Dairies                  47 327.52

91139           Walker Mfg. Ltd.                  7 047.23
96346           Woolworth, F.W.                       45.92
                Total                          $116 028.65
```

FIGURE 5-31   *Accounts receivable summary*

SENTENCE

Mrs. Buckley was brought to trial on criminal charges involving theft over $1 000, an indictable offence under Canadian criminal law. She was found guilty of the embezzlement, as outlined by the forensic accountants in their report to the court. A pre-sentence report documented her loyalty to the company, her efficiency, and her long service. As well, Mrs. Buckley was an exemplary citizen in the community, and an active participant in several community organizations.

Since this was her first offence, she was sentenced to two years less a day, in a minimum security institution. A program was also to be drawn up for her to make restitution to Upper Canada Transport for the funds embezzled. Mrs. Buckley can no longer be bonded. She found other employment which did not involve any access to the handling of cash.

QUESTIONS

1. Under what conditions should forensic accountants, or the police, be allowed to examine personal bank accounts?
2. How could Mrs. Buckley have been caught earlier in this lapping scheme?
3. How were the forensic accountants able to determine the actual loss to Upper Canada Transport?
4. Was the penalty appropriate? What would your sentence have been?

NAME

NO.

Career Profile

Liz McDannold had come a long way since starting to play golf at the age of 7. A strong academic student in school, and an all-around athlete throughout her high school career, Liz's favourite sport was golf. She competed in as many tournaments as she could, and at the age of 18 won the Alberta Ladies Amateur championship. She repeated this feat for the next two years, setting a new record for the province and ladies amateur golf. It was a natural course of events for Liz to be offered the chance to be Club Professional at the Banff Springs Golf Course.

Her new job involved giving lessons to club members, and hotel guests. In addition she was required to operate the pro shop for the course. Handling the business side of golf was not a problem for Liz. She had majored in recreational leadership at the University of Alberta, and minored in Business options. She had planned at one point to open her own store in Calgary, and wanted to be prepared for this eventuality.

The pro shop was a successful business venture during her first year. The members of the club and the hotel guests who used the facilities were wealthy customers who could afford luxury and were happy to pay for exclusive clubs, clothes, and golf accessories. Liz also found during that first year that her clients were people used to charging their purchases and paying for them later; or in the case of hotel guests, when they checked out of the hotel. Liz did all of her accounting work by hand that first year. She was able to keep her accounts receivable current but she felt that this particular task was taking too much of her valuable time. It was certainly more lucrative for Liz to be giving golf lessons than spending time keeping books for the pro shop.

During the winter hiatus from golf, Liz decided to improve her accounting skills. She bought an MS-DOS computer system with a

40 megabyte hard drive, dual floppy disks, a near-letter quality printer, and a computerized accounting package. She spent the winter months going through the training manuals, and learning enough to put her pro shop records on the computer. The general ledger was first. She was able to load in all her balance sheet and income statement accounts quite easily. Once they were stored, she could display a chart of accounts, an income statement for last year, and a balance sheet for last year.

The next step was to prepare the computer for her accounts receivable files. Since Liz's business is seasonal, she had no accounts receivable during the winter months. Nevertheless she needed practice. So she loaded 40 fictitious customer accounts into the accounts receivable module of the computer program. This module was able to handle 1 000 customer accounts, more than Liz had in one season of golf. She decided that the following data was needed for each customer — name, address, province, postal code, telephone number, and membership number.

Once the fictitious customers were loaded into the computer, she found that she could produce several accounts receivable documents:

- statements for each customer
- a trial balance of the accounts receivable ledger
- an accounts receivable aging analysis

The following golf season Liz used her new computer system and the computerized package for her pro shop. Her accounts receivable were always up-to-date. But more importantly, Liz found that the computer system did save her valuable time. Her revenue from golf lessons increased 25% over the previous year. Liz is already thinking about next year and is adding inventory and accounts payable to her computer program. There is one question in Liz's mind — How many more lessons can I teach next year?

FOR DISCUSSION

- How was Liz McDannold able to become proficient on the computer?
- Do you have any other suggestions on how Liz could use a computer for her golf business?

6

Accounts
Payable

OBJECTIVES

At the end of this chapter, you should be able to:

- **Journalize and post accounts payable transactions, and understand control procedures for purchases.**

- **Understand accounts associated with the purchasing routine of a merchandising firm.**

- **Understand terms, discounts, and shipping arrangements.**

- **Understand analysis and reporting techniques for accounts payable control.**

- **Operate a typical voucher system for a business.**

- **Use computer software for handling accounts payable activities.**

6.0

Overview

Accounts payable are payments due to creditors in the near future for **purchases** made on account. The phrase **on account** refers to purchasing goods or services from suppliers and paying for them at a later date. In this chapter the purchase transactions will relate to merchandise bought for resale.

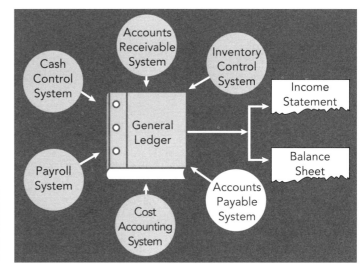

FIGURE 6-1   Flowchart of the accounting process

The purchasing routine for a business involves all of the accounting procedures needed to properly record the acquisition of goods and services by the business, and the cash payments for those purchases. All purchases and cash payments must be supported by proper source documents — purchase invoices, receiving reports, cheques, and credit invoices. **Source documents** are business forms that initiate an entry into a book of account. There should be a formal process for authorizing the purchase of goods. Once the purchase invoice is received by the business it should not be paid unless there is a receiving report to prove that the goods or services were actually received in good condition and as ordered. (A **receiving report** is a statement showing the description and quantity of goods received in a business from a supplier.) Creditors' records must be up-to-date at all times so that the business can take advantage of any supplier cash discounts offered. And finally, a voucher system is a useful alternative accounting tool for handling purchase routines.

6.1

Source Documents and Journalizing

Al Munro operates his own retail business, Munro's Jewellery, as a sole proprietorship in Vancouver, British Columbia. Munro's Jewellery was started by Al shortly after he completed college and it has been a family business for over 40 years. Goods bought for resale include diamonds, rings, watches, jewellery accessories, and giftware.

This section will describe the source documents used by Munro's Jewellery in handling its accounts payable activities. The accounting entries associated with the source documents will be journalized in general journal form; and in section 6.2, all the transactions affecting accounts payable will be recorded in a purchases journal, and in a cash payments journal.

Purchase orders are completed by the owner, Al, his daughter Phyllis, or his son Ross. All purchase orders must be approved by Al before being sent to the supplier. The supplier sends back the goods ordered, along with a purchase invoice, and expects payment from Munro's Jewellery within 30 days.

In larger businesses, there is a complex routine in place for handling accounts payable transactions. A simplified example of this procedure can be represented by the following flowchart.

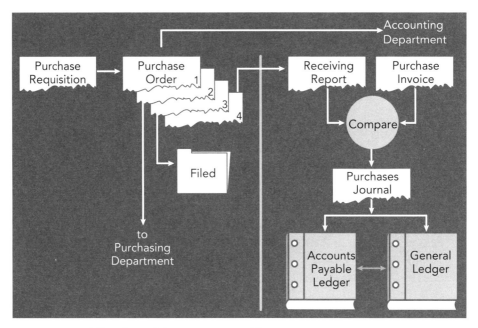

FIGURE 6-2   A flowchart of the accounts payable routine

There are many source documents and accounting entries associated with accounts payable. The main ones are:

(1) purchase requisition
(2) purchase order
(3) purchase invoice
(4) freight charges
(5) credit invoices
(6) payments on account
(7) monthly statements

PURCHASE REQUISITION

In a larger business or a business specializing in big-ticket items, departments wanting to order merchandise inventory will complete a form called a purchase requisition. The **purchase requisition** is a document which when completed is the basis for a formal purchase order.

In a smaller business, the purchase requisition might be just a note on a piece of paper stating the number of items needed, with a brief description about each one. Once the purchase requisition is checked, it is used to make the formal document, the purchase order.

Purchase Requisition		No. 112
		Date: July 20 **19 –**

Number of Items	Description
6	18" gold chains – #C68132 Crown Jewellery

Requested By _Lois_   Approved By _Al_

FIGURE 6-3   *A purchase requisition*

PURCHASE ORDER

Suppliers are chosen on the basis of their prices, delivery time, quality of goods, and credit terms. A purchase order is prepared once a supplier for the goods in question has been selected. Therefore, a **purchase order** is a formal document, prepared from a purchase requisition, which orders goods from another company.

MUNRO'S JEWELLERY
Box 100
1289 Burrard Street
Vancouver, BC   V7A 3T5

PURCHASE ORDER

No 112

Date July 20 19–

To Name _Crown Jewellery_
     Address _1605 Queen St. W._
     City _Toronto_
     Province _Ontario_   PC _M6R 3T5_

Quantity	Description	Unit Price	Amount
6	18" gold chains #C68132	15 –	90 –

Signature _Al Munro_

FIGURE 6-4   *A purchase order*

In larger businesses a purchase order will have several copies. A possible distribution of the copies might be:

Original — vendor (this is the best copy for reading)
Copy 1 — Accounting department (to journalize entry)
Copy 2 — Purchasing department (to authorize payment)
Copy 3 — filed alphabetically (for reference)
Copy 4 — Receiving department (to check when goods arrive)

	CROWN JEWELLERY 1605 Queen Street West Toronto, Ontario M6R 1A9		INVOICE Tel. No. (416) 555-0033 Fax No. (416) 555-9876	
Rings	Wedding Bands	Children's, Ladies', Gents' Jewellery		

Sold To Munro Jewellery
Box 100
1289 Burrard St.
Vancouver, BC   V7A 3T5

Ship To
--- same ---

Account # 1410	Our Order # CJ 1200	Ship Via Loomis	Ship Date July 25, 19–	Terms 4/10, n/30	Date July 25, 19–

Order	Shipped	Item No.	Description	Price	Amount
6	6	C68132	18" gold chains	15 –	90 –

All claims must be made within 5 days of receipt of goods from Crown Jewellery.	Sub Total	90 –
A service charge of 2% per month (26.82% per annum) is applied on overdue accounts.	GST	6 30
INVOICE # 33222	All prices f.o.b. shipping point	TOTAL	96 30

FIGURE 6-5   A purchase invoice

PURCHASE INVOICE

Suppliers who deliver goods to Munro's Jewellery send a purchase invoice in the mail when the goods have been shipped. All purchase invoices are unique and each supplier may have different payment terms. Figure 6-5 shows a sample purchase invoice received from one of the suppliers for Munro's Jewellery.

In this purchase invoice example, the business is buying some gold chains for resale. The invoice line labelled GST is important, since Munro's Jewellery is allowed an input tax credit for this amount. They are allowed to deduct the GST (goods and services tax) paid on purchases from the amount of GST they must submit to the federal government. Note that there is no PST charged on goods purchased for resale. The accounting entry for this purchase is:

GENERAL JOURNAL

PAGE 148

DATE 19–		PARTICULARS	PR	DEBIT	CREDIT
July	31	Purchases		90 –	
		GST Recoverable		6 30	
		A/P—Crown Jewellery			96 30
		To record invoice 33222			

FIGURE 6-6   *The general journal entry for a purchase invoice*

Strictly speaking the word *Purchases* refers to goods which are bought to be resold, i.e. rings, watches, gifts, etc. The entry for all of these types of invoices is a debit to Purchases, a debit to GST Recoverable, and a credit to Accounts Payable, or a credit to Bank if it is a cash purchase. This debit to Purchases records the "cost" of merchandise. Inventory items are then marked up to a retail price which is recorded in the "revenue" account, Sales, when these items are sold. Other invoices, for example, those for the purchase of non-inventory items such as office supplies, are also often handled as part of the purchase routine of a larger business.

FREIGHT-IN

Freight-In is the cost of transporting goods to the business when they are purchased. The phrase *shipping terms* indicates who pays the freight bill, the seller or the buyer. Some goods are shipped **f.o.b. shipping point**; in this case the buyer pays the freight, and title to the goods passes to the buyer at this time. Goods shipped **f.o.b. destination** means that the seller pays the freight bill, and the buyer takes title when the goods arrive. The journal entry for the freight bill for goods shipped f.o.b. shipping point is:

GENERAL JOURNAL

PAGE 148

DATE 19–		PARTICULARS	PR	DEBIT	CREDIT
July	31	Freight-In		18 –	
		GST Recoverable		1 26	
		A/P—Loomis Courier			19 26
		To record shipping charges re invoice			
		of this date from Crown Jewellers			

FIGURE 6-7   *The general journal entry for a freight bill*

If the freight cost is included on the creditor's bill, it should be recorded separately in the accounts. There is no journal entry for freight when the goods are shipped f.o.b. destination, since the seller pays the bill.

CREDIT INVOICES

Credit invoices are received from suppliers when defective goods are returned to creditors, or when an allowance is given on an amount owing to a supplier. When the goods are received by the supplier, a credit is issued to Munro's Jewellery and mailed back to the store. Credit invoices are designated as such by having "Credit Invoice" or "Credit Note" on the document.

It is important to note that when a credit invoice is received, part or all of the original accounting entry has to be reversed.

There are two choices that can be made. The credit side of the entry can be charged directly to the Purchases account, as in Figure 6-9. If this approach is taken, however, the dollar volume of goods returned to suppliers will be buried in the Purchases account, and important information about returned goods may be lost.

Alternately, the credit side of the entry can be charged to **Purchases Returns and Allowances**, a contra account that will offset the Purchases account on the income statement. **Contra accounts** are accounts which are paired with each other, each having an opposing balance.

	CROWN JEWELLERY 1605 Queen Street West Toronto, Ontario M6R 1A9	CREDIT INVOICE Tel. No. (416) 555-0033 Fax No. (416) 555-9876
Rings	Wedding Bands	Children's, Ladies', Gents' Jewellery

Credit	Munro Jewellery Box 100 1289 Burrard St. Vancouver, BC V7A 3T5	Our Order # CJ 4200 Invoice # 33222 Date Aug.2 19 –

Item No.	Description	Price	Amount
C68132	18" gold chain	15 –	15 –

Your account has today been credited with the items listed above, for the reason indicated:
- defective goods ✔
- pricing error ☐
- other _____

Credit Invoice No.
CR 339

Sub Total	15 –
GST	1.05
Credit	16.05

FIGURE 6-8   *A credit invoice*

GENERAL JOURNAL

PAGE 151

DATE 19–		PARTICULARS	PR	DEBIT	CREDIT
Aug.	2	A/P—Crown Jewellery		16 05	
		GST Recoverable			1 05
		Purchases			15 –
		To record credit invoice CR 339			

FIGURE 6-9   *The general journal entry for a credit invoice (credit to Purchases)*

GENERAL JOURNAL

PAGE 151

DATE 19–		PARTICULARS	PR	DEBIT	CREDIT
Aug.	2	A/P—Crown Jewellery		16 05	
		GST Recoverable			1 05
		Purchases Ret. and Allow.			15 –
		To record credit invoice CR 339			

FIGURE 6-10   *The general journal entry for a credit invoice (credit to Purchases Returns and Allowances)*

This method provides a record of the goods returned to suppliers in the course of one year. If the figure is high, it will be a signal to management that better control over the quality of goods being purchased should be sought, or a change in suppliers is needed.

In both cases the credit to the GST Recoverable account reduces that account's balance. The result of this entry is an increase in the store's liability to the federal government since there is a smaller input credit with which to offset GST Payable.

PAYMENTS ON ACCOUNT

If the supplier offers a trade discount, the bill should be paid within the time specified on the purchase invoice, to take advantage of the purchase discount. All payments from Munro's Jewellery are made by cheque, to provide a written record of the payment and better control over cash disbursements.

To pay for Al's last purchase from Crown Jewellery, the following items have to be taken into account:

Chains Purchased	$96.30
Less: Chains Returned	16.05
Still Owing	$80.25

The amount that will be remitted by Munro's Jewellery, after deducting the 4% discount allowed is:

Amount Available for Discount	$80.25
Less: 4% Discount	3.21
Remittance	$77.04

The accounting entry needed to record the remittance of the original invoice amount less the discount is:

GENERAL JOURNAL

PAGE 152

DATE 19–		PARTICULARS	PR	DEBIT	CREDIT
Aug.	4	A/P—Crown Jewellery		80 25	
		Discounts Earned			3 21
		Bank			77 04
		To record payment of inv. 33222			
		less credit inv. CR339 less 4%			

FIGURE 6-11   *The general journal entry for cash payment less discount*

"Make sure this one doesn't leave before he pays his bill."

MONTHLY STATEMENTS

A **monthly statement** is a report received from a supplier showing the activity in an account during the last month. Suppliers will remit monthly statements to Munro's, detailing the purchase(s) made and payment(s) received during the previous month. The statement shows a running balance of the account, all the debit entries (charges), and any credits (payments) made since the last statement. Here is a monthly statement from a supplier, Crown Jewellery.

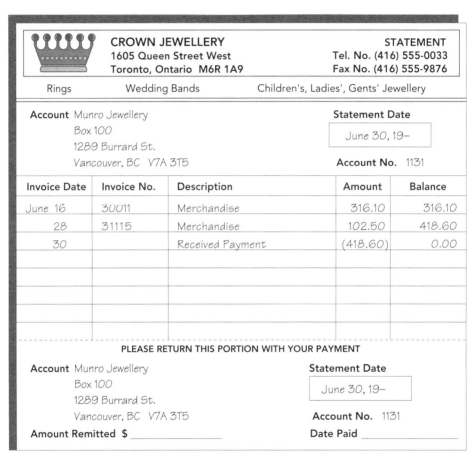

FIGURE 6-12 *A monthly statement*

Most creditor statements have a return portion or a duplicate copy, to mail back in with the payment. The original statement will be filed alphabetically by Munro's for future reference.

QUESTIONS

1. What two special journals are usually associated with accounts payable activities?

2. What is the main purpose of a purchase requisition?

3. What are the four qualities that a business will look for when choosing a supplier for its goods or services?

4. What do the shipping terms *f.o.b. shipping point*, and *f.o.b. destination* mean?

5. An invoice is dated July 4 and has terms of 2/10, n/30. What is the last day for paying and taking the discount?

6. What is the purpose of the return portion of a customer's statement?

7. Why would a business use a Purchases Returns and Allowances account, instead of just crediting Purchases with the value of the returned goods?

6.2

Journalizing and Posting Sales Invoices / Internal Control

Munro's uses a purchases journal to record all purchase invoices, and credit invoices; and a cash payments journal for payments on account and bank debit memos. The purchases journal and the cash payments journal used by Munro's Jewellery are typical of those found in many businesses, but they are tailored to suit the needs of the store. Standard journals could be used for purchases and payments, but an efficient business will shape the accounting records to suit its own needs.

THE PURCHASES JOURNAL

A **purchases journal** is a book of original entry for recording all charge purchases. Figure 6-13 shows the purchases journal that was specially designed for Munro's Jewellery.

The purchases journal for Munro's Jewellery has special columns for the accounts used most frequently: Purchases, GST Recoverable, Freight-In, and Accounts Payable. Most purchases will have an GST Recoverable component that Munro's Jewellery will eventually deduct from its GST liability, and so it is natural for GST Recoverable (Dr) to be one of the special columns. The

	DATE 19–		PARTICULARS	INV. NO.	OTHER ACCOUNTS DR			
					ACCOUNT	PR	AMOUNT	
1	July	2	Canada Gems	202				
2		8	Sterling Giftware	0067				
3		11	Canada Freight	8811				
4		12	Canada Gems	CR96				
5		18	Candec Jewels	746				
6		23	Singh Imports	333				
7		24	Exeter Mfg.	9-87				
8		28	Asian Jewellery	P111				
9		31	Singh Imports	C400				
10		31	Canada Gems	253				
11								
12								

FIGURE 6-13 Purchases journal with entries

purchases journal also has special columns for invoice numbers, and a tick column which is checked when the accounts payable credit entries are posted to the customers' accounts in the accounts payable subsidiary ledger.

There are two types of accounting transactions that affect accounts payable which are entered into the purchases journal — purchases on account and credit invoices received.

To study how the purchases journal is used by the business, assume that Munro's Jewellery had these sample transactions in July.

July   2: Purchase Invoice #202, from Canada Gems, $2 496.88 plus $174.78 GST; for rings for resale; terms 1/10, n/30.

8: Purchase Invoice #67, from Sterling Giftware, $814.20, plus $56.99 GST; for rings; terms 2/15, n/30.

11: Purchase Invoice #8811, from Canada Freight, $38, plus $2.66 GST; for shipping on goods from Sterling Giftware.

12: Credit Invoice #Cr96 from Canada Gems, $271.40, plus $19.00 GST; for a defective ring returned to them.

18: Purchase Invoice #746, from Candec Jewels, $1 460.13, plus $102.21 GST; for watches for resale; terms n/30.

23: Purchase Invoice #333, from Singh Imports, $3 412.53, plus $238.88 GST; for gold chain necklaces; terms 2/15, n/30.

PURCHASES JOURNAL

FOR THE Month ENDED July 31 19 – PAGE 7

FREIGHT-IN DR	MISCELL. EXPENSE DR	OFFICE EXPENSE DR	PURCHASES DR	GST RECOVERABLE DR	✔	ACCOUNTS PAYABLE CR	
			2 4 9 6 88	1 7 4 78		2 6 7 1 66	1
			8 1 4 20	5 6 99		8 7 1 19	2
3 8 –				2 66		4 0 66	3
			(2 7 1 40)	(1 9 –)		(2 9 0 40)	4
			1 4 6 0 13	1 0 2 21		1 5 6 2 34	5
			3 4 1 2 53	2 3 8 88		3 6 5 1 41	6
			3 0 3 9 68	2 1 2 78		3 2 5 2 46	7
			2 2 7 98	1 5 96		2 4 3 94	8
			(4 3 42)	(3 04)		(4 6 46)	9
			1 6 2 84	1 1 40		1 7 4 24	10
							11
							12

24: Purchase Invoice #9-87 from Exeter Mfg., $3 039.68, plus $212.78 GST; for a grandfather clock; terms n/30.

28: Purchase Invoice #P111, from Asian Jewellery, $227.98, plus $15.96 GST; for bracelets; terms 1/20, n/30.

31: Credit Invoice #C400, from Singh Imports, $43.42, plus $3.04 GST; for one defective chain.

31: Purchase Invoice #753, from Canada Gems, $162.84, plus $11.40 GST; for rings for resale; terms 1/10, n/30.

These source documents are all entered into the purchases journal for Munro's Jewellery. The credit invoices are opposite entries and are entered in the appropriate columns of the purchases journal with circles, or in red. See Figure 6-13.

Purchase invoices have a GST Recoverable component that is an input tax credit to Munro's Jewellery. The business can deduct the GST Recoverable account from the GST Payable account to calculate the net goods and services tax owing to the federal government.

The columns labelled "Other Accounts" will be used in the purchases journal for transactions which cannot be recorded in one of the special columns.

Figure 6-14 shows how the purchases journal for Munro's Jewellery would look after it has been balanced and posted at the end of the month.

	DATE 19–		PARTICULARS	INV. NO.	OTHER ACCOUNTS DR			
					ACCOUNT	PR	AMOUNT	
1	July	2	Canada Gems	202				
2		8	Sterling Giftware	0067				
3		11	Canada Freight	8811				
4		12	Canada Gems	CR96				
5		18	Candec Jewels	746				
6		23	Singh Imports	333				
7		24	Exeter Mfg.	9-87				
8		28	Asian Jewellery	P111				
9		31	Sing Imports	C400				
10		31	Canada Gems	253				
11								
12								
13								
14								

FIGURE 6-14   *Purchases journal posted*

The total of the Accounts Payable column must equal the totals of all of the debit columns. All of the column totals except for Other Accounts are posted to their respective accounts in the general ledger of the business at the end of the month. Amounts in the Other Accounts column are posted individually. In addition, the individual entries in the Accounts Payable credit column are all posted to the individual customer accounts in the accounts payable subsidiary ledger. (The **accounts payable ledger** is a group of accounts containing all the transactions for suppliers of a business.) This posting should be done on a daily basis so that the supplier account totals in the subsidiary ledger are always current. The posting references for the individual postings to the creditor accounts are a tick, while the references for the column totals are the general ledger account numbers inside the brackets at the bottom of each column.

Figure 6-15 gives a sample of 3-column accounts to show how the postings from the purchases journal (and the cash payments journal) are made to the general ledger control account, Accounts Payable, and to the accounts payable subsidiary ledger.

PURCHASES JOURNAL

FOR THE __Month__ ENDED __July 31_____ 19 – __ PAGE __7__

FREIGHT-IN DR	MISCELL. EXPENSE DR	OFFICE EXPENSE DR	PURCHASES DR	GST RECOVERABLE DR	✔	ACCOUNTS PAYABLE CR	
			2 4 9 6 88	1 7 4 78		2 6 7 1 66	1
			8 1 4 20	5 6 99		8 7 1 19	2
3 8 –				2 66		4 0 66	3
			⟨ 2 7 1 40 ⟩	⟨ 1 9 – ⟩		⟨ 2 9 0 40 ⟩	4
			1 4 6 0 13	1 0 2 21		1 5 6 2 34	5
			3 4 1 2 53	2 3 8 88		3 6 5 1 41	6
			3 0 3 9 68	2 1 2 78		3 2 5 2 46	7
			2 2 7 98	1 5 96		2 4 3 94	8
			⟨ 4 3 42 ⟩	⟨ 3 04 ⟩		⟨ 4 6 46 ⟩	9
			1 6 2 84	1 1 40		1 7 4 24	10
3 8 –	Ø	Ø	1 1 2 9 9 42	7 9 3 62		1 2 1 3 1 04	11
							12
(5 2 1)		(5 2 0)		(2 1 1)		(2 2 0)	13
							14

ACCOUNT Accounts Payable   **NO** 220

DATE 19–	PARTICULARS	PR	DEBIT	CREDIT	DR CR	BALANCE
June 30	Balance Forward	✔			CR	2 0 1 3 86
July 31				1 2 1 3 1 04	CR	1 4 1 4 4 90
31			1 0 1 5 0 52		CR	3 9 9 4 38

ACCOUNT Canada Gems   **NO**

DATE 19–	PARTICULARS	PR	DEBIT	CREDIT	DR CR	BALANCE
June 30	Balance Forward	–			–	Ø
July 2		PJ7		2 6 7 1 66	CR	2 6 7 1 66
12		PJ7	2 9 0 40		CR	2 3 8 1 26
14		CPJ11	2 3 8 1 26		–	Ø
31		PJ7		1 7 4 24	CR	1 7 4 24

FIGURE 6-15   3-column accounts

	DATE 19–		PARTICULARS	CH. NO.	OTHER ACCOUNTS DR			
					ACCOUNT	PR	AMOUNT	
1	July	3	City of Vancouver	200	Property Taxes	575	375 –	
2		5	BC Tel	201	Telephone Exp.	580	101 35	
3		8	A. Munro	202	Drawings	315	1000 –	
4		10	Sterling Giftware	203				
5		13	Canada Gems	204				
6		14	Canada Freight	205				
7		21	Pete's Garage	206	Auto Exp.	502	27 99	
8		21	Lewis & Bell	207	Accounting Exp.	501	150 –	
9		23	Vancouver PUC	208	Heat & Light Exp.	515	211 33	
10		24	Bank of B.C.	209	Loan Interest Exp.	520	125 –	
11		27	Exeter Mfg.	210				
12		28	Grand & Toy	211	Misc. Exp.	550	42 78	
13		31	Singh Imports	212				
14							2033 45	
15								
16								
17								

FIGURE 6-16   *Cash payments journal*

THE CASH PAYMENTS JOURNAL

When Al pays creditors by cheque, the payments are entered in the cash payments journal for the business. The **cash payments journal** is a book of original entry in which all cash payments of a business are first recorded (along with bank debit memos). Figure 6-16 shows a sample cash payments journal for the month of July. The entries indicating payments to suppliers are highlighted for you.

The total of the Accounts Payable column is posted into the control account in the general ledger at end of the month. The **control account** is the main Accounts Payable account in the general ledger. The other column totals are posted to their respective general ledger accounts as well, with the exception of the Other Accounts total. Any items recorded in the Other Accounts column are posted individually. The individual entries in the Accounts Payable column have already been posted to the individual supplier accounts in the accounts payable subsidiary ledger. These postings

CASH PAYMENTS JOURNAL

FOR THE ___Month___   ENDED ___July 31___   19– ___ PAGE ___11___

DISCOUNTS EARNED CR	GST RECOVERABLE DR	PURCHASES DR	FREIGHT-IN DR	ACCOUNTS PAYABLE DR	✔	BANK CR	
						375 –	1
	6 69					1 08 04	2
						1 0 00 –	3
1 7 42				87 1 19	✔	85 3 77	4
2 3 81				2 38 1 26	✔	2 35 7 45	5
				40 66	✔	40 66	6
	1 96					29 95	7
	10 50					1 60 50	8
	14 79					2 26 12	9
						1 25 –	10
				3 25 2 46	✔	3 25 2 46	11
	2 83					45 61	12
7 2 10				3 60 4 95	✔	3 53 2 85	13
1 1 3 33	36 77	Ø	Ø	10 1 50 52		12 1 07 41	14
							15
(5 1 1)	(1 1 8)			(2 2 0)		(1 1 0)	16
							17

should be done fairly often so that supplier account totals in the subsidiary ledger are always current. The posting references for the individual postings to the customer accounts are a tick, while the references for the column totals are the general ledger account numbers inside the brackets at the bottom of each column.

Internal Control refers to the methods used to ensure accurate recording of accounts payable transactions in the books of account. In a small retail store, such as Munro's Jewellery, internal control is not a problem because the business is family owned and operated. In larger businesses, there are procedures that can be established to help control purchasing and accounts payable:

Separating Requisitioning and Ordering

In a larger business where the purchase requisition triggers a purchase order, the requisition should be prepared by one person and the purchase order prepared (or approved) by another person. This prevents one person from ordering any items that will not be used by the business.

Matching Purchase Orders to Receiving Reports

Where a business uses purchase orders, it will also be completing formal receiving reports when goods arrive at the plant. Payment for merchandise purchased should not be made unless the purchase order matches the receiving report.

Payment Approval

All payments, whether for purchases or for other types of expenses, should be made by cheque, since this provides proof of payment when the cheque is returned to the business at the month end.

When suppliers are to be paid, one person should prepare the cheque, and present the documentation to the persons who have signing authority for the business. The person signing the cheque should make sure that the purchase order and the receiving report match before signing the cheque. The co-signor should do likewise.

Q U E S T I O N S

8. In the purchases journal, which column always has an entry? In the cash payments journal, which column always has an entry?

9. Explain the posting process that must be performed from a purchases journal for accounts payable entries.

10. Explain the posting process that must be performed from a cash payments journal for entries from the Other Accounts column.

11. What are two ways to record credit invoices in the purchases journal?

12. What does the term *internal control* mean?

13. Identify three methods of establishing control over the accounts payable of a business.

14. Could a computer be used for any of the internal control measures used for accounts payable? Explain.

6.3

Analysis and Reporting

The next important phases of accounts payable work are analysing the balances in the accounts payable ledger, determining if discounts have been taken on all accounts, and finding out whether the accounts are being paid within the time period allotted by the supplier.

Accounts Payable Trial Balance

At the end of every month, an accounts payable trial balance should be prepared. This is a listing of all supplier accounts in the accounts payable subsidiary ledger, and the balance due. The total of the supplier accounts must match the balance in the Accounts Payable control account. This schedule can be written with the same heading format as used for the trial balance of a general ledger. See Figure 6-17.

Accounts Payable usually have a credit balance but occasionally a debit balance appears. This can occur when a supplier account is overpaid. The debit balance should theoretically be shown as a current asset. In practice, the debit is simply netted against the other credit balances in the trial balance, unless the credit balance was a significant amount and misrepresented the accounts payable balance.

Munro's Jewellery Accounts Payable Trial Balance July 31, 19–		
Asian Jewellery	$ 243.94	
Barber Rings	110.35	
Blondell Imports	55.55	
Bulova	200.00	
Canada Gems	174.24	
Candec Jewels	1 562.34	
Willow Time Inc.	213.22	
Youngs of Canada	667.82	
Accounts Payable Control Account		$3 994.38
Total	$3 994.38	$3 994.38

FIGURE 6-17   *Accounts payable trial balance*

Reporting

Accounts Payable is shown as a current liability on the balance sheet because these debts are paid off in less than one year. In fact, creditors usually expect to be paid within a 30-day time period from the billing date.

Unlike accounts receivable, there is no contra account associated with accounts payable since the balances owing are firm commitments of the business. Here is a balance sheet illustration:

Munro's Jewellery
Partial Balance Sheet
July 31, 19–

Current Liabilities:	
Bank Loan	$12 000.00
Accounts Payable	3 994.38
GST Payable	885.67
Total Current Liabilities	$16 880.05

FIGURE 6-18   *Partial balance sheet*

It is possible for an account payable to be converted to a note payable, if the business needs an extension of time and the creditor agrees. A **note payable** is a promise, in writing, to pay over a long period of time for goods or services purchased. The advantage, for the vendor, of allowing this is that the note carries an interest charge which the open account payable may not have. If this happens, there will be a general journal entry to transfer the amount owing from Accounts Payable to Notes Payable.

GENERAL JOURNAL

PAGE 157

DATE 19–		PARTICULARS	PR	DEBIT	CREDIT
July	31	Accounts Payable		156234	
		Note Payable			156234
		To convert an open account to a			
		90-day note payable (Candec Jewels)			

FIGURE 6-19   *The general journal entry for a note payable*

Both Accounts Payable and Notes Payable will be shown as current liabilities on the balance sheet if they are due to be paid in less than one year.

The Discounts Earned account, associated with paying creditor accounts early, can be shown on the income statement as a reduction in the value of Purchases. **Discounts earned** is a percentage applied to a purchase to reduce the amount owed to a supplier.

Munro's Jewellery
Partial Income Statement
For the Year Ended July 31, 19-1

Revenue:			
Sales			$180 000
Less: Sales Returns and Allowances			2 500
Net Sales			$177 500
Cost of Goods Sold:			
Inventory, Aug. 19-0		$ 50 450	
Purchases	$85 550		
Add: Freight-In	3 450		
	89 000		
Less: Discounts Earned	1 700	87 300	
Goods Available for Sale		137 750	

Figure 6-20   Partial income statement

QUESTIONS

15. What is the accounting treatment for an account payable that has a debit balance at year end?

16. Why does the Accounts Payable account not have a contra account like the Accounts Receivable contra account?

17. Why would an account payable be converted by a creditor to a note payable?

18. What is the financial statement presentation for discounts earned?

6.4

Vouchers Payable I

Vouchers payable is a system of keeping track of accounts owing to suppliers which attaches a voucher to each payment of the business. A larger business requires a very formal process for handling and controlling accounts payable. The voucher system provides detailed records of purchases, and a system for ensuring that payments are authorized before being made to suppliers. In the voucher system, all payments, other than petty cash disbursements, must be made by cheque. And the cheque is issued only after an extensive series of verifications and/or approvals has been passed. A voucher system provides excellent control over payments but because of the paper-work involved, it is a costly program for smaller businesses to consider.

The voucher system involves two main steps:

(1) All payments must be formally authorized with a voucher.

(2) A cheque is made out only for an approved voucher.

The voucher system can be flowcharted so that it can be compared to the purchase routine outlined earlier (Figure 6-2) in this chapter.

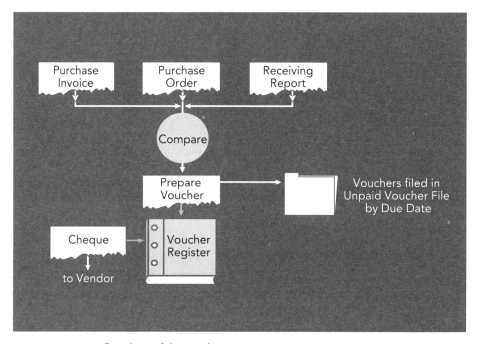

FIGURE 6-21   A flowchart of the voucher system

The starting point for a voucher system is the supplier's invoice for goods received. Figure 6-22 shows an invoice sent from a company called Off-shore Imports Limited to another company called Jewellery Distributors. Jewellery Distributors is a jewellery wholesale company that sells province-wide and uses a voucher system.

Once an invoice is received by a business, a voucher is prepared. A voucher is sometimes called a "voucher jacket" because it often folds in half and holds the invoice inside. All invoices that come into a larger business will receive a voucher, bills for purchases, utility bills, advertising expense bills, etc. See Figure 6-23.

offshore imports limited

200 5th St., Vancouver, BC, V5C 1L7
Tel. (416) 555-6721 Fax (416) 555-0012

INVOICE
#73621

Sold To	Jewellery Distributors	Ship To
	Box 3300	--- same ---
	2465 Pacific Ave.	
	Vancouver, BC V8B 4S6	

Date	Date Shipped	Ship Via	f.o.b.	Terms
July 4/ –	July 3/ –	Maas Freight	Destination	4/10, n/30

Quantity	Description	Price	Amount
120	Hawaiian Charms	18.50	2 220.00

OUR ORDER # OIL 6673
YOUR ORDER # 3784
SALESPERSON M. Muggins
THANK YOU

Sub Total	2 220.00
GST	155.40
TOTAL	2 375.40

FIGURE 6-22 Supplier's invoice

Once the voucher is complete, the information contained on it can be transferred to a voucher register. The **voucher register** is a book of original entry in which all vouchers payable of the business are first recorded. See Figure 6-24.

The voucher register is similar to a purchases journal except that the credit is to a new account called "Vouchers Payable". The data in the Paid column is only completed when the cheque is made out to pay the voucher.

The voucher register is a new special journal, that acts as a book of original entry for a business, and contains all vouchers issued. A firm using a voucher register will not have an Accounts Payable control account nor an accounts payable subsidiary ledger. The Vouchers Payable account will appear in the general ledger, and unpaid accounts will be kept in an Unpaid Vouchers file. The voucher register has special columns for accounts which are used frequently but all merchandising firms that use a voucher register will have a column for Purchases.

The posting process of the voucher register is similar to that for the purchases journal. The column totals for all but the Other Accounts column are posted to their respective general ledger accounts at month end. The individual amounts in the Other Accounts columns are posted to the correct account.

VOUCHER				Voucher No. 500	

Jewellery Distributors	Voucher Date	July 8, 19–
Box 3300	Terms	4/10, n/30
2465 Pacific Ave.	Discount Date	July 14, 19–
Vancouver, BC V8B 4S6	Due Date	Aug. 4, 19–

Payee Offshore Imports Limited, 200 5th St., Vancouver, BC V5C 1L7

Invoice Date	Invoice Number	Description		Amount
July 4	73621	120 Hawaiian Charms		2 220.00
		Plus GST		155.40
		Total		2 375.40
		Less: 4% Discount		95.02
			Payable	2 280.38

Account Distribution		Authorizations	
Acc. No.	**Amount**	**Description**	**Initials**
520	2 375.40	Price/Extensions OK	
		Order Received	
		Payment Approved	
		Cheque Number	
		Date Paid by Cheque	

FIGURE 6-23 A voucher

	DATE 19–		VO. NO.	PAYEE	PAID		PURCHASES DR	GST RECOVERABLE DR
					DATE	CH.		
1	July	2	496	CP Ships	7/8	842		18 82
2		4	497	A. Heng Chow	7/24	848	3 893 12	2 72 52
3		5	498	K. Low Holdings	7/11	844		56 –
4		7	499	B & B Supplies	7/10	843		2 23 9
5		8	500	Offshore Imports Ltd.	7/12	845	2 220 –	1 55 40
6		13	501	J. Bradford	7/15	846		
7		18	502	K. Lam Importing	7/25	849	4 002 10	2 80 15
8		20	503	CP Air	7/21	847		3 2 89
9		21	504	Eastern Traders	7/31	850	5 655 40	3 95 88
10		23	505	Pacific Jewel Co			1 122 33	7 8 56
11		24	506	BC Tel				1 8 56
12		31	507	J & B Jewels			10 800 –	7 56 –
13							27 692 95	20 87 17
14								
15							(520)	(211)
16								
17								

FIGURE 6-24 Voucher register

The voucher is completed with these pertinent details:

- name and address of the billing company
- description of the cost item
- the account to be charged (Purchases, Advertising, etc.)
- payment terms (4/10, n/30)
- the due date
- verification that

  quantity ordered = quantity received in good condition
  the arithmetic on the invoice is correct
  prices charged agree with the purchase order
  terms agree with the purchase order

- a place for authorization (signature of an official)
- the date the voucher was paid
- cheque number

VOUCHER REGISTER

FOR THE _Month_ ENDED _July 31_ 19 – PAGE _9_

FREIGHT-IN DR	SUPPLIES EXPENSE DR	VOUCHERS PAYABLE CR	OTHER ACCOUNTS			
			ACCOUNT	PR	AMOUNT DR	
268 83		287 65				1
		4165 64				2
		856 –	Rent Expense	570	800 –	3
	319 81	342 20				4
		2375 40				5
		2500 –	Drawings	315	2500 –	6
		4282 25				7
469 80		502 69				8
		6051 28				9
		1200 89				10
		299 66	Telephone Exp.	585	2811 10	11
		1155 6 –				12
738 63	319 81	34419 66			35811 0	13
						14
(521)	(572)	(220)				15
						16
						17

19. Why will a small business, such as a jewellery store, not consider using the voucher system?

20. What types of bills must have a voucher made out for them?

21. Refer to Figure 6-24 and answer these questions:
    (a) What is the difference between the discount date and the due date?
    (b) What is the area labelled "Account Distribution" for?
    (c) Where does the information from this voucher get entered?

22. Can a firm use an accounts payable subsidiary ledger system and a voucher system at the same time? Explain.

23. Why is there a column labelled "GST Recoverable" on the voucher register?

24. Explain, briefly, the posting process used in a voucher register.

6.5

Vouchers Payable II

When a cheque is issued in payment of a voucher, the date paid and the cheque number are recorded in the Paid column in the voucher register. Vouchers which have not yet been paid will have no entry in the Paid column of the voucher register, and will be filed in an Unpaid Vouchers file. In the voucher register shown in Figure 6-24, the last three vouchers have yet to be paid and therefore there is no notation in the Paid column for these entries.

Part Payment

One of the problems of the voucher register is its inability to handle a part payment of a voucher very efficiently. If a business wants to make a part payment on a voucher, the old voucher must be cancelled, and two or more new vouchers created to replace the old voucher. In the voucher register in Figure 6-24, the last amount owing is for $11 556. If the business wants to split this in two, then voucher 507 is cancelled and two new vouchers, 508 and 509, are made out for $5 778 each. A notation is made in the voucher register that voucher 507 has been cancelled, and the two new vouchers will be entered in the voucher register, as shown in Figure 6-25.

When the two new vouchers are paid, a notation will be made in the Paid column in the usual way.

CHEQUE REGISTER

A **cheque register** is a book of original entry used as part of the voucher system to record all cheques issued. When a voucher system is used, it requires that a cheque register also be used, to record the payments of the vouchers. The cheque register is similar to a cash payments journal. Cheques are written only for approved vouchers, so that each entry in the cheque register must have a voucher number. See Figure 6-26.

As soon as the cheque is written, a notation must be made in the voucher register indicating the date paid, and the cheque number. Since cheques are written only for vouchers payable, the only columns needed in the cheque register are Vouchers Payable, Discounts Earned, and Bank. The voucher number is needed to cross-reference to the original invoice in the voucher register. The columns are totalled and balanced at month end, and then posted to the correct account in the general ledger.

UNPAID VOUCHERS

When a voucher is prepared and not paid immediately, it is filed in an unpaid vouchers file. Unpaid vouchers can either be filed by their normal due date, or by the date they must be paid to take advantage of supplier discounts. The unpaid vouchers file is similar to the accounts payable subsidiary ledger mentioned earlier in this chapter. The total of all of the vouchers in the unpaid file must equal the amount due according to the Vouchers Payable account in the general ledger. This comparison should be done by the accountant at the end of every month, and a schedule of unpaid vouchers prepared. See Figure 6-27.

When an unpaid voucher is paid, the voucher is removed from the unpaid vouchers file, marked paid, and stored in a paid vouchers file.

	DATE 19–		VO. NO.	PAYEE	PAID		PURCHASES DR	GST RECOVERABLE DR
					DATE	CH.		
1	July	2	496	CP Ships	7/8	842		18 82
2		4	497	A. Heng Chow	7/24	848	3893 12	272 52
3		5	498	K. Low Holdings	7/11	844		56 –
4		7	499	B & B Supplies	7/10	843		22 39
5		8	500	Offshore Imports	7/12	845	2220 –	155 40
6		13	501	J. Bradford	7/15	846		
7		18	502	K. Lam Importing	7/25	849	4002 10	280 15
8		20	503	CP Air	7/21	847		32 89
9		21	504	Eastern Traders	7/31	850	5655 40	395 88
10		23	505	Pacific Jewel Co			1122 33	78 56
11		24	506	BC Tel				18 56
12		31	507	J & B Jewels	CANCELLED TO 508 509		10800 –	756 –
13							27692 95	2087 17
14								
15							(520)	(211)
16								
17								

FIGURE 6-25   *Voucher register revised*

CHEQUE REGISTER

FOR THE __Month__ ENDED __July 31__ 19– PAGE _07_

	DATE 19–		CH. NO.	PAYEE	VOU-CHER NO.	VOUCHERS PAYABLE DR	DISCOUNTS EARNED CR	BANK CR
1	July	8	842	CP Ships	496	287 65		287 65
2		10	843	B & B Supplies	499	342 20		342 20
3		11	844	K. Low Holdings	498	856 –		856 –
4		12	845	Offshore Imports	500	2375 40	95 02	2280 38
5		15	846	J. Bradford	501	2500 –		2500 –
6		21	847	CP Air	503	502 69		502 69
7		24	848	A. Heng Chow	497	4165 64	166 63	3999 01
8		25	849	K. Lam Importing	502	4282 25	171 29	4110 96
9		31	850	Eastern Traders	504	6051 28	121 03	5930 25
10						21363 11	553 97	20809 14
11								

FIGURE 6-26   *Cheque register*

VOUCHER REGISTER

FOR THE Month ENDED July 31 19– PAGE 9

FREIGHT-IN DR	SUPPLIES EXPENSE DR	VOUCHERS PAYABLE CR	OTHER ACCOUNTS			
			ACCOUNT	PR	AMOUNT DR	
268 83		287 65				1
		4165 64				2
		856 —	Rent Expense	570	800 —	3
	319 81	342 20				4
		2375 40				5
		2500 —	Drawings	315	2500 —	6
		4282 25				7
469 80		502 69				8
		6051 28				9
		1200 89				10
		299 66	Telephone Exp.	585	281 10	11
		11556 —				12
738 63	319 81	34419 66			3581 10	13
						14
(521)	(572)	(220)				15
						16
						17

Jewellery Distributors
Schedule of Unpaid Vouchers
July 31, 19–

Voucher No.	Payee	Amount
505	Pacific Jewel Co.	$ 1 200.89
506	BC Tel	283.75
507	J & B Jewels	11 556.00
	Total Unpaid	$13 040.64

FIGURE 6-27 *Schedule of unpaid vouchers*

QUESTIONS

25. How does a person know if a voucher has been paid or not by looking at the voucher register?

26. What has to be done when a business wants to pay only part of a voucher, instead of all of the amount owing?

27. How does a cheque register (in the voucher system) differ from a cash payments journal?

28. What is physically done with unpaid vouchers?

29. When a voucher system is used, what account appears as a current liability on the balance sheet?

6.6

Using the Computer

The computer can be used to prepare special reports relating to accounts payable by using an integrated software package that has spreadsheet, graphics, database, and word processing components.

Spreadsheets

An example of a spreadsheet activity in accounts payable would be the preparation of a cheque register for use with the voucher system. Figure 6-28 shows an example that might be used for Jewellery Distributors.

The headings are all a permanent part of the spreadsheet; the date, cheque number, voucher number, and vouchers payable amounts will have to be entered. The spreadsheet will calculate the discounts earned, complete the entry, and total all the columns automatically.

Graphics

Spreadsheets are used to produce graphs on the computer. Most integrated software packages have this feature. Once the spreadsheet is stored, one of several types of graphs can be produced. The three main types would be a bar graph, a line graph, or a pie graph. The example shown in Figure 6-29 is a line graph. It shows the accounts payable balances for Jewellery Distributors for the last three years, month by month.

A quick look indicates that the business has been very successful in reducing the accounts payable balances for three years in a row, assuming a constant or growing sales volume. The advantage of graphs is the quick visual impression that owners or managers obtain from them.

	A	B	C	D	E	F
1						
2	Jewellery Distributors					
3	Cheque Register					
4	July 19-					
5						
6				Vouchers	Discounts	
7				Payable	Earned	Bank
8	Date	Ch.No.	Vo.No.	Dr	Cr	Cr
9	Jul 08	842	499	287.65	0.00	287.65
10	Jul 10	843	499	342.20	0.00	342.20
11	Jul 11	844	498	856.00	0.00	856.00
12	Jul 12	845	500	2375.40	95.02	2280.38
13	Jul 15	846	501	2500.00	0.00	2500.00
14	Jul 21	847	503	502.69	0.00	502.69
15	Jul 24	848	497	4165.64	166.63	3999.01
16	Jul 25	849	502	4282.25	171.29	4110.96
17	Jul 31	850	504	6051.28	121.03	5930.25
18						
19	Balancing Totals			21363.11	553.97	20809.14
20						

FIGURE 6-28   *A spreadsheet cheque register*

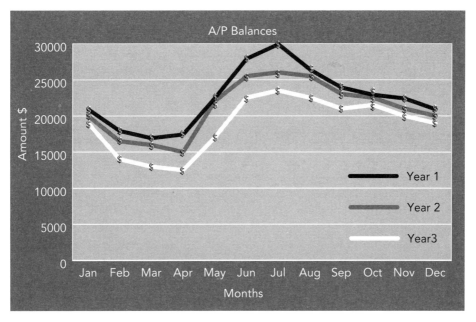

FIGURE 6-29   *A computer-generated line graph*

Databases

A good example of a database for Jewellery Distributors is a list of those suppliers who offer discounts to Jewellery Distributors.

```
Name:  Dickson Time
Address:  651 West Avenue
Town:  Calgary                      one record
PC:  T5T 2H3
Terms:  4/10, n/20
```

```
SUPPLIER DISCOUNT FILE
Name            Address           Town        PC        Terms
Amethyst Int.   45 6th Street     Vancouver   V8T 2J7   2/10, n/30
Bulova          667 rue Chause    Montreal    J7T 2G1   3/10, n/30
Caravel         1200 Yonge N.     Toronto     M2F 1S3   1/15, n/30
Dickson Time    651 West Ave.     Calgary     T5T 2H3   4/10, n/20
Emerson Ltd.    1190 Mason St.    Saskatoon   S9S 3L2   3/15, n/30
```

FIGURE 6-30   *A supplier discount file*

The top part of the diagram shows the form used when the database is set up and stored. The lower part is a listing of the suppliers' names, addresses, towns, and postal codes, along with the discount terms offered. This helps Jewellery Distributors compare suppliers and look to replacing those who do not offer good discount terms.

Word Processing

Jewellery Distributors uses a standard form letter that it mails to suppliers when it remits payments to them. The form details the invoice(s), and/or credit note(s) that the payment covers. See Figure 6-31.

The letter is stored on the computer using a word processing program, and only the supplier's name and address and the invoice details have to be changed for each letter. The letter is then printed and mailed to the customer. It also provides additional proof of payment (along with a copy of the cancelled cheque) when Jewellery Distributors files their copy by vendor name.

```
                    Jewellery Distributors
                         Box 3300
                    2465 Pacific Avenue
                 Vancouver, BC    V8T 2S9

Name of Supplier
Address
Town
Postal Code

Dear Sir/Madam

We are enclosing a cheque for your company in the amount of
$xxx.xx. This amount represents our payment for the following
invoices, and/or credit notes, from your company:

              Invoice #          Amount
                XXXXX          X XXX.XX
                XXXXX          X XXX.XX
                XXXXX          X XXX.XX
                XXXXX          X XXX.XX

Your company has offered us terms of sale which allow us to deduct a
discount of x%. We appreciate this discount and have taken advantage
of your terms in our payment calculations.

Yours truly



M. Fouse, President
Jewellery Distributors
Encl.
```

Figure 6-31   A form letter

Bedford Exercise 6 — Jordan Landscaping Revisited

Many of the accounting software packages on the market today offer accounts receivable and accounts payable as companion modules.

The **Payable** module of a computerized accounting system is used to record all the details of each credit purchase of goods and services of the company, and the subsequent cash payment to the supplier.

The accounts and all of the historical balances have been entered onto a data disk for you, and the computer accounting system only has to be set to **Ready** mode. The instructions for using *Bedford* are outlined in Chapter 1.

ACCESSING THE JORDAN LANDSCAPING GENERAL LEDGER

To retrieve the general ledger for Jordon Landscaping, you use the file name **jordlan6**. Key this name into the computer, insert the dates provided by your teacher, and set the program to **Ready**, as described in Chapter 1.

Enter the **Using** date provided by your teacher. Remember the sequence, mmddyy. As before, ignore the cautions and proceed.

This is a continuation of the exercise you completed in Chapter 5 for Jordan Landscaping. The chart of accounts presently being used for Jordan Landscaping is stored on the data disk. You can see the chart of accounts by accessing **GENERAL**, **Display** and **Chart**. Here is the chart without the special *Bedford* section headings.

Jordan Landscaping
Chart of Accounts

110	Bank	310	C. Jordan, Capital
120	A/R Control	315	C. Jordan, Drawings
130	GST Recoverable	356	Retained Earnings
140	Prepaid Office Supplies	410	Consulting Income
141	Prepaid Drafting Supplies	510	Advertising Expense
180	Drafting Equipment	515	CPP Expense
181	Acc. Dep. — Drafting Equipment	520	Dep. Exp. — Drafting Equip.
190	Truck	521	Dep. Exp. — Truck
191	Acc. Dep. — Truck	525	Drafting Supplies Expense
210	Bank Loan	530	Interest Expense
220	A/P Cano Drafting Supplies	540	Office Supplies Expense
221	A/P Abblass Office Supply	545	Rent Expense
230	GST Payable	570	Salaries Expense
240	CPP Payable	580	Telephone Expense
241	UI Payable	585	Truck Expense
242	Income Tax Payable	590	UI Expense
		595	Utilities Expense

CHANGING THE CHART OF ACCOUNTS

Before you journalize for this exercise, you must insert some new accounts into the general ledger.

The following new accounts can be inserted into the general ledger by accessing the **GENERAL** module, and the **Ledger** and **Insert** options.

185   Landscaping Equipment (**Type:** L   **Suppress:** N)
186   Acc. Dep.—Landscaping Equip. (**Type:** L   **Suppress:** N)
231   PST Payable (**Type:** L   **Suppress:** N)
411   Landscaping Services (**Type:** L   **Suppress:** N)
502   Landscaping Purchases (**Type:** L   **Suppress:** N)
522   Dep. Exp.—Landscaping Equip. (**Type:** L   **Suppress:** N)

In addition, account 220 must be changed from A/P Cano Drafting Supplies to 220 Accounts Payable. This can be done by selecting the **GENERAL** module and the **Ledger** and **Modify** options. Account 221 must be deleted, by selecting **GENERAL**, **Ledger**, and **Delete**.

SETTING UP THE ACCOUNTS PAYABLE LEDGER

For this exercise, you will be using the **GENERAL** Ledger module, the Accounts **PAYABLE** Ledger module, and the Accounts **RECEIVABLE** Ledger module in *Bedford*.

At this point in time, the company has only one supplier with an outstanding balance: Cano Drafting Supplies (Invoice #4496), $2 234.45.

The **PAYABLE** module will have to be made ready before you start to journalize any transactions. This involves three steps.

Step 1   *Enter the balance above into the Accounts* **PAYABLE** *sub-ledger.*
Select **PAYABLE**, **History**, and **Purchase**.

Step 2   *Set the integration accounts.*
Select **System, Integrate, Payable**, and key in the account numbers, as shown:

```
          Cash        110
          AccPay      220
```

Step 3   *Make the* **PAYABLE** *module ready.*
Select **SYSTEM, Default, Module**, and **Payable**.
Change **Ready** to **Yes**. Return to the main status line.

You will also have to make the **RECEIVABLE** module ready. Select **SYSTEM**, Default, Module, and Receivable. Change **Ready** to **Yes**. Return to the main status line.

JOURNALIZING TRANSACTIONS

To journalize general ledger transactions, access the **GENERAL** module and the **Journal** option.
To journalize accounts receivable transactions, access the **RECEIVABLE** module and the **Journal** option.
To journalize accounts payable transactions, access the **PAYABLE** module and the **Journal** option.

TRANSACTIONS

1. Cheque 557 (**GENERAL, Ledger**)   Dated: mm01yy
   Cheque for $4 500 plus GST $315 sent to Ontario Properties Ltd. for the monthly rent of office and plant facilities.

2. Cheque 558   Dated: mm01yy
   Cheque for $2 234.45 sent to Cano Drafting Supplies in payment of invoice 4496.

3. To record this transaction you will have to enter a new account in the **RECEIVABLE** sub-ledger. To do this, select **RECEIVABLE, Ledger,** and **Insert**; and key in this data: Las Margaritas Restaurant, 3344 Wessex Road, Ottawa, Ontario, K1E 3B7, 555-3851. (Answer Y to the **Purge** question and Y to the **Statement** question.)

   Sales Invoice S465 (**RECEIVABLE, Journal, Sale**)   Dated: mm01yy
   Invoice to Las Margaritas Restaurant, $1 890 plus GST $132.30, for consulting income. Terms n/30.

4. Purchase Invoice 986 (**PAYABLE, Journal, Purchase**)
   Dated: mm02yy
   Bought landscaping equipment from Westview Equipment, $13 200 plus GST $855.56. Balance is to be paid in three months.

5. Purchase Invoice 4589   Dated: mm03yy
   Bought drafting supplies, $3 456 plus GST $244.00, from Cano Drafting Supplies. Terms net 10.

6. Purchase Invoice 366   Dated: mm04yy
   Bought office supplies from Abblass Office Supply, $605 plus GST
   $39.21. Terms net 10.

7. Purchase Invoice 1003   Dated: mm05yy
   Bought decorative stone and masonry products (landscaping purchases)
   from Appian Stoneworks, $4 689 plus GST $328.23. Terms net 10.

8. Purchase Invoice 456   Dated: mm05yy
   Bought fencing materials (landscaping purchases) from Taku Fence
   Supplies, $5 800 plus GST $406.00. Terms net 15.

9. Cash Receipt (**RECEIVABLE**, **Journal**, **Payment**)
   Dated: mm06yy
   Cheque received from C. Therault, $1 712, in full payment of invoice
   S461; their cheque 1348.

10. Sales Invoice S466   Dated: mm07yy
    Invoice to M. Lawton, $13 000 plus GST $910 and PST $640, for
    landscaping services. Terms n/30.

11. To record this transaction you will have to enter a new account in the
    RECEIVABLE sub-ledger: Dr. P. Segal, 10 Royalmount Avenue,
    Ottawa, Ontario, K8Y 4T2, 555-3507. (Answer Y to the **Purge**
    question and Y to the **Statement** question.)

    Sales Invoice S467   Dated: mm08yy
    Invoice to Dr. P. Segal, $3 045 plus GST $213.15, for consulting
    income. Terms n/30.

12. Cash Receipt   Dated: mm10yy
    Cheque received from M. Lawton, $2 431.04, in full payment of invoice
    S462; their cheque 900.

13. Sales Invoice S468   Dated: mm12yy
    Invoice to C. Therault, $9 000 plus GST $630 and PST $480, for
    landscaping services. Terms n/30.

14. Cheque 559 (**PAYABLE**, **Journal**, **Payment**)   Dated: mm12yy
    Cheque for $3 680.00 sent to Cano Drafting Supplies in payment of
    invoice 4589.

15. Cheque 560   Dated: mm14yy
    Cheque for $202 plus GST $13.09 sent to Bell Canada for telephone expense.

16. Cheque 561   Dated: mm14yy
    Cheque for $644.21 sent to Abblass Office Supply in full payment of invoice 366.

17. Sales Invoice S469   Dated: mm14yy
    Invoice to P. Peterson, $16 000 plus GST $1 120 and PST $880, for landscaping services. Terms n/30.

18. Cheque 561   Dated: mm15yy
    Cheque for $3 660.40 for deductions withheld during the previous month: CPP $676, UI $842.40, Income Tax $2 142; payment to the Receiver General of Canada.

19. Cheque 563   Dated: mm15yy
    Cheque for $5 017.23 to Appian Stoneworks in full payment of invoice 1003.

20. Cash Receipt   Dated: mm16yy
    Cheque received from J. Lemieux, $1 872.50, in full payment of invoice S463; their cheque 650.

21. To record this transaction you will have to enter a new account in the **RECEIVABLE** sub-ledger and key in this data: Imperial Developments, 456 Manchester Crescent, Ottawa, Ontario, K4C 1S1, 555-0101. (Answer Y to the **Purge** question and Y to the **Statement** question.)

    Sales Invoice S470   Dated: mm18yy
    Invoice to Imperial Developments, $6 700 plus GST $469 and PST $400, for landscaping services. Terms n/30.

22. Cheque 564   Dated: mm19yy
    Cheque for $6 206 to Taku Fence Supplies in full payment of invoice 456.

23. Bank Debit Memo   Dated: mm21yy
    Loan payment for $2 000 plus interest of $87 to Bank of Nova Scotia.

24. Purchase Invoice 2390   Dated: mm22yy
    Bought landscaping materials for $3 890 plus GST $272.30 on account
    from Emerald Landscape Supplies. Terms n/30.

25. Sales Invoice S471   Dated: mm23yy
    Invoice to A. Suttcomb for $14 500 plus GST $1 015 and PST $848, for
    landscaping services. Terms n/30.

26. Purchase Invoice 8034   Dated: mm25yy
    Bought landscaping materials from Anderson's Sod Farm for $10 986
    plus GST $769.02. Terms n/30.

27. Purchase Invoice 666   Dated: mm26yy
    Bought landscaping materials from Sunrise Manufactured Products,
    $7 800 plus GST $546. Terms n/30.

28. Cheque 565   Dated: mm29yy
    Owner withdrew $4 000 from the business for his personal use.

29. Cash Receipt   Dated: mm29yy
    Cheque received from S. Chang, $1 917.44, in full payment of invoice
    S464; their cheque 3750.

30. Purchase Invoice 3390   Dated: mm30yy
    Bought concrete for various job sites from Trimark Concrete, $13 000
    plus GST $910. Terms n/30.

31. Cheque 566   Dated: mm30yy
    Payment to Ontario Hydro for utilities, $304 plus GST $21.28.

32. Purchase Invoice 7009   Dated: mm30yy
    Bought plants and shrubs for landscaping projects from Goldleaf
    Nurseries, $6 500 plus GST $455. Terms n/30.

33. Cash Receipt   Dated: mm30yy
    Payment received from Las Margaritas Restaurant, $2 022.30, in full
    payment of invoice S465; their cheque 8550.

34. Voucher 113   Dated: mm30yy
    Adjust the accounts for office supplies used, $715; drafting supplies
    used, $3 445; and landscaping materials used, $39 683.

35. Voucher 114   Dated: mm30yy
    Adjust the accounts for estimated depreciation expense incurred:
    Drafting Equipment, $469; Automobiles, $375; Landscaping
    Equipment, $667.

36. Voucher 115   Dated: mm30yy
    Record month-end payroll entry. Voucher showed Salaries Expense
    $22 500; CPP Payable $845; UI Payable $877; Income Tax Payable
    $5 355; net pay transferred to the payroll bank account, $15 423.

37. Voucher 116   Dated: mm30yy
    Record employer's payroll costs. CPP $845; UI $1 227.80.

38. Bank Credit Memo   Dated: mm30yy
    Bank loan $20 000.

39. Cash Receipt   Dated: mm30yy
    Owner invests $50 000.

DISPLAYING AND PRINTING

Select **Display**. Your teacher will advise you which of the six options to
preview. You may be prompted for dates. Remember, a date is entered in
the sequence mmddyy (month/day/year).

Print any statements requested by your teacher. Again, you may be
prompted for dates.

FINISHING A SESSION

Access the **SYSTEM** module and select the **Finish** option.

6.8

Dictionary of Accounting Terms

Accounts Payable   Payments due in the near future to creditors for purchases made on account.

Accounts Payable Ledger   A group of accounts containing all the transactions for suppliers of the business.

Cash Payments Journal   A book of original entry in which all cash paid out by business is first recorded, along with bank debit memos.

Cheque Register   A book of original entry used as part of the voucher system to record all cheques issued.

Contra Account   An account which is paired with another account and has an opposing balance.

Control Account   The main Accounts Payable account in the general ledger.

Credit Invoice   A document received from a supplier to reduce accounts payable, or issued to a customer to reduce accounts receivable.

Discounts Earned   A percentage applied to a purchase to reduce the amount paid to a supplier.

F.O.B. Destination   The vendor pays the cost of shipping the goods to the buyer's business.

F.O.B. Shipping Point   The buyer pays the cost of shipping the goods from the vendor's business.

Freight-In   The cost to the buyer of transporting goods from the supplier.

Internal Control   The methods used to safeguard assets and to ensure the accurate recording of transactions in the books of account.

Monthly Statement   A report received from a supplier or sent to a customer showing the purchases and payments made during the past month.

Note Payable   A promise in writing to pay a certain amount at a future time for goods or services purchased.

On Account   A term which refers to amounts owed to vendors for goods or services to be paid for at a later date.

Purchase Invoice   An accounting document received when goods or services are bought on account.

Purchases Journal   A book of original entry used to record the purchase of all items bought on account.

Purchase Order   A formal document, prepared from a purchase requisition, which orders goods from another company.

Purchase Requisition   A document which is the basis for a formal purchase order.

Purchases   Merchandise bought for resale.

Purchases Returns and Allowances   A contra account which offsets the Purchases account of a business.

Receiving Report   A statement showing the description and quantity of goods received in a business from a supplier.

Source Document   A document which is used to make an entry in a book of account.

Voucher Register   A book of original entry in which all vouchers payable of the business are first recorded.

Vouchers Payable   A system of keeping track of amounts owing to suppliers that attaches a voucher to each payment of the business.

MANUAL EXERCISES

1. Record these transactions on page 14 in a purchases journal for the month of February. Total and balance the journal.

Feb.   1:   Invoice #666 from Gard Supply, purchases; terms n/30; $404.46 (GST included $26.46).

3:   Invoice #P210 from Packo Ltd., purchases; terms 2/10, n/15; $231.12 (GST included $15.12).

5:   Credit Invoice #C88 from Packo Ltd.; defective goods returned to vendor, $57.78 (GST included $3.78).

10:   Invoice #8817 from Huang Importing; purchases, $1 386.72 (GST included $90.72); terms 1/10, n/30.

10:   Invoice #F398 from Freightway; freight-in on shipment from Huang Importing, $28.89 (GST included $1.89).

15: Invoice #91-5, from Wong Loo Ltd., purchases; $693.36 (GST included $45.36).

18: Invoice #691 from Gard Supply, purchases; n/30; $184.90 (GST included $12.10).

23: Credit Invoice #200 from Gard Supply, wrong goods; $57.78 (GST included $3.78).

24: Invoice #8823 from Huang Importing, purchases; $1 617.84 (GST included $105.84); terms 1/10, n/30.

28: Invoice #F444 from Freightway; freight-in on shipment from Huang Importing; $37.45 (GST included $2.45).

2. Record these transactions on page 17 in a purchases journal for the month of March. Total and balance the journal.

Mar. 2: Invoice #800 from Hill Bros., purchases; terms n/30; $808.92 (GST included $52.92).

4: Credit Invoice #C33 from Hill Bros., defective goods returned to vendor; $46.22 (GST included $3.02).

6: Invoice #333 from Ungaro Mfg., purchases; terms 2/10, n/15; $231.12 (GST included $15.12).

9: Invoice #901 from Teak Creations purchases; $2 426.76 (GST included $158.76). Terms n/30.

12: Invoice #F398 from Western Freight, freight-in on shipment from Teak Creations; $28.00 (GST included $1.83). Terms n/30.

14: Invoice #HT88 from Sai Woo Imports, purchases; $704.92 (GST included $46.12). Terms n/30.

18: Credit Invoice #66 from Sai Woo, goods scratched; $138.67 (GST included $9.70).

23: Invoice #840 from Hill Bros., purchases; terms n/30; $462.24 (GST included $30.24).

25: Invoice #367 from Ungaro Mfg., purchases; terms 2/10, n/15; $797.36 (GST included $52.16).

25: Invoice #555 from Trans-Canada Freight, freight-in on purchases; $130 (GST included $8.50).

31: Invoice #HT99 from Sai Woo Imports, purchases; $491.13 (GST included $32.13). Terms n/30.

3. Record the following transactions on page 46 in a purchases journal for the month of April. Label the extra column as "Supplies Expense". Total and balance the journal. The PST rate is 8% calculated on the base price only. GST of 7 % is included in all merchandise purchases and credit invoices.

Apr. 3: Invoice #220 from Grand & Toy, supplies, $254.23 (taxes included). Terms n/30.

4: Invoice #468 from Kam Enterprises, purchases; $924.48. Terms 2/10, n/30.

9: Invoice #777 from Tangerine Mfg., purchases; $1 627.84. Terms 1/15, n/30.

14: Credit Invoice #CR66 from Tangerine Mfg., purchases; $60.09.

15: Invoice #11-44 from Overland Transport, freight-in; $118.00 (GST included). Terms n/30.

15: Invoice #F889 from Lambert Mfg., purchases; $487.66. Terms 1/10, n/30.

15: Invoice #792 from Tangerine Mfg., purchases; terms 1/15, n/30; $2 137.86.

20: Invoice #9191 from Khanna Ltd., supplies; $381.35 (taxes included). Terms n/30.

24: Invoice #F902 from Lambert Mfg., purchases; $722.25. Terms 1/10, n/30.

27: Invoice #8531 from Taipei Imports, purchases; $548.91. Terms n/30.

28: Credit Invoice #CR96 from Taipei Imports, broken goods; $86.67.

30: Invoice #280 from Grand & Toy, supplies; $231.12 (taxes included). Terms n/30.

4. Record these transactions on page 16 in a cash payments journal for the month of May. Total and balance the journal. The PST rate is 8% and is calculated on the base price only. The GST is 7%.

May 1: Cheque #100 to Lan-Mar Holdings for monthly rent, $1 250, plus GST.

5: Cheque #101 to Brantford P.U.C. for utilities, $341.50, plus GST.

7: The owner, Peter Gugeler, withdrew $400 from the business for his personal use, cheque #102.

10: Cheque #103 to Ward Supply, paying invoice 666, $404.46; no discount terms.

14: Cheque #104 to Schultz Ltd, $231.12 on account, less a credit note for $57.78 and 2% discount.

15: Cheque #105 to Smith & Smith, Chartered Accountants for their accounting fees, $875, plus GST.

20: Cheque #106, European Importing, $1 386.72 less 1% discount.

21: Debit memo from Bank of Nova Scotia, interest on bank loan, $235.50.

30:     Cheque #107 to Wong Loo paying invoice #732, $693.36; no discount.

5. Record these transactions on page 12 in a cash payments journal for the month of June. Total and balance the journal. There is no PST. The GST is 7%.

June   1:   Cheque #470 to J.K. Sifton for monthly rent, $925, plus GST.

       3:   Cheque #471 to Canador Mfg. on account, $450.80, less 2% discount.

       7:   Cheque #472 to Harris Ltd., on account $1 029.87.

   11:   Cheque #473 to Pol Supply, on account $2 334.75, less 3% discount.

   12:   Cheque #474 to Orange Packers, $817.20 on account, less a credit note for $18.10 and 3% discount.

   13:   Cheque #475 to Fran Motors, $500 down payment on a new $20 500 truck for the business. Add GST. The balance is on account, to be paid in 30 days.

   19:   Cheque #476 to Indolay Mfg., $2 022.00 on account, less a credit note for $45.00 and 1% discount.

   22:   Cheque #477 to Nethercott Press for new letterhead for the office, $87.50, plus GST.

   29:   Cheque #478 to Y. Gianni, $808.08; no discount.

6. Record these transactions on page 18 in a cash payments journal for the month of July. Total and balance the journal. The PST rate is 6% calculated on the base price only. The GST is 7%.

July   2:   Cheque #1120 to the owner, J. Kupisz, for drawings, $850.00.

      4:   Cheque #1121 to Littler Co. on account, $615.28, less 2% discount.

      6:   Cheque #1122 to Briggs and Stratton, on account, $1 029.87, less 1% discount.

   10:   Cheque #1123 to Hyde Express, freight-in, $115.00, plus GST.

   11:   Cheque #1124 to Victoria PUC for utilities, $513.12, plus GST.

   13:   Cheque #1125 to Frames Ltd., $484.75, for the cash purchase of merchandise (GST included $31.71).

   13:   Cheque #1126 to Lamers Mfg., $1 352.70 on account, less a credit note for $75.00 and 2% discount.

   20:   Cheque #1127 to CompuSupply for computer supplies for the office, $118.90, plus taxes. (Charge to Prepaid Office Supplies.)

   31:   Cheque #1128 to Canadian Tire, $615.85, plus taxes; for new power tools. (Charge to Tools.)

7. Record these transactions on page 13 in a purchases journal or on page 17 in a cash payments journal for August. The PST rate is 7% calculated on the base price plus GST. The 7% GST is included in all merchandise purchases and credit invoices.

Aug. 2:   Invoice #899, from Johnson & King, $2 309.54, purchases. Terms n/30.

4:   Invoice #223 from Barrow Mfg., $1 505.05, purchases. Terms 2/15, n/30.

7:   Credit Invoice #555 from Barrow Mfg., $120.20, purchases.

8:   Cheque #450 to Gordon Ltd., for purchases on account, $2 143.66.

10:   Cheque #451 to Kip Lok Ltd., for purchases on account, $772.20, less 3% discount.

10:   Invoice #11-66 from Overland Transport, freight-in, $120.00. GST included. Terms n/30.

12:   Invoice #R338 from Pallamini Co., purchases, $556.93. Terms 1/10, n/30.

13:   Cheque #452 to Barrow Mfg. for purchases on account, $1 505.05, less credit invoice $120.20 and 2% discount.

16:   Invoice #753 from Radwanski Mfg., purchases, $2 434.34; Terms 1/15, n/30.

17:   Invoice #673 from Davis & Brown, purchases, $1 756.56. Terms 1/10, n/20.

18:   Cheque #453 to Heleniak Co., $432.32 on account, no discount.

20:   Credit Invoice #C271 from Davis & Brown, $80, on defective merchandise.

20:   Cheque #454 to Pallamini Co. to cover merchandise invoice #R338, less the discount.

22:   Cheque #455 to West Motors, $2 000 down payment on a new delivery van bought for $24 000, for the business. (Taxes included in price.) The balance is on account, to be paid in 30 days.

24:   Invoice #245 from Barrow Mfg., purchases, $1 667.30. Terms 2/15, n/30.

26:   Cheque #456 to Davis & Brown, $1 756.56 on account, less a credit note for $80.00 and 1% discount.

27:   Invoice #12-66 from Overland Transport, freight-in, $140.00. GST included. Terms n/30.

28:   Invoice #812 from Ambert Mfg., purchases, $880.60. Terms 1/10, n/30.

29:   Cheque #457 to Lariviere Press for new letterhead for the office, and envelopes, $112.56, plus taxes.

30:   Cheque #458 to A. Hishchak, $808.08, drawings.

8. Indicate how these accounts would be classified. For each account state whether current or long term for assets and liabilities; and whether balance sheet or income statement.

(a) accounts payable
(b) notes payable (due in 24 months)
(c) interest payable
(d) purchases

(e) discounts earned
(f) purchase returns and allowances
(g) freight-in

9. Journalize, on page 17 in a general journal, the transaction that converts a voucher payable balance of $12 000 into a note payable for the same amount, on July 1st. Journalize the interest on that note for 3 months at 14.5% per annum, and the payment of the note in full plus the interest on September 30.

10. Journalize on page 22 in a general journal, the transaction that converts a voucher payable balance of $18 500 into a note payable for the same amount, on June 1st. Journalize the interest on that note for 4 months at 12.5% per annum, and the payment of the note in full plus the interest on September 30.

11. Enter the following documents on page 14 in a voucher register for November. Assume the first source document number is the voucher number. Total and balance the voucher register. The PST rate is 8% calculated on the base price only. GST is 7%. Apply taxes as indicated.

Nov.   1:   #310 CP Ships, freight-in, $330.80 plus GST. Paid by cheque #675 on Nov. 14.

3:   #311 G. Ponti, drawings, $750. Cheque #671.

5:   #312 Gordon Chang, purchases, $2 445.65 (GST included $160). Paid by cheque #673 on Nov. 11.

6:   #313 Bank of Montreal for a loan payment, $1 800. (Interest included $742.50.) Paid by cheque #672 on Nov. 6.

12:   #314 Offshore Imports, purchases, $2 556.93 (GST included $167.28). Paid by cheque $676 on Nov. 19.

14:   #315 Benton-Ellis, for supplies, $304.02 (GST included $18.51). Paid by cheque #674 on Nov. 14.

17:   #316 Fred's Garage, for truck repairs, $135.00 (GST included $8.22). Paid by cheque #676 on Nov. 17.

22:   #317 Italia Jewels, purchases, $5 005.60 (GST included $327.47). Paid by cheque #678 on Nov. 30.

27:   #318 Hang Sen Imports, purchases, $4 004.18 (GST included $261.96).

28:   #319 Dulip & Drew for legal fees, $800 plus GST. Paid by cheque #677 on Nov. 28.

29:   #320 Broadhurst Advertising, for preparation of newspaper advertisements, $1 200 plus GST.

30:   #321 I. Scallopini, purchases, $3 556.77 (GST included $232.69).

31:   #322 Post Woodworks, $1 400 plus taxes, for new tools.

12. Enter the following documents into a voucher register for October. Assume the first source document number is the voucher number. Total and balance the voucher register. GST is 7% and PST is 6% calculated on the base price only.

Oct.   2:   #900 Gord Freight, freight-in, $220 (GST included). Paid by cheque #127 on Oct. 5.

4:   #901 Western Gas, for heat, $512.00 plus GST. Paid by cheque #128 on Oct. 5.

5:   #902 Alberta Pallets, for supplies, $1 022.34 (taxes included).

5:   #903 Bank of Nova Scotia, for interest on a bank loan, $885.43. Paid by cheque #129 on Oct. 5.

10:   #904 American Imports, purchases, $2 444.33 (GST included). Paid by cheque #131 on Oct. 18.

11:   #905 Computer Warehouse, for computer supplies, $734.55 (taxes included). Paid by cheque #132 on Oct. 19.

12:   #906 Wilson & Wist, for building repairs and maintenance, $970.00 (GST included). Paid by cheque #130 on Oct. 12.

18:   #907 Pacific Jewels, purchases, $4 442.22 (GST included). Paid by cheque #136 on Oct. 27.

22:   #908 Trumpf Holdings, for monthly rent, $1 500 plus GST. Paid by cheque #133 on Oct. 22.

23:   #909 Chiu & Singh, for legal fees, $1 500 plus GST. Paid by cheque #135 on Oct. 27.

25:   #910 The Calgary Herald, for newspaper advertisements, $660.50 plus GST. Paid by cheque #134 on Oct. 25.

29:   #911 Stormont Mfg., purchases, $3 449.87 (GST included).

30:   #912 Farrell Transport, for freight-in, $230.00 (GST included).

13. Enter the following documents on page 27 in a cheque register for October. Assume the first source document number is the cheque number, and the discounts are as shown. Total and balance the cheque register.

Oct. 1: #300 B & B Supplies $376.67, less 3%. Voucher #506.
      3: #301 Harold Holdings $4 750.00. Voucher #512.
      8: #302 Vasco Mfg. $2 449.85, less 1%. Voucher #507.
     12: #303 Quebec Metals Ltd. $1 009.08, less 2%. Voucher #510.
     12: #304 Canadian Imperial Bank of Commerce $500. Voucher #513.
     14: #305 A. Heng Chow $4 007.64, less 1%. Voucher #511.
     16: #306 Eastern Importing $6 770.88, less 1%. Voucher #514.
     19: #307 Hardy Fuels $650.00. Voucher #515.
     21: #308 Alf Lossing $410.00. Voucher #516.
     21: #309 PacWest Supplies $4 550.67, less 3%. Voucher #517.
     23: #310 B. Tyner $182.12. Voucher #518.
     28: #311 Victoria Imports $3 118.18, less 2%. Voucher #520.
     31: #312 Rupert Ltd. $889.90, less 1%. Voucher #519.

14. Enter the following documents into a cheque register for January. Total and balance the cheque register. Assume the first source document number is the cheque number, and the discounts are as shown. Total and balance the cheque register.

Jan. 1: #1000 Bradshaw Ltd. $900.00, less 2%. Voucher #672.
      3: #1001 V. Price $820.00. Voucher #676.
      8: #1002 Vecchio Mfg. $1 333.45, less 1%. Voucher #673.
     12: #1003 Regina Boxes $422.33, less 2%. Voucher #674.
     12: #1004 Royal Bank $3 000. Voucher #677.
     14: #1005 Tripp & Voigt $3 110.02, less 2%. Voucher #675.
     16: #1006 Drew Mfg. Ltd. $3 378.13, less 1%. Voucher #676.
     19: #1007 Sturdy Fuels $725.00. Voucher #678.
     21: #1008 Pete Williams $650.75. Voucher #677.
     21: #1009 Alberta Lock $1 003.03, less 2%. Voucher #679.
     23: #1010 A. Safari $203.64. Voucher #680.
     28: #1011 Far East Imports $2 211.66, less 2%. Voucher #681.
     30: #1012 Rupert Olyk Ltd. $116.54, less 1%. Voucher #682.

COMPUTER EXERCISES

SS1   Use a spreadsheet to produce this accounts payable listing.
Increase the width of Column A to 15 characters. Program the spreadsheet to calculate the total of the A/P column. Save your solution on disk
under the file name CH6SS1.

	A	B
1	ACCOUNTS PAYABLE	
2	August 31, 19-	
3	Supplier	A/P Cr.
4	Arc Welders	2333.76
5	Laker Bros.	5667.93
6	More Plating	740.77
7	Tower Ltd.	3245.66
8	Wilson & Zinn	1554.02
9		———
10	TOTAL	?
11		═══

SS2   Use a spreadsheet to produce this accounts payable listing. Increase the
width of column A to 20 characters. Program the spreadsheet to calculate the total of the A/P column. Save your solution on disk under the file
name CH6SS2.

	A	B
1	Accessories Unlimited	
2	ACCOUNTS PAYABLE	
3	January 31, 19-	
4	Supplier	A/P Cr.
5	Andrews & Holt	18665.44
6	Capiski Co.	2425.00
7	Fong Export	16777.23
8	Gibson Ltd.	334.09
9	Eversham, T.	10334.44
10	Fong, W.	9887.45
11		———
12	Total	?
13		═══

SS3   Create this cheque register template on the computer using a spread-sheet. Increase the width of column C to 15 characters. Program the cells in column G to calculate the Bank Cr. and to total all the columns in the cheque register. Save your template under the file code name CH6SS3.

	A	B	C	D	E	F	G
1	Name						
2	CHEQUE REGISTER						
3		Ch.			V/P	Disc.	Bank
4	Date	No.	Payee	Vo.No.	Dr.	Earn. Cr.	Cr.
5	xxx	x	x----x	xxx	xxx.xx	x.xx	
6		x	x----x	xxx	xxx.xx	x.xx	
7		xx	x----x	xxx	xxx.xx	xx.xx	

SS4   Recall the cheque register template CH6SS3, and insert this data. Obtain a printout of the cheque register. Save your solution under the file name CH6SS4.

	A	B	C	D	E	F	G
1	Wells Enterprises						
2	CHEQUE REGISTER						
3		Ch.			V/P	Disc.	Bank
4	Date	No.	Payee	Vo.No.	Dr.	Earn. Cr.	Cr.
5	Jan 3	81	Landon Ltd.	110	345.56	3.46	
6	8	82	CP Air	108	550.00		
7	11	83	Smith Bros.	106	815.56	16.31	
8	15	84	Royal Bank	111	800.00		
9	17	85	G. Lear	112	23.14		
10	18	86	Baystore	113	660.30	19.81	
11	20	87	Hesson Mfg.	105	560.00	5.60	
12	24	88	K. Jackson	114	115.12	2.30	
13	25	89	Xerxes ltd.	115	302.04	12.08	
14	30	90	M. Miller	116	34.34		

SS5   Use a spreadsheet to produce the following accounts payable discount calculation. Program the spreadsheet to calculate the net amount owing to suppliers after the discount is taken. Assume there is no PST. The first formula has been given to you as a pattern to follow. Save your solution under the file name CH6SS5.

```
            A           B           C           D           E
 1   ACCOUNTS PAYABLE DISCOUNT CALCULATION
 2   September 30, 19-
 3   Supplier        A/P Cr.     Discount %  Discount    Net
 4   Arc Welders     6456.86        2           ?          ?
 5   Laker Bros.     4978.34        1           ?          ?
 6   More Plating    7889.33        1.5         ?          ?
 7   Tower Ltd.      4354.00        3           ?          ?
 8   Wilson & Zinn   5339.11        2.5         ?          ?
 9                   ─────                     ─────      ─────
10   TOTAL             ?                         ?          ?
11                   ═════                     ═════      ═════
```

The formula for the discount is $\dfrac{\text{A/P Cr.} \times \text{Discount \%}}{100}$

Column B minus column E gives the net amount owing.

SS6   Use a spreadsheet to produce this accounts payable discount calculation.
      Program the spreadsheet to calculate the net amount owing to suppliers
      after the discount is taken. Assume there is no PST. Save your solution
      under the file name CH6SS6.

```
            A           B           C           D           E
 1   ACCOUNTS PAYABLE DISCOUNT CALCULATION
 2   February 28, 19-
 3   Supplier        A/P Cr.     Discount %  Discount    Net
 4   Glen Mfg. Ltd.   445.37        1           ?          ?
 5   Zavitz. Co.     1223.04        1           ?          ?
 6   Lasko           2227.75        2.5         ?          ?
 7   Rofalini Ltd.   3345.45        2           ?          ?
 8   Lewis & Stiedl   560.06        3.5         ?          ?
 9   Basko Bros.     6770.08        4           ?          ?
10   A.T. Harding    2000.00        2.5         ?          ?
11   Daskin Supply    445.95        1.5         ?          ?
12                   ─────                     ─────      ─────
13   TOTAL             ?                         ?          ?
14                   ═════                     ═════      ═════
```

Calculate the discount and the net as in question SS5.

DB1   Create a supplier database for Bargain Hal. Define the following fields
      for your file. Save your file under the name CH6DB1.

      Name   = 15 columns
      Address   = 18 columns
      Town   = 10 columns
      Postal Code   = 7 columns
      Balance Owing   = 10 columns

Enter the raw data shown below, and print a listing of the file.

Name	Address	Town	PC	Balance
Morlon Mfg.	23 Ontario St.	Toronto	M3G 2H1	
Ash & Beech	77 Spruce St.	Toronto	M5T 2H7	
Beecroft Co.	312 Parkside Dr.	Toronto	M7H 2G2	
Yong & Yong	75 Spadina Ave.	Toronto	M3D 2C6	
Crewson, Ed.	2 High Avenue	Markham	M9T 5A9	
Arus Corp.	944 Eglinton E.	Toronto	M4F 3L1	

DB2   Recall the database stored as CH6DB1 and insert these balances owing. Calculate the total balance owing and print a list of the supplier file.

Name	Balances
Morlon Mfg.	$12 335.46
Ash & Beech	$23 994.03
Beecroft Co.	$18 775.65
Yong & Yong	$ 3 558.44
Crewson, Ed.	$10 001.01
Arus Corp.	$ 6 778.86

DB3   Create a database for suppliers who offer discounts to your business. Define the following fields for your file.

Name	= 15 columns
Address	= 15 columns
Town	= 10 columns
Postal Code	= 7 columns
Terms	= 10 columns

Enter the raw data shown below, and print an alphabetized list of the file.

Name	Address	Town	PC	Terms
Babcock Ltd.	336 Fine Ave.	Regina	S2F 6T6	2/10, n/30
Zavitz Co.	88 Industy Dr.	Regina	S6G T7Y	1/10. n/30
Holt & Daw	200 5th Avenue	Regina	S56 3W4	3/15. n/30
Oleyn Co.	111 Lams Drive	Regina	S6W 7D1	2/15, n/30
King Ltd.	1400 Beechmont	Regina	S7Y 3L2	3/10, n/30
Chan, K.L.	300 Horning St.	Regina	S5R 2P8	2/20, n/30
Spectre Inc.	'55 Spectre Dr.	Regina	S4R 3D5	1/20, n/30

G1   Create a line graph for this purchase data.

	Year 1	Year 2
January	$44 500	$48 700
February	$36 700	$36 800
March	$78 000	$82 500
April	$34 500	$67 900
May	$ 7 800	$15 000
June	$ 2 500	$ 1 000

G2   Create a bar graph for this accounts payable data.

Store	Year 1	Year 2
Leduc	$12 300	$10 800
Calgary	$55 000	$60 000
Medicine Hat	$18 700	$24 500
Edmonton	$70 800	$90 200
Banff	$22 000	$28 000
Jasper	$16 500	$12 300

G3   Create a pie graph for this accounts payable data.

Store	
London	$234 567
Chatham	$112 337
Hamilton	$298 778
Kitchener	$334 465
Woodstock	$ 87 665
Stratford	$ 72 334

WP1   Use a word processor to send this letter to the manager of the Hamilton store. Save your work under the file name CH6WP1.

December 31, 19–

The Computer People
1212 Mountain Dr.
Hamilton, Ontario
N2S 3C5

Attention: Raymond Hunking, Manager

We have spent a great deal of time analysing our list of suppliers for our business. None of our suppliers up to this point in time has provided any discounts to us for volume purchases. We have talked to all of them in the past four months, and are happy to report that these suppliers will offer us volume discounts now:

Fong Ltd.	75 Henry Ave.	Toronto	M4K 2J1
Mabel Co.	24 Belton Avenue	Markham	M9T 5T8
DataMax	9944 Eglinton E.	Toronto	M4F 3L1

When you order new stock, please try to give these vendors as much of your store business as possible to take advantage of the new discount terms. This will assist your profit margins.

Yours truly

David Irving
President
The Computer People

WP2   Retrieve CH6WP1 and send a copy of the same letter to the store manager, Joe Palmer, at 1345 Downie St., Stratford, Ontario N5A 1W6.

R. v. WESTERN FUEL

BACKGROUND

Chris Hand was a graduate CMA when he was hired by the Red Valley School Board to act as the Assistant Business Manager. One of his areas of responsibility was the authorization and control of expenditures of the Board, including payments for all elementary and secondary schools. To acquaint himself with those expenditures, Chris performed what he thought were some routine checks on past expenditures "to get a feeling for the business of the Board". Chris gathered expenditure data for all elementary and secondary schools in the district, and fed the data into his computer for a percentage analysis scan. The results were fascinating.

INVESTIGATION

A cursory glance at his data and the resulting computer reports indicated that one of the schools, Red Deer Secondary School, had fuel expenses that seemed unreasonably high. This is not an expenditure that the school principal would have noticed, since the payment of fuel is centrally controlled at the board office. Chris suspected some form of fraud and called in a team of forensic accountants to investigate his finding. The accountants found that for three years Western Fuel Company had submitted the lowest tender to the Board for the delivery of fuel to the school, even though one of the tenderers was Gulf Oil Canada Limited, a supplier to Western Fuel Company itself. The school board accepted the Western Fuel tender since it was the lowest bid. The accountants found, however, that Western Fuel was charging for fuel it did not deliver to the school. The meter on the company's oil truck was rigged to continue running after the oil was shut off, and the school board was billed accordingly.

Before any evidence could be gathered, the head office of Western Fuel was destroyed by fire. The investigating team

looked for evidence to third parties: the supplier, Gulf, and the records of the school and its bank.

An engineer analysed the school's heating capacity and calculated the number of "degree days" of heat the school should have used for the past three school years, assuming that all doors and windows were *open* all winter. The amount of fuel required, according to this analysis, was much lower than the billing by Western Fuel.

An acccountant prepared line graphs comparing the amount of oil delivered according to school records — purchase invoices and cancelled cheques — and the maximum amount required as per the engineer's study.

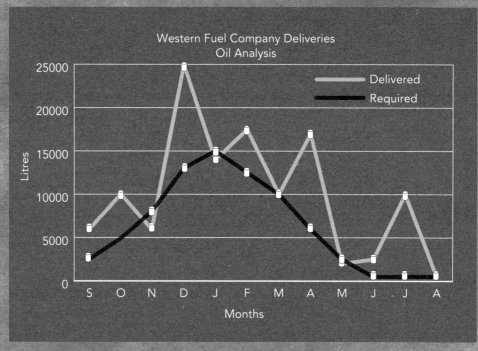

FIGURE 6-32   *Comparison line graphs*

A spreadsheet comparing the winter fuel deliveries of the past three years by Western Fuel with the winter fuel deliveries by Gulf Oil Canada in the following school year was also prepared by the forensic accountants. The amount of oil that Gulf delivered was consistent with the engineer's calculations.

```
        A      B       C       D       E       F       G       H       I
 1  Western Fuel Company
 2
 3  Comparison of Amount of Fuel Delivered by The
 4  Western Fuel Co. to Amount Deleivered by Gulf Oil Canada Ltd.
 5
 6          Western Fuel     Western Fuel     Western Fuel     Gulf Canada
 7             Year 1           Year 2           Year 3          Year 4
 9          Degree  Litres  Degree  Litres  Degree  Litres  Degree  Litres
10          Days    Del.    Days    Del.    Days    Del.    Days    Del.
11  Dec     1561    12916   1908    26959   1745    18883   1893    14691
12  Jan     2106    25555   2239    12447   2195     9953   1720    11467
13  Feb     1694    18595   1550    18618   1848    18475   1561     6000
14          ------  ------  ------  ------  ------  ------  ------  ------
15          5361    57066   5697    58024   5788    47311   5174    32158
16          ======  ======  ======  ======  ======  ======  ======  ======
Litres Required
Per Engineer        38599           41018           41674           37253
```

FIGURE 6-33   *Spreadsheet comparison of oil delivered*

FRAUD

The forensic accountants were able to satisfy the court that
fraud had taken place, even though the primary accounting
evidence from Western Fuel's records was not available
because of the fire. This illustrates an approach to be considered if available documentary evidence has been
destroyed, as is often the case when arson is committed to
cover up a crime. The sales invoices submitted by Western
Fuel Company were available from the school board's
department of supply and services, as were the cancelled
cheques and the agreement with Western Fuel Company.
Documents were made available to the court from Gulf Oil
Canada Ltd. as well, indicating their fuel deliveries initially
to Western Fuel and subsequently to the school.

SENTENCE

The president of Western Fuel, Nick Kowalchuk, was indicted for fraud after a preliminary hearing in court in Red Valley. Trial was held in County Court, because the theft involved exceeded $1 000.

Trial was held and the jury deliberated only two hours before bringing in a guilty verdict. Mr. Kowalchuk was sentenced to a prison term of two years less a day for his crime, to be served in a minimum security institution.

QUESTIONS

1. Could this fraud have gone undetected for a long time, or would it eventually have been caught by somebody?
2. What do you think the term *primary accounting evidence* probably refers to?
3. Which evidence do you think was more important in this case, that of the forensic accountants or that of the engineer?
4. What role did the computer play in this case?

NAME

NO.

Career Profile

Diane Anderson had been reading about cars since the age of seven. Since Diane's parents own a large new car dealership, Diane had long been exposed to new cars. Newly graduated from high school, Diane was now employed full time in her parents' business, starting at the bottom but with an eye to making it to the top some day. Diane enjoyed her daily work selling cars, but she wanted to start her own business to increase her income and have more practice at making management decisions. Diane read in an entrepreneurial magazine about a new business opening up in the United States called Car Detail. This was an expensive franchise and Diane felt that though the idea was great, she could do it more cheaply on her own. She bought some car-cleaning equipment through contacts her parents had with automobile suppliers, and opened her own business, Diane's Car Clean. For several months she operated in the evenings and on weekends from home, with sales steadily increasing from month to month. Part of Diane's success was due to her policy of picking cars up from clients at their homes, and part was due to the excellent quality of the work she did. Diane's service was convenient, fast, and expertly done.

A year later, Diane left her parents' business to strike out on her own with Diane's Car Clean. Diane was ready to rent a building and set up her own shop. Her banker advised her that she needed some cash flow projections for her business before a $20 000 loan would be granted. Diane had studied spreadsheets in high school and immediately went to her home computer. With the help of her mother she was able to project revenue and expenses for a two-year period. She was able to do a cash flow projection as well, with a payback schedule for the bank on their loan. The bank approved the loan over a five-year time period and Diane was in business.

Before the business opened, Diane carried her computer to the business and loaded an accounting program on the system. She felt that she might as well start with her general ledger on the computer, right from day one. Her brother Lee volunteered to enter the data for a few weeks "just to get the business going". Lee was such a good help that Diane eventually began to pay him an hourly salary. Both Diane and Lee became very computer-literate and were able to enter accounting documents with ease. At the end of the first year, Diane's Car Clean showed a healthy profit.

Diane has decided to keep the business running for a while, and has enrolled in some business and accounting courses at night school to polish off her business knowledge. Diane still thinks about joining her parents' business again, but she's already President of Diane's Car Clean, and that has a nice ring to it.

FOR DISCUSSION

- Diane "carried her computer to the business." Does that sound like a nuisance? What else should she have done?
- What software has Diane used on her computer already? What future use will Diane have for her computer?

7

Inventory Control

- Distinguish between a service business and a merchandise business in respect of their inventory control requirements.

- Complete all transactions related to the cost of goods sold section of an income statement.

- Understand periodic inventory systems.

- Understand perpetual inventory systems.

- Identify the need for inventory management in a business.

- Use computer software to handle inventory control activities.

7.0

Overview

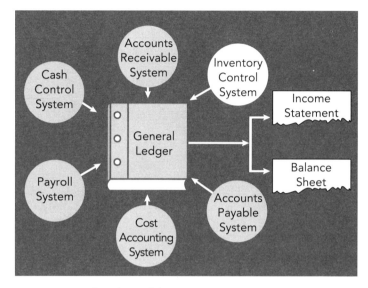

FIGURE 7-1   Flowchart of the accounting process

The inventory recording and control function of some businesses is responsible for a multi-million dollar operation. Many stores carry high priced merchandise — televisions, cars, furniture, furs, and jewellery, for example. This inventory must be properly recorded, valued and physically safe-guarded or substantial business losses can occur.

This chapter will detail the accounting procedures necessary to prepare the cost of goods sold section of an income statement for a merchandise business, and the special accounts associated with the inventory function. It will explain the two basic kinds of inventory accounting systems, periodic and perpetual, and the inventory applications where each system would be best suited. And it will outline the problems associated with the management, or internal control, of inventory.

7.1

Service v. Merchandise Businesses

There are differences required in the accounting systems used by service businesses, merchandise businesses, and manufacturing businesses. This section details the differences between a service business and a merchandise business with regard to inventory control, and its accounting effect on a balance sheet and an income statement.

Since this chapter focuses on inventory control, it is important to review briefly the difference between a service business and a merchandise business with regard to inventory.

The Service Business

A **service business** sells personal skills or the use of facilities as opposed to goods. A service business does not have inventory for resale. A clear example of this would be a dentist. A dentist has a skill learned through several years of education at a university dental school. A dentist sells professional services to people but does not keep an inventory of goods that are sold to clients.

The balance sheet of a dentist does not, therefore, have an asset account called Merchandise Inventory on the books. This partial balance sheet will indicate that a dentist's current asset list can be relatively simple.

```
                    Dr. A. Mowlar
                 Partial Balance Sheet
                  December 31, 19–

        Current Assets:
        Bank                           $ 7 000
        Accounts Receivable             20 000
        Supplies                         3 000
                                       ─────────
        Total Current Assets           $30 000
```

FIGURE 7-2   *A partial service balance sheet*

The supplies account refers to materials which the dentist uses in the course of her/his work, such as materials for filling teeth. Supplies are expected to be used up within a year and therefore, by definition, are a current asset.

The Merchandise Business

A **merchandise business** is a concern which sells goods to customers, as opposed to personal services. A good example is a sporting goods store. Sports Emporium is a chain of retail sporting goods stores that is located in 20 major shopping centres across Canada, from Halifax to Vancouver. It was started by John Kupisz, a high school physical education instructor, who became frustrated with the lack of a sports store that sold top quality sporting goods. He began selling goods in his spare time, and eventually opened his first store in Calgary.

The largest current asset of a merchandise concern will be its merchandise inventory. **Merchandise inventory** refers to the quantity of goods available for sale by a business. Figure 7.3 shows a partial balance sheet for one of Sports Emporium's smaller stores:

Sports Emporium	
Partial Balance Sheet	
December 31, 19–	
Assets	
Current Assets:	
Bank	$ 15 000
Accounts Receivable	43 000
Merchandise Inventory	60 000
Supplies	2 000
Total Current Assets	$120 000

FIGURE 7-3   *A partial merchandise balance sheet*

Merchandise inventory is a current asset because the store expects to sell all of its merchandise within a year. The supplies for Sports Emporium are the packaging materials used to wrap sports equipment sold to customers. Supplies differ from inventory because supplies are used up in the course of making a sale.

QUESTIONS

1. What account does a merchandise concern have on its balance sheet that a service business does not?

2. Why is Merchandise Inventory a current asset?

3. Name a business in your area that is a service business and another that is a merchandise concern.

4. How do supplies differ from merchandise inventory?

5. Given these business names, indicate the type of inventory one would expect each one to have: Dairy Queen; Danielle's Security Centre; Megavideo; 4 Baby; Compucentre; Great Frame Up; Wicks N' Sticks

7.2

Cost of Goods Sold

The phrase **cost of goods sold** refers to the laid-down cost of the goods which have already been sold by the business. Since a merchandise business adds cost items (such as purchases) to its general ledger accounts, the income statement setup is more complex than the one used for a service business. The format of an income statement for a service business is straightforward, and follows the abbreviated outline shown in Figure 7-4.

The income statement for a merchandise business is used to subtract both the cost of merchandise and operating expenses from revenue and therefore has an extra section called Cost of Goods Sold. A merchandising business generally uses an outline similar to Figure 7-5 for its income statement.

Note the Sales Returns and Allowances account used by the merchandise business. It is a contra account to Sales, and is shown directly underneath the Sales account. A Sales Returns and Allowances account keeps a separate record of customer returns and is a useful management tool to indicate bad products or service if the account gets unreasonably high.

Dr. A. Mowlar
Income Statement
For the Year Ended December 31, 19–

Revenue:		
Fees Income		$220 000
Expenses:		
Advertising	$ 1 500	
Bank Charges	3 500	
Rent	18 000	
Utilities	7 000	
Wages	90 000	120 000
Net Income		$100 000

FIGURE 7-4   *A partial service income statement*

Sports Emporium
Income Statement
For the Year Ended December 31, 19–

Revenue:		
Sales		$800 000
Less: Sales Returns and Allowances		3 700
Sales Discounts		6 300
Net Sales		790 000
Cost of Goods Sold:		
Opening Inventory	$ 50 000	
Add: Purchases	490 000	
Cost of Goods Available for Sale	540 000	
Less: Closing Inventory	60 000	
Cost of Goods Sold		480 000
Gross Profit		310 000
Expenses:		
Advertising	8 000	
Bank Charges	4 000	
Rent	24 000	
Utilities	4 000	
Wages	120 000	160 000
Net Income		$150 000

FIGURE 7-5   *An expanded merchandise income statement*

In actual practice the Cost of Goods Sold section of a merchandising business is more complicated than the outline shown in Figure 7-5. Figure 7-6 gives a model that shows all of the accounts that could be found in the Cost of Goods Sold section of an income statement of a real business.

Cost of Goods Sold:			
Inventory, January 1, 19–			$ 50 000
Add: Purchases		$490 000	
Freight-In		5 000	
		495 000	
Less: Purchases Returns and Allowances	$1 500		
Purchases Discounts	3 500	5 000	
Net Purchases			490 000
Cost of Goods Available for Sale			540 000
Inventory, December 31, 19–			60 000
Cost of Goods Sold			$480 000

FIGURE 7-6   *A cost of goods sold statement*

The Purchases and **Freight-In** (the cost of transporting goods to the business when they are purchased) accounts are added together since they represent the total cost of buying goods and shipping them into the store to be placed in inventory. The Purchases Returns and Allowances account and the Discounts Earned account have credit balances since they represent negative costs of the business. **Discounts earned** is a percentage applied to purchases that reduces the amount owing to a supplier.

The basic formula for the cost of goods sold section of the income statement is:

Opening Inventory + Net Purchases – Closing Inventory = Cost of Goods Sold

Opening inventory is the value of goods on hand at the start of a fiscal period; **closing inventory** is the value of goods on hand at the end of the same period. The term **net purchases** has four components to it: Purchases, Freight-In, Purchases Returns and Allowances, and Discounts Earned. (Discounts Earned can also be called Purchase Discounts on some financial statements, but the accounting treatment stays the same.)

The closing inventory in the Cost of Goods Sold section of the income statement also appears as a current asset on the balance sheet of the merchandise business. In the next fiscal period, last year's closing inventory balance will become the opening balance. This link of the financial statements from one year to the next means that the figure arrived at for the closing inventory must be as accurate as possible.

The format of financial statements will vary from one business to the next, but the general setup will be quite similar. Some businesses use an account called **Transportation-In** instead of the Freight-In account used in this text. Computer software packages also will not necessarily follow a given set of rules when producing their own particular financial statements.

QUESTIONS

6. What is the extra section found on the income statement of a merchandising business that is not found in a service business?

7. Indicate whether these accounts have debit or credit balances: purchases, freight-in, purchases returns and allowances, and discounts earned.

8. What is another name for freight-in?

9. Of the accounts used in a cost of goods sold section, which would you describe as contra accounts?

10. Does the cost of goods sold section follow the same format in every company? Explain.

7.3

Periodic Inventory Systems

A **periodic inventory** system debits all goods bought to a Purchases account and counts and values inventory only at the end of the fiscal period. Under a periodic system of inventory management, records are kept of the opening inventory, and of the purchases made during the year. The inventory at the beginning of the fiscal period is a debit balance in the Merchandise Inventory account.

FIGURE 7-7   T-account for Merchandise Inventory under a periodic inventory system

Merchandise Inventory	
50 000	

As merchandise is bought during the year, accounting entries are made to debit the Purchases account and credit either Accounts Payable (if the goods are bought on account), or Bank (if cash is paid for the goods). As of January 1, 1991, a federal GST (goods and services tax) has been imposed on most of the goods and services sold in Canada. This retail tax complicates the accounting for purchases, since any GST paid by a business becomes an input tax credit to that business. In this text, we have used an account called **GST Recoverable** to accumulate the amount of GST paid by a business. The purchasing firm will debit an account called GST Recoverable for the tax paid on its purchases and will eventually deduct the GST Recoverable (input tax credit) from its GST liability (which is a result of making retail sales) to the federal government. The purchase on account of $20 000 worth of goods for resale would be entered into the books of account this way:

GENERAL JOURNAL

PAGE 21

DATE 19–		PARTICULARS	PR	DEBIT	CREDIT
Feb.	10	Purchases		20 000 –	
		GST Recoverable		1 400 –	
		A/P—Wholesale Sports			21 400 –
		To record inventory purchase			
		Inv. WS865			

FIGURE 7-8   *The general journal entry for inventory purchase*

PHYSICAL INVENTORY

Taking a **physical inventory** is the process of physically counting goods on hand at the fiscal year end, attaching a cost value to them, and calculating the total dollar value of the inventory on hand. Most businesses that use the periodic inventory system only take inventory once a year, although it can be done more often.

The relationship between opening and closing inventories and the purchases during the fiscal period can be illustrated as shown in Figure 7-9.

There are two basic problems with determining inventory cost at the year end:
(1) calculating the inventory quantity
(2) assigning a cost to this quantity

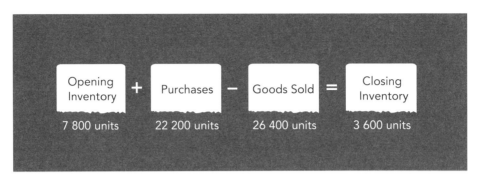

FIGURE 7-9   *Inventory flow*

Calculating inventory quantity is not usually difficult. An **inventory tag** is attached to each inventory item when it is physically counted. Information contained on the tag could include the retail price, a cost formula, date counted, and the signature of the person who tagged the inventory. After inventory items are tagged, the number sequence of the tags will be checked as a matter of control.

SPORTS EMPORIUM   **Tag No. 178**

Store Location _Calgary_   **Date** _Dec 31/ –_

Item Description _Footballs_

Cost Price _$26.00_   **Retail Price** _$50.00_

Quantity on Hand _1_   **Counted by** _JA_

Checked by _RL_

FIGURE 7-10   *An inventory tag*

Inventory is usually taken when the store is not open: nights, holidays, weekends, etc. One person calls out the inventory item while another records it on an **inventory sheet**, a document used to summarize the information contained on inventory tags.

The inventory sheet for Sports Emporium has several control checks built into it; one person calls the inventory from the tag, another records it on the sheet, another costs the inventory etc. Depending on the size of staff, some of these functions may have to overlap, but the more people involved the better the inventory control features.

SPORTS EMPORIUM		Inventory Sheet			Page ___3___
Date __Dec. 31___ 19 –		Store __Calgary__			
Description	Qty	Unit	Unit Cost	Extension	
Footballs	1	ea	28.56	28	56
Baseballs — hard	15	ea	6.07	91	05
" — soft	15	ea	5.28	79	20
Squash Balls	25	ea	3.00	75	00
Racquetballs	25	ea	3.06	76	50
Tennis Balls	20	/3	5.50	110	00
Called By __Claire__		Costed By __Fred__			
Recorded By __all__		Extended By __San__			
Checked By __LL__		Manager's Initials __JK__			

FIGURE 7-11   An inventory sheet

Physically counting inventory is not difficult, but assigning a cost to that inventory can be a problem. For example, assume that during one year Sports Emporium bought footballs at these prices:

Opening Inventory:	Jan. 2	0 Footballs
Purchases:	May 12	4 Footballs @ $27.00
	Aug. 30	8 Footballs @ $28.00
	Sept. 1	8 Footballs @ $29.00
	Oct. 31	5 Footballs @ $30.00

Further, assume that at the year end only one football is left in stock. Is it a $27.00 football or a $30.00 football? What is its cost?

There are four ways to determine which purchase cost should be attached to the one football left in inventory:

(1) Specific Identification
(2) FIFO
(3) LIFO
(4) Weighted Average Cost

Specific Identification

Specific identification is a method of pricing inventory by identifying the units in the ending inventory as coming from specific purchases during the year. This method means that the store owner can identify the specific inventory item which is still in stock. If the footballs above were coded, the owner could know, for instance, that the football still left in inventory was part of the September shipment. The cost would be $29.00.

This method is most useful and practical where the inventory consists of a small number of more expensive items, e.g. cars; and especially when the units can be identified by a serial number. The main flaw of this method is the accurate bookkeeping necessary to ensure that the correct price is identified for the article left in inventory at year end. An unscrupulous business person (perhaps badly in need of additional financing) can alter the income statement by choosing the wrong price for the ending inventory item. If ending inventory is higher than it should be, then the cost of goods sold will be lower than it should be and the gross profit higher than it should be. Profits will be artificially overstated.

Using the specific identification method the cost of goods sold for Sports Emporium would be:

Football Inventory	
Cost of Goods Sold:	
Opening Inventory	$ 0
Add: Purchases	714
Cost of Goods Available for Sale	714
Less: Closing Inventory	29
Cost of Goods Sold	$685

FIGURE 7-12   *Cost of goods sold following specific identification pricing*

FIFO

The acronym **FIFO** stands for First-In, First-Out; it assumes that the first item purchased is the first one sold. Think of the footballs being stored and sold in the order they are bought.

Under this method, the opening inventory and all of the purchases except one of the last lot purchased is assumed to have been sold. The closing inventory value, therefore, will be $30.00, the cost of one of the footballs in the October purchase.

Using the FIFO method of costing closing inventory, the cost of goods sold for Sports Emporium would be:

```
                    Football Inventory

        Cost of Goods Sold:
        Opening Inventory                    $  0
        Add: Purchases                        714
                                            _____
        Cost of Goods Available for Sale      714
        Less: Closing Inventory                30
                                            _____
        Cost of Goods Sold                   $684
                                            ======
```

FIGURE 7-13   *Cost of goods sold using FIFO pricing*

The FIFO method works very well in businesses where there are systems by which the oldest items are sold first. Grocery stores and pharmacies, for example, always stock fresher goods behind older goods so that the older stock is sold first. Eggs, milk, butter, drugs, films, and baked goods are dated stock that retailers will try to keep moving in the order bought.

LIFO
The acronym **LIFO** stands for Last-In, First-Out. It assumes that the last item purchased is the first one sold. In a hardware store selling nails in bulk quantities out of a bin, new nails purchased are simply dumped on top of the old nails. The nails at the top of the bin will be the first sold, and therefore LIFO is the most accurate way of costing this inventory.

If Sports Emporium used this method of costing inventory, it would attach a cost of $27.00 to the year-end football. The football still in stock would be presumed to have come from the opening inventory. All other footballs would have been sold.

Using the FIFO method of costing closing inventory the cost of goods sold for Sports Emporium would be:

```
                    Football Inventory

        Cost of Goods Sold:
        Opening Inventory                    $  0
        Add: Purchases                        714
                                            _____
        Cost of Goods Available for Sale      714
        Less: Closing Inventory                27
                                            _____
        Cost of Goods Sold                   $689
                                            ======
```

FIGURE 7-14   *Cost of goods sold using LIFO pricing*

Weighted Average Cost

Weighted average cost is the total cost of all items of a specific type or model available for sale divided by the number of units purchased. The weighted average cost method is used where it is difficult to determine specific costs of year-end inventory items using either FIFO or LIFO. In reality, it is hard for stores to keep their stock in the same order in which it is bought. Weighted average cost is a balance between FIFO and LIFO where it is difficult to determine the actual flow of goods.

In the example for Sports Emporium, divide the total cost of the footballs by the number of units available for sale.

	Qty	Cost	Total
Opening Inventory	0		
Purchases	4	$27.00	$108.00
	8	$28.00	$224.00
	8	$29.00	$232.00
	5	$30.00	$150.00
	25		$714.00

$$\frac{\text{Cost of Goods Available}}{\text{Number of Units}} = \text{Average Weighted Cost}$$

$$\frac{\$714}{25} = \$28.56$$

FIGURE 7-15   *Weighted average cost calculation*

Using the weighted average method of costing inventory, the cost of goods sold for Sports Emporium would be:

Football Inventory	
Cost of Goods Sold:	
Opening Inventory	$ 0.00
Add: Purchases	714.00
Cost of Goods Available for Sale	714.00
Less: Closing Inventory	28.56
Cost of Goods Sold	$685.44

Figure 7-16   Cost of goods sold using weighted average cost pricing

The method of inventory costing used varies among businesses. The table in Figure 7-17 attempts to summarize some of the key arguments for and against each costing method.

	Advantages	Disadvantages
(1) Specific Identification	is the most accurate because it uses the actual cost	is often impossible to use in a real inventory situation
(2) FIFO	assigns most recent prices to the ending inventory	cost of goods sold lower and net income higher; increases income tax payable.
(3) LIFO	realistic because it matches revenues with costs of replacing inventory sold	values the ending inventory at original cost i.e., low book value
(4) Weighted Average Cost	is the quickest and perhaps easiest method to use	not realistic since it assigns the same cost to each unit

FIGURE 7-17   *Comparison table of costing methods*

One of the most important accounting principles is that of consistency; the accounting procedures adopted by the firm should be the same from one fiscal period to the next, unless there is a special reason to change. This means that if a business uses the LIFO method for costing its closing inventory, the LIFO method must be used from one year to the next. The business cannot change from LIFO to FIFO to Weighted Average Cost as it wishes. The same inventory valuation method once adopted must be used consistently.

The impact of an error in valuing ending inventory can be seen if you examine these two abbreviated Cost of Goods Sold sections from a comparative income statement:

	19-0	19-1
Beginning Inventory	4 000	5 000
Purchases	56 000	55 000
Goods Available	60 000	60 000
Closing Inventory	5 000	6 000
Cost of Goods Sold	55 000	54 000

The closing inventory for year 19-0, $5 000, is also the opening inventory for year 19-1. Therefore, if the $5 000 is not correct, then the income statements for 19-0 and for 19-1 are affected.

Here are two income statements for 19-0 shown side by side to illustrate the effect of an inventory error on the income statement. The closing inventory should have been $7 000.

	Incorrect	Correct
Sales	$90 000	$90 000
Cost of Goods Sold		
Opening Inventory	4 000	4 000
Purchases	56 000	56 000
Goods Available	60 000	60 000
Closing Inventory	5 000	7 000
Cost of Goods Sold	55 000	53 000
Gross Profit	35 000	37 000
Other Expenses	15 000	15 000
Net Income	$20 000	$22 000

When the closing inventory is understated on the income statement, the cost of goods sold is overstated, and the net profit is understated. Conversely, when the closing inventory is overstated, cost of goods sold is understated, and net income is overstated. The valuation of closing inventory is critical because it directly affects net income in two consecutive accounting years.

A periodic system is useful where there are many different inventory items of low dollar value and keeping detailed records might be expensive. A hardware store is a good example of a merchandise concern that has this type of inventory. With the increase in computers, however, more firms will use perpetual inventory systems for their business. The next section deals with this type of system.

QUESTIONS

11. Under the periodic system of inventory what account is charged when goods are purchased for resale?

12. What does *input tax credit* mean? Explain.

13. List the accounting checks that might be found on a typical inventory sheet.

14. What are the four costing methods that can be used to calculate the value of a year-end inventory? Explain each method briefly.

15. Name four businesses that could use the specific identification method of costing quite easily.

16. Why is the word *weighted* used in the weighted average cost method of costing inventory?

17. What do the letters FIFO stand for?

18. Which of these businesses are most likely to use a FIFO method for costing inventory? grocery store; hardware store; donut shop; bakery

19. In what type of business does the FIFO system work well?

20. What do the letters LIFO stand for?

21. Give an example of two businesses where LIFO would be the most accurate inventory method to use.

22. In what type of business is the periodic system most useful?

23. Which inventory system would a business use if:
    (a) it wanted to assign the same inventory cost to each inventory unit?
    (b) the goods which were bought most recently are the first to be sold?
    (c) the business sold farm implements?
    (d) goods were stacked at the back of the shelf and the older goods were pushed to the front of the shelf every day?

24. Recommend an inventory costing system for each of these businesses: record store; heavy equipment dealer; candy store; jewellery store; sporting goods store; drug store

Perpetual Inventory Systems

A business that sells high value inventory items such as cars, farm implements, appliances, and stereo equipment often uses a perpetual inventory system. **Perpetual inventory** is a system in which inventory is debited to a Merchandise Inventory account and the value of the inventory is known at any given moment. Under this system, the opening inventory value is a debit balance in the Merchandise Inventory account. Purchases are also debited to this current asset account, and when inventory is sold, the account is credited with the cost of goods sold.

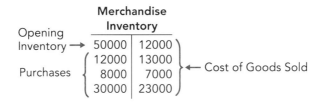

FIGURE 7-18   *T-account for Merchandise Inventory under a perpetual inventory system*

As merchandise is bought during the year, accounting entries are made to debit Merchandise Inventory (instead of Purchases as under the periodic system) and GST Recoverable, and credit either Accounts Payable or Bank. The purchase on account of $20 000 worth of goods under the perpetual system would be handled this way:

GENERAL JOURNAL

PAGE 21

DATE 19–		PARTICULARS	PR	DEBIT	CREDIT
Feb.	10	Merchandise Inventory		20000 –	
		GST Recoverable		1400 –	
		A/P—Wholesale Sports			21400 –
		To record purchase of inventory,			
		Inv. WS865			

FIGURE 7-19   *The general journal entry for purchase of merchandise inventory on account*

Under a perpetual system of inventory, a running balance of stock on hand is kept, both of quantity and of unit cost. In a manual inventory setup this can be done through an inventory ledger card. An **inventory ledger card** is a record of purchases and sales for one particular item of inventory. An example of such a card using the MaxiGym stock of Sports Emporium would be:

SPORTS EMPORIUM			Inventory Ledger Card			Store __Calgary__		
Item __MaxiGym 3000__			Maximum __8__			Minimum __2__		
	Purchased		Sold		Balance			
Date	Qty	Unit Cost	Qty	Unit Cost	Qty	Unit Cost	Total Cost	
1/18					2	478 50	957 –	
2/01	6	478 50			8	478 50	3828 –	
2/21			1	478 50	7	478 50	3349 50	
2/27			2	478 50	5	478 50	2392 50	
3/14			2	478 50	3	478 50	1435 50	
3/28			1	478 50	2	478 50	957 –	
4/16	6	490 –	1	478 50	1 / 6	478 50 / 490 –	3418 50	

FIGURE 7-20   *An inventory ledger card*

The inventory ledger card has notations on it for maximum and minimum quantities. When the stock on hand reaches the minimum level, a purchase requisition should be initiated for more stock, and just enough ordered to bring the item in question up to its maximum inventory level.

As purchases are received and are verified by packing slips and/or receiving reports, they are entered onto the card by quantity bought and unit cost. Each time a sale is made, as per a sales invoice copy, the quantity sold and the unit cost of those items sold is entered on the stock card. The Balance columns always have an up-to-date record of the value of the inventory on hand.

When inventory is sold under the perpetual inventory system, two accounting entries are required:

(1) to record the sale and corresponding accounts receivable
(2) to transfer the cost from the Merchandise Inventory account to a Cost of Goods Sold account

GENERAL JOURNAL

PAGE 24

DATE 19–		PARTICULARS	PR	DEBIT	CREDIT
Feb.	21	A/R—Marco Iannucci		1 0 2 3 9 9	
		Sales			9 5 7 –
		GST Payable			6 6 9 9
		To record the sale of one			
		MaxiGym 3000			
	21	Cost of Goods Sold		4 7 8 5 0	
		Merchandise Inventory			4 7 8 5 0
		To record cost of merchandise sold			

FIGURE 7-21   *The general journal entries for sale and cost of goods sold*

The Cost of Goods Sold account is an expense account that appears on the income statement and is closed out at the end of the fiscal period. There are no separate accounts for Purchases, Purchases Returns and Allowances, or Discounts Earned. Any transaction affecting these items is charged or credited to the Merchandise Inventory account directly. Here are two sample transactions to illustrate this point, in general journal form:

Purchase Return

A defective leather golf bag that cost $500 is returned to the supplier for credit:

GENERAL JOURNAL

PAGE 24

DATE 19–		PARTICULARS	PR	DEBIT	CREDIT
Feb.	22	A/P—Deluxe Leathercrafters		5 3 5 –	
		Merchandise Inventory			5 0 0 –
		GST Recoverable			3 5 –
		To record the return of inventory			

FIGURE 7-22   *The general journal entry for a purchase return*

Discounts Taken

Assume that merchandise costing $2 500 was purchased on Feb. 20 with terms of 2/10, n/30; the following entry would be made to record the payment and discount for the purchase:

GENERAL JOURNAL

PAGE 27

DATE 19–		PARTICULARS	PR	DEBIT	CREDIT
Feb.	26	A/P—Wholesale Sports		2675 –	
		Merchandise Inventory			53 50
		Bank			2621 50
		To record the payment of invoice			
		WS902 with a 2% discount			

FIGURE 7-23   *The general journal entry to record payment with purchase discount used to reduce the value of the inventory*

Under a perpetual inventory system, the balance of the Merchandise Inventory account in the general ledger always agrees with the cost of inventory actually on hand in the store. If it doesn't, then an investigation should take place to reveal the reason for the shortage (or overage). Assuming a shortage of $605, the following adjusting entry must be made to the books:

GENERAL JOURNAL

PAGE 27

DATE 19–		PARTICULARS	PR	DEBIT	CREDIT
Dec.	31	Inventory Shortage		605 –	
		Merchandise Inventory			605 –
		To adjust the inventory account for			
		a shortage			

FIGURE 7-24   *The general journal entry for a shortage adjustment*

Perpetual inventory systems are easy to operate with the assistance of a computer.

QUESTIONS

25. Name four examples of businesses that would be wise to use a perpetual system of inventory.

26. Under the perpetual system of inventory, what account is charged when goods are purchased for resale?

27. What information is found on an inventory ledger card?

28. What do the terms *maximum* and *minimum* mean on an inventory ledger card?

29. Maintaining an inventory ledger card is time-consuming if completed by hand. Of what practical use is it?

30. Where does the Cost of Goods Sold account appear?

31. What ledger accounts that are used in a periodic inventory system are not needed in a perpetual inventory system?

32. What is the main advantage of a perpetual inventory system?

33. What happens if a shortage is detected under the perpetual inventory system?

7.5

Inventory Management

The phrase **inventory management** refers to the methods used to ensure the accurate recording of inventory purchases in the books of account. A perpetual system of inventory management has the potential of providing excellent control over inventory, since management knows at all times what the particular inventory level of goods should be. By comparing the perpetual inventory records with the actual inventory on hand, management will be immediately aware of shortages or errors. However, a perpetual inventory system alone does not guarantee good management control over inventory. Other internal control measures (such as dividing duties between the handling and recording of goods, and using serially numbered documents) are still necessary for a strong control system. In addition, businesses with high value inventories on hand will want the physical protection provided by strong locks, bonded security personnel, and possibly an electronic alarm system that includes a hidden camera. Modern security systems can fill a warehouse or store with invisible laser beams that trigger an alarm system when intruders break into a designated area and attempt to steal inventory.

A small number of fast-moving inventory items is preferable to a larger, slower moving, inventory. It is costly to maintain a large inventory of goods for resale. But at the same time, a store needs to balance this cost against the need to have adequate stock to meet customer demands. This is the role of inventory management.

One way to manage inventory is through an analysis of certain information provided on the financial statements.

INVENTORY TURNOVER RATIO

One of the management tools for controlling inventory is the **inventory turnover ratio**. The following formula calculates by what factor the inventory has turned over, or sold, in a given fiscal period.

$$\text{Inventory Turnover Ratio} = \frac{\text{Costs of Goods Sold}}{\text{Average Merchandise Inventory}}$$

The average merchandise inventory is computed by adding the opening inventory and ending inventory, and dividing by 2.

For illustration purposes, the following sample data is provided covering three fiscal years:

Sports Emporium Costs of Goods Sold For the Years Ended December 31, 19-1 to 19-3			
	19-1	19-2	19-3
Opening Inventory	$ 72 000	$ 66 000	$ 70 000
Add: Purchases	490 000	520 000	490 000
Costs of Goods Available for Sale	562 000	586 000	560 000
Less: Closing Inventory	66 000	70 000	50 000
Cost of Goods Sold	$496 000	$516 000	$510 000

If you apply the inventory turnover ratio to data for 19-1, you see that

$$\text{Inventory Turnover Ratio} = \frac{\text{Costs of Goods Sold}}{\text{Average Merchandise Inventory}}$$

$$= \frac{496\ 000}{(72\ 000 + 66\ 000) \div 2}$$

$$= 7.2$$

The inventory ratio is most useful, however, when compared from one sales season to the next. Using the sample data provided:

19-1	19-2	19-3
$\dfrac{496\,000}{69\,000} = 7.2$	$\dfrac{516\,000}{68\,000} = 7.6$	$\dfrac{510\,000}{60\,000} = 8.5$

In this example, the inventory turnover ratio has increased from 7.2 in 19-1 to 8.5 in 19-3; this is favourable and a healthy sign for the business.

AVERAGE NUMBER OF DAYS

The **average number of days** formula is used to calculate the average length of time the inventory is on hand, in terms of days. The formula is:

365 days divided by the inventory turnover figure

Thus, for year 19-1

$$\frac{365}{7.2} - 51 \text{ days}$$

In 19-1 the inventory was on hand 51 days before it was sold. The set of ratios for the three years would be:

19-1	19-2	19-3
$\dfrac{365}{7.2} = 51$ days	$\dfrac{365}{7.6} = 48$ days	$\dfrac{365}{8.5} = 43$ days

These calculations can be compared over a period of time for the company, as seen above, or to the same data for similar businesses in the industry, if available. Detailed cost of goods sold information, however, does not always appear in the financial reports of other companies, so comparisons are sometimes difficult to make. The main objective in inventory management is to strike a reasonable balance between inventory, sales, and the financial ability of the company to maintain inventory levels.

The computer has proven to be an invaluable tool for some businesses for their inventory management. This will be dealt with in greater detail in the next section.

QUESTIONS

34. Name four ways to have good internal control over an expensive inventory system.

35. Explain what the phrase *inventory management* means.

36. What is the main objective of inventory management?

37. (a) Explain the term *inventory turnover ratio*.
    (b) Calculate the inventory turnover ratios for these companies:
    (c) Find the average number of days inventory for each company.

	A	B	C
Opening Inventory	$18 000	$ 55 000	$ 33 677
Closing Inventory	$22 000	$ 45 000	$ 38 994
Cost of Goods Sold	$84 000	$275 000	$190 651

7.6

Using the Computer

Using a computer to handle inventory control is almost a routine job. The computer can easily keep track of the number of units on hand of a given product, deduct units sold, and also cause an order message to be printed on the computer screen when stocks are low.

A customer enters one of the Sports Emporium stores (#1) and orders 12 footballs, but the store is out of stock. The clerk contacts another store (#2), through the computer modem, finds a store with 36 in stock, and processes an order to the other store for the sale. The computer deletes the footballs from store 2 inventory and sends a signal to ship the goods to store 1. Another message is sent to the accounts receivable ledger to charge the buyer for the 12 footballs, and the customer account is updated. An invoice is printed with the shipping date, and a printout of the customer's updated account if requested. The computer also triggers a purchase order to replenish the football inventory at store 1.

A good computer inventory control setup ensures that an optimum minimum inventory level is established. A message is sent to the store manager when inventory levels are below that minimum level.

On a simpler level, the computer can be used to prepare special reports relating to merchandise inventory by using an integrated software package that has spreadsheet, graphics, database, and word processing components.

Spreadsheets

An example of a spreadsheet activity in inventory would be the preparation of an inventory listing which extends the inventory by calculating the quantity on hand multiplied by the unit price of each item, and then totals the entire inventory listing for the business. Here is an example that might be used for Sports Emporium for golf set inventory:

	A	B	C	D	E
1					
2	Sports Emporium				
3	Inventory Listing — Golf Sets				
4	February		19-		
5					
6	No.	Description	Qty	Cost	Value
7					
8	203	Jack Nicklaus	5	920.00	4600.00
9	358	Lee Trevino	3	628.00	1884.00
10	444	Greg Norman	4	770.00	3080.00
11	569	Payne Stewart	1	500.00	500.00
12	660	Nick Faldo	4	820.00	3280.00
13	770	Ben Hogan	8	315.00	2520.00
14	990	Arnold Palmer	2	875.00	1750.00
15					
16				Total	17614.00
17					

FIGURE 7-25   A spreadsheet inventory listing

The headings are all a permanent part of the spreadsheet; only the data in columns C and D will change each month or each time the schedule is prepared. Once the new data is inserted in columns C and D, the rest of the spreadsheet is calculated automatically and the new product values and the total for the inventory arrived at.

Graphics

Spreadsheets are used to produce graphs on the computer. Most integrated software packages have this feature. Once the spreadsheet is stored, one of several types of graph can be produced. The main three types are a bar graph, a line graph, or a pie graph. The example here is a bar graph which shows the monthly inventory turnover ratios for Sports Emporium for its Manitoba stores, compared to Saskatchewan and Alberta over a six-month period.

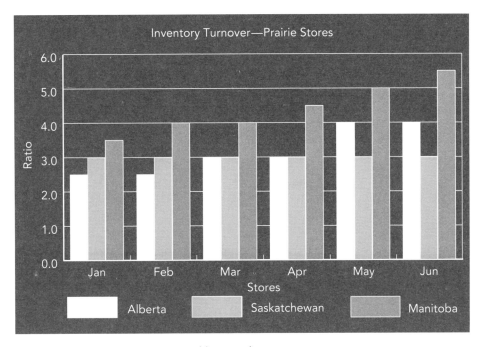

FIGURE 7-26   *A computer-generated bar graph*

A quick look indicates that the business has been very successful in increasing the inventory turnover ratios in Alberta and Manitoba, but not in Saskatchewan. There is work to be done for the Saskatchewan stores to improve the company's profit position.

Databases

The best example of a database for Sports Emporium is a list of all of the suppliers from whom inventory is purchased for the stores, and the credit terms offered by each supplier. The list is also categorized by territory to allow for cost comparisons of the database information. See Figure 7-27.

The top part of the diagram shows the form used when the database is set up and stored. The lower part is a listing of the supplier's name, address, town, postal code, and the discount terms usually offered to Sports Emporium. The code will help Sports Emporium add and delete suppliers to its database to take maximum advantage of the best terms and deals.

```
Name:  Sportswear
Address:  35 Fine Ave.
Town:  Winnipeg                   one record
Prov:  MB
PC:  R3G 2V6
Terms:  net 30
```

```
SUPPLIER DISCOUNT FILE
Name          Address           Town      Prov.   PC        Terms
Adidas        1210 Yonge St.    Toronto   ON      M2F 1S5   3/10, n/30
Jantzen       888 8th Street    Winnipeg  MB      R5T 6S9   net 30
Reebok        876 Tenth St.     Calgary   AB      T1D 3N7   2/15, n/30
Sportswear    35 Fine Ave.      Winnipeg  MB      R3G 2V6   net 30
Golf Supply   1400 Fairway Rd.  Regina    SK      S3S 5H8   1/20, n/30
```

FIGURE 7-27   *A supplier discount file*

Word Processing

Once the accountant for Sports Emporium has calculated the inventory turnover ratios, these statistics are made available to the stores in each region. This allows store managers to compare their results with each other, and acts as an incentive for them to improve their inventory positions.

February 28, 19–

Merrick McCall, Manager
Sports Emporium
Stampede Mall
Calgary, Alberta T3T 9S4

Dear Merrick

I have enclosed the inventory turnover ratio report for the first six months of the current year. As you can see by the statistics, your store has the best ratio of the three Prairie stores.

Congratulations on a fine performance! More extensive data will be coming your way when all the reports are in to the computer for processing. But we thought you might like an early look at your standings.

You will remember from our sales conference late last year that bonuses at year end will be based on sales, inventory turnover, and profit margins. It looks as if you are heading for a record year.

Well done!
Regards

John Kupisz, President
Sports Emporium Ltd.
Head Office

FIGURE 7-28   *An inventory letter*

The letter can be stored on the computer using a word processor since it will be used again, and since there are twenty stores to contact each time. The person inputting merely replaces the name and address of each store, and the inventory ratio data, each time a new letter is printed for the next store manager in the chain. Both the store address and the inventory ratios are kept as a database so that they can be drawn quickly into each new letter.

7.7

Bedford Exercise 7 — Scott Electronics

Scott Electronics is a retail consumer electronics dealership authorized to sell and service Sony, Panasonic, and RCA products, is owned and managed by Gail Scott who purchased the business ten years ago from her father. The business is located in Manitoba.

Gail and her husband Keith do the accounting for the business manually, utilizing a multipurpose journal and a general ledger and three subsidiary ledgers. Her sales policy is cash or credit card. Since her purchases of goods and services are usually on a credit basis she uses an accounts payable ledger, and because she sells many high-priced items she uses a perpetual inventory system. This entails the use of individual stock cards for each item she sells. On her accountant's advice, Gail has decided to convert her manual accounting records to a computerized system. The accounting firm has provided one of its students — you — to help the Scotts in the conversion process and to oversee the recording of transaction data for the first month.

The trial balance for Scott Electronics at the beginning of the new fiscal year is as shown.

The accounts and all of the general ledger balances have been entered onto a disk for you, and the computer accounting system only has to be set to **Ready** mode. The instructions for using *Bedford* and entering data are outlined in Chapter 1.

In this chapter, the asset account GST Recoverable has been replaced by a contra liability account, GST Paid, since this is the way *Bedford* computes GST. Only in this chapter is the GST automatic feature of *Bedford* used.

Scott Electronics
Beginning Trial Balance

No.	Account	Debit	Credit
105	Petty Cash	$ 100.00	
110	Bank	8 000.00	
120	Accounts Receivable	10 450.18	
124	Inventory — TVs	8 480.00	
125	Inventory — VCRs	3 550.00	
126	Inventory — Microwaves	700.00	
127	Inventory — Video Cameras	7 400.00	
128	Inventory — Audio Products	12 085.00	
140	Prepaid Store Supplies	424.30	
141	Prepaid Office Supplies	874.16	
142	Prepaid Repair Supplies	1 439.88	
180	Office Equipment	4 799.84	
181	Acc. Dep. — Office Equip.		$ 1 728.12
185	Store Equipment	6 400.00	
186	Acc. Dep. — Store Equip.		3 124.00
190	Delivery Truck	26 400.00	
191	Acc. Dep. — Delivery Truck		7 920.00
210	Bank Loan (Current)		2 500.00
220	Accounts Payable		21 160.79
230	GST Payable		1 424.07
231	GST Paid	992.83	
235	PST Payable		1 239.21
260	Bank Loan (Long-Term)		13 000.00
310	G. Scott, Capital		40 000.00
315	G. Scott, Drawings	0.00	
410	Sales — TVs		0.00
411	Sales — VCRs		0.00
412	Sales — Microwave Ovens		0.00
413	Sales — Video Cameras	0.00	
414	Sales — Audio Products		0.00
415	Sales Ret. & Allowances		0.00
416	Service Income		0.00
502	C.G.S. — TVs	0.00	
503	C.G.S. — VCRs	0.00	
504	C.G.S. — Microwave Ovens	0.00	
505	C.G.S. — Video Cameras	0.00	

506	C.G.S. — Audio Products	0.00
510	Advertising Expense	0.00
515	Bank Charges & Interest	0.00
520	Dep. Exp. — Office Equipment	0.00
521	Dep. Exp. — Store Equipment	0.00
522	Dep. Exp. — Del. Equipment	0.00
535	Mastercard Discount Expense	0.00
540	Miscellaneous Expense	0.00
560	Rent Expense	0.00
575	Salaries Expense	0.00
580	Telephone Expense	0.00
590	Utilities Expense	0.00

$92 096.19 $92 096.19

ACCESSING THE SCOTT ELECTRONICS GENERAL LEDGER

To retrieve the general ledger for Scott Electronics, you use the file name scotelec. Key this name into the computer, insert the dates provided by your teacher, and set the program to Ready, as before.

The GST feature of the program must also be activated. To do this, select SYSTEM, Default, Module, and System. Move the cursor down to GSTActive, press the right arrow ⟶ to change the choice to Yes.

Press the left arrow ⟵ key to save your choice. Exit *Bedford* by selecting SYSTEM, Finish.

Enter the Using data provided by your teacher. Remember the sequence, mmddyy. As before, ignore the cautions and proceed.

SETTING UP THE OTHER MODULES

For this exercise, you will be using the GENERAL, PAYABLE, RECEIVABLE, and INVENTORY modules in *Bedford*.

The accounts payable subsidiary ledger listing as of the beginning of the new fiscal year is as follows:

Scott Electronics
Accounts Payable Ledger Listing

Analytic Systems:	Invoice 432; mm04yy	$ 3 860.79
Atpac Distributors:	Invoice 289; mm14yy	4 690.00
	Invoice 395; mm28yy	2 840.00
Interworld Electronics:	Invoice 1140; mm10yy	4 400.00
Tracan Electronics:	Invoice 1002; mm21yy	3 500.00
	Invoice 2432; mm29yy	1 870.00
	Total Accounts Payable	$21 160.79

The **PAYABLE** module will have to be made ready before you start to journalize any transactions. This involves three steps.

Step 1   *Enter the balances above into the Accounts* **PAYABLE** *sub-ledger.*
Select **PAYABLE**, **History**, and **Purchase**.

Step 2   *Set the integration accounts.*
Select **SYSTEM**, **Integrate**, **Payable** and key in the account numbers as shown:

```
Cash      110
AccPay    220
GSTPaid   231
```

Step 3   *Make the* **PAYABLE** *module ready.*
Select **SYSTEM**, **Default**, **Module**, and **Payable**.
Change **Ready** to **Yes**. Return to the main status line.

The accounts receivable subsidiary ledger listing as of the beginning of the new fiscal year is as follows:

```
                        Scott Electronics
                Accounts Receivable Ledger Listing

Arnold, A.B.           Invoice S345; mm06yy          $  1 450.18
Dunn, G.C.             Invoice S340; mm03yy              760.00
                       Invoice S349; mm20yy            1 420.00
Meadows, D.B.          Invoice S342; mm04yy            2 840.00
                       Invoice S347; mm12yy            1 280.00
Sanderson, O.T.        Invoice S346; mm08yy              900.00
Zawicky, R.C.          Invoice S348; mm15yy            1 800.00
                                                      ──────────
                       Total Accounts Receivable      $10 450.18
                                                      ══════════
```

The **RECEIVABLE** module will have to made ready before you start to journalize any transactions. This involves three steps.

Step 1   *Enter the balances above into the Accounts* **RECEIVABLE** *sub-ledger.*
Select **RECEIVABLE**, **History**, and **Sale**.

Step 2   *Set the integration accounts.*
Select **SYSTEM**, **Integrate**, **Receivable**, and key in the account numbers, as shown:

```
            Cash        110
            AccRec      120
            GSTRate1    230
            PSTPay      235
```

Step 3   *Make the* **RECEIVABLE** *module ready.*
Select **SYSTEM**, **Default**, **Module**, and **Receivable**.
Select **GSTRate1**: key in 7, for 7%.
Select **PST**: key in 7, for 7%.
Change **Ready** to **Yes**. Return to the main status line.

To see the inventory listing, select **INVENTORY**, **Display**, **Stock**, and the default option **All**.

The **Inventory** module must be made ready. Select **SYSTEM**, **Default**, **Module**, and **Inventory** Change **Ready** to **Yes**.

JOURNALIZING TRANSACTIONS

To journalize general ledger transactions, access the **GENERAL** module and the **Journal** option.

To journalize accounts payable transactions, access **PAYABLE**, **Module**, **Journal**, and **Inventory**.

To journalize accounts receivable transactions, access **RECEIVABLE**, **Journal**, and **Inventory**.

TRANSACTIONS

1. Sales Invoice S350 (**RECEIVABLE**, **Journal**, **Sale**, **Inventory**)
   Dated: mm02yy
   Sold 1 microwave oven to G.C. Dunn on account, $300.00 plus $21 GST and $21 PST.
   Follow this guide when entering your data:

Customer	2
Invoice	S350
Date	mm02yy
Row	1 (Select the default here. The reference **Row** when you journalize will always be 1 since your invoices only have one line each.)
Item	7 (Microwave — Panasonic)
Quantity	1
Price	Select the default price, $300.
GSTCode	3 (GST is not included in the price.)
PST	Y (to have PST calculated automatically)
Amount	This will be filled in automatically.

   (Note: The *Bedford* file has been programmed to calculate GST and PST components on this invoice automatically.)

Account	Select the default account, Sales — Microwave Ovens.

   You should press ⌷F2⌷ to check the journal entry before posting.

   The program automatically calculates the transfer from the Inventory account to the Cost of Goods Sold account.

   Press ⌷Enter⌷ (to finish entering the data.)

2. Purchase Invoice 1116 (**PAYABLE**, Journal, Purchase, Inventory)
   Dated: mm02yy
   Bought 4 NEC portable cellular phones from Tracan Electronics, $1 900
   plus $133 GST; net 30.

Vendor	4
Invoice	1116
Date	mm02yy
Item	1
Quantity	4
Amount	1900

   Press ⌈Enter⌉

GST	133

3. Cheque 401 (**GENERAL**, Journal)   Dated: mm02yy
   To Alpine Properties, $800 plus $56 GST for store rent.

4. Cash Receipt 403 (**RECEIVABLE**, Journal, Payment)
   Dated: mm02yy
   From G.C. Dunn, $760, in full payment of invoice S340; cheque 1380.

   (Note: Press ⌈Enter⌉ twice after you enter the $760, then enter the cheque
   number.)

5. Sales Invoice S351   Dated: mm03yy
   1 RCA video camera to D.B. Meadows, $1 670 plus $116.90 GST and
   $116.90 PST. (Note: use transaction 1 as a guide here.)

6. Cheque 402 (**PAYABLE**, Journal, Payment)   Dated: mm03yy
   To Analytic Systems, $3 860.79, in payment of invoice 432.

7. Cash Receipt 404 (**RECEIVABLE**, Journal, Payment)
   Dated: mm03yy
   From D.B. Meadows, $2 840, in full payment of invoice S342, his cheque
   00369.

8. To record this transaction you will have to enter this new vendor in the
   PAYABLE sub-ledger: CMS Office Products, 456 Hornby Street,
   Brandon, MB, R5P 2C9, 555-1289; **Purge Y**.

   Purchase Invoice C2025 (**PAYABLE**, Journal, Purchase, Other)
   Dated: mm05yy
   Bought office supplies from CMS Office Products, $128.40 plus $8.40
   GST; terms n/30.

9. Cash Receipt 405   Dated: mm05yy
   From A.B. Arnold, $1 450.18, in full payment of invoice S345;
   cheque 12.

10. Sales Invoice S352   Dated: mm06yy
    Sold 1 Panasonic TV to A.B. Arnold, $700 plus $49 GST and $49 PST;
    net 30.

11. Purchase Invoice 1289   Dated: mm07yy
    Bought 2 Sony TVs from Interworld Electronics, $480 plus $33.60 GST;
    net 30.

12. Cheque 403   Dated: mm08yy
    To Manitoba Hydro & Power Authority for utilities, $340 plus
    $23.80 GST.

13. Cash Receipt 406   Dated: mm08yy
    From O.T. Sanderson, $200, in part payment of invoice S346,
    cheque 10.

14. Bank Debit Memo   Dated: mm09yy
    From the Bank of Montreal, $1 000 payment on the bank loan
    (current portion) plus $148 interest.

15. Sales Invoice S353   Dated: mm10yy
    Sold 1 Panasonic CD Player to R.C. Zawicky, $550 plus $38.50 GST
    and $38.50 PST.

16. Cheque 404   Dated: mm10yy
    To Manitoba Telephone Company, $190.46 plus $12.46 GST.

17. Cheque 405   Dated: mm10yy
    To Interworld Electronics, $4 400, in full payment of invoice 1140.

18. Cash Receipt 407   Dated: mm11yy
    From D.B. Meadows, $1 280, in full payment of invoice S347;
    cheque 48.

19. Purchase Invoice 512   Dated: mm12yy
    Bought 1 Panasonic Microwave Oven from Analytic Systems,
    $140 plus $9.80 GST.

20. Cheque 406 (**PAYABLE, Journal, Payment**)   Dated: mm13yy
    To Atpac Distributors, $4 690, in full payment of invoice 289.

21. Cash Receipt 408   Dated: mm14yy
    From R.C. Zawicky, $1 800, in full payment of invoice S348;
    cheque 102.

22. Sales Invoice S354   Dated: mm15yy
    Sold 1 RCA CD Player to G.C. Dunn, $490 plus $34.30 GST and
    $34.30 PST.

23. Cash Receipt 409   Dated: mm15yy
    Cheque received from O.T. Sanderson, $700; final payment on invoice
    S346; cheque 18.

24. Purchase Invoice 1380   Dated: mm16yy
    Bought 1 Sony Video Camera from Interworld Electronics, $750 plus
    $52.50 GST.

25. Sales Invoice S355   Dated: mm19yy
    Sold 1 Panasonic VCR to O.T. Sanderson, $400 plus $28 GST and
    $28 PST.

26. Cheque 407   Dated: mm20yy
    To Tracan Electronics, $3 500, in full payment of invoice 1002.

27. Cash Receipt 410   Dated: mm20yy
    From G.C. Dunn, $1 420, in full payment of invoice S349; cheque 75.

28. Purchase Invoice 1349   Dated: mm25yy
    Bought 2 cellular phones from Tracan Electronics, at a total cost of
    $950 plus $66.50 GST.

29. Sales Invoice S356   Dated: mm26yy
    Sold 1 RCA TV, $300 plus $21 GST and $21 PST to D.B. Meadows;
    net 30.

30. Cheque 408   Dated: mm27yy
    To Atpac Distributors, $2 840, in full payment of invoice 395.

31. To record this transaction you will have to enter a new vendor in the
    PAYABLE sub-ledger: Delta Publishing Ltd., 44 Willis Avenue,
    Brandon, MB, R8A 2O3, 555-5432; **Purge Y**.

    Billing Statement 99 (**PAYABLE, Journal, Purchase, Other**)
    Dated: mm28yy
    From Delta Publishing Ltd., $420 plus $29.40 GST, for product
    catalogues (advertising); net 30.

32. Cheque 409   Dated: mm28yy
    To Tracan Electronics, $1 870, in full payment of invoice 1032.

33. Cash Receipt 411 (**GENERAL, Journal**)   Dated: mm30yy
    Owner invested $10 000 into the business from a personal bank account.

34. To record the next entry you will have to enter a new account in the **GENERAL** ledger: 530 Inventory Shrinkage, **Type L, Suppress Y**.

    Inventory Shrinkage (**INVENTORY, Journal, Adjust**)
    Dated: mm30yy

Comment	Inventory Shrinkage
Source	Voucher 100
Item	3
Quantity	1
Amount	180-
Account	530

    Press Enter .

    Press F2 to see how this journal entry looks before posting it.

35. To record the next entry you will have to enter a new account in the Accounts Receivable ledger: Brandon Cable TV, 1370 Main Street, Brandon, MB, R7N 1E6, 555-0101. **Purge Y, Statement Y**.

    Sales Invoice S357   Dated: mm30yy
    Sold 3 RCA Video Cameras to Brandon Cable TV, $5 010 plus $350.70 GST and 350.70 PST.

DISPLAYING AND PRINTING

Select **Display**. Your teacher will advise you which of the six options to preview. You will be prompted for dates. Remember, a date is entered in the sequence mmddyy (month, date, year).

Print any statements requested by your teacher. Again, you may be prompted for dates.

FINISHING A SESSION

Access the **SYSTEM** module and select the **Finish** option.

7.8

Dictionary of Accounting Terms

Average Number of Days   A formula that calculates the average length of time the inventory is on hand, in terms of days.

Closing Inventory   The goods on hand at the end of a fiscal period.

Cost of Goods Sold   The laid-down cost of the goods which have already been sold by the business.

Discounts Earned   A percentage applied to purchases that reduces the amount owing to a supplier.

FIFO   First-in first-out; products which were bought first are assumed to have been sold first by the business.

Freight-In   The cost to the business of transporting goods from the supplier.

Inventory Control   The methods used to safeguard assets and ensure the accurate recording of inventory in the books of account.

Inventory Ledger Card   A document containing purchase and sales data for one particular item of inventory.

Inventory Sheet   A document used to summarize the information contained on inventory tags.

Inventory Tag   Information attached to each inventory item when it is physically counted.

Inventory Turnover Ratio   A formula that determines by what factor an inventory has sold in a one-year time period.

LIFO   Last-in first-out; products which were bought last are assumed to have been sold first by the business.

Merchandise Inventory   The quantity of goods available for sale.

Opening Inventory   The goods on hand at the beginning of a fiscal period.

Periodic Inventory   An inventory system which debits all goods bought to a Purchases account and counts and values inventory only at the end of the fiscal period.

Perpetual Inventory   An inventory system in which inventory is debited to a merchandise inventory account and the value of inventory is known at any given moment.

Physical Inventory   The process of physically counting goods on hand at year end and attaching a cost value to them, and then calculating the total dollar value.

Specific Identification   A method of valuing inventory by identifying the units in the ending inventory as coming from specific purchases during the year.

Transportation-In   Another name for Freight-In.

Weighted Average Cost   A method of valuing inventory which totals the costs of items purchased and divides by the number of units purchased.

MANUAL EXERCISES

1. From the following information, set up the cost of goods sold section of the income statement for Yogie's Yogurt.

Inventory Jan. 1, 19–	$ 25 000
Purchases	165 000
Freight-In	3 200
Purchases Returns and Allowances	400
Discounts Earned	3 650
Inventory Dec. 31, 19–	22 000

2. From the following information, set up the cost of goods sold section of the income statement for Habbu Optical.

Inventory Jan. 1, 19–	$ 72 000
Purchases	138 000
Freight-In	4 100
Purchases Returns and Allowances	700
Discounts Earned	4 280
Inventory Dec. 31, 19–	81 500

3. Fast Track Audio had these transactions relating to compact disk player inventory during January 19–.

Jan. 1:   Balance 100 units @ $500 each. (Lot 1)
       4:   Purchased 28 units @ $510 each. (Lot 2)
     10:   Sold 33 units @ $700 each. (30 units from Lot 1; 3 units from Lot 2)
     15:   Purchased 7 units @ $520 each. (Lot 3)
     23:   Sold 40 units @ $720 each. (20 units from Lot 1; 20 units from Lot 2)
     31:   Sold 48 units @ $720 each. (43 units from Lot 1; 5 units from Lot 2)

The company uses periodic inventory. Compute the following under Specific Identification, Weighted Average Cost, FIFO, and LIFO.
(a) inventory at the end of the month
(b) cost of goods sold for the month

4. Faxination had these transactions relating to their fax machine inventory during February 19–.

Feb. 2:   Balance 70 units @ $800 each. (Lot 1)
      7:   Purchased 28 units @ $820 each. (Lot 2)
     11:   Sold 60 units @ $1 000 each. (40 units from Lot 1;
           20 units from Lot 2)
     18:   Purchased 32 units @ $820 each. (Lot 3)
     24:   Sold 30 units @ $1 020 each. (25 units from Lot 1;
           5 units from Lot 2)
     28:   Sold 15 units @ $1 020 each. (3 units from Lot 1;
           2 units from lot 2; 10 units from Lot 3)

The company uses periodic inventory. Compute the following under Specific Identification, Weighted Average Cost, FIFO and LIFO:
(a) inventory at the end of the month
(b) cost of goods sold for the month

5. The Miller Nut House had an inventory of $16 000 on June 1, 19–. The other information for June is:

Sales	$ 8 000
Sales Returns and Allowances	120
Discounts Allowed	80
Purchases	12 000
Purchases Returns and Allowances	180
Discounts Earned	250

If the gross profit averages 40% of net sales, find the estimated inventory on June 30, 19–.

6. Georgia's Jeans had an inventory of $90 000 on May 1, 19–. The other information for May is:

Sales	$ 74 000
Sales Returns and Allowances	625
Discounts Allowed	3 250
Purchases	148 000
Purchases Returns and Allowances	1 235
Discounts Earned	2 875

If the gross profit averages 30% of net sales, find the estimated inventory on May 31, 19–.

7. Bregman & Company had a beginning inventory of 100 units of Item A costing $12.75 per unit on July 1, 19–. The July purchases were:

	Quantity	Unit Cost
July 4	80	$13.00
10	100	13.10
20	70	13.20
31	30	13.40

At the end of the month, there were 80 units on hand in the inventory.
Determine the ending inventory under:
(a) Weighted Average Cost
(b) FIFO
(c) LIFO

8. Canadian Billiards had a beginning inventory of 30 tables costing $800 per unit on Nov. 1, 19–. The purchases were:

	Quantity	Unit Cost
Nov. 3	8	$800.00
17	12	820.00
22	20	820.00
30	10	850.00

At the end of the month, there were 25 units on hand in the inventory.
Determine the ending inventory under:
(a) Weighted Average Cost
(b) FIFO
(c) LIFO

9. Prepare an income statement for Connie's Cookies for the year ended March 31, 19-1, given this information:

Sales	$280 000
Purchases	215 000
Purchases Returns and Allowances	12 200
Discounts Earned	6 800
Freight-In	1 500
Inventory April 1, 19-0	32 500
Inventory March 31, 19-1	28 500
Other Expenses	44 400

10. Prepare an income statement for Shoes & Bags for the year ended June 30, 19–1, given this information:

Sales	$182 765
Purchases	102 919
Purchases Returns and Allowances	2 104
Discounts Earned	3 373
Freight-In	2 667
Inventory July 1, 19-0	18 564
Inventory June 30, 19-1	21 979
Other Expenses	44 400

11. If the merchandise inventory determined on December 31, 19-0, is overstated by $1 700, what is the effect of this error on the gross profit for the year 19-1?

12. On December 31, 19-0, the company failed to count $350 worth of merchandise when the ending inventory was taken. On December 31, 19-1, the company counted some inventory twice and the inventory was overvalued by $920. If these errors are not discovered until 19-2, what is the effect on the gross profit in 19-2?

13. In January 19–, Rainbow Paints had the following merchandise inventory transactions. The PST rate is 6%, calculated on the base price only. The GST rate is 7%. Record them on page 79 in a general journal:
    (a) using the periodic system of inventory
    (b) using the perpetual system of inventory

    Jan.   3:   Sold merchandise on account to Joe Stinson, $650 plus taxes. The cost of the merchandise was $390.
           10:   Bought paint on account from BC Manufacturing, $9 124.56 plus GST. Terms were 2/15, n/30.
           19:   Sold merchandise on account to Ann Briar, $690 plus taxes. The cost of the merchandise was $414.

23: Wrote a cheque (#788) to pay for the merchandise bought from BC Manufacturing on January 10th. Took the discount.

27: Bought merchandise from Benjamin Parents, $10 003 plus GST. Wrote cheque #795 to pay for the merchandise immediately. There was a 5% discount for the immediate cash payment.

14. In October 19–, Auto Supply Store had the following merchandise inventory transactions. Record them on page 59 in a general journal. The PST rate is 12%, calculated on base price plus GST (7%). Record them on page 59 in a general journal:
(a) using the periodic system of inventory
(b) using the perpetual system of inventory

Oct. 7: Sold merchandise on account to Greg Bukta, $1 234 plus taxes. The cost of the merchandise was $925.50.

12: Bought merchandise on account from Nova Supply, $6 334.77 plus GST. Terms were 3/10, n/30.

20: Sold merchandise on account to David Henhawk, $456.17 plus taxes. The cost of the merchandise was $342.13.

21: Wrote a cheque (#334) to pay for the merchandise bought from Nova Supply on October 12th. Took the discount.

26: Bought merchandise for cash from Barr Ltd., $8 007.07 plus GST. Wrote cheque #348 to pay for the merchandise. There was a 4% discount for the immediate cash payment.

15. On January 1, 19–, Northwood Supply had merchandise inventory of $19 550. The PST rate is 8% calculated on the base price only. The GST rate is 7%. The January transactions were:

Jan. 6: Bought merchandise on account from A & B Ltd., $12 300 plus GST. Terms 2/10, n/30.

12: Bought merchandise on account from Gordons Inc., $9 000 plus GST. Terms 2/10, n/30.

14: Cheque #1212 to A & B Ltd. to pay in full, less the discount earned.

18: Sold goods to B. Neale on account $3 900 plus GST, and PST. The cost of the merchandise was $2 300.

20: Cheque #1213 to Gordons Inc. to pay in full, less the discount earned.

24:   Bought merchandise from King & Cong Ltd., $6 300 plus GST. Cheque #1220.

31:   Sold goods to Church Construction, on account $6 740 plus GST, and PST. The cost of the merchandise was $4 100.

On January 31, the physical inventory value was $39 194.

Required:
Record the transactions on page 32 in a general journal (including adjusting entries needed on January 30) under:
(a) the periodic system of inventory
(b) the perpetual system of inventory

16. On March 1, 19–, Farm-Agri Ltd., had merchandise inventory of $42 800. The PST is 10% calculated on base price plus GST. The GST rate is 7%. The March transactions were:

Mar.   3:   Bought merchandise on account from Ralston Co., $28 600 plus GST. Terms 1/25, n/30.

8:   Bought merchandise on account from Farm Wholesale, $11 500 plus GST. Terms 2/20, n/30.

20:   Sold goods to J. Meyer on account, $4 690 plus GST, and PST. The cost of the merchandise was $3 730.

21:   Cheque #089 to Ralston to pay in full, less the discount earned.

27:   Cheque #090 to Farm Wholesale to pay in full, less the discount earned.

30:   Bought merchandise from Power Tools Inc., $9 125 plus GST. Cheque #091.

31:   Sold goods to Ralph Kent on account, $3 118 plus GST, and PST. The cost of the merchandise was $2 575.

On March 31, the physical inventory value was $85 720.

Required:
Record the transactions on page 47 in a general journal, (including adjusting entries needed on March 31) under:
(a) the periodic system of inventory
(b) the perpetual system of inventory

COMPUTER EXERCISES

SS1   Use a spreadsheet to produce this inventory listing. Program the spread-sheet to calculate the inventory value for each item and the total of the inventory list. Save your solution under the file name CH7SS1.

	A	B	C	D	E
1	INVENTORY LISTING				
2	AUGUST 31, 19-				
3	No.	Description	Quantity	Cost	Value
4	23	B/W Television	18	79.95	
5	28	B/W Television	7	139.95	
6	52	Colour TV	20	415.00	
7	55	Colour TV	13	675.00	
8	58	Colour TV	16	1020.50	
9					
10				TOTAL	?
11					

SS2   Use a spreadsheet to produce this inventory listing. Program the spread-sheet to calculate the value of each item of inventory and the total of the inventory list. Save your solution under the file name CH7SS2.

	A	B	C	D	E
1	Johnson Jewellery				
2	INVENTORY LISTING				
3	No.	Description	Quantity	Cost	Value
4	667	Timex Watches	15	15.80	
5	223	Bulova Watches	18	175.00	
6	096	Seiko Watches	11	230.50	
7	883	Caravel Watches	9	75.10	
8	545	Swatches	22	24.75	
9					
10				TOTAL	?
11					

SS3   Use a spreadsheet to produce the following inventory ledger card tem-plate. Save the template under the file name CH7SS3. Set each column width to 6 characters.

	A	B	C	D	E	F	G	H	I	J
1	Campus Sporting Goods									
2	INVENTORY LEDGER CARD									
3	Item:									
4	Max:			Min:						
5		Purchased				Sold			Balance	
6	Date	Units	Cost	Total	Units	Cost	Total	Units	Cost	Total
7	XX	XX	XX	XXX	XX	XX	XXX	XX	XX	XXX
8										
9										
10										
11										

SS4   Recall the inventory ledger card template CH7SS3 and insert this data.
Program the spreadsheet to perform the total calculations.

	A	B	C	D	E	F	G	H	I	J
1	Campus Sporting Goods									
2	INVENTORY LEDGER CARD									
3	Item: Badminton Racquets #330									
4	Max: 20			Min: 2						
5		Purchased				Sold			Balance	
6	Date	Units	Cost	Total	Units	Cost	Total	Units	Cost	Total
7	1/5							10	20	?
8	1/8	3	20	?				?	20	?
9	1/10				2	20	?	?	20	?
10	1/20				6	20	?	?	20	?
11	1/31				3	20	?	?	20	?

SS5   Recall the inventory ledger card template CH7SS3 and insert this data.

	A	B	C	D	E	F	G	H	I	J
1	Campus Sporting Goods									
2	INVENTORY LEDGER CARD									
3	Item: Golf Shoes #20									
4	Max: 10			Min: 2						
5		Purchased				Sold			Balance	
6	Date	Units	Cost	Total	Units	Cost	Total	Units	Cost	Total
7	1/3							7	50	?
8	1/6	13	50	?				?	50	?
9	1/13				18	50	?	?	50	?
10	1/24	8	50	?	4	50	?	?	50	?
11	1/30				3	50	?	?	50	?

SS6 Prepare a spreadsheet for this inventory report and have the computer calculate the turnover ratio.

	A	B	C	D
1	Campus Sporting Goods — Western Stores			
2	INVENTORY TURNOVER RATIOS			
3		Cost of	Average	Turnover
4	Store	Goods Sold	Inventory	Ratio
5	Victoria	240000	62000	
6	Vancouver	320000	85000	
7	Calgary	300000	60000	
8	Edmonton	275000	75000	
9	Regina	189000	36000	
10	Saskatoon	164000	47000	
11	Brandon	165000	52000	
12	Winnipeg	415000	56000	

SS7 Prepare a spreadsheet for this inventory report and have the computer calculate the turnover rate.

	A	B	C	D
1	Campus Sporting Goods — Ontario Stores			
2	INVENTORY TURNOVER RATIOS			
3		Cost of	Average	Turnover
4	Store	Goods Sold	Inventory	Ratio
5	Thunder Bay	125000	30000	
6	Owen Sound	145000	41000	
7	London	410000	58000	
8	Windsor	220000	44000	
9	Hamilton	340000	89000	
10	Waterloo	380000	76000	
11	Kingston	240000	44000	
12	Ottawa	375000	68000	

SS8 Complete the following inventory listing for the Maritime stores for Campus Sporting Goods, by having the computer calculate both the turnover ratio and the average number of days (365 divided by column D).

	A	B	C	D	E
1	Campus Sporting Goods — Maritime Stores				
2	AVERAGE NUMBER OF DAYS OF INVENTORY				
3		Cost of	Average	Turnover	Avg. #
4	Store	Goods Sold	Inventory	Ratio	of Days
5	Fredericton	115000	30000		
6	Moncton	128000	34000		
7	Charlottetown	110000	40000		
8	St. John	127000	36000		
9	Halifax	210000	41000		
10	Antigonish	98000	33000		
11	St. John's	176000	42000		

DB1   Create a supplier database for Boyd's Appliances. Define the following fields for your file. Save your file under the name CH7DB1.

Name	= 20 columns
Address	= 18 columns
Town	= 10 columns
Postal Code	= 7 columns
Balance Owing	= 10 columns

Enter the raw data shown below, and print a listing of the file.

Name	Address	Town	PC
Inglis Mfg.	328 Rowley Ave.	Toronto	M4P 2T3
Saddler Can	45 Price St.	Toronto	M4W 1Z2
Royal Craft	99 Melgund Rd.	Toronto	M5R 1Z9
Davis & Davis	75 Spadina Ave.	Toronto	M3E 2C7
Tech Electric	117 Regina Ave.	Toronto	M6A 1R8
Fox & Wall	1 Leduc Dr.	Toronto	M9W 2A6

DB2   Recall the database stored as CH7DB1 and insert a column showing these balances owing. Calculate the total balance owing and print a list of the supplier file in alphabetical order.

Name	Balance
Inglis Mfg.	$2 346.17
Saddler Can	$1 118.19
Royal Craft	$ 334.59
Davis & Davis	$2 009.02
Tech Electric	$1 094.55
Fox & Wall	$1 884.32

DB3   Create a database for suppliers who offer discounts to Campus Sporting Goods. Define the following fields for your file.

Name	= 15 columns
Address	= 15 columns
Town	= 10 columns
Postal Code	= 7 columns
Terms	= 10 columns

Enter the raw data shown below, and print an alphabetized listing of the file.

Name	Address	Town	PC	Terms
Golf Supply	100 Conway Dr.	Calgary	T1A 5T2	4/10, n/30
Rod & Reel	333 Halton Ave.	Regina	S4S 4D3	3/10. n/30
Babby Shirt	1200 Camp Ave.	Calgary	T3G 3V2	2/15. n/30
Western Link	6 Lams Drive	Winnipeg	R6F 7R4	1/15, n/30
Pacific Rim	87 Victoria	Vancouver	V7T 3T4	2/10, n/30
CMC Cycle	50 Vanier Dr.	Vancouver	V8R 2P8	3/20, n/30
Racquet Whse.	51 Pearen Ave.	Edmonton	T2E 1E7	4/20, n/30

G1   Create a bar graph for this inventory data.

Description	Store 1	Store 2
Roland Printers	$15 000	$18 000
286 Computers	$38 000	$34 000
386 Computers	$42 000	$50 000
Laser Printers	$16 000	$10 000
Mouses	$ 1 400	$ 2 000
Laptops	$12 000	$18 000

G2   Create a line graph for this inventory data.

Month	19-0	19-1
January	$45 000	$48 000
February	$42 000	$46 000
March	$38 000	$39 000
April	$40 000	$35 000
May	$50 000	$45 000
June	$60 000	$55 000

G3   Create a pie graph for this inventory data.

Product	19-0
Laser Printers	$ 23 465
Software	$ 46 775
Computers	$178 907
Dot Matrix Printers	$ 44 001
5.25 Disk Drives	$ 16 338
3.50 Disk Drives	$ 34 654

WP1   Use a word processor to send this letter to the manager of the Edmonton Store. Save it under the file name CH7WP1.

December 31, 19–

Campus Sporting Goods
1242 Airport Rd.
Edmonton, Alberta
T5S 2R6

Attention: Jane Spek, Store Manager

Our head office accountant has recently obtained computer printouts of the inventory turnover ratios of all of the stores in our company, as well as the average number of days of inventory levels. I am happy to report to you that your store has the highest inventory turnover ratio in the Prairie Province Region. Your turnover ratio was 5.5, which incidentally is also a record high for the six-year history of your store. The average number of days for your inventory levels is 66.4. I will be contacting you soon about giving a presentation at our annual store conference to be held in March.

Congratulations on a fine report!

Yours truly

Veronica Chan
President, Campus Sporting Goods

WP2   Retrieve CH7WP1 and send a copy of a similar letter to the store manager, Jill Cervini, at the Vancouver store, 2310 Burrard St., Vancouver, V6T 3H7. Substitute 5.3 for the inventory turnover ratio and 68.9 for the average number of days.

R. v. BEATON

BACKGROUND

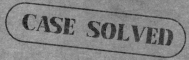

As the president of Construct Rental Equipment, David Beaton was held in high regard by the president of the parent company, Thunder Heavy Equipment. According to the computerized accounting reports from Beaton, the subsidiary business was both active and profitable. Beaton was a prime candidate to become a vice-president of the parent company at the start of the new fiscal year.

INVESTIGATION

In September, one of the mechanics in the Construct Rental Equipment repair shop was asked to transfer a serial number from a new machine just purchased to an old reconditioned machine. This mechanic had been an employee at Construct for ten years, and this was the first time he had been asked to do such a thing. Since it didn't sound right, he reported it to a mechanic friend at Thunder Heavy Equipment, who passed the information up through the system to the president, Jim Brown. Brown phoned his accountant immediately, who in turn suggested that a team of forensic accountants be called in to investigate. An examination of the books of Construct Rental Equipment indicated that the following series of events had taken place within that company.

1. A back hoe, serial number 01E0607, was purchased on September 28 by Construct for $9 100.
2. That same day a company called Aurora Rentals leased a back hoe, serial number 01E0607, to a company called Voght Construction.
3. The inventory listing of rental heavy equipment for Construct at the end of September showed this back hoe on its books, when it was in reality being used by Voght Construction.

NAME

NO.

CRIMEBUSTERS

4. On October 14 Construct sold the back hoe to a company called McManus Construction for $10 000, $3 000 in cash plus a trade-in earth mover supposedly valued at $7 000.
5. McManus Construction is a company which did not exist. McManus is the maiden name of Beaton's wife.
6. An independent appraisal of the trade-in earth mover suggested a value of $4 500, not $7 000.

FRAUD

The accused, David Beaton, had abused his power as president of Construct to approve the acceptance of the earth mover at an inflated value of $7 000 rather than the appraised value of $4 500. Further, he had caused the back hoe to be included in the inventory listing of Construct at the end of September, when the back hoe in question, 01E0607, had already been sold to Aurora Rentals, who had leased it to Voght Construction. And he had asked a shop foreman to have a mechanic change the serial number plate of the new back hoe, 01E0607, to cover up the sale. Beaton also abused his powers as president to have the back hoe included in inventory, when in fact it had been sold and was physically elsewhere, generating rental income for another company. Finally, as president, he was able to tell Construct's regular customer Voght Construction to deal with Aurora Rentals.

The books of Construct showed a profit on the sale of the back hoe of $900, the sale price to McManus Construction (the bogus company) of $10 000, minus the purchase price of $9 100. In fact, Construct lost $8 500 on these events:

Profit on sale of back hoe to Aurora	$6 900
Overvaluation of trade-in	2 500
Less profit recorded on sale to McManus	(900)
Actual loss to Construct Rental Equipment	$8 500

The investigation revealed how David Beaton, as a result of his position of power and control, overrode the existing accounting controls with regard to inventory control, customers, and employees. This act is an example of front-end fraud.

SENTENCE

David Beaton was clearly guilty of fraudulent activities with regard to the operations of Construct Rental Equipment. He was charged with fraud under the appropriate sections of the Criminal Code of Canada. The forensic accountants were called to court to testify because of the complexity of the accounting involved in Beaton's fraudulent dealings. Beaton tried to hide behind the corporate veil of limited liability, but the court had no difficulty finding him personally responsible for the fraud that occurred.

Because the fraud involved several transactions by the president, and because it involved his coercion of employees, the recognition of a bogus company, and the breaking of existing accounting controls of the company, the court felt Beaton's offences were extremely serious. He was given a jail term of four years for his crimes.

QUESTIONS

1. How could the back hoe be shown on the month-end inventory of Construct Rental Equipment when another company had it?
2. How much was the original profit that was shown on the books for 01E0607? What was the true loss?
3. Who had to be in collusion with David Beaton to help cover up the fraud he was trying to perpetrate on Construct Rentals?
4. Did the accounting system reveal this fraud? Why or why not?

Career Profile

Darrell Marshall had thought someday he might be a disk jockey on radio. Throughout high school he played for as many student dances as he could, and worked part time at Top 10 Records in the local mall. When he graduated from high school, the manager wanted Darrell to work full time, but Darrell had been accepted into a radio and television arts program at a nearby community college. Three years later, the manager still needed help and offered Darrell a job as assistant manager at a good salary. Two years later, the head office of the record chain was impressed enough by Darrell's job performance reports to offer him a position as the manager of a new store about to be opened in the West Edmonton Mall. The position offered an excellent salary, good fringe benefits, and a commission on all record sales in the store.

Before Darrell started managing the store he was sent to the head office of Top 10 Records in Calgary. He was given a one-month training course on store operations and bookkeeping. One week of that time was devoted to learning the basics of accounting and the *Bedford* computer accounting software. Darrell realized the immediate benefits of putting his record inventory on the computer. In the store, he would be able to call up any request by customers for specific records. This would save the customers' time, particularly the many customers who came during their lunch hour, and whose time was limited.

He purchased an MS-DOS computer system with a dot matrix printer and had it installed at the front desk of the store for immediate access. He bought two pieces of software: a well-known database, and the *Bedford* accounting package.

All the music in the store was divided into four types — compact disks (CDs), cassette tapes (Tapes), long-playing records (LPs) and 45 rpms (Singles). Darrell knew from industry releases that long-playing records were on their way out, but he felt that a certain inventory was still necessary for customers who had not converted to compact disk. Each type of music was catalogued by classification, title, artist, recording studio, cost, and store bin number.

The inventory was all stored on the computer using the database. Here is a sample listing of that database.

```
#   Title         Artist            Studio      Cost    Bin
1   Adorable      BJ Guru           Capitol     10.50    8
4   Afro Jazz     Kenya 5           Zahili      14.50    6
3   Ahead of Me   Sutherland        National    12.00    4
2   American Pie  Beach Band        LA Wild     10.50    4
1   As You Take   Willson Sisters   Symphony    14.50    4
2   At The Cave   Maynard Po        Fast Fast   14.50    6
```

FIGURE 7-29 *Inventory*

The general ledger for the store was put into the computer using the *Bedford* accounting package. Darrell felt that initially he would not use the accounts receivable, nor accounts payable modules with *Bedford*, since his sales were all cash and there were few suppliers. And the database seemed to be very efficient for the store music inventory.

Bedford was used to produce his income statement and balance sheet at year end, and Darrell was more than satisfied with the accounting results obtained from his computer. The area manager has asked Darrell to prepare a report for head office on his use of the computer so that other store managers can see the benefits. Darrell could soon be number one at Top 10.

FOR DISCUSSION

- Did Darrell have to know any accounting to get his job managing a record store?
- Assuming you were going to use a database for the inventory of this record store, what groups would you divide your music inventory into?

8

Payroll

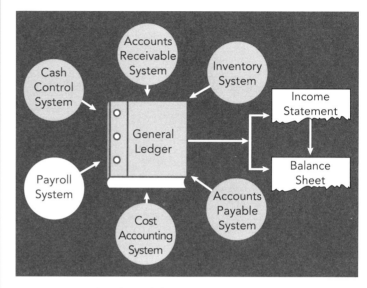

OBJECTIVES

At the end of this chapter, you should be able to:

- Recognize source and output documents for payroll.

- Master various methods of paying employees.

- Calculate statutory and voluntary payroll deductions.

- Complete, journalize, and post a payroll journal.

- Use computer software to assist in payroll applications.

8.0

Overview

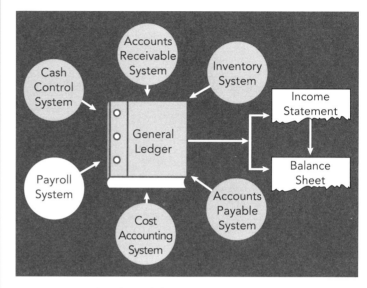

FIGURE 8-1   Flowchart of the accounting process

The preparation and recording of the payroll is one of the most important accounting functions that a business performs. The employees expect the employer to be accurate in the calculation of their paycheques. The government insists on accurate payroll deductions being made from paycheques. And the business itself wants to ensure that accounting entries associated with payroll procedures are recorded correctly. This chapter will show all the key aspects of the payroll function.

8.1

Source Documents

A source document is a business form that provides the accounting information that is to be entered into the company's books of account.

Figure 8-2 is a flowchart of the source documents for the payroll procedure for a business. Some of the documents (such as the employee earnings record card) are ongoing documents which are used from one year to the next. Other documents (such as the employee's time card for a pay period, and the TD1 form) are used once and then filed for later reference.

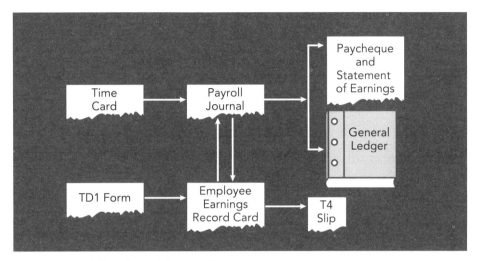

FIGURE 8-2   *A flowchart of the payroll process*

The two main source documents are the time card and the TD1 form. These will be discussed in detail shortly. But first, here is a brief description of all of the documents in the payroll process.

(1) The **time card** is a document used to record regular and overtime hours for hourly rated employees.

(2) The **TD1 form** is a Revenue Canada form filled out by employees when they start work and used to determine an employee's income tax exemption status.

(3) The **payroll journal** is used to record the gross pay, deductions, and net pay for each employee at the end of a pay period.

(4) The **employee earnings record card** contains a record of each employee's earnings, deductions, and net pay for a year.

(5) A **T4 slip** is a record of the year's income, and deductions taken from that income, for an employee.

(6) A **paycheque** and statement of earnings is given to each employee at the end of every pay period (weekly, bi-weekly, semi-monthly, or monthly).

(7) The **general ledger** has payroll data posted to it from the payroll journal (or general journal where a business is small) at the end of each pay period.

The source documents used by various businesses for payroll procedures will differ, but the flowchart above will cover most of the payroll procedures used in a manual accounting environment.

Two important payroll documents for many businesses are the time card and the TD1 Form. These are now discussed in detail.

THE TIME CARD

A time card is a document used for recording the hours worked by an employee in a given time period, assuming that a business has hourly rated employees. Time cards may be manually prepared or punched by a mechanical time clock. Figure 8-3 shows an example of a time card completed manually.

TIME CARD

Employee No.   1
Name   Deward Yates
Week Ended   May 15   19 –

Day	a.m.		p.m.		EXTRA		TOTAL HOURS	
	IN	OUT	IN	OUT	IN	OUT	REG.	O.T.
M	8:00	12:00	1:00	5:00			8	Ø
T	8:00	12:00	1:00	5:00			8	Ø
W	7:59	12:00	1:00	5:01			8	Ø
T	8:00	12:01	1:00	5:02	6:00	10:00	8	4
F	8:00	12:00	1:00	5:00			8	Ø
S								
S								
						TOTALS	40	4

	HOURS	RATE	GROSS PAY	
REGULAR	40	12 –	$ 480	–
OVERTIME	4	18 –	$ 72	–
		TOTAL	$ 552	–

FIGURE 8-3   *A manually completed time card*

The overtime rate used is time-and-a-half, i.e., the regular hourly rate multiplied by a factor of 1.5, or one-and-a-half times the regular rate ($12.00 × 1.5 = $18.00/h). In the situation in Figure 8-3, employees are required to work eight hours each day. Any time worked over eight hours is paid at overtime rates, i.e., at time-and-a-half. Employees may be paid double time under certain conditions, such as working on a holiday.

Time cards should be checked for accuracy by a supervisor, or the employer, before they are processed for payment. Even time cards run through a mechanical time clock should be checked for accuracy and/or reasonableness. This practice is good internal accounting control.

The rules for overtime and lateness will vary from one business to another. In addition, rules for paying employees overtime are subject to employment standards legislation in each province. Labour legislation is very specific with regard to minimum hours and statutory holidays. For the purposes of this book, overtime is to be any hours worked beyond eight hours in a day and 40 hours a week.

THE TD1 FORM

Revenue Canada requires that a TD1 form be filled out by an employee when he or she starts work for a company. TD1 is the code name for the form used by Revenue Canada. Its real name is the Personal Tax Credit Return. The PTCR (or TD1 form) indicates to the employer which column to use in the tax deduction tables, and hence, how much tax to deduct from the employee's earnings for the period. If a person fails to file this form, the employer will make deductions as though the employee were single and allowed only the basic personal amount. An example of the TD1 form used in 1991 has been reproduced for you to see. (Figures 8-4 and 8-5)

Do not worry too much about the fine details of the TD1. Only the basic points of this form will be covered in this text material. For 1991, the following data applies to income tax claims:

Basic Personal Amount	$6 280
Married, and supporting a spouse	$5 233
1st and 2nd dependant (under 19)	$ 406 (each)
3rd and additional dependants (under 19)	$ 812 (each)

These amounts are used to calculate an employee's net claim code to determine the income tax deductions that an employer will have to make from an employee's gross pay.

Revenue Canada Taxation	Revenu Canada Impôt		page 1 TD1 (E) Rev.91

1991 PERSONAL TAX CREDIT RETURN

FAMILY NAME (Please print): **KALD**	USUAL FIRST NAME AND INITIALS **KATHRYN A.**	EMPLOYEE NUMBER
ADDRESS **26 MOORE CRES**	For NON RESIDENTS ONLY Country of permanent residence	SOCIAL INSURANCE NUMBER **244976197**
NORWICH Postal code **N0J 1P0**		DATE OF BIRTH Day **16** Month **04** Year **56**

Instructions

- Please fill out this form so your employer or payer will know how much tax to deduct regularly from your pay. Otherwise, you will be allowed only the basic personal amount of $6,280. Regular deductions will help you avoid having to pay when you file your income tax return.
- **You must complete this form if you receive** • salary, wages, commissions or any other remuneration;
  - superannuation or pension benefits including an annuity payment made under a superannuation or pension fund or plan;
  - Unemployment Insurance benefits including training allowances.
- You may also complete this form if you receive payments under registered retirement income funds and/or registered retirement savings plans.
- Give the completed form to your employer or payer. Pensioners who receive Canada Pension Plan benefits, Old Age Security or Guaranteed Income Supplements should send the completed form to the Regional Office of Health and Welfare Canada.
- **Need help?** If you need help to complete this form, **you** may ask your employer or payer, or call the Source Deductions section of your local Revenue Canada district taxation office. Before you do this, see the additional information on page 2 under "Notes to Employees and Payees."

1. **Are you a non-resident of Canada?** (see note 1 on page 2). If so, and **less than** 90 per cent of your 1991 total world income will be included when calculating taxable income earned in Canada, enter claim code 0 in the box on line 17 and sign the form. If you are a resident of Canada, go to item 2.

2. **Basic personal amount.** (everyone may claim $6,280). ▶ $6,280. 2

3. (a) **Are you married and supporting your spouse?** (see notes 4 and 5 on page 2).
   or
   (b) **Are you single, divorced, separated or widowed and supporting a relative who lives with you who is either your parent or grandparent, OR who is under 19 at the end of 1991, OR 19 or older and infirm?** (see notes 2, 3 and 4 on page 2).

   Note: A spouse or dependant claimed here cannot be claimed again on lines 4 or 5.
   If you answered yes to either (a) or (b) and your spouse's or dependant's 1991 net income will be
   - under $524, CLAIM $5,233
   - between $524 and $5,757, CLAIM (e) ▶
   - over $5,757, CLAIM $0

	$5,757 (c)
Minus: spouse or dependant's net income	(d)
Claim (c minus d)	(e)
   ▶ _____ 3

4. **Do you have any dependants who will be under 19 at the end of 1991?** (see notes 2 and 4 on page 2). If so, and your 1991 net income will be **higher** than your spouse's, calculate the amount to claim for **each** dependant. If you are not married, please see notes 2, 3 and 4 on page 2.

   Note: If you have three or more dependants who will be under 19 at the end of the year, you do not have to claim them in the order they were born. You may claim them in the **most beneficial** order. For example, a dependant who is 16 with a net income of $3,500 could be claimed as the first dependant (claim 0) while the other two, with no income, could be claimed as second and third dependants.

   First and second dependant:
   If your dependant's 1991 net income will be
   - under $2,617, CLAIM $406
   - between $2,617 and $3,023, CLAIM (e) ◄
   - over $3,023, CLAIM $0

	$3,023 (c)	dependants
Minus: dependant's net income	(d)	1st **406**
Claim (c minus d)	(e)	2nd **406**
		3rd _____
		4th _____

   Third and each additional dependant:
   If your dependant's 1991 net income will be
   - under $2,617, CLAIM $812
   - between $2,617 and $3,429, CLAIM (e) ◄
   - over $3,429, CLAIM $0.

	$3,429 (c)	5th _____
Minus: dependant's net income	(d)	6th _____
Claim (c minus d)	(e) Total **812**	▶ **812** 4

5. **Do you have any infirm dependants who will be 19 or older at the end of 1991?** (see notes 2 and 4 on page 2). If so, and your dependant's net income will be
   - under $2,617, CLAIM $1,540
   - between $2,617 and $4,157, CLAIM (e) →
   - over $4,157, CLAIM $0

	$4,157 (c)	dependants
Minus: dependant's net income	(d)	1st _____
Claim (c minus d)	(e)	2nd _____
		3rd _____
		Total _____
   ▶ _____ 5

6. **Do you receive eligible pension income?** (see note 6 on page 2). If so, claim your pension income amount or $1,000, whichever is less. ▶ _____ 6

7. **Will you be 65 or older at the end of 1991?** If so, claim $3,387. ▶ _____ 7

8. **Are you disabled?** (see note 7 on page 2). If so, claim $3,387. ▶ _____ 8

9. **Are you a student?** If so, claim
   - tuition fees paid for courses you take in 1991 to attend either a university, college or a certified educational institution. If you receive any scholarships, fellowships or bursaries in 1991, subtract the amount over $500 from your tuition fees before you claim them.
   - $60 for each month in 1991 that you will be enrolled in a qualifying program, full-time, at either a university, college or a school offering job retraining courses or correspondence courses. Total _____ ▶ _____ 9

10. Total (add 2 to 9 — please enter this amount on line 11 on page 2) **7092** 10
    (See reverse)

FIGURE 8-4 TD1 form — front

page 2

11. Total (from line 10 on page 1) **7092** 11.

12. Are you claiming any transfers of unused pension income, age, disability, tuition fees and education amounts from your spouse and/or dependants? (see note 10 below)

- If your **spouse receives eligible pension income**, you may claim any unused balance to a maximum of $1,000 (see note 6 below). $
- If your **spouse will be 65 or older in 1991**, you may claim any unused balance to a maximum of $3,387.
- If your **spouse and/or dependants are disabled**, you may claim any unused balance to a maximum of $3,387 for each (see note 7 below).
- If you are supporting a **spouse and/or dependants who are attending either a university, college or a certified educational institution**, you may be entitled to claim the unused balance to a maximum of $3,529 for each (see item 9 on page 1). Total ▶ 12.

13. Total claim amount – Add lines 11 and 12. ▶ **7092** 13.

14. Will you or your spouse receive **family allowance (baby bonus) payments in 1991?** If so, and your 1991 net income will be **higher** than your spouse's, enter the amount of family allowance payments you will receive in 1991. If you are not married, see note 3 below. ▶ **792** 14.

Voluntary: If your 1991 taxable income will be more than $28,784, and you have **reported** family allowance income, not enough tax will be withheld by your employer. If you wish to have this additional tax withheld, use the following table to calculate the amount and enter the result on line 18. If you already have additional tax withheld, only show the total of both amounts on line 18.

Pay period		Number of children		Enter this amount on line 18
Weekly	$1 X		=	$
Bi-weekly or semi-monthly	$2 X		=	$
Monthly	$5 X		=	$

15. NET CLAIM AMOUNT – Line 13 minus line 14. ▶ **6300** 15.

16. Is your estimated total income for 1991 (excluding family allowance payments) less than your net claim amount on line 15? If so, enter E in the box on line 17 and tax will **not** be deducted from your pay. Otherwise, go to line 17.

17. NET CLAIM CODE – Match your net claim amount from line 15 with the table below to determine your net claim code, and enter this code in the box. If you already have a code, go to line 18. **2** 17.

18. Do you want to **increase the amount of tax to be deducted from your salary or from other amounts paid to you** such as pensions, commissions etc.? (see note 8 below). If so, state the amount of additional tax you wish to have deducted from each payment. ▶ 18.

19. Will you be **living in the Yukon, Northwest Territories or another prescribed area for more than six months in a row beginning or ending in 1991?** If so, claim $225 for each 30-day period that you live in a prescribed area, **or** if you maintain a "self-contained domestic establishment" in a prescribed area and you are the only person within that establishment claiming this deduction, claim $450 for each 30-day period. You **cannot** claim more than 20 per cent of your net income for 1991 (see note 9 below). ▶ 19.

I HEREBY CERTIFY that the information given in this return is correct and complete.

Signature *K. Kald*   Date *Jan. 29/91*

Complete a new return within seven days of any change in your claim. It is an offence to make a false return.

NOTES TO EMPLOYEES AND PAYEES

1. If you are in doubt about your **non-resident** status, please contact the Source Deductions section of your local district taxation office. If you are a **non-resident and 90 per cent or more** of your 1991 world income will be included in determining your taxable income earned in Canada, you are entitled to claim certain personal amounts. Again for more information contact your district taxation office.

2. A **dependant** is an individual who is dependent on you for support and is either under 19, OR 19 or older and physically or mentally infirm. This includes a child, grandchild, parent, grandparent, brother, sister, aunt, uncle, niece or nephew (including in-laws). Except in the case of a child or grandchild, this individual must also be living in Canada.

3. Except for married individuals, the person who receives the **family allowance** must report the benefits and claim the amount for dependent children. Whoever claims the dependant for an equivalent-to-married amount must report the family allowance for that dependant regardless of who receives the family allowance benefits.

4. Your spouse's or dependant's **net income**, for tax withholding purposes, is the total annual income from all sources including salary, pensions, Old Age Security, UI benefits, workers' compensation and social assistance (welfare) payments minus annual deductions for registered pension plan and registered retirement savings plan contributions.

5. If you **marry** during the year, your spouse's net income will include the income before and during marriage.

6. **Eligible pension income** includes pension payments received from a pension plan or fund as a life annuity and foreign pension payments. It does not include payments from Canada or Quebec Pension plans, Old Age Security, guaranteed income supplement and lump-sum withdrawals from a pension fund.

7. To claim a **disability**, you must be severely impaired (mentally or physically) in 1991 and have a Disability Credit Certificate. Such an impairment must markedly restrict you in your daily living activities. The impairment must have lasted or be expected to last for a continuous period of at least 12 months.

8. You may find it convenient to deduct additional tax on line 18 for other income you receive that has little or no tax deducted from it. For example, UI benefits, Old Age Security, investment or rental income.

9. **"Self-contained domestic establishment"** means the dwelling house, apartment or similar place where you sleep and eat. It does not include a bunkhouse, dormitory, hotel room or rooms in a boarding house. For more information, including the list of prescribed areas, see the *Northern Residents Deductions Tax Guide*, available at any district taxation office.

10. Your spouse and/or dependants must first use their pension income, age, disability, tuition fees and education amounts as applicable to reduce their federal tax to zero before they can **transfer** any unused balance of these amounts to you.

Cette formule est disponible en français.

1991 NET CLAIM CODES

Net claim amount		claim code
over	not over	
NO claim amount		0
$0 -	$6,280	1
6,280 -	7,818	2
7,818 -	9,357	3
9,357 -	10,897	4
10,897 -	12,435	5
12,435 -	13,973	6
13,973 -	15,512	7
15,512 -	17,050	8
17,050 -	18,589	9
18,589 -	20,129	10
20,129 and over		X
NO tax withholding required		E

FIGURE 8-5   TD1 form — back

Assume that you have just hired Joyce Jackson. Joyce is married and supports a spouse at home who has no earnings. There are three children in the family and all are claimed as dependants on Joyce's tax return at year end. The family allowance payments for the three children reduce Joyce's payroll claim. Her current TD1 payroll claims (rounded to the nearest dollar) are:

Basic Personal Amount	$ 6 280
Married, supporting spouse	5 233
Dependants 1 and 2 (2 × $406)	812
Dependant 3 (1 × $812)	812
Total Claim Amount	13 137
Less: Family Allowance Payments	
(3 × $33/month × 12 months)	1 188
Net Claim Amount	$11 949

This amount is then compared to the net claim codes table (Figure 8-6) to determine Joyce's net claim code.

1991 NET CLAIM CODES	
Net claim amount over · not over	**claim code**
NO claim amount	0
$ 0 - $6,280	1
6,280 - 7,818	2
7,818 - 9,357	3
9,357 - 10,897	4
10,897 - 12,435	5
12,435 - 13,973	6
13,973 - 15,512	7
15,512 - 17,050	8
17,050 - 18,589	9
18,589 - 20,129	10
20,129 and over	X
NO tax withholding required	E

The **net claim code** is based on personal exemptions and is used to determine an employee's income tax deduction. Joyce's total claim is $11 949. If you look up this amount in the net claim codes table, you find that Joyce's net claim code is 5.

FIGURE 8-6   Net claim codes table

QUESTIONS

1. Why is payroll accounting important to a business? Give three reasons.

2. Use Figure 8-2, the payroll flowchart, to find the names of these documents:
   (a) Where does the information for the payroll journal come from?
   (b) What two documents are produced using the payroll journal?
   (c) What document does a business use to prepare an employee's T4 slip?

3. Indicate which payroll documents are being described in each of these:
   (a) used to record the gross pay, deductions, and net pay for all employees for a pay period
   (b) accumulates hours worked by employees
   (c) given to an employee as the source of data from which to prepare his or her income tax returns
   (d) data from the payroll journal is posted here
   (e) completed for every employee showing earnings, deductions, and net pay
   (f) given to an employee at the end of every pay period, with the paycheque

4. In what two ways are time cards completed?

5. Why are employees often given payroll numbers?

6. Are time-card rules the same for all businesses?

7. Who completes a TD1 form?

8. What is another name for the TD1?

9. What is the purpose of filling out a TD1 form?

10. When is a TD1 form completed?

11. What is the income tax "claim" for each of these people? Use Figures 8-4 and 8-5.
    (a) an employee who is single
    (b) an employee who is married and supports a spouse
    (c) a married employee whose husband works (She claims two children as dependants.)
    (d) a married employee whose spouse has no earnings and who has five dependants under the age of 18
    (e) an employee who is divorced and supports four children as dependants

12. Use the net claim codes table to find the claim code for each of the employees in question 11.

13. If an employee claims $6 280 as his basic personal amount, does this mean his income tax is reduced by $6 280? Explain.

14. Look at the sample TD1 form given in this section. List some of the other possible deductions that can be claimed by taxpayers.

8.2

Methods of Paying Employees

There are four basic methods of paying employees: hourly rate, salary, piece rate, and commission rate.

Hourly Rate

In the **hourly rate** method, employees are paid a set amount per hour according to the hours worked. This is often split between regular hours and overtime hours. Overtime hours are usually paid at a multiple of the regular hourly rate.

Example:

Regular Pay	40 hours × $8.00/hour	= $320.00
Overtime Pay	4 hours × $12.00/hour	= $48.00

The overtime rate used above is at time-and-a-half the regular hourly rate. You saw this type of calculation earlier, in Figure 8-3.

Salary

In the **salary** method of payment, employees are hired at a set daily, monthly, or annual rate of pay (for example, $150 a day, $3 000 a month, or $36 000 a year). An annual salary will be paid in instalments that match the type of pay period followed by the employer.

Example 1: Monthly Salary
Annual Salary   = $36 000 a year
Monthly Pay   = $36 000/12 months   = $3 000/month

Salaried employees may also be paid **bi-weekly** (every two weeks).

Example 2: Bi-Weekly Salary
Annual Salary   = $36 000 a year
Bi-Weekly Pay   = $36 000/26 pay periods   = $1384.62 each payday

Information for calculating salaried amounts can be taken from the employee earnings record card.

Piece Rate

Employees who are paid on a **piece rate** basis are paid according to how many pieces they produce each pay period.

Example:
   2 000 pieces × $.30 each = $600

Information for calculating piece rate payroll would be taken from a piece rate schedule which would be similar to the time card used for hourly rated employees.

Commission Rate

Commission rate employees are often salespersons who are paid a percentage of the sales dollars they earn for the company. A computer salesperson is a good example.

Example:
   Monthly Computer Sales $100 000
   Commission: $100 000 × 6% = $6 000

The information for calculating commission payroll is taken from sales records for a business.

The method of payment used depends on the nature of the business. Many service businesses have hourly rated employees. An office employee, such as an accounting clerk, could be salaried or paid an hourly rate. Factory and farm workers are often paid an hourly rate or a piece rate. And salespersons who sell expensive items are most likely paid on a commission basis, while salespersons in department stores might receive an hourly rate plus a commission.

There are also other methods of providing incentives to employees. Some businesses, for example, have profit sharing plans which they use to increase the pay of their salaried, hourly rated, or piece work employees. In this case, if the business has had a successful year, then part of the net income is turned over to the employees as a bonus.

Q U E S T I O N S

15. Name the four basic methods of paying employees.

16. Indicate which method is being used in each of these employment situations.

(a) Alex receives 5% of all his monthly sales.

(b) Gwen is paid according to the number of computer chips installed by her in calculators each day.

(c) Lisa earns $8.00 an hour and is paid time-and-a-half for overtime.

(d) Arjit was hired as an accounting assistant at $32 000 a year.

17. In the hourly rate method of payroll, how is overtime usually calculated?

18. Ask one of your classmates how she or he is paid when overtime is worked. Find out what the pay rate is if the person works on a holiday such as Thanksgiving or Christmas Day.

19. Some salaried employees are paid bi-weekly. What does this mean?

20. Name a job that you know is paid by the piece rate method.

21. Give three examples where employees are paid using the commission rate method.

22. What does the term *profit sharing* mean?

23. Do you know any other payroll methods used by employers as incentives for employees?

8.3

Payroll Deductions

There are two main groups of payroll deductions: those which are remitted to Revenue Canada, and those which are not.

Revenue Canada deductions are sometimes called **statutory deductions** since they must be taken from employees' paycheques by law. There are three statutory payroll deductions that must be remitted to Revenue Canada: Income Tax, Canada Pension Plan, and Unemployment Insurance. Each of these will be dealt with for an employee, Joyce Jackson, whose regular weekly pay is $600.

INCOME TAX

The booklet *Source Deductions Tables*, supplied by Revenue Canada, is used by employers to determine the income tax to be withheld from employees. Employers must use these tables to deduct income tax from:

• salary, wages, and commissions (including pay advances, the value of free board and lodging, and any other taxable benefits and allowances)
• bonuses, vacation pay, and gratuities (tips)
• benefits under a supplementary unemployment benefit plan
• pensions, retiring allowances, and death benefits

Employers must next subtract from the gross pay either of these two items if they occur:

• the employee's contribution to a Registered Pension Plan (RPP)
• any dues deducted from a paycheque and paid to a union

The calculation for Joyce Jackson, using the above rules, is as follows:

Regular Pay		$600.00
Taxable Benefits		55.00
Gross Pay		655.00
Less:		
RPP Contribution	$25.00	
Union Dues	5.50	30.50
Remuneration subject to tax		$624.50

The word **remuneration** is another term used for the gross or net pay paid to an employee.

How to Use the Income Tax Deduction Tables

In order to calculate Joyce's income tax deduction, you have to know her gross pay and net claim code. Her gross pay is $655.00 per week, but her remuneration subject to tax is $624.50. The net claim code calculated earlier for Joyce was 5. Now look at Table 1, Weekly Tax Deductions.

TABLE 1											
WEEKLY TAX DEDUCTIONS Basis — 52 Pay Periods per Year					RETENUES D'IMPÔT PAR SEMAINE Base — 52 périodes de paie par année						
WEEKLY PAY Use appropriate bracket	IF THE EMPLOYEE'S "NET CLAIM CODE" ON FORM TD1 IS *SI LE "CODE DE DEMANDE NETTE" DE L'EMPLOYE SELON LA FORMULE TD1 EST*										
PAIE PAR SEMAINE *Utilisez le palier approprié*	0	1	2	3	4	5	6	7	8	9	10
From-*De* Less than *Moins que*	DEDUCT FROM EACH PAY – *RETENEZ SUR CHAQUE PAIE*										
613.- 621.	167.75	135.30	131.35	123.40	115.45	107.50	99.55	91.60	83.65	75.70	67.75
621.- 629.	171.00	138.55	134.55	126.60	118.65	110.70	102.80	94.85	86.90	78.95	71.00
629.- 637.	174.20	141.80	137.80	129.85	121.90	113.95	106.00	98.05	90.10	82.15	74.20
637.- 645.	177.45	145.00	141.05	133.10	125.15	117.20	109.25	101.30	93.35	85.40	77.45
645.- 653.	180.70	148.25	144.30	136.35	128.40	120.45	112.50	104.55	96.60	88.65	80.70

FIGURE 8-7   *Weekly Tax Deductions — Table 1*

The first column on the left of the table shows various amounts of weekly pay. Run your finger down the column to the range $621 – $629. Then run another finger over to net claim code column 5. The tax deduction for Joyce this week is $110.70.

There are similar tax deduction tables for various pay periods: weekly, bi-weekly, semi-monthly, monthly, etc. The tax tables are updated periodically by Revenue Canada as tax laws change, and new tables are automatically sent to all business employers registered with Revenue Canada.

CANADA PENSION PLAN

The booklet *Source Deduction Tables*, supplied by Revenue Canada, is also used by employers to determine the Canada Pension Plan (CPP) amount payable by employees who are paid on a weekly, bi-weekly, semi-monthly, or monthly basis.

Employers must deduct the required Canada Pension Plan contribution from the gross pay of each employee who meets all three of these criteria:

- is 18 years of age and has not reached 70 years of age
- is employed in pensionable employment during the year
- is not receiving a Canada or a Quebec Pension Plan retirement or disability pension

Some types of employment are excepted, that is, they are not subject to Canada Pension Plan contributions. Here is a partial list for your information and interest:

- employment of a casual nature
- employment of a member of a religious order who has taken a vow of perpetual poverty
- employment, except as an entertainer, at a circus, fair, or carnival, if the employee is not a regular employee and works less than seven days in the year

The types of income that must be included when calculating Canada Pension Plan contributions are:

- salary and wages, commissions, bonuses, value of board and lodging
- certain rent free and low rent housing, interest free and low interest loans, personal use of employer's automobile, certain gifts, prizes and awards, holiday trips, provincial medical insurance premiums, and subsidized meals
- honoraria or profit shares from a company

In the case of Joyce Jackson you have the following situation:

Regular Pay	$600.00
Taxable Benefits	55.00
Gross Pay	$655.00

How to Use the Canada Pension Plan Contribution Tables

In order to calculate the Canada Pension Plan contribution for any employee you only have to know the gross pay.

CANADA PENSION PLAN CONTRIBUTIONS				COTISATIONS AU RÉGIME DE PENSIONS DU CANADA					
WEEKLY PAY PERIOD — *PÉRIODE HEBDOMADAIRE DE PAIE* 558.35—2807.03									
Remuneration *Rémunération*		C.P.P. R.P.C.	Remuneration *Rémunération*		C.P.P. R.P.C.	Remuneration *Rémunération*		C.P.P. R.P.C.	Remuneration *Rémunération*		C.P.P. R.P.C.
From-*de*	To-*à*		From-*de*	To-*à*		From-*de*	To-*à*		From-*de*	To-*à*	
558.35 -	558.77	11.52	647.04 -	657.03	13.67	1367.04 -	1377.03	30.23	2087.04 -	2097.03	46.79
558.78 -	559.21	11.53	657.04 -	667.03	13.90	1377.04 -	1387.03	30.46	2097.04 -	2107.03	47.02
559.22 -	559.64	11.54	667.04 -	677.03	14.13	1387.04 -	1397.03	30.69	2107.04 -	2117.03	47.25
559.65 -	560.08	11.55	677.04 -	687.03	14.36	1397.04 -	1407.03	30.92	2117.04 -	2127.03	47.48
560.09 -	560.51	11.56	687.04 -	697.03	14.59	1407.04 -	1417.03	31.15	2127.04 -	2137.03	47.71
560.52 -	560.95	11.57	697.04 -	707.03	14.82	1417.04 -	1427.03	31.38	2137.04 -	2147.03	47.94
560.96 -	561.38	11.58	707.04 -	717.03	15.05	1427.04 -	1437.03	31.61	2147.04 -	2157.03	48.17
561.39 -	561.82	11.59	717.04 -	727.03	15.28	1437.04 -	1447.03	31.84	2157.04 -	2167.03	48.40
561.83 -	562.25	11.60	727.04 -	737.03	15.51	1447.04 -	1457.03	32.07	2167.04 -	2177.03	48.63

FIGURE 8-8   Canada Pension Plan Contributions — Weekly Pay Period

In this example the gross pay is $655 per week. Run your finger down the Remuneration column of the weekly CPP contribution table until you see the pay range $647.04 – $657.03. The amount to be deducted from the employee's paycheque for CPP is in the column to the right, $13.67.

There are also Canada Pension Plan contribution tables for employees who are paid on a bi-weekly, semi-monthly, and monthly basis. The CPP tables too are updated periodically by Revenue Canada as pension laws change, and new CPP tables are automatically sent to employers registered with Revenue Canada. CPP contributions are remitted to the government along with the income tax deductions on a regular basis, and by law the employer must match the CPP contributions made by the employees. In this example, the employee's Canada Pension Plan contribution of $13.67 will be matched by the employer with another $13.67.

Unemployment Insurance

Generally, all employment in Canada is insurable employment and subject to Unemployment Insurance premiums. Some types of earnings are excluded, however, and not subject to regular Unemployment Insurance contributions, for example:

- payments made by an employer on behalf of an employee under a supplemental unemployment benefit plan
- where no cash remuneration is paid by the employer for a pay period, value of board, lodging or other benefits received or provided in the pay period
- travelling, personal, or living expenses.

The types of income that must be included in a calculation of Unemployment Insurance premiums include:

- salaries and wages
- overtime pay
- taxable benefits
- vacation and holiday pay
- retroactive pay increases
- statutory holiday pay
- bonuses and gratuities
- accumulated sick leave credits
- shift premiums
- incentive payments
- cost of living allowances
- separation payments
- wages in lieu of notice

How to Use the Unemployment Insurance Premium Tables

In order to calculate the deduction for Unemployment Insurance premiums, you only have to know the gross pay for the employee. In this example the gross pay is $655 per week.

UNEMPLOYMENT INSURANCE PREMIUMS		COTISATIONS À L'ASSURANCE-CHÔMAGE	
For minimum and maximum insurable earnings amounts for various pay periods see Schedule II. For the maximum premium deduction for various pay periods see bottom of this page.		Les montants minimum et maximum des gains assurables pour diverses périodes de paie figurent en annexe II. La déduction maximale de primes pour diverses périodes de paie figure au bas de la présente page.	

Remuneration Rémunération	U.I. Premium Prime d'a-c	Remuneration Rémunération	U.I. Premium Prime d'a-c	Remuneration Rémunération	U.I. Premium Prime d'a-c	Remuneration Rémunération	U.I. Premium Prime d'a-c
From-de To-a		From-de To-à		From-de To a		From-de To-à	
652.23 - 652.66	14.68	684.23 - 684.66	15.40	716.23 - 716.66	16.12	748.23 - 748.66	16.84
652.67 - 653.11	14.69	684.67 - 685.11	15.41	716.67 - 717.11	16.13	748.67 - 749.11	16.85
653.12 - 653.55	14.70	685.12 - 685.55	15.42	717.12 - 717.55	16.14	749.12 - 749.55	16.86
653.56 - 653.99	14.71	685.56 - 685.99	15.43	717.56 - 717.99	16.15	749.56 - 749.99	16.87
654.00 - 654.44	14.72	686.00 - 686.44	15.44	718.00 - 718.44	16.16	750.00 - 750.44	16.88
654.45 - 654.88	14.73	686.45 - 686.88	15.45	718.45 - 718.88	16.17	750.45 - 750.88	16.89
654.89 - 655.33	14.74	686.89 - 687.33	15.46	718.89 - 719.33	16.18	750.89 - 751.33	16.90
655.34 - 655.77	14.75	687.34 - 687.77	15.47	719.34 - 719.77	16.19	751.34 - 751.77	16.91
655.78 - 656.22	14.76	687.78 - 688.22	15.48	719.78 - 720.22	16.20	751.78 - 752.22	16.92

FIGURE 8-9   Unemployment Insurance Premiums

Run your finger down the Remuneration column of the Unemployment Insurance Premiums table until you see the pay range $654.89 – $655.33. The amount to be deducted from the employee's paycheque for UI is in the next column, $14.74. (The maximum deduction per pay period is shown at the foot of each page of the UI tables. The weekly maximum is $15.30.)

Unemployment Insurance Premium tables are updated periodically by Revenue Canada as unemployment insurance regulations change. UI deductions are remitted to the government along with the income tax deductions, and CPP contributions on a regular basis; however, as of January 1991, the employer must pay 1.4 times the UI contributions made by the employees. In the example here, the employee's Unemployment Insurance payment is $14.74. This amount will be multiplied by 1.4 to get the employer's share for Unemployment Insurance, i.e., $20.64.

Income tax deductions, Canada Pension Plan contributions, and Unemployment Insurance premiums must be received by Revenue Canada on or before the 15th day of the month immediately following the month in which the remuneration was paid to the employees. Employers whose monthly withholding amounts average more than $15 000 must remit on a more frequent basis:

- amounts deducted during the first 15 days of the month must be received by the Receiver General by the 25th of the same month
- amounts deducted for the rest of the month are due by the 10th of the following month

QUESTIONS

24. Name the three compulsory payroll deductions to be remitted to the Receiver General.

25. List seven types of income on which employees must pay income tax.

26. Name the two pieces of information an employer needs in order to use the Revenue Canada tax deduction tables.

27. Where does an employer find the information needed to determine an employee's net claim code?

28. Many employees are paid weekly. List three other common pay periods.

29. When does an employer have to remit income tax deductions to the government (Revenue Canada)?

30. Only employees who meet three conditions will have CPP deducted from their paycheques. Name the conditions.

31. Indicate if these types of income are included in the CPP calculation by an employer, or not: board and lodging; bonuses; prizes

32. If an employer deducted $23.00 from an employee for a CPP contribution, what would be the employer's contribution to CPP?

33. Name three types of income that are not included when an employer calculates the deduction for unemployment insurance.

34. Overtime pay, holiday pay, and wages in lieu of notice are all types of income on which employees pay unemployment insurance. Name five other types of income which are included to calculate unemployment insurance.

35. If an employee contributed $15.90 to the Unemployment Insurance fund, how much would the employer have to contribute as his or her share?

OTHER PAYROLL DEDUCTIONS

There can be many other types of payroll deductions. Some are compulsory while others are purely voluntary. Some additional examples of compulsory deductions might be union dues, payments for life insurance, supplementary medical insurance (the so-called drug plans), long-term disability insurance, a dental plan, and contributions to a registered pension plan. Whether a benefit deduction is compulsory is usually established by the insurance carrier offering certain types of benefits in agreement with the employer and the union or the employees' representatives.

Voluntary deductions are optional and vary depending on the choices that individual employees make. Some examples of voluntary deductions are the Canada Savings Bond payroll plan, supplementary life insurance plans, and charitable donations such as the United Way. Here are some deductions discussed in more detail for you.

Union Dues
Union Dues are generally mandatory for all union members and are often a set dollar figure per pay period. For example, if the union contract specified that each employee was to have dues of $5 per week deducted from the weekly paycheque, the employer would deduct this and remit all collected dues to the treasurer of the union. The employee has no control over this deduction.

Registered Pension Plans
Some businesses provide registered pension plans for their employees. Both the employer and the employee often contribute to this plan on behalf of

the employee. The amounts deposited to this plan are usually established through contract negotiations and are usually expressed as a percentage of gross pay. Contributions to an RPP are deducted from gross pay to arrive at the amount of taxable income for an employee.

Canada Savings Bonds

Some employees ask their employers to deduct a certain sum from their gross pay each pay period for the purchase of Canada Savings Bonds. The bonds are turned over to the employee for her/his safekeeping when they have been fully paid for.

Long-Term Disability

Long-term disability plans (LTDs) provide earnings for employees unable to work because injuries or illness. These plans usually provide for a percentage of earnings to be paid as a disability income, and the payments are made on proof of medical disability. If LTD premiums are paid by the employer, then benefits from the plan are taxable to the employee. If LTD premiums are made by the employee, then benefits are not taxable.

In some provinces there are worker's compensation plans which provide disability benefits for injuries directly related to the job. In these provinces the employer must, by law, pay premiums to these worker compensation plans. Premiums are based on the total annual payroll and the risk of injury for a particular industry, as well as the job-related injury record of the firm itself. Worker's compensation protection is not identical to long-term disability, and hence there is a need for both plans.

"If you don't think you can make it into work tomorrow, give me a call."

Dental and Supplementary Medical Plans

Some businesses may provide dental and/or supplementary medical plans for their employees. Deductions for these plans are submitted to the insuring company by the employer. The division of the payment of the premiums for these plans is often the subject of intense negotiation, and that division of payment becomes part of a union contract if the business is unionized.

It is important to note that, when the employer pays part or all of a benefit plan (for example, a dental plan) the employer's share becomes a taxable benefit to the employee. That is, the employer's share of the premium paid on behalf of the employee will be included in the calculation of taxable income and included on the employee's T4 slip at the end of the year.

QUESTIONS

36. Talk to a member of a union, and find out:
    (a) whether or not the union dues are voluntary
    (b) how much that person pays in union dues
    (c) whether the employer matches the union dues that employees pay

37. What do the letters RPP stand for? Ask a parent or guardian if they belong to an RPP. List some of the details about the plan.

38. Do employers usually contribute to Canada Savings Bond plans?

39. Is there a government-run provincial health insurance plan in your province? If so, find the rates for single and married people for your provincial health insurance plan.

40. What kind of coverage does long-term disability provide?

41. Are premiums paid to a dental plan by the employer a taxable benefit?

42. Name any other payroll deductions made from you or any member of your family.

8.4

Journalizing Payroll

If you refer to the flowchart of the payroll process (Figure 8-2), you will see that one of the main documents used is the **payroll journal**. This is the book of original entry where payroll data is first recorded. In some businesses this document is referred to as a payroll register; however, this text will use the term payroll journal.

THE PAYROLL JOURNAL

A payroll journal is completed at the end of a pay period. It is used to calculate gross pay, deductions, and net pay for all the employees. Figure 8-10 shows a basic model which might be used by a very small proprietorship.

PAYROLL JOURNAL
FOR THE Week   ENDED Apr. 30   19 –

EMP. NO.	EMPLOYEE NAME	NET CLAIM CODE	GROSS PAY	DEDUCTIONS				NET PAY
				INCOME TAX	CPP	UI		
1	Adams, J.R.	3	600 –	116 90	12 52	13 50		457 08
2	Brunel, J-P.	10	750 –	123 25	15 97	15 30		595 48
3	Costas, A.P.	2	648 –	144 30	13 67	14 58		475 45
	Totals		1998 –	384 45	42 16	43 38		1528 01

FIGURE 8-10   *A basic payroll journal*

The payroll journal is always dated; in this case it covers the week ended April 30, 19–. The payroll data for each employee is entered into the journal: employee number, employee name, net claim code, gross pay, deductions, and net pay.

In this basic model there are no deductions other than those taken for the government (Revenue Canada). The most important thing to note about the payroll journal is that it must be added and cross-balanced after it is completed. In this example, the total of the Gross Pay column minus the totals of the three Deductions columns must equal the total of the Net Pay column. This is called **cross-balancing**.

Payroll journals in larger businesses will probably look more like the one shown in Figure 8-11.

	EMP. NO.	EMPLOYEE NAME	NET CLAIM CODE	EARNINGS					
				TOTAL	TAXABLE BENEFITS	GROSS	UNION DUES		RPP
1	1	Barnard, D.	1	580 –	2050	60050	750		1
2	2	Bauer, J.	1	595 –	2570	62070	750		1
3	3	Cassone, M.	3	67950	2050	700 –	750		2
4	4	Horvath, H.	5	66010	2050	68060	750		2
5	5	Leung, L.	1	655 –	2570	68070	750		2
6	6	McLean, P.	2	62430	2570	650 –	750		1
7				379390	13860	393250	45 –		11
8									
9									

FIGURE 8-11   *An advanced model payroll journal*

In this model, taxable benefits are added to the total earnings to arrive at gross pay. Union dues and RPP (Registered Pension Plan) contributions are then deducted to arrive at the taxable income. Income tax is calculated on the taxable income using the Revenue Canada table, *Income Tax Deductions at Source*. The rest of the deductions are calculated — CPP, UI, LTD, and Dental — and the net pay is arrived at. There is also a Total column for the total of all deductions, and a column at the right hand side to record the cheque number for each employee. The cheque number is useful data for reconciling the bank account at month end.

A payroll journal must be accurate. Government auditors may visit a business and perform an audit on payroll records to see if deductions for income tax, CPP, and UI are being correctly made. The payroll journal is also important because it will be used for posting the accounting entries into the general ledger. The journal entries generated by the payroll journal will be covered next.

QUESTIONS

43. Where does the information for the payroll journal come from?

44. What is another common name for the payroll journal?

45. How often would a Payroll Journal be completed?

46. What does *cross-balancing* the payroll journal refer to?

47. A payroll journal has three deduction columns for statutory Revenue Canada deductions. Name these three deductions.

PAYROLL JOURNAL

FOR THE _Week_ ENDED _Apr. 30_ 19 –

DEDUCTIONS							NET PAY	CH. NO.
TAXABLE GROSS / INCOME TAX DEDUCTION	CPP	UI	LTD	DENTAL	TOTAL			
574 98	119 15	12 52	13 51	2 –	2 50	175 20	425 30	110	1
594 58	125 60	12 98	13 97	2 –	2 50	183 17	437 53	111	2
671 50	146 05	14 82	15 30	2 –	5 –	211 67	488 33	112	3
652 68	120 45	14 36	15 30	2 –	5 –	185 03	495 57	113	4
652 78	148 25	14 36	15 30	2 –	2 50	210 33	470 37	114	5
623 –	134 55	13 67	14 63	2 –	5 –	196 85	453 15	115	6
3769 52	794 05	82 71	88 01	12 –	22 50	1162 25	2770 25		7
									8
									9

48. Look at the advanced model payroll journal. What two figures are added together to arrive at the gross pay?

49. List the three statutory deductions that appear on the advanced model payroll journal.

50. List the voluntary deductions that appear on the advanced model payroll journal.

51. Why is the cheque number column useful on a payroll journal?

PAYROLL ENTRIES IN THE GENERAL JOURNAL

There are several accounting entries generated by the payroll journal. The basic general journal entries needed to record the entire cost of the payroll at the end of each pay period are:

1. the original payroll
2. the employer's share of CPP
3. the employer's share of UI
4. the employer's share of other deductions
5. the remittance of statutory deductions to Revenue Canada
6. the remittance of other deductions to the appropriate organizations

1. The Original Payroll

The journal entry shown in Figure 8-12 is taken from the bottom line of the more detailed payroll journal in the previous section.

DATE 19–		PARTICULARS	PR	DEBIT	CREDIT
Apr.	30	Wage Expense		3 9 3 2 5 0	
		Income Tax Payable			7 9 4 0 5
		CPP Payable			8 2 7 1
		UI Payable			8 8 0 1
		Union Dues Payable			4 5 –
		RPP Payable			1 1 7 9 8
		LTD Payable			1 2 –
		Dental Insurance Payable			2 2 5 0
		Bank			2 7 7 0 2 5
		To record the payroll for the week			
		ended April 30			

FIGURE 8-12   *The general journal entry to record the payroll journal totals*

The debit to Wage Expense is the total of the Gross Earnings column in the payroll journal. The Income Tax, CPP, UI, Union Dues, RPP, LTD, and Dental columns in the Payroll Journal are liabilities (amounts deducted from employees and owing to Revenue Canada and to the other organizations for which payments are being collected). The Net Pay total, which is the amount to be paid to the employees, appears in this case as a credit to Bank. The payroll journal may be posted directly to the general ledger.

As shown above, some businesses issue a single cheque for the total net pay and deposit it into a special payroll account. Individual paycheques are then written on this special payroll bank account. This process makes the payroll bank account easier to reconcile because it contains only payroll cheques.

2. The Employer's Share of CPP

The next general journal entry recognizes the need for the employer to match the amount deducted from employees for Canada Pension Plan contributions. From the general journal entry in Figure 8-12, you see that the employees contributed $82.71 to the Canada Pension Plan. According to law, the employer must put in another $82.71 as the business' share. The employer's share is an operating expense to the business and is recorded by the entry shown in Figure 8-13.

GENERAL JOURNAL

PAGE _17_

DATE 19–		PARTICULARS	PR	DEBIT	CREDIT
Apr.	30	CPP Expense		82 71	
		CPP Payable			82 71
		To record employer's CPP contribution			

FIGURE 8-13   The general journal entry for employer's share of CPP

3. The Employer's Share of UI

The employer also has to pay Unemployment Insurance premiums on behalf of the employees, but the employer's share is calculated by multiplying the employees' deduction by a factor of 1.4. In this example, the employees paid $88.01 in Unemployment Insurance premiums. The employer's contribution will be $123.21 ($88.01 × 1.4). As with the Canada Pension Plan contribution, the employer's share of Unemployment Insurance premiums is an operating expense. The general journal entry to record the employer's share of Unemployment Insurance is:

GENERAL JOURNAL

PAGE _17_

DATE 19–		PARTICULARS	PR	DEBIT	CREDIT
Apr.	30	UI Expense		123 21	
		UI Payable			123 21
		To record employer's UI contribution			

FIGURE 8-14   The general journal entry for employer's share of UI

You may have noticed that there is no employer's share for the income tax deducted from employees. The Canada Pension Plan contribution is matched, the Unemployment Insurance deduction is increased by a factor of 1.4, but the income tax deduction is remitted as is to Revenue Canada.

4. The Employer's Share of Other Deductions

According to the payroll journal, $12 has been deducted from employees as their weekly contribution to the Long-Term Disability plan (LTD). Because of an agreement with this employer, employees pay only 25% of the cost. The employer pays the other 75%, or $36.

This company has collected deposits to the Registered Pension Plan in the amount of $117.98. It happens that the agreement with the employees is for this company to match the employees' deposits, $117.98.

The other benefit that is partly paid for by this company is the dental plan. The agreement is that the company pays 60% of the premiums while the employees pay 40%. The amount collected for dental insurance premiums according to the payroll journal is $22.50. Therefore, the amount the employer owes for dental insurance premiums is $33.75 ($22.50 × 1.5 = $33.75).

The entry to record the employer's share of these benefit premiums is:

GENERAL JOURNAL

PAGE 17

DATE 19–		PARTICULARS	PR	DEBIT	CREDIT
Apr.	30	LTD Expense		36 –	
		LTD Payable			36 –
		To record employer's share of			
		provincial health plan premium for			
		week ended April 30			
	30	RPP Expense		117 98	
		RPP Payable			117 98
		To record employer's share of RPP			
		for the week ended April 30			
	30	Dental Insurance Expense		33 75	
		Dental Insurance Payable			33 75
		To record the employer's share of			
		dental insurance for the week ended			
		April 30			

FIGURE 8-15   The general journal entry for employer's share of other deductions

These entries are very similar to the ones for the employer's share of CPP and UI. The employer's share of the cost is an expense and there is also a liability created for the amount owing to the various benefit plans.

The deductions from employees and the additional premiums from the employer are sent off to the various government and private agencies on a monthly basis. Figure 8-16 shows the general ledger accounts that have been involved in payroll, with the transactions for the month of April. No payments have been made yet on behalf of the employees for April.

Look at the entries carefully. Do you understand where each entry comes from? Test yourself by explaining what each entry represents.

GENERAL LEDGER

Bank		Income Tax Payable		CPP Payable	
	2 746.08		787.24		82.05
	2 731.82		783.20		82.05
	2 811.99		805.88		81.63
	2 761.21		791.52		81.63
	2 770.25		794.05		83.97
	(13 821.35)		(3 961.89)		83.97
					82.49
					82.49
					82.71
					82.71
					(825.70)

UI Payable		Union Dues Payable		RPP Payable	
	87.31		45.00		116.97
	122.23		45.00		116.97
	86.87		45.00		116.38
	121.62		45.00		116.38
	89.35		45.00		119.71
	125.09		(225.00)		119.71
	87.78				117.60
	122.89				117.60
	88.01				117.98
	123.21				117.98
	(1 054.36)				(1 177.28)

LTD Payable		Dental Insurance Payable		CPP Expense	
	12.00		22.50	82.05	
	36.00		33.75	81.63	
	12.00		22.50	83.97	
	36.00		33.75	82.49	
	12.00		22.50	82.71	
	36.00		33.75	(412.85)	
	12.00		22.50		
	36.00		33.75		
	12.00		22.50		
	36.00		33.75		
	(240.00)		(281.25)		

Dental Insurance Expense		LTD Expense		RPP Expense	
33.75		36.00		116.97	
33.75		36.00		116.38	
33.75		36.00		119.71	
33.75		36.00		117.60	
33.75		36.00		117.98	
(168.75)		(180.00)		(588.64)	

UI Expense		Wage Expense	
122.23		3 899.15	
121.62		3 879.40	
125.09		3 990.40	
122.89		3 920.10	
123.21		3 932.50	
(615.04)		(19 621.55)	

FIGURE 8-16
Payroll T-accounts

5. The Remittance of Revenue Canada Deductions

The final accounting entry for government deductions for April takes place when the employer remits the amount owing to the Receiver General at the beginning of the following month.

The amount deducted from all employees for Income Tax is $3 961.89; the CPP Payable total of $825.70 represents the employees' and employer's contribution to Canada Pension Plan; the $1 054.36 total is the employees' and the employer's share of the Unemployment Insurance premium. The general journal entry that clears out these liability accounts when the employer remits the balance owing to the Receiver General is:

GENERAL JOURNAL

PAGE 18

DATE 19–		PARTICULARS	PR	DEBIT	CREDIT
May	1	Income Tax Payable		3 961 89	
		CPP Payable		825 70	
		UI Payable		1 054 36	
		Bank			5 841 95
		To record the remittance of deductions			
		to the Receiver General of Canada for			
		for the month of April			

FIGURE 8-17   *The general journal entry for payment to the Receiver General*

6. The Remittance of Other Deductions

When it comes to remitting the other deductions, separate entries are usually required for each one. The journal entries are shown in Figure 8-18.

The set of T-accounts in Figure 8-19 shows the posted entries. Examining them carefully will give you a better understanding of the payroll procedure.

The entries are numbered as follows so that you can track them more easily.

(1) the original entries from the payroll journal;
(2) the employer's share of CPP for each pay period;
(3) the employer's share of UI for each pay period;
(4) the employer's share for the other deductions;
(5) the remittance to the Receiver General; and
(6) the remittance of the other deductions.

GENERAL JOURNAL

PAGE 18

DATE 19–		PARTICULARS	PR	DEBIT	CREDIT
May	1	Union Dues Payable		225 –	
		Bank			225 –
		To remit union dues collected in April			
	1	RPP Payable		1 177 28	
		Bank			1 177 28
		To remit RPP contributions for April			
	1	LTD Payable		240 –	
		Bank			240 –
		To remit LTD premiums to NuWest Ins.			
		for April			
	1	Dental Insurance Payable		281 25	
		Bank			281 25
		To remit dental insurance premiums to			
		Confederation Life for April			

FIGURE 8-18   *The general journal entry for remittance of other deductions*

Notice that the liability accounts relating to payroll are now all cleared out to zero. For the month of April, the business is left with the following net payroll entry:

Account	Debit	Credit
CPP Expense	$ 412.85	
Dental Insurance Expense	168.75	
LTD Expense	180.00	
RPP Expense	588.64	
UI Expense	615.04	
Wages Expense	19 621.55	
Bank		$21 586.83
	$21 586.83	$21 586.83

The total payroll cost for the sample case above is the original gross pay figure $19 621.55 plus the employer's share of Canada Pension Plan, Unemployment Insurance, and all other benefits, which have cost the employer an additional $1 965.28. As you can see, payroll actually costs a business more than it appears to when we just look at the payroll journal.

GENERAL LEDGER

Bank		Income Tax Payable		CPP Payable	
	2 746.08 (1)	(5) 3 961.89	787.24 (1)	(5) 825.70	82.05 (1)
	2 731.82 (1)		783.20 (1)		82.05 (2)
	2 811.99 (1)		805.88 (1)		81.63 (1)
	2 761.21 (1)		791.52 (1)		81.63 (2)
	2 770.25 (1)		794.05 (1)		83.97 (1)
	5 841.95 (5)				83.97 (2)
	225.00 (6)		0		82.49 (1)
	1 177.28 (6)				82.49 (2)
	240.00 (6)				82.71 (1)
	281.25 (6)				82.71 (2)
	21 586.83				0

UI Payable		Union Dues Payable		RPP Payable	
(5) 1 054.36	87.31 (1)	(6) 225.00	45.00 (1)	(6) 1 177.28	116.97 (1)
	122.23 (3)		45.00 (1)		116.97 (4)
	86.87 (1)		45.00 (1)		116.38 (1)
	121.62 (3)		45.00 (1)		116.38 (4)
	89.35 (1)		45.00 (1)		119.71 (1)
	125.09 (3)		0		119.71 (4)
	87.78 (1)				117.60 (1)
	122.89 (3)				117.60 (4)
	88.01 (1)				117.98 (1)
	123.21 (3)				117.98 (4)
	0				0

LTD Payable		Dental Insurance Payable		CPP Expense	
(6) 240.00	12.00 (1)	(6) 281.25	22.50 (1)	(2) 82.05	
	36.00 (4)		33.75 (4)	(2) 81.63	
	12.00 (1)		22.50 (1)	(2) 83.97	
	36.00 (4)		33.75 (4)	(2) 82.49	
	12.00 (1)		22.50 (1)	(2) 82.71	
	36.00 (4)		33.75 (4)	412.85	
	12.00 (1)		22.50 (1)		
	36.00 (4)		33.75 (4)		
	12.00 (1)		22.50 (1)		
	36.00 (4)		33.75 (4)		
	0		0		

Dental Insurance Expense		LTD Expense		RPP Expense	
(4) 33.75		(4) 36.00		(4) 116.97	
(4) 33.75		(4) 36.00		(4) 116.38	
(4) 33.75		(4) 36.00		(4) 119.71	
(4) 33.75		(4) 36.00		(4) 117.60	
(4) 33.75		(4) 36.00		(4) 117.98	
168.75		180.00		588.64	

UI Expense		Wage Expense	
(3) 122.23		(1) 3 899.15	
(3) 121.62		(1) 3 879.40	
(3) 125.09		(1) 3 990.40	
(3) 122.89		(1) 3 920.10	
(3) 123.21		(1) 3 932.50	
615.04		19 621.55	

FIGURE 8-19
T-accounts for payroll procedure

QUESTIONS

52. Of the three deductions taken for Revenue Canada, which require the employer to make a contribution as well?

53. What is the difference between a debit to Wage Expense and a debit to Salaries Expense?

54. If employees had $75.65 deducted from their pay for Canada Pension Plan contributions, what would the employer's share be?

55. If employees had $82.40 deducted from their pay for Unemployment Insurance contributions, what would the employer's share be?

56. Does a business always have to pay a share of other employee benefits such as an LTD insurance plan? Explain.

57. What is special about the three accounts, Income Tax Payable, Canada Pension Plan Payable, and Unemployment Insurance Payable?

58. The total cost of wages in the payroll journal is not really the total cost of payroll to a business. Does this statement make sense? Explain.

59. Where are other payroll deductions remitted?

8.5

Payroll Documents

There are four main documents generated by the payroll procedure in a business. The first of these is the payroll journal which you have already seen in section 8.4. The other main documents are the employee's paycheque with the accompanying statement of earnings, the T4 slip, and the employee's earnings record card. Each of these other documents will be shown to you in this section, together with a short explanation of its purpose.

THE PAYCHEQUE AND STATEMENT OF EARNINGS

Paying employees by cheque, as opposed to cash, provides better document support for the accounting system, and makes the business less vulnerable to cash losses through carelessness or theft. The paycheque also provides written proof that a business has actually paid a certain employee.

Bruna's Classic Giftware Mfg.		No. 8233

Bruna's Classic Giftware Mfg.
7041 Industrial Drive
Timmins, Ontario
P0N 2H0

No. 8233

Date April 30 19 –

Pay to the order of _____ Jackie Bauer _____ $ 437.53

---------------- Four Hundred and Thirty-seven ---------------- 53 /100 Dollars

Bank of Nova Scotia
2122 Pine Street
Timmins, ON P2H 1N2

Bruna Riley

Mobarok Ahmed

President
Treasurer

⑆12345⑈678⑆ 1234⑈678⑈

Employee Statement of Earnings
Detach and retain this statement.

No. 8233

Period Ending	Earnings			Deductions			Net Pay	
04/30/–	Regular	595	–	Union Dues		7	50	
	Taxable Benefits	25	70	RPP		18	62	
				Income Tax		125	60	
				CPP		12	98	
				UI		13	97	
				LTD Ins.		2	–	
				Dental		2	50	
	Gross Pay	620	70	Total Ded.		183	17	437	53

FIGURE 8-20 *A paycheque with a statement of earnings*

Most companies today attach a statement of earnings to the paycheque so that the employee can see all of his or her pay calculations. The **statement of earnings** below the cheque resembles a line in the payroll journal, since it has all of the same information and shows the employee exactly how the gross wage was calculated, the amount of the deductions, and the net pay for the time period. The employee detaches the statement of earnings before cashing the cheque and should keep it for future reference. It is a useful document that can be used to verify the data on the T4 slip which the employer issues to the employee at year end.

As mentioned earlier, some businesses use a separate payroll bank account to handle all the paycheques. A single cheque from the business is deposited in this payroll bank account to handle the exact amount of the payroll at the end of the pay period. The payroll bank account is reconciled regularly as an accounting control in the payroll procedure.

THE T4 SLIP

T4 slips must be completed by the employer and given to the employees by February 28th of the year following the taxation year in question.

The employee needs the T4 slip to prepare her or his tax return. The T4 slip shows the employee's gross pay for the year; the income tax deducted by the employer; the employee's contributions to the Canada Pension Plan and Unemployment Insurance; the employee's tax deductible contributions to a Registered Pension Plan; and Union Dues deducted from the employee's paycheque, if applicable.

One copy of the T4 slip is filed with the employee's income tax return and another copy is kept by the employee in her or his files. The employer, of course, keeps a copy of each T4 slip with the other payroll records on file, and one copy is sent to Revenue Canada.

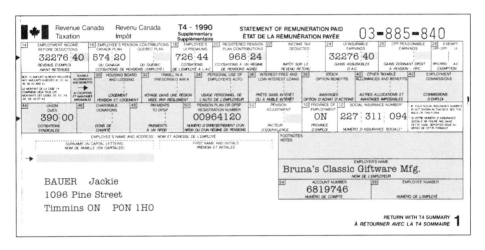

FIGURE 8-21 A T4 slip

THE EMPLOYEE EARNINGS RECORD CARD

An employee earnings record card (E.E.R.C.) is prepared for each employee when hired. It is used to accumulate the total of all the earnings of a particular employee and the information is used at the end of the year to prepare the T4 slip for that employee. See Figure 8-22 overleaf.

The business must ensure that the E.E.R.C. for each employee is accurately prepared from the information provided in the payroll journal for each pay period.

EMPLOYEE EARNINGS RECORD CARD

Bauer	Jackie		1
Last Name	First Name	Initial	Employee No.

1096 Pine Street			227 311 094
Street		Apt.	S.I.N.

Timmins	ON	PON 1HO	28/03/60
City	Province	Postal Code	Birthdate (d/m/y)

555-8973			28/03/25
Telephone			Normal Retirement Date (d/m/y)

PAY PERIOD ENDING (d/m/y)	EARNINGS			DEDUCTIONS		
	REGULAR	TAXABLE BENEFITS	GROSS	UNION DUES	RPP	INCOME TAX
Bal. Fwd.	7735 –	334 10	8069 10	97 50	24 206	1632 80
2/4/ –	595 –	25 70	620 70	7 50	18 62	125 60
9/4/ –	595 –	25 70	620 70	7 50	18 62	125 60
16/4/ –	595 –	25 70	620 70	7 50	18 62	125 60
23/4/ –	595 –	25 70	620 70	7 50	18 62	125 60
30/4/ –	595 –	25 70	620 70	7 50	18 62	125 60
TOTAL						

FIGURE 8-22   An employee earnings record card

One-Write Payroll

Payroll can also be prepared using a one-write system. This is useful for smaller businesses that may have a limited number of payroll entries. With the **one-write** method, three payroll output documents are produced simultaneously: the payroll journal, a paycheque for the employee, and an updated employee earnings record card. The specially coated documents are placed onto a hard writing board, one on top of the other. A payroll entry is then made onto the first document, and is automatically recorded on the two documents beneath; in other words, one writing operation does the job for the payroll. The one-write method can be very efficient (if no mistakes are made when recording the payroll) since it cuts the processing time for the payroll operation considerably.

Position: Accounts Receivable Supervisor
Department: Accounting

Marital Status: Single
Standard Earnings: $14.88

Employment Date (d/m/y): 30/01/86
Standard Deductions: all benefits/single coverage

Net Claim Code: 1

DEDUCTIONS					NET PAY	CCP TO DATE *
CPP	UI	LTD	DENTAL	TOTAL		
16 8 74	1 81 61	26 –	3 250	23 81 21	56 87 89	1 68 74
1 2 98	1 3 97	2 –	250	1 83 17	4 37 53	1 81 72
1 2 98	1 3 97	2 –	250	1 83 17	4 37 53	1 94 70
1 2 98	1 3 97	2 –	250	1 83 17	4 37 53	2 07 68
1 2 98	1 3 97	2 –	250	1 83 17	4 37 53	2 20 66
1 2 98	1 3 97	2 –	250	1 83 17	4 37 53	2 33 64

* Maximum annual contribution to CPP $ 632.50

QUESTIONS

60. Name the four output documents generated by a payroll procedure.

61. The payroll journal is both an input document and an output document in the payroll process. Explain this statement.

62. Why is it a good idea to pay employees by cheque, rather than cash?

63. What payroll information is contained on a statement of earnings?

64. What does a business use the statement of earnings for at the end of the calendar year?

65. (a) What does an employee do with his or her T4 slip?
    (b) What is the last date on which employers must give employees their T4 slips each year?

66. What three documents are prepared simultaneously when using a one-write for payroll?

8.6

Using the Computer

Computer software can be used in various aspects of the payroll operation. This section will provide examples using spreadsheet, database, graphics, and word processing software for payroll accounting.

Spreadsheets

The first spreadsheet example from the computer is an employee time card.

```
           A            B            C            D
    1  TIME CARD
    2  NAME:     Dave Quarrie
    3
    4  Week Ending           May 15, 19-
    5
    6  DAY           HOURS         REG          OT
    7
    8  Mon            8.00         8.00         0.00
    9  Tue           10.00         8.00         2.00
   10  Wed            9.00         8.00         1.00
   11  Thu            8.50         8.00         0.50
   12  Fri            8.00         8.00         0.00
   13  Sat            4.00         0.00         4.00
   14  Sun
   15             _____     _____     _____
   16  Totals        47.50        40.00         7.50
   17
   18
   19  Regular       40.00         8.50       340.00
   20  Overtime       7.50        12.75        95.63
   21                                        _____
   22                             Gross      435.63
   23                                        ========
```

FIGURE 8-23   *A spreadsheet time card*

The format of the time card is permanent, as are the title, employee name, week ending and other headings. All an accounting clerk has to do is enter onto the spreadsheet (time card) the number of hours worked during the week from Monday to Friday. The spreadsheet is programmed to calculate the regular and overtime hours, and the total hours at the bottom of the time card.

It will then calculate the regular and overtime pay, and the gross pay for the employee for the week.

Graphics
Payroll graphs can be prepared using different formats: bar graph, line graph, or pie chart. The example used here is a commission report for an office products firm which uses the bar graph form for the commission data. The graph shows the commissions paid to seven salespersons during the month of July.

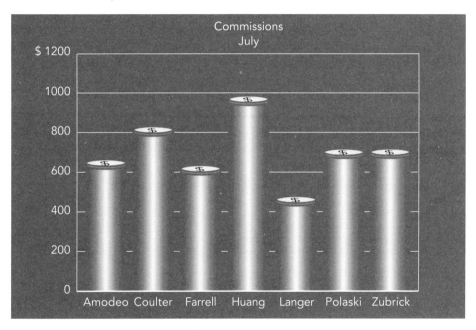

FIGURE 8-24   *A computer-generated bar graph*

By taking a quick look at the graph you can easily determine who sold the most or the least, assuming an indentical rate of commission. In a larger firm, you can see what an impact a graph would have on a person reading it.

Database
In the example that follows, the Payroll Information file has seven fields: Name, Address, Town, PC, Telephone Number, Salary, and Net Claim Code. Each field varies in width because the data to be entered is different

each time. The address field usually has to be quite long, and the phone field is always 8 characters.

```
Name: Rosita Suarez
Address: 2300 Friar Street
Town: Lethbridge
PC: T6T 3R1
Tel. No.: 555-0983
Salary: $680.00
Net Claim Code: 1
```

one record

FIGURE 8-25   *A payroll information record*

With more expensive database software, the payroll clerk can change the widths of the field to accommodate longer items of data than originally planned for. Once the data for all the employees has been entered and saved, the database can be used to generate payroll documents. It would be very useful for preparing the T4 slips at the end of the year, for example.

Word Processing

A good example of the use of word processing for payroll would be an exception report to the president, or owner, of a company that detailed overtime worked by employees in a given time period. Here is an example:

To: Ms. Vanita Pradesh, President
From: Ms. May Wong, Controller
Re: Employee Overtime, week ending March 20
Date: Wed. Mar. 27, 19–

Last week was particularly heavy for overtime pay due to a breakdown in two of the computerized embroidery machines. The schedule outlined below is from Department D where the breakdown occurred. Departments A, B, and C reported normal wage patterns with no variances above 1% of gross pay.

Employee	OT	Rate	OT Pay
Stephen Saelen	10	$16.00	$160.00
Cheng Chan	10	$15.00	$150.00
Shawn Morgan	8	$15.00	$120.00
Julie Sandham	8	$14.00	$112.00
Total Overtime Pay			$542.00

I will continue to monitor the weekly reports from the payroll department for your information.

Word processed documents are quick to prepare and can be easily spell-checked by the computer. In addition, they can be stored on floppy disks or the hard disk drive for instant recall later on.

Bedford Exercise 8 — Langley Campground

Relax for a Day, Come Camping Our Way is the slogan that is prominent on the brochures advertising the Langley's campground near Haliburton, Ontario. The Langley family have created a family vacation resort. Whether you prefer tenting in the bush, camping beside a lake, staying in a rustic cabin, or setting up your RV on a concrete pad, complete with all the amenities, this campground has it. Included in its fees, the resort offers row-boats, canoes, fishing, miniature golf, and the use of a play area. There is a variety store and bait shop on an adjacent property, which allows the Langleys to be free to concentrate on the rental of their facilities and developing fun activities for their clients.

As one can imagine, the largest recurring expense is the monthly payroll. Because the recreation industry is seasonal, most of the employees work only in the peak months of May through the end of September. Many of the employees are high school and college students.

Peter Langley is responsible for the accounting work and over the past winter he purchased a microcomputer system and the *ACCPAC Bedford Integrated Accounting* software. He has already set up the **General** module of accounts and has asked you to continue the computerizing of the accounting system by preparing the **Payroll** module so it will be ready for the coming tourist season. As part of your summer job you have been designated to enter the accounting data as required. Langley's fiscal year begins when the tourist season starts.

The trial balance for Langley Campground at the beginning of the season is as shown.

The accounts and all of the historical balances have been entered onto a disk for you, and the computer accounting system only has to be set to **Ready** mode. The instructions for using *Bedford* and entering data are outlined in Chapter 1.

Langley Campground
Trial Balance
at the beginning of the season

No.	Account	Debit	Credit
110	Bank	$30 000	
130	GST Recoverable	217	
135	Prepaid Insurance	5 000	
140	Prepaid Maintenance Supplies	3 000	
141	Prepaid RV Supplies	800	
142	Prepaid Taxes	2 700	
180	Equipment	48 700	
181	Acc. Dep. — Equipment		$ 7 920
185	Trucks	54 000	
186	Acc. Dep. — Trucks		19 760
190	Buildings	147 000	
191	Acc. Dep.—Buildings		14 550
195	Land Improvements	62 000	
198	Land	400 000	
210	Bank Loan		70 000
220	A/P Municipality of Haliburton		1 700
221	A/P Canadian Sanitation Supply		2 875
222	A/P Kost Kut RV Supplies		690
230	GST Payable		0
310	P. Langley, Capital		635 922
315	P. Langley, Drawings	0	
410	Site Rentals		0
412	Cabin Rentals		0
510	Advertising Expense	0	
515	Bank Charges	0	
520	Dep. Exp. — Buildings	0	
521	Dep. Exp. — Trucks	0	
522	Dep. Exp. — Equipment	0	
525	Equipment Repairs Expense	0	
530	Gasoline Expense	0	
535	Insurance Expense	0	
538	Interest Expense	0	
540	Maint. Supplies Expense	0	
545	Property Tax Expense	0	
547	RV Supplies Expense	0	
550	Salaries Expense	0	
565	Telephone Expense	0	
570	Truck Repairs Expense	0	
580	Utilities Expense	0	
		$753 417	$753 417

Accessing the Langley Campground General Ledger

To retrieve the general ledger for Langley Campground, you use the file name **langcamp**. Key this name into the computer, insert the dates provided by your teacher, and set the program to **Ready** as described in Chapter 1.

Enter the **Using** date provided by your teacher. Remember the sequence, mmddyy. As before, ignore the cautions, and proceed.

Journalizing Transactions

To journalize general ledger transactions, access the **GENERAL** module and the **Journal** option.

To journalize payroll transactions, access the **PAYROLL** module, and the **Journal** option, as follows.

Step 1 *Create employee files.*
        The payroll data for Langley Campground has been stored for you in the **PAYROLL** module. There are five employees at Langley. Their names and addresses can be seen by accessing **PAYROLL**, **Display**, and **Summary**.

Step 2 *Enter the necessary integration accounts in the general ledger chart of accounts.*
        Select **GENERAL**, **Ledger**, and **Insert**.

121	Advances Receivable	(select **R** for **Type** and **Y** for **Suppress**)
235	Vacation Pay Payable	(" " " " " " " ")
236	CPP Payable	(" " " " " " " ")
237	UI Payable	(" " " " " " " ")
238	Income Tax Payable	(" " " " " " " ")
240	WCB Payable	(" " " " " " " ")
517	CPP Expense	(select **L** for **Type** and **Y** for **Suppress**)
575	UI Expense	(" " " " " " " ")
590	WCB Expense	(" " " " " " " ")

Step 3 *Set the integration accounts.*
        Access **SYSTEM**, **Integrate**, and **Payroll**, and key in the account numbers, as shown:

Cash	110
AdvRec	121
VacPay	235

UIPay	237
CPPPay	236
TaxPay	238
WCBPay	240
Wages	550
UIExp	575
CPPExp	517
WCBExp	590

Step 4   *Make the* **Payroll** *module ready.*
Access the **SYSTEM** module, **Default**, **Module**, and **Payroll**.
Change **Ready** to **Yes**. Return to the main status line.

TRANSACTIONS

1. Cheque 101 (**GENERAL**, **Journal**)   Dated: mm01yy
To the Municipality of Haliburton, $1 700, payment of property tax bill owing.

2. Purchase Invoice 3221   Dated: mm01yy
Maintenance supplies, $1 080 plus GST $70, from Canadian Sanitation Supply.

3. Purchase Invoice 234   Dated: mm03yy
RV supplies, $1 296 plus $84 GST, from Kost Kut RV Supplies.

4. Cash Receipts Summary 001   Dated: mm07yy
Cash receipts for the week, $5 462.35. All cash is deposited daily to the bank account. Cabin Income, $3 475; Site Rental Income, $1 630; GST $357.35.

5. Cheque 102   Dated: mm09yy
To Kost Kut RV Supplies, $690 on account.

6. Cash Receipts Summary 002   Dated: mm14yy
Cash receipts for the week, $5 729.85. Cabin rental income, $3 800; Site Rental Income, $1 555; GST $374.85.

7. Cheque 103   Dated: mm15yy
To the Toronto Star for advertising, $950 plus GST $66.50.

8. Cheque 104 (**PAYROLL**, **Journal**)   Dated: mm16yy
To Mary-Ann Pollen, $240. Paid middle of the month advance.
Follow this guide.

Employee	1	(Mary-Ann Pollen)
Ending	mm16yy	
Regular		
Overtime		
Salary	Enter	
Commission	Enter	
Benefit	Enter	
Vacation	Enter	
Release	Enter	
Advance	240	
Pension		
Union		
Medical		
Project		
Amount		
Cheque	104	

9. Cheque 105 (**PAYROLL, Journal**)   Dated: mm16yy
   To Hans Geisbrecht, $300. Paid middle of the month advance.

10. Cheque 106 (**PAYROLL, Journal**)   Dated: mm16yy
    To Rai Kaljit, $210. Paid middle of the month advance.

11. Cheque 107 (**PAYROLL, Journal**)   Dated: mm16yy
    To Heidi Van Tol, $360. Paid middle of the month advance.

12. Cheque 108 (**PAYROLL, Journal**)   Dated: mm16yy
    To Curt Wytenbroek, $225. Paid middle of the month advance.

13. Cheque 109   Dated: mm19yy
    To Esso Canada, $680 plus $47.60 GST, for gasoline.

14. Cash Receipts Summary 003   Dated: mm21yy
    Cash receipts for the week, $6 260.57. Cabin rental income, $4 156;
    Site Rental Income, $1 695; GST $409.57.

15. Cheque 110   Dated: mm24yy
    To Kost Kut RV Supplies, $1 380 payment on account.

16. Cash Receipts Summary 004   Dated: mm28yy
    Cash receipts for the week, $9 837.58. Cabin rental income, $6 400;
    Site rental income, $2 794; GST $643.58.

17. Cheque 111   Dated: mm30yy
    To Canadian Sanitation Supply, $2 875 on account.

18. Cheque 112   Dated: mm30yy
    To The Royal Bank, $2 000 payment on the bank loan plus $700 interest.

19. Cheque 113 (**PAYROLL, Journal**)   Dated: mm30yy
    Paid month-end payroll to Mary-Ann Pollen.
    Note: The *Bedford* program will generate the other deductions and net
    pay automatically. The program also will generate the employer's payroll
    taxes internally to save you making these as entries. Follow this guide
    when you make this entry:

Employee	1
Ending	Select Default data
Regular	
Overtime	
Salary	Select Default data
Commission	⌷Enter⌷
Benefit	⌷Enter⌷
Vacation	Select Default
Release	⌷Enter⌷
Advance	Select Default
Pension	
Union	
Medical	
Project	
Amount	
Cheque	113

20. Cheque 114 (**PAYROLL, Journal**)   Dated: mm30yy
    Paid month-end payroll to Hans Geisbrecht.

21. Cheque 115 (**PAYROLL, Journal**)   Dated: mm30yy
    Paid month-end payroll to Rai Kaljit.

22. Cheque 116 (**PAYROLL, Journal**)   Dated: mm30yy
    Paid month-end payroll to Heide Van Tol.

23. Cheque 117 (**PAYROLL, Journal**)   Dated: mm30yy
    Paid month-end payroll to Curt Wytenbroek.

24. Voucher 117   Dated: mm30yy
    Adjusting entry for maintenance supplies expense incurred, $2 120.

25. Voucher 118   Dated: mm30yy
    Adjusting entry for RV supplies used, $2 960.

26. Cheque 118   Dated: mm30yy
    Payment of $40 000 to the bank to make a major reduction in the bank loan; $25 000 to reduce the long-term portion and $15 000 to reduce the current portion.

27. Voucher 119   Dated: mm30yy
    Adjustment for monthly taxes, $550.

28. Voucher 120   Dated: mm30yy
    Adjustment for prepaid insurance expired, $500.

DISPLAYING AND PRINTING

Select **Display**. Your teacher will advise you which of the options to preview. You will be prompted for dates. Remember, a date is entered in the sequence mmddyy (month, day, year).

Print any statements requested by your teacher. Again, you may be prompted for dates.

FINISHING A SESSION

Access the **SYSTEM** module and select the **Finish** option.

8.8

Dictionary of Accounting Terms

Bi-Weekly Pay Period   Payment is made every two weeks to the employee.

Commission Rate   A method of pay based on a percentage of sales volume.

Employee Earnings Record Card   A record of each employee's earnings, deductions, and net pay for the year.

Hourly Rated   Refers to employees who are paid a set rate per hour according to the hours worked.

Net Claim Code   Based on personal exemptions, it is used to determine an employee's income tax deduction.

One-write   A system that produces several documents using only one writing entry.

Payroll Journal   A book of original entry where payroll data is first recorded.

Piece Rate   A method of pay by which employees are paid according to how many pieces they produce each day or week.

Remuneration   Another term used for the gross or net pay paid to an employee.

Salary   A method of pay for employees who are hired at a daily, monthly, or annual rate of pay.

Statement Of Earnings   A summary of an employee's gross pay, deductions, and net pay for a specific pay period.

Statutory Deductions   Those deductions which must be taken from employees' paycheques by law.

T4 Slip   A record of the year's income, and deductions taken from that income, for an employee.

TD1 Form   A Revenue Canada form (also called a PTCR form) filled out by employees when they start work for a company and used to determine an employee's income tax exemption status.

Time Card   A document for recording the hours worked by an employee in a given time period.

Voluntary deductions   Those deductions which are optional.

MANUAL EXERCISES

1. Complete the four time cards below in your working papers. Assume that any time worked over eight hours per day, and any time worked on Saturday, is paid at the overtime rate, time-and-a-half.

TIME CARD

Employee No ___1___
Name ___Irene Bruggeman___
Week Ended ___March 13___ 19 –

Day	am IN	am OUT	pm IN	pm OUT	EXTRA IN	EXTRA OUT	TOTAL HOURS REG.	TOTAL HOURS O.T.
M	8	12	1	5				
T	8	12	1	5				
W	8	12	1	5				
T	8	12	1	5				
F	8	12	1	5				
S								
S								
						TOTALS		

	HOURS	RATE	GROSS PAY
REGULAR		10 50	$
OVERTIME			$
		TOTAL	$

TIME CARD

Employee No ___4___
Name ___Jamie Martin___
Week Ended ___March 13___ 19 –

Day	am IN	am OUT	pm IN	pm OUT	EXTRA IN	EXTRA OUT	TOTAL HOURS REG.	TOTAL HOURS O.T.
M	8	12	1	5				
T	8	12	1	5				
W	8	12	1	5				
T	8	12	1	5				
F	8	12	1	5				
S	8	12						
S								
						TOTALS		

	HOURS	RATE	GROSS PAY
REGULAR		10 70	$
OVERTIME			$
		TOTAL	$

TIME CARD

Employee No ___5___
Name ___Tracey Orth___
Week Ended ___March 13___ 19 –

Day	am IN	am OUT	pm IN	pm OUT	EXTRA IN	EXTRA OUT	TOTAL HOURS REG.	TOTAL HOURS O.T.
M	8	12	1	5				
T	8	12	1	5				
W	8	12	1	5				
T	8	12	1	5				
F	8	12	1	5				
S	8	12	1	3				
S								
						TOTALS		

	HOURS	RATE	GROSS PAY
REGULAR		10 80	$
OVERTIME			$
		TOTAL	$

TIME CARD

Employee No ___8___
Name ___Jennifer Arthur___
Week Ended ___March 13___ 19 –

Day	am IN	am OUT	pm IN	pm OUT	EXTRA IN	EXTRA OUT	TOTAL HOURS REG.	TOTAL HOURS O.T.
M	8	12	1	5				
T	8	12	1	5	7	10		
W	8	12	1	5	7	9		
T	8	12	1	5				
F	8	12	1	5				
S								
S								
						TOTALS		

	HOURS	RATE	GROSS PAY
REGULAR		10 95	$
OVERTIME			$
		TOTAL	$

FIGURE 8-26 *For exercise 1*

2. Complete the four time cards below in your working papers. Assume that any time worked over eight hours per day is paid at the overtime rate, time-and-a-half. Time worked on Saturday is paid at double-time rate.

TIME CARD

Employee No ___1___
Name ___Adam Cornwell___
Week Ended ___June 21___ 19—

Day	am IN	am OUT	pm IN	pm OUT	EXTRA IN	EXTRA OUT	TOTAL HOURS REG.	TOTAL HOURS O.T.
M	8	12	1	5	6	6		
T	8	12	1	5	9	9		
W	8	12	1	5				
T	8	12	1	5				
F	8	12	1	5				
S			1	5				
S								
						TOTALS		

	HOURS	RATE	GROSS PAY
REGULAR		10 60	$
OVERTIME			$
		TOTAL	$

TIME CARD

Employee No ___2___
Name ___Jodi Smith___
Week Ended ___June 21___ 19—

Day	am IN	am OUT	pm IN	pm OUT	EXTRA IN	EXTRA OUT	TOTAL HOURS REG.	TOTAL HOURS O.T.
M	8	12	1	5	6	10		
T	8	12	1	5	6	9		
W	8	12	1	5	6	9		
T	8	12	1	5				
F	8	12	1	5				
S			1	5				
S								
						TOTALS		

	HOURS	RATE	GROSS PAY
REGULAR		10 65	$
OVERTIME			$
		TOTAL	$

TIME CARD

Employee No ___3___
Name ___Heather Picknell___
Week Ended ___June 21___ 19—

Day	am IN	am OUT	pm IN	pm OUT	EXTRA IN	EXTRA OUT	TOTAL HOURS REG.	TOTAL HOURS O.T.
M	8	12	1	5	6	8		
T	8	12	1	5	6	8		
W	8	12	1	5				
T	8	12	1	5				
F	8	12	1	5				
S	8	12	1	3				
S								
						TOTALS		

	HOURS	RATE	GROSS PAY
REGULAR		10 80	$
OVERTIME			$
		TOTAL	$

TIME CARD

Employee No ___4___
Name ___Stuart Harrison___
Week Ended ___June 21___ 19—

Day	am IN	am OUT	pm IN	pm OUT	EXTRA IN	EXTRA OUT	TOTAL HOURS REG.	TOTAL HOURS O.T.
M	8	12	1	5	5:30	8		
T	8	12	1	5	5:30	8		
W	8	12	1	5	5:30	8		
T	8	12	1	5				
F	8	12	1	5				
S								
S								
						TOTALS		

	HOURS	RATE	GROSS PAY
REGULAR		11 00	$
OVERTIME			$
		TOTAL	$

FIGURE 8-27   For exercise 2

3. Donna Yuen earns a salary of $48 000 a year. What is her gross pay if calculated
   (a) weekly?   (b) bi-weekly?   (c) semi-monthly?   (d) monthly?

4. Holt Ritter earns a salary of $37 500 a year. What is his gross pay if calculated
   (a) weekly?   (b) bi-weekly?   (c) semi-monthly?   (d) monthly?

5. Calculate the gross pay for these office employees, first monthly and then
   bi-weekly.
   (a) Mike Fischer $28 000/year
   (b) Alice Gamble $30 000/year
   (c) Allison Zadow $35 000/year
   (d) Donna Newton $43 500/year

6. Calculate the gross pay for each employee.
   (a) Adam worked 36 hours at $9.63 per hour.
   (b) Joan earns $35 000 a year. How much is this per month?
   (c) Karma assembled 1 975 toys this week at a pay rate of $.29 per toy.
   (d) Karin sold $17 654 worth of goods and receives a sales commission of
       2.5% on her sales.

7. Calculate the overtime rates for these hourly-rated employees, assuming
   overtime is paid at time-and-a-half:
   (a) Josh $9.00 (b) Ryan $10.50 (c) Sara $8.12 (d) Ben $9.37 (e) Jodi $10.10

8. Calculate the gross pay for these six employees. All overtime is paid at time-
   and-a-half.

Employee	Rate	Hours
Diane Proper	$11.00	40
Dorothy Christo	10.50	42
Karen Avey	9.75	44
Anna Carrini	8.40	40
Jomar Fallina	7.15	35
Ted Morgan	7.00	20

9. Find the gross pay for the following piece rate employees.

Name	Pieces	Rate
Nancy Hagerman	800	$.75
Lynn Kehler	615	.60
Angela Gorvett	700	.73
Joel Miller	685	.70

10. The sales people for Hill Pharmaceuticals are paid a weekly commission of 2% of sales. Find their gross pay for last week.

Name	Sales
Trevor Czader	$44 200
Dan Trickett	$48 600
Abe Hiebert	$50 700
Duncan Singh	$47 300

11. Using the tables provided at the end of this chapter, find the employee's CPP contributions for these gross weekly wages.
(a) $465.20   (b) $800.00   (c) $501.10   (d) $773.12
(e) $1 556.34   (f) $1 943.11

12. Using the tables provided at the end of this chapter, find the UI deductions for these gross wages.
(a) $590.00   (b) $738.00   (c) $521.10   (d) $600.00
(e) $665.38   (f) $702.40

13. Using the tables provided at the end of this chapter, complete this payroll journal. Time worked over 40 hours is overtime and is paid at time-and-a-half the regular hourly rate. Cross-balance the journal.
(NCC = Net Claim Code for income tax deduction)

#	Employee Name	Hours	Rate	NCC
1.	Monica Sousa	43	$14.00	1
2.	Vicki Walker	42	$14.00	5
3.	Scott Vitias	40	$13.50	1
4.	Tim Harvey	44	$13.80	1
5.	Jamie Toth	42.5	$14.00	2

14. Using the tables provided, complete this salary payroll journal. Cross-balance the payroll journal. (NCC = Net Claim Code)

#	Employee Name	Weekly Salary	NCC
1.	Christine Thompson	$530	8
2.	Doug Nuyan	$540	1
3.	Mike Verboom	$610	4
4.	Jackie Cartier	$580	1
5.	Jay Taylor	$595	10

15. Using the tables provided, complete this piece rate payroll journal. Cross-balance the payroll journal.

#	Employee Name	Pieces	Rate	NCC
1.	Chris Lenardon	4 000	$.16	10
2.	Lisa Daniels	3 800	$.15	8
3.	Carin Hishchak	3 750	$.15	6
4.	Dave Milton	4 120	$.16	1
5.	Anthony Yang	4 300	$.16	1

16. Using the tables provided, complete the following commission payroll journal. The gross pay is obtained by multiplying the weekly sales by the rate. Cross-balance the payroll journal.

#	Employee Name	Sales	Rate	NCC
1.	Nijola Sernas	12 800	5%	1
2.	Krista Eslin	12 450	5%	5
3.	Fatuma Ahmed	11 900	4.5%	1
4.	Tahseen Ali	11 890	4.5%	1
5.	Joanne Paulionis	11 950	4.5%	2

17. Given the following payroll information for the Tillsonburg Parts Manufacturing Company, you are to:
   (a) Complete a payroll journal for the week ending September 12th using the Revenue Canada Source Deduction Tables for income tax, CPP, and UI. Employees are paid at time-and-a-half for all hours over 40 worked each week. Each employee has $6.00 per week deducted from gross pay for union dues, and $8.00 per week deducted for LTD.
   (b) Journalize all the payroll entries required to:
      (i) record the original pay.
      (ii) record the employer's share of Canada Pension Plan and Unemployment Insurance.
      (iii) remit the income tax, CPP, and UI deductions to the Receiver General.
      (iv) remit union dues to the Canadian Auto Workers Union.
      (v) remit the LTD to HealthPro Insurance.

Emp.No.	Employee Name	Hours	Rate	NCC
1.	Rajiv Nehru	42.0	$13.50	1
2.	Stu Huan	40.0	$14.00	2
3.	Chris Bradford	40.0	$14.00	8
4.	Saya Burghardt	44.0	$13.80	4
5.	Curtis Mervin	42.5	$14.00	1

18. Given this payroll information for Calgary Packaging Co., you are to:
   (a) Complete a payroll journal dated July 17th for the following employees using the Revenue Canada Source Deduction Tables for income tax, CPP, and UI. Employees are paid at the piece rates shown. Each employee has $20 per week deducted for LTD insurance, $8.00 per week for union dues, and 5% of gross pay for RPP contributions.
   (b) Journalize all the payroll entries required to:
      (i) record the original pay.
      (ii) record the employer's share of CPP and UI.
      (iii) record the employer's share of RPP (the employee's deduction is matched.)
      (iv) record the employer's share of LTD Insurance (twice the employee's contribution.)
      (v) remit the deductions to the Receiver General.
      (vi) remit union dues to the Canadian Auto Workers Union.
      (vii) remit LTD and RPP to Gore Mutual Ltd.

#	Employee Name	Pieces	Rate	NCC
1.	Keshav Chari	4 000	$.16	1
2.	Norm Collins	4 292	$.16	1
3.	Lisa Haupt	4 300	$.16	1
4.	Marisa Rossi	3 990	$.15	4
5.	Tom Mercredi	3 800	$.15	7

19. Given this payroll information for Wyley Publishing, you are to:
   (a) Complete a payroll journal dated Nov. 30th for the following employees using the Revenue Canada Source Deduction Tables for income tax, CPP, and UI. Each employee has 5% of gross pay deducted for RPP contributions, $25 per week deducted for LTD insurance, and $8.00 per week for the company dental plan.
   (b) Journalize all the payroll entries required to:
      (i) record the original pay.
      (ii) record the employer's share of CPP and UI.
      (iii) record the employer's share of RPP (the employee's deduction is matched).
      (iv) record the employer's share of LTD insurance (twice the employee's contribution).
      (v) record the employer's share of the dental plan (twice the employee's contribution).
      (vi) remit the deductions to the Receiver General.
      (vii) remit dental contributions to Mutual Life.
      (viii) remit LTD and RPP to Gore Mutual Ltd.

#	Employee Name	Salary	Taxable Benefits	NCC
1.	Connie Bigras	$560	$20	1
2.	Heather Hackney	580	$35	4
3.	Jerome Van De Slyke	580	$35	6
4.	Jason Huang	600	$20	6
5.	Phan Donc	600	$20	1

20. Given this payroll information for PennShirt Ltd., you are to:
    (a) Complete a payroll journal dated Aug. 7th for the following employees using the Revenue Canada Source Deduction Tables for income tax, CPP, and UI. Employees are paid a commission of 5% on sales. Each employee has 5% of gross pay deducted for RPP contributions, $20 per week deducted for LTD insurance, and $6.00 per week for the company dental plan.
    (b) Journalize all the payroll entries required to:
        (i) record the original pay.
        (ii) record the employer's share of CPP and UI.
        (iii) record the employer's share of RPP (the employee's deduction is matched).
        (iv) record the employer's share of LTD insurance (twice the employee's contribution).
        (v) record the employer's share of the dental plan (twice the employee's contribution).
        (vi) remit the deductions to the Receiver General.
        (vii) remit dental contributions to Mutual Life.
        (viii) remit LTD and RPP to Gore Mutual Ltd.

Name	Taxable Sales	Net Claim Benefits	NCC
Agatha Hiebert	$11 000	$40	3
Rose Couse	11 600	$40	5
Scott Moggach	11 800	$50	1
Chris Fish	11 400	$50	6
Rob Kelly	11 000	$60	1
Michael Wezse	11 900	$60	3

COMPUTER EXERCISES

SS1   Create the lookup table below for Income Tax.
  (i) Set column A and B widths to 5 characters.
  (ii) Keep the rest of the columns to a width of 10 characters.
  (iii) Columns C to G should be formatted to 2 decimal places.
  (iv) Use the wage figures in Column B of the Weekly Pay Range and the following tax rates to calculate the income taxes in Net Claim Code columns 1 to 5. Print your results.

The tax rates for the various Net Claim Codes are:

Net Claim Code 1	21%
Net Claim Code 2	20%
Net Claim Code 3	19%
Net Claim Code 4	18%
Net Claim Code 5	17%

	A B	C	D	E	F	G
1	Weekly			Net Claim Code		
2	Pay Range	1	2	3	4	5
3						
4	550 560	xx.xx	xx.xx	xx.xx	xx.xx	xx.xx
5	560 570	xx.xx	xx.xx	xx.xx	xx.xx	xx.xx
6	570 580	xx.xx	xx.xx	xx.xx	xx.xx	xx.xx
7	580 590	xx.xx	xx.xx	xx.xx	xx.xx	xx.xx
8	590 600	xx.xx	xx.xx	xx.xx	xx.xx	xx.xx

SS2   Create the following payroll journal template. Save your template on disk under the file name CH8SS2.
  (i) Set the Name column to 20 characters; set money columns to 10.
  (ii) Your money columns should be formatted to 2 decimal places.
  (iii) The Gross Pay column is to contain formulas in cells D3, D4, D5, D6, and D7 which will multiply the Hours in column B by the Rate in column C.
  (iv) Cell D9 should contain a formula which will automatically add the Gross Pay column (column D).

```
          A                    B                 C              D
 1  PAYROLL  JOURNAL
 2         Name              Hours              Rate        Gross Pay
 3  xxxxxxxxxxxxxxxxxxxxx     xx               x.xx          xxx.xx
 4  xxxxxxxxxxxxxxxxxxxxx     xx               x.xx          xxx.xx
 5  xxxxxxxxxxxxxxxxxxxxx     xx               x.xx          xxx.xx
 6  xxxxxxxxxxxxxxxxxxxxx     xx               x.xx          xxx.xx
 7  xxxxxxxxxxxxxxxxxxxxx     xx               x.xx          xxx.xx
 8                                                          ‾‾‾‾‾‾‾‾
 9                                           Total         xxxx.xx
10                                                         ========
```

SS3   Using the template from CH8SS2:
      (a) Insert the following data into the spreadsheet template.
          Save your solution under the file name CH8SS3.

Name	Hours	Rate
Jay Hoekstra	40	$12.00
Jennie Schmidt	39	$12.10
Cecilia Van Egmond	40	$12.50
Michael Sung	40	$11.75
Jennifer Symons	35	$11.40

      (b) Print a copy of the payroll journal.

SS4   Using the payroll journal from CH8SS3, insert two new columns in your
      spreadsheet, at the right; one for income tax, "Inc.Tax"; another for net
      pay, "Net".
      The Income Tax column can be programmed with this formula:
      Inc. Tax = Gross * .20
      The Net column can be programmed with this formula:
      Net = Gross – Inc. Tax
      Cells E9 and F9 are to be programmed with formulas to add them.
      Print your results.

SS5   (a) Create and use a template for time cards.
         (i) Create a time card template as shown.
        (ii) Program the spreadsheet so that the hours in column B are divided
             into regular hours (column C), or overtime hours (column D). Any
             hours over 8 each day are overtime.
       (iii) Program the spreadsheet so that it automatically adds the HRS
             (hours) column, the R (regular hours) column, and the OT (overtime
             hours) column.

	A	B	C	D
1	TIME CARD			
2	Name:			
3	Date:			
4				
5	DAY	HRS	R	OT
6	Monday	XX	XX	XX
7	Tuesday	XX	XX	XX
8	Wednesday	XX	XX	XX
9	Thursday	XX	XX	XX
10	Friday	XX	XX	XX
11		___	___	___
12	TOTALS	?	?	?
13		═══	═══	═══

(b) Use your template and enter the data given below.

Name: Jaren Penny   Date: August 12, 19–
Hours worked: M   T   W   Th   F
                  8   9   12   8   9

SS6   Set up a payroll journal with Revenue Canada deductions.
(i) Set up the template shown below, using your work from CH8SS3.
(ii) Program the spreadsheet so that the following are used to
calculate the data required in columns C, D, and E.
Income Tax = 20.00% of Gross Pay
CPP   =   2.10% of Gross Pay
UI   =   1.95% of Gross Pay
(iii) Program cells F3 to F7 to find each employee's net pay.
(iv) Program the spreadsheet to total columns B, C, D, E, and F.

	A	B	C	D	E	F
1	PAYROLL JOURNAL					
2	Name	Gross	Inc.Tax	CPP	UI	Net Pay
3	XXXXXXXXXXXXXX	XXX.XX	XX.XX	XX.XX	XX.XX	XXX.XX
4	XXXXXXXXXXXXXX	XXX.XX	XX.XX	XX.XX	XX.XX	XXX.XX
5	XXXXXXXXXXXXXX	XXX.XX	XX.XX	XX.XX	XX.XX	XXX.XX
6	XXXXXXXXXXXXXX	XXX.XX	XX.XX	XX.XX	XX.XX	XXX.XX
7	XXXXXXXXXXXXXX	XXX.XX	XX.XX	XX.XX	XX.XX	XXX.XX
8		___	___	___	___	___
9	Totals	XXXX.XX	XXX.XX	XXX.XX	XXX.XX	XXXX.XX
10		═══	═══	═══	═══	═══

DB1 Create an employee data file with these fields:

No.	=	3 columns
Last Name	=	15 columns
First Name	=	10 columns
SIN	=	11 columns
NCC	=	3 columns
Hours	=	3 columns
Rate	=	2.2 columns
Gross	=	3.2 columns

  (i) Enter the raw data shown below.
  (ii) Program the database to produce the Gross Pay.
  (iii) Put the title on your file.

No.	Last Name	First Name	SIN	NCC	Hrs	Rate
1	Ratz	Diana	344-356-901	1	40	$ 9.10
2	Daigle	Allan	777-001-192	2	40	$ 9.00
3	Brown	Dwight	202-101-663	10	40	$ 9.50
4	George	Brian	576-553-121	1	35	$ 8.50
5	Horvath	Lisa	486-897-002	3	40	$10.00
6	Jetz	Susan	543-333-644	4	38	$ 9.30
7	Ng	Abner	675-113-060	5	40	$ 9.45
8	Millson	Clyde	473-222-999	10	35	$ 9.75
9	Evans	Millie	666-343-676	10	40	$ 9.10
10	Piper	Starr	271-127-555	1	37	$ 9.00

DB2 Create a commission payroll table with these fields:

No.	=	3 columns
Name	=	20 columns
Sales	=	5.2 columns
Rate	=	1.3 columns
Commission	=	5.2 columns

  (i) Enter the following raw data.
  (ii) Program the database to calculate the Commission column.
  (iii) Program the database to add the Commission column.
  (iv) Put the title on the file.

No.	Name	Sales	Rate
1	Sebok, Jonathon	$33 456.78	.045
2	Zavitz, Jacob	$38 555.02	.050
3	Dwindler, Cynthia	$20 400.00	.040
4	Estuary, Barbara	$32 800.78	.045
5	Flagstaff, Pete	$40 200.60	.055
6	Coldwell, Lucy	$25 666.80	.040
7	Fazakas, Wayne	$37 333.54	.045
8	Morrison, Gary	$42 600.20	.045
9	Anderson, Jodi	$30 005.05	.040
10	Watling, Sonya	$37 340.40	.050

DB3   Create a piece rate payroll table with these fields:

No.	=	3 columns
Name	=	20 columns
Mon	=	3 columns
Tue	=	3 columns
Wed	=	3 columns
Thu	=	3 columns
Fri	=	3 columns
Total	=	5 columns
Rate	=	1.2 columns

(i)   Enter the raw data shown below.

(ii) Program the database to calculate the Total pieces.

(iii) Add a new field called Gross to the database; define it as 4.2 columns and program the database to calculate each employee's Gross Pay (Total * Rate).

(iv) Put the title on the file.

No.	Name	Mon	Tue	Wed	Thu	Fri	Rate
1	Johnson, R.	175	212	190	200	202	$.50
2	Arnd, V.	188	210	199	198	220	$.45
3	Van Winden, S.	190	190	195	195	200	$.50
4	VerBruggen, R.	180	200	180	200	190	$.50
5	Corbeil, J.	200	204	206	208	210	$.60
6	Kirktown, H.	210	220	225	225	230	$.60
7	Wright, T.	175	175	175	180	180	$.40
8	Stone, T.	150	150	152	160	154	$.35

GR1   Create a line graph for this payroll data for Jerome Black. Your vertical axis should read $400, $450, $500, $550, $600, $650, $700, $750. Your horizontal axis should be the months January to June.

Jan.	$720.00
Feb.	$525.00
Mar.	$600.00
Apr.	$412.00
May	$675.00
June	$449.00

GR2   Create a bar graph for this payroll data. Your vertical axis should read $1 000, $1 500, $2 000, $2 500, $3 000, $3 500, $4 000, $4 500.

Payroll Commissions Paid — January

Arnold, Jason	$4 013.00
Barnard, Derek	$1 015.00
Cattrys, Mark	$2 875.00
Hackney, Heather	$3 333.00
Harper, Andrea	$3 875.00
Lu, Lisa	$1 840.00

GR3   Create a pie graph for this payroll data.

Blaster Fireworks Ltd.
Commissions Paid — By Territory

Ontario	$120 000
Quebec	$ 85 000
British Columbia	$ 60 000
Prairie Provinces	$ 40 000
Maritimes	$ 25 000
Newfoundland	$ 7 000

WP1   As the president of Purrfect Cat Food, write a letter to your top salesperson for the month congratulating him on his sales efforts. Jason
earned commissions of $4 013 for the month. This is a new company
record. Tell him that his picture will be published in the monthly
newsletter that goes to all sales units across Canada.

Employee Data:
Jason Arnold
1231 Fairview Crescent
Lindsay, Ontario N6G 1K7

WP2   As the president of Purrfect Cat Food, draft a letter to Derek Barnard
indicating that his sales for the month are the lowest. Include a copy of
the graph from exercise GR2 above if possible. Tell him that he is affecting company profits and that unless he improves, he will have to be dis-
missed from the company.

Employee Data:
Derek Barnard
121 Don Vale Road
Toronto, Ontario M4K 2J2

WP3   As the president of Purrfect Cat Food, draft a letter to the shareholders
indicating:
(i) This year has been record-breaking for sales (up 18%).
(ii) The company is expanding its product line. This will be discussed at
the next A.G.M., to be held in Winnipeg, three months hence.

R. v. KRANSZ

BACKGROUND

Gabriella Kransz was the office manager of Divine Drilling Limited. Any one of the office manager, the president, or the vice-president was authorized to sign payroll cheques for the company. During the time that Gabriella was office manager, the auditors had difficulty checking the financial statements at year end because the books of account were poorly maintained. The president finally fired Gabriella and a new office manager assumed her duties. The new office manager, Judy, suspected that Gabriella had received unauthorized payments from Divine Drilling Limited over a five-year period. These unauthorized payments were covered up by using the payroll data for the company.

INVESTIGATION

Divine Drilling used a payroll bank account for its weekly payroll accounting. The payroll journals for Divine Drilling were examined and it was found that ten cheques totalling $20 000 were paid to Gabriella but were not recorded in the company's payroll journal.

FRAUD

The cover up routine used by Gabriella was the same on all ten occasions. Here is an example of the technique used.

A payroll cheque dated June 1 in the amount of $1 800 was paid to Gabriella, but not recorded in the payroll journal. A note was put in with the December bank statement that said, "This is to certify that Gabriella Kransz received a loan of $1 800 from Divine Drilling Limited; to be repaid by the end of the year." In red ink on the note was this comment "Repaid December 1."

In the same month a special journal entry was recorded in the general journal of the business, as shown.

DATE 19–		PARTICULARS	PR	DEBIT	CREDIT
Dec.	31	Salespersons' Salaries—Montreal		2 3 4 67	
		Salespersons' Salaries—Calgary		4 1 8 44	
		Delivery Salaries—Toronto		6 1 2 03	
		Salespersons' Salaries—Vancouver		5 3 4 86	
		Bank			1 8 0 0 00
		To record cheques cashed but not			
		recorded in the payroll records for			
		the year			

The only cheque not recorded was a cheque made out to, and cashed by, Gabriella Kransz for $1 800.00.

SENTENCE

Gabriella's case was heard in Provincial Court in Montreal. Evidence was heard that this was her first criminal offence; that she supported two young daughters on her own and that money was scarce. She was ordered to repay the money, and because of the extenuating circumstances described above, she was put on probation for a period of two years. As a result of this conviction, however, Gabriella is no longer bondable (i.e. insurable for handling money), and her reputation as a reliable office manager has suffered considerably. Gabriella will have to seek work in another line of employment.

QUESTIONS

1. How would this fraud have been caught in a normal business that had proper internal control over its payroll recording function?
2. How many signing officers are normal for company paycheques?
3. Why would a company use a payroll bank account, instead of its regular bank account, to pay employees?
4. How could the auditors tell if the general journal entry was fraudulent or not?

NAME

NO.

Career Profile

Sara Chu joined Oxford Consolidated Insurance the month after she graduated from high school. Sara's father had sold general insurance all his life and had built up a solid group of clients by providing excellent service over a period of 35 years. Sara joined her father in his insurance agency and five years later took over the business. Sara was even better than her father at making business contacts, and under her guidance the agency grew and profits soared. Clients were happy with the service provided and word of mouth quickly added more clients to the business.

Sara's only concern was her lack of accounting skills and knowledge. She knew all about selling insurance, providing service to clients, and checking the "bottom line" on the income statements for profits; but she felt that the manual way of keeping the books was outdated, and that the agency should be computerizing its accounting records.

Since Sara now had seven agents working for her in the general insurance business, she wanted to computerize all the payroll records first. Her agents were paid a base salary and commission. The commissions were easy enough to calculate but doing the calculations, recording the entries, posting the payroll journal, preparing the T4s and keeping up the employee earnings record cards took a lot of time.

So Sara signed up for two evening courses at a local community college. The first was an Accounting Fundamentals course that taught her all about journalizing, posting, preparing worksheets, and producing financial statements for a business. By the time she had completed this, Sara had a very firm understanding of the accounting cycle for a small business such as her insurance agency.

The next course in the winter was a Computerized Accounting course. This course used IBM computers with 20 megabyte hard drives hooked up to printers so that hard copies of financial statements could be produced. The accounting software used had several major components to it: accounts receivable, accounts payable, payroll, and inventory. The payroll portion was of particular interest to Sara. After the course was completed, she discussed the purchase of a microcomputer with her accountant, and together they bought one for Sara's business.

Sara doesn't feed the payroll data into the machine; her sister, Sheri, does this on Saturday morning for her. Sheri enters the sales data for each insurance agent and the computer does the rest. It calculates commissions, adds in the base salary, takes the required deductions, prepares the payroll journal entry, posts to the general ledger, produces the payroll commission cheques for the agents, updates their employee earnings record cards, and outputs all of this on hard copy for Sara and Sheri to analyse.

More importantly, Sara understands the role of accounting for her business now. She can concentrate on servicing the insurance needs of her clients, and she does not have to worry about the accounting records balancing each month. Computerized accounting has streamlined Sara's office operations.

The other night at dinner, Sheri asked her father, "How does a person get started in the insurance business anyway?"

FOR DISCUSSION

- How has Sara's computer system saved her time?
- Can a person run an insurance business today without the help of a computer?

ONTARIO — TABLE 1 — ONTARIO

WEEKLY TAX DEDUCTIONS
Basis — 52 Pay Periods per Year

RETENUES D'IMPÔT PAR SEMAINE
Base — 52 périodes de paie par année

IF THE EMPLOYEE'S "NET CLAIM CODE" ON FORM TD1 IS
SI LE «CODE DE DEMANDE NETTE» DE L'EMPLOYÉ SELON LA FORMULE TD1 EST

DEDUCT FROM EACH PAY – *RETENEZ SUR CHAQUE PAIE*

WEEKLY PAY / PAIÉ PAR SEMAINE From-De	Less than Moins que	0	1	2	3	4	5	6	7	8	9	10
233.-	237.	60.60	28.15	24.20	16.25	5.50	.25					
237.-	241.	61.65	29.20	25.20	17.25	6.20	.90					
241.-	245.	62.65	30.20	26.25	18.30	7.65	1.60					
245.-	249.	63.70	31.25	27.25	19.30	9.35	2.25					
249.-	253.	64.70	32.25	28.30	20.35	11.10	2.95					
253.-	257.	65.75	33.30	29.30	21.40	12.80	3.65					
257.-	261.	66.75	34.30	30.35	22.40	14.45	4.30					
261.-	265.	67.80	35.35	31.35	23.45	15.45	5.00					
265.-	269.	68.80	36.35	32.40	24.45	16.50	5.70	.40				
269.-	273.	69.85	37.40	33.40	25.50	17.55	6.35	1.10				
273.-	277.	70.85	38.40	34.45	26.50	18.55	8.10	1.75				
277.-	281.	71.90	39.45	35.50	27.55	19.60	9.80	2.45				
281.-	285.	72.90	40.45	36.50	28.55	20.60	11.50	3.15				
285.-	289.	73.95	41.50	37.55	29.60	21.65	13.20	3.80				
289.-	293.	74.95	42.50	38.55	30.60	22.65	14.70	4.50				
293.-	297.	76.00	43.55	39.60	31.65	23.70	15.75	5.15				
297.-	301.	77.00	44.60	40.60	32.65	24.70	16.75	5.85	.55			
301.-	305.	78.05	45.60	41.65	33.70	25.75	17.80	6.80	1.25			
305.-	309.	79.05	46.65	42.65	34.70	26.75	18.80	8.50	1.95			
309.-	313.	80.10	47.65	43.70	35.75	27.80	19.85	10.25	2.60			
313.-	317.	81.10	48.70	44.70	36.75	28.80	20.85	11.95	3.30			
317.-	321.	82.15	49.70	45.75	37.80	29.85	21.90	13.65	4.00			
321.-	325.	83.15	50.75	46.75	38.80	30.85	22.90	14.95	4.65			
325.-	329.	84.20	51.75	47.80	39.85	31.90	23.95	16.00	5.35	.05		
329.-	333.	85.20	52.80	48.80	40.85	32.90	24.95	17.00	6.05	.75		
333.-	337.	86.25	53.80	49.85	41.90	33.95	26.00	18.05	7.25	1.45		
337.-	341.	87.25	54.85	50.85	42.90	34.95	27.00	19.05	8.95	2.10		
341.-	345.	88.30	55.85	51.90	43.95	36.00	28.05	20.10	10.65	2.80		
345.-	349.	89.30	56.90	52.90	44.95	37.00	29.05	21.10	12.35	3.45		
349.-	353.	90.35	57.90	53.95	46.00	38.05	30.10	22.15	14.10	4.15		
353.-	357.	91.35	58.95	54.95	47.00	39.05	31.10	23.15	15.20	4.85	.25	
357.-	361.	92.40	59.95	56.00	48.05	40.10	32.15	24.20	16.25	5.50	.90	
361.-	365.	93.40	61.00	57.00	49.05	41.10	33.15	25.20	17.25	6.20	1.60	
365.-	369.	94.45	62.00	58.05	50.10	42.15	34.20	26.25	18.30	7.65	2.30	
369.-	373.	95.45	63.05	59.05	51.10	43.15	35.20	27.25	19.30	9.35	2.30	
373.-	377.	96.50	64.05	60.10	52.15	44.20	36.25	28.30	20.35	11.10	2.95	
377.-	381.	97.50	65.10	61.10	53.15	45.20	37.25	29.30	21.35	12.80	3.65	
381.-	385.	98.55	66.10	62.15	54.20	46.25	38.30	30.35	22.40	14.45	4.30	
385.-	389.	99.55	67.15	63.15	55.20	47.25	39.30	31.35	23.40	15.50	5.00	
389.-	393.	100.60	68.15	64.20	56.25	48.30	40.35	32.40	24.45	16.50	5.70	.40
393.-	397.	101.65	69.20	65.20	57.25	49.30	41.35	33.40	25.50	17.55	6.35	1.10
397.-	401.	102.65	70.20	66.25	58.30	50.35	42.40	34.45	26.50	18.55	8.10	1.75
401.-	405.	103.70	71.25	67.25	59.30	51.35	43.40	35.45	27.55	19.60	9.80	2.45
405.-	409.	104.70	72.25	68.30	60.35	52.40	44.45	36.50	28.55	20.60	11.50	3.15
409.-	413.	105.75	73.30	69.30	61.35	53.40	45.45	37.50	29.60	21.65	13.25	3.80
413.-	417.	106.75	74.30	70.35	62.40	54.45	46.50	38.55	30.60	22.65	14.70	4.50
417.-	421.	107.80	75.35	71.35	63.40	55.45	47.50	39.60	31.65	23.70	15.75	5.15
421.-	425.	108.80	76.35	72.40	64.45	56.50	48.55	40.60	32.65	24.70	16.75	5.85
425.-	429.	109.85	77.40	73.40	65.45	57.50	49.55	41.65	33.70	25.75	17.80	6.80
429.-	433.	110.85	78.40	74.45	66.50	58.55	50.60	42.65	34.70	26.75	18.80	8.50
433.-	437.	111.90	79.45	75.45	67.50	59.55	51.60	43.70	35.75	27.80	19.85	10.20
437.-	441.	112.90	80.45	76.50	68.55	60.60	52.65	44.70	36.75	28.80	20.85	11.95
441.-	445.	113.95	81.50	77.50	69.55	61.60	53.65	45.75	37.80	29.85	21.90	13.65
445.-	449.	114.95	82.50	78.55	70.60	62.65	54.70	46.75	38.80	30.85	22.90	14.95
449.-	453.	116.00	83.55	79.55	71.65	63.65	55.70	47.80	39.85	31.90	23.95	16.00

ONTARIO										ONTARIO	
TABLE 1											
WEEKLY TAX DEDUCTIONS Basis — 52 Pay Periods per Year						RETENUES D'IMPÔT PAR SEMAINE Base — 52 périodes de paie par année					

WEEKLY PAY Use appropriate bracket		IF THE EMPLOYEE'S "NET CLAIM CODE" ON FORM TD1 IS SI LE «CODE DE DEMANDE NETTE» DE L'EMPLOYÉ SELON LA FORMULE TD1 EST										
PAIE PAR SEMAINE Utilisez le palier approprié		0	1	2	3	4	5	6	7	8	9	10
From - De	Less than Moins que		DEDUCT FROM EACH PAY – RETENEZ SUR CHAQUE PAIE									
453.-	461.	117.50	85.10	81.10	73.15	65.20	57.25	49.30	41.35	33.40	25.50	17.50
461.-	469.	119.55	87.15	83.15	75.20	67.25	59.30	51.35	43.40	35.45	27.55	19.60
469.-	477.	121.60	89.20	85.20	77.25	69.30	61.35	53.40	45.45	37.55	29.60	21.65
477.-	485.	123.65	91.25	87.25	79.30	71.35	63.40	55.45	47.50	39.60	31.65	23.70
485.-	493.	125.75	93.30	89.30	81.35	73.40	65.45	57.50	49.55	41.65	33.70	25.75
493.-	501.	127.80	95.35	91.35	83.40	75.45	67.50	59.55	51.65	43.70	35.75	27.80
501.-	509.	129.85	97.40	93.40	85.45	77.50	69.55	61.60	53.70	45.75	37.80	29.85
509.-	517.	131.90	99.45	95.45	87.50	79.55	71.60	63.65	55.75	47.80	39.85	31.90
517.-	525.	133.95	101.50	97.50	89.55	81.60	73.65	65.75	57.80	49.85	41.90	33.95
525.-	533.	136.00	103.55	99.55	91.60	83.65	75.70	67.80	59.85	51.90	43.95	36.00
533.-	541.	138.05	105.60	101.60	93.65	85.70	77.75	69.85	61.90	53.95	46.00	38.05
541.-	549.	140.10	107.65	103.65	95.70	87.75	79.80	71.90	63.95	56.00	48.05	40.10
549.-	557.	142.15	109.70	105.70	97.80	89.80	81.85	73.95	66.00	58.05	50.10	42.15
557.-	565.	145.25	112.80	108.80	100.85	92.90	84.95	77.05	69.10	61.15	53.20	45.25
565.-	573.	148.40	116.00	112.00	104.05	96.10	88.15	80.20	72.25	64.30	56.40	48.40
573.-	581.	151.60	119.15	115.20	107.25	99.30	91.35	83.40	75.45	67.50	59.55	51.60
581.-	589.	154.80	122.35	118.40	110.45	102.50	94.55	86.60	78.65	70.70	62.75	54.80
589.-	597.	158.05	125.60	121.60	113.65	105.70	97.75	89.80	81.90	73.95	66.00	58.05
597.-	605.	161.25	128.85	124.85	116.90	108.95	101.00	93.05	85.10	77.15	69.20	61.25
605.-	613.	164.50	132.05	128.10	120.15	112.20	104.25	96.30	88.35	80.40	72.45	64.50
613.-	621.	167.75	135.30	131.35	123.40	115.45	107.50	99.55	91.60	83.65	75.70	67.75
621.-	629.	171.00	138.55	134.55	126.60	118.65	110.70	102.80	94.85	86.90	78.95	71.00
629.-	637.	174.20	141.80	137.80	129.85	121.90	113.95	106.00	98.05	90.10	82.15	74.20
637.-	645.	177.45	145.00	141.05	133.10	125.15	117.20	109.25	101.30	93.35	85.40	77.45
645.-	653.	180.70	148.25	144.30	136.35	128.40	120.45	112.50	104.55	96.60	88.65	80.70
653.-	661.	183.95	151.50	147.50	139.55	131.60	123.65	115.75	107.80	99.85	91.90	83.95
661.-	669.	187.15	154.75	150.75	142.80	134.85	126.90	118.95	111.00	103.05	95.10	87.15
669.-	677.	190.40	157.95	154.00	146.05	138.10	130.15	122.20	114.25	106.30	98.35	90.40
677.-	685.	193.65	161.20	157.25	149.30	141.35	133.40	125.45	117.50	109.55	101.60	93.65
685.-	693.	196.95	164.50	160.55	152.60	144.65	136.70	128.75	120.80	112.85	104.90	96.95
693.-	701.	200.20	167.80	163.80	155.85	147.90	139.95	132.00	124.05	116.15	108.20	100.25
701.-	709.	203.50	171.05	167.10	159.15	151.20	143.25	135.30	127.35	119.40	111.45	103.50
709.-	717.	206.80	174.35	170.40	162.45	154.50	146.55	138.60	130.65	122.70	114.75	106.80
717.-	725.	210.10	177.65	173.65	165.75	157.75	149.80	141.90	133.95	126.00	118.05	110.10
725.-	733.	213.35	180.95	176.95	169.00	161.05	153.10	145.15	137.20	129.25	121.35	113.35
733.-	741.	216.65	184.20	180.25	172.30	164.35	156.40	148.45	140.50	132.55	124.60	116.65
741.-	749.	219.95	187.50	183.55	175.60	167.65	159.70	151.75	143.80	135.85	127.90	119.95
749.-	757.	223.25	190.80	186.80	178.85	170.90	162.95	155.05	147.10	139.15	131.20	123.25
757.-	765.	226.50	194.10	190.10	182.15	174.20	166.25	158.30	150.35	142.40	134.45	126.50
765.-	773.	229.80	197.35	193.40	185.45	177.50	169.55	161.60	153.65	145.70	137.75	129.80
773.-	781.	233.10	200.65	196.70	188.75	180.80	172.85	164.90	156.95	149.00	141.05	133.10
781.-	789.	236.35	203.95	199.95	192.00	184.05	176.10	168.15	160.20	152.30	144.35	136.40
789.-	797.	239.65	207.20	203.25	195.30	187.35	179.40	171.45	163.50	155.55	147.60	139.65
797.-	805.	242.95	210.50	206.55	198.60	190.65	182.70	174.75	166.80	158.85	150.90	142.95
805.-	813.	246.25	213.80	209.80	201.90	193.90	185.95	178.05	170.10	162.15	154.20	146.25
813.-	821.	249.50	217.10	213.10	205.15	197.20	189.25	181.30	173.35	165.40	157.50	149.50
821.-	829.	252.80	220.35	216.40	208.45	200.50	192.55	184.60	176.65	168.70	160.75	152.80
829.-	837.	256.10	223.65	219.70	211.75	203.80	195.85	187.90	179.95	172.00	164.05	156.10
837.-	845.	259.40	226.95	222.95	215.00	207.05	199.10	191.20	183.25	175.30	167.35	159.40
845.-	853.	262.65	230.25	226.25	218.30	210.35	202.40	194.45	186.50	178.55	170.60	162.65
853.-	861.	265.95	233.50	229.55	221.60	213.65	205.70	197.75	189.80	181.85	173.90	165.95
861.-	869.	269.25	236.80	232.85	224.90	216.95	209.00	201.05	193.10	185.15	177.20	169.25
869.-	877.	272.55	240.10	236.10	228.15	220.20	212.25	204.30	196.35	188.45	180.50	172.55
877.-	885.	275.80	243.35	239.40	231.45	223.50	215.55	207.60	199.65	191.70	183.75	175.80
885.-	893.	279.10	246.65	242.70	234.75	226.80	218.85	210.90	202.95	195.00	187.05	179.10

CANADA PENSION PLAN CONTRIBUTIONS — COTISATIONS AU RÉGIME DE PENSIONS DU CANADA

WEEKLY PAY PERIOD — *PÉRIODE HEBDOMADAIRE DE PAIE*

433.13—558.34

Remuneration / Rémunération From-de	To-à	C.P.P. R.P.C.	Remuneration / Rémunération From-de	To-à	C.P.P. R.P.C.	Remuneration / Rémunération From-de	To-à	C.P.P. R.P.C.	Remuneration / Rémunération From-de	To-à	C.P.P. R.P.C.
433.13	433.55	8.64	464.43	464.86	9.36	495.74	496.16	10.08	527.04	527.47	10.80
433.56	433.99	8.65	464.87	465.29	9.37	496.17	496.60	10.09	527.48	527.90	10.81
434.00	434.42	8.66	465.30	465.73	9.38	496.61	497.03	10.10	527.91	528.34	10.82
434.43	434.86	8.67	465.74	466.16	9.39	497.04	497.47	10.11	528.35	528.77	10.83
434.87	435.29	8.68	466.17	466.60	9.40	497.48	497.90	10.12	528.78	529.21	10.84
435.30	435.73	8.69	466.61	467.03	9.41	497.91	498.34	10.13	529.22	529.64	10.85
435.74	436.16	8.70	467.04	467.47	9.42	498.35	498.77	10.14	529.65	530.08	10.86
436.17	436.60	8.71	467.48	467.90	9.43	498.78	499.21	10.15	530.09	530.51	10.87
436.61	437.03	8.72	467.91	468.34	9.44	499.22	499.64	10.16	530.52	530.95	10.88
437.04	437.47	8.73	468.35	468.77	9.45	499.65	500.08	10.17	530.96	531.38	10.89
437.48	437.90	8.74	468.78	469.21	9.46	500.09	500.51	10.18	531.39	531.82	10.90
437.91	438.34	8.75	469.22	469.64	9.47	500.52	500.95	10.19	531.83	532.25	10.91
438.35	438.77	8.76	469.65	470.08	9.48	500.96	501.38	10.20	532.26	532.68	10.92
438.78	439.21	8.77	470.09	470.51	9.49	501.39	501.82	10.21	532.69	533.12	10.93
439.22	439.64	8.78	470.52	470.95	9.50	501.83	502.25	10.22	533.13	533.55	10.94
439.65	440.08	8.79	470.96	471.38	9.51	502.26	502.68	10.23	533.56	533.99	10.95
440.09	440.51	8.80	471.39	471.82	9.52	502.69	503.12	10.24	534.00	534.42	10.96
440.52	440.95	8.81	471.83	472.25	9.53	503.13	503.55	10.25	534.43	534.86	10.97
440.96	441.38	8.82	472.26	472.68	9.54	503.56	503.99	10.26	534.87	535.29	10.98
441.39	441.82	8.83	472.69	473.12	9.55	504.00	504.42	10.27	535.30	535.73	10.99
441.83	442.25	8.84	473.13	473.55	9.56	504.43	504.86	10.28	535.74	536.16	11.00
442.26	442.68	8.85	473.56	473.99	9.57	504.87	505.29	10.29	536.17	536.60	11.01
442.69	443.12	8.86	474.00	474.42	9.58	505.30	505.73	10.30	536.61	537.03	11.02
443.13	443.55	8.87	474.43	474.86	9.59	505.74	506.16	10.31	537.04	537.47	11.03
443.56	443.99	8.88	474.87	475.29	9.60	506.17	506.60	10.32	537.48	537.90	11.04
444.00	444.42	8.89	475.30	475.73	9.61	506.61	507.03	10.33	537.91	538.34	11.05
444.43	444.86	8.90	475.74	476.16	9.62	507.04	507.47	10.34	538.35	538.77	11.06
444.87	445.29	8.91	476.17	476.60	9.63	507.48	507.90	10.35	538.78	539.21	11.07
445.30	445.73	8.92	476.61	477.03	9.64	507.91	508.34	10.36	539.22	539.64	11.08
445.74	446.16	8.93	477.04	477.47	9.65	508.35	508.77	10.37	539.65	540.08	11.09
446.17	446.60	8.94	477.48	477.90	9.66	508.78	509.21	10.38	540.09	540.51	11.10
446.61	447.03	8.95	477.91	478.34	9.67	509.22	509.64	10.39	540.52	540.95	11.11
447.04	447.47	8.96	478.35	478.77	9.68	509.65	510.08	10.40	540.96	541.38	11.12
447.48	447.90	8.97	478.78	479.21	9.69	510.09	510.51	10.41	541.39	541.82	11.13
447.91	448.34	8.98	479.22	479.64	9.70	510.52	510.95	10.42	541.83	542.25	11.14
448.35	448.77	8.99	479.65	480.08	9.71	510.96	511.38	10.43	542.26	542.68	11.15
448.78	449.21	9.00	480.09	480.51	9.72	511.39	511.82	10.44	542.69	543.12	11.16
449.22	449.64	9.01	480.52	480.95	9.73	511.83	512.25	10.45	543.13	543.55	11.17
449.65	450.08	9.02	480.96	481.38	9.74	512.26	512.68	10.46	543.56	543.99	11.18
450.09	450.51	9.03	481.39	481.82	9.75	512.69	513.12	10.47	544.00	544.42	11.19
450.52	450.95	9.04	481.83	482.25	9.76	513.13	513.55	10.48	544.43	544.86	11.20
450.96	451.38	9.05	482.26	482.68	9.77	513.56	513.99	10.49	544.87	545.29	11.21
451.39	451.82	9.06	482.69	483.12	9.78	514.00	514.42	10.50	545.30	545.73	11.22
451.83	452.25	9.07	483.13	483.55	9.79	514.43	514.86	10.51	545.74	546.16	11.23
452.26	452.68	9.08	483.56	483.99	9.80	514.87	515.29	10.52	546.17	546.60	11.24
452.69	453.12	9.09	484.00	484.42	9.81	515.30	515.73	10.53	546.61	547.03	11.25
453.13	453.55	9.10	484.43	484.86	9.82	515.74	516.16	10.54	547.04	547.47	11.26
453.56	453.99	9.11	484.87	485.29	9.83	516.17	516.60	10.55	547.48	547.90	11.27
454.00	454.42	9.12	485.30	485.73	9.84	516.61	517.03	10.56	547.91	548.34	11.28
454.43	454.86	9.13	485.74	486.16	9.85	517.04	517.47	10.57	548.35	548.77	11.29
454.87	455.29	9.14	486.17	486.60	9.86	517.48	517.90	10.58	548.78	549.21	11.30
455.30	455.73	9.15	486.61	487.03	9.87	517.91	518.34	10.59	549.22	549.64	11.31
455.74	456.16	9.16	487.04	487.47	9.88	518.35	518.77	10.60	549.65	550.08	11.32
456.17	456.60	9.17	487.48	487.90	9.89	518.78	519.21	10.61	550.09	550.51	11.33
456.61	457.03	9.18	487.91	488.34	9.90	519.22	519.64	10.62	550.52	550.95	11.34
457.04	457.47	9.19	488.35	488.77	9.91	519.65	520.08	10.63	550.96	551.38	11.35
457.48	457.90	9.20	488.78	489.21	9.92	520.09	520.51	10.64	551.39	551.82	11.36
457.91	458.34	9.21	489.22	489.64	9.93	520.52	520.95	10.65	551.83	552.25	11.37
458.35	458.77	9.22	489.65	490.08	9.94	520.96	521.38	10.66	552.26	552.68	11.38
458.78	459.21	9.23	490.09	490.51	9.95	521.39	521.82	10.67	552.69	553.12	11.39
459.22	459.64	9.24	490.52	490.95	9.96	521.83	522.25	10.68	553.13	553.55	11.40
459.65	460.08	9.25	490.96	491.38	9.97	522.26	522.68	10.69	553.56	553.99	11.41
460.09	460.51	9.26	491.39	491.82	9.98	522.69	523.12	10.70	554.00	554.42	11.42
460.52	460.95	9.27	491.83	492.25	9.99	523.13	523.55	10.71	554.43	554.86	11.43
460.96	461.38	9.28	492.26	492.68	10.00	523.56	523.99	10.72	554.87	555.29	11.44
461.39	461.82	9.29	492.69	493.12	10.01	524.00	524.42	10.73	555.30	555.73	11.45
461.83	462.25	9.30	493.13	493.55	10.02	524.43	524.86	10.74	555.74	556.16	11.46
462.26	462.68	9.31	493.56	493.99	10.03	524.87	525.29	10.75	556.17	556.60	11.47
462.69	463.12	9.32	494.00	494.42	10.04	525.30	525.73	10.76	556.61	557.03	11.48
463.13	463.55	9.33	494.43	494.86	10.05	525.74	526.16	10.77	557.04	557.47	11.49
463.56	463.99	9.34	494.87	495.29	10.06	526.17	526.60	10.78	557.48	557.90	11.50
464.00	464.42	9.35	495.30	495.73	10.07	526.61	527.03	10.79	557.91	558.34	11.51

CANADA PENSION PLAN CONTRIBUTIONS   COTISATIONS AU RÉGIME DE PENSIONS DU CANADA

WEEKLY PAY PERIOD — PÉRIODE HEBDOMADAIRE DE PAIE

558.35—2807.03

Remuneration From-de	To-à	C.P.P. R.P.C.	Remuneration From-de	To-à	C.P.P. R.P.C.	Remuneration From-de	To-à	C.P.P. R.P.C.	Remuneration From-de	To-à	C.P.P. R.P.C.
558.35	558.77	11.52	647.04	657.03	13.67	1367.04	1377.03	30.23	2087.04	2097.03	46.79
558.78	559.21	11.53	657.04	667.03	13.90	1377.04	1387.03	30.46	2097.04	2107.03	47.02
559.22	559.64	11.54	667.04	677.03	14.13	1387.04	1397.03	30.69	2107.04	2117.03	47.25
559.65	560.08	11.55	677.04	687.03	14.36	1397.04	1407.03	30.92	2117.04	2127.03	47.48
560.09	560.51	11.56	687.04	697.03	14.59	1407.04	1417.03	31.15	2127.04	2137.03	47.71
560.52	560.95	11.57	697.04	707.03	14.82	1417.04	1427.03	31.38	2137.04	2147.03	47.94
560.96	561.38	11.58	707.04	717.03	15.05	1427.04	1437.03	31.61	2147.04	2157.03	48.17
561.39	561.82	11.59	717.04	727.03	15.28	1437.04	1447.03	31.84	2157.04	2167.03	48.40
561.83	562.25	11.60	727.04	737.03	15.51	1447.04	1457.03	32.07	2167.04	2177.03	48.63
562.26	562.68	11.61	737.04	747.03	15.74	1457.04	1467.03	32.30	2177.04	2187.03	48.86
562.69	563.12	11.62	747.04	757.03	15.97	1467.04	1477.03	32.53	2187.04	2197.03	49.09
563.13	563.55	11.63	757.04	767.03	16.20	1477.04	1487.03	32.76	2197.04	2207.03	49.32
563.56	563.99	11.64	767.04	777.03	16.43	1487.04	1497.03	32.99	2207.04	2217.03	49.55
564.00	564.42	11.65	777.04	787.03	16.66	1497.04	1507.03	33.22	2217.04	2227.03	49.78
564.43	564.86	11.66	787.04	797.03	16.89	1507.04	1517.03	33.45	2227.04	2237.03	50.01
564.87	565.29	11.67	797.04	807.03	17.12	1517.04	1527.03	33.68	2237.04	2247.03	50.24
565.30	565.73	11.68	807.04	817.03	17.35	1527.04	1537.03	33.91	2247.04	2257.03	50.47
565.74	566.16	11.69	817.04	827.03	17.58	1537.04	1547.03	34.14	2257.04	2267.03	50.70
566.17	566.60	11.70	827.04	837.03	17.81	1547.04	1557.03	34.37	2267.04	2277.03	50.93
566.61	567.03	11.71	837.04	847.03	18.04	1557.04	1567.03	34.60	2277.04	2287.03	51.16
567.04	567.47	11.72	847.04	857.03	18.27	1567.04	1577.03	34.83	2287.04	2297.03	51.39
567.48	567.90	11.73	857.04	867.03	18.50	1577.04	1587.03	35.06	2297.04	2307.03	51.62
567.91	568.34	11.74	867.04	877.03	18.73	1587.04	1597.03	35.29	2307.04	2317.03	51.85
568.35	568.77	11.75	877.04	887.03	18.96	1597.04	1607.03	35.52	2317.04	2327.03	52.08
568.78	569.21	11.76	887.04	897.03	19.19	1607.04	1617.03	35.75	2327.04	2337.03	52.31
569.22	569.64	11.77	897.04	907.03	19.42	1617.04	1627.03	35.98	2337.04	2347.03	52.54
569.65	570.08	11.78	907.04	917.03	19.65	1627.04	1637.03	36.21	2347.04	2357.03	52.77
570.09	570.51	11.79	917.04	927.03	19.88	1637.04	1647.03	36.44	2357.04	2367.03	53.00
570.52	570.95	11.80	927.04	937.03	20.11	1647.04	1657.03	36.67	2367.04	2377.03	53.23
570.96	571.38	11.81	937.04	947.03	20.34	1657.04	1667.03	36.90	2377.04	2387.03	53.46
571.39	571.82	11.82	947.04	957.03	20.57	1667.04	1677.03	37.13	2387.04	2397.03	53.69
571.83	572.25	11.83	957.04	967.03	20.80	1677.04	1687.03	37.36	2397.04	2407.03	53.92
572.26	572.68	11.84	967.04	977.03	21.03	1687.04	1697.03	37.59	2407.04	2417.03	54.15
572.69	573.12	11.85	977.04	987.03	21.26	1697.04	1707.03	37.82	2417.04	2427.03	54.38
573.13	573.55	11.86	987.04	997.03	21.49	1707.04	1717.03	38.05	2427.04	2437.03	54.61
573.56	573.99	11.87	997.04	1007.03	21.72	1717.04	1727.03	38.28	2437.04	2447.03	54.84
574.00	574.42	11.88	1007.04	1017.03	21.95	1727.04	1737.03	38.51	2447.04	2457.03	55.07
574.43	574.86	11.89	1017.04	1027.03	22.18	1737.04	1747.03	38.74	2457.04	2467.03	55.30
574.87	575.29	11.90	1027.04	1037.03	22.41	1747.04	1757.03	38.97	2467.04	2477.03	55.53
575.30	575.73	11.91	1037.04	1047.03	22.64	1757.04	1767.03	39.20	2477.04	2487.03	55.76
575.74	576.16	11.92	1047.04	1057.03	22.87	1767.04	1777.03	39.43	2487.04	2497.03	55.99
576.17	576.60	11.93	1057.04	1067.03	23.10	1777.04	1787.03	39.66	2497.04	2507.03	56.22
576.61	577.03	11.94	1067.04	1077.03	23.33	1787.04	1797.03	39.89	2507.04	2517.03	56.45
577.04	577.47	11.95	1077.04	1087.03	23.56	1797.04	1807.03	40.12	2517.04	2527.03	56.68
577.48	577.90	11.96	1087.04	1097.03	23.79	1807.04	1817.03	40.35	2527.04	2537.03	56.91
577.91	578.34	11.97	1097.04	1107.03	24.02	1817.04	1827.03	40.58	2537.04	2547.03	57.14
578.35	578.77	11.98	1107.04	1117.03	24.25	1827.04	1837.03	40.81	2547.04	2557.03	57.37
578.78	579.21	11.99	1117.04	1127.03	24.48	1837.04	1847.03	41.04	2557.04	2567.03	57.60
579.22	579.64	12.00	1127.04	1137.03	24.71	1847.04	1857.03	41.27	2567.04	2577.03	57.83
579.65	580.08	12.01	1137.04	1147.03	24.94	1857.04	1867.03	41.50	2577.04	2587.03	58.06
580.09	580.51	12.02	1147.04	1157.03	25.17	1867.04	1877.03	41.73	2587.04	2597.03	58.29
580.52	580.95	12.03	1157.04	1167.03	25.40	1877.04	1887.03	41.96	2597.04	2607.03	58.52
580.96	581.38	12.04	1167.04	1177.03	25.63	1887.04	1897.03	42.19	2607.04	2617.03	58.75
581.39	581.82	12.05	1177.04	1187.03	25.86	1897.04	1907.03	42.42	2617.04	2627.03	58.98
581.83	582.25	12.06	1187.04	1197.03	26.09	1907.04	1917.03	42.65	2627.04	2637.03	59.21
582.26	582.68	12.07	1197.04	1207.03	26.32	1917.04	1927.03	42.88	2637.04	2647.03	59.44
582.69	583.12	12.08	1207.04	1217.03	26.55	1927.04	1937.03	43.11	2647.04	2657.03	59.67
583.13	583.55	12.09	1217.04	1227.03	26.78	1937.04	1947.03	43.34	2657.04	2667.03	59.90
583.56	583.99	12.10	1227.04	1237.03	27.01	1947.04	1957.03	43.57	2667.04	2677.03	60.13
584.00	584.42	12.11	1237.04	1247.03	27.24	1957.04	1967.03	43.80	2677.04	2687.03	60.36
584.43	584.86	12.12	1247.04	1257.03	27.47	1967.04	1977.03	44.03	2687.04	2697.03	60.59
584.87	585.29	12.13	1257.04	1267.03	27.70	1977.04	1987.03	44.26	2697.04	2707.03	60.82
585.30	585.73	12.14	1267.04	1277.03	27.93	1987.04	1997.03	44.49	2707.04	2717.03	61.05
585.74	586.16	12.15	1277.04	1287.03	28.16	1997.04	2007.03	44.72	2717.04	2727.03	61.28
586.17	586.60	12.16	1287.04	1297.03	28.39	2007.04	2017.03	44.95	2727.04	2737.03	61.51
586.61	587.03	12.17	1297.04	1307.03	28.62	2017.04	2027.03	45.18	2737.04	2747.03	61.74
587.04	597.03	12.29	1307.04	1317.03	28.85	2027.04	2037.03	45.41	2747.04	2757.03	61.97
597.04	607.03	12.52	1317.04	1327.03	29.08	2037.04	2047.03	45.64	2757.04	2767.03	62.20
607.04	617.03	12.75	1327.04	1337.03	29.31	2047.04	2057.03	45.87	2767.04	2777.03	62.43
617.04	627.03	12.98	1337.04	1347.03	29.54	2057.04	2067.03	46.10	2777.04	2787.03	62.66
627.04	637.03	13.21	1347.04	1357.03	29.77	2067.04	2077.03	46.33	2787.04	2797.03	62.89
637.04	647.03	13.44	1357.04	1367.03	30.00	2077.04	2087.03	46.56	2797.04	2807.03	63.12

UNEMPLOYMENT INSURANCE PREMIUMS   COTISATIONS À L'ASSURANCE-CHÔMAGE

For minimum and maximum insurable earnings amounts for various pay periods see Schedule II. For the maximum premium deduction for various pay periods see bottom of this page.

Les montants minimum et maximum des gains assurables pour diverses périodes de paie figurent en annexe II. La déduction maximale de primes pour diverses périodes de paie figure au bas de la présente page.

Remuneration / Rémunération From-de — To-à	U.I. Premium / Cotisation d'a.-c.	Remuneration / Rémunération From-de — To-à	U.I. Premium / Cotisation d'a.-c.	Remuneration / Rémunération From-de — To-à	U.I. Premium / Cotisation d'a.-c.	Remuneration / Rémunération From-de — To-à	U.I. Premium / Cotisation d'a.-c.
512.23 - 512.66	11.53	544.23 - 544.66	12.25	576.23 - 576.66	12.97	608.23 - 608.66	13.69
512.67 - 513.11	11.54	544.67 - 545.11	12.26	576.67 - 577.11	12.98	608.67 - 609.11	13.70
513.12 - 513.55	11.55	545.12 - 545.55	12.27	577.12 - 577.55	12.99	609.12 - 609.55	13.71
513.56 - 513.99	11.56	545.56 - 545.99	12.28	577.56 - 577.99	13.00	609.56 - 609.99	13.72
514.00 - 514.44	11.57	546.00 - 546.44	12.29	578.00 - 578.44	13.01	610.00 - 610.44	13.73
514.45 - 514.88	11.58	546.45 - 546.88	12.30	578.45 - 578.88	13.02	610.45 - 610.88	13.74
514.89 - 515.33	11.59	546.89 - 547.33	12.31	578.89 - 579.33	13.03	610.89 - 611.33	13.75
515.34 - 515.77	11.60	547.34 - 547.77	12.32	579.34 - 579.77	13.04	611.34 - 611.77	13.76
515.78 - 516.22	11.61	547.78 - 548.22	12.33	579.78 - 580.22	13.05	611.78 - 612.22	13.77
516.23 - 516.66	11.62	548.23 - 548.66	12.34	580.23 - 580.66	13.06	612.23 - 612.66	13.78
516.67 - 517.11	11.63	548.67 - 549.11	12.35	580.67 - 581.11	13.07	612.67 - 613.11	13.79
517.12 - 517.55	11.64	549.12 - 549.55	12.36	581.12 - 581.55	13.08	613.12 - 613.55	13.80
517.56 - 517.99	11.65	549.56 - 549.99	12.37	581.56 - 581.99	13.09	613.56 - 613.99	13.81
518.00 - 518.44	11.66	550.00 - 550.44	12.38	582.00 - 582.44	13.10	614.00 - 614.44	13.82
518.45 - 518.88	11.67	550.45 - 550.88	12.39	582.45 - 582.88	13.11	614.45 - 614.88	13.83
518.89 - 519.33	11.68	550.89 - 551.33	12.40	582.89 - 583.33	13.12	614.89 - 615.33	13.84
519.34 - 519.77	11.69	551.34 - 551.77	12.41	583.34 - 583.77	13.13	615.34 - 615.77	13.85
519.78 - 520.22	11.70	551.78 - 552.22	12.42	583.78 - 584.22	13.14	615.78 - 616.22	13.86
520.23 - 520.66	11.71	552.23 - 552.66	12.43	584.23 - 584.66	13.15	616.23 - 616.66	13.87
520.67 - 521.11	11.72	552.67 - 553.11	12.44	584.67 - 585.11	13.16	616.67 - 617.11	13.88
521.12 - 521.55	11.73	553.12 - 553.55	12.45	585.12 - 585.55	13.17	617.12 - 617.55	13.89
521.56 - 521.99	11.74	553.56 - 553.99	12.46	585.56 - 585.99	13.18	617.56 - 617.99	13.90
522.00 - 522.44	11.75	554.00 - 554.44	12.47	586.00 - 586.44	13.19	618.00 - 618.44	13.91
522.45 - 522.88	11.76	554.45 - 554.88	12.48	586.45 - 586.88	13.20	618.45 - 618.88	13.92
522.89 - 523.33	11.77	554.89 - 555.33	12.49	586.89 - 587.33	13.21	618.89 - 619.33	13.93
523.34 - 523.77	11.78	555.34 - 555.77	12.50	587.34 - 587.77	13.22	619.34 - 619.77	13.94
523.78 - 524.22	11.79	555.78 - 556.22	12.51	587.78 - 588.22	13.23	619.78 - 620.22	13.95
524.23 - 524.66	11.80	556.23 - 556.66	12.52	588.23 - 588.66	13.24	620.23 - 620.66	13.96
524.67 - 525.11	11.81	556.67 - 557.11	12.53	588.67 - 589.11	13.25	620.67 - 621.11	13.97
525.12 - 525.55	11.82	557.12 - 557.55	12.54	589.12 - 589.55	13.26	621.12 - 621.55	13.98
525.56 - 525.99	11.83	557.56 - 557.99	12.55	589.56 - 589.99	13.27	621.56 - 621.99	13.99
526.00 - 526.44	11.84	558.00 - 558.44	12.56	590.00 - 590.44	13.28	622.00 - 622.44	14.00
526.45 - 526.88	11.85	558.45 - 558.88	12.57	590.45 - 590.88	13.29	622.45 - 622.88	14.01
526.89 - 527.33	11.86	558.89 - 559.33	12.58	590.89 - 591.33	13.30	622.89 - 623.33	14.02
527.34 - 527.77	11.87	559.34 - 559.77	12.59	591.34 - 591.77	13.31	623.34 - 623.77	14.03
527.78 - 528.22	11.88	559.78 - 560.22	12.60	591.78 - 592.22	13.32	623.78 - 624.22	14.04
528.23 - 528.66	11.89	560.23 - 560.66	12.61	592.23 - 592.66	13.33	624.23 - 624.66	14.05
528.67 - 529.11	11.90	560.67 - 561.11	12.62	592.67 - 593.11	13.34	624.67 - 625.11	14.06
529.12 - 529.55	11.91	561.12 - 561.55	12.63	593.12 - 593.55	13.35	625.12 - 625.55	14.07
529.56 - 529.99	11.92	561.56 - 561.99	12.64	593.56 - 593.99	13.36	625.56 - 625.99	14.08
530.00 - 530.44	11.93	562.00 - 562.44	12.65	594.00 - 594.44	13.37	626.00 - 626.44	14.09
530.45 - 530.88	11.94	562.45 - 562.88	12.66	594.45 - 594.88	13.38	626.45 - 626.88	14.10
530.89 - 531.33	11.95	562.89 - 563.33	12.67	594.89 - 595.33	13.39	626.89 - 627.33	14.11
531.34 - 531.77	11.96	563.34 - 563.77	12.68	595.34 - 595.77	13.40	627.34 - 627.77	14.12
531.78 - 532.22	11.97	563.78 - 564.22	12.69	595.78 - 596.22	13.41	627.78 - 628.22	14.13
532.23 - 532.66	11.98	564.23 - 564.66	12.70	596.23 - 596.66	13.42	628.23 - 628.66	14.14
532.67 - 533.11	11.99	564.67 - 565.11	12.71	596.67 - 597.11	13.43	628.67 - 629.11	14.15
533.12 - 533.55	12.00	565.12 - 565.55	12.72	597.12 - 597.55	13.44	629.12 - 629.55	14.16
533.56 - 533.99	12.01	565.56 - 565.99	12.73	597.56 - 597.99	13.45	629.56 - 629.99	14.17
534.00 - 534.44	12.02	566.00 - 566.44	12.74	598.00 - 598.44	13.46	630.00 - 630.44	14.18
534.45 - 534.88	12.03	566.45 - 566.88	12.75	598.45 - 598.88	13.47	630.45 - 630.88	14.19
534.89 - 535.33	12.04	566.89 - 567.33	12.76	598.89 - 599.33	13.48	630.89 - 631.33	14.20
535.34 - 535.77	12.05	567.34 - 567.77	12.77	599.34 - 599.77	13.49	631.34 - 631.77	14.21
535.78 - 536.22	12.06	567.78 - 568.22	12.78	599.78 - 600.22	13.50	631.78 - 632.22	14.22
536.23 - 536.66	12.07	568.23 - 568.66	12.79	600.23 - 600.66	13.51	632.23 - 632.66	14.23
536.67 - 537.11	12.08	568.67 - 569.11	12.80	600.67 - 601.11	13.52	632.67 - 633.11	14.24
537.12 - 537.55	12.09	569.12 - 569.55	12.81	601.12 - 601.55	13.53	633.12 - 633.55	14.25
537.56 - 537.99	12.10	569.56 - 569.99	12.82	601.56 - 601.99	13.54	633.56 - 633.99	14.26
538.00 - 538.44	12.11	570.00 - 570.44	12.83	602.00 - 602.44	13.55	634.00 - 634.44	14.27
538.45 - 538.88	12.12	570.45 - 570.88	12.84	602.45 - 602.88	13.56	634.45 - 634.88	14.28
538.89 - 539.33	12.13	570.89 - 571.33	12.85	602.89 - 603.33	13.57	634.89 - 635.33	14.29
539.34 - 539.77	12.14	571.34 - 571.77	12.86	603.34 - 603.77	13.58	635.34 - 635.77	14.30
539.78 - 540.22	12.15	571.78 - 572.22	12.87	603.78 - 604.22	13.59	635.78 - 636.22	14.31
540.23 - 540.66	12.16	572.23 - 572.66	12.88	604.23 - 604.66	13.60	636.23 - 636.66	14.32
540.67 - 541.11	12.17	572.67 - 573.11	12.89	604.67 - 605.11	13.61	636.67 - 637.11	14.33
541.12 - 541.55	12.18	573.12 - 573.55	12.90	605.12 - 605.55	13.62	637.12 - 637.55	14.34
541.56 - 541.99	12.19	573.56 - 573.99	12.91	605.56 - 605.99	13.63	637.56 - 637.99	14.35
542.00 - 542.44	12.20	574.00 - 574.44	12.92	606.00 - 606.44	13.64	638.00 - 638.44	14.36
542.45 - 542.88	12.21	574.45 - 574.88	12.93	606.45 - 606.88	13.65	638.45 - 638.88	14.37
542.89 - 543.33	12.22	574.89 - 575.33	12.94	606.89 - 607.33	13.66	638.89 - 639.33	14.38
543.34 - 543.77	12.23	575.34 - 575.77	12.95	607.34 - 607.77	13.67	639.34 - 639.77	14.39
543.78 - 544.22	12.24	575.78 - 576.22	12.96	607.78 - 608.22	13.68	639.78 - 640.22	14.40

Maximum Premium Deduction for a Pay Period of the stated frequency.
Déduction maximale de prime pour une période de paie d'une durée donnée.

Weekly - Hebdomadaire	15.30	10 pp per year - 10 pp par année	79.56
Bi-Weekly - Deux semaines	30.60	13 pp per year - 13 pp par année	61.20
Semi-Monthly - Bi-mensuel	33.15	22 pp per year - 22 pp par année	36.16
Monthly - Mensuellement	66.30		

| 72 | UNEMPLOYMENT INSURANCE PREMIUMS | | COTISATIONS À L'ASSURANCE-CHÔMAGE |

For minimum and maximum insurable earnings amounts for various pay periods see Schedule II. For the maximum premium deduction for various pay periods see bottom of this page.

Les montants minimum et maximum des gains assurables pour diverses périodes de paie figurent en annexe II. La déduction maximale de primes pour diverses périodes de paie figure au bas de la présente page.

Remuneration / Rémunération From-de	To-à	U.I. Premium / Prime d'a.-c.	Remuneration / Rémunération From-de	To-à	U.I. Premium / Prime d'a.-c.	Remuneration / Rémunération From-de	To-à	U.I. Premium / Prime d'a.-c.	Remuneration / Rémunération From-de	To-à	U.I. Premium / Prime d'a.-c.
640.23	640.66	14.41	672.23	672.66	15.13	704.23	704.66	15.85	736.23	736.66	16.57
640.67	641.11	14.42	672.67	673.11	15.14	704.67	705.11	15.86	736.67	737.11	16.58
641.12	641.55	14.43	673.12	673.55	15.15	705.12	705.55	15.87	737.12	737.55	16.59
641.56	641.99	14.44	673.56	673.99	15.16	705.56	705.99	15.88	737.56	737.99	16.60
642.00	642.44	14.45	674.00	674.44	15.17	706.00	706.44	15.89	738.00	738.44	16.61
642.45	642.88	14.46	674.45	674.88	15.18	706.45	706.88	15.90	738.45	738.88	16.62
642.89	643.33	14.47	674.89	675.33	15.19	706.89	707.33	15.91	738.89	739.33	16.63
643.34	643.77	14.48	675.34	675.77	15.20	707.34	707.77	15.92	739.34	739.77	16.64
643.78	644.22	14.49	675.78	676.22	15.21	707.78	708.22	15.93	739.78	740.22	16.65
644.23	644.66	14.50	676.23	676.66	15.22	708.23	708.66	15.94	740.23	740.66	16.66
644.67	645.11	14.51	676.67	677.11	15.23	708.67	709.11	15.95	740.67	741.11	16.67
645.12	645.55	14.52	677.12	677.55	15.24	709.12	709.55	15.96	741.12	741.55	16.68
645.56	645.99	14.53	677.56	677.99	15.25	709.56	709.99	15.97	741.56	741.99	16.69
646.00	646.44	14.54	678.00	678.44	15.26	710.00	710.44	15.98	742.00	742.44	16.70
646.45	646.88	14.55	678.45	678.88	15.27	710.45	710.88	15.99	742.45	742.88	16.71
646.89	647.33	14.56	678.89	679.33	15.28	710.89	711.33	16.00	742.89	743.33	16.72
647.34	647.77	14.57	679.34	679.77	15.29	711.34	711.77	16.01	743.34	743.77	16.73
647.78	648.22	14.58	679.78	680.22	15.30	711.78	712.22	16.02	743.78	744.22	16.74
648.23	648.66	14.59	680.23	680.66	15.31	712.23	712.66	16.03	744.23	744.66	16.75
648.67	649.11	14.60	680.67	681.11	15.32	712.67	713.11	16.04	744.67	745.11	16.76
649.12	649.55	14.61	681.12	681.55	15.33	713.12	713.55	16.05	745.12	745.55	16.77
649.56	649.99	14.62	681.56	681.99	15.34	713.56	713.99	16.06	745.56	745.99	16.78
650.00	650.44	14.63	682.00	682.44	15.35	714.00	714.44	16.07	746.00	746.44	16.79
650.45	650.88	14.64	682.45	682.88	15.36	714.45	714.88	16.08	746.45	746.88	16.80
650.89	651.33	14.65	682.89	683.33	15.37	714.89	715.33	16.09	746.89	747.33	16.81
651.34	651.77	14.66	683.34	683.77	15.38	715.34	715.77	16.10	747.34	747.77	16.82
651.78	652.22	14.67	683.78	684.22	15.39	715.78	716.22	16.11	747.78	748.22	16.83
652.23	652.66	14.68	684.23	684.66	15.40	716.23	716.66	16.12	748.23	748.66	16.84
652.67	653.11	14.69	684.67	685.11	15.41	716.67	717.11	16.13	748.67	749.11	16.85
653.12	653.55	14.70	685.12	685.55	15.42	717.12	717.55	16.14	749.12	749.55	16.86
653.56	653.99	14.71	685.56	685.99	15.43	717.56	717.99	16.15	749.56	749.99	16.87
654.00	654.44	14.72	686.00	686.44	15.44	718.00	718.44	16.16	750.00	750.44	16.88
654.45	654.88	14.73	686.45	686.88	15.45	718.45	718.88	16.17	750.45	750.88	16.89
654.89	655.33	14.74	686.89	687.33	15.46	718.89	719.33	16.18	750.89	751.33	16.90
655.34	655.77	14.75	687.34	687.77	15.47	719.34	719.77	16.19	751.34	751.77	16.91
655.78	656.22	14.76	687.78	688.22	15.48	719.78	720.22	16.20	751.78	752.22	16.92
656.23	656.66	14.77	688.23	688.66	15.49	720.23	720.66	16.21	752.23	752.66	16.93
656.67	657.11	14.78	688.67	689.11	15.50	720.67	721.11	16.22	752.67	753.11	16.94
657.12	657.55	14.79	689.12	689.55	15.51	721.12	721.55	16.23	753.12	753.55	16.95
657.56	657.99	14.80	689.56	689.99	15.52	721.56	721.99	16.24	753.56	753.99	16.96
658.00	658.44	14.81	690.00	690.44	15.53	722.00	722.44	16.25	754.00	754.44	16.97
658.45	658.88	14.82	690.45	690.88	15.54	722.45	722.88	16.26	754.45	754.88	16.98
658.89	659.33	14.83	690.89	691.33	15.55	722.89	723.33	16.27	754.89	755.33	16.99
659.34	659.77	14.84	691.34	691.77	15.56	723.34	723.77	16.28	755.34	755.77	17.00
659.78	660.22	14.85	691.78	692.22	15.57	723.78	724.22	16.29	755.78	756.22	17.01
660.23	660.66	14.86	692.23	692.66	15.58	724.23	724.66	16.30	756.23	756.66	17.02
660.67	661.11	14.87	692.67	693.11	15.59	724.67	725.11	16.31	756.67	757.11	17.03
661.12	661.55	14.88	693.12	693.55	15.60	725.12	725.55	16.32	757.12	757.55	17.04
661.56	661.99	14.89	693.56	693.99	15.61	725.56	725.99	16.33	757.56	757.99	17.05
662.00	662.44	14.90	694.00	694.44	15.62	726.00	726.44	16.34	758.00	758.44	17.06
662.45	662.88	14.91	694.45	694.88	15.63	726.45	726.88	16.35	758.45	758.88	17.07
662.89	663.33	14.92	694.89	695.33	15.64	726.89	727.33	16.36	758.89	759.33	17.08
663.34	663.77	14.93	695.34	695.77	15.65	727.34	727.77	16.37	759.34	759.77	17.09
663.78	664.22	14.94	695.78	696.22	15.66	727.78	728.22	16.38	759.78	760.22	17.10
664.23	664.66	14.95	696.23	696.66	15.67	728.23	728.66	16.39	760.23	760.66	17.11
664.67	665.11	14.96	696.67	697.11	15.68	728.67	729.11	16.40	760.67	761.11	17.12
665.12	665.55	14.97	697.12	697.55	15.69	729.12	729.55	16.41	761.12	761.55	17.13
665.56	665.99	14.98	697.56	697.99	15.70	729.56	729.99	16.42	761.56	761.99	17.14
666.00	666.44	14.99	698.00	698.44	15.71	730.00	730.44	16.43	762.00	762.44	17.15
666.45	666.88	15.00	698.45	698.88	15.72	730.45	730.88	16.44	762.45	762.88	17.16
666.89	667.33	15.01	698.89	699.33	15.73	730.89	731.33	16.45	762.89	763.33	17.17
667.34	667.77	15.02	699.34	699.77	15.74	731.34	731.77	16.46	763.34	763.77	17.18
667.78	668.22	15.03	699.78	700.22	15.75	731.78	732.22	16.47	763.78	764.22	17.19
668.23	668.66	15.04	700.23	700.66	15.76	732.23	732.66	16.48	764.23	764.66	17.20
668.67	669.11	15.05	700.67	701.11	15.77	732.67	733.11	16.49	764.67	765.11	17.21
669.12	669.55	15.06	701.12	701.55	15.78	733.12	733.55	16.50	765.12	765.55	17.22
669.56	669.99	15.07	701.56	701.99	15.79	733.56	733.99	16.51	765.56	765.99	17.23
670.00	670.44	15.08	702.00	702.44	15.80	734.00	734.44	16.52	766.00	766.44	17.24
670.45	670.88	15.09	702.45	702.88	15.81	734.45	734.88	16.53	766.45	766.88	17.25
670.89	671.33	15.10	702.89	703.33	15.82	734.89	735.33	16.54	766.89	767.33	17.26
671.34	671.77	15.11	703.34	703.77	15.83	735.34	735.77	16.55	767.34	767.77	17.27
671.78	672.22	15.12	703.78	704.22	15.84	735.78	736.22	16.56	767.78	768.22	17.28

Maximum Premium Deduction for a Pay Period of the stated frequency.
Déduction maximale de prime pour une période de paie d'une durée donnée.

Weekly - Hebdomadaire	14.40	10 pp per year · 10 pp par année	74.88
Bi-Weekly · Deux semaines	28.80	13 pp per year · 13 pp par année	57.60
Semi-Monthly · Bi-mensuel	31.20	22 pp per year · 22 pp par année	34.04
Monthly - Mensuellement	62.40		

9

Cost Accounting

Overview

OBJECTIVES

At the end of this chapter, you should be able to:

- Identify job cost components: direct materials, direct labour, and factory overhead.

- Complete a job calculation of material, labour, and overhead costs.

- Complete financial statements for a manufacturing concern.

- Understand a process cost system.

- Use computer software for handling cost accounting activities.

- Journalize source documents and prepare financial statements on a computer using the ACCPAC Bedford Integrated Accounting software.

Cost accounting is one of six major accounting systems that may be important to a business.

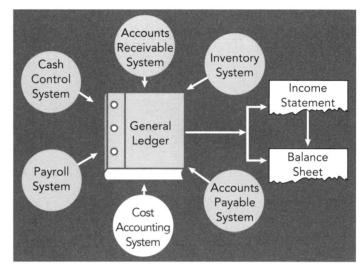

FIGURE 9-1   Flowchart of the accounting process

Unlike the other systems discussed in this text, cost accounting is applicable mainly to manufacturing concerns, businesses that transform materials into other goods through the use of labour and factory facilities.

There are essentially three main types of business that operate in our society: service, merchandising, and manufacturing businesses. The accounting treatment for each of these is similar in their use of books of original entry, journalizing, posting, adjusting entries, and the preparation of financial statements. Manufacturing businesses differ in their use of special cost accounts, and their need for a different type of information for management. The main emphasis in this chapter will be on a firm which uses *job costing*, but section 9.5 describes another type of costing called *process cost accounting*.

9.1

Manufacturing Businesses

Manufacturing concerns take materials and, using labour and plant facilities, produce a new product which is then sold. An example of a typical manufacturing concern is a steel mill: it purchases iron ore, coke, and metals to produce different types, or alloys, of steel. Varying amounts of human and machine labour must be applied to these materials to produce each alloy. Costs (operating the plant, and value of raw materials), amount of end product, and profit requirements all determine the selling price.

These alloys, the end product of the steelmaking process, become the "raw" material for a further stage of development. A manufacturer of parts for the automobile industry, for example, would apply further human and machine labour, to produce another end product, a moulded floor for the trunk of a particular make and model of car. The process of pricing this end product would be the same as for the steelmaker. The trunk floor will become a "raw" material at an auto assembly plant, where it will be one of the pieces assembled to make the final end product, the consumer product. Once again, the manufacturer would price the product following the same types of considerations as the steelmaker and the component manufacturer.

The same type of manufacturing sequence is followed for most consumer products: cameras, video cassette recorders, cellular telephones, computers, clothes, paint brushes, earrings, and other manufactured goods.

COST OF GOODS SOLD

The Cost of Goods Sold section on an income statement of a manufacturing business follows this format:

Cost of Goods Sold	
Beginning Finished Goods Inventory	$ 19 000
Cost of Goods Manufactured	121 000
Merchandise Available for Sale	140 000
Ending Finished Goods Inventory	10 000
Cost of Goods Sold	$130 000

Notice the terminology in the Cost of Goods section shown above. Beginning Finished Goods Inventory represents the opening inventory of manufactured goods for the new fiscal period. (**Finished Goods** is the cost of all products which have been manufactured and are ready for sale.) The Cost of Goods Manufactured represents the additions to the inventory of manufactured goods, and Ending Finished Goods Inventory represents the inventory of manufactured goods at the end of the fiscal period.

The Cost of Goods Manufactured is set out in detail in another statement that is needed by a manufacturing concern. It looks like this:

Statement of Cost of Goods Manufactured For the Year Ended December 31, 19–			
Work in Process Inventory, Jan. 1, 19–			$ 9 000
Direct Materials:			
Inventory, Jan. 1	$ 2 000		
Direct Materials Purchases	63 000		
Materials Available for Use	65 000		
Inventory, Dec. 31	5 000	$60 000	
Direct Labour		60 000	
Factory Overhead:			
Indirect Materials	3 500		
Indirect Labour	7 500		
Other Overhead Costs	19 000	30 000	150 000
			159 000
Work in Process Inventory, Dec. 31, 19–			4 000
Cost of Goods Manufactured			$155 000

FIGURE 9-2   *A statement of cost of goods manufactured*

As can be seen from Figure 9-2, the **Statement of Cost of Goods Manufactured** details the manufacturing costs associated with the goods available for sale. The most important accounting problem for manufacturing concerns is the calculation of the cost of all of the components that go into a finished product: direct materials, direct labour, and factory overhead. These three costs are added together and the total cost of manufacturing the product is obtained.

There are two main methods used by manufacturing businesses to accumulate (calculate) the costs of manufacturing a product: job costing, and process cost accounting.

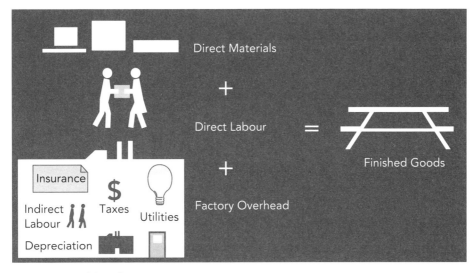

FIGURE 9-3   Manufacturing costs

Job Costing

Job Costing assumes that each job has three major cost components to it: direct materials, direct labour, and factory overhead. **Direct materials** refers to all of the raw materials used to make the finished product. **Direct labour** is the wages and salaries and related costs of all employees who are *directly* involved in working the raw materials into their finished form. **Factory overhead** is all of the other costs that are necessary to keep a plant or workshop running — depreciation, supplies used, electricity, property taxes, indirect labour, indirect supplies, and management salaries, for example.

The accounting concepts behind job costing are especially important to a manufacturing concern that has to quote on jobs for customers. The example used for a job costing manufacturer is Wayne Hopkins, a small independent carpenter who builds outdoor decks, swings, garden chairs, and picnic tables, in Alberta.

Wayne has to know exactly what the cost of the materials for each project is. He must add in an hourly labour rate, a rate that will cover overhead expenses, and a profit margin. Once these costs are calculated, Wayne can give a job quote.

Process Cost Accounting

Process costing is used in a manufacturing business where there is an ongoing production of finished goods, and the costing process must be "stopped" at some point in time to measure the product costs. A clear example is an assembly line for making golf balls — they are assembled, covered with their heavy outer shell, and painted various colours then stamped with the brand name.

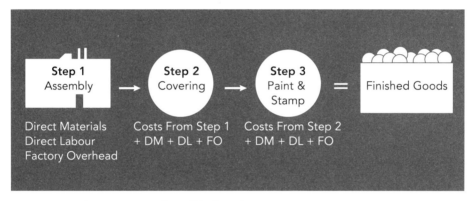

FIGURE 9-4   *Process costing for golf ball production*

Assuming that the plant that makes the golf balls runs 24 hours a day, it is hard to know where the costs for one job begin and end. The process of making golf balls is ongoing; the production line never stops. There is a special way to accumulate these costs — called *process cost accounting* — and to cut off the accounting at the appropriate time to produce the financial statements. Process cost accounting will be discussed in greater detail in section 9.5 of this chapter.

QUESTIONS

1. What are some of the special problems that are created when a manufacturing business has to deal with inventory?

2. There are three main cost categories on a statement of cost of goods manufactured, other than the Work in Process account. Name these three major costing categories.

3. What are the two main methods used by manufacturing businesses to accumulate the costs of manufacturing a product?

4. Explain the terms *direct materials, direct labour,* and *factory overhead* as they would apply to a company manufacturing blue jeans.

5. Think about a factory that produces bicycles. What kinds of factory overhead costs would such a business have? Compile as large a list of costs as you can.

6. What is *process costing*?

7. How does a company that makes golf balls differ from one that makes picnic tables?

9.2

Job Costing

When customers order special products that are made to specifications, a job cost system must be used. A **job cost system** enables the manufacturer to calculate all the direct and indirect costs of a project, and add a suitable profit margin to arrive at the selling price. There are three main cost components to costing a job: direct materials, direct labour, and factory overhead.

The costing of ending inventory is also important in a job cost system. There are three inventories in a job cost system: direct materials inventory, work in process inventory, and finished goods inventory. In a job cost system, the perpetual inventory method must be used to keep track of these inventory costs. In a manufacturing concern's **perpetual inventory method**, materials move through the three inventory accounts just as they move through the manufacturing process itself, and the value of each type of inventory is known at any given moment.

DIRECT MATERIALS

The direct materials cost is the cost of the materials that become a physical part of the finished product, for example, the wood used for garden furniture.

A perpetual inventory method must be used with job costing, and therefore the accounting entry for the purchase of direct materials is a debit to Direct Materials Inventory, a debit to GST Recoverable, and a credit to Accounts Payable or Bank.

Most purchases and sales are subject to the federal Goods and Services Tax (GST), currently 7%. When GST is paid, this amount is used as an **input tax credit** to reduce the amount of GST owing.

Direct Materials Purchased

The accounting entry for direct materials purchased is:

GENERAL JOURNAL

PAGE 29

DATE 19–		PARTICULARS	PR	DEBIT	CREDIT
Aug.	5	Direct Materials Inventory		5700 –	
		GST Recoverable		399 –	
		A/P—Supplier (or Bank)			6099 –
		To record the purchase of direct			
		materials using the perpetual			
		inventory system			

FIGURE 9-5   *The general journal entry for purchase of direct materials*

Direct Materials Used

Subsidiary ledger accounts are kept for each different direct material used in the production process. When the direct materials are transferred to work in process, a **materials requisition form** is completed to indicate which jobs the materials were used for. See Figure 9-6.

When materials are issued to production, a journal entry is made to record the use of those direct materials. The journal entry (Figure 9-7) transfers the cost of materials used into a costing account called Work in Process.

DIRECT LABOUR

Direct labour cost is the wages paid to the employees who work directly on the product being manufactured. In an automobile plant, direct labour costs would be the wages of the assembly line workers. In a meat packing plant, the butchers' wages would be direct labour.

In a small woodworking shop, the direct labour costs can be allocated to specific jobs through an employee **time card** that details the hours and jobs worked on by the employee.

Wayne's Woodworking	Materials Requisition Form			
Job No. 238				
Customer K. Van De Slyke		**Date** Aug. 5	**19 –**	
Material #	**Description**	**Qty**	**Unit Cost**	**Total Cost**
212	cedar 4 X 4 X 8	36	6 02	2 1 6 72
217	cedar 1 X 6 X 8	100	4 91	4 9 1 –
232	cedar 2 X 4 X 8	70	4 87	3 4 0 90

FIGURE 9-6   *A materials requisition form*

GENERAL JOURNAL

PAGE 29

DATE 19–		PARTICULARS	PR	DEBIT	CREDIT
Aug.	9	Work in Process		1 8 90 –	
		Direct Materials Inventory			1 8 90 –
		To transfer raw materials from			
		inventory to work in process			

FIGURE 9-7   *The general journal entry to debit Work in Process*

WAYNE'S WOODWORKING			TIME CARD					
Employee Kevin Haggith				**SIN** 398-681-426				
For The Week Ended August 9 **19 –**				**Rate** $10.00				
Date	**Job**	**Customer**	**Morning**		**Afternoon**		**Rate**	**Labour Cost**
			In	**Out**	**In**	**Out**		
Aug. 5	232	J. Peazel	8:00	12:00	1:00	5:00	10 –	80 –
6	232	J. Peazel	7:59	12:01	1:00	5:00	10 –	80 –
7	232	J. Peazel	8:00	12:00	—	—	10 –	40 –
7	233	C. Yuen	—	—	1:00	5:00	10 –	40 –
8	233	C. Yuen	8:00	12:00	1:00	5:00	10 –	80 –
9	234	J. Miller	7:45	11:45	12:30	4:30	10 –	80 –

FIGURE 9-8   *A time card*

The weekly summary for this employee is:

Kevin Haggith
Weekly Job Summary Per Time Card

Job	Hours	Rate	Debit
232	20	$10.00	$200.00
233	12	10.00	120.00
234	8	10.00	80.00
	Total Billings		$400.00

The time card summary results in two journal entries for the week: one to record the direct labour charges to Work in Process, and a second to record the employer's contributions to CPP and UI.

GENERAL JOURNAL

PAGE _29_

DATE 19—		PARTICULARS	PR	DEBIT	CREDIT
Aug.	12	Work in Process		400 —	
		CPP Payable			7 87
		UI Payable			9 30
		Income Tax Payable			50 35
		Bank			332 48
		Cheque 313 to Kevin Haggith for			
		wages up to August 9			
	12	Work in Process		20 89	
		CPP Payable			7 87
		UI Payable			13 02
		To record the employer's share of			
		CPP and UI			

FIGURE 9-9   The general journal entries to record allocation of direct labour costs to work in process

FACTORY OVERHEAD

The term factory overhead, sometimes just called overhead, refers to three types of costs, all of which can be charged directly into an account called Factory Overhead Control.

Indirect Materials
These are materials that are not used directly in producing the finished product, but that do support the manufacturing process as a whole. A good example is any lubricants used to keep the machinery running, or the maintenance materials used to keep the manufacturing area clean, or the packaging materials. These costs are not directly associated with the finished product but they become part of the final cost through their contribution to the overhead costs.

The accounting entry that transfers the cost of indirect materials used into the production process is:

GENERAL JOURNAL

PAGE 30

DATE 19–		PARTICULARS	PR	DEBIT	CREDIT
Aug.	14	Factory Overhead Control		2 4 9 5 0	
		GST Recoverable		1 7 4 7	
		A/P—Supplier (or Bank)			2 6 6 9 7
		To record purchase of indirect			
		materials			

FIGURE 9-10   *The general journal entry for purchase of indirect materials*

Indirect Labour
This refers to the labour costs that are not directly associated with the cost of the product being produced. Some examples of indirect labour costs would be the cost of the maintenance staff, and any plant supervisors who do not work directly on the finished product.

The accounting entry that transfers the cost of indirect labour into the production process is as shown in Figure 9-11.

GENERAL JOURNAL

PAGE 31

DATE 19–		PARTICULARS	PR	DEBIT	CREDIT
Aug.	13	Factory Overhead Control (indirect		1 1 4 3 –	
		labour)			
		CPP Payable			2 3 61
		UI Payable			2 5 72
		Income Tax Payable			2 2 4 45
		Bank			8 6 9 22
		To record payment of indirect labour			
	13	Factory Overhead Control (indirect		5 9 62	
		labour)			
		CPP Payable			2 3 61
		UI Payable			3 6 01
		Employer's portion of CPP and UI			

FIGURE 9-11   The general journal entries for indirect labour cost

Other Overhead Costs

This includes other plant expenses that can not be tied directly to the finished product either, but that have to be paid. Examples would be depreciation on the plant equipment, property taxes on the plant, and utilities such as plant heat and light costs.

The accounting entry that transfers the cost of these overheads into the production process is:

GENERAL JOURNAL

PAGE 31

DATE 19–		PARTICULARS	PR	DEBIT	CREDIT
Aug.	18	Factory Overhead Control		3 6 9 57	
		GST Recoverable		2 5 87	
		Bank			3 9 5 44
		Cheque 421 to Ontario Hydro			
		To record other overhead costs			

FIGURE 9-12   The general journal entry for other overhead costs

APPLYING FACTORY OVERHEAD

It is difficult to tie factory overhead costs in to specific jobs, and therefore a pre-determined overhead rate is used, often based on direct labour costs. Wayne Hopkins uses a factory overhead rate of 50% of his direct labour cost. This rate was determined using the following formula:

$$\text{factory overhead rate} = \frac{\text{total overhead costs}}{\text{direct labour costs}}$$

$$= \frac{\$30\,000}{\$60\,000}$$

$$= 0.5, \text{ that is, } 50\%$$

If we round Wayne's labour cost to $10.00 per hour, his factory overhead rate is $5.00 per hour. The use of this pre-determined rate can best be explained with an extended illustration in which Wayne's business makes a product on request for a customer.

Extended Illustration

Wayne Hopkins has been asked to make an octagonal picnic table for Newman's Garden Centre. He has assigned this job to his employee, Becky, who will see the project through from start to finish. Here are the steps this project will take to completion, and the accounting entries that will be journalized for the production of this picnic table.

Step 1   A materials requisition form is completed for the lumber and bolts that will be used, $54.00.

Step 2   Becky's time card shows that 6.4 hours were taken to make this particular table; her hourly rate is $10.00.

Step 3   The pre-determined factory overhead rate for Wayne's business is 50% of direct labour cost. Therefore, $32.00 is transferred to the Work in Process account.

Step 4   The table is transferred from work in process inventory to finished goods inventory when it is done. Total cost, $150.

Step 5   The table is sold to the customer for the $150 cost plus a markup of 20% on cost, i.e. $180. The customer paid cash.

Step 6   The cost of the table sold is removed from the finished goods inventory, $150.

Figure 9-13 shows the accounting entries necessary from the start of production right through to the sale of the manufactured product. The last two entries are important because they are related: entry #5 recording the sale at retail price, and entry #6 recording the specific cost of the sale. Study these entries carefully for a firm understanding of the job costing process.

GENERAL JOURNAL

PAGE _____

DATE 19–		PARTICULARS	PR	DEBIT	CREDIT
①		Work in Process		54 –	
		Direct Materials Inventory			54 –
		To transfer raw materials used to			
		Work in Process			
②		Work in Process		64 –	
		Payroll			64 –
		To record direct labour used			
		(6.4 hours @ $10.00/hour)			
③		Work in Process		32 –	
		Factory Overhead Control			32 –
		To record overhead @ 50% of direct			
		labour cost			
④		Finished Goods Inventory		150 –	
		Work in Process			150 –
		To transfer completed table to			
		Finished Goods Inventory			
⑤		A/R—Customer		192 60	
		GST Payable			12 60
		Sales			180 –
		To record the sale of the table			
		@ cost plus 20%			
⑥		Cost of Goods Sold		150 –	
		Finished Goods Inventory			150 –
		To transfer the cost of the table			
		to Cost of Goods Sold			

FIGURE 9-13   *The general journal entries for picnic table production*

QUESTIONS

8. What are the three main cost components to costing a job?

9. There are three types of inventories in a manufacturing concern. What are they?

10. List as many direct materials as you can that would be needed to manufacture an in-ground, 20 × 40, vinyl-lined pool.

11. What is the purpose of a materials requisition form?

12. What is the purpose of a Work in Process account?

13. How do we differentiate between direct materials and indirect materials in the manufacturing process?

14. How do we differentiate between direct labour and indirect labour in the manufacturing process?

15. If the total overhead costs of a business are $45 000 and the labour costs are $436 000, what is the pre-determined factory overhead rate?

9.3

Adjustments and the Worksheet

At the end of the accounting period, a worksheet is prepared to facilitate the preparation of the financial statements for the fiscal period. A **worksheet** is an accounting form used to make adjusting entries to the accounts and assist in the preparation of financial statements. Many of the adjustments are already known to you, for example: depreciation, prepaid insurance, prepaid supplies, accrued wages, etc.

But there are special adjustments for a manufacturing business that must be done carefully, and these involve the three inventories on hand mentioned earlier — direct materials, work in process, and finished goods.

Figure 9-14 shows a sample worksheet for Wayne's Woodworking for the year ended December 31, 19–. The trial balance is kept small and some ledger accounts have been eliminated to keep the illustration clear. This worksheet has two extra columns that have not been used before in this text, namely, Cost of Goods Manufactured. All of the accounts in these two columns will appear as part of a statement of cost of goods manufactured. The use of these two columns will make it easier to prepare the financial statements once the worksheet is completed.

There are eight adjustments that will be made for Wayne's Woodworking on the worksheet. Study them carefully, along with these notes:

(1) Prepaid Insurance: Half of the $480 in prepaid insurance has been used up and is charged to the Insurance Expense account. Since the insurance is all on the shop building and equipment, and therefore a part of factory overhead, the $240 expense is also extended to the Cost of Goods Manufactured columns.

(2) Shop Supplies: $320 of supplies are still on hand, and the $480 used up is charged to Factory Supplies Used, a cost account that also belongs in the Cost of Goods Manufactured as part of overhead.

(3) Depreciation: The shop has to be depreciated for the year. The declining-balance method is used, and the shop is depreciated 10%.

	ACCOUNTS	ACCT. NO.	TRIAL BALANCE		ADJUSTMENTS	
			DEBIT	CREDIT	DEBIT	CREDIT
1	Bank	110	6500 –			
2	Accounts Receivable	120	1800 –			
3	GST Recoverable	130	500 –			
4	Direct Materials Inventory	140	4000 –		⑥ 3500 –	⑥ 4000 –
5	Work in Process Inventory	141	2000 –		⑦ 1000 –	⑦ 2000 –
6	Finished Goods Inventory	142	3000 –		⑧ 5000 –	⑧ 3000 –
7	Prepaid Insurance	150	480 –			① 240 –
8	Factory Supplies	160	800 –			② 480 –
9	Shop	170	50000 –			
10	Accumulated Depreciation—Shop	171		5000 –		③ 4500 –
11	Equipment	180	15000 –			
12	Accumulated Depreciation—Equip.	181		3000 –		④ 2400 –
13	Accounts Payable	210		2000 –		
14	GST Payable	220		900 –		
15	W. Hopkins, Capital	310		34100 –		
16	W. Hopkins, Drawings	320	20000 –			
17	Sales	410		85000 –		
18	Direct Labour	530	8000 –		⑤ 800 –	
19	Indirect Labour	550	2200 –		⑤ 200 –	
20	Other Expenses	570	6720 –			
21	Purchases	580	9000 –			
22			130000 –	130000 –		
23	Insurance Expense	560			① 240 –	
24	Factory Supplies Used	540			② 480 –	
25	Depreciation Expense—Shop	520			③ 4500 –	
26	Depreciation Expense—Equip.	510			④ 2400 –	
27	Accrued Wages	230				⑤ 1000 –
28	Manufacturing Summary				⑥ 4000 –	⑥ 3500 –
29					⑦ 2000 –	⑦ 1000 –
30	Income Summary				⑧ 3000 –	⑧ 5000 –
31					27120 –	27120 –
32	Cost of Goods Manufactured					
33						
34	Net Income					
35						
36						

Depreciation is the process of allocating the cost of an asset over its useful life. It is an expense chargeable to factory overhead, and therefore this amount is extended to the Cost of Goods Manufactured columns.

(4) Depreciation: The equipment has to be depreciated also. The declining-balance method is used, the equipment is depreciated 20%. Depreciation is an expense chargeable to factory overhead, and therefore this amount is extended to the Cost of Goods Manufactured columns.

(5) Accrued Wages: There are wages owing that have to be charged to Direct Labour ($800), and Indirect Labour ($200). The totals for direct and indirect labour are extended to the Cost of Goods Manufactured debit column.

WORKSHEET

FOR THE _Year_ ENDED _Dec. 31_ 19 —

COST OF GOODS MANUFACTURED		INCOME STATEMENT		BALANCE SHEET		
DEBIT	CREDIT	DEBIT	CREDIT	DEBIT	CREDIT	
				6500 –		1
				1800 –		2
				500 –		3
				3500 –		4
				1000 –		5
				5000 –		6
				240 –		7
				320 –		8
				50000 –		9
					9500 –	10
				15000 –		11
					5400 –	12
					2000 –	13
					900 –	14
					34100 –	15
				20000 –		16
			85000 –			17
8800 –						18
2400 –						19
		6720 –				20
9000 –						21
						22
240 –						23
480 –						24
4500 –						25
2400 –						26
					1000 –	27
4000 –	3500 –					28
2000 –	1000 –					29
		3000 –	5000 –			30
33820 –	4500 –					31
	29320 –	29320 –				32
33820 –	33820 –	39040 –	90000 –	103860 –	52900 –	33
		50960 –			50960 –	34
		90000 –	90000 –	103860 –	103860 –	35
						36

FIGURE 9-14
Worksheet

For the next three adjustments, a new account will be used called Manufacturing Summary.

(6) Direct Materials Inventory: is $3 500. This requires two adjustments, a credit of $4 000 to Direct Materials Inventory (and a debit to Manufacturing Summary) to eliminate the old balance, and a debit of $3 500 to Direct Materials Inventory (and a credit to Manufacturing Summary) to set up the new inventory.

(7) Work in Process Inventory: is $1 000. This requires two adjustments, a credit of $2 000 to Work in Process Inventory (and a debit to Manufacturing Summary) to eliminate the old balance, and a debit of $1 000 to Work in Process Inventory (and a credit to Manufacturing Summary) to set up the new inventory.

(8) Finished Goods Inventory: is $5 000. This requires two adjustments, a credit of $3 000 to Finished Goods Inventory (and a debit to Income Summary) to eliminate the old balance, and a debit of $5 000 (and a credit to Income Summary) to set up the new inventory.

The adjustments to both columns of Direct Materials Inventory and Work in Process Inventory belong on the statement of cost of goods manufactured, and therefore these adjustments are transferred to the Manufacturing Summary account. The entries to both columns of Finished Goods Inventory belong on the income statement, and are therefore extended to the Income Statement columns. The Purchases must also be extended to the Cost of Goods Manufactured debit column.

In summary, all manufacturing costs are extended to the Cost of Goods Manufactured columns, and all revenue and non-manufacturing expenses are extended to the Income Statement columns. At the bottom of the worksheet, the Cost of Goods Manufactured is extended to the Income Statement debit column, and the Net Income is extended to the Balance Sheet credit column.

Q U E S T I O N S

16. How often is a worksheet prepared for a manufacturing business?

17. What extra columns appear on the worksheet of a manufacturing concern that do not appear for a merchandise business?

18. An adjustment for accrued wages can affect two possible accounts. Name the two accounts.

19. There are four possible inventory adjustments on the worksheet of a manufacturing concern. What are the four?

20. Which manufacturing accounts are extended from the trial balance columns to the CGM columns?

21. What three financial statements are prepared from the worksheet for a manufacturing concern?

9.4

Preparing the Financial Statements

Once the worksheet has been totalled and cross-balanced, the financial statements can be prepared for the fiscal period. The **fiscal period** is the period of time over which the net income of a (manufacturing) business is measured. In a manufacturing concern, since the cost of goods manufactured is transferred from its statement to the income statement, and the net income is transferred from the income statement to the balance sheet, this means that there are three formal statements, and they are should be prepared in this order:

1. statement of cost of goods manufactured
2. income statement
3. balance sheet

Here are the three statements for Wayne's Woodworking for the year ended December 31, 19–. These are prepared in the order that the columns appear on the worksheet; the statement of cost of goods manufactured is, therefore, first.

Wayne's Woodworking Statement of Cost of Goods Manufactured For the Year Ended December 31, 19–			
Work in Process Inventory, Jan. 1, 19–			$2 000
Direct Materials:			
Inventory, Jan. 1	$ 4 000		
Direct Materials Purchases	9 000		
Materials Available for Use	13 000		
Inventory, Dec. 31	3 500	$9 500	
Direct Labour		8 800	
Factory Overhead:			
Indirect Labour	2 400		
Insurance Expense	240		
Depreciation Expense — Shop	4 500		
Depreciation Expense — Equipment	2 400		
Factory Supplies Used	480	10 020	28 320
			30 320
Work in Process Inventory, Dec. 31, 19–			1 000
Cost of Goods Manufactured			$29 320

FIGURE 9-15   *Statement of cost of goods manufactured*

The final figure on this statement is transferred to the income statement where it becomes part of the Cost of Goods Sold calculation.

Wayne's Woodworking		
Income Statement		
For the Year Ended December 31, 19–		
Revenue:		
Sales		$85 000
Cost of Goods Sold:		
Finished Goods Inventory, January 1, 19–	$ 3 000	
Cost of Goods Manufactured	29 320	
Finished Goods Available for Sale	32 320	
Finished Goods Inventory, December 31, 19–	5 000	
Cost of Goods Sold		27 320
Gross Profit		57 680
Operating Expenses:		
Other Expenses		6 720
Net Income		$50 960

FIGURE 9-16   *Income statement*

In this income statement, the other expenses are lumped into one category. In reality, there would be several expenses detailed here such as advertising, bank charges, heat and light, telephone, etc. These accounts are not shown here since the main purpose of this chapter is to highlight the new cost accounts for a manufacturing concern. As with service businesses and merchandising businesses, the net income is transferred to the balance sheet where it is added to the owner's capital balance from the start of the year. If a net loss were incurred, it would be subtracted from the old capital.

Notice on the balance sheet (Figure 9-17) that the three ending inventory accounts used on the statement of cost of goods manufactured and the income statement appear as current assets on the balance sheet.

Once the financial statements are prepared, the adjustments should be journalized in general journal form, as shown in Figure 9-18.

Wayne's Woodworking
Balance Sheet
December 31, 19–

Assets

Current Assets:

Bank			$6 500
Accounts Receivable			1 800
GST Recoverable			500
Inventories: Direct Materials		$3 500	
Work In Process		1 000	
Finished Goods		5 000	9 500
Prepaid Insurance			240
Factory Supplies			320
Total Current Assets			18 860

Fixed Assets:

	Cost	Acc. Dep.	N.B.V.	
Shop	$50 000	$9 500	$40 500	
Equipment	15 000	5 400	9 600	50 100
				$68 960

Liabilities

Current Liabilities:

Accounts Payable	$2 000
GST Payable	900
Accrued Wages	1 000
Total Current Liabilities	3 900

Owner's Equity

W. Hopkins, Capital

Balance, January 1, 19–	$34 100	
Add: Net Income	50 960	
	85 060	
Less: Drawings	20 000	
Balance, December 31, 19–		65 060
		$68 960

FIGURE 9-17   Balance sheet

DATE 19–		PARTICULARS	PR	DEBIT	CREDIT
Dec.	31	ADJUSTING JOURNAL ENTRIES			
		①			
		Insurance Expense		2 4 0 –	
		Prepaid Insurance			2 4 0 –
		To adjust for insurance expense			
		②			
		Factory Supplies Used		4 8 0 –	
		Factory Supplies			4 8 0 –
		To adjust for factory supplies used			
		③			
		Dep. Expense—Shop		4 5 0 0 –	
		Acc. Dep.—Shop			4 5 0 0 –
		To adjust for shop depreciation			
		④			
		Dep. Expense—Equipment		2 4 0 0 –	
		Acc. Dep.—Equipment			2 4 0 0 –
		To adjust for equipment expense			
		⑤			
		Direct Labour		8 0 0 –	
		Indirect Labour		2 0 0 –	
		Accrued Wages			1 0 0 0 –
		To adjust labour costs			
		⑥			
		Manufacturing Summary		4 0 0 0 –	3 5 0 0 –
		Direct Materials Inventory		3 5 0 0 –	4 0 0 0 –
		To adjust direct materials costs			
		⑦			
		Manufacturing Summary		2 0 0 0 –	1 0 0 0 –
		Work in Process Inventory		1 0 0 0 –	2 0 0 0 –
		To adjust for work in process			
		⑧			
		Income Summary		3 0 0 0 –	5 0 0 0 –
		Finished Goods Inventory		5 0 0 0 –	3 0 0 0 –
		To adjust finished goods inventory			

FIGURE 9-18   *Adjusting journal entries*

These adjustments are taken directly from the worksheet. The adjusting entries must be formally journalized and posted into the general ledger accounts to revise them to their correct balances at year end.

Then the closing entries should be journalized and posted to the general ledger accounts, and a post-closing trial balance prepared. (**Closing entries** are prepared at the end of a fiscal period to close out the Drawings account, and all revenue, cost, and expense accounts.)

GENERAL JOURNAL

PAGE 72

DATE 19–		PARTICULARS	PR	DEBIT	CREDIT
		CLOSING JOURNAL ENTRIES			
		①			
Dec.	31	Manufacturing Summary		27820 –	
		Direct Labour			8800 –
		Indirect Labour			2400 –
		Purchases			9000 –
		Insurance Expense			240 –
		Factory Supplies Used			480 –
		Dep. Expense—Shop			4500 –
		Dep. Expense—Equipment			2400 –
		To close out Cost accounts			
		②			
	31	Income Summary		29320 –	
		Manufacturing Summary			29320 –
		To close out Manufacturing Summary			
		③			
	31	Sales		85000 –	
		Other Expenses			6720 –
		Income Summary			78280 –
		To close out Expense accounts			
		④			
	31	W. Hopkins, Capital		20000 –	
		W. Hopkins, Drawings			20000 –
		To close out Drawings accounts			
		⑤			
	31	Income Summary		50960 –	
		W. Hopkins, Capital			50960 –
		To close out Income Summary			

FIGURE 9-19 Closing journal entries

In the closing out process for a manufacturing concern, there are five steps:

Step 1   Close out the cost accounts to the Manufacturing Summary account. (The cost accounts are found in the Cost of Goods Manufactured columns).

Step 2   Close out the Manufacturing Summary account to the Income Summary account.

Step 3   Close out all Revenue and Expense accounts to the Income Summary account.

Step 4   Close out the Drawings account to Capital.

Step 5   Close out the Income Summary account to Capital.

The closing journal entries are posted to the general ledger accounts and a post-closing trial balance prepared of the general ledger.

Wayne's Woodworking Post-Closing Trial Balance December 31, 19–		
Bank	$ 6 500	
Accounts Receivable	1 800	
GST Recoverable	500	
Direct Materials Inventory	3 500	
Work in Process Inventory	1 000	
Finished Goods Inventory	5 000	
Prepaid Insurance	240	
Factory Supplies	320	
Shop	50 000	
Accumulated Depreciation — Shop		$ 9 500
Equipment	15 000	
Accumulated Depreciation — Equipment		5 400
Accounts Payable		2 000
GST Payable		900
Accrued Wages		1 000
W. Hopkins, Capital		65 060
	$83 860	$83 860

FIGURE 9-20   *Post-closing trial balance*

The only accounts remaining after the post-closing trial balance are the balance sheet accounts. The general ledger is ready for the next fiscal period.

22. Is there a specific order in which the financial statements for a manufacturing concern should be prepared? Why?

23. What is the link between:
    (a) The Statement of Cost of Goods Manufactured and the Income Statement?
    (b) The Income Statement and the Balance Sheet?

24. Once the worksheet has been totalled and balanced, what are the next three accounting operations that should be performed?

25. What types of accounts will carry over and be used in the next fiscal year of a manufacturing concern?

9.5

Process Cost Accounting

Process cost accounting is a cost system that recognizes a continuous flow-through of a product from one manufacturing department in a company to another.

A process cost system is used in a manufacturing concern where the products made have similar specifications — golf balls, cereal, soft drinks, televisions, etc. Plants that manufacture these produce a continuous stream of goods. As with job costing, process cost accounting has three main elements: direct materials, direct labour, and factory overhead. Under process costing, however, the costs are accumulated as the product moves through a series of stages in the manufacturing process.

Let's assume that you are a manufacturer of golf balls, and that the production process has three stages: assembly, covering, and paint and stamp. Assembly is the main production stage where the raw materials are compressed together to shape the golf ball. Covering is the process of putting the outer layer on the golf ball. Painting is coating the ball with white, yellow, pink, or orange colours, and stamping is placing the name description on the ball, e.g., Fairway 1. The costing of the golf ball can be shown in a step diagram, Figure 9-21.

Process costing assumes that costs are transferred from one department to another and once the total cost has been established, it can be divided by the total number of units produced to arrive at the per unit cost.

Golf Ball Production
Process Costing
June figures

Step 1: ASSEMBLY	
Direct Materials	$ 35 000
Direct Labour	$ 10 000
Factory Overhead	$ 5 000
Total Cost	$ 50 000
Golf Balls Produced	50 000
Unit Cost/Golf Ball	$1.00

Step 2: COVERING	
Costs From Step 1	$ 50 000
Direct Materials	$ 5 000
Direct Labour	$ 3 000
Factory Overhead	$ 2 500
Total Cost	$ 60 500
Golf Balls Produced	50 000
Unit Cost/Golf Ball	$1.21

Step 3: PAINT & STAMP	
Costs From Step 2	$ 60 500
Direct Materials	$ 1 700
Direct Labour	$ 1 300
Factory Overhead	$ 2 500
Total Cost	$ 66 000
Golf Balls Produced	50 000
Unit Cost/Golf Ball	$1.32

FIGURE 9-21   *Golf ball production*

Process costing is an accounting system whereby the materials, labour, and factory overhead costs are averaged over the number of units produced; in this case, over the number of golf balls. Under process costing there is no attempt to distinguish between direct and indirect materials costs, or direct and indirect labour costs, since all costs are charged directly to a specific department.

In Figure 9-21, for example, costs are all accumulated in the assembly operation, step 1, and then the total costs are transferred to step 2, the covering process. Costs are kept track of by department. Step 2 adds the costs for the covering department to those transferred from assembly. And step 3 adds the paint and stamp costs to the costs transferred from step 2, the covering department.

From an accounting perspective, the finished goods from step 1 become the raw materials for step 2, and the finished goods from step 2 become the raw materials for step 3. Once the golf balls have passed through step 3 of production, the final unit cost of a golf ball can be determined, i.e. $1.32.

The example as shown in Figure 9-21 assumes that no units were lost during the production cycle, and also that there were no beginning or ending work in process inventories during that manufacturing period. (Treatment of units lost is a special problem and is left for another, more detailed, course in cost accounting.)

There is one more issue in process costing that must be outlined here, and that is the costing of production in any given manufacturing period. The existence of inventories in various stages of completion is a reality since process costing is used for a continuous manufacturing process. Accountants use a technique called equivalent units for this calculation. The term equivalent units means "How many units would have been produced if one unit (golf ball) had been finished before another one was started?"

Equivalent units are the number of fractional units that equate to one whole unit. This concept assumes, for example, that four golf balls which are 25% completed are the same as one completed golf ball. The best way to understand this concept is through a costing illustration.

Assume that the golf ball plant (Figure 9-21) had these inventory statistics for June:

Beginning Work in Process Inventory	2 000	(25% completed)
Started and Completed During Period	50 000	
Ending Work in Process Inventory	4 000	(50% completed)

The calculation of equivalent units of *production* for June must reflect the amount of labour, materials, and overhead *needed to complete* the beginning work in process inventory.

Beginning Work in Process Inventory	2 000 × 75% =	1 500
Started and Completed During Period	50 000 × 100% =	50 000
Ending Work in Process Inventory	4 000 × 50% =	2 000
Equivalent Units		53 500

Using the final total cost from Figure 9-21, the per unit cost of the golf balls now will be calculated this way:

Total Cost	$66 000
Golf Balls Produced	53 500
Unit Cost/Golf Ball	$1.23

The concept of equivalent units is more complex than indicated here, since there can be both beginning and ending inventories for each stage of the production process. Again, a more detailed analysis is left to another textbook. Indeed, whole courses revolve around the idea of job and process costing, and our purpose here is to gain only a brief insight into the complexities of cost accounting.

QUESTIONS

26. The textbook lists four examples of businesses that use process costing. See if you can think of another six.

27. What are the three main elements of process costing?

28. How does process costing differ from job costing, if the three main elements are the same?

29. What happens to such costs as indirect materials, and indirect labour, under process costing?

30. In the golf ball production example, by how much would the unit cost of a golf ball change if the direct labour in step 3 was doubled?

31. Two assumptions were made in the golf ball example that do not hold true in a real manufacturing process. What were these two problems?

32. Define the term *equivalent units*.

9.6

Using the Computer

Computers can be used for either job costing or process costing. They can store costs relating to all three of the major cost components — direct materials, direct labour, and factory overhead. If a perpetual inventory method is being used, the computer can keep track of the cost of units transferred to the production process.

On a simpler level, the computer can be used to prepare special reports relating to cost accounting by using an integrated software package that has spreadsheet, graphics, database, and word processing components.

Spreadsheets

An example of a spreadsheet activity in cost accounting would be the preparation of a schedule showing the calculation of the costs for a product under process costing. Figure 9-22 shows an example that might be used for the golf ball production plant discussed in section 9.5.

The costs can be inserted for the three departments. The spreadsheet is programmed to find the total cost per department, to calculate the unit cost per golf ball, and to transfer the costs from one department to the next.

	A	B	C	D
				Paint &
1	Golf Ball Production			
2	Process Costing			
3				Paint &
4		Assembly	Covering	Stamp
5				
6	Cost Forward	0	50000	60500
7	Direct Materials	35000	5000	1700
8	Direct Labour	10000	3000	1300
9	Factory Overhead	5000	2500	2500
10	Total Cost	50000	60500	66000
11				
12	Golf Balls Produced	50000	50000	50000
13	Unit Cost/Golf Ball	1.00	1.21	1.32
14				

FIGURE 9-22   *A spreadsheet of costs under process costing*

Graphics

A good example of a graphics application in cost accounting is a pie graph that indicates the percentage of costs produced by various departments in a job cost situation.

Once the pie graph has been prepared, it provides a quick visual analysis for management of the cost components of the product.

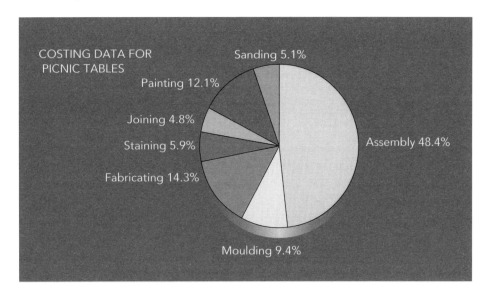

FIGURE 9-23   *A computer-generated pie graph*

Databases

An example of a database for Wayne's Woodworking is a inventory list of the raw materials (wood) used in his shop, along with the supplier names. This can be used for reference when Wayne is providing a cost estimate for a customer.

```
Stock Number: 1210
Description: 1 x 4 x 8 Pine
Cost: $1.30
Supplier: Franklin Home Centre
```
                                                    one record

```
RAW MATERIALS INVENTORY
Stock No.   Description            Cost     Supplier
1200        2 x 4 x 8 Pine         $2.45    Franklin Home Centre
1202        1 x 6 x 8 Cedar        $3.15    Canada Buildall
1204        4 x 4 x 8 Pressure Tr. $5.05    Northern Lumber
1206        2 x 4 x 8 Pressure Tr. $3.75    Northern Lumber
1208        1 x 8 x 8 Spruce       $1.90    West Lumber
1210        1 x 4 x 8 Pine         $1.30    Franklin Home Centre
```

FIGURE 9-24   *An inventory listing*

The top part of the diagram shows the form used when the database is set up and stored. The lower part is a listing of the inventory stock number, description, cost, and supplier name. The database could be added to by including the supplier's mailing data — address, town, and postal code, and/or any discount information applicable to each creditor.

Word Processing

The golf ball company mentioned in the process cost section uses word processing for interdepartmental memos from the Cost Accounting department. Each department manager is informed about the costs accumulated in that department from one month to the next.

The basic form can be stored on the computer. The operator merely adds the name of the department and the manager, and the date of the memo. The form is then printed and mailed to the department manager.

Interdepartmental Memo

To: J. McMillen, Manager
Assembly Department

From: Head Office, Costing Department

Re: COSTING DATA

Date: Wednesday, July 4, 19–

Our costing data is now complete for the first six months of this fiscal year. Costing data for your department for the same period last year is also included in this memo for your information and analysis. Data is expressed as cost per golf ball.

	19–0	19–1
Jan	$.97	$ .99
Feb	.97	.99
Mar	.97	.99
Apr	.98	1.00
May	.98	1.00
Jun	.98	1.00

This data will be discussed at our regular monthly cost meeting which will take place on Monday next.

Jim Hill
Costing Department Manager

FIGURE 9-25   *An interdepartmental memo*

9.7

Bedford Exercise 9 — Locomotion Unlimited

Locomotion Unlimited, an Alberta company, was the brainchild of Rob di Vincenzo who had been a skateboarding enthusiast for a number of years. During that time he had used a number of different brands and models of skateboards, many of which he had subsequently modified to suit his own tastes. He felt that he could build a skateboard that would incorporate a number of design characteristics that would enable the user to be more creative in the stunts that could be performed, yet retain ultimate control. Rob convinced his father of the viability and marketability of his new skateboard design and persuaded him to invest in Locomotion Unlimited.

A pro forma (projected) monthly income statement was prepared to determine projected costs and profits. This plan listed projected sales, the cost of raw materials, direct labour, factory overhead, and selling and administration costs. Costing data revealed these figures:

Costs Involved In Manufacturing Skateboards

Schedule A: Raw Material Cost

Plastic	$ 8.40
Wheels	11.20
Supports	8.12
Rubber grometts	1.12
Polypropylene ball socket supports	.21
Screws	.49
Bolts and washers	.42
Decals	.70
Cost Per Unit	$30.66
Raw Materials Cost for Monthly Production of 12 000 units	$367 920

Schedule B: Direct Labour Cost Per Month
(Assuming 22 working days per month @ 8h each)

5 hourly assembly line workers ($13.30/h)	$11 704.00
1 moulding machine operator ($14.00/h)	2 464.00
Health Insurance ($38 per person per month)	228.00
Workers Compensation (2.1%)	297.53
Canada Pension Plan (1.8%)	255.02
Unemployment Insurance	476.04
Total Direct Labour Cost	$15 424.59

Shedule C: Factory Overhead Per Month

Depreciation — Manufacturing Equipment:

Injection moulding machine, $75 000 (5-year life)	$1 250	
Mould $20 000 (1-year life)	1 670	
Storage tanks $6 000 (5-year life)	100	
Fork lift $21 000 (5-year life)	350	
Assembly Line $42 000 (5-year life)	700	
Tools $8 400 (1-year life)	700	
Total Manufacturing Equipment Depreciation Costs		$ 4 770.00
Rent: (464.5 m^2 @ $103.34 m^2/year)		3 200.00
Utilities: gas, electric		800.00
Insurance on property and inventory		1 000.00
Interest and bank charges		4 800.00
Packaging costs		18 480.00
Transportation and Warehousing		15 120.00

Indirect Labour:

2 shipping and receiving clerks ($9.00/h)	3 168.00	
1 maintenance repairman ($16.50/h)	2 904.00	
1 manufacturing supervisor ($18.00/h)	3 168.00	
Health Insurance ($38 per person per month)	152.00	
Workers Compensation (2.1%)	194.04	
Canada Pension Plan (1.8%)	166.32	
Unemployment Insurance	310.46	
Total Indirect Labour Cost		10 062.82
Total Factory Overhead		$58 232.82

Schedule D: Administration Costs

Accounting clerk	$1 900.00	
Secretary	1 600.00	
Benefits	332.10	
Total wages and benefits		$3 832.10
Telephone		800.00
Office supplies		1 315.87
Depreciation of office equipment		150.00
Rent		800.00
Total Administration		$6 897.97

Locomotion Unlimited
Pro Forma Monthly Income Statement

Sales:
(12 000 skateboards/month × $50.40/skateboard) $604 800.00

Cost of Goods Sold:
Raw Materials (Schedule A)	$367 920.00	
Direct Labour (Schedule B)	14 948.55	
Factory Overhead (Schedule C)	58 232.82	
Total Manufacturing Cost		441 101.37
Gross Profit		163 698.63
Selling Expenses (.06 × $604 800)	36 288.00	
Administration	6 897.97	43 185.97
Net Income		$120 512.66
Profit as % of Sales		19.93%
Profit/Skateboard		$10.04

You have been hired on a short term basis to help the accounting clerk make the computer accounting system ready for the first day of business. The chart of accounts for Locomotion Unlimited can be seen by accessing **GENERAL**, **Display**, and **Chart**. The instructions for using *Bedford* and entering data are outlined in Chapter 1.

ACCESSING THE LOCOMOTION UNLIMITED GENERAL LEDGER

To retrieve the general ledger for Locomotion Unlimited, you use the file name **locomote**. Key this name into the computer, insert the data provided by your teacher, and set the program to **Ready**, as described in Chapter 1.

Enter the **Using** date provided by your teacher. Remember the sequence, mmddyy. As before, ignore the cautions and proceed.

ACTIVATING THE JOBCOST MODULE

For this exercise you will be using the **GENERAL** and **JOBCOST** modules in *Bedford*. The **JOBCOST** module needs to have three cost centres recorded in it. To do this, access **JOBCOST**, **Project**, and **Insert**. The three cost centres for Locomotion Unlimited are:

1. Administration
2. Manufacturing
3. Selling

When you create job cost centres you are able to track daily transactions for revenue and expenses associated with these centres.

JOURNALIZING TRANSACTIONS

To journalize general ledger transactions, access the **GENERAL** module and the **Journal** option.

TRANSACTIONS

1. Voucher 001 (**GENERAL, Journal**)   Dated: mm01yy
   Record the opening position of Rob di Vincenzo in Locomotion Unlimited:
   Bank, $500 000; Note Payable — W. di Vincenzo, $80 000;
   Bank Loan (long term), $400 000; R. di Vincenzo, Capital, $20 000.

2. Purchase Invoice 4098   Dated: mm01yy
   Invoice received for manufacturing equipment installed, $172 400 plus
   GST Recoverable $12 068. Cheque 100 for $84 468; balance owing to
   Highland Equipment.

3. Cheque 101   Dated: mm01yy
   Rent for office and manufacturing facilities, $4 000 (Project 1:
   Administration 800; Project 2: Manufacturing 3 200) plus $280 GST
   Recoverable. Cheque mailed to Great West Properties for $4 280. (Rent
   payments started when plant was ready to operate.)

4. Cheque 102   Dated: mm01yy
   Office Equipment purchased from Office Outfitters Ltd., $6 770.40 plus
   $473.93 GST Recoverable. Paid in full.

5. Purchase Invoice 2489   Dated: mm02yy
   Purchased plastic, $100 800 (Project 2: Manufacturing 100 800), plus
   GST Recoverable $7 056, from Poly-Chlor Industries; terms n/30.

6. Purchase Invoice 223   Dated: mm02yy
   Purchased raw materials, $258 720 plus GST Recoverable $18 110.40,
   from O E M Industrial Supply, terms n/30 (Project 2).

7. Purchase Invoice 2259   Dated: mm02yy
   Purchased decals (raw materials), $8 400 plus GST Recoverable $588,
   from Ad-Print Decals Ltd.; terms n/20 (Project 2).

8. Purchase Invoice 667   Dated: mm02yy
   Purchased packaging, $18 480 plus GST Recoverable
   $1 293.60, from Varco Packaging Ltd.; terms n/10 (Project 2).

9. Purchase Invoice 446   Dated: mm02yy
   Purchased office supplies, $1 676.55 plus GST Recoverable $117.36,
   from Cascade Office Supply; terms n/15 (Project 1).

10. Voucher 002   Dated: mm05yy
    2 725 skateboards were completed and packaged for delivery in the first
    week of production at total raw material cost of $83 548.50. Transfer this
    cost from Inventory — Raw Materials to Inventory — Finished Goods.

11. Cheque 103   Dated: mm11yy
    $19 773.60, to Varco Packaging Ltd. in full payment of Invoice 667.

12. Voucher 003   Dated: mm12yy
    2 725 skateboards were completed and packaged for delivery in the second
    week of production at total raw material cost of $83 548.50. Transfer
    this cost from Inventory — Raw Materials to Inventory — Finished
    Goods.

13. Sales Invoices   Dated: mm12yy
    Skateboards were shipped to the following customers with sales terms
    at n/15. Shipments of the same quantity are to be made every other
    week as per contractual arrangements for distribution.

    - S101 to Brian Adrell Agencies, $32 356.80; Sales $30 240
      (Project 3: 30 240), GST Payable $2 116.80.
    - S102 to DTU Sports Supplies, $64 713.60; Sales $60 480, GST
      Payable $4 233.60.
    - S103 to Ingenius Sports, $62 017.20; Sales $57 960, GST Payable
      $4 057.20.
    - S104 to Northern Sports, $21 571.20; Sales $20 160, GST Payable
      $1 411.20.
    - S105 to Western Sports, $53 928; Sales $50 400, GST Payable $3 528.
    - S106 to PD's Hot Shop, $16 178.40; Sales $15 120, GST Payable
      $1 058.40.
    - S107 to Ontario Skateboards, $43 142.40; Sales $40 320, GST
      Payable $ 2 822.40.

14. Voucher 004   Dated: mm12yy
    Record the decrease to Inventory — Finished Goods, $167 097. The amount should be transferred to Cost of Goods Sold.

15. Cheque 104   Dated: mm12yy
    Paid Sports Marketing Group their commission, Selling Expenses $16 480.80 (Project 3) plus GST Recoverable $1 153.66.

16. Cheque 105   Dated: mm15yy
    Record the bi-weekly payroll for the ten hourly rated employees and the two office salaried persons. Wages Expense $11 065.60 (Project 2), Salaries Expense $1 820 (Project 1), CPP Payable $564.01, UI Payable $468.02, Income Tax Payable $2 354.86. Credit Bank for the net pay, $9 498.71.

17. Voucher 005   Dated: mm16yy
    Employer's share of payroll deductions: CPP Expense $564.01 (Project 1: 56.41; Project 2: 507.60); UI Expense $902.42 (Project 1: 90.24; Project 2: 812.18). Credit CPP Payable and UI Payable.

18. Voucher 006   Dated: mm16yy
    Workers Compensation payment owing $396.49 (Project 1: 39.65; Project 2: 356.84). Debit WCB Expense and credit WCB Payable.

19. Cheque 106   Dated: mm16yy
    $1 793.91, to Cascade Office Supply in full payment of Invoice 446.

20. Voucher 007   Dated: mm19yy
    2 725 skateboards were completed and packaged for delivery in the third week of production at total raw material cost of $83 548.50. Transfer this cost from Inventory — Raw Materials to Inventory — Finished Goods.

21. Cash Receipts   Dated: mm21yy
    Received on account from customers in full payment of Invoices S101-107.

    • R101, Brian Adrell Agencies, $32 356.80.
    • R102, DTU Sports Supplies, $64 713.60.
    • R103, Ingenius Sports, $62 017.20.
    • R104, Northern Sports, $21 571.20.
    • R105, Western Sports, $53 928.
    • R106, PD's Hot Shop, $16 178.40.
    • R107, Ontario Skateboards, $43 142.40.

22. Cheque 107   Dated: mm22yy
    $8 988, to Ad-Print Decals Ltd. in full payment of Invoice 2259.

23. Voucher 008   Dated: mm26yy
    2 725 skateboards were completed and packaged for delivery in the fourth
    week of production at total raw material cost of $83 548.50. Transfer this
    cost from Inventory — Raw Materials to Inventory — Finished Goods.

24. Sales Invoices   Dated: mm26yy
    Skateboards were shipped to the following customers with sales terms
    at n/15.

    - S108 to Brian Adrell Agencies, $32 356.80; Sales $30 240 (Project 3:
      30 240), GST Payable $2 116.80.
    - S109 to DTU Sports Supplies, $64 713.60; Sales $60 480; GST
      Payable $4 233.60.
    - S110 to Ingenius Sports, $62 017.20; Sales $57 960, GST Payable
      $4 057.20.
    - S111 to Northern Sports, $21 571.20; Sales $20 160, GST Payable
      $1 411.20.
    - S112 to Western Sports, $53 928; Sales $50 400, GST Payable
      $3 528.
    - S113 to PD's Hot Shop, $16 178.40; Sales $15 120, GST Payable
      $1 058.40.
    - S114 to Ontario Skateboards, $43 142.40; Sales $40 320, GST
      Payable $2 822.40.

25. Voucher 009   Dated: mm26yy
    Record the decrease to Inventory — Finished Goods, $167 097. The
    amount should be transferred to Cost of Goods Sold.

26. Cheque 108   Dated: mm26yy
    Paid Sports Marketing Group their commission, Selling Expenses
    $16 480.80 (Project 3) plus GST Recoverable $1 153.66.

27. Cheque 109   Dated: mm28yy
    Record the bi-weekly payroll for the ten hourly rated employees and
    the two office salaried persons. Wages Expense $11 065.60 (Project 2),
    Salaries Expense $1 820 (Project 1), CPP Payable $564.01, UI Payable
    $468.02, Income Tax Payable $2 354.86. Credit Bank for the net pay,
    $9 498.71.

28. Voucher 010   Dated: mm28yy
    Employer's share of payroll deductions, CPP Expense $564.01
    (Project 1: 56.41; Project 2: 507.60); UI Expense $902.42 (Project 1:
    90.24; Project 2: 812.18). Credit CPP Payable and UI Payable.

29. Voucher 011   Dated: mm28yy
Workers Compensation payment owing, $396.49 (Project 1: 39.65; Project 2: 356.84). Charge this to WCB Expense and credit WCB Payable.

30. Cheque 110   Dated: mm29yy
Paid Utilities Expense to Alberta Power Authority, $789 and GST Payable $55.23 (Project 1: 78.90; Project 2: 710.10).

31. Voucher 012   Dated: mm30yy
Costs associated with packaging the product were $16 786. Transfer this amount from Inventory — Raw Materials to Cost of Goods Sold.

32. Voucher 013   Dated: mm30yy
Record adjusting entry for depreciation expense incurred: Manufacturing Equipment, $4 770 (Project 2); Office Equipment, $150 (Project 1).

33. Voucher 014   Dated: mm30yy
Record adjusting entry for Office Supplies Expense, $1 315.87 (Project 1).

DISPLAYING AND PRINTING

Select **Display**. Your teacher will advise you which of the six options to preview. You may be prompted for dates. Remember, a date is entered in the sequence mmddyy (month/day/year).

Print any statements requested by your teacher. Again, you may be prompted for dates.

FINISHING A SESSION

Access the **SYSTEM** module and select the **Finish** option.

9.8

Dictionary of Accounting Terms

Closing Entries   Journal entries which close out certain accounts to nil balances at year end.

Depreciation   The method of allocating an asset's cost over its useful life.

Direct Labour   The cost of labour that can be traced directly to the product.

Direct Materials   The cost of materials used which can be traced directly to the production process.

Equivalent Units   The number of fractional units that equate to one whole unit.

Factory Overhead   All manufacturing costs, except direct materials and direct labour, that are not directly traced to the manufacturing process.

Finished Goods   The cost of all products which have been manufactured and are ready for sale.

Fiscal Period   The period of time over which the net income of a business is measured.

Indirect Labour   Labour costs that are not directly associated with the cost of the product being produced.

Indirect Materials   Materials that are not used directly in producing the finished product, but that do support the manufacturing process as a whole.

Input Tax Credit   The GST paid for purchases which can be subtracted from the GST otherwise payable.

Materials Requisition Form   A form completed when direct materials are transferred to work in process.

Perpetual Inventory   An inventory system in which inventory is debited to a merchandise inventory account and the value of inventory is known at any given moment.

Process Costing   A cost system that recognizes a continuous flow-through of a product from one manufacturing department in a company to another.

Statement of Cost of Goods Manufactured   A financial statement for a manufacturing business that details the manufacturing costs associated with the cost of goods sold.

MANUAL EXERCISES

1. Indicate whether these accounts would be found on the financial statements of a merchandising business (MB), or a manufacturing company (MC).
   (a) Ending Finished Goods Inventory
   (b) Purchases
   (c) Direct Labour
   (d) Beginning Merchandise Inventory
   (e) Indirect Materials

2. Indicate whether each of these accounts would be found on a Statement of Cost of Goods Manufactured (CGM), or on an Income Statement (IS).
   (a) Beginning Finished Goods Inventory   (f) Factory Supplies
   (b) Depreciation — Automobiles   (g) Direct Labour
   (c) Ending Work in Process Inventory   (h) Direct Materials
   (d) Ending Finished Goods Inventory   (i) Sales
   (e) Depreciation Expense — Machinery   (j) Indirect Labour

3. Classify each of these items as (1) direct material, (2) direct labour, or (3) factory overhead.
   (a) factory foreperson's salary
   (b) wood used in making the product
   (c) wages of the machine operators
   (d) depreciation on plant
   (e) supplies used to clean the shop
   (f) rent for two machines

4. Journalize these transactions on page 17 of a general journal for the DeClerc Manufacturing Company at the end of August.
   (a) Bought raw materials for $6 000 plus $420 GST, on account.
   (b) Bought supplies to clean the shop floor, $248.40 plus $16.10 GST Recoverable; paid by cheque #323.
   (c) Workers were paid $48 000 for the month.
   (d) The labour cost was allocated: $42 000 for direct labour and the rest for indirect labour.
   (e) Actual factory overhead paid for the month was $9 000, of which $2 000 was for rent, $4 500 for machine repairs, and $2 500 for shop utilities.

5. Journalize these transactions on page 22 of a general journal for Balazs Fabricating at the end of September.

(a) Bought raw materials for $5 786 plus $405.02 GST Recoverable, on account.

(b) Wrote a cheque for shop utilities, $615 plus $43.05 GST Recoverable. Cheque #228.

(c) Workers were paid $24 570 for the month.

(d) The labour cost was allocated: $24 000 for direct labour and the rest for indirect labour.

(e) Actual factory overhead paid for the month was $4 023, of which $1 400 was for rent, $1 614 for machine repairs, and $1 009 for shop utilities.

5. Prepare a cost of goods sold statement for Opeechee Manufacturing, given this raw data:

Inventory, July 1, 19–1	$12 625
Inventory, June 30, 19–2	9 715
Purchases	76 225
Freight-In	4 095

6. Prepare a cost of goods sold statement for Amazing Mfg. Ltd., given this raw data:

Inventory, April 1, 19–1	$ 24 536
Inventory, March 31, 19–2	28 797
Purchases	114 330
Freight-In	8 018

7. Prepare a cost of goods sold statement for Alberta Form Tool Manufacturing Ltd., given this data:

Finished Goods Inventory, Jan. 1, 19–1	$ 45 600
Finished Goods Inventory, Dec. 31, 19–2	36 775
Cost of Goods Manufactured	210 665

8. Prepare a cost of goods sold statement for Hawkins Ltd., given this data:

Finished Goods Inventory, Jan. 1, 19–1	$ 67 867
Finished Goods Inventory, Dec. 31, 19–2	65 760
Cost of Goods Manufactured	243 654

9. Prepare a statement of cost of goods manufactured for the month of April, using this data:

Materials:

Opening Inventory	$ 8 000
Ending Inventory	7 000

Work in Process

Opening Inventory	2 500
Ending Inventory	3 500
Direct Materials	12 000
Direct Labour	18 000
Indirect Labour	4 000
Factory Supplies	600

10. Prepare a statement of cost of goods manufactured for the month of July, using this data:

Materials:

Opening Inventory	$ 7 650
Ending Inventory	6 220
Work in Process	
Opening Inventory	1 845
Ending Inventory	1 530
Direct Materials	23 675
Direct Labour	43 335
Indirect Labour	6 215
Factory Supplies	719

11. The Battle Creek Cereal Company had these cost statistics for its production of Choco-Wheats. Prepare a schedule of process costing that calculates the unit cost of each cereal box.

	Mixing	Packaging	Stamping
Direct Materials	$38 000	$3 800	$2 000
Direct Labour	17 000	1 200	600
Factory Overhead	5 000	1 000	400
Number of boxes 30 000			

12. Mountain Cola had these cost statistics for its production of cola soft drinks. Prepare a schedule of process costing that calculates the unit cost of each can of soft drink.

	Mixing	Bottling	Capping
Direct Materials	$ 34 000	$13 800	$2 000
Direct Labour	8 200	2 200	500
Factory Overhead	17 800	14 000	7 500
Number of cans 300 000			

13. Daniel Manufacturing has the following unadjusted trial balance as of December 31, 19–.

Bank	$ 6 000	
Accounts Receivable	1 700	
Direct Materials Inventory	2 450	
Work in Process Inventory	1 140	
Finished Goods Inventory	3 860	
Prepaid Insurance	600	
Factory Supplies	550	
Machinery	40 000	
Accumulated Depreciation — Machinery		$ 8 000
Accounts Payable		1 000
D. Van Winden, Capital		39 000
D. Van Winden, Drawings	14 000	
Sales		152 000
Materials Purchases	44 100	
Direct Labour	34 000	
Indirect Labour	18 000	
Factory Rent	7 200	
Utilities	8 400	
Sales Salaries	18 000	
	$200 000	$200 000

Given this data, and the adjustment information below, prepare:
(a) a worksheet
(b) a statement of cost of goods manufactured
(c) an income statement and balance sheet
(d) adjusting journal entries, and closing journal entries

Adjustments:
 (i) insurance expired, $500
 (ii) factory supplies used, $250
(iii) depreciation of machinery is at 20%, declining-balance rate
(iv) accrued wages are $900 direct labour and $100 indirect labour
 (v) direct materials inventory, $940; work in process inventory, $380; finished goods inventory, $3 270

14. Durst Fabricating has the following unadjusted trial balance as of December 31, 19–.

Bank	$ 4 200	
Accounts Receivable	8 920	
Direct Materials Inventory	3 140	
Work in Process Inventory	3 640	
Finished Goods Inventory	4 440	
Prepaid Insurance	1 200	
Factory Supplies	1 800	
Building	90 000	
Accumulated Depreciation — Building		$ 8 775
Machinery	60 000	
Accumulated Depreciation — Machinery		21 600
Accounts Payable		2 375
Mortgage Payable		67 250
D. Durst, Capital		60 000
D. Durst, Drawings	28 000	
Sales		190 000
Materials Purchases	42 990	
Direct Labour	44 000	
Indirect Labour	10 470	
Factory Rent	8 125	
Utilities	9 075	
Sales Salaries	30 000	
	$350 000	$350 000

Given this data, and the adjustment information below, prepare:
(a) a worksheet
(b) a statement of cost of goods manufactured
(c) an income statement and balance sheet
(d) adjusting journal entries, and closing journal entries

Adjustments:
 (i) insurance expired, $200
 (ii) factory supplies used, $1 430
 (iii) depreciation of building is at 5%, and machinery is at 20%; both are declining-balance rates
 (iv) accrued wages are $1 600 direct labour and $500 indirect labour
 (v) direct materials inventory, $2 422; work in process inventory, $2 390; finished goods inventory, $2 970

COMPUTER EXERCISES

SS1   Use a spreadsheet to produce this cost of goods sold statement. Set Column A to a width of 30 characters and column B to a width of 12. Program the spreadsheet to perform the addition and subtraction needed. Save your solution on disk under the file name CH9SS1.

	A	B
1	COST OF GOODS SOLD	
2	Inventory, Jan. 1, 19-	34365.78
3	Purchases	135678.04
4		
5	Goods Available For Sale	?
6	Inventory, Dec. 31, 19-	28112.06
7		
8	Cost of Goods Sold	?
9		

SS2   Use a spreadsheet to produce this cost of goods sold statement. Set the width of column A to 30 characters, column B to 12 and column C to 12. Program the spreadsheet to perform the calculation required. Save your solution on disk under the file name CH9SS2.

	A	B	C
1	COST OF GOODS SOLD		
2	Inventory, Jan. 1, 19-		15667.98
3	Purchases	114564.43	
4	Freight-In	8778.02	
5			
6	Goods Available For Sale		?
7	Inventory, Dec. 31, 19xx		17776.57
8			
9	Cost of Goods Sold		?
10			

SS3 Prepare this Materials Requisition spreadsheet template. Set the width of column A to 12 characters, column B to 14, and columns C, D, and E to 8 each. Save your template on disk under the file name CH9SS3.

```
        A            B           C          D           E
1   MATERIALS REQUISITION FORM
2   Job:
3   Customer:                            Date:
4   Material #   Description     Qty      Cost        Total
5   xxxxx          x------x      xxx      x.xx        xxx.xx
```

SS4 Recall the requisition template CH9SS3 and insert this data. Program the spreadsheet to calculate the total cost of each item and to total the material costs. Print out the resulting schedule.

Job: 555
Customer: Joy Lowrie
Date: 02/08/–

Material #	Description	Qty	Cost
102	2 × 4s	6	$8.45
104	1 × 2s	8	$5.05
150	2 × 2s	14	$6.25

SS5 Recall the requisition template CH9SS3 and insert this data. Program the spreadsheet to calculate the total cost of each item and to total the material costs. Print out the resulting schedule.

Job: P-12
Customer: Chris Gosso
Date: 02/15/–

Material #	Description	Qty	Cost
665	Steel	14	$20.34
719	Hinges	12	$ 3.28
881	Tie rods	28	$ 7.72
1010	Tin	38	$10.23

SS6   Use a spreadsheet to set up this process costing summary. Set column A to 20 characters. Insert any formulas required to provide the missing information. Print the solution and save this template under CH9SS6.

	A	B	C	D
1	Chocolate Bar Production-Nutso			
2	Process Costing			
3				
4		1st Mix	2nd Mix	Package
5	Costs Forward		?	?
6	Direct Materials	17589	16774	2873
7	Direct Labour	14556	3247	887
8	Factory Overhead	26887	8885	123
9				
10	Total Cost	?	?	?
11				
12				
13	Bars Produced	160000	160000	160000
14	Unit Cost	?	?	?

SS7   Use the template saved as CH9SS6 to set up this process costing summary. Enter the necessary changes and save as CH9SS7.

	A	B	C	D
1	Soap Production-Savour Spring			
2	Process Costing			
3				
4		Mixing	Drying	Package
5	Costs Forward		?	?
6	Direct Materials	6552	7009	2445
7	Direct Labour	4567	5787	1678
8	Factory Overhead	7456	3333	304
9				
10	Total Cost	?	?	?
11				
12				
13	Bars Produced	170000	170000	170000
14	Unit Cost	?	?	?

SS8   Use Figure 9-14 as a model and prepare a worksheet for a manufacturing business. Program the spreadsheet so that when adjustments are entered they are automatically extended, and the worksheet is automatically totalled and balanced. Print a copy of the spreadsheet. Save your work as CH9SS8.

DB1 Create a supplier database for Canco Manufacturing. Define the following fields for your file. Save your file under the name CH9DB1.

Name	=	20 columns
Address	=	18 columns
Town	=	10 columns
Postal Code	=	7 columns
Balance	=	12 columns

Enter the raw data shown below, and print a listing of the file.

Name	Address	Town	PC	Balance
Wong & Herbert	9 Douglas Ave.	Vancouver	V6T 2N5	$1 073.21
PacWest Mfg.	12 Victor Dr.	Vancouver	V7R 3S6	$6 721.93
D & G Mfg.	444 Sandway Dr.	Vancouver	V2D 2A4	$2 002.02
Keewating Ltd.	50 Fawcett Ave.	Vancouver	V3D 7T3	$ 321.11
McMillan & Co.	88 Bank Street	Vancouver	V6T 8B3	$ 742.07
Chong Import	908 Wharf Dr.	Vancouver	V4G 5H9	$2 126.97

DB2 Create a database for (inventory) costing information. Define the following fields for your file. Save your file under the name CH9DB2.

Stock Number	=	8 columns
Description	=	20 columns
Cost	=	7 columns
Quantity	=	7 columns
Value	=	10 columns

Enter the raw data shown below. Calculate the value of each inventory item. Print a listing of your file.

Stock No.	Description	Cost	Quantity	Value
1212	Tubing #2	$ 3.54	178	?
1214	Tubing #4	$5.919	212	?
1220	Steel Sheets	$ 8.19	66	?
1226	Hollow Tubing	$2.761	132	?
1230	Angle Iron	$ 5.21	99	?
1240	Welding Rods	$ 4.56	304	?

DB3 Create a database for (inventory) costing information. Define the following fields for your file. Save your file under the name CH9DB3.

Description	=	20 columns
Bin No.	=	5 columns
Cost	=	7 columns
Quantity	=	8 columns
Value	=	10 columns

Enter the raw data shown below. Calculate the value of each inventory item. Print a listing of your file.

Description	Bin No.	Cost	Quantity	Value
Handles	23	$12.13	34	?
Small Frame	24	$ 8.98	44	?
Large Frame	25	$10.00	83	?
Insert	26	$ 2.16	67	?
Flange	27	$ 2.17	52	?
Flat Pieces	28	$ 7.21	91	?
Angle Hinges	29	$ 4.44	70	?

G1   Create a pie graph for this costing data.

Department	Cost
Fabricating	$56.75
Welding	$ 7.65
Moulding	$12.43
Assembly	$ 6.66
Painting	$ 4.02
Packaging	$ 3.79

G2   Create a bar graph for this direct materials data.

Warehouse	19-0	19-1
Niagara Falls	$43 456	$42 365
North Bay	$18 765	$16 777
London	$22 887	$29 968
Ottawa	$35 665	$36 665
Toronto	$48 976	$48 977
Thunder Bay	$30 062	$38 808

G3   Create a line graph for this costing data.

Storage Cost Per Unit

Warehouse	19-0	19-1	19-2
Niagara Falls	$6.17	$6.30	$6.65
North Bay	$5.78	$5.82	$5.90
London	$4.44	$4.44	$4.50
Ottawa	$5.90	$6.00	$6.40
Toronto	$8.12	$8.50	$9.00
Thunder Bay	$3.88	$3.93	$4.02

WP1   Set up this Interdepartmental memo for Waddo Gum Company. Save your work under the file name CH9WP1.

Interdepartmental Memo

To: L. Birdie, Manager
Assembly Department

From: Costing Department — Waddo Gum Co.

Re: COSTING DATA

Date: Wednesday, January 7, 19–

Our costing data is now complete for the first six months of operations. Costing data for your department for the same period last year is also included in this memo for your information and analysis.

	19-0	19-1
Jan	$.042	$.070
Feb	$.044	$.074
Mar	$.044	$.080
Apr	$.050	$.092
May	$.053	$.094
Jun	$.061	$.096

This data will be discussed at our regular monthly cost meeting which will take place on Monday next.

Albert Runnymede
Cost Accountant

WP2   Retrieve CH9WP1 and send a copy of the same memo to the manager of the packaging department, Heather Lemon, with this data.

	19-0	19-1
Jan	$.112	$.137
Feb	$.112	$.137
Mar	$.115	$.137
Apr	$.120	$.150
May	$.126	$.150
Jun	$.127	$.160

R. v. DUBRINAN & VITTORIO

BACKGROUND

Jackie Dubrinan and Sal Vittorio were cashiers at the Ministry of Transportation and Communication, Queen's Park office, handling collection of Ontario Retail Sales Tax. During a four-month period, thirteen people paid the ORST relating to their purchase of cars, but did not receive receipts for their sales tax payments. Two of the thirteen people talked to a senior supervisor at the MTC to inquire as to why they did not receive receipts. The supervisor decided to investigate and asked a team of forensic accountants to assist.

INVESTIGATION

The official receipt that should be issued to show payment of the sales tax is called an MV1. All of the MV1s for the period were examined for possible omissions or discrepancies. Investigators found that:

1. all the serially pre-numbered MV1s were accounted for during the period under investigation; none were missing.
2. during the four-month period there were thirteen sales tax payments made that had no supporting MV1 receipts issued.
3. all of the MV1s issued for the four months had cash and cheques for the correct amount deposited to the MTC's bank account.
4. cash totalling $4 600 was deposited to personal bank accounts controlled by Jackie Dubrinan during the same time period.

FRAUD

The accused persons had perpetrated an embezzlement scheme which resulted in $4 600 in cash and cheques being stolen from the MTC. A list was prepared for the court which showed the thirteen payments that had no sales tax receipts issued. The list was prepared from ministry vehicle permits issued during that time period. The schedule also listed the days that Dubrinan and Vittorio were present or absent when receipts were not issued.

R. v. Dubrinin and Vittorio
Schedule of Known Persons Who Reportedly Paid Ontario
Retail Sales Tax During January and February 19–
For Which an Official Receipt Has Not Been Issued

Permit Date	Name	Retail Sales Tax Paid	Payment Method	Present (P) Absent (A)	
01/16/–	Henry Simpson	$ 267.75	Cash	Dubrinin	(P)
				Vittorio	(A)
01/24/–	Peter Cuelo	$ 175.00	Cash	Dubrinin	(P)
				Vittorio	(P)
01/29/–	Susie Bartlett	$ 84.00	Cash	Dubrinin	(P)
				Vittorio	(P)
01/30/–	Sal Baretta	$ 133.00	Cheque	Dubrinin	(P)
				Vittorio	(P)
02/05/–	Paula Klein	$ 315.00	Cash	Dubrinin	(P)
				Vittorio	(P)
02/28/–	Brent Rockus	$ 504.00	Cheque	Dubrinin	(P)
				Vittorio	(A)
02/28/–	Michel Moulon	$ 182.00	Cheque	Dubrinin	(P)
				Vittorio	(A)
	Total	$4 600.00			

FIGURE 9-26   ORST schedule

Some of the items on the MTC list are denoted as having been paid by cheque. This presents a problem for embezzlers since cheques must be endorsed by the payee on the back of the cheque to be cashed. In this fraud case, Dubrinan and Vittorio took the cheques and substituted them for (retail sales tax) cash payments from other motorists. The cash-paying customers were issued receipts and the cheques substituted for the cash.

The MTC schedule also proved that Dubrinan and Vittorio had conspired together in the scheme to defraud the MTC, since Dubrinan was present at all fraudulent transactions, and Vittorio was present for most of them.

The information that disclosed the fraud was obtained from information relating to the permits issued to owners when new vehicles are bought or old vehicles change hands. The registration of motor vehicles is separate from the retail sales tax entries relating to the ownership changes. This basic internal control principle of separating duties enabled this fraud to be discovered fairly easily once the initial complaint was launched.

SENTENCE

Both Dubrinan and Vittorio stood trial on charges of embezzling funds from the Ministry of Transportation and Communications. Dubrinan received the heavier sentence since she was the main clerk on duty at all times, had handled most of the money, and ended up with the embezzled funds in her personal bank accounts. She received a sentence of one year, and was ordered to make restitution for the embezzled funds. Vittorio was given a 30-day jail term by the courts and a stern warning about future involvement in cash embezzlement schemes. Neither will be able to be bonded again for handling cash transactions.

QUESTIONS

1. How was this embezzlement scheme discovered? Is there a chance it could have gone undiscovered forever?
2. Were there any internal controls in place to help prevent a cash embezzlement such as this?
3. How were the forensic accountants able to determine the actual loss to the Ministry of Transportation and Communication?
4. Were the penalties appropriate? What would your sentence have been?

Usha Naik began sewing in her home part-time to earn some extra income. She had made canvas bags for her family to use for school and work. Friends and relatives liked her work and asked her to make a few more as favours to them. Usha took their orders, added a profit margin, and made her first sales.

Word spread in the small community of Tillsonburg, and Usha was soon besieged by orders for special canvas bags of all kinds. For the first three years there was never any need to advertise, since word of mouth brought just enough orders to keep Usha busy in her spare time.

Once her two daughters were in school, Usha had more spare time and decided that her business could handle a full work week. She advertised in the local paper, and orders began to trickle in. Her biggest break came when local farmers began to order canvas products for their work. People who owned their own boats and recreational vehicles also called to ask about new canvas tarpaulins and canvas repairs for their vehicles.

Two years ago, Usha opened her new business, *Naik Canvas and Tarpaulin Ltd.* The shop is located in an industrial complex near Tillsonburg, and readily accessible to customers. There is enough room to spread out large tarpaulins for sewing work, and the workers are keeping up with all orders.

One month later, Usha bought her first computer for the business. Her evenings, and some weekends, were taken up with studying the new system. Her raw materials inventory has been stored on the computer, using the inventory module. The business can now operate a perpetual inventory system with the use of the computer. At the stroke of a key, Usha can call up information about quantities of canvas on hand in the shop. The system also prepares a report, when requested, indicating which inventory stocks are running low, and which should be re-ordered.

The next step for *Naik Canvas & Tarpaulin Ltd.* was to store the general ledger for the business on the computer. Usha's neice Seema studied accounting at Glendale High School last year, and wants to learn more about computerized accounting. She promised her aunt that the general ledger would be on the computer by summer's end.

Seema kept her promise and by the start of school in September she had the business accounts on the computer. In addition, she surprised her aunt and loaded all the customer and supplier accounts on the system as well. On the last day of work, before returning to grade 12, Seema had a present for her aunt:

(1) a Chart of Accounts for *Naik Canvas & Tarpaulin Ltd.*
(2) an up-to-date balance sheet.
(3) an income statement for the first eight months of the year.
(4) accounts receivable reports which included an updated schedule as of August 31st, and a list of customer names and addresses.
(5) accounts payable reports which included an updated schedule as of August 31st, and a list of vendor names and addresses.

Naik Canvas & Tarpaulin Ltd. has entered the computer age and prospects for an efficient operation are excellent.

Seema has returned to school but has revised her timetable. She has opted for a special course in computer accounting to expand her knowledge in this area. And she has now set her sights on more education than she originally planned. She thinks that many business jobs will require computer training and she is checking out both college and university brochures to see where she can best be trained for her career choice — computer accounting.

FOR DISCUSSION

- How did Usha find time to master the computer?
- What accounting applications do you think would be most important for a business like *Naik Canvas and Tarpaulin Ltd.* — cash control, inventory, payroll, etc. Why?

Index

Photo Credits

CHAPTER 1:
p. 5: Cannon Canada Inc. **p. 7**: IBM Canada Ltd. **p. 8**: IBM Canada Ltd.
p. 9 (up. l): IBM Canada Ltd. **p. 9 (up. r)**: Universal Press Syndicate. **p. 9 (lw.r)**:
Digital Equipment of Canada.
p. 57: John Wiley and Sons Canada Ltd.

CHAPTER 2:
p. 60: Universal Press Syndicate. **p. 61**: First Light. **p. 68**: Universal Press Syndicate.
p. 124: Robert W. Allen/ First Light.

CHAPTER 3:
p. 128: Ron Cougler. **p. 203**: First Light.

CHAPTER 4:
p. 207 Major Video Canada Inc. **p. 223**: Universal Press Syndicate.
p. 239: Universal Press Syndicate.

CHAPTER 5:
p. 268: University of Waterloo. **p. 273**: Land of Software. **p. 292**: Universal Press
Syndicate. **p. 327**: T. Bruckbauer/First Light.

CHAPTER 6:
p. 331: Lee White/First Light. **p. 339**: Universal Press Syndicate.
p. 389: Jessie Parker/First Light.

CHAPTER 7:
p. 394: Doug Nichols – Photography **p. 445**: Steve Strickland/First Light.

CHAPTER 8:
p. 465: Universal Press Syndicate. **p. 509**: Lee White/First Light.

CHAPTER 9:
p. 521: Ron Cougler. **p. 571**: Jim Russell/First Light.